1985

The Puerto Rican Community and Its Children on the Mainland

A Source Book for Teachers, Social Workers and Other Professionals

Third Revised Edition

by

Francesco Cordasco and
Eugene Bucchioni

The Scarecrow Press, Inc.
Metuchen, N.J., & London
1982

Library of Congress Cataloging in Publication Data
Main entry under title:

The Puerto Rican community and its children on the
    mainland.

    Bibliography: p.
    Includes index.
    1. Puerto Ricans--Education--United States.   2. Bi-
lingualism.   3. Students--United States--Socioeconomic
states.   4. Education, Urban--United States.   I. Cordasco, Francesco, 1920- .   II. Bucchioni, Eugene.
III. Title.
LC2692. P8   1982   305. 8'687295'073   81-21250
ISBN 0-8108-1506-0   AACR2

To

LEONARD COVELLO

for over one-half century of dedicated
service to youth and the schools

iii

TABLE OF CONTENTS

Part III: PUERTO RICAN CHILDREN IN MAINLAND
         SCHOOLS

The favorable reception of this book by the professional constituen-
cies by whom it has been used has prompted the editors to assemble
a third expanded and revised edition. The successful use of the
earlier editions by many individuals working with the Puerto Rican
community on the mainland has made clear that its readership has
not been limited to teachers and to educational contexts. Actually,
as initially projected (and as its use over the years has affirmed),
the volume is a sociological sourcebook for the Puerto Rican community on the mainland; it provides resources not only to teachers,
but to social workers, psychologists, medical personnel, social historians, and other professionals whose work with Puerto Ricans
makes necessary a convenient collection of documents and related
materials that place in perspective the multi-dimensional experience
(and reaction) of a growing mainland community. Most importantly,
the text has underscored the needs, both socio-political and educational, of Puerto Ricans on the mainland, and the greatest plaudits
for the book have come from the Puerto Rican community itself at
all levels of articulation. At the time of its initial appearance (1968),
the text provided the first systematic effort to delineate the needs of
the growing Puerto Rican mainland community, with particular reference to Puerto Rican children and their experiences in the schools.

The structure of the text has been recast, with some materials
deleted, and new materials (reflecting recent developments) added.
Part I (The Puerto Rican Family and Island Backgrounds) affords a
politico-cultural kaleidoscope of island life; Part II (Conflict and Acculturation on the Mainland) provides a multi-faceted portraiture of
mainland life as perceived by Puerto Ricans, and is further strengthened by the statistical profile of the Puerto Rican community of New
York City (assembled by the Puerto Rican Forum), an invaluable
register of data which remains unequalled by any other extant resource; Part III (Puerto Rican Children in Mainland Schools) includes
materials both retrospective (e. g. , the unpublished memoranda of
Messrs. Covello, Monserrat, Oliveras, and Osuna) and current, and
furnishes a dimensional overview of the needs of Puerto Rican youth
in continental schools. The Appendix (Puerto Ricans on the United
States Mainland: A Summary in Facts and Figures) assembles the
most recent demographic and related data.

The editors are keenly aware of the fact that no clear consensus can exist (either within or outside a community) on what
should be included in a collection of documents, and it is hardly
necessary to add that the editors do not subscribe to all of the statements recorded herein. However, the materials have all been carefully chosen so that the multi-dimensional portrait remains unambig-
uous and historical canons are not violated. The editors have in-
curred many obligations, both within and outside the academic community, and these are gratefully acknowledged.

F. C.   E. B.
New York City
September 1981

vii

Urban education in many parts of the United States is confronted by a variety of seemingly overwhelming problems. There are serious shortages of teachers, overcrowded classes, an inadequate supply of instructional materials and inadequate space. Alarmingly high rates of academic retardation among urban children and adolescents, especially in reading and mathematics, are of special concern. Greater numbers of high school students in the inner city are leaving school before receiving their diplomas, and those who complete the secondary school program find that they are not as well prepared for employment as they should be.

Urban education in the last few decades has become sharply characterized by two patterns of development that have affected the traditional program--indeed, the very structure and function--of urban education. The schools are becoming increasingly segregated on the basis of social class. That is, middle class children and adolescents, because of housing patterns in the city, tend to go to certain schools while lower class children and adolescents and other students from poverty areas attend other schools. The general movement of middle class people out of the cities is further contributing to segregation by social class because fewer middle class people are living in the cities and sending their children to urban schools.

The second major pattern of development in urban education that has vital sociological significance is the increased ethnic segregation. White students tend to go to school in predominantly white residential areas. Discriminatory housing patterns in most American cities have contributed to the increased de facto segregation in urban education.

The heavy influx of Puerto Ricans into some cities such as New York, Philadelphia, Chicago and Newark, presents the schools with the additional important task of assisting the newcomers in adjusting to a new society: a society that generally demands that they function inconspicuously, a society that equates inconspicuousness with adjustment and which tends to suppress, as a mechanism of adjustment, the existing problems within the ethnic group.

The schools in these cities can play an important part in the orientation of Puerto Ricans to North American society as well as providing them with education in the traditional sense. That is, Puerto Rican students can be helped to understand and learn the values, the norms, the culture patterns and the language of urban North America as transmitted by the schools in addition to being taught to read and write English and to master all the other subjects that comprise the elementary and secondary school curricula.

Schools with large Puerto Rican enrollments, however, have become the "difficult" schools in the view of many teachers and urban boards of education. Classes are heavily weighted with transients, with children and adolescents from economically depressed families, with students from broken homes and with "problem" students. In these schools, the reported average I.Q.'s and levels of achievement in reading and mathematics are low. Teachers are reluctant to teach in these schools because they consider that such schools present unrewarding, and even dangerous, teaching situations. As a result, schools with large Puerto Rican enrollments are unable to attract sufficient numbers of qualified teachers and they have extremely high rates of teacher transfer and resignation.

Most Puerto Rican students who come to urban schools are members of lower classes, and they demonstrate characteristic social patterns. In addition, social class patterns are combined with Puerto Rican culture patterns. The result is a social and cultural milieu that is neither understood nor accepted by the middle-class North American teacher. This lack of understanding is evidenced by the failure to modify instruction for Puerto Rican students. The lack of understanding and acceptance of social and cultural patterns that are different is further evidenced through the attitudes of suspicion, hostility, animosity and fear expressed by many teachers.

Many middle class teachers and principals view Puerto Ricans in terms of the prevailing prejudices, clichés and stereotypes. Puerto Ricans are "dirty, lazy, wiry, treacherous, aggressive, 'spics,' potential rapists, and knife wielders." They are viewed as rapidly "taking over" some cities. Many Puerto Ricans are Negro. In the world of many middle class teachers, Puerto Ricans are dark, unintelligible, ominous and threatening. All this is contrary to middle class experience; middle class individuals are not like this. It is much better to teach one's own. If it is not possible to teach one's own, then every attempt must be made to pattern members of the out-group upon models found within one's own group.

The middle class perspective of teachers and principals is reinforced by that of boards of education whose members reflect middle class norms and values. The result is the development of the school as an institution that teaches lower class Puerto Rican students only from its perspective. This middle class orientation of education has so influenced many urban schools that Puerto Rican students lose interest in the programs offered.

Urban education tends to push ahead the mobile middle class individual. Puerto Ricans, however, are not similarly selected and trained for mobility. For most Puerto Rican students, emphasis is placed upon learning the values and norms of middle class people, rather than upon the academic and other related knowledge and skills that are necessary if lower class Puerto Rican students are to compete with middle class North American students.

As a result of the middle class nature of the urban school, a sharp clash of cultural and class values, identifications and loyalties, develops. The meaning of this clash becomes clear when Puerto Ricans are encouraged to shed their identifications and loyalties as Puerto Ricans and assume those of middle class North Americans. In a sense, the school, in requiring Puerto Ricans to suppress and reject their values, loyalties and identifications, is engaging in a direct assault upon the personal and cultural identities of Puerto Rican students.

The education of Puerto Ricans must be understood within the context of this conflict in cultural and social class values. North American middle class teachers like to teach students who are well dressed, well behaved, who study a great deal, and who will follow obediently whatever instructions are given. Teaching is less difficult and students seem to be learning with ease. When lower-class Puerto Rican students are taught, however, the teachers are confronted with many different social and cultural patterns of behavior. Lower class Puerto Rican students are not always oriented to school and they often attend school only because their parents send them to school or because of compulsory education laws. To many Puerto Rican students, much of North American middle class teaching is uninteresting and unrealistic. North American middle class teachers attempt to motivate Puerto Rican students and reward them in an effort to secure their attention and interest. Brightly colored stars or pictures of animals are distributed to reward good work in the elementary school. In the high school there may be talk of future work as doctors or lawyers. But Puerto Rican students are not always motivated by these techniques, partly because of the seeming impossibility of attainment of these goals, and partly because they may not have appropriate parental or other family models that they can emulate. For many Puerto Rican students the urban school becomes a marketplace of unreality and alienation.

Puerto Rican students attempt to escape from the urban classroom through inattention, daydreaming, talking, playing in the classroom, and absenteeism, especially in the high school. Many Puerto Rican students become hostile and resistant to the unrealities in the urban schools and to the assaults made upon their personal and cultural identities by teachers and principals. When resistance and hostility are expressed in the classroom, the urban school teacher reprimands and punishes, often at great length. In addition, certain moral connotations are added to the teacher's response to resistance and hostility and Puerto Rican students learn, either overtly or subtly, that they are considered bad, immoral, disorderly, evil and unable to succeed in school. When the urban teacher does this, he is exhibiting, in a sociological sense, symbols of higher status, and he is requesting, at the same time, the prestige and deference he believes should be accorded to him by his students.

As the culture conflict in the schools becomes more pronounced, a complex arrangement of rhetoric, myth and reality emerges. The rhetoric describes the optimum program of education that is to be provided for Puerto Rican students. The rhetoric further describes the problems that exist in educating Puerto Rican students and the efforts that are being made to resolve those problems. The result, in fact, is widespread academic retardation among Puerto Rican students, failure of the schools to come to grips with the problems and conflicts in the education of Puerto Rican students, and, in general, a breakdown in education for Puerto Ricans. As rhetoric and reality confront one another, a dangerous myth emerges. This myth holds that education for Puerto Rican students is highly successful and that, while there are many problems and difficulties, these problems are the result of inadequate family experience, deprived home conditions and unsatisfactory and hostile attitudes of the students. The myth further states that education for Puerto Rican students is at least as good as, and generally much better than, the education offered to the immigrants who came from Europe decades ago.

What, then, is urban education accomplishing? Insofar as Puerto Rican students are concerned, it is excluding them from the academic channel that is essential if they are to compete with more privileged middle class students. Urban education, as currently constituted, holds Puerto Rican students at a lower class level and prevents upward social mobility that could improve their life chance. A concomitant of this process is increasing social divisiveness and discontent, a result of the inequality in education opportunity offered to Puerto Rican students.

Teachers, principals, school guidance personnel, social workers and other professionals responsible for school programs represent key factors in the education of Puerto Rican students. All too often, however, these professionals lack the sociological sophistication that could improve the teaching of Puerto Ricans. As a result, educational programs often reflect and are built upon stereotypes, misconceptions, prejudicial attitudes and a general lack of knowledge of the realities and significance of social class and cultural differences. Students of the social and behavioral sciences have not given sufficient attention to the specific problems posed by the relationships between the Puerto Rican lower-class culture and the middle class North American urban education programs.

We have reached an impasse built upon ignorance, suspicions and fear. If we begin to learn what we need to know about the realities of the Puerto Rican experience, our ignorance, suspicions and fears can be reduced somewhat, and we may begin to extricate ourselves and the urban schools from their current untenable plight --the failure of North American education to provide effectively for the education of Puerto Ricans.

THE PUERTO RICAN FAMILY AND ISLAND BACKGROUNDS

C. J. Bodarsky

CHAPERONAGE AND THE PUERTO RICAN MIDDLE CLASS

[Abstract: Attitudes toward the custom of chaperonage are examined in a sample of Puerto Rican students and their parents. Predominantly favorable attitudes indicate that the custom, although more relaxed, still persists and is viewed as functional by its adherents despite the influence of American culture.]

A frequently expressed belief in Puerto Rico is that the traditional Spanish customs are disappearing under the onslaught of the American cultural invasion. Although the precise nature of chaperonage has been modified to meet the needs of the current tempo of Puerto Rican life,[2] the custom of chaperonage, as a psychological commitment to external controls to assure acceptable behavior, does not appear to be an immediate victim.

Methodology and Sample. A sample of 10 Puerto Rican high school seniors, half boys and half girls, was selected for participation in a cross-culture study. All students chosen for the study had demonstrated superior competence in academic, extracurricular, and social behavior during high school. The students were interviewed four times during their senior year in order to determine psychological factors influencing their superior performance. During their freshman year at college, an interview was conducted with the students' parents, focusing upon areas such as their goals for the son or daughter, changes in the student since college, and how the college was chosen. Several additional interviews with the students were conducted during freshman and sophomore years. The author visited the 18 Puerto Rican families in the study (two students had North American parents residing in Puerto Rico) over a period of almost two years (1960-62). These visits took place in the families' homes and afforded an opportunity for an intensive introduction to a

Puerto Rican cultural stratum which has not been significantly studied: the middle class.

Results. Only one of the fathers in the study said that he disapproved of the custom of chaperoning; only two mothers stated that they did not approve of it. The one mother who disapproved of the custom had been divorced and was interviewed at her home in the United States where she and the student were living. The other couple who disapproved of chaperonage consisted of a Puerto Rican husband and his American wife who had resided for some time in the United States. The remaining parents, irrespective of the sex of their children, were clearly in favor of the custom and expressed themselves at various levels of enthusiasm and sophistication.

All of the parents who expressed approval of chaperonage actually practiced it. The mothers of the girls expected to accompany their daughters on dates or to arrange for some member of the family or friend to do so. In some instances, the father accompanied the young people. The parents of sons expected that their sons would have chaperoned dates. Frequently, mothers arranged the dates for both girls and boys, especially if an important dance was scheduled.

The male students were almost equally divided in their acceptance and rejection of being chaperoned, and all but one of the girls accepted and approved of being chaperoned. The one disapproving girl was also the one female Puerto Rican student attending a university in the United States, and her mother was the only parent who disapproved of chaperonage.

Four themes were presented by the parents as rationale for continuing the custom of chaperoning their young people. The most frequently expressed were: (a) the fear that people would gossip if it were not done; (b) young people were considered less responsible now; (c) it was necessary to teach good behavior and how to control oneself; and (d) since Latins are more passionate by nature, the girls require protection.

The concern that people would gossip was generally accepted as sufficient reason for protecting the girl's reputation by chaperoning her. This anxiety about gossip was often presented as being so strong that only a native Puerto Rican could appreciate its importance. The most meaningful way to appreciate the intensity and tenacity of these families' feelings about chaperonage is to consider their often passionately expressed comments.

The point was frequently made that the parents trusted their son or daughter but did not feel comfortable about "other young people." These "other young people" were considered to be wild and dangerous, and it was against them that their own sons and daughters had to be protected:

"I think chaperoning is necessary because it seems to me boys behave differently now from when I was a boy. There is more drinking, and they drive cars very wildly, and as you know, I think that Latins are more passionate than North Americans, and if you mix this with alcohol. . . . "

Another couple indicated their trust in their daughter, their concern about gossip, and the mother's general wariness of boys:

"My daughter has been chaperoned by me up to last year, but now I permit her to go out in groups, never alone. Sometimes we permit her to go to a dance in groups, and chaperoning is necessary or one's daughter will be free on the lips of everyone. We are sure she wouldn't do anything wrong, but the harmful gossip. . . . If I lived in New York City, I would want to chaperone her. I know that I couldn't but I would have to know the boy very well, because I trust girls but not boys. "

The study did not attempt to study the frequency with which chaperonage was practiced throughout the island and among various classes of Puerto Ricans. Most of the parents did report that the precise nature of chaperonage was changing in the direction of less restrictiveness. Groups of girls may now go to the movies or a dance together, and a girl may go unchaperoned to the library or a church activity during daylight hours with a boy friend. The rigidity of the process which many parents described as characteristic of their own youth (for example, a daylight trip to the drugstore by a young girl occasioned parental involvement) no longer seems representative of the custom, and this former fierce protectiveness and total control has been ameliorated.

Conclusions. The custom of chaperonage may have become, for this class of Puerto Ricans, a status symbol which represents their aspirations in society. Chaperonage does require leisure time, money, an automobile, and access to clubs, and it assures the social movement of the young people within an acceptable group. Its practice could be considered as evidence of the family's socio-economic level. Chaperonage frequently requires that the parents socialize with each other while the young people dance, and these occasions probably provide reassuring contacts for the parents.

The ideology of freedom of mate selection with its corresponding courtship practices does not appear to be characteristic of this sample. However, it should not be assumed that the chaperonage system necessarily militates against a self-expressive process of mate selection. Most of the dates of the subjects reflected personal preference and choice. Within the dating experience, however, experimentation is limited and privacy curtailed. This tends to limit interpersonal experiences and to surround them with obstacles which act to discourage the less aggressive youth.

Notes

1. Supported by USPH (NIMH) Grant No. 3M9175 (C1) at the Puerto

Rico Institute of Psychiatry. E. D. Raldonado-Sierra,
C. J. Bodarky, P. B. Field, S. E. Wallace, R. Fernandez-
Marina, G. V. Coelho, Richard D. Trent, Arlene Cohen,
and Francisco J. Umpierre constituted the professional research team for the project. Carol De Dov has aided in
the preparation of this paper. See E. Silber, G. V. Coelho,
E. B. Murphey, D. A. Hamburg, L. I. Pearlin, and M. Rosenberg, "Competent Adolescents Coping with College Decisions,"
AMA Archives of General Psychiatry, 5 (1961), pp. 517-527;
and E. Silber, D. A. Hamburg, G. V. Coelho, E. B. Murphey, M. Rosenberg, and L. I. Pearlin, "Adaptive Behavior
in Competent Adolescents," Ibid., pp. 354-365.
2. Reuben Hill, "Courtship in Puerto Rico: An Institution in
Transition," Marriage and Family Living, 17 (February
1955), pp. 26-35.

THE LOWER STATUS PUERTO RICAN FAMILY

(1) In discussing the Puerto Rican family, one must remember at all times that the society of this West Indian island is part of a wider Spanish-speaking world, which in turn is part of our Western civilization. Thus, in the final analysis, the family in Puerto Rico should be expected to have a great deal in common with the family in Spain, Ireland, Sweden, the United States, et al.

Our interest in this discussion, however, is focused on Puerto Rico, and consequently we shall deal with specific local-historical percularities found in Puerto Rican society. In so doing one should be careful not to overstate the significance of these peculiarities, as over against the more widely shared characteristics of family life in the total European-American culture area.

(2) In concentrating on one particular national society out of several dozen constituting the European-American world one runs into more differences of degree than those of structure. Thus all societies of that area are monogamous. Some of them, however, are more rigorous in opposing adultery, concubinage, divorce and pre-marital experimentation than others. None of the Western societies has placed the wife's and mother's authority legally or socially above that of the father's and husband's. Yet it is known that male authority is weaker in Denmark than, let us say, in Greece.

(3) It is also important to keep in mind that statements regarding national or class characteristics are at best probabilistic in nature. When we say that the cult of gastronomy is typically French, we actually mean that we are likely to find more individuals valuing the refinements of cuisine among the French than, for in-

---

Unpublished paper, Graduate School of Arts and Sciences, New York University (March 1963).

7

stance, in England. Thus all statements about Puerto Rican modes of behavior made in this essay must be understood as referring to their relative frequencies.

(4) The title of this article points out that our concern here is with the lower status Puerto Rican family. One knows that comparative social status can be defined in terms of numerous criteria, such as income, housing, occupation, education, clothes, manners, peculiarities of speech, racial origins, church membership, etc. In most cases the identification of social status must be based on several such criteria, which occur in consistent and meaningful clusters.

(5) When dealing with the social status of an immigrant group one must consider one at a time the standards of status rating applied to it by the majority society (mainland Americans in our case) and those of the immigrant group itself. To many prejudiced mainland Americans all Puerto Ricans in the United States are low status people with just a few individual exceptions. A member of the Puerto Rican community, on the other hand, may be keenly aware of a wide range of status differences among his fellow islanders.

(6) The status rating of individual immigrant families by their own community is never identical with the one they enjoyed on native grounds. When moving from the island to New York City many a Puerto Rican family undergoes a loss of "accumulated social assets." In its new position as occupant of a cold-water flat on Tenth Avenue in Manhattan it finds itself down-graded, with no neighbors aware of the good social standing it enjoyed in the native environment.

(7) The same process, however, may operate in reverse and be described in terms of a loss of "accumulated social blemishes." Thus a family which at home had labored under an established unfavorable reputation, may, under the protection of metropolitan anonymity, be able to make a fresh start and move upwards on the socio-economic ladder.

(8) Of the many criteria of lower social status listed above, poverty seems to us the most significant one. If one excepts the cases of recent and accidental reverses of fortune, poverty is most meaningfully related to other such earmarks as housing, clothes, manners, level of literacy, etc.

(9) How much poverty is there on the island of Puerto Rico today? The economic advances made by the island society since the establishment of the semi-autonomous Commonwealth of Puerto Rico in 1952 have been quite spectacular. At the same time, the well-deserved publicity given them by the press has obscured the picture of mass destitution which remains widespread. Here are some figures based on the population census of 1960: (Based on Boricua, La Revista de Puerto Rico. Diciembre 1962, p. 31)

18.2 per cent of the families have an
    annual income of more than $3,000

33.8 per cent of the families have an
    annual income between $3,000-$1,000

16.9 per cent of the families have an
    annual income between $1,000-$ 500

31   per cent of the families have an
    annual income of less than $500

The extreme forms of poverty are alleviated by various Commonwealth programs: free school lunches, free shoes for impecunious school children, free outpatient clinics, free hospitalization, visiting nursing services, pension and relief plans, low income housing and the distribution of surplus food made available by the Federal Government.

Well-planned and generous as these policies have been they have not done away with mass poverty and all its usual concomitants.

(10) It is sometimes assumed that the cost of living in Puerto Rico must be much lower than in the continental United States. This is only partially true. The climate of the island, of course, makes it unnecessary to own warm clothes or to spend money on heating the homes. The alimentary needs of the body are also somewhat lower in the sub-tropical Caribbean area. On the other hand, Puerto Rico is dependent on imported foods including such national staples as rice, beans, wheat flour and dried codfish (bacalao). The cost of freight is added to the prices of these staples. Clothes, domestic appliances and cars also cost more on the island than in the United States.

(11) One could claim, nevertheless, that extreme poverty is a bit more bearable in a place where temperature is never below 68°. Children have no lack of natural playgrounds; the aged lounge on benches around the plaza of their community, neighbors spend long hours socializing outside their small and inadequate dwellings, and many a homeless man may find a shed or a driveway where no one would disturb his sleep. Streams and water-holes in the mountain areas and the beaches along the coast provide accessible facilities for bathing and swimming. Cooking can be done on open-air improvised stoves (fogon). Furthermore starchy fruits such as panapen (breadfruit) are plentiful and inexpensive as emergency resources. There is no intent in these remarks to play down the drama of poverty, disease and loneliness to which many human beings fall prey in Puerto Rico. Yet for purely comparative purposes attention is being called to the relatively less tragic fate of the poor in the less inclement climate of the Caribbean area.

(12) The poor of Puerto Rico are of two basic types--urban

and rural. Rural folk are in turn divided into those of the lowlands of the coast, and the dwellers of the highlands. The urban poor may be either of recent rural origin or with an older urban background.

Town people tend to call all rural folk jíbaros. Coastal rural groups feel insulted by this term and apply it to the farmers of the mountainous interior. But even these farmers would sometimes use the term in referring to another hamlet or community while excluding themselves from this category. Thus not many people openly identify themselves as jíbaros while the term is used loosely with regard to a wide range of socio-economic types.

(13) The reluctance to regard oneself as a jíbaro conflicts with the idealization of this type by the literati and intellectuals of the island. The jíbaro has been portrayed by them as the true carrier of the Puerto Rican folk tradition. He was the authentic native "son of the earth" marked off by his own inimitable sense of humor, practical wisdom, shrewdness in his dealings with city people, and a strong spirit of independence. All jíbaro proverbs, sayings, songs, games, superstitions, tales of supernaturalism and works of craftsmanship (e.g. home-made string instruments, figures of saints, i.e. santos, carved out of wood, et al.) have been reverentially collected and enshrined in the public mind or in public collections.

(14) What sober statements can one make about this sizeable and yet elusive element in the population of Puerto Rico? "True" jíbaros appear to be descended from the predominantly white early settlers of the interior of the island. Geographical isolation combined with poverty has made them the least literate element in the insular society, and the least familiar with the urban way of life. Not many true jíbaros have had the daring, for instance, to migrate to New York City. Those who did had spent first a few years in one of the coastal shanty-towns or slum suburbs in Puerto Rico, where they underwent a bit of acculturation to city ways.

The well-known drama La Carreta (1952) by René Marqués portrays the social fate of such a family. In the first act they are shown leaving their home in the mountains under the pressure of economic circumstances. In the second act we witness their trials and tribulations in the coastal slums of Puerto Rico. The third and last act of the play portrays them as "adjusted" to the urban ways of The Bronx as well as victims of unscrupulous individuals and of industrial accidents.

(15) Many jíbaros are landless and propertyless agricultural workers who meet their subsistence needs by selling their labor power. Some of them own their homes but do not always own the lot on which the dwelling is located. Others live rent-free in the home provided by their employer. Occupying a house erected on lands belonging to another person qualifies them as "squatters"

(agregados) and implies various customary obligations with regard to the owner of the holding.

Those jíbaros who are agricultural wage-earners without property or any outside income are often forced to play a subservient role with regard to their potential or virtual employers, the store-keeper from whom they buy their groceries on credit between the harvest seasons (zafras), the wealthier neighbors who may give a temporary job to their wife or son, and to many others. They teach their children to behave with proper humility and to render services to their more powerful neighbors and even playmates.

(16) In a somewhat different category are those jíbaros who own enough land to depend for survival on subsistence farming. They raise marketable crops of fluctuating value (such as tobacco or coffee) and supplement cash income with some vegetables, fruit, chickens and pigs grown and raised by their own efforts. In jíbaro families of this type the father finds himself in the role of taskmaster and foreman, whose job is to extract as much work as he can from his small family group. At the same time, he also controls the family expenditures and is thus cast in the role of an occasional "kill-joy." The same function, however, gives him a chance to make a show of generosity and affection by buying things for the home or clothes for his wife and children.

(17) Halfway between the wage-earner and the small land holder is the share-cropper. In the tobacco area he splits with the owner of the land the costs of production and shares in the half of the proceeds. Traditionally share-croppers press the members of their family into work in the fields or into services to the landlord and thus again they are found in the role of taskmasters and disciplinarians.

(18) As elsewhere in the Spanish-speaking world, the Puerto Rican jíbaro family is also governed by male authority. The jíbaro man who has limited claims to social and economic prestige is strongly dependent on his wife's and children's deferential attitudes (particularly in the presence of outside observers) for his ego-gratification. Many a jíbaro's wife does not begrudge her husband this privilege since indirectly it enhances her own social standing as well. She feels that there is no honor attached to being married to a weak and unmanly husband. In fact, she may even tend to exaggerate his dictatorial masculinity and portray herself as a masochistic victim in the hands of a strong virile tyrant.

(19) Where male authoritarianism appears to be a socially recognized norm, women quite commonly evolve indirect methods of defense and compensation. The ailing wife and mother (without being an outright malingerer) often uses her afflictions to secure sympathy and a more lenient treatment. Threats of suicide and frequent unsuccessful attempts at suicide (suicides manqués) by Puerto Rican women have been diagnosed by careful observers as attention-getting devices. Quite often, however, suicide in Puerto Rico is committed in an irretrievable manner. The Anglo-American

imagination is particularly struck by those cases where the victim soaks her clothes in gasoline and sets herself on fire. Several such cases occur every year along with more numerous but less spectacular forms of self-destruction.

(20) The jíbaro mother makes up for her inferior social position by gaining her children's (her sons' in particular) affection and attachment. She may do that by protecting the guilty boy from his father's anger, by passing small amounts of spending money to him and in many other ways. The image of his "suffering mother" has been found deeply embedded in the mind of many a Puerto Rican adolescent boy or grown man. Most Puerto Rican men regard themselves as natural protectors of their mothers when they are victims of desertion, widowhood, poverty or social abuse.

(21) The jíbaros are known to be proud of their numerous progeny, which symbolizes the father's procreative vigor and also represents the poor man's only "wealth." It is indeed a proud day in an individual jíbaro's life when he walks to a fiesta in the nearest center surrounded by his small flock of four or five children.

(22) The rural folk of the coastal plains are not drastically different from the jíbaros of the highlands. Nevertheless, several points of distinction should be brought out. To begin with, most of them are employed by either government operated or privately owned sugar cane plantations. They thus are landless laborers entirely dependent on their wages for a living. They more than often live in primitive barracks where each family occupies a one or two-room dwelling (without cooking or toilet facilities) or a section in a similarly inadequate multiple dwelling. They are surrounded on all sides by temporary tenants like themselves and have no illusions of independence that go along with the ownership (by a jíbaro) of a small home in the relatively inaccessible mountain fastness. The comparative crowding which characterizes their life deprives them of all privacy and affects their sense of dignity.

(23) The family of a sugar cane worker is more a unit of consumption than of production. The head of the family does not have to act as a task-master since he rarely has access to any gardening or poultry raising facilities where members of his family might be engaged in productive work. As soon as his sons or daughters reach the age of marriage or become employable they tend to strike out for themselves and drift away to wherever work can be secured.

(24) Workers in the cane and their families are also in a much less personal relationship with their employers (private owners, corporation representatives, supervisers, foremen, et al) than the rural folk of the highlands. For practical and traditional reasons the jíbaros of the interior have to live up to the standards of conduct acceptable to wealthier neighbors on whose goodwill they ofen depend, i. e. the store-keepers who sell to them on credit, landowners on whose land they build their homes, local politicians

and other power-wielders. This may account for a somewhat higher rate of the more respectable church weddings and for more regular attendance at church services in the mountain area, also for a somewhat stronger resistance to the inroads of Protestantism.

Correspondingly, the sugar-cane workers of the coast have a much higher incidence of the less respectable consensual or common-law unions and have proven more receptive to the appeals of Protestant proselytizers.

(25) The urban poor of the island are much more open to observation on the part of the middle class and upper class people of the cities than are the jíbaros. The slums and shanty-towns of Puerto Rico are adjacent to the more respectable neighborhoods and no one can escape the sight of human misery which they harbor. The city poor more often come to the attention of medical men, hospital personnel, social workers, police authorities, school teachers, members of the clergy and other professional people. This being the case it is rather surprising to discover that sociologists and other researchers in Puerto Rico have given them less attention than rural populations.

(26) This element in the population of the island is of course much more diversified than anything one would observe in the countryside. We find among them widows with or without dependent children, abandoned wives, jilted girls, orphans, invalids subsisting on small pensions, uprooted jíbaros, unemployed and unemployable individuals of every possible origin, mentally inadequate persons, women of easy virtue, and many aged people (single or in couples), et al. They survive by engaging in a wide variety of small and often temporary occupations as pedlars, delivery men, unskilled repairmen, gardeners, part-time domestics, lottery ticket salesmen, newsboys, etc. Some of their activities conflict with municipal regulations, police rules and law in general. This would be true of illegal number games (bolita), the sale of privately manufactured rum (canita), prostitution, etc. Centuries of existence under indifferent and inefficient administrations combined with widespread poverty have resulted in much more lenient attitudes toward these "marginal" and outlawed occupations than a moralist conditioned by life in prosperous democratic communities would expect. Here is an area where one has to approach human behavior with a bit of historical perspective and the faculty of empathy.

(27) Government relief, municipal aid, private charity and sporadic contributions by relatives keep many of these city poor not only alive but less unhappy than one might imagine them to be. In part this is due, as pointed out earlier, to the climate of the island, but also to the gift of sociability with which the people of Puerto Rico are so richly endowed.

(28) One of its expressions is their extreme fondness for children. In giving their care and affection to children, the Puerto Ricans are less proprietary than other Europeans and Americans.

They easily make room in their poor and crowded homes for children of divorced parents, illegitimate offspring, orphans, abandoned children and foster children (hijos de crianza) in general. Many people enter marriage while having children by previous common law or legalized marriages. It is not unusual to have a family with three or four children none of whom are the offspring of the married couple. As a rule such adopted children or children by previous marriages are treated as well as their adoptive parents' joint progeny.

(29) A special type of relationship known as godparenthood (compadrazgo) can also be considered as a partial corrective to poverty and loneliness among lower status Puerto Ricans. A person sponsoring a child at baptism and christening becomes his life-long godfather (padrino) or godmother (madrina). Where two godparents (compadres) preside over the same ritual this co-participation establishes a special social tie between them. Similarly all godparents are bound in a special way to the biological parents of their godchild. Thus most Puerto Ricans have ritually sanctioned friends, allies, protectors and confidants. The practical value of such a relationship may vary from case to case. Nevertheless, the institution of godparenthood obviously extends the individual's trust and reliance beyond the immediate family, and in some cases provides a person with a substitute for a defaulting family group.

(30) The love of children so common in Puerto Rico appears in a somewhat less idyllic light if viewed against the background of demographic statistics. In 1940 the population of the island was 1,869,255. In 1950 it had reached the figure of 2,210,703 and in 1960 it was 2,349,544. The total land area of the island being 3,421 square miles, the population density of Puerto Rico is nearing the ratio of 700 per square mile, one of the highest in the world. Considering the slender natural resources of the island, the situation is rapidly reaching the point of critical intensity.

(31) There are three basic ways of relieving this growing population pressure: birth control through contraception, emigration and industrialization. All three have been encouraged by the government of the Commonwealth, unfortunately with inconclusive results. Contraception has met with strong opposition on the part of the Roman Catholic Church, which has, however, failed to reverse its growing popularity. Industrialization, combined with tourism, has created numerous jobs and indirect sources of income for the island treasury with its heavy programs of social welfare. And, finally, emigration has relieved some of the immediate pressure on the island economy by reducing the number of unemployed and encouraging the flow of subsidies by emigrants to their needy kin.

(32) The advocacy of contraception has also run into non-religious opposition. Some Puerto Rican men have been reported as feeling that the use of contraceptives was humiliating to their wives or to their own male dignity (or both). Other observers have claimed that shyness and awkwardness in communication

between married people made the use of contraception difficult. The provisional figures of birth rate for 1961 give 23.4 (per 1,000 population) for the United States, 31.0 for Puerto Rico. Nevertheless there has been a steady decline in the successive birth rate figures over ten years. The much sharper rate of decline in the rates of mortality, however, has neutralized the limited gains made by the application of birth control.

(33) We have mentioned earlier the frequency of common law (consensual) marriages among lower status Puerto Ricans. Dr. Sidney Mintz in focusing on one specific rural area (which he calls Barrio Jauca) has established the fact that out of 183 marital unions 134 were of the consensual variety. [1] For the island at large the ratio of such common law marriages has been variously estimated between 25 per cent and 35 per cent of the total. The historical roots of this practice go too far to be examined here. The phenomenon is not restricted to Puerto Rico but has been observed throughout the Caribbean area and in parts of South America.

(34) Dr. Mintz shows very clearly that such marriages are as a rule initiated by means of a socially standardized procedure (a "ritualized elopement") which is viewed by the community as equivalent to more traditional legal and religious observances. [2]

(35) Children born to such unions suffer only minor social disadvantages in their home areas, but run into inconveniences and embarrassments when they migrate to the cities or to the mainland of the United States. This is due to the growing importance of pension plans, social security benefits, veteran pensions and insurance policies, all of which have to rely on properly legalized relationships between spouses and between parents and children.

(36) In the meantime people say that "vale más un buen amancebado que un matrimonio mal llevado" (a good consensual union is worth more than a bad marriage). The prohibition of divorce by the Roman Catholic Church has also been used to justify consensual unions where the two parties are not tied to each other for life. The growth of Protestant congregations in Puerto Rico may be in part due to the toleration of divorces by most of them, even though their strong emphasis on personal morals obviously checks the trend toward easy divorces.

(37) From the Anglo-American point of view one of the striking features of Puerto Rican marriage relationship is the prevalence of jealousy. As could be expected, male infidelities are somewhat more frequent and less rigorously condemned by the community. When the woman's husband shows a decline of personal interest in his wife, she is likely to seek "professional" advice from a spiritualist medium or a practitioner of folk-medicine (or folk-magic).

When a man suspects his wife of growing indifference he looks around for a possible rival and is very likely to challenge and even assault the presumed seducer. Painful and dramatic as they

are these tensions and actions are indicative of somewhat higher
romantic and erotic expectations on the part of married lower status
Puerto Ricans than what we observe in our more placid and sedate
society.

(38)   The Puerto Rican family as we find it in New York
(or Philadelphia, Chicago, Boston, etc.) should not be expected to
be a duplicate of its counterpart on the island.   To begin with,
mainland Puerto Ricans are keenly aware of the social prejudice
they encounter on the mainland.   Two conflicting reactions to social
hostility may take place.   The members of a family group may, so
to say, "close their ranks," i.e. experience an intensified sense of
solidarity and view their home as a haven of refuge.   The other
possible reaction is that of resentment against the group to which
they belong, whose characteristics are the alleged cause of its rejection by the outside world.

(39)   Where local prejudice against Puerto Ricans assumes
racialist undertones (which seems to be always the case), it may
have a divisive effect on family unity and solidarity.   Puerto Rico
is a land of racially mixed marriages (particularly in the lower
social strata), and children in many homes run the whole gamut of
pigmentation from the very dark to the Mediterranean light.   In the
North American social environment lighter-complexioned youngsters
have a better chance of social and occupational acceptance than their
darker siblings.   Brothers and sisters are thus separated by differential opportunities, and envy and resentment enter their life.

The same factors may invade the relationship between two
differently colored spouses or in-laws, or grandparents and grand-
children.   The dark grandmother who hides in the kitchen while her
lighter granddaughter, a high school girl, entertains her classmate
in the living room, could serve as a symbol of the impact of race
prejudice on the Puerto Rican family in New York.

(40)   Another source of anxieties among mainland Puerto
Ricans is constituted by their gradual loss of influence over their
children.   In the natural course of events, Puerto Rican children
learn English better and faster than their parents.   With the language they acquire a whole world of values, attitudes and rules of
adolescent etiquette which remain incomprehensible to their elders.
Before long, the English-speaking child may serve as an interpreter
in his mother's or father's dealings with the outside world and may
come to feel that his parents are unsuited to the American way of
life, or even "inferior."

(41)   Quite often Puerto Rican women have an easier chance
of finding employment than their husbands in our city economy, and
thus become principal family providers.   With this economic change
goes a re-definition of male authority, and many a family head feels
that something has gone wrong in his domestic life.   Some accept
their new dependence on their more successful wives and turn to a
half-way justifiable idleness.   In the meantime, the unemployed man's

children lose their traditional respect for him, and refuse to accept his attempts at reasserting his authority.

(42) Many other changes take place in Puerto Rican family life in the new social environment. At home they lived under what sociologists call "primary social controls," i.e. in small close-knit communities, where neighbors, relatives, storekeepers, school teachers and all others exercised a restraining influence on individual behavior. The anonymity of New York life makes them feel uncomfortably free, "on their own," and also fearful of how this might affect those loved ones (wife, daughters, sons, etc.) whose behavior they would like to supervise.

(43) The easy and casual sociability of the island has also been affected by the new urban world. The climate of the mainland and big city traffic have made street life of the Caribbean type next to impossible. Instead of occupying small family homes with doors and windows open on the outside world, New York Puerto Ricans find themselves living in isolated apartments behind closed doors.

(44) Numerous other material details undergo far-reaching changes, e.g. methods of laundering, patterns of cooking, sleeping arrangements, shopping practices, etc. ad infinitum. None of these taken by itself may be viewed as profoundly significant; in combination they change the whole style of living. Eventually the values of the island give way to something new and different.

(45) When an entire ethnic group is undergoing such a change, it should not be assumed that its individual members will move along at the same pace or will react to the challenges of transformation in the same manner. Family circles may thus be expected to be torn between nostalgic homesick old-timers, ambitious and pushing opportunists and the more rational synthesizers between the old and the new. The island home which was left behind becomes idealized and/or vilified quite realistically, just as the urban world of mainland America is extolled or run down in accordance with the fluctuating circumstances and changing moods. The influx of new migrants from the island keeps alive the overall ambivalent attitudes of the Puerto Rican community. Numerous individuals get tempted by the short distance and the low airplane fares and go home, only to turn around and come back to New York.

(46) Trying to describe and understand the lower status Puerto Rican family of our day is on the whole not easy. The island society is undergoing numerous changes, briefly identifiable by such terms as urbanization, industrialization, secularization, welfare economy, diffusion of literacy, growing life span, increasing population, etc. When individual Puerto Rican families fly over to the mainland and attempt an adjustment to the new socio-economic world of the United States, they find themselves subjected to numerous additional pressures. Neither back home nor here in the States can their existence be described as stable and secure. Thus in

order to understand any specific Puerto Rican family group one has to "locate" it on the total map of social change which this national society is undergoing at this time.

Selected Bibliography

Bram, Joseph	Spirits, Mediums and Believers in Contemporary Puerto Rico, <u>Transactions of the New York Academy of Sciences</u>, Ser. II, Vol. 20, No. 4, pp. 340-347, February 1958
Hansen, E.	<u>Transformation: The Story of Puerto Rico, 1955</u>
Hatt, R. K.	<u>Backgrounds of Human Fertility in Puerto Rico, 1952</u>
Landy, David	<u>Tropical Childhood,</u> Cultural Transmission and Learning in a Rural Puerto Rican Village, 1959
Mills, C. W. , C. Senior and R. Goldsen.	<u>The Puerto Rican Journey,</u> 1950.
Mintz, Sidney W.	<u>Worker in the Cane. A Puerto Rican Life Story,</u> 1960
Roberts, L. J. and R. L. Stefani	<u>Patterns of Living in Puerto Rican Families,</u> 1949
Rogler, Charles	<u>Comerio. A Study of a Puerto Rican Town,</u> 1940.
Sereno, R.	Cryptomelanism: A Study of Color Relations and Personal Insecurity in Puerto Rico. <u>Psychiatry</u> 10: 261-269, 1947
Steward, J. H. et al	<u>The People of Puerto Rico,</u> 1956
Stycos, J. M.	<u>Family and Fertility in Puerto Rico,</u> 1955
Tugwell, R. G.	<u>The Stricken Land,</u> 1947
Wolf, K. L.	Growing Up and Its Price in Three Puerto Rican Subcultures. <u>Psychiatry</u> 15:401-433, 1952

Notes

1. Sidney W. Mintz, - <u>Worker in the Cane. A Puerto Rican Life Story.</u> Yale University Press. 1960. pp. 89-92.
2. <u>Ibid.</u>

Ceferino Carrasquillo

HISTORICAL DEVELOPMENT OF THE PUERTO RICAN
SPANISH LANGUAGE CURRICULUM
DURING THE TWENTIETH CENTURY
(1900-1965)

[Abstract: The Puerto Rican Spanish language curriculum has been
confronted with many problems and approaches since the United
States' domination began there in 1898.   The imposition of the
English language in Puerto Rico had contributed, in part, to creating controversies and misunderstandings among the people.   Puerto
Rican society has placed great emphasis on the educational system
of the Island.   The history of the twentieth century reveals a period
of efforts to improve the quality and quantity of the educational level
of the people of Puerto Rico.]

Educational Languages Policies and Changes

Before 1898, the Spanish language was used as a medium of instruction in Puerto Rican schools.   It was also studied as a subject.
After the American domination which began on May 12, 1898, differ-
end approaches came into effect depending on who was Commissioner
of Education at that time.   John R. Brook became the first military governor of Puerto Rico.   He was succeeded by General Guy
V. Henry, who eliminated the Spanish Administration.   Brigadier
General George W. Davis succeeded Henry and remained in office
until May 1, 1900.   In 1900, the United States conceded the Foraker Act to Puerto Rico, creating a Civil Government and making
provisions for the creation of a Commissioner of Education.   It is
stated in the same Act:

> ... That the Commissioner of Education shall super-
> intend public instruction throughout Puerto Rico and all
> disbursements on account thereof must be approved by
> him, and he shall perform such other duties as may be
> required by the Commissioner of Education of the United
> States. ... [1]

Mr. Martin G. Braumbaugh was appointed on August 8, 1900, as the first Commissioner of Education. Dr. Braumbaugh's language policy recognized the importance of preserving the Spanish language while the students acquired knowledge of English. He introduced English as a subject in all the grades of the elementary school, and English became the language of instruction in the high school.[2] Dr. Braumbaugh left Puerto Rico in 1902 and was succeeded by Samuel McCune Lindsay who followed the educational language policy of Dr. Braumbaugh. Mr. Lindsay left Puerto Rico in 1904 and Roland P. Falkner became Commissioner and remained such until 1907. Upon his arrival on the island, great language changes occurred in the Puerto Rican educational system. He made English the official language of the school.[3] English was the medium of instruction in all the subjects of the curriculum except Spanish.[4] Falkner explained his language policy in the following words:

> As outlined in my last report, we adopted a new plan in the teaching of English. Being fully convinced that no really practical results in this work could be obtained until instruction in all subjects was given in English, I put all grades above the first on the English basis, the work in all subjects except Spanish being given in that language.[5]

According to Pedro A. Cebollero, the Falkner policy was used in Puerto Rico until 1916.[6] However, the Puerto Rican community disagreed with it. Educational organizations and political groups protested the use of English as the medium of instruction.

Another means to solve the language controversy was implemented in 1916 when Paul G. Miller was appointed Commissioner of Education. He proposed the use of both languages in the fifth grade. Spanish was used as a medium of instruction in the first four grades. English became the complete medium of instruction from the sixth grade up, and Spanish was then taught only as an independent subject. As stated in his annual report:

> Spanish was used as the medium of instruction in the first four grades, English being taught as a special subject. Oral English was taught in the first grade ... The emphasis is now placed on instruction through the medium of the mother tongue in the four lower grades.[7]

Juan B. Huyke was appointed in 1921 to succeed Dr. Miller as Commissioner of Education. He continued Miller's language policy. Juan J. Osuna stated that: "In his desire to americanize Puerto Rico, he pushed the teaching of English as the means to achieve his end."[8] The Miller-Huyke policy was in practice until 1934. During this time several studies were conducted in Puerto Rico to study the language problem. In 1916, José A. Padín, Assistant Commissioner of Education, in a study titled <u>The Problem</u>

of Teaching English to the People of Puerto Rico, concluded that:
"English should not be used as a medium of instruction until the
seventh grade."[9]   On March 20, 1925 the Legislature of Puerto
Rico demanded an investigation of the organization and methods used
in the University of Puerto Rico and in the public school.   The
Commission concluded that: " ... the schools are not justified in
making English the medium of instruction until the seventh grade."
[10]   However, in spite of all recommendations, the Miller-Huyke
language policy remained in Puerto Rico until 1934.

In 1925, the University of Puerto Rico created the Department of Hispanic Studies for the purpose of teaching the Spanish
language employing the best possible methods and techniques.   The
Department offered specialized instruction in linguistics, Spanish
literature, Spanish American literature and Puerto Rican literature.
Teachers used to take courses in this Department, despite the
policies of the Department of Education minimizing the importance
of the knowledge of the Spanish language.

José A. Padín was appointed Commissioner of Education in
1930. [11]   During his four years in this position he studied the
situation and consulted with teachers and Puerto Rican leaders.
The Teachers' Association of Puerto Rico conducted a referendum
among its members concerning the language of instruction, and, an
overwhelming majority voted for the substitution of Spanish for
English. [12]

In 1934 Dr. Padín sponsored a series of studies which pointed out the need to use Spanish as the medium of instruction in the
elementary school, grades one to eight.[13]   He invited Dr. William
S. Gray, the great linguist from the University of Chicago, to study
the language problems of Puerto Rico.   Dr. Gray went to Puerto
Rico in the Spring of 1936 and among his recommendations were
the following:

1.   The major change adopted at the beginning of the cur-
     rent school year--that is, providing for the use of the
     vernacular as the sole medium of instruction (outside of
     English classes) in the first eight grades of the urban
     and rural school--represents a significant step in the
     right direction.

2.   The program outline should be revised somewhat to in-
     sure more rapid growth in the command of oral English,
     if pupils are to be prepared by the beginning of the high
     school period to use English as the medium of instruc-
     tion. [14]

José A. Padín also invited Dr. Michael West, a well-known
English educator, to Puerto Rico in the summer of 1936.   His most
significant recommendation was: "It would clearly be better to devote the English periods of first and second grades to reading in the
mother tongue, and to begin reading English when the children have

established a sound foundation of reading ability in their own language. "[15]

Padín's policy recommending the use of Spanish as the medium of instruction in the first eight grades was welcomed by a great majority of the people of Puerto Rico. However, the United States government disagreed with his policy. Dr Padín resigned in 1936 and the language questions remained unanswered. Although the Padín policy did not last many years (1934-36), it influenced the teaching of Spanish as a subject.

In 1937, José M. Gallardo became Commissioner of Education. In the academic year 1940-41, he stated:

> The teaching of English in the elementary schools of Puerto Rico has been marked during the past year by the introduction of a new distribution of the time allocated to instruction in English and Spanish. All teaching in grades one and two was in Spanish, except for one period of English conversation. [16]

Commissioner Gallardo gave certain freedom to the classroom teacher in the use of Spanish as the language of instruction. In 1942, Gallardo established that in the elementary school, grades one through six, Spanish would be the vehicle of instruction and English was to be taught as a special subject. [17] Osuna says that: "This freedom stimulated the use of vernacular more and more. "[18] However, on April 8, 1937 President Franklin D. Roosevelt sent a letter to Gallardo emphasizing the need to intensify the teaching of English in Puerto Rico. The letter says:

> Dear Mr. Gallardo:
> I have decided to appoint you Commissioner of Education of Puerto Rico, ... I desire at this time to make clear the attitude of my Administration to the extremely important matter of teaching English in Puerto Rico. ... It is regrettable that today hundreds of thousands of Puerto Ricans have little enough and virtually no knowledge of the English language ... It is an indispensable part of American policy that the coming generations of American citizens in Puerto Rico grow up with complete facility in the English tongue. It is the language of our nation. Only through the acquisition of this language will Puerto Ricans and Americans secure a better understanding of American ideals and principles. [19]

With this letter, it was understood that the President of the United States wanted English as a medium of instruction in Puerto Rico. Dr. Gallardo abandoned the policy of Dr. Padín and began a series of trial and error. [20] The years 1937 to 1942 were characterized by the absence of a clear language policy for Puerto Rican schools. The Commissioner was pressured by the Puerto

Rican Teachers' Association [21] and by the Consejo Superior de Enseñanza (Superior Educational Council--an organization created by the Law Number 135 of 1942, known as the Leyes de Reforma Universitaria, which adopted a resolution stating that Spanish was the preferable vehicle of instruction in the University of Puerto Rico)[22] encouraging the use of Spanish as the means of instruction in all levels of education including the University. More and more teachers began using Spanish and Osuna says that "by 1944-45, it was unofficially understood that there was no harm in using the native language when the children did not understand English." Slowly, Spanish became the language of instruction, while English was taught as a subject. [23] Dr. Gallardo resigned in 1945 and Mariano Villaronga, a professor in the University of Puerto Rico, was appointed the new Commissioner of Education. His language policy could be summarized in his own words:

> ... These facts clearly demonstrate that, for maximum results, English should be taught at all levels of our school system. However, for such teaching to be effective, English should be considered as a school subject and not as the medium for teaching all other subjects. [24]

In 1947, the Superior Educational Council conducted a study of the educational problems of Puerto Rico. This study was entitled Problemas de educación en Puerto Rico (Problems of Education in Puerto Rico). In it, the Commission highly favored the use of the Spanish language in the teaching process. An analysis of the available Spanish textbooks for all curricula during 1944-47 was undertaken as well. The Commission found that few books written in Spanish were available. [25] Those books were not written with the students' interests and culture in mind. [26] In 1947, the Department of Education created a Committee for the preparation of textbooks and courses of study adapted to the cultural, political, social and economic needs of the Puerto Rican children. [27]

Since the Mariano Villaronga period, Spanish as medium of instruction was firmly incorporated into the Puerto Rican educational system. After a series of studies done in some Puerto Rican schools in 1947-48, acting Commissioner Francisco Collazo stated that Spanish was the medium of instruction in the intermediate schools of Puerto Rico. In August 1948, Spanish was used from the first to ninth grades. In November 1948, the first gubernatorial elections were held, according to the Organic Law approved by the Congress of the United States. Luis Muñoz Marín was elected governor of Puerto Rico. He took office in January of 1949 and reappointed Mariano Villaronga Commissioner of Education. Villaronga confronted the seemingly interminable language problem of Puerto Rican Education. He stated that Spanish would be the medium of instruction at all school levels in Puerto Rico beginning with the school year of 1949-50. [28] After fifty years of facing a language problem characterized by misunderstanding and confusion among educational leaders, teachers and others, Puerto Rico has solved its problems by deciding that Spanish is the language of instruction in the classroom and that English should be taught as a subject. This policy responds to the exigencies of Puerto Rico's socioeconomic evolution, "provides for the teaching of English as a second language and provides education in the other subjects in the pupil's native language."[29] Therefore, teachers received technical training in the methods of teaching English as a second language to a Spanish speaking population.

The Spanish Language Elementary School Curriculum

Before 1898, Puerto Rico did not have a specific Spanish language curriculum. The curricular programs consisted of a group of different methods and techniques with few books in use.

At the beginning of the century, Manuel Fernández Juncos, among others, translated and adapted a series of books in use at that time in the United States. Among these books were: Libro primero de lectura by Arnold and Gilbert (1899), Libro segundo de lectura and Libro tercero de lectura by Arnold and Gilbert (1901), and Libro cuarto de lectura by Keith McDermott (1902).

In 1905, a Committee appointed by Commissoner Falkner recommended, in addition to these books, the following: Cartilla by Arnold and Gilbert, Libro primero and Libro segundo by the American Book Company, three books from the series Lector Moderno by J. García Purón The Spanish Readers by Matzke and Loiseus, El pájaro verde by Juan Valera. For the teaching of grammar: Gramática castellana by Enrique C. Hernandez, Los primeros pasos en castellano and an adaptation made by Manuel Fernández Juncos of First Steps in English by Albert Le Roy Bartlett were the two books commonly used for the development of the Spanish language. These unrelated books formed the curricular Spanish program during the first years of the century.

In preceding pages it was mentioned that the language affected the development of the Spanish language curriculum. It was also mentioned that great demands were made by the Teachers' Association on the Puerto Rican Legislature. In 1914 to satisfy these demands, the Legislature created the position of "Superintendente General de Español" (General Spanish Superintendent). Enrique C. Hernández became the first Puerto Rican Spanish superintendent.[30]

In 1914, the Department of Education published the pamphlet Course of Study in Spanish for the Grade Schools of Puerto Rico. It was prepared by Pedro P. Arán under the Paul G. Miller administration. In this publication the following books were recommended to be used in the Spanish curriculum: Libro fundamental by Aldine, Lecturas hispanas modernas, Antología puertorriqueña and Enigmas de la naturaleza by H. W. Shephard-Walwyng.

In 1916, the Department of Education incorporated into its

Spanish language curriculum the Spanish reading program El método racional para enseñar a leer y escribir el castellano simultáneamente (The Rational Method for Teaching Reading and Writing Castillian Simultaneously), written by José Gonzáles Ginorio (appointed General Spanish Superintendent in 1918). This program was a valuable contribution to the history of the methodology of reading in Puerto Rico. Furthermore, for the first time in the history of the Spanish language in Puerto Rico, Spanish was systematized in the first grades of the elementary school. The program consisted of two books: Lectura infantil I and Lectura infantil II, accompanied by an explanatory teachers' manual entitled Método racional para aprender a leer y escribir el castellano.

The method was a combination of phonetic analyses and recognition of words. The whole program made use of twenty words: mesa (table), bola (ball), tina (bathtub), mula (mule), dedo (finger), pavo (turkey), farol (street lamp), jarro (jar), caballo (horse), niño (boy), zapato (shoe), gato (cat), buey (ox), yugo (yoke), coche (coach), quinqué (lantern), guineo (banana), cielo (sky), ángel (angel) and hombre (man). These twenty words were used in nineteen lessons. Each lesson consisted of five steps: presentation of the word, analysis of the structure of the word, study of the syllable and sounds, composition of new words and a summary of the whole process. The first four lessons took approximately one week. At the end of the fourth lesson, the student was able to compare both the printed and the cursive written styles of the word. After the fifth lesson, each succeeding lesson took two days to present and one day to review. After the eighth lesson, the review day was dedicated to reading in Lectura infantil I. After lesson nineteen the rest of the time was devoted to completing the textbook material. The Program emphasized the need for phonetic analysis: As stated in the manual: "perception of sounds rather than visual symbols."[31] The student was also guided to consider the whole sentence before reading it orally, thus reinforcing the sight-seen ability. Commissioner Paul G. Miller in the Preface of the book states its cultural relevance in the following words: "I am convinced that if the book is going to be used in the schools of Puerto Rico, it should be used by those persons familiar with Puerto Rican life, the school and its problems.[32] The Program represented the first attempt to write reading books with insight to Puerto Rican culture.

In 1920-21, a new list of recommended books was published. The list included the following books for the elementary school: Sonriendo by Carlos Wagner, La alegría de vivir by Orison Sween Marden, Biografía de Luis Muñoz Rivera by José Gonzalez Ginorio. The Department of Education prepared a series of courses of study up to the sixth grade.[33] Three years later Rimas infantiles by Juan B. Huyke and Los mejores cuentos de Andersen by Carmen García Méndez were added to the list.

In 1927, the second attempt to present a Spanish reading program for first graders appeared. Encarnación and Juana Alicea published Método fonético para enseñar a leer y escribir [34] (Phonetic Method to Teach Reading and Writing). The program consisted of thirty-six lessons. Each lesson consisted of a story to be presented by the teacher who would then introduce the sound, letter (small or capital, printed and cursive) and syllable to be taught. The method recommended the teaching of sounds, letters and words. At the end of each lesson, La cartilla was used as the reading book. The authors recommended frequent dictation to create sound association through oral, visual and motor perception. Upon completion of the book, students were required to pronounce and recognize letters of the alphabet. The Ginorio reading program and the Alicea program had in common the simultaneous use of reading and writing and the introduction of phonics concurrent with reading.

Regarding the Language Arts curriculum of the different grades, it was unrelated and books were very scarce. Lenguaje castellano, written by Gerardo Sellés Solá (Spanish Superintendent from 1921-1926) in 1926, emphasized the teaching of vocabulary, oral and written composition, dictation and grammatical rules.[35] This book, in addition to Gramática castellana (1915) by Felipe Janer and El buen castellano (1920) were primary language sources for teachers. Under Sellés Solá's direction, a series of pamphlets were published--one for each grade--containing lesson plans and course content regarding the teaching of the Spanish language.

During 1928-29 the Spanish curriculum did not undergo major changes.[36] The following books were added: Libro primero by Alfredo M. Aguayo, Libro primero by R. Guerra Sánchez and Un libro para mis nietos, a collection of children's poems by Virgilio Dávila. Most of these were reading books for the first and second grades. At that time a definition of curriculum included only textbooks. No teachers' manuals were available to guide the teachers in the use of these books. The position of the Commissioner of Education was as follows:

> In regard to the conservation of Spanish, it is well to note here that it is not the mere conservation of the language, which would require no effort on the part of the schools. The Spanish-speaking population of the Island is so large that the language itself will take care of its own preservation.[37]

It could be said that the most complete methodological Spanish language curriculum appeared in Puerto Rico in 1929. It was Lectura y lenguaje, a Spanish course of study for the rural schools of Puerto Rico. It was prepared under the guidance of Pedro P. Arañ, Spanish General Superintendent.[38]

In the school year 1931, the following books were adopted: Libro primero de lectura and Libro segundo de lectura by Manuela Dalmau and Herminia Acevedo, Páginas de color rosa by Luis Rechani Agrait written for second graders and Libro tercero and Libro cuarto de lectura by Carolina Marcial Dorado.

In the following three years there were not many changes in the teaching of the Spanish language in the elementary school. New books were recommended: Selección de leyendas puertorriqueñas by Cayetano Coll y Toste and Leamos y juguemos by Angela L. Muñoz de Rodriguez and Herminia Acevedo.

In 1931, Carmen Gómez Tejera was appointed Supervisor of Spanish in the Department of Education by Commissioner of Education, José A. Padín. Under her direction, a study was conducted in the school district of San Juan to investigate the deficiencies and problems in the teaching of Spanish in the elementary school. This study was based on a curriculum prepared years before--Programa de lengua española para la escuela elemental (Spanish Language Program for the Elementary School) in the Elementary School of the University of Puerto Rico in the years 1926-1931.

Another attempt to develop Spanish curricular material was the analysis of the teaching of reading in the first grade. The study described the reading method called Manual del método de rimas y fonética para enseñar a leer en primer grado (Phonetical and Rhyme Method to Teach Reading in the First Grade).[39] As the title indicates, rhymes were the starting point in the reading process. The following rhyme is an example of those used in the method.

> Mamá mía, mamá mía
> adorada mamá mía
> bésame, bésame.
> Bésame todos los días.

The authors realized the importance of phonics, and the recognition of printed words. The Program offered the introductory rhyme lessons in which students were to acquire reading readiness. After this preparatory phase the students would be able to read any of the assigned first grade books: La nueva cartilla by Juan B. Huyke, El libro primero translated by Manuel Fernández Juncos, and Libro natural by Isabel Keith McDermott.

In the school year of 1935-36, a pamphlet entitled "Observaciones y comentarios sobre el método de rimas y fonética" was written explaining the methodological approach of the reading program. The program was implemented for several years, after which it was discontinued. In 1941, the Department of Education sent a circular letter stating that this modern method should be used in the teaching of reading.[40]

In 1935, the Department of Education was interested in increasing the amount of supplementary reading materials for the elementary schools. A collection of poems and selections written by Rubén Darío was prepared, titled Rubén Darío--Selecciones en verso y prosa para niños. This book was very useful in increasing the children's awareness of the literature. In 1935 in its desire to augment and prepare poetic selections liked by the Puerto

Rican children, the Department of Education of Puerto Rico began an educational study to determine the poetical preferences of the students. The results of this study was the publication of a book in 1937 Suplemento al programa de lengua española para la escuela elemental that includes the children's preferred poems.[41]

In May of 1936, a study was conducted throughout the schools of Puerto Rico to determine the extent of the vocabulary of first grade children. This project was not completed and the only step taken was the tabulation of the vocabulary expressed by children in some school districts of the Island.[43]

In 1936, invited by Commissioner of Education José A. Padín, William S. Gray visited the Island. He lectured on the teaching of reading in various towns of Puerto Rico. Among his recommendations were to prepare basal readers geared toward centers of interest and to publish more supplementary readers. A revision of Programa de lengua española para las escuelas elementales were prepared following one of Dr. Gray's recommendations. Dr. Gray concluded that:

> The major change adopted at the beginning of the school year--that is providing for the use of the vernacular as the sole medium of instruction (outside of English classes) in the first eight grades represents a significant step in the right direction. It is based on the assumption that the primary function is to broaden and enrich the lives of children and to promote the development of happy, efficient individuals and intelligent citizens rather than to teach subjects or develop specific skills.[43]

To the same purpose Dr. Michael West, the famous bilingual researcher, came to the Island to assess the language needs and problems. This period was characterized by the implementation of Spanish as a medium of instruction until the intermediate grades. Dr. West's recommendations contributed to the acceptance and validation of the need for the use of the Spanish language in the school curriculum.[44]

With these recommendations toward the effective use and study of the Spanish language, the Puerto Ricans and the mainland Americans concerned with the public school system were accepting the idea of preparing more and better Spanish language materials and curricula. In 1936, Juan Ramón Jiménez was invited to Puerto Rico to aid the Department of Education in the preparation of a collection of his poems. He resided in Puerto Rico several years and established the "Fiesta por la Poesía y el Niño de Puerto Rico" (Festival for the Poetry and Child of Puerto Rico). For several years, this organization prepared poetical festivals for children. This organization also published Poesía Puertorriqueña--Antología para niños.[45]

Methodological books were needed in Puerto Rico in order to help teachers develop effective reading and language lessons. With this purpose in mind, the School Administration and Supervision Circle of Puerto Rico published La lectura en la escuela y en la vida in 1940. Five years later (1945) Antonia Sáez published Las Artes del lenguaje en la escuela elemental. Both books helped Puerto Rican Spanish language teachers by presenting methodological procedures and guidelines.

During the school year of 1942-43, the traditional 8-4 plan of school organization (transplanted from United States) was changed to 6-3-3 plan. The former had suffered severe criticism beginning in 1920 when the majority of students attended only four years or less of school. In 1937, serious deliberations began toward the acceptance of the 6-3-3 plan. In 1942-43 it was accepted as the standard organization for the school system of Puerto Rico.[46] With the establishment of the 6-3-3 plan, the Department of Education was forced to create curricular materials according to this school organization. Programa de lengua española para las escuelas elementales written in 1933, was revised in 1945 to include the entire reading method. The student was guided toward the recognition of the whole unit, phrases, sentences and words. The sight-seen reading method was recommended in Actividades de lengua española para principiantes.[47] The following books were recommended as part of the Spanish language curriculum: Con mis amigos (Isabel Ereyre de Matos), Oye un secreto (Patricia Rivera de Roy), A caza de aventuras (Dalia Ruiz de Rodríguez), Un Mundo para tí (Blanca Pesquera Hernández), Luis y Lola (M. Evelyn Craigs) and Secretos y maravillas (Elena Ayala García). Silver Burdett Publishing Company published three books written by Francisco Gaztambide that were accepted as textbooks in the elementary school curriculum: Jugando y riendo, Los niños se divierten and A Viajar y a gozar. These three books were highly recommended since they included characteristics of the books in series or basal readers in use in the United States during that time: controlled vocabulary, thematic units, dialogues and elements of humor and surprise. However, these books did not include a teacher's manual indicating the author's philosophy of reading education and appropriate methodological techniques.

Another important aspect of the history of the Puerto Rican language curriculum is the fact that until 1948, Puerto Rico had not published any particular research on the scientific study of the Spanish language of the Island. El español de Puerto Rico is the first linguistic study which describes the linguistic variables of the people of Puerto Rico.[48] The master's and doctoral theses written for the Hispanic Department of the University of Puerto Rico have augmented the knowledge and characteristics of the Island's language, two important elements of which teachers of the Spanish language must be aware. In 1947, the central office of the Department of Education was reorganized. In this reorganization a curriculum division was created.[49] Osuna pointed out the plan for this division:

a. To attempt to make the curriculum of the school function
    in accordance with the most modern conception of the
    word curriculum--"the dynamics of the educational ex-
    periences that the school offers both in and out of the
    classroom"; "the result of a series of factors, including
    the physical environment, and the desires, beliefs, knowl-
    edge, attitudes, and skills of the persons served by and
    serving the school."

b. To cooperate with the teaching and administrative per-
    sonnel of our school system and with the Puerto Rican
    community in bringing about the solution of some of the
    educational problems of Puerto Rico insofar as it is
    possible, especially those urgent problems that are most
    directly related to the curriculum.

c. To culivate likewise a comprehensive attitude toward
    international problems which will serve in the orienta-
    tion of the curriculum. [50]

With the creation of this division, the preparation of text-
books was one of the major preoccupations of the Department of
Education.   The plan established was for the preparation of text-
books in accordance with modern practices, and related to the Puerto
Rican environment, customs, traditions, language and ways of life.
To accomplish this goal, the Curriculum Division in collaboration
with the Consejo Superior de Enseñanza of the University of Puerto
Rico began a series of investigations.

In the school year of 1948-49, the Department of Education,
conscious of the lack of Spanish reading materials, agreed to publish them in some Puerto Rican newspapers and magazines. El
Mundo, Diario de Puerto Rico, El Día, Puerto Rico Illustrado and
Alma Latina published educational materials sent to them by the
Department of Education.   Children identified these reading materials
in the newspapers by the title "Página de la escuela." This page
appeared for the first time in December 12, 1949 and continued to
appear until May 19, 1950. [51] It was discontinued when the Department of Education organized its own newspaper, in the school
year of 1948-49. In September 1950, the weekly newspaper Escuela
went to press for the first time. [52] It had the same objectives as
"Página de la escuela." Rodríguez Bou cited the newspaper's director, Rafael Pont Flores, who stated the main purpose of the
publication of Escuela. Pont Flores said:

> The basic reason for this weekly newspaper is to develop
> readers with the periodistic approach to themes and tasks
> related to the classroom, that will complement or supple-
> ment the textbooks, but will not substitute them. [53]

The Printing Office of the Department of Education was in
charge of the distribution of this material. The material was subdivided according to the children's reading levels. Escuela for the

elementary school had two editions: Level I, distributed among first to third grade students, and Level II for students in fourth to sixth grade. Another two editions were published; one for intermediate level students and another for high school students. Students received the newspaper every two weeks, since its preparation and distribution was alternated by levels.[54] The Escuela reading materials could be of great advantage for the classroom teachers. However, in spite of the quality of material, few teachers took advantage of the newspaper nor did the libraries recompile them.

In the school year of 1951-52, the necessity for more Spanish language textbooks increased, because the Department finally determined that Spanish was to be used as the medium of instruction.[55]

Since 1953, Educación a teachers' monthly newspaper has been published. It was published to be used by the teachers as a means of information and orientation. Through Educación, teachers became knowledgeable of methodological techniques, educational legislative matters and general topics related to the teaching profession. Educación is still in circulation.

Semana was another newspaper publication to be used as a medium of instruction and culture. The purpose of this publication was to inform the Puerto Rican people about the week's most important news. It was written for adults to whom newspapers or other periodicals were not available.[56] The newspapers were distributed to the students who took them home. This material could be used for the Spanish language class since it was written entirely in Spanish. The first edition appeared on September 10, 1955.

In the school year 1956-57, a group of New York University students conducted a study to determine which Spanish textbooks were in use in the elementary school in Puerto Rico. The following list was compiled: first grade: Luis y Lola (M. Evelyn Craigs), Jugando y riendo (Gaztambide), and Con mis amigos (Department of Education). Second grade: Juego de niños (Candido Ibarra), Oye un secreto (Department of Education) and Nuestro mundo tropical (Pedro A. Cebollero). Third grade: Los niños se divierten (Gaztambide). Fourth grade: A viajar y a gozar (Gaztambide) and A caza de aventuras (Dalia Ruiz de Rodríguez). Fifth grade: Un Mundo para tí (Blanca Pesquera Hernández). This book consisted of seventy eight selections grouped into five units: "Las murallas de San Juan," "Tierra, mar y cielo," "Nuestra isla," "Nuestros amigos," and "Días que no se olvidan." Vidas heroicas (Department of Education), which is a collection of twenty one biographies. Sixth grade: Mundo sin geografía (Carmen A. Cadilla), a collection of pictures of a jíbaro child praising Puerto Rican nature. La canción verde is a Spanish translation of the Doris Troutman book. España pintoresca (Carolina Marcial Dorado), was written for English speaking children. The book presents a panoramic view of Spain and its culture.

In 1960 the Curriculum and Supervision Division of the Department of Education published Manual para la enseñanza de lectura.[57] This reading manual offered valuable information to teachers about the reading process; steps in reading readiness, systematic approach and reading for entertainment. The book presents suggestions for the evaluation of the reading readiness period and systematic reading. It also contains example lesson plans.

The basic reading program Por el mundo del cuento y la aventura prepared by Carmen Gómez Tejera, Angeles Pastor and Rosa Guzmán Vda. de Capó is the first basic reading series organized in Puerto Rico. A study was conducted to determine the needs of the Spanish language curriculum, that includes: analysis of the current Spanish curriculum, a questionnaire that was sent to a representative group of teachers. Also the Consejo Superior de Enseñanza report about the educational system of the Island and the analysis of the publications prepared by the Department of Education for the teachers' use were also studied. This series covers all the grades of the elementary school. The preparation of these books was sponsored by the Department of Education and published by Laidlaw Brothers Publishing Company. A group of Puerto Rican teachers worked together with the authors. Kathleen B. Hester was the linguistic consultant. The series consisted of ten books. The first books were published in the school year 1960-61. They were put to use in the school year of 1962-63. The series was prepared using United States reading standard guidelines: controlled vocabulary, organization of selections by units or interest centers, systematic and sequential skills, variety of material in terms of style and content. The first three books were for the first grade and the other grades were assigned one book each. Teachers' manual and students' workbooks were included, also.

Por el mundo de la palabra were the three language books used in the last grades of the elementary school (4, 5, and 6). Dictation, outline organization and dictionary use were studied in conjunction with the speaking and reading skills. The vocabulary of the readings is not controlled, although the 10,000 words most commonly used in the Spanish language appear. Each book has a teacher's manual, Por el mundo de la palabra and Por el mundo del cuento y la aventura were planned separately. There is no correlation between the books in these two series. Apuntes sobre la enseñanza de la lengua hablada y escrita en la escuela elemental was another book used by the elementary teachers.[58] All aspects related to the teaching of language are discussed in this manual.

The Spanish Language Secondary School Curriculum

Secondary education was new to the Island when the American occupation took place. Before 1898, secondary centers or schools existed for the few students whose families could afford it. Schools in those days made no attempt to reach all of the children and secondary education especially was for the very few. However, the idea of offering secondary education to a large group of students became a reality after the first two decades of the twentieth century. Juan José Osuna explains what was called secondary education in Puerto Rico until 1942. He says:

> Until recently, secondary education in Puerto Rico, since its organization, included educational training given to pupils who had completed an eight year elementary course or its equivalent.
> ... The high school in Puerto Rico was the same as the traditional high school in the United States, that institution offering a four year course of study beyond the elementary school of eight grades. [59]

Later, Dr. Osuna defines the objectives of secondary education. He says that the special talents, aptitudes, and social needs of the children must be noted and allowances made for individual differences, both cultural and vocational. From the above philosophy the following functions are derived:

1. To promote good health, social consciousness based on democratic principles, good use of leisure time and the development of creative capacities for the enrichment of both the individual and society.

2. To guide the pupil in the exploration of scientific, literary, artistic, and occupational fields so that, through the discovery of his innate abilities, he may be helped to come to a decision concerning his life's work. [60]

In 1920, Puerto Rico had not developed a philosophy of education. The secondary school goals, curriculum, and methodology were an imitation of what was done in the United States. Spanish was not considered an important subject. During the school year 1926-27, the Commissioner of Education appointed a committee composed of high school principals and teachers instructed to undertake a complete revision of the general course of the high school curriculum. [61] Under Gerardo Sellés' (Spanish Supervisor) direction, a Spanish teachers assembly was organized, and for the first time, the problems of teaching Spanish as a subject in the secondary school were discussed. The Department of Hispanic Studies influenced a discussion of the possibility of creating a Spanish program for secondary schools. Spanish was studied simply as a subject. [62]

Between 1900 to 1928, the following books were recommended by the Department of Education: El capitán veneno (Pedro A. de Alarcón), Compendio de moral para las escuelas (Manuel Fernández Juncos), María (Jorge Isaac) and Antología puertorriqueña (Manuel Fernández Juncos). It was not specified in which grades these books could be used nor were the specific objectives stated.

During 1926-1931, a formal secondary Spanish curriculum did not exist in Puerto Rico. The curriculum consisted of a series of unrelated books without any specific instructional methodology. In actuality, history of the secondary Spanish curriculum began in 1931 when Carmen Gómez Tejera, Supervisor of Spanish, tested the secondary students to determine the students' Spanish academic achievement. In 1932 under her direction, a pamphlet suggesting effective methods to correct the students' deficiencies was published.[63] In February of 1932, Carmen Gómez Tejera wrote "Apuntes para la enseñanza de español en la escuela superior (Comments of the Teaching of Spanish in the High School)." It is an attempt to explain the role of the supervisor of Spanish language, adolescent psychology related to the teaching of Spanish, objectives of the teaching of reading, literature and language; and principles of language methodology. The teachers of Spanish expressed a need for training and materials in the Spanish language curriculum. On June 28, 1932, a central committee composed of the Department of Hispanic Studies from the University of Puerto Rico and members of the Department of Education was organized. The result of these meetings was the publication of Programa de lengua y literatura española para la escuela superior in 1938. Also, university courses dealing with methods and techniques of teaching Spanish were offered to the teachers. The classes were held on Saturdays or during the summers. Spanish conferences, workshops and seminars were organized throughout the Island, as well. In 1934, the Círculo Cultural de Maestros de Español (Cultural Circle of Teachers of Spanish) was organized to promote awareness and interest among the teachers regarding the learning and the teaching of Spanish. The organization's magazine Brújula was publishedffrom 1934 to 1937.

In the early thirties, the following books were added to the Spanish curriculum: Leyendas puertorriqueñas (Cayetano Coll y Toste), Hace falta un muchacho (Arturo Cuyas), Páginas escogidas (Manuel Fernández Juncos), Marianela (Benito Pérez Galdós), Consejo a la juventud and Cuentos Populares (Pablo Morales Cabrera), Juan R. Jiménez--Verso y prosa para niños (Gómez, Tejera), and Rabindranath Tagore--Verso y prosa para niños (Gómez Tejera and Alvarez-Torre.)

In 1939, the revision of Programa de lengua y literatura española para la escuela superior was initiated. This revision, however was not completed due to Miss Gómez Tejera's return to the faculty of the University of Puerto Rico.

With the establishment of the 6-3-3 plan in 1942, the Department of Education was forced to create certain curricular materials. In 1945, six units were prepared for each grade on the intermediate level (seventh, eighth and ninth grades). These units were organized into six themes: "Desarrollo personal," "Lengua," "Vida en el hogar," "Vida en Puerto Rico," "Goce y enriquecimiento de la salud" and "Lectura." Several years later these units were organized into five areas: "Desarrollo personal," "Desarrollo de destrezas lingüísticas, " "Vida en Puerto Rico, " "Estudio de la obra literaria" and "Enriquecimiento cultural. "

"Desarrollo personal" (Personal Development) was the first unit of the three grades of the intermediate school. Its purpose was the creation of a favorable environment in which to conduct Spanish classes. [64] Each unit included diagnostic tests to determine the language level of the students. Antonia Sáez described this unit's importance in the following words: "It is in reality an exploration of the linguistic abilities and interests of the students. "[65]

The formal study of language was conducted through the unit "Desarrollo de destrezas lingüísticas. " (Development of Linguistic Skills). Each grade emphasized different language skills. "Vida en Puerto Rico" covered specific topics of Puerto Rican life and culture. In the seventh grade, songs, folklore and poems were the areas of study. Puerto Rican contributors to the Island's life and culture were the center of discussion in ninth grade. Ninth grade topics were centered around the Puerto Rican life during the nineteenth and twentieth centuries. The three units formed an entire thematic unit of which the final purpose was to interest students in the different aspects of the Puerto Rican life in order to become better citizens. [66] "Estudio de la obra literaria" was the third unit. Its purpose was stated in the following words: "That it will continue familiarizing the students with the different literary genres (story, novel, poem, and drama), specifically and in depth. "[67] During this period the teaching of Spanish was alternated with social studies in many intermediate schools.

The books assigned to the study of these units were the following. Seventh grade: Cuentos y leyendas (Juan Valera), El final de Norma and Novelas cortas (Pedro A. de Alarcón), Flor de leyendas (Department of Education), El genio alegre and Amores y amoríos (Hnos. Alvarez Quintero), Lecturas hispanas modernas (Department of Education), Leyendas puertorriqueñas (Cayetano Coll y Toste), and Selección de leyendas puertorriqueñas (Department of Education). Eighth grade: Cuentos españoles (Enrique A. Laguerre), Marianela (Benito Pérez Galdós), Isla cerrera (Manuel Méndez Ballester), Juan R. Jiménez--Verso y prosa para niños (Gómez Tejera), La muela del rey Farfán (Hnos. Alvarez Quintero) and Le reja (Hnos. Alvarez Quintero). Ninth grade: Rabindranath Tagore-- Verso y prosa para niños (Gómez Tejera and Alvarez-Torre), Rimas y leyendas (Gustavo Adolfo Bécquer), El genio alegre (Hnos. Alvarez Quintero) and Medallas de oro (Augusto Malaret). Despite the fact that these were the textbooks assigned to the units described, many classrooms did not have all the books or did not have a book for each child.

After these units were in use for a while, some limitations were discovered: the unit content was entirely in the teacher's hands, students had access only to textbooks--no workbooks were available, and many schools did not have the resources to duplicate the necessary materials.

In order to revise the intermediate Spanish program of 1945, the Central Program administration organized a curriculum committee. After a few meetings, the committee agreed to start the revision of the Spanish program from the first to the twelfth grades. Teachers from all school levels were represented on this committee as were professors from the University of Puerto Rico. In 1961, a questionnaire was administered to all Spanish language teachers. The results revealed a need to revise the Spanish curriculum. During this time, the teachers received Síntesis del programa del español de escuela intermedia (Synthesis of the Spanish Program for the Junior High School) the purpose of which was to give the teachers, methodological ideas related to old units that were still in use. Among the many recommendations sent by the Spanish language teachers was the incorporation of the following aspects into the curriculum: understanding of adolescent's psychology, student's needs and individual differences, general objectives of the teaching of Spanish, communication with the University of Puerto Rico, and knowledge of values and characteristics of Puerto Rican culture.[68]

The high school used Programa de lengua y literatura española para la escuela superior (Language and Literature Program for the High School) from 1938 until 1945. In 1945, the teaching of Spanish for high school was organized in terms of the major areas of language arts: listening, speaking, reading and writing. The objectives of the program were:

1. Effective use of the language as a medium of communication and culture. Three factors are involved in its use. These are psychological and social adjustment and skills development.
2. Good utilization of the following communication sources: radio, printing and motion pictures.
3. Development of good study habits.
4. Promotion of human relations for productive and happy lives.
5. Development of spiritual and moral values.
6. Cultivation of aesthetic appreciation and creativity.[69]

The teaching of Spanish in high school was organized into six areas: 1) Exploration and orientation, 2) Language, 3) Communication, 4) Puerto Rican culture, 5) American culture, 6) Spanish culture.[70] In the three grades of the high school these units were studied. In twelfth grade an essay unit was added. With the establishment of the "Morovis Plan," [71] the units were organized into book tasks or tareas. In the introduction of each book, the purpose of the unit content is explained. The following paragraph is part of the introduction of the book used in tenth grade.

These units are prepared in the form of work tasks, prepared in such a way that, little by little, you could be more independent of the teacher, who will be a counselor.... The content of the book tasks is divided as

follows: 1) Student's introduction 2) Individual activities
3) Group activities 4) Evaluation. [72]

The six units discussed before were also subdivided into
small thematic topics.   In tenth grade the discussion topics were
the following: 1) Exploration and orientation, 2) How to better express ourselves, 3) The importance of the radio in the community,
4) How the people's way of life reflects the Puerto Rican folklore,
5) Let's know our America, 6) Spanish life through the literature
of the nineteenth century (Romanticism). [73]

The textbooks used with the task books or tareas were:
Antología de prosa hispanoamericana (Department of Education)
Terrazo (Abelardo Díaz Alfaro), El trovador and Los amantes de
Teruel (A. García Gutierrez and Juan E. Hartzembush), Misericor-
dia (Benito Pérez Galdós) and Teatro y poesía del siglo dieciocho
(L. Fernandez de Moratín).

The Spanish program for the eleventh grade was organized
according to the following topics: 1) Exploration and orientation,
2) How to better express ourselves with appropriateness and accuracy, 3) The movie in the contemporary world, 4) The modern
novel in Latin America, 5) Spanish culture through the Golden Age
drama. [74]   The two books used were subdivided into units.   These
units followed the following sequential order: 1) Exploration and
orientation, 2) How to better express ourselves, 3) The movie in
the contemporary world, 4) Art in Puerto Rico, 5) The modern
novel in Latin America, 6) Spanish culture in the Golden Age, 7)
History of the Spanish theater (until Lope de Vega) and 8) The
Spanish drama (Calderón de la Barca).

The textbooks used were: 1) Doña Bárbara (Rómulo Gallegos), Peribáñez, Las estrellas de Sevilla, El caballero de Olmedo
(Lope de Vega), La verdad sospechosa, Las paredes oyen, Mudarse
por mejorarse (Juan Ruiz de Alarcón), El burlador de Sevilla and
La prudencia en la mujer (Tirso de Molina).

The six units covered in the twelfth grade are as follows:
1) Exploration and orientation, 2) How to better express ourselves,
3) Importance of the press in the community, 4) Puerto Rican literature, 5) The essay, 6) American contribution to lyric poetry,
7) Spanish life style in the Golden Age novel.

The units discussed were in accordance with the areas described here.   The textbooks used for the study of these topics
were: La llamarada (Enrique A. Laguerre), Tiempo muerto, El
clamor de los surcos (M. Méndez Ballester), La charca (M. Zeno
Gandía), Antología de ensayos (Department of Education), Poesía
hispanoamericana (Félix Franco Oppenheimer), El lazarillo de Tor-
mes (anonymous) and Don Quijote de la Mancha (Miguel de Cervantes).   The twelfth grade Spanish course was not required for
graduation.   In addition to these units and textbooks Normas de
aprovechamiento progresivo en la escuela secundaria (Achievement

Progress Norms in the Secondary School), published in 1960, was used as guideline in the development of linguistic skills.[75]

During the sixties, various attempts were made to revise the Spanish language program. One of these attempts was to organize the curriculum into five areas: language, grammar, style, Puerto Rican literature and general or universal literature.[76] Books were added or eliminated accordingly. It was not until 1966 that a formal plan was organized called Plan de Desarrollo Curricular (Curricular Development Plan). Its goals were to create an educational philosophy for the teaching of Spanish in the secondary school.[77] Curriculum was to be based on the following objectives:

1. To correspond to the environment of the community that the school serves.
2. To be selective and interpretive.
3. To be developed through a previous diagnostic survey.[78]

The result of all committees' questionnaires, studies and revisions is the new Spanish language program in effect in Puerto Rico since 1970.

References

1. Puerto Rico, Department of Education, The School Laws of the Island of Puerto Rico (Washington, D. C. : Government Printing Office, 1899, Part II), p. 36.
2. Juan J. Osuna, A History of Education in Puerto Rico (Río Piedras: Editorial de la Universidad de Puerto Rico, 1949), p. 343.
3. Luis Muñiz Suffront, El problema del idioma en Puerto Rico (San Juan: Biblioteca de Autores Puertorriqueños, 1950), p. 18.
4. Emilio Delgado, El destino de la lengua española en Puerto Rico (New York: Hispanic Publisher, 1945), p. 10.
5. Puerto Rico, Department of Education, Annual Report of the Commissioner of Education (Washington, D. C. : Government Printing Office, 1906), p. 34.
6. Pedro A. Cebollero, A School Language Policy for Puerto Rico (San Juan: Imprenta Baldrich, 1954), p. 11.
7. Puerto Rico, Department of Education, Report of the Commissioner of Education to the Governor of Puerto Rico (Washington, D. C. : Government Printing Office, 1917), p. 464.
8. Osuna, A History of Education in Puerto Rico, p. 351.
9. Cited by Carmen Gómez Tejera and David Cruz López in La escuela puertorriqueña (Sharon, Conn. : Troutman Press, 1970), p. 167.
10. International Institute of Teachers College, Columbia University, A Survey of the Public Educational System of Puerto Rico (New York: Bureau of Publications, Teachers College, Columbia University, 1926), p. 10.
11. Muñiz Suffront, El problema del idioma en Puerto Rico, p. 19.

12. Cebollero, A School Language Policy for Puerto Rico, p. 23.
13. Puerto Rico, Department of Education, Circular Letter no. 10, year 1934-35.
14. William S. Gary, "Report to the Commissioner of Education," April 1936, in Ismael Rodríguez Bou, Problemas de lectura en Puerto Rico (Río Piedras: Universidad de Puerto Rico, 1948), pp. 99 and 103.
15. Michael West, Memorandum "The Language Problem and the Teaching of English in Puerto Rico" in Rodríguez Bou, Problemas de lectura y lengua en Puerto Rico, p. 109.
16. Annual Report of the Commissioner of Education 1937-38, p. 29.
17. Circular Letter no. 1, 1 July 1942.
18. Osuna, A History of Education in Puerto Rico, p. 408.
19. Muñiz Suffront, El problema del idioma en Puerto Rico, pp. 65-66.
20. Ibid.
21. Ibid.
22. Consejo Superior de Enseñanza, Memoria anual, 1942-43, p. 7.
23. Osuna, A History of Education in Puerto Rico, p. 408.
24. Mariano Villaronga, "The Teaching of English in the Public Schools of Puerto Rico," An excerpt from the address of the Commissioner of Education of Puerto Rico, before the Annual Convention of the Teachers Association of Puerto Rico, 26 December 1946.
25. Ismael Rodríguez Bou, Problemas de educación en Puerto Rico (San Juan: Imprenta Venezuela, 1947, pp. 100-101.
26. Ibid.
27. Tania Viera Martínez, "Textbooks Used in the Public Schools of the Commonwealth of Puerto Rico," Report submitted as part of the survey of the school system of Puerto Rico, n. d. (Mimeographed.)
28. Circular Letter no. 10, 6 August 1949.
29. Pauline M. Rojas, "Conference on the Teaching of Language," Conference at Rotary Club of San Juan. 28 September 1954.
30. Rodríguez Bou, Problemas de lectura y lengua en Puerto Rico, p. 54.
31. José Gonzalez Ginorio, El método racional para enseñar a leer y escribir el castellano simultáneamente, Libro primero (Boston: Heath y Compañia, 1916), p. 23.
32. Ibid, p. 6.
33. Gerardo Sellés Solá, Lenguaje castellano, San Juan: Bureau of Supplies, Printing and Transporation, 1922.
34. Encarnación Alicea and Juana Alicea, Método fonético para enseñar a leer y escribir, Guía del maestro, Chicago: Rand McNally and Company, 1927.
35. Gerardo Sellés Solá, Lenguaje castellano.
36. Puerto Rico, Department of Education, Español de grados primarios en matrícula doble (San Juan: Negociado de Materiales, Imprenta y Transporte, 1928), p. 4.
37. Second Annual Report of the Governor of Porto Rico, Fiscal year ended June 30, 1929, p. 286.
38. Puerto Rico, Department of Education, Lectura y lenguaje, San

Juan: Bureau of Supplies, Printing and Transportation, 1929.

39. Josefita Monserrate, el al., Manual del método de rimas y fonética para enseñar a leer en primer grado. San Juan: Negociado de Materiales, Imprenta y Transporte, 1934.

40. Puerto Rico, Department of Education, "Enseñanza de lectura," Circular Letter no. 56, 21 December 1941.

41. Carmen Gómez Tejera, Suplemento al programa de lengua española para la escuela elemental, San Juan: Universidad de Puerto Rico, 1937.

42. Ismael Rodríguez Bou, "Las 105 palabras de mayor frecuencia" in Problemas de lectura y lengua en Puerto Rico, pp. 93-94.

43. William S. Gray, "Report to the Commissioner of Education of Puerto Rico," p. 99.

44. Michael West, "The Language Problem and the Teaching of English in Puerto Rico," p. 7.

45. Carmen Gómez Tejera and Juan Asencio Alvarez-Torre, Poesía puertorriqueña Antología para niños, La Habana, Cuba: n. p., 1938.

46. Osuna, A History of Education in Puerto Rico, p. 280.

47. Josefita Monserrate de Sellés and Carmen Gómez Tejera, Actividades de lengua española para principiantes, San Juan: Departamento de Instrucción Pública, 1948.

48. Tomás Navarro, El español de Puerto Rico, Río Piedras, Puerto Rico: Editorial de la Universidad de Puerto Rico, 1948.

49. "Implantarán enseñanza en español a partir del próximo curso escolar, Carmen Gómez Tejera va a dirigir nueva división en vías de crearse," El Mundo, 4 May 1947, p. 1.

50. Osuna, A History of Education in Puerto Rico, pp. 479-480.

51. Ismael Rodríguez Bou, "Libros de texto y otros materiales," in Estudio del sistema educativo de Puerto Rico, 3 vols. (Universidad de Puerto Rico, 1960), 2:1496.

52. Ibid.

53. Ibid.

54. Circular Letter No. 12, 1 September 1950.

55. Circular Letter No. 10. 6 August 1949.

56. Puerto Rico, Department of Education, "Memorandum del Director de Semana a la señora Daisy Molina, Información sobre Semana," 10 December 1958, p. 1.

57. Puerto Rico, Department of Education, Manual para la enseñanza de lectura, San Juan: Editorial Departmento de Instrucción Pública, 1960.

58. Consejo Superior de enseñanza, Apuntes sobre la enseñanza de la lengua hablada y escrita en la escuela elemental, Río Piedras: Universidad de Puerto Rico, 1954.

59. Osuna, A History of Education in Puerto Rico, pp. 246-247.

60. Ibid., pp. 466-467.

61. Puerto Rico, Department of Education, Course of Study for the High School of Puerto Rico, Bulletín No. 28 (San Juan: Bureau of Supplies, Printing and Transportation, 1928), p. 3.

62. Puerto Rico, Department of Education, "The Teaching of Spanish," General Survey of the Secondary School System of Puerto Rico, San Jaun: Government Printing Office, 1932.

63. Carmen Gómez Tejera, "Apuntes para la enseñanza de español en la escuela superior," February 1932. (Mimeographed.)

64. Consejo Superior de Enseñanza, "El currículo de la escuela puertorriqueña," in Estudio del sistema educativo de Puerto Rico, 2:1216.

65. Antonia Sáez, "Informe de las observaciones de la enseñanza del vernáculo en las escuelas intermedias y secundarias de ciertas poblaciones de Puerto Rico," n. d., p. 6 (Mimeographed).

66. Puerto Rico, Department of Education, "Vida en Puerto Rico," ninth grade unit, n. d., p. 3. (Mimeographed).

67. Puerto Rico, Department of Education, "Estudio de la obra literaria." Eighth grade unit, n. d., p. 3. (Mimeographed).

68. Puerto Rico, Department of Education, "Programa de educación secundaria," 1952, pp. 67-80. (Mimeographed).

69. Rodríguez Bou, "La escuela superior de Puerto Rico," in Estudio del sistema educativo, 2:1334.

70. Puerto Rico, Department of Education, "Programa de educación secundaria," 1952, pp. 67-68. (Mimeographed).

71. "The Morovis Plan" was a high school program initiated in the town of Morovis. In this program, students and adults had flexible schedules in accordance with their working hours. It was a program in which the teacher assumed the role of advisor while the students had the option to take most of the basic courses by independent study. It was created for those students who could not attend school during regular school hours.

72. Puerto Rico, Department of Education, "Programa de español 10, Tareas de español 10, First Semester (San Juan: Editorial del Departamento de Instrucción Pública, 1958), p. 2.

73. Puerto Rico, Department of Education, "Programa de español 10, Tareas de español 10, Second Semester, 1958, Table of Contents.

74. Puerto Rico, Department of Education, Tareas de español 11, First Semester, 1958, p. i.

75. Puerto Rico, Department of Education, Normas de aprovechamiento progresivo en la escuela secundaria (Hato Rey: Editorial del Departamento de Instrucción Pública, 1960), pp. 9-11.

76. Carmen Lugo Filippi and Carmen Puigdollers, "El programa de español en las escuelas de Puerto Rico," Educación 23-24, p. 109.

77. Laura, Gallegos, "La integración de las artes del lenguaje en la escuela secundaria," Educación 23-24, p. 109.

78. Ibid., p. 112.

Bibliography

Alicea, Encarnación and Alicea, Juana. Método fonético para enseñar a leer y escribir--Guía del maestro. Chicago: Rand McNally and Company, 1927.

Babín, María Teresa. Panorama de la cultura puertorriqueña.

San Juan: Instituto de Cultura Puertorriqueña, 1958.
Cebollero, Pedro A. A School Language Policy for Puerto Rico.
San Juan: Imprenta Baldrich, 1954.
Consejo Superior de Enseñanza. Apuntes sobre la enseñanza de la
lenguaje hablada y escrita en la escuela elemental. Río
Piedras: Universidad de Puerto Rico, 1954.
_____. Memoria anual, 1942-1943.
Delgado, Emilio, El destino de la lengua española en Puerto Rico.
New York: Hispanic Publisher, 1945.
Gómez Tejera, Carmen. Suplemento al programa de lengua es-
pañola para la escuela elemental. San Juan: Universidad
de Puerto Rico, 1937.
_____ and Alvarez-Torre, Juan Asencio. Poesía puertorriqueña-
Antología para niños. La Habana, Cuba: n.p., 1938.
_____. Rabindranath Tagore--Verso y prosa para niños. Méjico:
Editorial Orión, 1958.
_____ and Cruz Lopez, David. La escuela puertorriqueña.
Sharon, Conn.: Troutman Press, 1970.
González Ginorio, José. El método racional para enseñar a leer
y escribir el castellano simultáneamente, Libro primero.
Boston: Heath and Company, 1916.
Government of Puerto Rico. Second Annual Report of the Governor
of Porto Rico, Fiscal Year Ended June 30, 1929. Washing-
ton, D.C.: Government Printing Office, 1929.
"Implantarán enseñanza en español a partir del próximo curso es-
colar. Carmen Gómez Tehera va a dirigir nueva división
en vías de crearse," El Mundo, May 1947, p.1.
International Institute of Teachers College, Columbia University.
A Survey of the Public Educational System of Puerto Rico.
New York: Bureau of Publications, Teachers College,
Columbia University, 1926.
Lugo Filippi, Carmen and Puigdollers, Carmen. "El programa de
español en las escuelas de Puerto Rico." Educación 23-24.
p.39.
Monserrate de Sellés, Josefita and Tejera, Carmen. Actividades
de lengua española para principiantes. San Juan: Departa-
mento de Instrucción Pública, 1948.
Muñiz Suffront, Luis. El problema del idioma en Puerto Rico.
San Juan: Biblioteca de Autores Puertorriqueños, 1950.
Navarro, Tomás. El español de Puerto Rico. Río Piedras: Edi-
torial de la Universidad de Puerto Rico, 1948.
Osuna, Juan José. A History of Education in Puerto Rico. San
Juan: Editorial de la Universidad de Puerto Rico, 1949.
Puerto Rico, Department of Education. Annual Report of the
Commissioner of Education. Washington, D.C.: Govern-
ment Printing Office, 1937-38.
_____. Circular Letter no. 49, 2 November 1934.
_____. Circular Letter 12, 1 September 1950.
_____. Course of Study for the High Schools of Puerto Rico.
San Juan: Bureau of Supplies, Printing and Transportation,
1928.
_____. Español de grados primarios en matrícula doble. San
Juan: Negociado de Materiales, Imprenta y Transporte, 1928.
_____. General Survey of the Secondary School System of Puerto

Rico. San Juan: Government Printing Office, 1932.

_____. Lectura y lenguaje. San Juan: Bureau of Supplies, Printing and Transportation, 1929.

_____. Manual para la enseñanza de lectura. San Juan: Editorial del Departamento de Instrucción Pública, 1960.

_____. Normas de aprovechamiento progresivo en la escuela secundaria. Hato Rey: Editorial del Departamento de Instrucción Pública, 1960.

_____. Report of the Commissioner of Education to the Governor of Puerto Rico. Washington, D. C.: Government Printing Office, 1917.

_____. Tareas de español 10. Hato Rey: Editorial del Departamento de Instrucción Pública, 1958.

_____. The School Laws of the Island of Puerto Rico. Washington, D. C.: Government Printing Office, 1899.

Rodríguez Bou, Ismael. Problemas de lectura y lengua en Puerto Rico. Río Piedras: Universidad de Puerto Rico, 1948.

_____. Problemas de educación en Puerto Rico. San Juan: Imprenta Venezuela, 1947.

Rojas, Pauline M. "The Teaching of Language." Conference at the Rotary Club of San Juan, 28 September, 1954.

Sáez, Antonia. "Informe de las observaciones de la enseñanza del vernáculo en las escuelas intermedias y secundarias de ciertas poblaciones de Puerto Rico." n. d. (Mimeographed).

Sellés Solá, Gerardo. Lecturas históricas de la educación en Puerto Rico. San Juan: Biblioteca de Autores Puertorriqueños, 1943.

_____. Lenguaje Castellano. San Juan: Bureau of Supplies, Printing and Transportation, 1922.

Viera Martínez Tania. "Textbooks Used in the Public Schools of the Commonwealth of Puerto Rico," Report Submitted as part of the Survey of the School System of Puerto Rico, n. d. (Mimeographed).

Francesco Cordasco

THE PUERTO RICAN FAMILY AND THE ANTHROPOLOGIST: OSCAR LEWIS, LA VIDA, AND THE CULTURE OF POVERTY

Few European scholars (and fewer American savants) have managed to scale the ramparts of academe and carry their intellectual wares into the lay market place: those who have, almost inevitably, have earned the envy and suspicion of their professional confrères, and the countless dollars of dilettantish lay readers who have acquired fashion and prized erudition in frenzied pursuit of the erstwhile academicians. Most often, historians and sociologists (Cesare Lombroso, Guglielmo Ferero, Oswald Spengler, H. G. Wells, and W. G. Sumner come easily to mind) have made the trek from Parnassus into the valley of discord. Successively, they have titillated, infuriated, amused and mesmerized their lay audiences: they have cast dazzling pearls before raucous crowds, and they have counted ducats; and few have remembered to return home to their Olympian lairs. The latest of the academic itinerants is the anthropologist Oscar Lewis, who has studied Blackfeet Indians in Canada, farmers in Texas, and the culture of the Indian subcontinent. And all of this he has done well; but with the publication of La Vida,[1] Professor Lewis has disappeared into the lay gethsemane to which, with some timorous flirtation, his Five Families (1959), The Children of Sanchez (1961) and Pedro Martinez (1964) had earlier brought him.

La Vida (an enormously thick, nondescripto Teutonic volume) is the first of a series on Puerto Rican slum families in San Juan and New York which Professor Lewis plans. It is part of the burgeoning literature on the Puerto Rican community, and beyond the accolades it has received from book distribution clubs (which have been ecstatic in their praises), La Vida has been hailed as "... one of the most important books published in the United States this year;" cautioned against, in that "(its) insights ... will depend upon the com-

Reprinted by permission from Urban Education 3:32-38, 1967.

passion and perception of the reader;" and energetically questioned: "Is he (Professor Lewis) describing Puerto Ricans, ... or is he describing exceptional people, leading exceptional lives, who resemble their fellow Puerto Ricans only in limited ways?"[2]

The Plan of LA VIDA

Basic to any of these considerations is Professor Lewis' plan for La Vida, and his theory of the "culture of poverty" out of which the plan evolves. If the plan of La Vida is deceptively simple, Professor Lewis' "culture of poverty" is not; yet one is meaningless without the other, and it is not the portraiture of La Vida (a vast pathological Eloge) which gives validity to the theory, but rather the theory which is the deus ex machina of Professor Lewis' vast social tableau.

The plan for La Vida takes on Zolaesque proportion: some three hundred individuals cross its pages. While preparing the volume, Professor Lewis studied nineteen related households, eleven in San Juan and eight in New York; and data on twelve other households appear in the book. The Ríos family which is presented "consists of five households, a mother and two married daughters in Puerto Rico and a married son and daughter in New York. The mother, Fernanda Fuentes ... is now living with her sixth husband in La Esmeralda, a San Juan slum. Her children--Soledad, twenty-five; Felicita, twenty-three; Simplicio, twenty-one; and Cruz, nineteen--were born to Fernanda while she was living in free union with her first husband, Cristobal Ríos, a light-skinned Puerto Rican." Professor Lewis' family kaleidoscope revolves about Fernanda in San Juan; Soledad in New York; Felicita in San Juan; Simplicio in New York; and Cruz in San Juan. It is a harrowing tale of two cities of life-styles largely recorded on tape which Professor Lewis has edited to present the details of the way of life of the Ríos family with Karamazovian affectlessness. And there is no absence of detail. What emerges is a vast panorama of social and psycho-pathology: cruelty and violence; deceit; the subtleties of human degradation; endemic social deviance; the "game" of prostitution; consensual unions; and abandonment; and omnipresent sex, never missing from the lives of the protagonists, and recorded with such literalness of language and an unrestrained abundance of detail by Professor Lewis that it initially shocks and, then, revolts the reader. [3] The Ríos family are a dramatis personae in search of an author and in a curious Pirandellean twist, Professor Lewis not only furnishes a play, but a theory as well. It is this theory (the "Culture of Poverty") which translates La Vida into Balzacian reality or into grotesque illusion.

Professor Lewis and The Culture of Poverty

Professor Lewis (by his own statement) originated the concept of the "Culture of Poverty"; as a conceptual model, he has attempted its precise definition. The trick lies in distinguishing between "poverty" and the "culture of poverty": for the Ríos family is not representative of the poor, but rather of the subculture of poverty (Professor Lewis uses the shorter form); and this subculture of poverty focuses upon the individual personality rather than upon the group (that is, upon the family and the slum community).[4] Lewis defines the "culture of poverty" as,

> "... both an adaptation and a reaction of the poor to their marginal position in a class-stratified, highly individuated, capitalistic society. It represents an effort to cope with feelings of hopelessness and despair which develop from the realization of the improbability of achieving success in terms of the values and goals of the larger society. Indeed, many of the traits of the culture of poverty can be viewed as attempts at local solutions for problems not met by existing institutions and agencies because the people are not eligible for them, cannot afford them or are ignorant or suspicious of them." (p. xliv)

However, Professor Lewis is quick to add that the "culture of poverty" is "... not only an adaptation to a set of objective conditions of the larger society. Once it comes into existence it tends to perpetuate itself from generation to generation because of its effects on the children. By the time slum children are age six or seven, they have usually absorbed the basic values and attitudes of their subculture and are not psychologically geared to take full advantage of changing conditions or increased opportunities which may occur in their lifetime." (p. xiv). Daniel Moynihan refines the theory and adds still other ingredients: "... these families and the communities they make up (in the culture of poverty) tend to transmit from one generation to the next, traits and circumstances which help perpetuate their condition. There is nothing absolute about this: as many individuals, no doubt, leave the culture as remain in it, and on one level the proposition amounts to little more than the assertion that the poor rarely inherit large estates." (Commentary, February 1967, p. 36. The emphasis has been added.)

This adaptive ambience, Professor Lewis finds both creative and the source of great strengths (with its own structure and rationale, as a way of life), but with the key traits of fatalism and a low level of aspiration, "(which) helps to reduce frustration, (and with) the legitimization of short-range hedonism (which) makes possible spontaneity and enjoyment." Within these theoretic constructs, Professor Lewis analyzes the "culture of poverty" against four sets of characteristics: (1) the lack of effective participation and integration of the poor in the major institutions of the larger society; (2) poor housing, crowding, gregariousness, and a minimum of organization beyond the level of the nuclear and extended family; (3) the absence of childhood as a specially prolonged and protected stage in the life cycle; early initiation into sex, free unions or consensual marriages, high incidence of abandonment of wives and children, female-centered families, lack of family stability, authoritarianism; (4) marginality, helplessness, dependence and inferiority. In essence, if one is disposed to accept the thesis, Professor Lewis' discussion is a major contribution to the "culture of poverty."

Lewis develops the thesis and basic methodology in a lengthy introduction (pp. iv-ix) which must be read if the book is to be kept in its proper setting. The socio-economic correlates of the theory, mutatis mutandis, vis à vis the Negro community were developed by Daniel Moynihan in The Case For National Action (1965). Although Lewis, at no point in any substance, relates his "culture of poverty" to the schools and education, Moynihan does. In a review of the controversy spawned by The Negro Family (the Moynihan Report), he gives the theory a significant and new dimension: "At the moment Negroes are placing enormous confidence in the idea that quality education can transform their situation. But it is not at all clear that education has this potential. Last summer, the U.S. Office of Education issued its report on "Equality of Educational Opportunity" based on the study ... ordered by the Civil Rights Act of 1964 of the educational facilities available to Negroes and other minority groups as compared with the white majority. The report (The Coleman Report) ... radically confounded expectation. Negroes, it turned out, tested badly at the outset of their schooling, and worse at the end of it. But the quality of the schools they attended--shockingly segregated schools--was not in fact significantly different from that of schools attended by whites and others. More important, the regression analysis carried out for the study produced the astounding proposition that the quality of the schools has only a trifling relation to achievement ... the two great determinants of outcome turned out to be family background and social peer group." (Commentary, February 1967, p. 44)

The Vast Slough of LA VIDA

Caught in the vast slough of La Vida, the central question for the Ríos family is their typicality: is Professor Lewis describing exceptional people, leading exceptional lives, who resemble their fellow Puerto Ricans in only limited ways? The very viability of Lewis' theory of "the culture of poverty" depends on the answer to this crucial question. Unfortunately, Professor Lewis is ambiguous in his answer. Although he disclaims the representativeness of the Ríos family ("I should like to emphasize that this study deals with only one segment of the Puerto Rican population and that the data should not be generalized to Puerto Rican society as a whole"), he still claims a much larger significance and typicality: "The Ríos family would probably be classified as a multi-problem family by most social workers, but it is by no means an extreme example nor is it the worst I have encountered in the Puerto Rican slums;" and he extends his observation by noting, "The history of the Ríos family ... suggests that the pattern of free unions and multiple spouses was not limited to the poor. It has been a widespread pattern among wealthy rural families." (pp. xxviii-xxix). In much of the data, the tendency is always the cultivation of a special perspective even if this leads Professor Lewis to distortion.

Continuing Doubts

Clearly, continuing doubt frames a crucial question: is La Vida a study of the culture of lower-class Puerto Rican life; or is it a study of the culture of radically disorganized forms of slum life? Does all poverty lead to Professor Lewis' culture of poverty? For the theory must, if it has any validity, be more than the adaptation to the urban ambience which is its nexus: is it (for Professor Lewis) culture itself? All of the indices of Professor Lewis' "culture of poverty" (its marginality, and its helplessness, its sex and its prostitution) are related to poverty, but is the microcosm which Professor Lewis sketches in the macabre vignettes of the Ríos family the very substance of poverty itself?

The controversy which surrounds La Vida will obscure many of the important questions it raises. It will, unhappily, overshadow the tremendous struggle of the Puerto Rican community (both on the mainland and in the island) to confront the realities of the grim social and economic problems;[5] it will minimize the gains achieved in mainland schools;[6] it will register as crude parodies the poetic pathos of the Puerto Rican poor. [7] And it will be widely read, misinterpreted and misused.

References

1. La Vida: A Puerto Rican Family in the Culture of Poverty--San Juan and New York. By Oscar Lewis. Random House (1966). 669 pp.
2. See the reviews, respectively, of Michael Harrington, New York Times Book Review, November 20, 1966, p. 1; Rev. Joseph P. Fitzpatrick, America, December 10, 1966, p. 778; and Nathan Glazer, Commentary, February, 1967, p. 83. See also the negative sentiments in the review by Joseph Monserrat, "A Puerto Rican Family," Natural History (April 1967).
3. See the description of Soledad's relationship with Benedecto as an illustration of the pervasive luridity, pp. 217 ff.
4. Cf. Michael Harrington's definition of the "culture of poverty" in his The Other America (1961). See also Elizabeth Herzog, "Some Assumptions About the Poor." The Social Service Review, December 1963, pp. 389-402; and Nathan Glazer, loc. cit., supra. Professor Lewis is not without historical predecessors who have attempted to fashion a viable theory out of the poignant evocations and delineations of human misery: Henry Mayhew's London Labour and the London Poor (1861-62) is an analogous tableau; and so is the literary and sociological canon of Mid-Victorian England.
5. See particularly, Dorothy D. Bourne and James R. Bourne, Thirty Years of Change in Puerto Rico (New York: Frederick A. Praeger 1966); and The Puerto Rican Community Development Project: Un Proyecto Puertorriqueño De Ayuda Mutua Para El Desarrollo De La Communidad (New York: The Puerto Rican Forum 1964).

6. "Most of our children are brought up in homes where the language and culture is still mostly shaped along the way of life parents lived in Puerto Rico. This is good and positive and it has to be so because parents themselves cannot transmit what they do not know, but here is where the school enters as the institution that will help transmit the new culture into a child's life, and for that matter into the home as a whole. We pledge our support in all aspects where community support will be needed." Statement of Carmen Dinos (Supervisor of the Education Program of the Migration Division of the Commonwealth of Puerto Rico) before the Board of Education of New York City, March 11, 1966. See also, F. Cordasco, "Puerto Rican Pupils and American Education," School and Society, vol. 95 (February 18, 1967), pp. 116-119.

7. "Ricardo Sanchez came from where the sugar cane is higher than a man to the plaza in old San Juan where the buses marked Aeropuerto stop. He came with his wife and two daughters and three suitcases and a paper bag and the promise from a brother in Harlem, New York, that there was work to be found in fabrica. The work in the sugar cane was over for the season and Ricardo had found nothing else. The government would pay him $7 every two weeks for thirteen weeks before the season began again, and then with the season he would get $3.60 a day for eight hours in the sun. He had done it before, as his fathers had done it but this time he told himself he wanted something more. 'It is,' he said, 'no good to be poor.'" Dan Wakefield, Island in the City. The World of Spanish Harlem (New York: Houghton Mifflin, 1959), p. 23.

TRANSITION TO THE MAINLAND

The institution which faces the most direct shock in the migration to the mainland is the family, and the progress of Puerto Ricans can be measured to a large extent by a study of the family. First a statistical description of Puerto Rican families can be presented, followed by an analysis of the effect of migration on the family.

It has long been recognized that the migration of Puerto Ricans is a family migration, in the sense that they either come as families, or expect to stay and found their families here. This is reflected in the percentage of the population on the mainland which is married. According to the 1960 census, of all Puerto Rican males over 14 years of age, 70 per cent were married; of females, about 80 per cent.[1] Age at marriage shows a sharp decline from first generation to second generation, indicating an adaptation to mainland patterns.

Type of Ceremony

Another indication of change can be found in the type of religious ceremony of Puerto Rican marriages on the mainland. As indicated before, this varies considerably from one area of Puerto Rico to another. Comparison of type of religious ceremony for all marriages in Puerto Rico for 1960 with type of religious ceremony for Puerto Rican marriages in New York City for 1959 brings results as shown in Table 1 [from J. P. Fitzpatrick, "Intermarriage of Puerto Ricans in New York City," Amer. J. of Sociol., 71, 4(1966), 403].

Two things are evident from Table 1. The pattern of marriage ceremony differs considerably between Puerto Rico and New York, and

Table 1
Type of Religious Ceremony for All Marriages
in Puerto Rico and All Puerto Rican Marriages
in New York City for Selected Years

	Civil (%)	Catholic (%)	Protestant (%)
Puerto Rico, 1949	24. 3	61. 4	14. 3
Puerto Rico, 1960	36. 2	45. 8	17. 6
New York City, 1949 (n. 4514)*	20. 0	27. 0	50. 0
New York City, 1959 (n. 9370)	18. 0	41. 0	38. 0

*A small number of other types of ceremonies are included in this total.

the pattern in New York, as in Puerto Rico, changed greatly between 1949 and 1959. The increase in Catholic ceremonies can be explained by the widespread efforts of the Catholic Archdioceses of New York and Brooklyn to develop special programs for the religious care of Puerto Rican people between 1949 and 1959. In addition, ceremonies in Pentecostal and Evengelical Churches declined from 1949 to 1959, particularly between first and second generation. If the Protestant marriages performed by ministers of Pentecostal and Evangelical sects are taken separately, the decline is very evident. In 1959, 38. 4 per cent of first generation grooms were married by Pentecostal minis-ters, but only 33. 3 per cent of second generation grooms; among brides, 37 per cent of first generation, but only 30. 1 per cent of the second generation were married by Pentecostal ministers. [2] The implica-tions of this for religious practice will be discussed in Chapter Eight. The consistent drop from first to second generation tends to confirm the theory that association with sects and storefront religious groups is a first generation phenomenon. When the second generation be-comes more familiar with American life, they tend to withdraw from the sects.

Out-Group Marriage

The most significant evidence of adjustment to life on the mainland has been the increase of marriage of Puerto Ricans with non-Puerto Ri-cans. In his study of New York marriages, 1949 and 1959, Fitzpa-trick established that there is a significant increase in the rate of out-group marriage among second generation Puerto Ricans over the first. The data are presented in Table 2 [from J. P. Fitzpatrick, "Intermarriage of Puerto Ricans in New York City," Amer. J. of Sociol. , 71, 4(1966), 398].

The increase in the rate of out-group marriage among Puerto Ricans in both 1949 and 1959 between the first and second generation was as great as was the increase for all immigrants in New York City in the years 1908 to 1912. [3] It is legitimate to conclude from this that, if out-group marriage is accepted as an index of assimilation, the assimilation of Puerto Ricans in New York is moving as rapidly as the assimilation of all immigrant groups during the years 1908-1912.

Table 2
Rate of Out-Group Marriage of Puerto Ricans
in New York City, 1949 and 1959, by Generation;
and of All Immigrants in New York City, 1908-1912

| | First Generation | | Second Generation | | Increase in Second Generation |
	%	No.	%	No.	%
Grooms:					
Puerto Rican, 1949	5. 2	3,079	28. 3	378	23. 1
Puerto Rican, 1959	3. 6	7,078	27. 4	638	23. 8
1908-1912	10.39	64,577	32. 4	12,184	22.01
Brides:					
Puerto Rican, 1949	8. 5	3,077	30. 0	523	21. 5
Puerto Rican, 1959	6. 0	7,257	33. 1	717	27. 1
1908-1912	10. 1	61,823	30. 12	14,611	20. 02

Changes in Values

Much more important than the statistical description of the Puerto Rican families in the United States or in New York City is the study of the changes in values which they face. Probably the most serious is the shift in roles of husband and wife. There is abundant evidence that this is a common experience of immigrants. It is provoked by a number of things. First, it is frequently easier for Puerto Rican women to get jobs in New York rather than Puerto Rican men. This gives the wife an economic independence which she may never have had before, and if the husband is unemployed while the wife is work-ing, the reversal of roles is severe. Second, the impact of American culture begins to make itself felt more directly in New York than on the Island. Puerto Rican women from the poorer classes are much more involved in social, community, and political activities than they are in Puerto Rico. This influences the Puerto Rican wife gradually to adopt the patterns of the mainland.

Even more direct and difficult to cope with is the shift in role of the Puerto Rican child. Puerto Rican families have frequently la-mented the patterns of behavior of even good boys in the United States. Puerto Rican parents consider them to be disrespectful. American children are taught to be self-reliant, aggressive, and competitive, to ask "why," and to stand on their own two feet. A Puerto Rican child is generally much more submissive. When the children begin to behave according to the American pattern, the parents cannot understand it. A priest who had worked for many years with migrating Puerto Ricans remarked to the writer: "When these Puerto Rican families come to New York, I give the boys about 48 hours on the streets of New York, and the difference between his behavior and what the family expects, will have begun to shake the family."

The distance which gradually separates child from family is indicated in much of the literature about Puerto Ricans in New York. In the autobiography of Piri Thomas, Down These Mean Streets,[4] it is clear that his family--and it was a good, strong family--had no way of controlling him once he began to associate with his peers on the streets. The sharp contrast of two life histories, Two Blocks Apart,[5] also demonstrates the difficulties of a Puerto Rican family in trying to continue to control the life of a boy growing up in New York. His peers become his significant reference group. A considerable number of scholars and social workers attribute much of the delinquency of Puerto Ricans to the excessive confinement which the Puerto Rican families impose in an effort to protect their children. Once the children can break loose in the early teens, they break completely. When Julio Gonzalez was killed in a gang fight on the lower East Side in reprisal for the murder of a Negro girl, Theresa Gee, in 1959, he was buried from Nativity Church. Julio's father, a poor man from a mountain town in Puerto Rico, was like a pillar of strength during the wake. He was a man of extraordinary dignity and self-possession. After the funeral Mass, he went to the sacristy of the Church, embraced each of the priests who had participated, and thanked them. Here was a man who sought to pass on to his son the qualities of loyalty, dignity, and strength. But when the son reached the streets, different definitions of loyalty and dignity took over. As Julio was dying, after the priest had given him the last rites of the Catholic Church, he fell into unconsciousness, mumbling: "Tell the guys they can count on me; tell them I'll be there."[6]

Probably the most severe problem of control is the effort of families to give their unmarried girls the same kind of protection they would have given them in Puerto Rico. When the girls reach the early teens, they wish to do what American girls do--go to dances with boys without a chaperone, and associate freely with girls and boys of the neighborhood or school. For a good Puerto Rican father to permit his daughter to go out unprotected is a serious moral failure. In a Puerto Rican town, when a father has brought his daughters as virgins to marriage, he can hold up his head before his community; he enjoys the esteem and prestige of a good father. To ask the same father to allow his daughters to go free in New York is to ask him to do something which the men of his family have considered immoral. It is psychologically almost impossible for him to do this. This tension between parents and daughter(s) is one of the most difficult for Puerto Rican parents to manage. It is frequently complicated because Americans, including school teachers and counsellors, who are not aware of the significance of this in the Puerto Rican background, advise the parents to allow the girls to go out freely. [7]

Finally, the classic tension between the generations takes place. The parents are living in the Puerto Rican culture in their homes. The children are being brought up in an American school where American values are being presented. The parents will never really understand their children; the children will never really understand the parents.

Weakening of Extended Kinship

Apart from the conflict between generations, the experience of migration tends to weaken the family bonds that created a supporting network on which the family could always rely. To a growing extent, the family finds itself alone. This is partly the result of moving from place to place. It is also due to the fact that the way of life in mainland cities is not a convenient environment for the perpetuation of family virtues and values. The Department of Social Services provides assistance in time of need, but not with the familiar, informal sense of personal and family respect. Regulations in housing, consumer loans, schools, and courts create a requirement for professional help, and the family is less and less effective.

Replacement of Personalist Values

Closely related to all the above difficulties, and creating difficulties of its own, is the slow and steady substitution of impersonal norms, norms of the system rather than norms of personal relationships. The need to adjust to the dominant patterns of American society requires a preparation to seek employment and advancement on the basis of merit or ability. To people for whom the world is an extensive pattern of personal relationships, this is a difficult adjustment.

This process of uprooting has been described before in the extensive literature about immigrants. It leads to three kinds of adjustments. The first involves escape from the immigrant or migrant group and an effort to become as much like the established community as possible in as short a time as possible. These people seek to disassociate themselves from their past. They sometimes change their name, they change their reference groups, and seek to be accepted by the larger society. They are in great danger of becoming marginal. Having abandoned the way of life of their own people, in which they had a sense of "who they were," there is no assurance that they will be accepted by the larger community. They may find themselves in a no man's land of culture. In this stage, the danger of personal frustration is acute.

A second reaction is withdrawal into the old culture, a resistance to the new way of life. These people seek to retain the older identities by locking themselves into their old way of life.

The third reaction is the effort to build a cultural bridge between the culture of the migrants and that of the mainland. These are the people who have confidence and security in their own way of life, but who realize that it cannot continue. Therefore, they seek to establish themselves in the new society, but continue to identify themselves with the people from whom they come. These are the ones through whom the process of assimilation moves forward.

Present Situation of Puerto Rican Families

In view of the above discussion, it is important to discover at what level of assimilation the Puerto Rican family now stands, and how it is affected by the problem of identity. In terms of intermarriage, the data indicate that the increase in the rate of out-group marriage between first and second generation is as great as it was for all immigrants to New York, 1908-1912. Replication of the study for 1969 which is now in progress at Fordham University, New York, will involve many more first and second generation marriages, and will give a much more reliable indication of the trend. In this regard, Puerto Ricans are simply repeating the consistent pattern of immigrants who preceded them.

Second, in view of the character of the migration from Puerto Rico (i. e. , the return of many Puerto Ricans from the mainland and the continuing movement of large numbers of new migrants to the mainland), there continue to be large numbers of Puerto Rican families in the early and difficult stages of adjustment to New York, struggling for a satisfactory cultural adjustment as defined by Gordon and Eisenstadt.

The increase in the number of second generation Puerto Ricans indicates that the classical problems of newcomers, the problems of the second generation, are very likely at a serious level and will continue to be so for a considerable length of time. It is not clear just how family difficulties contribute to the larger problems of education, mental illness, need for public assistance, and drug addiction, but it is certain that these problems contribute immeasurably to family difficulties. In the early 1960's, a group of Puerto Rican social workers founded the Puerto Rican Family Institute in an effort to assist Puerto Rican families in New York. The objective of the Institute was not simply to provide family casework, but rather to identify well established Puerto Rican families in New York and match them as compadres to newly arrived families which showed signs of suffering from the strains of adjustment to the city. This was an attempt to use the traditional forms of neighborhood and family help which were characteristic of Puerto Rico. Where families could be matched, the program has been very helpful. But recently the Institute has found that the percentage of families with serious and immediate problems has been increasing. This may reflect the fact that, as agencies around the city learn of a Puerto Rican Institute, they refer their Puerto Rican problem cases to it; it may also reflect the shock of uprooting upon the newly arriving families, or the disruption which occurs as the numbers in the second generation increase. The growth of militancy among the young will be another factor which will increase tension. However, in the demonstrations at City College of New York in the Spring of 1969, in which militant Puerto Rican students played a major part, observers commented that the parents of the Puerto Rican students were very much on hand supporting their sons and daughters, bringing them food, clothing, and supplies.

In the period during which the Puerto Ricans struggle for greater solidarity and identity as a community, the family remains the major psychosocial support for its members. In many cases it is a broken family; in others it is hampered by poverty, unemployment, illness; but it remains the source of strength for most Puerto Ricans in the process of transition. In the turbulent action of the musical West Side Story, when Bernardo, leader of the Puerto Rican gang, sees Tony, a youth of another ethnic group, approaching his sister Maria, Bernardo pulls Maria away from Tony to take her home; he then turns to Tony in anger and shouts: "You keep away from my sister. Don't you know we are a family people!"

During 1966 the first presentation in New York of The Ox Cart took place. This is a play by a Puerto Rican playwright, René Marques, which presents a picture of a simple farm family in the mountains of Puerto Rico, struggling to survive but reflecting the deep virtues of family loyalty and strength. Under the influence of the oldest son, the family moves to a slum section of San Juan in order to improve itself. But deterioration sets in as the slum environment begins to attack the solidarity and loyalty of the family members. The family then moves to New York, where the strain of the uprooting becomes worse, the gap between mother and children more painful, and the virtues of the old mountain family seem even more distant. After the violent death of the son, the play ends with the valiant mother setting out to go back to the mountains of Puerto Rico, where she hopes to regain the traditional values of Puerto Rican family life which were destroyed in San Juan and New York.

This is an ancient theme, and it may be as true for Puerto Ricans as it was for earlier newcomers. But if the Puerto Ricans make it on the mainland, it will be through the same source of strength which supported the immigrants of earlier times--the solidarity of the family.

References

1. J. P. Fitzpatrick, "Intermarriage of Puerto Ricans in New York City," Amer. J. of Sociol., 71, 4(1966), 401, Tables 4 and 5.
2. Ibid., 404, Table 10.
3. The data for marriages of immigrants, 1908-1912, which were used in the Fitzpatrick study were taken from Julian Drachsler, Intermarriage in New York City (New York: Columbia University Press, 1921).

4. Piri Thomas, Down These Mean Streets (New York: Alfred A. Knopf, 1967).

5. Charlotte Leon Mayerson, ed. , Two Blocks Apart (New York: Holt, Rinehart and Winston, 1965).

6. For a lengthy discussion of this change of values and its relation to delinquency, see J. P. Fitzpatrick, "Crime and Our Puerto Ricans," in Catholic Mind, LVIII (1960), 39-50. This is reprinted in Gus Tyler, Organized Crime in America (Ann Arbor: University of Michigan Press, 1962), p. 415-421.

7. Protection of the girls generates its own problems in Puerto Rico, a form of "cloister rebellion" which may lead to escape from the home or elopement. It is well described in Stycos, Family and Fertility, op. cit. , Chap. 5.

RESPETO, RELAJO AND INTERPERSONAL
RELATIONS IN PUERTO RICO

Every universe of discourse has its clichés. [2]   Ordinary speech is full of trite statements which describe and evaluate the behavior of individuals.   Among these cultural forms are two poorly explored classes: one refers to the way in which all roles must be played; the other refers to the way in which kinds of individuals play all their roles--that is, to a general styling of all their interaction.   The first class refers to the characteristics which any encounter between all persons must possess, and which any actor must demonstrate; the second class refers to the characteristics of specific personae, or social personality types.   Students of Latin American anthropology have not devoted enough discussion to this type of analysis[3] with one significant exception: Edwin Seda's codification of Puerto Rican social personality types (1957: 32-63).

Our examination of some of these clichés utilizes a conceptual scaffolding derived from Erving Goffman's work, [4] who in turn builds upon earlier insights provided by G. H. Mead (1934).   In ordinary social intercourse, the participants mutually present and maintain a certain image of self which pertains to each of them.   Men seek to communicate certain information about themselves and each other; they establish and convey impressions about certain qualities of the self. In this process, men give each other value: "the person ... is allotted a kind of sacredness that is displayed and confirmed by symbolic acts." (Goffman 1956b:473) The self, and the image of self built up in action is endowed with the sort of ritual value discussed by Radcliffe-Brown (1939).   This is accomplished through the use of a ceremonial or ritual idiom, by which individuals express their character and also convey their appreciation of the other participants in the encounter.   If, through the proper use of this idiom, a man shows himself as committed to, and capable of, maintaining another person's

Reprinted by permission from Anthropological Quarterly 37:53-67, April 1964.   Published by The Catholic Univ. of America Press.

image of himself, he demonstrates what Goffman terms proper demeanor. In doing so, he will use a component of the ceremonial idiom which serves to express the positive value with which the participants in any situation endow each other. Goffman describes this component of activity as "deference" (op. cit. 477). The idiom also provides for profaning the self; it contains equally elaborate rituals of defamation.

1. Seda's analysis of a number of clichés of Puerto Rican speech ordered them into sets delineating social personae.[5] Our discussion begins with another of these linquistic labels, respeto. Rather than being associated with a specific social personality type, respeto is a quality of self which must be presented in all interpersonal treatment.

In attempting to describe this self, we must have recourse to an additional set of clichés. Besides the set containing those of Puerto Rican social discourse, we add that of many observers of Puerto Rican social discourse. Such commentators have placed considerable emphasis on the folk aspects of dignidad (literally, "dignity"), honor ("pride," "honor"), upon the courtesy of adult males, upon the impression given that each man seems to conceive of himself as always being primus inter pares; the image of the haughty Hispanic individualist, conserving within himself an inviolable residue of pride. Many of these comments appear in discussions which implicitly or explicitly postulate a uniform Puerto Rican "national character."[6] They are hackneyed comments, but we submit that they can be endowed with heuristic value precisely because they are hackneyed. They are clichés because they refer to clichés; i.e., the most general definition of a social situation which Puerto Ricans present to each other is also presented to outsiders. Both sets overlap.

Respeto is a quality ascribed to the properties. It signifies proper attention to the requisites of the ceremonial order of behavior, and to the moral aspects of human activities. This quality is an obligatory self-presentation; no Puerto Rican is considered properly socialized unless he can comport himself with respeto.

The verb form, respetar, indicates that in any encounter, one expresses deference to the person whom he confronts. Failure to convey this is termed una falta de respeto ("lack of respeto").

Un hombre de respeto is a man who projects the kind of self which is capable of maintaining the ceremonial order. He demonstrates proper demeanor; his comportment gives the impression that he can be a proper "interactant," committed to, and capable of, maintaining another man's image of himself. He is said to be un hombre de consideración--one who has consideration for the self-images of others.

But the quality of possessing proper demeanor is also something which must be presented to the individual; he alone cannot legitimize his claim to it. Others' communication of their regard for him in turn endow his self with proper demeanor. It is frequently said "Hay que darse a respetar antes de ser respetado," alternatively, "El que no se da a respetar, no lo respetan"--one must evidence proper demeanor, show oneself worthy of being respected before another will defer to him; he who shows no respect will not receive it. When a man does show it, él considera--he shows "personalized deference,"[7] he is de carácter ("of character"), possessing the requisite self-attributes. He is also de vergüenza, capable of knowing shame, of taking responsibility for his acts. Carácter and vergüenza denote "self-respect"; one shows that one has sufficient regard for one's self, to be allocated a self in society.

Thus, in their daily intercourse, Puerto Rican men give each other value; they treat each other as if they were sacred. Through their mutual enactment of the ritual, they establish and convey impressions concerning certain highly valued self-qualities. And it is here that the clichés of Puerto Rican social discourse coincide with the clichés of those who have commented upon this discourse. Both sets overlap. We have the picture of men who stand off from each other, players in an elaborate game where no one may come too close for fear of offending, who treat each other as potential duelists, ferocious in self-defense. And the man who is indeed de respeto, possessing dignidad, or who is truly macho,[8] who is serio, taking the moral and ceremonial order seriously, and cumplidor, who complies with the obligations of proper inter-personal treatment, is the hombre completo, the integral or complete man. He possesses, as one Puerto Rican anthropologist has described this, "an almost fanatical conviction of his self value" (Seda 1957:40).

In treating with others, one is always careful not to step on the other's dignidad. Men might kill for many reasons in Puerto Rico, but their reasons are usually phrased in this idiom; violations of the basic right to respeto, either in personam or in rem, can lead this far.

Further, one must treat all men with respeto. To be sure, the concrete deferential acts of respeto communicate many kinds of regard in which a person may be held--awe, trust, esteem for technical capacity, recognition of superior rank, and affection. But the element of respeto which must be communicated in the most minimal message of this ceremonial idiom concerns the person's basic right to a self. This element of respeto obtains between those who are, otherwise, social equals, superiors, and subordinates. One's very social existence is predicated upon the bonds of respeto.

However, respeto is a homonym. In describing this term, it is necessary to differentiate between the sort of generalized deference which we have been discussing, and various particularized forms of respeto which are the concomitants of particular kinds of social relations in Puerto Rico. The two categories must not be confused. The first category of respeto is that which must be present as a quality of all social relations, regardless of their content. The second category contains a wide variety of kinds of regard, all defined as respeto. One deserves special mention: deference in the ordinary sense of the term, as we use it--giving place to a person of superior authority or prestige. But no matter how much the subordinate is expected to respetar his superior, in this sense, the latter must always express deference as well, using the first form of respeto. Even if the superior comports himself with an overbearing hauteur, he is obligated to express his deference to the subordinate's self through the proper symbolic acts.[9]

Just as the kinds of regard which are expressed through respeto vary, so do the symbolic forms which communicate them. There is a universal ceremonial idiom, in which all adult Puerto Ricans can communicate; there are other idioms which are more specific to certain segments of Puerto Rican society. In either case, respeto is the basic prop of the deference game. But not all Puerto Ricans are capable of manipulating the forms of all of the special idioms. Embarrassment, loss of face, shaming, and other breaks in communication are created by the contact of these differing ceremonial orders. The well-known examples of the peasant who cannot mesh with the bureaucracy of the State; and the nouveau riche who cannot get on with the visiting technical specialist from the capital are illustrations. Yet both these examples of dissonance are evaluated in terms of the universal idiom. The peasant avoids the use of State services because the clerks do not express respeto properly: "no consideran a uno"; the nouveau riche is "misunderstood" and refuses to take the advice of the specialist.

2.   As Puerto Ricans have developed an elaborate set of honorific rituals around the conveyance of respeto, so have they developed an equally elaborate idiom of defamation. We may examine one aspect of this idiom in considering the semantics of the verb relajar and the associated noun el relajo. They have a wide variety of behavioral referents, a few of which we will briefly illustrate before examining one set of these referents in detail.

Most usages of relajar refer to joking, and to a kind of joking interaction whose elements parallel the content of the classical joking relationship--privileged insult, banter, and so forth. The topics are numerous; reference can be made to the personal, political, occupational idiosyncrasies and sexual habits of a participant in the interchange, or some close relative or friend, or of some absent person. Ribbing, riding, kidding all come under the purview of un relajo. The derogatory nickname with which a person is endowed may sometimes be used. Many Puerto Ricans have two nicknames: one, the apodo or sobrenombre serves as an alternate, or sometimes the only name by which a person is addressed; the other, the mal nombre, is wounding and derogatory, unless the situation in which it is used is otherwise carefully defined. Use of either type of nickname is a relajo. One may also "put one over" on another man, making him swallow a tall story, or cogerle de bobo (take him for a sucker, make a fool out of him); an alternate form is to catch him out in some set joking gambit. If a man falls for the gambit, the reply is "Me cogiste" ("you caught me off guard," "my face slipped"), and/or a sally in kind.[10]

The telling of jokes, obscene or otherwise, the use of obscenity regardless of the interactive context is described as están diciendo relajos. Friendly grappling, punching, slapping also rate this epithet, which also serves to describe a somewhat unruly or disorderly gathering or party, ("se formó el gran relajo en el baile"). Sexual intercourse is also described--e.g., "Cogieron a Chuito y Pepa en el relajo en el monte" ("they found Chuito and Pepa making out in the bush"). Impious or inappropriate behavior with reference to religion is another example. In one case, a man described what he deemed to be a faked trance on the part of a young member of a certain revivalistic sect as "el niño estaba relajando con los ojos abiertos. Estaba relajando con la religión." ("the kid was faking it with his eyes wide open; he was fooling around with religion").

There are more neutral uses; an excessively sweetened cup of coffee will evoke the comment "Este café relaja"; a woman, commenting on a dress which is in fashion, but owned by too many women, may say "Esa moda está relajada." The connotation, in common with most uses of the term, is of excess.

Cogen las cosas a relajo is said of those who do not take things seriously, of those who fool around, in our parlance. Some men can take nothing seriously; they attempt to turn everything into a joke; such a one is described as un relajón. Frequently, the adjective un exagerado is added, signifying one who always exaggerates some aspect of behavior, some aspect of his role playing--one who continually and consistently goes too far.

The full array of meanings assignable to relajar and un relajo may be paralleled, in colloquial New York speech, by the full array of uses of "to fool with/to fool around/to fool around with"; "to mess with/to mess around/to mess around with"....

Space permits the detailing of only one of these behavioral complexes: the confrontational joking game, where the object of the relajo is a direct participant in a social encounter. The behavior which constitutes part of a joking game, in which all adult male Puerto Ricans are seemingly capable of participating, may be observed to take place between the occupants of practically any position in the structure of any Puerto Rican social grouping. Such passages may occur between any type of kinsmen, peers, colleagues, "buddies," friends, and neighbors, and even between compadres (cogodparents), subordinates and superordinates, and men of quite disparate ages. It occurs among and between representatives of any segment of Puerto Rican society. Only one significant difference is notable; where the overall social position of the participants is symmetrical, then any one has the right to initiate the relajo; where the overall status is asymmetrical, only the superior may generally initiate the game.

The settings and occasions for such interaction are legion. They occur in bars, in the plaza, at race-tracks and cockpits, around baseball diamonds, in clubrooms, in private homes, in the streets, or any place of work. Indeed, any place where men congregate is an appropriate context. The joking most often takes place when men are at their leisure, or where the place of work is in a temporary locus of "leisure" activity. We must emphasize that joking, riding, kidding, banter, the ironic sally, are among the salient characteristics of all encounters between men, except in the courtroom, in churches, and during parts of the work process.

When the content of the message would be considered offensive or insulting, a consensus must be established between the participants, allowing someone to begin the relajo, knowing that the person he confronts will maintain a poised line of action--that he will take it as a joke. A rich vocabulary of speech and gesture aids in so defining the situation. Tone, gesture, laughter, and the time and place of the confrontation convey the impression that the statement is not meant as an affront. The other will immediately indicate just how he accepts the sally. In general, he is obliged to accept it--cogerlo como relajo; he may laugh at his own expense, and usually returns the treatment in kind. From there, the game continues. If he is angered, he is obliged not to express it.

Sometimes, he cannot reply--the sally may have hit him too hard, or his repertoire of retorts is exhausted. He may say "Ah, deja eso" or "Deja el relajito ese" ("Ah, cut it out, get off my back!"), making it clear that he is not offended. He may attempt to stop the interchange by expressing the faintest hint of anger via intonation and a stiffening of the body. Or he says "tumba ese relajo," a usage specifically showing that he means it this time; "no relajes más commigo," "don't mess around with me anymore."

The mutual "fooling around," described as "se relajaban uno al otro" (kidding each other) can occur as a sustained interchange, remaining at the level of a simple game whose vocabulary is part of the ritual of defamation and humiliation, but no one takes it seriously. At other times, the participants may take it very seriously, yet maintain the façade of the friendly joke. For analytical purposes, two categories may be distinguished: a simple "joking game" and the much more serious, and consequently infrequent "joking contest." In the second case, the mutual relajo becomes a joking contest, a full-blown contest of defamation, a ritual of degradation whose players are aggressively engaged in scoring points against each other, in seeing how far they can go and still retain the superficial consensus of amiability. All the devices, gambits and insults are used, successively becoming more dangerous. The winners are those who do not express their anger, who do not become embarrassed or flustered. In such a contest, the self maintained in interaction is attacked on two levels: its positive qualities are assailed; in addition, one is treated by the rest of the participants, not as a participant, a full social person, but as a mere focus of attention.[11]

In the contest, the standardized techniques of withdrawal from the particular line of interaction cannot be used without losing face.

One cannot become embarrassed, nor can one demand, with various degrees of severity or mock-severity, that the opponent stop there, or stomp out in a righteous rage, or become angry and curse, or even resort to the ultimate sanction of violence. The game continues until someone breaks, or the participants are somehow satisfied that they cannot break through the other's reserve, or some witness succeeds in intervening. Such intervention takes numerous forms; frequent tactics include outright criticism of the line of interaction being followed by one of the participants; re-direction of the joking at a different level, with different objects and referents; a new alliance between those who are temporarily onlookers; an attempt to shift the focus of attention to matters outside the frame of the relajo. Of course, the game may end in mutual recrimination and fighting.

The obligation to take it as a joke can produce different lines of interaction: the joking game, and the much less frequent joking contest. Either one may terminate in a serious rupture of relations, or in actual fighting. As the limits of tolerance are approached, el asunto coge calor (things get hot), the participants ponen color al asunto--they color it red-hot. If the limits are passed, men storm at each other, fight, or retire from the scene. Others comment on the incident: it has gone beyond joking; the relajo has been converted into un abuso, una ofensa; una falta de respeto has been committed. Se han pasado de la raya.[12]

Defamation contests, or profanation games, are described for several cultures, the best known being several varieties of "the dozens" and "jiving" among North American Negroes, and La Passategla of Southern Italy.[13] Both examples seem to be examples of a defamation contest that, as recurrent types of social situations, are more formally instituted than the relajo "contest." The rules of the "dozens" and La Passategla constitute sets which contrast sharply from milder forms of profanation. But the difference between the Puerto Rican joking game and joking contest is less a matter of special rules and symbolic forms and more the way in which the rules are manipulated. Joking game and joking contest are analytic constructs, in this case; Puerto Ricans do not define this as a game.

3. To indulge in relajos of any sort in the presence of anyone is to engage in a relation of confianza--of trust and familiarity with that person. The significance of confianza is quite complex, since it does not merely denote an absence of formality as it would amongst North Americans. Thus, certain kinds of social relations are characterized by a great degree of both respeto and confianza. In general, however, confianza refers to an invasion of that social space surrounding the self which is demarcated by the ritual avoidances enjoined by the maintenance of generalized respeto. And confianza implies that one's image of self is even more committed into the hands of others. Conflict, or its threat, follows upon an abuse of such trust, or when one presumes to inject an element of confianza in a relationship where there should be none. And the relajón is frequently called un confianzudo, one who presumes too much familiarity.

4. The aspects of the ceremonial order discussed above are symbolically coherent. Respeto refers to a set of deferential rituals; relajo subsumes, among other things, the symbols of defamation, counters in transactions of mutual degradation and profanation. Respeto and relajo are sometimes seen as antithetical; "si tú no respetas y te pones a relajar con cualquiera, nunca te respetarán a tí " ("if you do not defer properly to others and fool around with everyone, no one will respect you") is a statement frequently made to children--and to ethnographers.

Considering the standard meaning of relajar (to relax, to stretch, to loosen) the choice of this term to describe rituals of defamation becomes significant. A man who indulges in such behaviors figuratively does just that to the obligation of respeto which should rigidly bind the confrontational self-presentations of Puerto Ricans. The rule of conduct is stretched; avoidances are relaxed; the precincts of the self are invaded. In acceptable joking, one presumes upon the respeto due to one's self and that of another; and one can, relajando, stretch things too far. One can pasarse del límite and commit a true falta de respeto. In such cases so much metaphoric strain, in the logic of the ceremonial order, has been placed upon the rule of conduct that it ceases to obtain. The consensus which maintains the worth of each participant's social image is disrupted, and can no longer be restored through embarrassment or further banter. Only withdrawal, violence, rupture of relations or apology can restore the situation.

Other uses of relajar are consistent with the metaphor of strain upon the proper order of things or of excess beyond that which is seemly or satisfactory.[14]

5. We have stated that all adult male Puerto Ricans are capable of manipulating the symbols of respeto and relajo. In generalizing about elements which pertain, at least as a minimal or background element to all interaction among all Puerto Ricans, we introduce considerations which raise the same thorny problems presented by the national character studies. In discussing problems met in the study of Mexico as a complex society, Wolf (1956:1075) suggested:

> It seems possible to define "national character" operationally as those cultural forms or mechanisms which groups involved in the same overall web of relations can use in their formal and informal dealings with each other. Such a view need not imply that all nationals think or behave alike, nor that the forms used may not serve different functions in different social contexts. Such common forms must exist if communication between the different constituent groups of a complex society are [sic] to be established and maintained.

The ceremonial idiom under discussion is one such device. In Puerto Rico, we can demonstrate the existence of different cultural codes for various segments of the society. We postulate that all male adult Puerto Ricans, regardless of character or personality type, or the specific symbolic idiom of their particular social segment, are capable of communicating in a common ceremonial idiom. Each of the sub-groups of the society has its own ritual idiom, part of a symbolic order reflecting the peculiar social structure of the group; a symbolic order which produces differing cognitive models of the structure of the total society. But, using the symbolic small change of the universal ritual idiom, all Puerto Ricans may make statements to each other concerning their ceremonial and moral worth as social persons. Although, at times, the different orders may clash, the clash is evaluated in the same terms by the participants, using the idiom of respeto. They can tune in on a common network. Representatives of different segments of the society can converge upon one another, regardless of cognitive and emotional differences presupposed by the idiom of their particular social segment. Thus the element of respeto and the associated ceremonial order is one of a number of forms which allow us to speak of Puerto Rico as constituting a single society, as well as being a relatively homogeneous socio-cultural system. [15]

We have not attempted here any psychodynamic analysis of these situations. The image of self predicated upon respeto is an outcome of the confrontation of men in society; there is no need to postulate a particular set of psychic mechanisms at this level of analysis.

It is possible that the segment of the network which turns upon respeto may cease to be a stable mechanism in the articulation of Puerto Rico as a single society. New ritual forms, and a new symbolic idiom are apparently emerging. Through migration to the mainland, through the new educational system, and especially through the emergence of new religious systems, individual Puerto Ricans are differentially exposed to alternative symbol systems. The nature of the self which will be a product of the new systems of ceremonial discourse is changing; new sets of self-presentations are emerging. And the code built upon respeto, as well as the concept itself, may well become one of several partly antagonistic idioms mediating relations in the same social field. [16]

6. Summary. Respeto and relajo have been discussed as composing a symbolic idiom that serves to integrate Puerto Rican society. The relation of the term relajo to the crucial self-property of respeto has been demonstrated. This included showing why Puerto Ricans use relajo to designate those behaviors to which it refers. The conceptual scheme developed by Erving Goffman has proven useful in ordering data from another culture, although a systematic test of his formulations in cross-cultural perspective was not attempted. Using Goffman's framework, it is possible to operationalize at least some aspects of the notion of national character. The framework conveniently orders data in an attempt to delineate the kinds of messages which constitute the universal components of the circulation of symbols, cartes d'identité and self-presentations through a complex society. Further, the approach used in this paper seems to allow

the anthropologist to bring together the microstructural and the macrostructural aspects of the study of complex societies. On the basis of this tentative analysis, a uniquely Puerto Rican symbolic idiom is postulated. In the absence of comparative studies of sufficient rigor, it is not yet possible to specify the degree to which the idiom is unique.

References

Abrahams, R.
    1962--"Playing the Dozens." Journal of American Folklore 75:209-220.
Albizu Miranda, C. & H. Marty Torres
    1958--Atisbos de la personalidad puertorriqueña. Revista de Ciencias Sociales 2:383-403.
Berreman, Gerald D.
    1962--Behind many masks: ethnography and impression management in a Himalayan village. Monograph No. 4, Society for Applied Anthropology.
Brameld, T.
    1959--The remaking of a culture. New York
Cochran, T.
    1959--The Puerto Rican businessman. Philadelphia.
Dexter, L.
    1949--A dialogue on certain Puerto Rican personality patterns and the social psychology of colonialism. Human Relations 2:49-64.
Dollard, J.
    1939--The Dozens: dialect of insult. American Imago 1:3-25.
Goffman, Erving
    1955--On face-work: an analysis of ritual elements in social interaction. Psychiatry 18:213-231.
    1956a--Embarrassment and social organization. American Journal of Sociology 62:246-271.
    1956b--The nature of deference and demeanor. American Anthropologist 58:472-502.
    1959--The presentation of self in everyday life. Garden City.
    1962--Encounters: two studies in the sociology of interaction. Indianapolis.
Hotchkiss, J. C.
    1962--Children errand-runners: their roles in the social life of a small Mexican community. Paper read at the '61st annual meeting of the American Anthropological Association, Chicago, Illinois, Nov. 1962.
Hymes, D.
    1962--The enthnography of speaking. In T. Gladwin and W. C. Sturtevant (eds.) Anthropology and Human Behavior. Washington: Anthropological Society of Washington, 13-53.
Kany, Charles
    1960--American-Spanish euphemism. Berkeley.

Kaplan, B. (ed.)
    1961--Studying personality cross-culturally. Evanston.
Lauria, A.
    1960--The effects of migration on the processes of
          cultural stability and cultural change in contemporary
          Puerto Rico. MS.
Luquïn, E.
    1961--Análisis espectral del mexicano: el lambiscón, el
          madrugador, el pica-pedrero, el pistolero. México,
          D. F.
Manners, R. M.
    1956--Tabara: subcultures of a tobacco and mixed crops
          municipality. In Steward 1956:93-170.
Marqués, R.
    1962--El puertorriqueño dócil. Cuadernos Americanos 120:
          140-195.
Mead, G. H.
    1934--Mind, self, and society. Chicago.
Mintz, S. W.
    1956--Cañamelar: the subculture of a rural sugar plantation
          proletariat. In Steward, 1956:314-417.
Padilla, E.
    1956--Nocorá: the subculture of workers on a government
          owned sugar plantation. In Steward, 1956:265-313.
    1958--Up from Puerto Rico. New York.
Paz, Octavio
    1950--El laberinto de la soledad. México, D. F.
Pedreira, A. S.
    1934--Insularismo. Madrid.
Petrullo, V.
    1947--Puerto Rican paradox. Philadelphia.
Radcliffe-Brown, A. R.
    1939--Taboo. Reprinted In Structure and function in primi-
          tive society, 1952:133-152. Glencoe.
Reuter, E. B.
    1946--Culture contacts in Puerto Rico. American Journal of
          Sociology 52:91-101.
Seda Bonilla, Edwin
    1957--Normative patterns of the Puerto Rican family in var-
          ious situational contexts. Unpublished doctoral disser-
          tation, Department of Anthropology, Columbia University.
Steward, J. H. (et. al.)
    1956--The people of Puerto Rico. Urbana.
Stycos, J. M.
    1955--Family and fertility in Puerto Rico. New York.
Tugwell, R.
    1947--The stricken land. Garden City.
Vailland, R.
    1959--The Law. (P. Wiles, trans.) New York.
Wallace, A. F. C.
    1961--The psychic unity of human groups. In Kaplan 1961:
          129-164.
    1962--Culture and personality. New York.

Wolf, Eric R.
  1956--Aspects of group relations in a complex society: Mexico. American Anthropologist 58:1065-1078.
  1962--Cultural dissonance in the Italian Alps. Comparative Studies in Society and History 5:1-14.
  1963a--Review of M. Kenny, A Spanish Tapestry. American Anthropologist 65:432-434.
  1963b--Kinship, friendship, and patron-client relations in complex societies. Read at the Conference on New Approaches to the Study of Social Anthropology, Cambridge, U.K.
Wolf, Kathleen L.
  1952--Growing up and its price in three Puerto Rican subcultures. Psychiatry 15:401-433.

Notes

1. A shorter version of this paper was selected by The Central States Anthropological Society as the outstanding student paper presented at its annual meeting held in May, 1963 at Detroit, Michigan.

2. This study is based upon field materials gathered in Puerto Rico during the summer of 1958 and the period from August 1960 to August 1962. I am deeply indebted to Esther Santiago Lauria, my wife and colleague, for her advice and comments and suggestions of John C. Hotchkiss, Irving L. Horowitz, Julian Pitt-Rivers, James Silverberg, Eric R. Wolf, and Alvin W. Wolfe.

3. Anthropologists have generally left this to the belle-lettrists, who sometimes systematize the linguistic labels into types of personnae, and dialectologists and folklorists, who do not. See for example Luquïn (1961), Paz (1950). An interesting compendium of the terminology associated with aspects of self in American Spanish is found in Kany (1960).

4. This brief exposition of Goffman (esp. 1955, 1956a, 1956b, 1959, 1962) serves only to introduce our discussion; it does not do justice to the value of his work. His ideas were developed in the study of North American behavior; we are attempting to utilize his ideas in ordering data on another culture, as have Berreman (1962) and Hotchkiss (1962). However, this paper does not attempt a systematic test of all his formulations in cross-cultural perspective.

5. He shows certain sets of these clichés to be descriptions and evaluations of the individual "... not as an actor in a particular social role but generalized to apply to the personal stylization of the individual in all life activities ... and person playing roles ... may be described not with reference to a particular role but rather to a general description of his actions. Examination of these overall descriptions used in a culture may spell out clusters of attributes of high or low desirability. Such social personality forms provide ready-made styles in which individuals portray themselves and by

which they 'size-up' and accordingly respond to others."
(1957:32-33) In our terms, these are "self-attributes." Without Seda's codification, the present analysis could never have
been written.

6. Almost everything written about Puerto Rico touches on this.
The more important statements are to be found in: Brameld
(1959) Cochran (1959) Dexter (1949) Petrullo (1947) Tugwell
(1947) and a host of cultural nationalist exegises. The im-
agery of passivity employed by Albizu and Marty (1958) and
Marqués (1962) contrasts with the picture painted by the first
group. K. Wolf (1952) and Landy (1960) present analysis of
personality systems per se.

7. Seda's rendering (1957:42).

8. For present purposes, the usual translation labels "He-man,"
"real man" may be used to render macho.

9. This point is best documented in studies of the relations between
workers and their superiors. Cf. Mintz (1956:368) who men-
tions that a mayordomo should show workers on a sugar plantation "the respect (respeto, not deference) they believe appropriate." Generally the treatment of the concept of respeto
in the literature consists of noting nothing more than the concomitant of respeto peculiar to a specific social relation.
(Eg. Padilla 1956:292, 295; 1958:177; Stycos 1955:38n, 75,
79, 122-123; Mintz 1956:386). Manners (1956:144-45) apparently recognized some of the elements stressed in this paper:
a "word generally used to describe the proper behavior and
response to others in social situations ... there are no ab-
solutes determining what constitutes respectful behavior in all
situations.... When the forms are observed, the participants
in the vis-à-vis situation are said to be behaving properly
towards one another. When they are violated it is because
either or both behaved with falta de respeto."

10. The usual translation equivalent of bobo is "fool." The term
is used throughout Puerto Rico to describe a baby's rubber
pacifier. This is perhaps significant, since the term in e.g.
Northern Mexico is the more neutral chupón. This makes
our rendering--"sucker"--doubly significant.

11. Compare Goffman 1962:58-59.

12. Of course, these matters are extremely subtle; the cues, the
messages, which convey various degrees of relajo, intent,
and reaction cannot be expressed in a paper of this length.
Nor was I equipped to record them adequately. All of the
methodological problems posed by this paper are reviewed
in Hymes, 1962.

13. For "The Dozens," see Dollard, 1939; Abrahams, 1962. For
La Passategla, see Vailland, 1959. Among whites of various
ethnic groups in New York City, "ranking" or "sounding" an
individual represents a similar phenomenon.

14. There are a number of labels which are partial or complete
synonyms for relajo and relajar. Some are as yet imper-
fectly understood. The following are listed as examples only:
(subs.) un pasamacho, un chacoteo, una burla, una broma;
(verb) pasar el macho, burlar, bromear, molestar, chavar,
joder, chacotear.

15. See also Wolf, 1962, 1963a, 1963b, and parallel discussions by Wallace 1961, and 1962, Chapter 1.

16. An analysis of changes in the idiom of personal confrontation resulting from conversion to the Pentecostal church is currently in preparation. We do not mean to imply that, e.g., migration necessarily changes the idiom which a person uses; migrant returnees use the old patterns. Certain aspects of this problem are analyzed by Lauria (1960).

CULTURE OF POVERTY

Poverty and the so-called war against it provide a principal theme for the domestic program of the present Administration. In the midst of a population that enjoys unexampled material well-being-- with the average annual family income exceeding $7,000--it is officially acknowledged that some 18 million families, numbering more than 50 million individuals, are below the $3,000 "poverty line. " Toward the improvement of the lot of these people some $1,600 million of Federal funds are directly allocated through the Office of Economic Opportunity, and many hundreds of millions of additional dollars flow indirectly through expanded Federal expenditures in the fields of health, education, welfare and urban affairs.

Along with the increase in activity on behalf of the poor indicated by these figures there has come a parallel expansion of publication in the social sciences on the subject of poverty. The new writings advance the same two opposite evaluations of the poor that are to be found in literature, in proverbs and in popular sayings throughout recorded history. Just as the poor have been pronounced blessed, virtuous, upright, serene, independent, honest, kind and happy, so contemporary students affirm their great and neglected capacity for self-help, leadership and community organization. Conversely, as the poor have been characterized as shiftless, mean, sordid, violent, evil and criminal, so other students point to the irreversibly destructive effects of poverty on individual character and emphasize the corresponding need to keep guidance and control of poverty projects in the hands of duly constituted authorities. This clash of viewpoints reflects in part the infighting for political control of the program between Federal and local officials. The confusion results also from the tendency to focus study and attention on the personality of the individual victim of poverty rather than on the slum community and family and from the consequent failure to distinguish between poverty and what I have called the culture of poverty.

The phrase is a catchy one and is used and misused with some frequency in the current literature. In my writings it is the label for a specific conceptual model that describes in positive terms a subculture of Western society with its own structure and rationale, a way of life handed on from generation to generation along family lines. The culture of poverty is not just a matter of deprivation or disorganization, a term signifying the absence of something. It is a culture in the traditional anthropological sense in that it provides human beings with a design for living, with a ready-made set of solutions for human problems, and so serves a significant adaptive function. This style of life transcends national boundaries and regional and rural-urban differences within nations. Wherever it occurs, its practitioners exhibit remarkable similarity in the structure of their families, in interpersonal relations, in spending habits, in their value systems and in their orientation in time.

Not nearly enough is known about this important complex of human behavior. My own concept of it has evolved as my work has progressed and remains subject to amendment by my own further work and that of others. The scarcity of literature on the culture of poverty is a measure of the gap in communication that exists between the very poor and the middle-class personnel--social scientists, social workers, teachers, physicians, priests and others--who bear the major responsibility for carrying out the antipoverty programs. Much of the behavior accepted in the culture of poverty goes counter to cherished ideals of the larger society. In writing about "multiproblem" families social scientists thus often stress their instability, their lack of order, direction and organization. Yet, as I have observed them, their behavior seems clearly patterned and reasonably predictable. I am more often struck by the inexorable repetitiousness and the iron entrenchment of their lifeways.

The concept of the culture of poverty may help to correct misapprehensions that have ascribed some behavior patterns of ethnic, national or regional groups as distinctive characteristics. For example, a high incidence of common-law marriage and of households headed by women has been thought to be distinctive of Negro family life in this country and has been attributed to the Negro's historical experience of slavery. In actuality it turns out that such households express essential traits of the culture of poverty and are found among diverse peoples in many parts of the world and among peoples that have had no history of slavery. Although it is now possible to assert such generalizations, there is still much to be learned about this difficult and affecting subject. The absence of intensive anthropological studies of poor families in a wide variety of national contexts--particularly the lack of such studies in socialist countries--remains a serious handicap to the formulation of dependable cross-cultural constants of the culture of poverty.

My studies of poverty and family life have centered largely in Mexico. On occasion some of my Mexican friends have suggested delicately that I turn to a study of poverty in my own country. As a first step in this direction I am currently engaged in a study of Puerto Rican families. Over the past three years my staff and I have been assembling data on 100 representative families in four slums of Greater San Juan and some 50 families of their relatives in New York City.

Our methods combine the traditional techniques of sociology, anthropology and psychology. This includes a battery of 19 questionnaires, the administration of which requires 12 hours per informant. They cover the residence and employment history of each adult; family relations; income and expenditure; complete inventory of household and personal possessions; friendship patterns, particularly the compadrazgo, or godparent, relationship that serves as a kind of informal social security for the children of these families and establishes special obligations among the adults; recreational patterns; health and medical history; politics; religion; world view and "cosmopolitanism." Open-end interviews and psychological tests (such as the thematic apperception test, the Rorschach test and the sentence-completion test) are administered to a sampling of this population.

All this work serves to establish the context for close-range study of a selected few families. Because the family is a small social system, it lends itself to the holistic approach of anthropology. Whole-family studies bridge the gap between the conceptual extremes of the culture at one pole and of the individual at the other, making possible observation of both culture and personality as they are interrelated in real life. In a large metropolis such as San Juan or New York the family is the natural unit of study.

Ideally our objective is the naturalistic observation of the life of "our" families, with a minimum of intervention. Such intensive study, however, necessarily involves the establishment of deep personal ties. My assistants include two Mexicans whose families I had studied; their "Mexican's-eye-view" of the Puerto Rican slum has helped to point up the similarities and differences between the Mexican and Puerto Rican subcultures. We have spent many hours attending family parties, wakes and baptisms, responding to emergency calls, taking people to the hospital, getting them out of jail, filling out applications for them, hunting apartments with them, helping them to get jobs or to get on relief. With each member of these families we conduct tape-recorded interviews, taking down their life stories and their answers to questions on a wide variety of topics. For the ordering of our material we undertake to reconstruct, by close interrogation, the history of a week or more of consecutive days in the lives of each family, and we observe and record complete days as they unfold. The first volume to issue from this study is to be published next month under the title of La Vida, a Puerto Rican Family in the Culture of Poverty--San Juan and New York (Random House).

There are many poor people in the world. Indeed, the poverty of the two-thirds of the world's population who live in the underdeveloped countries has been rightly called "the problem of problems." But not all of them by any means live in the culture of poverty. For this way of life to come into being and flourish it seems clear that certain preconditions must be met.

The setting is a cash economy, with wage labor and production for profit and with a persistently high rate of unemployment and underemployment, at low wages, for unskilled labor. The society fails to provide social, political and economic organization, on either a voluntary basis or by government imposition, for the low-income population. There is a bilateral kinship system centered on the nuclear progenitive family, as distinguished from the unilateral extended kinship system of lineage and clan. The dominant class asserts a set of values that prizes thrift and the accumulation of wealth and property, stresses the possibility of upward mobility and explains low economic status as the result of individual personal inadequacy and inferiority.

Where these conditions prevail the way of life that develops among some of the poor is the culture of poverty. That is why I have described it as a subculture of the Western social order. It is both an adaptation and a reaction of the poor to their marginal position in a class-stratified, highly individuated, capitalistic society. It represents an effort to cope with feelings of hopelessness and despair that arise from the realization by the members of the marginal communities in these societies of the improbability of their achieving success in terms of the prevailing values and goals. Many of the traits of the culture of poverty can be viewed as local, spontaneous attempts to meet needs not served in the case of the poor by the institutions and agencies of the larger society because the poor are not eligible for such service, cannot afford it or are ignorant and suspicious.

Once the culture of poverty has come into existence it tends to perpetuate itself. By the time slum children are six or seven they have usually absorbed the basic attitudes and values of their subculture. Thereafter they are psychologically unready to take full advantage of changing conditions or improving opportunities that may develop in their lifetime.

My studies have identified some 70 traits that characterize the culture of poverty. The principal ones may be described in four dimensions of the system: the relationship between the subculture and the larger society; the nature of the slum community; the nature of the family, and the attitudes, values and character structure of the individual.

The disengagement, the nonintegration, of the poor with respect to the major institutions of society is a crucial element in the culture of poverty. It reflects the combined effect of a variety of factors including poverty, to begin with, but also segregation and discrimination, fear, suspicion and apathy and the development of alternative institutions and procedures in the slum community. The people do not belong to labor unions or political parties and make little use of banks, hospitals, department stores or museums. Such involvement as there is in the institutions of the larger society--in the jails, the army and the public welfare system--does little to suppress the traits of the culture of poverty. A relief system that barely keeps people alive perpetuates rather than eliminates poverty and the pervading sense of hopelessness.

People in a culture of poverty produce little wealth and receive little in return. Chronic unemployment and underemployment, low wages, lack of property, lack of savings, absence of food reserves in the home and chronic shortage of cash imprison the family and the individual in a vicious circle. Thus for lack of cash the slum householder makes frequent purchases of small quantities of food at higher prices. The slum economy turns inward; it shows a high incidence of pawning of personal goods, borrowing at usurious rates of interest, informal credit arrangements among neighbors, use of secondhand clothing and furniture.

There is awareness of middle-class values. People talk about them and even claim some of them as their own. On the whole, however, they do not live by them. They will declare that marriage by law, by the church or by both is the ideal form of marriage, but few will marry. For men who have no steady jobs, no property and no prospect of wealth to pass on to their children, who live in the present without expectations of the future, who want to avoid the expense and legal difficulties involved in marriage and divorce, a free union or consensual marriage makes good sense. The women, for their part, will turn down offers of marriage from men who are likely to be immature, punishing and generally unreliable. They feel that a consensual union gives them some of the freedom and flexibility men have. By not giving the fathers of their children legal status as husbands, the women have a stronger claim on the children. They also maintain exclusive rights to their own property.

Along with disengagement from the larger society, there is a hostility to the basic institutions of what are regarded as the dominant classes. There is hatred of the police, mistrust of government and of those in high positions and a cynicism that extends to the church. The culture of poverty thus holds a certain potential for protest and for entrainment in political movements aimed against the existing order.

With its poor housing and overcrowding, the community of the culture of poverty is high in gregariousness, but it has a minimum of organization beyond the nuclear and extended family. Occasionally slum dwellers come together in temporary informal groupings; neighborhood gangs that cut across slum settlements represent a considerable advance beyond the zero point of the continuum I have in mind. It is the low level of organization that gives the culture of poverty its marginal and anomalous quality in our highly organized

society. Most primitive peoples have achieved a higher degree of
sociocultural organization than contemporary urban slum dwellers.
This is not to say that there may not be a sense of community and
esprit de corps in a slum neighborhood. In fact, where slums are
isolated from their surroundings by enclosing walls or other physical
barriers, where rents are low and residence is stable and where the
population constitutes a distinct ethnic, racial or language group, the
sense of community may approach that of a village. In Mexico City
and San Juan such territoriality is engendered by the scarcity of low-
cost housing outside of established slum areas. In South Africa it
is actively enforced by the apartheid that confines rural migrants to
prescribed locations.

The family in the culture of poverty does not cherish childhood as a specially prolonged and protected stage in the life cycle.
Initiation into sex comes early. With the instability of consensual
marriage the family tends to be mother-centered and tied more
closely to the mother's extended family. The female head of the
house is given to authoritarian rule. In spite of much verbal emphasis on family solidarity, sibling rivalry for the limited supply
of goods and maternal affection is intense. There is little privacy.

The individual who grows up in this culture has a strong feeling of fatalism, helplessness, dependence and inferiority. These
traits, so often remarked in the current literature as characteristic
of the American Negro, I found equally strong in slum dwellers of
Mexico City and San Juan, who are not segregated or discriminated
against as a distinct ethnic or racial group. Other traits include a
high incidence of weak ego structure, orality and confusion of sexual
identification, all reflecting maternal deprivation; a strong present-
time orientation with relatively little disposition to defer gratification
and plan for the future, and a high tolerance for psychological path-
ology of all kinds. There is widespread belief in male superiority
and among the men a strong preoccupation with _machismo_, their
masculinity.

Provincial and local in outlook, with little sense of history,
these people know only their own neighborhood and their own way of
life. Usually they do not have the knowledge, the vision or the ideology to see the similarities between their troubles and those of their
counterparts elsewhere in the world. They are not class-conscious,
although they are sensitive indeed to symbols of status.

The distinction between poverty and the culture of poverty is
basic to the model described here. There are numerous examples
of poor people whose way of life I would not characterize as belonging to this subculture. Many primitive and preliterate peoples that
have been studied by anthropologists suffer dire poverty attributable
to low technology or thin resources or both. Yet even the simplest
of these peoples have a high degree of social organization and a relatively integrated, satisfying and self-sufficient culture.

In India the destitute lower-caste peoples--such as the Chamars, the leatherworkers, and the Bhangis, the sweepers--remain integrated in the larger society and have their own panchayat institutions of self-government. Their panchayats and their extended unilateral kinship systems, or clans, cut across village lines, giving them a strong sense of identity and continuity. In my studies of these peoples I found no culture of poverty to go with their poverty.

The Jews of eastern Europe were a poor urban people, often confined to ghettos. Yet they did not have many traits of the culture of poverty. They had a tradition of literacy that placed great value on learning; they formed many voluntary associations and adhered with devotion to the central community organization around the rabbi, and they had a religion that taught them they were the chosen people.

I would cite also a fourth, somewhat speculative example of poverty dissociated from the culture of poverty. On the basis of limited direct observation of one country--Cuba--and from indirect evidence, I am inclined to believe the culture of poverty does not exist in socialist countries. In 1947 I undertook a study of a slum in Havana. Recently I had an opportunity to revisit the same slum and some of the same families. The physical aspect of the place had changed little, except for a beautiful new nursery school. The people were as poor as before, but I was impressed to find much less of the feelings of despair and apathy, so symptomatic of the culture of poverty in the urban slums of the U.S. The slum was now highly organized, with block committees, educational committees, party committees. The people had found a new sense of power and importance in a doctrine that glorified the lower class as the hope of humanity, and they were armed. I was told by one Cuban official that the Castro government had practically eliminated delinquency by giving arms to the delinquents!

Evidently the Castro regime--revising Marx and Engels--did not write off the so-called lumpenproletariat as an inherently reactionary and antirevolutionary force but rather found in them a revolutionary potential and utilized it. Frantz Fanon, in his book The Wretched of the Earth, makes a similar evaluation of their role in the Algerian revolution: "It is within this mass of humanity, this people of the shantytowns, at the core of the lumpenproletariat, that the rebellion will find its urban spearhead. For the lumpenproletariat, that horde of starving men, uprooted from their tribe and from their clan, constitutes one of the most spontaneous and most radically revolutionary forces of the colonized people."

It is true that I have found little revolutionary spirit or radical ideology among low-income Puerto Ricans. Most of the families I studied were politically conservative, about half of them favoring the Statehood Republican Party, which provides opposition on the right to the Popular Democratic Party that dominates the politics of the commonwealth. It seems to me, therefore, that disposition for protest among people living in the culture of poverty will vary considerably according to the national context and historical circumstances. In contrast to Algeria, the independence movement in

Puerto Rico has found little popular support. In Mexico, where the cause of independence carried long ago, there is no longer any such movement to stir the dwellers in the new and old slums of the capital city.

Yet it would seem that any movement--be it religious, pacifist or revolutionary--that organizes and gives hope to the poor and effectively promotes a sense of solidarity with larger groups must effectively destroy the psychological and social core of the culture of poverty. In this connection, I suspect that the civil rights movement among American Negroes has of itself done more to improve their self-image and self-respect than such economic gains as it has won although, without doubt, the two kinds of progress are mutually reinforcing. In the culture of poverty of the American Negro the additional disadvantage of racial discrimination has generated a potential for revolutionary protest and organization that is absent in the slums of San Juan and Mexico City and, for that matter, among the poor whites in the South.

If it is true, as I suspect, that the culture of poverty flourishes and is endemic to the free-enterprise, pre-welfare-state stage of capitalism, then it is also endemic of colonial societies. The most likely candidates for the culture of poverty would be the people who come from the lower strata of a rapidly changing society and who are already partially alienated from it. Accordingly the subculture is likely to be found where imperial conquest has smashed the native social and economic structure and held the natives, perhaps for generations, in servile status, or where feudalism is yielding to capitalism in the later evolution of a colonial economy. Landless rural workers who migrate to the cities, as in Latin America, can be expected to fall into this way of life more readily than migrants from stable peasant villages with a well-organized traditional culture, as in India. It remains to be seen, however, whether the culture of poverty has not already begun to develop in the slums of Bombay and Calcutta. Compared with Latin America also, the strong corporate nature of many African tribal societies may tend to inhibit or delay the formation of a full-blown culture of poverty in the new towns and cities of that continent. In South Africa the institutionalization of repression and discrimination under apartheid may also have begun to promote an immunizing sense of identity and group consciousness among the African Negroes.

One must therefore keep the dynamic aspects of human institutions forward in observing and assessing the evidence for the presence, the waxing or the waning of this subculture. Measured on the dimension of relationship to the larger society, some slum dwellers may have a warmer identification with their national tradition even though they suffer deeper poverty than members of a similar community in another country. In Mexico City a high percentage of our respondents, including those with little or no formal schooling, knew of Cuauhtémoc, Hidalgo, Father Morelos, Juárez, Diaz, Zapata, Carranza and Cárdenas. In San Juan the names of Rámon Power, José de Diego, Baldorioty de Castro, Rámon Betances, Nemesio

Canales, Llorens Torres rang no bell; a few could tell about the late Albizu Campos. For the lower-income Puerto Rican, however, history begins with Muñoz Rivera and ends with his son Muñoz Marin.

The national context can make a big difference in the play of the crucial traits of fatalism and hopelessness. Given the advanced technology, the high level of literacy, the all-pervasive reach of the media of mass communications and the relatively high aspirations of all sectors of the population, even the poorest and most marginal communities of the U.S. must aspire to a larger future than the slum dwellers of Ecuador and Peru, where the actual possibilities are more limited and where an authoritarian social order persists in city and country. Among the 50 million U.S. citizens now more or less officially certified as poor, I would guess that about 20 per cent live in a culture of poverty. The largest numbers in this group are made up of Negroes, Puerto Ricans, Mexicans, American Indians and Southern poor whites. In these figures there is some reassurance for those concerned, because it is much more difficult to undo the culture of poverty than to cure poverty itself.

Middle-class people--this would certainly include most social scientists--tend to concentrate on the negative aspects of the culture of poverty. They attach a minus sign to such traits as present-time orientation and readiness to indulge impulses. I do not intend to idealize or romanticize the culture of poverty--"it is easier to praise poverty than to live in it." Yet the positive aspects of these traits must not be overlooked. Living in the present may develop a capacity for spontaneity, for the enjoyment of the sensual, which is often blunted in the middle-class, future-oriented man. Indeed, I am often struck by the analogies that can be drawn between the mores of the very rich--of the "jet set" and "café society"--and the culture of the very poor. Yet it is, on the whole, a comparatively superficial culture. There is in it much pathos, suffering and emptiness. It does not provide much support or satisfaction; its pervading mistrust magnifies individual helplessness and isolation. Indeed, poverty of culture is one of the crucial traits of the culture of poverty.

The concept of the culture of poverty provides a generalization that may help to unify and explain a number of phenomena hitherto viewed as peculiar to certain racial, national or regional groups. Problems we think of as being distinctively our own or distinctively Negro (or as typifying any other ethnic group) prove to be endemic in countries where there are no segregated ethnic minority groups. If it follows that the elimination of physical poverty may not by itself eliminate the culture of poverty, then an understanding of the subculture may contribute to the design of measures specific to that purpose.

What is the future of the culture of poverty? In considering this question one must distinguish between those countries in which it represents a relatively small segment of the population and those in which it constitutes a large one. In the U.S. the major solution proposed by social workers dealing with the "hard core" poor has been slowly to raise their level of living and incorporate them in the middle class. Wherever possible psychiatric treatment is prescribed.

In underdeveloped countries where great masses of people live in the culture of poverty, such a social-work solution does not seem feasible. The local psychiatrists have all they can do to care for their own growing middle class. In those countries the people with a culture of poverty may seek a more revolutionary solution. By creating basic structural changes in society, by redistributing wealth, by organizing the poor and giving them a sense of belonging, of power and of leadership, revolutions frequently succeed in abolishing some of the basic characteristics of the culture of poverty even when they do not succeed in curing poverty itself.

Michael Meyerson

PUERTO RICO: OUR BACKYARD COLONY

Citizens of San Juan were not surprised when they awakened one morning early this February to find that the Selective Service office, the local branch of General Electric and a portion of the El San Juan Hilton Hotel had all been bombed. Such attacks, carried out by a group calling itself Armed Commandos for Liberation (CAL), have become a fact of daily life in Puerto Rico. As the movement for independence from the U.S. has gained in momentum, more than a hundred bombings, the majority aimed at American corporations, have shaken the island over the past year alone. Of all the targets for this assault, one of the most obvious has been the popular image of Puerto Rico as the "happy commonwealth"--a sultry playground for American tourists and the showcase of U.S.-guided progress in the Caribbean. While the dust from the first pro-independence explosions was still settling, more and more Puerto Ricans, especially the young, were beginning to see how this tourbook rhetoric was used to conceal the bitter fact that their island was and is the only classic colony in the American experience.

For Puerto Ricans, colonial status is nothing new. They have spent the last five centuries under the rule of one Western country or another. Puerto Rico came close to achieving independence in the late 1800s, winning an autonomous constitution from Spain, only to lose it a year later when the island was "ceded" to the U.S. as part of the spoils of victory in the Spanish-American War. Ruled first by the U.S. military, then by presidential appointees and only recently by an elected governor, Puerto Ricans have had little power over the fate of their island; they were even made U.S. citizens over the objection of their one elected body.

Today the island legislature's powers are limited to traffic

Reprinted by permission from _Ramparts_, June 1970.

regulations and the like. Real political power resides in the U.S.
House Committee on Insular Affairs and the Senate Committee on
Territorial and Insular Affairs, both of which meet in Washington,
D.C., some 1500 miles from San Juan. Appeals from Puerto Rican
courts are decided in Boston and final jurisdiction rests with the
U.S. Supreme Court.

U.S. federal agencies control the country's foreign relations,
customs, immigration, post office system, communications, radio,
television, commerce, transportation, maritime laws, military service, social security, banks, currency and defense--all of this without
the people of Puerto Rico having a vote in U.S. elections.

The extent of U.S. military control of the country is particularly striking. One cannot drive five miles in any direction without running into an army base, nuclear site or tracking station.
Green Berets were recently discovered in the famed El Yunque National Rain Forest, presumably using the island as a training ground.

The Pentagon controls 13 per cent of Puerto Rico's land and
has five atomic bases, including Ramey Air Base. A major base
for the Strategic Air Command, Ramey includes in its confines everything from guided missiles to radio jamming stations which prevent
Radio Havana from reaching Puerto Rico and Santo Domingo. In addition to the major bases, there are about 100 medium and small
military installations, training camps, and radar and radio stations.

In the late 1940s, Puerto Rico became the target of Operation
Bootstrap. Hailed as an economic "New Deal" for the island, Bootstrap bore the kind of name that encourages Americans to believe
unquestioningly in their country's selfless generosity to other peoples.
In truth, the new program was a textbook perfect example of imperialism, guaranteeing tax-free investment to U.S. firms developing
the island as a market for U.S. goods. (As the Wall Street Journal
put it: "Two million potential customers live on Puerto Rico, but
the hopeful industrial planners see it as the shopping center for the
entire Caribbean population of 13 million.") While it fed America's
sense of self-righteousness and brought profits to U.S. investors,
Bootstrap left untouched the misery of the majority of Puerto Rico's
2.5 million inhabitants. In fact, by limiting the development of the
island's economy and forcing continual dependence on the U.S., Bootstrap deepened the cycle of poverty in Puerto Rico.

Over one million boriqueños have left their native land for the
barrios of East Harlem and South Bronx. That one-third of a nation
would escape into exile to the slums of New York testifies to the
living conditions in the Caribbean "paradise."

Four out of every five Puerto Rican families earn less than
$3,000 per year; one half receive less than $1,000 annually. Oscar
Lewis puts unemployment at 14 per cent; knowledgeable Puerto Ricans insist that a figure as high as 30 per cent is more realistic.
That is a permanent condition twice as bad as the depths of the Great

Depression in this country. Per capita income in Mississippi, our poorest state, was 81 per cent higher than in Puerto Rico in 1960. Whereas wages are a fraction of those on the mainland, the cost of living on the island is higher. Most statistics place island costs at 25 per cent higher than those in New York, Chicago or Boston.

Housing for most Puerto Ricans is abominable. In many a rural town, the only livable building is the town jail. Even government agencies consider 46 per cent of Puerto Rico's housing to be inadequate. Not atypical is the Los Chinos district of Ponce (Puerto Rico's second largest city), one of several slum areas, made up of thousands of one-room dirt-floor shacks inhabited by eight-and ten-member families. Groups of these families share a single outdoor toilet.

To most tourists, San Juan is Puerto Rico, and the Condado district (the strip of luxury hotels that accommodate tourists in increasing numbers each year) is San Juan. But within walking distance of the Caribe Hilton and the Flamboyan Hotel on the Condado are some of the worst slums in the Americas. Their picturesque names throw into bold relief the horror of their reality--La Perla (The Pearl), Los Bravos de Boston, etc. One slum, El Fangito, stretches for five miles along a rat-infested swamp which seeps with San Juan's sewage.

On a walk through Los Bravos de Boston, I met a woman standing outside what can only euphemistically be called a house. Made of bulletin board, sealed together with bailing wire and topped by a sheet of tin, the shack would have been blown over by a healthy gust of wind. The wretched home, six by six feet, housed the woman, her husband and two babies. As we spoke, an infant slept outside at our feet, his bed the basket of a rusty shopping cart. The mother, in a state of dispair, had learned only that morning that the government was going to move the shack elsewhere that day, and there was no way to contact her husband, a construction worker, to tell him where to come when his day ended.

If it does little to improve the lot of the poor, Bootstrap has by any standards been a bargain for investors. Offering U.S. firms cheap labor and tax "holidays" of 10 to 17 years, Bootstrap was hailed by Hubert Humphrey as the "miracle of the Caribbean."

As the colonial government reports: "Manufacturers average 30 per cent on their investment--thanks to the productivity of Puerto Rico's three-quarter million willing, able workers. Profits in electronics run 10.8 times those of the mainland industry's average." Every dollar invested has brought a profit of 30 cents during the first year. U.S. investments in Puerto Rico are the highest--after Venezuela--in all of Latin America.

For every dollar produced in the island's industrial system, only 17 cents is left in Puerto Rico. Only Britain, Canada, Japan and West Germany import more U.S. goods. This island of fewer than three million people buys more from us than do Spain, Portugal, Austria, Ireland and the four Scandinavian nations combined.

Sugar and petroleum account for most of the country's industry. The sugar industry, controlled by three U.S. companies (the Central Aguirre Sugar Company, owned by the First National Bank of Boston; C. Brewer & Company; and the South Puerto Rico Sugar Company of New Jersey, the largest owner of cane plantations in the world), is a classroom model of neo-colonialism. It accounts for half the island's agricultural income--a fact determined not by the agricultural needs of the island but by the U.S. sugar quota. Impoverished Puerto Rican plantation workers chop the cane for tax-free U.S. companies, ship the raw product to the States where it is refined, packaged and taxed, and then buy back the finished product at exorbitant prices.

Only the petrochemical industry has seen a bigger growth in Puerto Rico, with heavy investments from every major U.S. petroleum corporation--Phillips, Union Carbide, Texaco, Standard, etc. Virtually ringing the Caribbean coast of the island in search of off-shore oil, they have caused severe pollution in some of the best fishing waters in the world. This, together with the fact that the federal government prohibits Puerto Rico from maintaining its own fishing fleet, has resulted in the island's being forced to import 95 per cent of the fish it consumes.

Early in the 1950s, huge copper deposits were discovered in the interior. American Metal Climax and Kennicott Copper, operating through subsidiaries, moved in, taking exclusive rights to the deposits. Comparable in size to the largest deposits in this country, their ore value is higher than any in the United States. The deposits are worth at least $1.5 billion; American Metal Climax paid Puerto Rico just ten dollars for an exploration permit.

News of the deposits and of the negotiations between the two companies and the government was kept secret until the Pro-Independence Movement got word of the talks and began a public campaign. Through picketing, diplomatic protests and local organizing, the independentists have for four years successfully prevented the companies from starting production. Although the contract has not been signed yet, speculation is that with 64-year-old millionaire industrialist Luis Ferré as the new governor, the signing is imminent.

Washington propaganda has always held that Puerto Rico has no riches, that it needs the United States, hence independence is unreasonable. Now Japan has offered the country a better deal on its copper than have the U.S. companies, but its colonial position prohibits Puerto Rico from engaging in foreign trade. Undoubtedly, its oil, sugar, tobacco and coffee could also attract better prices if offered competitively. There seems no way to check or reverse the depletion of Puerto Rico's riches other than independence. The major argument against independence, aside from lack of natural wealth, has been the size of the country. But Puerto Rico has more people than the island nations of Cyprus and Jamaica; than eight Latin American countries, including Paraguay, Costa Rica and Panama; than some 32 member states of the United Nations, including Laos, Israel, Jordan, Albania and Lebanon.

Leading the drive for independence from U.S. domination is the Movimiento Pro-Independencia of Puerto Rico (MPI). A prominently displayed painting dominates the offices of the MPI in San Juan. The picture, depicting the Ponce Massacre of March 1937 when police beat and killed nationalist demonstrators, was painted by Fran Cervoni, one of Puerto Rico's most important artists and a member of MPI's Political Commission. Only part of the painting remains as the artist rendered it, the canvas having been salvaged from the fire which destroyed the MPI headquarters in November 1965. Nobody one encounters has the slightest doubt that the arsonists were agents of the U.S. Central Intelligence Agency.

Today, new fires are being set in Puerto Rico, but this time the flames are spreading in a different direction. Since New Year's Eve 1967, at least 75 fires aimed at North American properties have caused damage ranging in estimates from 25 to 75 million dollars. No one has been caught; no evidence has been found; no witnesses have come forth. But a group calling itself the Armed Commandos for Liberation (CAL) has taken credit for the action. To the chagrin of the propertied, no one can prove who belongs to CAL, although the press has attempted to tie the group to MPI. Police have even arrested local MPI leaders in connection with the bombings, but were forced to release them for lack of anything resembling evidence.

The island, already blanketed by CIA and FBI agents, has practically suffocated with the massive invasion of reinforcements from those two agencies. The Wackenhut Corporation, a Miami-based security firm, boosted its guard force by 40 per cent in less than a year, the bulk going to watch over U.S. holdings in Puerto Rico. Bargain Town, one of whose stores was fire-bombed, now has Burns Agency guards, equipped with fire masks and with fire-fighting equipment, both inside and outside its stores 24 hours a day. Still the bombings continue.

The goal, says CAL leader Alfonso Beal, is to make it so costly to stay in Puerto Rico that they leave. "We are in the first stage of operations," he says, "and in this phase we intend to cause $100 million worth of damage to U.S. concerns. Our idea is to inflict such heavy losses on these enterprises that the insurance companies will have to pay more money in indemnity than they have received in payment, thus upsetting the economy."

On September 23, 1968, the centenary of the Grito de Lares, the rebellion against Spanish colonialism, CAL issued a statement declaring the tourist strip of Condado a "zone of war" and asking Puerto Ricans to stay out, "especially in the evening hours." At an open-air ceremony commemorating the Grito de Lares that same afternoon, attended by some 20,000 independentistas, Juan Mari Bras, MPI general secretary, paid tribute to those who have begun to engage in "the highest form of struggle, armed struggle." The crowd took up the chant: "Fuego! Fuego! Fire! Fire! Fire!"

The cadres of MPI are serious revolutionaries. They are dedicated, committed to the long-range struggle, have very few illusions about their "objective reality" and are terribly energetic. This is true both of the top leadership and of the activists.

In Aguadilla, a town 60 miles west of San Juan, in the northwest corner of the rectangular island, MPI has established the José de Diego Mission. There are some two dozen such central missions scattered throughout Puerto Rico supported by twice as many "patriotic missions." A central mission is one with its own headquarters, the facilities to print leaflets and the organization to distribute literature. Patriotic missions are groups of cadres in the surrounding towns who, working out of the central missions, strive to expand their organization to the point that they have strength enough to become central missions themselves.

The Aguadilla mission has, in addition to the familiar posters of Latin revolutionary heroes, the slogan in large black letters: "Diablos, No! No Iremos!" (Hell No, We Won't Go!). The town is located on the coast, and the shacks pile on top of one another, ascending to the peak of the hill overlooking the Atlantic. The slums get poorer as the landscape rises. At the top stands the pride of the Diego Mission--the first zona libre (free zone) of Puerto Rico. Made up of clusters of the worst shanties in Aguadilla, the zone's official name is Cerra Villa Nuevo. It has been organized by MPI, which now has the near-unanimous backing of the people there. Today, the police no longer venture into Cerra Villa Nuevo.

Many hundreds of families populate the free zone (the total population of Aguadilla is placed at around 50,000). The dirt paths that pass for roads are filled with mangy, limping dogs, pigs and goats. Due to the continuing expansion of U.S. military bases, tracking stations and radio intelligence centers, land is becoming scarce and the rural poor are being forced off their land and herded into already overcrowded city slums. Aguadilla is faced with massive unemployment and the figures extend far above the estimated 30 per cent for the whole of the island.

On the day I met him, Julio Alvarez, one of Cerra Villa Nuevo's most active MPI cadres, was on trial for burning the U.S. flag. In contrast to the severe penalties dealt out to Julio's contemporaries in the States for similar offenses, the young man only received a fine of $25. The courts apparently fear to tread on Puerto Rican national feeling.

Julio's shack in the free zone, perhaps a dozen feet square, contains a kitchen with a mini-stove and an outdoor sink which one

must stretch out of the window to reach. Boiling on the stove was
a pot of yucca root, Julio's dinner. One wall features a half-dozen
water colors painted by Julio. His bookshelf, a made-over produce
crate, contains Dostoyevsky's House of the Dead, The Idiot and The
Brothers Karamazov; some works of Cervantes; and books on Monet,
Manet and Turner. Whatever else life denies him, Julio Alvarez's
intellectual pursuits will continue. It is Julio and hundreds of his
neighbors who comprise the population of the island's first zona
libre.

Women are conspicuously few in the movement's leadership,
not an uncommon situation on the Latin continent. One of the exceptions is Lucila Andino, the 25-year-old director of the Carolina
Mission. Her district stretches perhaps 25 miles east to Luquillo,
the town surrounding Puerto Rico's most famous and luscious strip
of beach. Included in the area is the village of Loiza Aldea, which
must be reached by raft. Loiza is populated almost entirely by black
Puerto Ricans, and the origin of this ethnic make-up is a subject of
constant speculation. Consensus generally holds that a slave ship
capsized off Loiza's coast and the slaves that made it to shore settled in the area; it then became a haven for runaway slaves.

Lucila is one of two female mission directors of MPI; the
second heads the organization in Mayaguez, Puerto Rico's fourth
largest city. Perhaps a major reason for this lack of women cadres
in the movement, aside from the obvious one of the general status
of women in Puerto Rican society, is that much of the recent growth
of MPI has come through its anti-draft activities. In 1966, a young
worker named Sixto Alvelo became the colony's first draft resister.
Within a year, MPI's newspaper Claridad printed a full-page adver-
tisement listing the signatures of 1000 Puerto Rican youths who joined
the Resistance. They stated their refusal to recognize what they
consider to be a colonial draft, to serve in a foreign army, and they
expressed their solidarity with the South Vietnam National Liberation
Front. (In 1965, MPI had established a fraternal relationship with
the NLF.) The ranks of the thousand have since been swelled much
beyond that. Rarely does a day go by when a young resister is not
arrested.

*   *   *

One of MPI's most encouraging recent developments is the
success of FEPI, the high school independence movement. The high
school organization serves not only to radicalize the hundreds of
thousands of young people (half the island's population is under 25);
it also provides the movement with a major wedge into the working
class and peasantry.

Ponce is Governor Ferré's town and main base. In addition
to his cement factories and his newspaper, El Día, he has uncounted
real estate holdings, foundries and much of the most costly land in
the city. Yet here too the MPI is extremely active.

In the slums of Los Chinos, and in La Playa near the Caribbean, as throughout the city of Ponce, the MPI mission conducts nightly "ciné-meetings." In the twilight hours, portable bulletin boards filled with news, posters and photographs are set up at a given intersection. As night falls, speakers make a brief presentation of the movement's program and ask for support, and then projectors show films, imported from Cuba and Vietnam, projected onto the wall of a windowless building. As many as 600 neighbors come to these meetings, even though chances are good that they will be interrogated by the FBI the following day.

*　　　　*　　　　*

MPI insists that social justice and independence will not be achieved through the established electoral process, for whatever laws are passed in San Juan are subject to approval by Washington. At election time, the movement is actively engaged in promoting the boycott as a political weapon. There are the remnants still of the independentist electoral party, PIP, but it has pretty much deteriorated as MPI gains strength and as the reality of the colonial situation becomes ever more apparent. Little more than 40 per cent of the eligible voters are registered and of that number only perhaps half bother to cast their ballots.

While MPI is firm in its principled opposition to the colonial establishment, it maintains active supporters within the establishment. These are referred to as its segundo nivel, its second-level membership. In the political parties, the government and the press, the second level acts as a source of intelligence for MPI, letting it know of impending arrests or shady government dealings. In 1967, for example, Claridad, the movement's weekly paper, broke the story of the hitherto undisclosed discovery of copper in the center of the island.

It is the work in the copper areas and the slums, and similar organization among the petroleum workers, that has brought about the radicalization of MPI and the search for fundamental social change, say movement spokesmen. In April 1968, Juan Mari Bras announced that MPI would uphold the right of Puerto Rico to use any methods, including armed struggle, to achieve its independence. In the midst of a press campaign to determine who was behind the recent wave of bombings, and attempts to tie MPI to CAL, the announcement caused a sensation.

MPI calls itself the "patriotic vanguard" of Puerto Rico. That is to say, it is the nationalist cause and urge that gives it life. But it is internationalist in outlook. Besides its pact of solidarity with the NLF in South Vietnam, the movement has representatives on the executive committees of the Organization of Solidarity with the Peoples of Asia, Africa and Latin America, and the Latin American Students' Organization, both based in Havana.

As Mari Bras says, "Puerto Rico is battling against time in

its struggle to save its nationhood. " Only a crisis in the U. S. colonial system will force independence. The sort of crisis MPI speaks of in this regard is a massive unified demand by the island's people that makes their outright colonial status an embarrassment to the United States. The only force that can create the crisis, MPI believes, is the working class when it is organized. The development of workers' cadres is to be a main focus of the organization from now on.

The United States does not want a Puerto Rico free and independent to determine its own course. Nor, says Mari Bras, does it want a state with its own nationality. But the Yankees too see the possibility of a crisis developing in its system. So it attempts to destroy the Puerto Rican nationality through its military-economic-cultural penetration of the island. If the United States should succeed in its offensive, it could then grant Puerto Rico statehood at the point of crisis.

Meanwhile, the Movimiento Pro-Independencia organizes in the slums of the cities and the hovels of the countryside, among university and high school students, and in the growing industrial working class. They are, they say, a patriotic vanguard leading a national struggle of survival. While nationalism is the cause and self-reliance the urgent need, MPI is by no means unaware of the role of anti-imperialist North Americans. In fact, they see it as our responsibility to fight with them for independence. Ultimately, says one MPI leader, "What you do in the United States may well determine the fate of Puerto Rico's nationhood. "

THE PUERTO RICANS

Puerto Rico, the smallest of the Greater Antilles, is located roughly midway between the southern tip of Florida and the north coast of Venezuela.[1] Its north coast faces the Atlantic Ocean and its southern shores face the Caribbean Sea.

The island is rectangular, about 100 miles long and 35 miles wide, with a rugged mountain range running east-west along its length. A few small offshore islands and keys are within Puerto Rico's jurisdiction; two of them, Vieques and Culebra, are inhabited and are considered municipalities of Puerto Rico.[2]

On November 19, 1493, during his second voyage to the New World, Christopher Columbus landed at Puerto Rico and claimed it for Spain. At the time, the island was called Boriquen by the several thousand Taino Indians who lived there.

In 1508 Juan Ponce de Leon was named governor, and established the first European settlement on the island at Caparra, across the bay from modern San Juan.

Spain's initial interest in Puerto Rico centered on tales of huge gold deposits. The few existing lodes were quickly depleted, however, and the Indians who had been forced to work them either died or fled the island. Spain then turned to agriculture, introducing a plantation economy. The few remaining Indians proved unsuited to field labor and slaves were imported in ever-increasing numbers from West Africa to take their place. (The institution of slavery was maintained in Puerto Rico until 1873.)

During the 19th century, Puerto Rico's population soared from

(Washington: United States Commission on Civil Rights, 1976, p. 11-43).

about 150,000 persons to nearly one million. After nearly four centuries of Spanish colonial rule, the island developed into a multi-racial Hispanic society. A 1787 census revealed that there still remained more than 2,000 pure-blood Indians in Puerto Rico, and that thousands of other Puerto Ricans were of partial Indian origin. In 1875, when abolition went into effect, more than 30,000 black slaves were freed. Thousands of others--blacks and mulattoes--lived as free men during the period of slavery. During the 19th century, the white community of Spanish settlers was augmented by continued migration from Spain. Many Spanish loyalists came to Puerto Rico from Central and South America in the wake of a series of pro-independence revolutions. Frenchmen came from Louisiana when it was purchased by the United States and from Haiti when the slaves revolted. In the 1840s labor shortages brought Chinese workers to Cuba and Puerto Rico. Italians, Corsicans, Lebanese, Germans, Scots, and Irish also spiced the melting pot.

As the 20th century approached, the racial composition of Puerto Rican society covered the spectrum from whites (blancos) to blacks (prietos or negros), with a large in-between category known as the trigueno ("tan," "olive-skinned," "swarthy"), and very fuzzy lines dividing the groups because of racial intermarriage.

By then, the island had developed its own unique culture and sense of nationhood. When most of Central and South America bubbled with pro-independence ferment, there was similar ferment in Puerto Rico. In 1868 a major rebellion (El Grito de Lares) that briefly established an independent republic was quashed by the Spanish military. There was also a loyalist movement that argued for full assimilation with Spain. Midway between these two diametrically opposed factions was the autonomista movement, which sought to establish home rule without a complete break from Spain.

In 1897, the Puerto Rican leadership, headed by Luis Muñoz Rivera, negotiated a Charter of Autonomy with the Spanish Government. [3] This gave the island an unprecedented degree of freedom. Elections would be held for all members of the island's House of Representatives, a majority of the members of the insular Administrative Council (equivalent to a senate) and also voting delegates to both houses of the Spanish Cortes (Spain's national legislative body). The island's legislature won the power to fix the budget, determine tariffs and taxes, and accept or reject any commercial treaties concluded by Spain without local participation.

But on July 25, 1898 (just a few months after the first autonomous government was formed), U.S. troops landed on Puerto Rico's south coast in one of the final engagements of the Spanish-American War. The United States--at the time seeking to expand its presence in the Pacific and Caribbean--viewed Puerto Rico as a profitable area for agriculture and as a coaling station for its warships (plans were already underway for the building of the Panama Canal).

Under the Treaty of Paris of 1899, Puerto Rico was ceded by Spain to the United States, with the provision that the civil rights and political status of the native inhabitants of the territory be determined by the U.S. Congress. [4]

These negotiations were between representatives of the Spanish and U.S. Governments. No Puerto Ricans were consulted or included in the negotiations. Political expectations on the island were varied. Some anticipated that the island would temporarily be a territory and that, in a matter of time, there would be a transition to full U.S. statehood. Others hoped for the granting of independence, as occurred in Cuba, where the United States evacuated its forces following the war. Others sought a form of autonomy under U.S. rule, similar to the terms of the 1897 Charter of Autonomy with Spain.

For the first two years, the island was ruled by the U.S. military. The Foraker Act of 1900 [5] established a civil government. But the Governor was an American, appointed by the U.S. President. The 11-member Executive Council contained an American majority. The laws passed by the 35 elected Puerto Ricans in the insular House of Delegates were subject to veto by the U.S. Congress. Speaking for Puerto Rico in the U.S. House of Representatives was an elected Resident Commissioner, who had no vote. English was imposed as the language of instruction in the schools, on an island where few people, including teachers, knew English. This situation was widely criticized in Puerto Rico.

In 1917 a Revised Organic Act (popularly known as the Jones Act) [6] increased the insular role in government. It included a bill of rights and an elective Senate of 19 members.

But at the same time, the Jones Act also conferred U.S. citizenship on all Puerto Ricans, with the concomitant requirement of obligatory military service. The conferral of citizenship was criticized by some groups in the United States as being a "war measure" since it was shortly before America's entry into the First World War, and German ships were prowling the Atlantic.

The conferral of U.S. citizenship met with mixed feelings in Puerto Rico. The Republican Party (not affiliated with the Republican Party in the United States) constituted a minority, and welcomed the move because its members aspired to eventual U.S. statehood. But the majority Unionist Party favored increased autonomy, and many of its members preferred eventual independence. During the floor debate in Congress, Resident Commissioner Munoz Rivera (Head of the Unionist Party) said that his party sought autonomy, and that U.S. citizenship conflicted with the long-range goals of the people. He asked that a plebiscite be held to determine whether or not Puerto Ricans desired American citizenship. The request was denied.

It was believed in some quarters that the grant of citizenship

Elections in Puerto Rico

(In thousands of votes)

Party	1948	1952	1956	1960	1964	1968	1972
Popular Democratic Party	392.0	429.0	433.0	457.8	487.2	367.3	609.6
Statehood Republican Party	88.1	85.1	172.8	252.3	284.6	4.3	—
Independence Party	66.1	125.7	86.3	24.1	22.1	25.3	52.1
Christian Action Party	—	—	—	52.1	26.8	—	—
Socialist Party	64.1	21.6	—	—	—	—	—
Reformist Party	28.2	—	—	—	—	—	—
New Progressive Party	—	—	—	—	—	390.9	524.0
People's Party	—	—	—	—	—	384.1	2.9
Authentic Sovereignty Party	—	—	—	—	—	—	0.4
Puerto Rico Unionist Party	—	—	—	—	—	—	1.6
Total	638.6	661.6	692.2	786.4	820.9	871.9	1190.6

Source: Board of Elections, Commonwealth of Puerto Rico. Cited in Kal Wagenheim, *Puerto Rico: A Profile*, 2d. ed. (New York: Praeger, 1975), p. 155.

implied the incorporation of Puerto Rico in the Union as a territory. But the U.S. Supreme Court eventually decided that it did not.[7]

For the next three decades, Puerto Rico's relationship with the United States continued unchanged. In 1948, however, Puerto Rico was allowed, for the first time, to elect its own Governor (Luis Munoz Marin). In 1950, the Congress passed Public Law 600, which authorized Puerto Rico to draft its own Constitution.[8] Two years later, on July 25, 1952 (exactly 54 years to the day, after U.S. troops invaded the island), the Commonwealth of Puerto Rico was inaugurated.

Under this new arrangement, Puerto Rico acquired a considerable degree of home rule. It would continue to elect its own Governor and Resident Commissioner in Congress, and all members of the insular House and Senate. It would appoint all judges, cabinet officials, and lesser officials in the executive branch. It would set its own educational policies (Spanish became the language of instruction in the public schools, with English a required second language, in 1948), determine its own budget, and amend its own civil and criminal code.

The Commonwealth was described as "a permanent union between the United States and Puerto Rico on the basis of common citizenship, common defense, common currency, free market, and a common loyalty to the value of democracy," with the Federal Government retaining specifically defined powers, "essential to the Union." In practical terms, the Federal Government retained powers over military defense and foreign affairs, and Federal agencies (such as the postal system, the Federal Communications Commission, and others) operated as they did in the States of the Union.

This political arrangement has gone unchanged since 1952.

The Popular Democratic Party, which won power in 1940 and has been the proponent of Commonwealth status, has remained in power since that time, except for a 4-year period (1969-1972), when a pro-statehood government won the election. (See Table 1 for election results from 1948 through 1972.)

In 1967 a plebiscite on political status was held. Nearly 60 percent of the voters favored continuation of Commonwealth status, with the aim of gradually increasing the island's powers of home rule. About 39 percent favored statehood. Less than 1 percent voted for independence, but the major pro-independence groups abstained from participation in the plebiscite. (Although the independence movement has not made strong showings in elections, it continues to be a prominent--albeit fragmented--force. Independence advocates cover the entire range of the ideological spectrum. Tactics have ranged from participation in elections, to militant protest, to occasional outbursts of violence.) As a result of the 1967 plebiscite and the reelection of the Popular Democratic Party in 1972, an ad hoc committee of U.S. and Puerto Rican members has developed proposals to increase Puerto Rico's autonomy in specific areas. Some of these proposals were submitted to Congress in 1975.[9]

While the island's political status has remained the same for the past 23 years, Puerto Rico has undergone radical socioeconomic change since the end of the Second World War.

The development strategy of the Puerto Rican leadership was to industrialize the island by attracting outside capital with long-term industrial tax exemptions, lower wage rates, government low-interest loans, and other types of incentives.

By the mid-1950s, manufacturing replaced agriculture as the island's principal source of income. There was also a shift in living patterns, as the island grew increasingly urban. A large urban and suburban middle class was created. Concrete homes replaced wooden shacks. Miles of new roads were built. Factories sprang up in fields once devoted to sugar cane. Remote areas were linked to major cities and the rest of the world by telephones, radio, and television. Table 2 gives some idea of the radical shift to modernization that has taken place in Puerto Rican society during the past few decades.

By 1970 Puerto Rico remained far poorer than the mainland United States. But it had leaped well ahead of many nations. A considerable sector of the island's populace enjoyed a living standard comparable to that of the United States and Western Europe. Advances in public health had made significant inroads in infant mortality and deaths from infectious diseases or malnutrition. A people that had once traveled on foot, or horseback, was now a people on wheels, as hundreds of thousands of cars clogged new highways. In a few decades, Puerto Rico had become, in the words of former Governor Roberto Sanchez Vilella, "a demi-developed society."

Table 2

Puerto Rico, 1940-1970

	1940	1950	1960	1970
Population (millions)	1.8	2.2	2.3	2.7
Birth rate per 1,000 Population	38.7	38.5	33.5	25.8
Life expectancy (years)	46	61	69	72
School enrollment (thousands)	302	475	718	809
University students (thousands)	5.2	12.5	24.5	256.9
Net per capita income	121	279	582	1417
Labor force (thousands)	602	686	685	827
Unemployed (thousands)	66	88	83	89
Unemployment rate (%)	11	13	11	11
Jobs (thousands) in:				
Manufacturing	56	55	81	141
Agriculture	230	216	125	74
Commerce	54	90	97	138
Government	19	45	62	113
Other fields	177	190	177	272
Number of registered motor vehicles (thousands)	26.8	60.7	179.6	614.0
Number of telephones (thousands)	17.4	34.4	82.4	319.2
Annual value of construction (millions)	—	$78.5	$131.9	$323.3

Source: Commonwealth of Puerto Rico Planning
Board, *Socioeconomic Statistics of Puerto Rico.*
Fiscal Years 1940, 1948, 1950, 1960, to 1973.

Despite this progress, major problems remained. One was the continuing debate over the political status of the island and its relationship to the United States. Although a majority of the voters continue to support the Commonwealth status, a strong minority advocates statehood, and a smaller (but no less vociferous) third group insists that independence should be the island's destiny.

Coupled with this perennial (often bitter) debate over political status are severe, chronic problems of poverty, unemployment, and underemployment.[10]

While the industrialization program permitted undeniable improvement in the quality of life for thousands of families, it was unable to keep pace with the island's growing needs. A high birth rate and the loss of jobs in agriculture (farm jobs dropped from 230,000 in 1940 to 74,000 in 1970) swelled the ranks of the unemployed.[11] In 1970 the executive director of the Puerto Rico Manufacturers Association estimated that real unemployment (as opposed to the official unemployment figure of 11 percent) was nearly 30 percent.[12]

For many, the sole hope for socioeconomic mobility was to migrate. Between 1940 and 1970, about three-quarters of a million Puerto Ricans left their island to seek better opportunities on the U.S. mainland.[13] (Considering Puerto Rico's population size, this would be equivalent to 50 million Americans leaving the United States to settle elsewhere.) It is doubtful that a single Puerto Rican family was left unaffected by this massive exodus.

Table 3

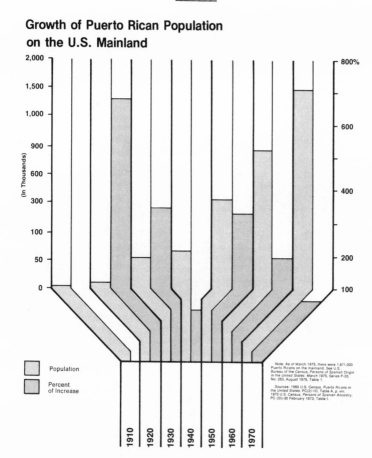

Growth of Puerto Rican Population on the U.S. Mainland

Note: As of March 1975, there were 1,671,000 Puerto Ricans on the mainland. See U.S. Bureau of the Census, Persons of Spanish Origin in the United States: March 1975, Series P-20, No. 283, August 1975, Table 1.

Sources: 1960 U.S. Census, Puerto Ricans in the United States, PC(2)-1D, Table A, p. viii; 1970 U.S. Census, Persons of Spanish Ancestry, PC (SI)-30 February 1973, Table I.

Migration to the Mainland

Puerto Ricans were living on the United States mainland more than 140 years ago, when the island was still a secure part of the Spanish colonial empire. During the 1830s, the founding members of a Spanish benevolent society in New York City included several Puerto Rican merchants.[14] By the middle of the 19th century, Puerto Rico was engaged in more commerce with the United States than it was with Spain, and the sea route between San Juan and New York (as well as other mainland ports) was well traveled. In the late 19th century, the movement for independence from Spain was being planned in New York City by groups of Puerto Rican and Cuban patriots. A dozen years after the U.S. takeover of Puerto Rico in 1898, the Bureau of the Census noted 1,513 Puerto Ricans on the mainland.

Table 4

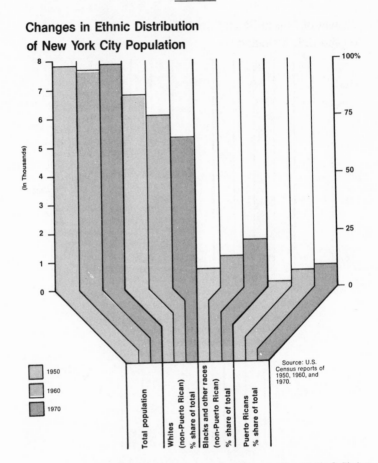

**Changes in Ethnic Distribution
of New York City Population**

Source: U.S. Census reports of 1950, 1960, and 1970.

But large-scale Puerto Rican migration to the United States mainland is a post-World War II phenomenon. As one observer has noted:

> The Puerto Ricans have come for the most part in the first great airborne migration of people from abroad; they are decidedly newcomers of the aviation age. A Puerto Rican can travel from San Juan to New York in less time than a New Yorker could travel from Coney Island to Times Square a century ago. They are the first group to come in large numbers from a different cultural background, but who are, nevertheless, citizens of the United States.[15]

In 1940 fewer than 70,000 Puerto Ricans lived on the U.S. mainland. Ten years later, the migrant community had more than quadrupled to 300,000 persons, and in the following decade, the population nearly tripled, to 887,000. By 1970, persons of Puerto Rican birth or parentage living in the United States numbered at least 1.4 million, and the figure grew to 1.7 million by 1975. (See Table 3.)

New York City, the first home for millions of immigrants to this country, now became the new home for a massive influx of U.S. citizens from other areas: Puerto Ricans from the West Indies and blacks from the Southern States.

Between 1950 and 1970, the population size of New York City remained stable at 7.9 million, but the city's racial-ethnic composition changed. In those two decades, the Puerto Rican community grew from 3 percent to better than 10 percent of the city's population. In turn, the number of blacks and persons of other races (Asian Americans, Native Americans, etc.) grew from 10 percent to 23 percent of the population. The city's white (non-Puerto Rican) population share dropped from 87 percent to 67 percent. (See Table 4.)

The earliest Puerto Rican migrants had settled in the East Harlem sector of Manhattan, which came to be known as El Barrio (a Spanish word meaning, roughly, "The Neighborhood"). In 1940 about 70 percent of New York's 61,000 Puerto Ricans lived in Manhattan. But the migrants soon began to fan out to the city's other four boroughs. By 1970, El Barrio was still an important Puerto Rican enclave, but the thrust of movement was elsewhere. The Manhattanites comprised only 23 percent of the city's 811,000 Puerto Ricans. By then, the Bronx was the largest Puerto Rican borough (39 percent of the population), followed by Brooklyn (with 33 percent). The outlying boroughs of Queens and Richmond were the homes of 5 percent of the city's Puerto Ricans. (See Table 5.)

Between 1960 and 1970, the Puerto Rican community in Manhattan dropped by 18 percent, to 185,000 persons. In the meantime, the Bronx community grew by nearly 70 percent (to 316,000 persons), Brooklyn saw an almost 50 percent increase (to 268,000 persons), and the small communities in Queens and Richmond (about 40,000 persons combined) grew by more than 120 percent. (See Table 5.)

While Puerto Ricans dispersed among the city's five boroughs, they were also moving outside of the city. In 1940, New York City was the home for nearly 90 percent of the migrants from the island. By 1970, only 57 percent of the Puerto Ricans lived there.[16]

There were substantial Puerto Rican communities in Yonkers, Long Island, and further upstate in Buffalo, Rochester, and Newburgh. Across the Hudson River, the Puerto Rican population of New Jersey grew to 137,000, more than double the figure of a decade previous.

Cities such as Newark, Jersey City, Paterson, and Hoboken

Table 5

Dispersion of Puerto Ricans Among New York City Boroughs

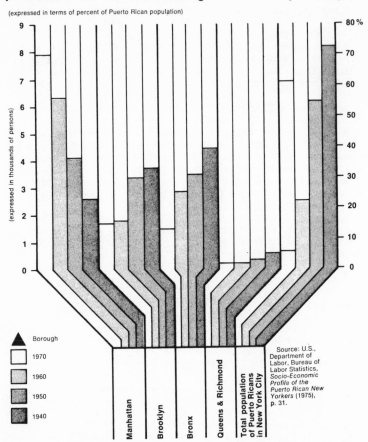

(expressed in terms of percent of Puerto Rican population)

Borough
1970
1960
1950
1940

Manhattan
Brooklyn
Bronx
Queens & Richmond
Total population of Puerto Ricans in New York City

Source: U.S., Department of Labor, Bureau of Labor Statistics, *Socio-Economic Profile of the Puerto Rican New Yorkers* (1975), p. 31.

all had Puerto Rican communities of more than 10,000 persons by 1970. In New England, large communities evolved in Boston, Bridge-port, and Hartford. Moving westward, the migrants established themselves in Philadelphia, Chicago, Cleveland, Lorain, and Gary. Large communities also developed in Miami and Los Angeles. (See Table 6.) By 1970, more than 30 U.S. cities had Puerto Rican communities of 5,000 or more persons. In some smaller towns, Puerto Ricans are now an important sector of the population.

Reasons for Migration: Although economics is almost always a key factor in the movement of peoples from their native land, hu-man motivation is never that simple or simplistic. Puerto Ricans fled neither political nor religious persecution, but life on the island for many young adults, particularly in rural areas, may have seemed

Table 6

Population Trends of Puerto Ricans on the U.S. Mainland, by Region, State, and City, 1950, 1960, 1970

	1950	1960	1970
United States			
Total	301,375	892,513	1,391,463
Northeast	264,530	740,813	1,126,410
New York	252,515	642,622	878,980
New York City	245,880	612,574	817,712
Buffalo	–	2,176	6,090
Rochester	–	1,990	5,916
New Jersey	5,640	55,351	136,937
Newark	545	9,698	27,663
Jersey City	655	7,427	16,325
Paterson	–	5,123	12,036
Hoboken	–	5,313	10,047
Passaic	–	–	6,853
Pennsylvania	3,560	21,206	44,947
Philadelphia	1,910	14,424	26,948
Connecticut	1,305	15,247	38,493
Bridgeport	590	5,840	10,048
Hartford	–	–	8,631
Massachusetts	1,175	5,217	24,561
Boston	–	995	7,335
Regional Balance	335	1,170	2,492
North Central	10,675	67,833	135,813
Illinois	3,570	36,081	88,244
Chicago	2,555	32,371	79,582
Ohio	2,115	13,940	21,147
Cleveland	–	4,116	8,104
Lorain	–	3,799	6,031
Indiana	1,800	7,218	9,457
Gary	–	2,946	5,228
Regional Balance	3,190	10,594	16,965
South	13,480	45,876	69,742
Florida	4,040	19,535	29,588
Miami	–	6,547	6,835
Regional Balance	9,440	26,341	40,154
West	12,690	38,030	59,498
California	10,295	28,108	46,955
Los Angeles	–	6,424	10,116
San Francisco	–	–	5,037
Regional Balance	2,395	9,922	12,543

intolerable. As is the case in many parts of the world, rural Puerto Rico offered a static environment, with few visible avenues for upward social mobility.

In the years following the Second World War, the urban parts of the island began to modernize, offering access to modern homes, automobiles, and other lures of modern life. Television and radio (which became ubiquitous by the 1950s) tempted rural viewers with scenes of life elsewhere. Thousands of Puerto Ricans had served in World War II and later in Korea. They came home with tales of their travels throughout the world and on the U.S. mainland. In other cases, Puerto Rican rural laborers were recruited for seasonal work on U.S. farms and gained a taste of mainland life. Air travel between San Juan and New York was quick and economical (as recently as the early 1960s the roundtrip economy flight between San Juan and New York was less than $100 and it still remains below $200). In many cases, migrants first moved from their rural homes to the island's cities, and then continued northward to the U.S. mainland.[17]

The hardships endured by the earliest migrants became less harsh for the later arrivals, who found relatives and friends waiting, stores that sold familiar vegetables and fruits, and even Spanish-language newspapers and radio and television programs. Migration nourished itself, to the point where some made the 3-hour flight to another world on a whim, or in reaction to some personal setback. If one can sum up motivations, they could all be equated with the search for a better life.

The question of economics was, of course, ever present and probably decisive. Wage levels on the U.S. mainland were higher than those in Puerto Rico. The opportunities for employment were more numerous and more varied. Joseph Monserrat, former director of the Migration Division of the Commonwealth of Puerto Rico, has observed that:

> The size of the Puerto Rican migration varies closely with job opportunities in the United States; i.e., when job opportunities increase, migration increases; when job opportunities decline, migration declines.[18]

This fact was confirmed in a recent study by a Puerto Rican economist, Dr. Rita M. Maldonado. Her study indicated that "Puerto Ricans emigrate to the U.S. mainland primarily for economic reasons ... specifically ... (1) if the job market in the U.S. is relatively better than that in Puerto Rico, [and] (2) if the average wage in the U.S. is higher relative to that in Puerto Rico...."[19] Her study also appears to indicate that the level of welfare payments and unemployment compensation in the United States is not a decisive factor in encouraging Puerto Ricans to emigrate.[20]

Since the Second World War, there have been three distinct trends in Puerto Rican migration, and all three have responded to job opportunities on the mainland and the island.

1. In the 1950s, an average of 41,000 Puerto Ricans migrated to the United States each year. The U.S. economy was booming, and job recruiters came to the island in search of workers for the sweatshops in the needlework industry. During this period, Puerto Rico, unlike the mainland, offered few urban jobs, particularly in factories, that could serve as a social step upward in comparison to field labor. At the same time, thousands of Puerto Rican farmworkers were afflicted by unemployment or had seasonal work (such as sugar cane cultivation) that left them idle for several months of the year. This was the single biggest decade of Puerto Rican migration, as more than 400,000 persons (nearly 20 percent of the island's population) moved to the U.S. mainland.

Table 7

Migration Between Puerto Rico
and the United States Mainland

Fiscal Year	Traveled to U.S. Mainland	Traveled to Puerto Rico	Net Migration to U.S. Mainland[1]
1920	19,142	15,003	4,139
1921	17,137	17,749	−612
1922	13,521	14,154	−633
1923	14,950	13,194	1,756
1924	17,777	14,057	3,720
1925	17,493	15,356	2,137
1926	22,010	16,389	5,621
1927	27,355	18,626	8,729
1928	27,916	21,772	6,144
1929	25,428	20,791	4,637
1930	26,010	20,434	5,576
1931	18,524	20,462	−1,938
1932	16,224	18,932	−2,708
1933	15,133	16,215	−1,082
1934	13,721	16,687	−2,966
1935	19,944	18,927	1,017
1936	24,145	20,697	3,448
1937	27,311	22,793	4,518
1938	25,884	23,522	2,362
1939	26,653	21,165	4,488
1940	24,932	23,924	1,008
1941	30,916	30,416	500
1942	29,480	28,552	928
1943	19,367	16,766	2,601
1944	27,586	19,498	8,088
1945	33,740	22,737	11,003
1946	70,618	45,997	24,621
1947	136,259	101,115	35,144
1948	132,523	104,492	28,031
1949	157,338	124,252	33,086
1950	170,727	136,572	34,155
1951	188,898	146,978	41,920
1952	258,884	197,226	61,658
1953	304,910	230.307	74,603
1954	303,007	258,798	44,209
1955	315,491	284,309	31,182
1956	380,950	319,303	61,647
1957	439,656	391,372	48,284
1958	467,987	442,031	25,956
1959	557,701	520,489	37,212
1960	666,756	643,014	23,742
1961	681,982	668,182	13,800
1962	807,549	796,186	11,363
1963	930,666	925,868	4,798
1964	1,076,403	1,072,037	4,366
1965	1,265,096	1,254,338	10,758
1966	1,475,228	1,445,139	30,089
1967	1,628,909	1,594,735	34,174
1968	1,858,151	1,839,470	18,681
1969	2,105,217	2,112,264	−7,047
1970	1,495,587	1,479,447	16,140
1971	1,566,723	1,605,414	−38,691
1972	–	–	−19,462
1973	1,780,192	1,799,071	−18,879
1974	1,622,001	1,630,525	−8,524

[1] A minus sign (−) denotes return migration.

Source: Data from Commonwealth of Puerto Rico Planning Board, published by Migration Division, Commonwealth of Puerto Rico, Department of Labor (Nov. 4, 1975).

Note: Figures from 1920 through 1969 are for total passenger traffic between Puerto Rico and all other destinations (U.S. mainland, U.S. Virgin Islands, and foreign nations), but the net migration figures accurately reflect migratory trends between Puerto Rico and the U.S. mainland.

Table 8

Return Migration from U.S. Mainland
to Puerto Rico, 1965-1970[1]

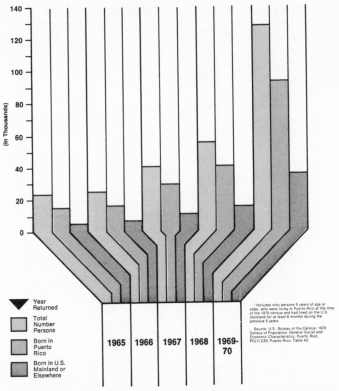

(In Thousands)

▼ Year
Returned

▢ Total
Number
Persons

▢ Born in
Puerto
Rico

▢ Born in U.S.
Mainland or
Elsewhere

| 1965 | 1966 | 1967 | 1968 | 1969-70 |

[1] Includes only persons 5 years of age or older, who were living in Puerto Rico at the time of the 1970 census and had lived on the U.S. mainland for at least 6 months during the previous 5 years.

Source: U.S., Bureau of the Census, 1970 Census of Population, General Social and Economic Characteristics, Puerto Rico, PC(1)-C53, Puerto Rico, Table 43.

2. By the 1960s, life had changed in Puerto Rico. While the U. S. economy was still vigorous, the island itself had begun to industrialize; hundreds of new factories opened, offering jobs and the chance for a life of modest comfort in Puerto Rico. Although these opportunities blunted the migratory thrust somewhat, the new factories could absorb neither all of the young persons entering the labor force nor the farm workers idled by the shrinkage of agricultural jobs. During the decade, an average of 20,000 persons migrated to the United States each year.

3. The U. S. economy began to turn sour in the early 1970s. Unemployment became widespread. Many factories closed in the New York City area. Despite the fact that Puerto Rico, too, was severely lashed by the recession of the 1970s (unemployment on the island soared to 19 percent by 1975), prospects for mainland jobs were so bleak that

Table 9

Combined Populations of Puerto Rico and Puerto Ricans on the U.S. Mainland, 1950, 1960, 1970[1]

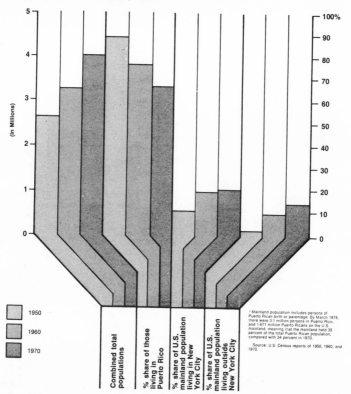

1950

1960

1970

Combined total populations

% share of those living in Puerto Rico

% share of U.S. mainland population living in New York City

% share of U.S. mainland population living outside New York City

[1] Mainland population includes persons of Puerto Rican birth or parentage. By March 1975, there were 3.1 million persons in Puerto Rico, and 1.671 million Puerto Ricans on the U.S. mainland, meaning that the mainland held 35 percent of the total Puerto Rican population, compared with 34 percent in 1970.

Source: U.S. Census reports of 1950, 1960, and 1970.

the migration flow was reversed. Since 1970 there has been a consistent trend of net return migration to the island each year. This is the first time that such a reverse migration trend has sustained itself over a prolonged period, except for the years 1931-1934, when the United States was in the midst of the Great Depression.[21] (See Table 7.)

It should be noted at this point that return migration to Puerto Rico is not just a phenomenon of the 1970s. There has always been constant return migration to Puerto Rico, but in previous years the number of migrants to the U.S. has almost invariably exceeded the number of return migrants. In 1965, for example, more than 22,000 persons moved back to Puerto Rico. In 1969--70, nearly 129,000 persons returned. All of these persons had lived on the mainland for at least 6 months, and a third of them had lived there for more than 6 years. (See Table 8.)

With such constant back-and-forth movement, it is difficult to find a Puerto Rican adult on the island who has not spent at least some time in the United States. Some observers have perceived the two Puerto Rican communities (on the island and on the mainland) as two parts of the same organism, linked by a highway in the air. By 1970, the combined population of Puerto Ricans on the island and the U.S. mainland was in excess of 4.1 million, with 66 percent residing in Puerto Rico, 20 percent in New York City, and 14 percent living elsewhere on the U.S. mainland. (See Table 9.)

According to the Migration Division of the Commonwealth of Puerto Rico:

> In addition to the 1.7 million year-round Puerto Rican residents of the U.S. mainland, several thousand migratory workers came each spring and summer, to fill seasonal farm labor shortages in many states along the Eastern seaboard and in the Midwest. Most of these workers return to Puerto Rico at the end of the farm season. Since the slack season in sugar cane (which is the winter crop in Puerto Rico) coincides with the peak of the farm season in the United States, this arrangement enables U.S. farmers to obtain much needed manpower; it also enables Puerto Rican agricultural workers, who might otherwise be unemployed during the summer months, to obtain work. Last year in New Jersey alone, Puerto Rican farm workers harvested crops worth more than $100 million.[22]

The focus of this report is not on this migratory farm labor population. However, Puerto Rican migrant farm workers have problems similar to those of Puerto Ricans residing permanently on the mainland. These include discrimination, low wages, inadequate housing, and poor educational facilities for their children.

Who Are the Migrants? According to the 1970 census, mainland Puerto Rican women slightly outnumbered men, 707,000 to 685,000.[23] Nearly 93 percent of the mainland Puerto Ricans were described as "white," while 5 percent were classified as "Negro," and the remaining 2 percent fell into the category of "other."[24] However, the simple black-white racial criteria commonly used in the United States are wholly inadequate when applied to the multiracial Puerto Rican society. In Puerto Rico, many persons describe themselves as "trigueno," which is neither Negroid nor Caucasian by U.S. standards. This is just one example of the type of cultural shock encountered by Puerto Rican migrants, who are not accustomed to such sharp-edged racial divisions. Puerto Rican scholar Frank Bonilla has observed:

> We live in a society that knows only black and white. Puerto Rican complacency and equivocation with respect to race and even our more genuine accommodations of racial differences have little place here. As we have discovered, here one is black, white, or a nonsomething. Still, Puerto

Ricans--white or black--have little comprehension of the
deep racial animosities that divide mainland Americans.
Many are understandably reluctant to become part of a fight
that is to them ugly and meaningless. [25]

More recently, a Puerto Rican professor at Pace University,
New York City, Clara Rodriguez, stated that:

> [W]ithin the U.S. perspective, Puerto Ricans, racially speak-
> ing, belong to both groups [black and white]; however, eth-
> nically, they belong to neither. Thus placed, Puerto Ricans
> find themselves caught between two polarities and at a dia-
> lectical distance from both. Puerto Ricans are between
> white and black. [26]

She noted, "Perhaps the primary point of contrast is that, in
Puerto Rico, racial identification is subordinate to cultural identification, while in the U.S., racial identification, to a large extent, determines cultural identification. Thus, when asked that decisive question, 'Who are you?' Puerto Ricans of all colors and ancestry answer,
'Puerto Rican,' while most New Yorkers answer, black, Jewish, or
perhaps 'of Italian descent.' This is not to say that Puerto Ricans
feel no racial identification, but rather that cultural identification
supercedes it."[27]

No recent studies have been made of Puerto Ricans at the moment of their departure for the U.S. mainland. But between the years
1951 and 1961, the Commonwealth of Puerto Rico government conducted
periodic surveys at San Juan International Airport, and came up with
the following profile of migrants:

●More than half were in the 15-24 age group and more than 85
percent were under age 35. Young children and older persons were
very much underrepresented.

●In terms of educational achievement, the migrants were slightly
above the island average. Three-fourths of them had completed 8
years or less of school. About one-third had attended high school,
but those with college experience were underrepresented.

●Most migrants were unskilled or semiskilled. While many
had been previously employed, and some had held professional or managerial jobs, more than half reported no work experience at all. Farm
laborers and factory workers represented the two largest groups with
job experience. [28]

A recent U.S. Department of Labor report has observed that:

> Puerto Ricans who migrate are better equipped for find-
> ing a job on the mainland than their counterparts in the
> Puerto Rican population. They tend to move at the beginning
> of their work careers, age 15-24; and almost half have some
> previous work experience. Their level of education and skill

Table 10

Population by Age, March 1975

	Total U.S. Pop.	Mexican American	Puerto Rican	Cuban
Total (thousands)	209,572	6,690	1,671	743
Percent	100.00	100.0	100.0	100.0
Under 5 years	7.7	13.7	13.0	4.6
5 to 9 years	8.3	12.5	13.0	6.5
10 to 17 years	15.7	19.5	20.7	16.7
18 to 20 years	5.7	6.6	6.2	4.0
21 to 24 years	6.9	7.8	5.8	5.4
25 to 34 years	14.4	13.8	15.9	9.3
35 to 44 years	10.8	10.7	12.8	15.6
45 to 54 years	11.3	8.1	7.0	18.6
55 to 64 years	9.3	3.8	4.1	10.7
65 years and over	10.1	3.3	1.5	8.6
18 years and over	68.3	54.3	53.3	72.2
21 years and over	62.6	47.7	47.1	68.2
Median age (years)	28.6	19.8	19.4	37.3

Source: U.S., Bureau of the Census, *Persons of Spanish Origin in the United States: March 1975*, Series P-20, No. 283, August 1975, Table 2.

is at or above the island average. Yet they face the competitive labor market of the mainland with several handicaps. Most have only a grade school education and are unable to speak English. The work experience which they have for example, farm labor, does not qualify them to compete for better jobs in urban areas. Even those who come from skilled occupations face the prospect that mainland employers will not consider their experience transferable. All share the disadvantage of newcomers in ability to cope with customs, practices and institutional arrangements in a new location. [29]

Age Differences: While the median age for the 209 million people of the United States is 28.6 years, the typical Puerto Rican is 9 years younger (and 18 years younger than the typical Cuban migrant to the United States). The proportion of Puerto Rican children in the preschool years is nearly double the national average (see Table 10.) Only 1.5 percent of mainland Puerto Ricans are age 65 or older, compared with 10.1 percent of all Americans. There appears to be a tendency for the Puerto Rican population to stay relatively young, because many of its older members return to the island. Between 1965 and 1970, for example, more than half of the return migrants were age 25 and older, and only one-fourth were in the age 15-24 bracket (whereas about half of the migrants to the mainland are age 15-24).

Language: More than 83 percent of mainland Puerto Ricans report that Spanish is their mother tongue, compared with 72 percent of Mexican Americans and 95 percent of Cuban Americans. [30] As for "language usually spoken in the home," only 27 percent of the

Table 11

Reporting Ability to Read and Write English, Total U.S. Population, Mainland Puerto Ricans, and All Persons of Spanish Origin, 1969

	Total U.S. Pop.	Puerto Ricans	Total Spanish Origin
Percent, age 10 and over	95.0	69.4	80.2
age 10 to 24	96.8	80.6	91.1
age 25 and over	94.2	59.7	71.9
Percent males, age 10 and over	95.3	72.9	82.8
males, age 10 to 24	96.7	82.3	91.7
males, age 25 and over	94.6	65.1	75.9
Percent females, age 10 and over	94.8	66.1	77.9
females, age 10 to 24	96.9	79.1	90.6
females, age 25 and over	93.9	55.6	68.1

Source: U.S., Bureau of the Census, *Persons of Spanish Origin in the United States, November 1969*, Series P-20, No. 213, February 1971, Table 17.

Table 12

Family Characteristics of Total U.S. Population, Mainland Puerto Ricans, Mexican Americans, 1972

	Total U.S. Population	Puerto Ricans	Mexican Americans
Families (in thousands)	53,296	363	1,100
Percent with own children under age 18	55.2	75.8	77.0
Average number of own children under age 18 per family	1.22	1.97	2.11
Percent families with:			
1 own child	18.9	19.2	19.8
2 own children	17.6	22.7	21.3
3 own children	10.2	13.9	12.5
4 own children	4.9	10.1	10.7
5 own children	2.1	4.8	6.9
6 or more own children	1.6	5.0	5.9
Percent families headed by a woman (one-parent families)	11.6	28.9	14.1

Source: U.S., Bureau of the Census, *Persons of Spanish Origin, March 1972*, Series P-20, No. 238, July 1972.

Puerto Ricans reported that it was English. More than 72 percent usually spoke Spanish at home, compared with 47 percent of the Mexican Americans and 87 percent of the Cuban Americans. [31]

However, younger mainland Puerto Ricans demonstrate far more facility in English. While less than 60 percent of the mainland Puerto Ricans age 25 and over report that they are able to read and write

Table 13

Relative Growth of Island-born and U.S.-born Puerto Rican Populations on the U.S. Mainland

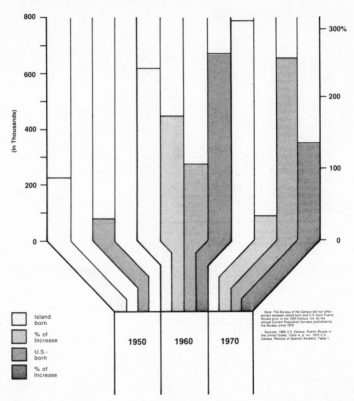

English, more than 80 percent of those in the age 10-24 bracket can do so. Males tend to be more able to read and write English, perhaps because their occupations thrust them into English-speaking environments (see Table 11).

Family Characteristics: Puerto Ricans have younger, larger families than the U. S. average. More than three-fourths of the Puerto Rican families have children under age 18, compared with slightly more than half of all U. S. families. Nearly 10 percent of the Puerto Rican families have five or more children, compared with under 4 percent of all U. S. families. Also, while 11 percent of U. S. families are headed by a woman (one-parent families), this was the case for nearly 30 percent of Puerto Rican families. [32] (See Table 12.)

Table 14

Age of Mainland Puerto Ricans, by Birthplace, 1970

Age	Born in Puerto Rico	Born in U.S.
Under 5 years	25,535	163,038
5 to 9 years	42,767	147,622
10 to 14 years	51,967	117,326
15 to 19 years	72,171	66,447
20 to 24 years	108,191	28,940
25 to 29 years	103,642	15,797
30 to 34 years	92,505	11,289
35 to 39 years	79,797	11,066
40 to 44 years	64,568	7,779
45 to 49 years	51,455	4,410
50 to 54 years	37,007	2,368
55 to 59 years	28,625	1,808
60 to 64 years	20,306	1,287
65 to 69 years	13,575	981
70 to 74 years	8,190	394
75 to 79 years	4,870	320
80 to 84 years	2,602	186
85 years and older	2,314	321
Totals	810,087	581,376
Median age (years)	30.0	9.3
Persons under age 18	159,900	474,496
Persons age 18 and over	650,187	106,880
Persons age 65 and over	31,551	2,202

Mainland-Born Puerto Ricans

While the mainland Puerto Rican population has grown rapidly in recent years, its composition has undergone radical change. In 1950, only about one-fourth of the 300,000 mainland Puerto Ricans had been born there. But by 1970, the U.S.-born had multiplied to 646,000, compared with 783,000 island-born migrants. In a decade, they had grown by 111 percent, compared to only 31 percent for their island-born parents. (See Table 13.)

The two groups (U.S.-born and island-born) can, at this point in history, already be perceived as quite different. The median age for migrants from the island is 30 years, which approximates the median for all Americans. But the median age for U.S.-born Puerto Ricans is only 9.3 years.

While only 25,000 of the migrants are under age 5, more than 163,000 of the U.S.-born are in this preschool category. While more than 650,000 of the migrants are over age 18, only 106,000 of the U.S.-born are over age 18. (See Table 14.)

The importance of these figures should not be overlooked. The typical Puerto Rican adult on the mainland was born in Puerto Rico.

Table 15

Ethnic Intermarriage of Puerto Ricans in the United States, 1970

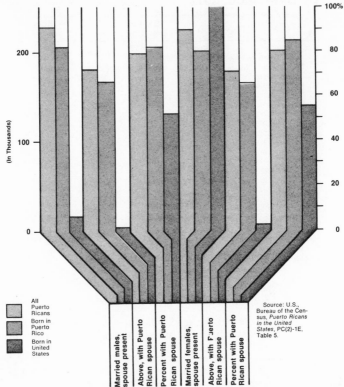

The great bulk of the U.S.-born are still of preschool or elementary school age, and have yet to make their impact upon the community.

Some trends, however, can already be ascertained. Relatively few U.S.-born Puerto Ricans are of marrying age, but they display a much faster rate of cultural mobility in comparison with their island-born parents. For example, while more than 80 percent of the married migrants have Puerto Rican spouses, only slightly more than 50 percent of the married U.S.-born have married within their ethnic group. (See Table 15.)

The U.S.-born Puerto Ricans seem to be conforming to many of the characteristics of American families. For example, the number of children per 1,000 American women age 25 to 34 is 2,374. Among migrant Puerto Rican women, the number is 2,812 children. For U.S.-

Table 16

Number of Children Born to all U.S. Women
and to Mainland Puerto Rican Women, 1970

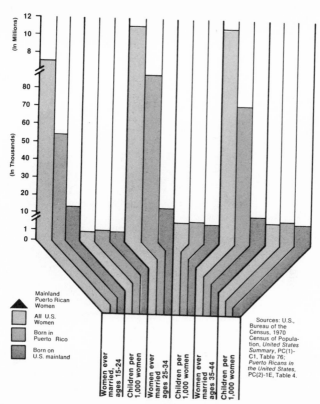

Mainland
Puerto Rican
Women

All U.S.
Women

Born in
Puerto Rico

Born on
U.S. mainland

Women ever married, ages 15-24 · Children per 1,000 women · Women ever married ages 25-34 · Children per 1,000 women · Women ever married ages 35-44 · Children per 1,000 women

Sources: U.S., Bureau of the Census, 1970 Census of Population, *United States Summary*, PC(1)-C1, Table 76; *Puerto Ricans in the United States*, PC(2)-1E, Table 4.

born Puerto Rican women, the number is 2,272, which is below the national average. The same holds true for women in the age 35-44 bracket. (See Table 16.)

Cultural adaptation is often a sign of upward socio-economic mobility, and these trends offer some cause for optimism. This does not mean that second-generation Puerto Ricans are not confronted with problems similar to those of their island-born parents. Even though their socioeconomic characteristics appear to be higher, when compared to those characteristics of the total U.S. population, even second-generation Puerto Ricans lag behind significantly. But we should not lose sight of the fact that the U.S.-born portion of the Puerto Rican mainland community is still extremely young. Most of the adults, responsible for family support in this crisis-ridden economy, are migrants from Puerto Rico, handicapped by language and a shrinking job market. They have immediate problems which must be addressed now, if their U.S.-born children (who hold such great promise for the future) are not to be irremediably scarred by poverty.

References

1. Puerto Rico lies 1,600 miles southeast of New York City, a $3\frac{1}{2}$ hour trip via jet plane.
2. See Bibliography for selection of books that offer socioeconomic and historical background data on Puerto Rico.
3. At the time, only Puerto Rico and Cuba remained of Spain's once vast empire in the Western Hemisphere, and the Cubans were engaged in a bloody, protracted war for independence.
4. Art. II and Art. IV, Treaty of Paris, 30 Stat. 1754 (1899).
5. 48 U.S.C. § 733 et seq. (1970) originally enacted as Act of Apr. 12, 1900, 31 Stat. 77).
6. 48 U.S.C. § 731 et seq. (1970) (originally enacted as Act of Mar. 2, 1917, 39 Stat. 951).
7. The Insular Cases: De Lima v. Bidwell, 182 U.S. 1 (1901); Downes v. Bidwell, 182 U.S. 244 (1901); Dooley v. United States, 182 U.S. 222 (1901); and Armstrong v. United States, 182 U.S. 243 (1902).
8. 48 U.S.C. §§ 731 (b)-(e)(1970)(originally enacted as Act of July 3, 1950, 64 Stat. 319).
9. Ad Hoc Advisory Group on Puerto Rico, Compact of Permanent Union Between Puerto Rico and the United States (San Juan, P.R.:GSA, 1975). House Resolution 11200 was introduced in the U.S. House of Representatives by Resident Commissioner from Puerto Rico Jaime Benitez in December 1975, for the purpose of codifying this compact. Hearings were held in February 1976.
10. Puerto Rico's political and socioeconomic tensions are very complex and cannot be adequately summarized in this volume, which focuses upon the U.S. mainland Puerto Rican community. The reader is advised to consult books listed in the Bibliography for background on Puerto Rico itself.
11. See Table 3.
12. New York Times, May 8, 1971.
13. U.S. census data cited in Kal Wagenheim, A Survey of Puerto Ricans on the U.S. Mainland in the 1970s (New York: Praeger, 1975), Table 1, p. 71.
14. Robert Ernst, Immigrant Life in New York City, 1825-1863 (New York: King's Crown Press, 1949).
15. Joseph Fitzpatrick, Puerto Rican Americans: The Meaning of Migration to the Mainland (Prentice-Hall, 1971), p. 2. Passage by ship between San Juan and New York City was another important means of transportation, especially in the early years.
16. 1960 U.S. Census, Puerto Ricans in the United States, Table A, p. viii; and 1970 U.S. Census, Persons of Spanish Ancestry in the United States, Table I, p. 1.
17. The strong lure of city life is reflected in 1970 figures showing that 1,358,987 mainland Puerto Ricans lived in urban areas,

compared with only 32,000 in U.S. rural areas. U.S. Bureau of the Census, 1970 Census of Population, Puerto Ricans in the United States, PC(2)-1E, Table 2, p. 4.

18. Joseph Monserrat, "Puerto Rican Migration: The Impact on Future Relations," Howard Law Journal (Fall 1968).

19. Rita Maldonado, "Determinants of Puerto Rico-United States Migration, 1947 to 1973," (Manuscript, 1975), p. 143. This study was supported by a grant from the U.S. Equal Employment Opportunity Commission. The study does not necessarily reflect the views of the EEOC.

20. Ibid.

21. The phenomenon of return migration in the 1970s is perhaps the best answer to uninformed allegations that many Puerto Ricans migrate to the mainland to collect welfare, since these payments are more generous on the mainland than they are in Puerto Rico.

22. Commonwealth of Puerto Rico, Department of Labor, Migration Division, Puerto Ricans in the United States (Pamphlet, 1975) (unpaged).

23. 1970 U.S. Census, Puerto Ricans in the United States. Table 1, p. 1.

24. Ibid.

25. Aspira, Inc., Hemos Trabajado Bien, a report on the first National Conference of Puerto Ricans, Mexican Americans, and Educators on "The Special Educational Needs of Urban Puerto Rican Youth," (May 14-15, 1968), p. 7.

26. Clara Rodriguez, "Puerto Ricans: Between Black and White," New York Affairs, vol. 1, no. 4 (1974), p. 94.

27. Ibid.

28. Commonwealth of Puerto Rico, Airport Survey, 1957, 1961.

29. U.S. Department of Labor, A Socio-Economic Profile of Puerto Rican New Yorkers: 1975, p. 18.

30. U.S., Bureau of the Census, Persons of Spanish Origin in the United States, November 1969, Series P-20, No. 213, February 1971, Table 6, p. 10.

31. Ibid., Table 10, p. 14.

32. These figures are for March 1972. Two years later, the Bureau of the Census reported that 33.2 percent of Puerto Rican families were headed by a woman (Persons of Spanish Origin in the United States, March 1974). In times of crisis, family stability is threatened. As Irving Howe has noted of immigrant Jewish families in the early 1900s, "The most severe sign of disturbance was the persistent desertion of families by immigrant husbands. Records of the United Hebrew Charities in New York for fiscal years 1903 and 1904 show that 1,052, or about 10 percent, of the applications for relief came from deserted women.... For years, the Forward (a Yiddish newspaper) ran a feature, Gallery of Missing Husbands." Howe, World of Our Fathers, p. 62.

L. H. Rogler and A. B. Hollingshead

PUERTO RICAN SPIRITUALIST
AS A PSYCHIATRIST

[Abstract: Preliminary study of schizophrenia in the lower class in
San Juan, Puerto Rico, suggests that spiritualists often serve as psychiatrists and that spiritualism functions as a therapeutic outlet for
mental illnesses. A mentally afflicted individual, alienated from his
social groups by his deviant and enigmatic behavior may find that a
group of spiritualists accepts his behavior. Participation in a spiritualist group serves to structure, define, and render the aberrant behavior institutionally meaningful. Spiritualism serves the afflicted
without the stigma of attending a psychiatric clinic.]

In recent years social scientists have made a number of studies of interrelations between the social system and mental illness,
some of which discuss the role the psychiatrist plays in society. [2]
This paper focuses on the therapeutic role of a quasi-professional
group only rarely thought of as being in the medical sphere--the spiritualists. [3]

Currently, we are doing research on mental illness in the lower
classes of the San Juan metropolitan area of Puerto Rico. Early in
our study we learned that persons afflicted with mental illness frequently come into contact with spiritualist mediums before, during,
and after their visits to psychiatrists. Local psychiatrists are aware
of these folk therapists. Likewise, spiritualist mediums have some
understanding of the functions of psychiatrists. In some cases, a
psychiatrist and a medium may share a patient: one psychiatrist, for
example, told us that relatives brought a patient to him for a "special"
purpose--they wanted him calmed so that he could be taken to a "genuine" therapist, a spiritualist medium! Psychiatric clinics in the San

Reprinted by permission from American Journal of Sociology 67:17-21,
July 1961. [1]   University of Chicago Press.

Juan area are known to have been used surreptitiously by local mediums to treat ambulatory patients. Furthermore, outpatients at one
psychiatric clinic have been heard to refer to psychotherapy as pases.
(Pases are the symbolic gestures performed by mediums for curative
purposes; the term is rich in connotation.)

Our experiences have led us to the tentative conclusion that
persons in the lower class rely upon spiritualist beliefs and practices
as therapeutic outlets for mental illnesses. We hope to furnish here
illustrative materials on the interrelations between the culture of the
lower class and the identification and treatment of mental illnesses by
non-medical practitioners. The materials are drawn from systematic
interviews with mentally ill persons, ranging from mild neurotics to
severe psychotics, with their spouses, and with a series of individuals
diagnosed by qualified psychiatrists as having "no mental illness." In
addition, we have interviewed spiritualist mediums and participated in
many of their sessions in order to observe their patients acting and
being reacted to in these settings.

Spiritualism is the belief that the visible world is surrounded
by an invisible world populated by spirits. The latter are "good" or
"bad."[4] Spirits have the power to penetrate the visible world and to
attach themselves to human beings. They may manifest themselves
as a reincarnation of some other person or thing. As metaphysical
beings they are able to coerce and influence human affairs, often very
dramatically. Persons may develop special faculties (facultades),
"mystical antennas," which enable them to communicate with spirits.
In this sense the person with facultades has gained a measure of control over the spirits. Consequently, an individual with facultades may
influence human affairs by commanding the obedience or favor of the
spirits.

The beliefs and practices of spiritualism are distributed throughout the society with, perhaps, a relatively pronounced tendency to concentrate in the lower classes. However, spiritualists and their followers in the upper classes are careful to distinguish their type of spiritualism from that of the lower classes. Upper-class spiritualists insist on the scientific and experimental character of their beliefs, ar-
guing that lower-class spiritualism is irrational and superstitious.[5]

Spiritualism actively provides social meanings to its troubled
participants. In the lower class, it is coterminous with social life,
woven into the intimate trials, strife and personal turmoil that en-
mesh the members of a socially and economically deprived stratum,
where its function is to discharge the tensions and anxieties generated
in other areas of social life. For example when, as often happens
in spiritualists' sessions, a married woman complains of the infidelity
of her husband, the medium may call upon the spirit of her rival and
assume her role. The medium indicates this change in her personality by gesticulating, changing the quality of her voice, and in general acting "como una mujer de la calle" (like a woman of the street),
it being assumed that that is the kind of woman that would lure married men from their spouses. The troubled wife then attempts to

convince the spirit that she should leave the husband alone and cease causing untold suffering. The effect of the dramatic exchange appears to be that the wife believes she has begun to cope with the problem.

"Crazy" (loco), "bad in the mind" (mal de la mente), and "weak in the brain" (débil del cerebro) are common expressions for mental illness in the vernacular of the persons studied. The words denote unusual and idiosyncratic behavior. One of our schizophrenic subjects said:

"A mentally ill person is one who has no control and can kill someone else. It is a person who is irrational, like an animal, one who does not use his mind. Such a person can do any horrible thing. They must be treated like children, otherwise they may fall upon you like a ray of lightning. Would I marry such a person? Absolutely not. Why would I want to bring a piece of worthless furniture into my house? It would be best to put such a person in a hospital where she could die."

"I am uncomfortable when I speak to [friends] about my illness. They may misinterpret what I say about my illness. They will laugh at me. They will not trust me. They will avoid me." This man, and others, realize that the very act of going to a psychiatric clinic may be the first step in the assumption of this feared role, for the psychiatric clinic is known as a place where locos go.

The spiritualist, as believer and participant, takes the stigma from an afflicted person. The spiritualist may announce to the sick man, his family, and friends that the patient is endowed with special psychic faculties, a matter of prestige in this social class. Spiritualism is a form of folk psychiatry. It serves its believers without their suffering the stigma associated with psychiatric agencies.

Spiritualism claims competence in the interpretation and treatment of pathological symptoms. Does the individual report hallucinations? This clearly indicates to the believer in spiritualism that he is being visited by spirits who manifest themselves visually and audibly. [6] Does he have delusions? He is told that evil spirits are deceiving him about himself as well as others. His thoughts are being distorted by interfering bad spirits. Or, through the development of his psychic faculties, spirits have informed him of the true enemies in his environment. Is his talk incoherent, rambling, and cryptic? This indicates that he is undergoing a test, an experiment engineered by the spirits to see if he is of the right moral fiber. Does he wander aimlessly through the neighborhood? He is being pursued by ambulatory spirits, unmercifully tormenting him. To illustrate: a thirty-seven-year-old woman, subject, according to the psychiatric diagnosis, to "hysterical hyperkinetic seizures," stated:

"Yes, I went to consult a spiritualist to see what the attacks meant. The medium told me that there was a young man who was in love with me. The mother-in-law of this young man bewitched me through an evil spirit. This evil spirit takes me over in a violent way."

"Did I believe the medium? Of course I did. She described many events in my life that were true. When I would see the mother-in-law of this young man I would get an attack. This proves that she [the medium] was right."

The basis for the medium's claims of competence is the assumption that all individual problems are material, or spiritual, or a combination of both material and spiritual things. The latter may have little or nothing to do with the outstanding complaint; rather, it classifies the source of the problem. Consequently, if the etiology of the illness is traced to the invisible world, it is a spiritual problem and, as such, within the control of the medium. Material problems, in contrast, have their causes in the visible world of "hard" facts. These, consequently, fall within the competence of doctors, druggists, nurses, and other professionals.

Few behavioral or medical problems have a conspicuous "material cause," immediately apparent to the subject, to the medium, or to others; therefore, problems are classified invariably as spiritual by the medium. Thus, the spiritualist medium effects a rough division of labor, relegating to herself (mediums are usually women) therapeutic competence to deal with a vast range of problems, many of which are disorders of personality in the broad, non-technical sense of the term.

The contacts between the medium and a patient take place variously in, to mention two possibilities, a private consultation or a session involving, usually, from fifteen to twenty participants. These meetings are organized explicitly to serve the participants; social interaction, consequently, is channeled toward the solution of problems they bring.

The room in which the session is held may be decorated with portraits of Franklin D. Roosevelt, Mahatma Gandhi, and banners of "Charity and Humility." A sober-faced, almost life-sized figure of a cigar-store Indian with arms crossed, looking ominously to the ceiling, may be a part of the setting. The odor of burning incense may pervade the room. The head medium opens the session with a long prayer, frequently from one of Allan Kardec's works,[7] directs herself to the auxiliary medium(s), and asks them to concentrate. Preparations are designed to develop the "correct" mood to welcome the spirits. As the session develops, the head medium may direct her attention to the participants' order of seating as they face the table where she and the auxiliary medium(s) are seated. The head medium then proceeds to probe, interpret, treat, and prescribe for the ills and maladies afflicting the individual. Prescriptions include a variety of herbs, ointments, medicated hot baths, massages with symbolic meaning, and prayers. The session generally requires intense participation by the members, which the medium frequently relieves by joking.

Participants who have developed psychic faculties show through their contortions, spasms, screeching, babbling, and deep breathing

that they have been possessed: the behavior varies in accordance
with the kind of spirit that has communicated with the one possessed.

The group meeting then is structured around four social roles:
those of the head medium, the auxiliary medium(s), and participants
with and those without faculties,[8] the four being arrayed according
to the participants' alleged degree of influence over spirits. The
roles are differentiated and co-ordinated by the charisma imputed to
the incumbents: we have observed psychiatrically diagnosed schizo-
phrenics effectively play each role.[9] Moreover, their performance
was enthusiastically received by the others at the session.

Although we lack direct evidence bearing on the therapeutic
effect on mental illness of participation in spiritualist sessions, we
have abundant information describing the manner in which participation served to cope with specific problems. To illustrate: the wife
of a paranoid schizophrenic described to us the disrupting effect her
husband's incessant and pervasive suspicions were having on her.
Were she to get up during the evening to take one of their children
to the outside toilet, her husband would accuse her of conspiring to
see a lover, waiting outside. Were she to leave the house to feed
the chickens, a similar charge would be made. In short, she had
to be within the radius of her husband's vision or suffer accusations
of unfaithfulness. As she says:

"Then I decided to take him to see a spiritualist medium since
his suspicions had created an impossible situation. She [the medium]
and the other people in the session advised him. He has not been
suspicious since then. They explained to him that it was a test that
he was undergoing since he was in the process of developing facultades. They told him that he should devote himself to charity and
to the good and that he should concentrate on the development of his
facultades. My husband is now a medium, and when he does not
feel well he performs pases on himself in front of the mirror. He
feels better afterward."

Another schizophrenic reports that, when he feels restless and
fearful inside, dissatisfied with himself and others, and not wanting
to see anyone, he turns to the spiritualist for help:

"I go to sessions because they make me feel good and rested
inside. They bring me peace. I go to them because the medium
is the maximum authority in knowing how to rid one of those evil
spirits and demons that upset one inside."

Another with a severe psychotic illness reports:

"Before I go to a session I feel very unhappy. When I get
to the group I talk to the medium and the others, and I feel good.
When the others begin to talk about their problems I feel as if I
am not alone. They [the group] make me feel sure of myself."

Such reports so often come from the mentally afflicted individuals in our study that we are led to the conclusion that attending group sessions serves, at least, to ease and alleviate personal stresses.

We do not have the research design to test the proposition that spiritualist sessions alter the personality of the mental patient in the direction of mental health. However, we believe that spiritualist sessions have a good many of the therapeutic advantages of group psychotherapy.[10] In addition to the presumed advantages of group psychotherapy as practiced in clinical settings, spiritualist sessions are coterminous with the values, beliefs, aspirations, and problems of the participants: no discontinuity in social contacts is required or participation. Little social distance separates the afflicted person from the medium, but, in contrast, visiting a psychiatrist involves bringing persons together who are separated by a vast social gulf. The others in the session are often neighbors, and so the spiritualist and her followers form a primary group where problems are discussed in the convivial setting, classified, interpreted, and rendered understandable within a belief system that is widely accepted even by those who profess not to believe in it.[11]

Persistent hallucinations to the believer in spiritualism are not symptoms of a deranged mind experiencing things unperceived by others, a definition which serves to isolate the sick. Rather, they demonstrate the development of psychic faculties that may eventually put the lucky person in more permanent contact with the invisible world. Thus, participation in a spiritualist group serves to structure, define, and render behavior institutionally meaningful that is otherwise perceived as aberrant.

References

1. Expanded and revised version of a paper read before the Section on the Sociology of Medicine at the annual meeting of the American Sociological Association held in New York City, 1960. The research reported here is being done by the Social Science Research Center of the University of Puerto Rico and is supported in part by a research grant, M-1750, from the National Institute of Mental Health, United States Public Health Service. We wish to acknowledge our debt to the members of the staff responsible for the interviews: Eugenia D'Acosta Ruiz, Francisca Santos de Limardo, Esperanza Acosta, Ricardo Márquez Rivera, Elsa Torres de Dávila, and Juan Muñoz Valentín. We would like to thank Dr. Charles Rogler, Mrs. Margot P. de la Cruz, and Mrs. Ann Richardson for reading and criticizing this article.

2. Ivan Belknap, Human Problems of a State Mental Hospital (New York: McGraw-Hill Book Co., 1956), pp. 205-7; G. Morris Carstairs, The Twice Born (London: Hogarth Press, 1957); Elaine Cumming and John Cumming, Closed Ranks (Cambridge, Mass.: Harvard University Press, 1957), pp. 36-44; Joseph W. Eaton and Robert J. Weil, Culture and Mental Disorders

(Glencoe, Ill.: Free Press, 1955); August B. Hollingshead and Frederick C. Redlich, Social Class and Mental Illness (New York: John Wiley & Sons, 1958), pp. 161-67, 353-55; Melvin L. Kohn and John A. Clausen, "Parental Authority Behavior and Schizophrenia," American Journal of Orthopsychiatry, XXVI (April, 1956), 297-313; Alexander H. Leighton, My Name Is Legion (New York: Basic Books, Inc., 1959); Alexander H. Leighton, John A. Clausen, and Robert N. Wilson, Explorations in Social Psychiatry (New York: Basic Books, Inc., 1957); Jerome K. Myers and Bertram H. Roberts, Family and Class Dynamics in Mental Illness (New York: John Wiley & Sons, 1959); Alfred H. Stanton and Morris S. Schwartz, The Mental Hospital (New York: Basic Books, Inc., 1954), pp. 143-44; Marion Radke Yarrow, Charlotte Green Schwartz, Harriet S. Murphy, and Leila Calhoun Deasy, "The Psychological Meaning of Mental Illness in the Family," Journal of Social Issues, XI (September, 1955), 12-24.

3. Joseph Bram, "Spirits, Mediums, and Believers in Contemporary Puerto Rico," Transactions of the New York Academy of Sciences, 1957, pp. 340-47; also Morris Siegel, "A Puerto Rican Town" (unpublished manuscript).

4. See Allan Kardec, El libro de los espiritus (Mexico City: Editorial Orion, 1951), pp. 147-80.

5. The type of data required to determine the prevalence of spiritualism and its class distribution is unavailable.

6. Allan Kardeck discusses the different ways in which the spirits may communicate and the corresponding facultades that spiritualists may have in El libro de los mediums (Mexico City: Editorial Orion, 1951), pp. 183-224.

7. For an official biography of Kardec see Henri Sausse, Biografia de Allan Kardec (Buenos Aires: Editorial Victor Hugo, 1952). This biography contains its own review (pp. 138-39), allegedly provided by Kardec's spirit, which spoke through one of the participants in a session attended by the author of the biography.

8. This fourfold role structure has been derived from observations of problem-oriented sessions in small spiritualist groups; other spiritualist groupings may be different.

9. Lee R. Steiner, who has made the same observations in New York City, says: "I've encountered psychopathic personalities with Jehovah complexes, at the lowest rung in both integrity and knowledge, who have effected emotional cures. It is my very definite impression that there is not very much correlation between validated knowledge and emotional cures. And I feel that this same condition obtains, at the moment, in professional therapy as well as in the occult" ("Why Do People Consult the Occult?" The Humanist, XIX [January-February, 1959], 27).

10. On the therapeutic advantages of group therapy see Marvin Opler, "Values in Group Psychotherapy." International Journal of Social Psychiatry, IV (Spring, 1959), 196.

11. "If you ever talk to a Puerto Rican who says he doesn't believe in spirits, you know what that means? It means you haven't

talked to him long enough"--statement attributed to a Puerto Rican in Dan Wakefield's Island in the City (Boston: Houghton Mifflin Co., 1959), p. 59. Though an exaggeration, it offers a very valuable hint to the interviewer. Often respondents will deny their belief in spiritualism when first questioned. However, once the interviewer has established a warm relationship with the respondent, the latter may not only admit his belief but may describe incidents that substantiate it dramatically. It is our impression that members of the upper class are more hesitant to admit to such beliefs than are lower-class individuals.

Part II

CONFLICT AND ACCULTURATION ON THE MAINLAND

Angela Carrasquillo and Ceferino Carrasquillo

THE NEO-RICAN: UNWELCOMED IN TWO WORLDS

The Puerto Rican Migration: Causes and Effects

On May 12, 1898, the city of San Juan, Puerto Rico was bombarded under the direction of Admiral William Sampson, and on July 15, American forces occupied Guanica and, three days later, Ponce. On October 18, the last of the Spanish troops to sail embarked for Spain. The forces of the United States occupied San Juan, raised the flag on the Fortaleza, and proclaimed United States sovereignty and the end of the Spanish rule. In 1900, the island of Puerto Rico was confronted with a new government, a new culture, and new language. During the first decades of United States domination, many crucial decisions affecting native Puerto Ricans were made without their expressed consent.

In 1917, the Jones Act was approved by Congress, giving American citizenship to all Puerto Ricans with no quota restriction or visa requirements on Puerto Rican migrants. Puerto Ricans were free to travel between the island and the mainland without any migration inconvenience. According to Adalberto López (1974), this United States action increased the Puerto Rican migration. He says: "By 1920, the Puerto Rican population on the United States mainland had risen to almost 12,000.... Ten years later, there were some 53,000 Puerto Ricans on the mainland; by 1940 the figure was close to 70,000."

Puerto Ricans came to the United States with the great hope of "making it" in the American mainland. Many Puerto Ricans came to the mainland with the idea of staying for a few years. The majority of them were rural people, poor, unskilled, relatively young, and seldom with more than a few years of elementary school education. Why did Puerto Ricans migrate to the United States? Among the causes of the Puerto Rican migration are:

1. Economic reasons: This is a key reason for the migration of Puerto Rican people to the mainland. In 1940,

Puerto Rico had a large population per square mile, a high rate of unemployment, and poverty was in all places. For Puerto Ricans, ways for economic improvement did not exist. Puerto Ricans thought of moving to the United States as the panacea for their financial problems. At the same time, the United States had a great demand for unskilled or semi-skilled labor in industries, and in jobs like janitors, dishwashers, and hotel maids.

2. A search for a better life: In the rural areas of Puerto Rico there was no hope of upward social mobility. Studies of Puerto Rican migration to the United States indicate that Puerto Ricans did not come to the mainland only to get a job. They also were seeking a better life than they had in Puerto Rico. For Puerto Ricans, a better life meant water and electricity in the apartment, stores around the neighborhood, radio and other available types of amusement, like the theater. It also meant furniture and food for their children.

3. The Puerto Rican Government's attitude toward the migration: The government of Puerto Rico did not discourage the migration (Fernando Sierra Berdecía, 1956), as shown by the arrangements the Government made to get low rates of air transportation between the island and the mainland. Therefore, Puerto Ricans found it relatively easy to move from Puerto Rico to the mainland. The Puerto Rican Government did not make explicit the poor life conditions that these people will find in the United States. Since people did not receive accurate information from governmental agencies, they continue to move to the United States.

In a document published by the Office of Civil Rights, Puerto Ricans in the Continental United States: An Uncertain Future (1976), it is stated that New York City became the home for thousands of Puerto Rican migrants. The report says: "Between 1950 and 1970, the population size of New York City remained stable at 7.9 million, but the City's racial-ethnic composition changed. In those two decades, the Puerto Rican community grew from three per cent to better than ten per cent of the City's population (p. 19)." The East Harlem sector of the borough of Manhattan known as "El Barrio" was one of the first areas to be settled by Puerto Ricans. In 1960, about seventy per cent of New York's 61,000 Puerto Ricans lived in Manhattan. But very soon, Puerto Ricans went out to other boroughs of New York City, such as the Bronx and Brooklyn. In the Bronx, Puerto Ricans moved to the south, to Hunts Point and Morrisania. In Brooklyn, Puerto Ricans settled in Williamsburg, Greenpoint, and South Brooklyn. Today, Puerto Ricans are found in large numbers in most of the big cities of the United States. In 1970, the Office of the United States Census reported that by 1970 there were 1,391,463 Puerto Ricans on the mainland. The following table, compiled in 1970, shows the concentration of Puerto Ricans in eleven American cities (see Table 1).

Table 1

City	State	Number of Puerto Ricans
New York	New York	817,712
Chicago	Illinois	78,582
Newark	New Jersey	27,663
Philadelphia	Pennsylvania	26,948
Jersey City	New Jersey	16,325
Paterson	New Jersey	12,036
Los Angeles	California	10,116
Hartford	Connecticut	8,631
Boston	Massachusetts	7,335
Buffalo	New York	6,090
San Francisco	California	5,037

Educational Language Policies in Puerto Rico and
Their Effects on the Puerto Rican Migration

In order to understand the attitudes of Puerto Ricans on the Island to-ward the Neo-Ricans, it is imperative to turn to the history of language policies on the island. In 1900, the island of Puerto Rico was faced, in theory, by a new and entirely different educational system: the North American system which had absolutely no relation to the culture and language of the Island. After 1898, different language approaches came into effect, depending on who the Commissioner of Education was at that time. Dr. Martin Braumbaugh was appointed on August 8, 1900, as the first Commissioner of Education. Dr. Braumbaugh's language policy recognized the importance of preserving the Spanish language while the students acquire knowledge of English. But this policy changed in 1904 when Commissioner Roland Falkner made English the official language of Puerto Rico (Luis Muñiz Suffront, 1950). According to Pedro A. Cebollero (1954), the Falkner policy was used in Puerto Rico until 1916. In 1916, José A. Padín, Assistant Commissioner of Education, in his The Problems of Teaching English to the People of Puerto Rico concluded that "English should not be used as a medium of instruction until the seventh grade (p. 67)."

On March 20, 1925, the Legislature of Puerto Rico demanded an investigation into the organization and methods used in the University of Puerto Rico and in the public schools. The Commission concluded that, "The schools are not justified in making English the medium of instruction until the seventh grade." In 1934 Dr. José Padín, Commissioner of Education, sponsored a series of studies which pointed out the need to use Spanish as the medium of instruction in the elementary school, grades one to eight. Dr. Padín's policy, recommending the use of Spanish as the medium of instruction in the first eight grades, was welcomed by a great majority of the people of Puerto Rico; but the United States government disagreed with it.

The years 1937 to 1942 were characterized by the absence of a clear language policy for Puerto Rican schools. In 1947, the Consejo

Superior de Enseñanza (Superior Educational Council) conducted a study of the educational problems of Puerto Rico entitled Problems of Education in Puerto Rico. In it, the Commission highly favored the use of the Spanish language in the teaching process. The conclusions of the study also pointed to the need for the introduction of English through more scientific methods.

In November 1948, the first gubernatorial elections were held, according to the Organic Law approved by the United States Congress. Luis Muñoz Marín was elected governor of Puerto Rico. He took office in January, 1949, and appointed Mariano Villaronga as Commissioner of Education. Villaronga confronted the seemingly interminable language problem of Puerto Rican education. He stated that Spanish would be the medium of instruction at all school levels in Puerto Rico beginning with the school year of 1949-50 (Circular Letter No. 10, August 6, 1949). After fifty years of facing a language problem characterized by misunderstandings and confusion among educational leaders, teachers, and others, Puerto Rico solved its problems by deciding that Spanish was the language of instruction in the classroom and that English should be taught as a subject. This policy responded to the exigencies of Puerto Rico's socioeconomic evolution. It provided for the teaching of English as a second language and provided education in the other subject areas in the pupil's native language.

Today Puerto Rico has 710,000 students in kindergarten through the twelfth grades. The median years of schooling is 6.9 years for the Puerto Rican adult of twenty one years or more. The drop out rate is 5.1 per cent (Baltasar Corrada, 1976). Instruction in English is developed as a priority and as a special subject. Spanish is used as the language of instruction throughout all grades, and English is introduced orally in grades one and two; reading and writing skills are developed in English in grades three and beyond.

Puerto Ricans on the Mainland

Puerto Ricans did not find the hopes they had expected. They are the minority group that benefits the least from educational programs, health, housing and political involvement in the United States (Cordasco, 1970). Puerto Ricans suffer during the winters because of lack of heat in the apartments and inadequate clothes. In the summer, they have reverse conditions; apartments are extremely hot, and they do not have air conditioning like most of the rest of the population. Their apartments are not safe; these residences are deteriorated and infested with roaches and often owned by inconsiderate or absentee landlords.

The Puerto Rican family's life style has suffered too. There are many broken families, as well as hopeless and unemployed youngsters who are driven to crime and drug addiction. Most of the Puerto Ricans migrate in family groups; and when they arrive in the United States, many conflicts of values and roles emerge that tend to weaken the family ties (Fitzpatrick, 1970). For example, employment is easier for women than for men. This aspect reverses the husband-wife roles and affects the children's mother and father role images, since these children are accustomed to seeing their mother at home while the father works. Nieves Colón and Acosta Belén (1973) pointed out that one of the most difficult things for the Puerto Rican parents to accept is the way that American children are reared. While the American child is taught to be aggressive, self-reliant, and competitive, the Puerto Rican child is taught to be humble and dependent; and when he starts to behave according to American patterns, the parents consider him disrespectful. The values of the parents are not always shared by the children, since they are learning other values and attitudes in school. These changes in behavior affect the family life style, resulting in broken families.

Puerto Ricans are among the lowest paid workers. They are unemployed or hold lower paying jobs. Many of them get jobs which require relatively little skills. They are handicapped in the competition for better employment by a poor educational background. Poor education and low-skill, low-stature jobs have made for poor earnings. In 1975, the median income for Puerto Ricans was $7,629; the lowest salary level of all Hispanic populations in the United States. In the case of the Puerto Rican women, it could be stated that they are overworked and underpaid. The 1975 United States Census Bureau reported that the median annual income of a Puerto Rican woman was only $3,889.

Puerto Ricans have one of the lowest levels of formal education among the ethnic and racial minorities in the nation. According to the 1970 United States Census, among persons aged 25 years and older, whites have a median of 12.1 school years completed, blacks have 9.8 school years, and mainland Puerto Ricans have 8.7 school years. The dropout rate among Puerto Ricans is still another problem, which becomes evident for ages 14 to 17. Nationwide, 93 per cent of all youngsters in this age range remain in school, compared with 85 per cent of Puerto Rican youngsters (Office of Civil Rights, 1976).

Neo-Ricans on the Mainland

Although the majority of Puerto Ricans had intended to come to the mainland for a few years, they stayed and raised their children in the United States. Most of the second or third generation Puerto Ricans on the mainland are from New York. This is the reason they are called "New Yoricans" or "Neo-Ricans." Often the term is used to designate loud, pushy and uncultured people. Actually the term "Neo-Rican" or "New Yorican" is a sociological one, employed to identify the thousands of Puerto Ricans who were born and reared in the United States. The following are characteristics applicable to the Neo-Ricans:

1. Among second and third generation Puerto Ricans, back-and-forth travel between the Island and the mainland is not common. Such communication applies mostly to the

first generation who look back to Puerto Rico with nostalgia.
The typical Neo-Rican does not know much about the history and culture of the island and his ancestors.

2. Neo-Ricans receive inadequate education on the mainland.
The educational inadequacy is seen in the curricula of the
school which is far apart from the student's culture, attitudes and values. The teachers do not show awareness of
and interest in the Neo-Ricans' ethnic background. The
testing mechanism used to assess their needs and improvement is biased and unrelated to the student's cultural and
historical reality. The general school environment does
not serve as an incentive for Puerto Ricans. The Office
of Civil Rights (1976) reported that "Of the 30 percent of
United States high school students who drop out each year,
one-third are in their senior year and have already completed most of the required courses. Most dropouts are
bored and find the school unresponsive to their cultural
backgrounds, or feel compelled to obtain a job." (p.96)
Many Puerto Rican dropouts felt that the school did not
understand and respect the culture from which they came.

Puerto Ricans born on the mainland will not show the
same attitudes and behaviors of Puerto Rican students born
on the island. Mainland Puerto Ricans have been conditioned to the life styles of slums in large cities. These
youngsters will show rebellion against the authority of parents and teachers. The teacher is not his or her "second
parent", as newly arrived Puerto Rican students would say.
Therefore, the behavior of the Neo-Rican is frequently
quite different from the humbleness exhibited by the youngster who has come directly from Puerto Rico. Acosta
Belén (1974) stated: "Teachers and school authorities initially blamed this failure on the students (because of their
supposed non-communicative posture, lack of interest, low
I.Q. inferiority, and number of deficiencies) and on the
community (because of lack of communication with the
school, and negative influences upon the students." (p.88-89))

3. Neo-Ricans show social and emotional disorientation, inferiority, and poor self-image. These psychological problems affect their academic performance and their development within the society. Most Puerto Rican youngsters
come from the lower socio-economic class and they show
these social class patterns in their behavior. These social class patterns are combined with various ethnic and
cultural patterns, making more difficult for these youngsters, the task of self-analysis and identification. In
many instances, the Neo-Ricans do not know to which
group they really belong.

4. There is growing Puerto Rican participation in higher education. Puerto Rican students have demanded that the

history and culture of Puerto Rico be included in the university curricula. This agitation has resulted in the creation of Puerto Rican Studies programs in some New York
City and New York State universities. These programs
have been received with enthusiasm and have improved the
American interest in Puerto Rican history and culture. The
Office of Civil Rights (1976), noted that "an estimated
25,000 mainland Puerto Ricans were enrolled as full-time
college undergraduates in 1972." (p. 119) In 1974, Puerto
Ricans and other Hispanic groups represented 13.4 per
cent of freshmen students in the CUNY system, compared
with 6.0 per cent five years earlier. In 1976, three million dollars were authorized to Hostos Community College
for the Spanish speaking students' educational needs (New
York Times, 1976). The Office of Civil Rights (1976)
made the following generalization about the mainland Puerto
Rican college student: "The student is more likely to be
male than female and from a low-income family. He is
the first in his family to go to college and is somewhat
older than the average student, as he may have worked or
completed military service prior to entering college. He
is likely to be a first-year student at a relatively low-cost
two year or community college...." (p. 123) Puerto Ricans
enrolled in schools of education tend to be single female
students; most of the time with the responsibility of being
a parent and the home's financial head. These statements
show that in spite of the marked progress, Puerto Ricans
are still behind academically.

5. English is used by Neo-Ricans in every day situations. The
political status of Spanish (especially in New York City) is
that of a migrant language (Milán, 1976). Mainland-born
Puerto Ricans tend to place a high value on English, since
it is their primary medium of communication. Although
their parents speak to them in Spanish, Neo-Ricans do not
respond in Spanish. They ask and answer questions in
English, watch English television programs, and listen to
English language radio stations. The Neo-Ricans' Spanish
vocabulary is very limited. Today, however, Neo-Ricans
are showing more interest in knowing the Spanish language
and using it as a medium of communication.

From the above characteristics it could be concluded that Neo-
Ricans are a group of Puerto Ricans who, little by little, are becoming conscious that they are Puerto Ricans, that they have to prepare
themselves educationally to improve the image of Puerto Rico on the
mainland. They are also going back to study the history and culture
of Puerto Rico and are coming to realize that the knowledge of the
vernacular language of Puerto Rico will put them close to the island.

Neo-Ricans in Puerto Rico

Today the Puerto Rican nation is receiving thosands of returning

Puerto Ricans. This reverse migration includes second and third generation Puerto Ricans who were born on the mainland. The seventies has not been a good decade for the United States; and for Puerto Ricans it has been even worse. The rate of migration to the Island has increased considerably. One reason is the difficulty in getting jobs on the mainland in an economy where there is a declining demand for unskilled labor in urban industries. Another reason is the deterioration of living conditions in the United States. Although Puerto Ricans have jobs, they realize that it is not worth remaining on the mainland when they consider the price they have to pay in terms of intolerable living conditions. These people cannot tolerate continued living in the ghettos and in an environment where crime and drugs are part of the daily life.

Many more Puerto Ricans are returning to Puerto Rico than are arriving in the United States. Statements from the Department of Labor reported in the (New York Times, October 3, 1975) indicated: "Nevertheless, the pattern of migration in recent years has been toward the Island from the mainland. In 1972, a total of 33,596 more people came here than left. In 1973, the net inflow rose to 34,492. Last year the net inflow fell to 18,378."

The following table indicates the Puerto Rican areas with the greatest concentration of returning Public School students (see Table 2).

Table 2

REGIONS SHOWING CONCENTRATION OF RETURNING
PUBLIC SCHOOL STUDENTS

Region	Enrollment	Per Cent
Arecibo	11,000	16%
Caguas	7,138	11%
Humacao	7,852	12%
Mayagüez	13,522	20%
Ponce	10,442	15%
San Juan	17,437	26%
Total	67,391	100%

Estudio Sobre Estudiantes Procedentes de Estados Unidos, Departamento de Instrucción de Puerto Rico, Mayo de 1978, p. 7.

In the school year of 1977-78, the Department of Education in Puerto Rico had an enrollment of 727,718 students. From this enrollment, 67,391 students (9.2%) had lived in the United States. A total of 11,517 (17%) had lived in the United States for three years and less, and 55,874 had lived in the United States more than three years. The following table shows this distribution (see Table 3).

Table 3

STUDENTS ENROLLED IN THE PUBLIC SCHOOLS OF PUERTO RICO
WHO HAD LIVED IN THE UNITED STATES

Years in The United States	Amount of Students	Per Cent
0--1 year	289	4%
1 year, 1 day--2 years	5,560	8.3%
2 years 1 day--3 years	5,668	8.5%
3 years 1 day--4 years	6,052	8.9%
4 years 1 day--5 years	5,786	8.6%
more than 5 years	44,036	65.3%
Total	67,391	100.0%

Censo Bilingüe, Departamento de Instrucción Pública, 1978

A New York Times reporter stated in 1976: "In recent years, the massive migration of Puerto Ricans to the mainland has been reversing itself, and in the last five years (of 1976) alone, more than 90,000 people have returned to the Island ... many of them, second or third generation Puerto Ricans, with limited, nonexistent Spanish-speaking ability, who often find academic and social problems as severe as those faced by earlier non-English speaking pupils in New York City.

Neo-Ricans in Puerto Rico and Neo-Ricans on the mainland have certain problems, although both groups share psychological attitudes and sociological circumstances. The following are some of the aspects that should be considered when analyzing the actual situation of Neo-Ricans in Puerto Rico.

1. Neo-Ricans go to Puerto Rico in search of their cultural roots. There is an increasing desire of second and third generation Puerto Ricans to know more about their ancestors, their culture, their mother tongue, etc. These Puerto Ricans make plans to go to Puerto Rico forever. Regarding their plans, they have ideas of getting a job, getting involved in cultural organizations, learning the Spanish language with fluency and becoming "real" Puerto Ricans. When they return to Puerto Rico, they often find that the homeland of their parents or grandparents no longer is theirs. As Adalberto López (1973) observed: "Most of these students like Puerto Rico and find their experiences there valuable, but they are often made to realize that they are not 'real' Puerto Ricans. The following paragraph (New York Times, October 3, 1975) is a clear example of the problems these youngsters confronted: 'Edward Mackey Colón, who is 15 years old, was in the ninth grade at Brooklyn Technical School when suddenly, family problems took him from his home in Corona, Queens, back to the Island of his mother's birth. He knew a little Spanish from home, but was not really fluent in the language, and soon he felt lost in his new surroundings.'" Another example of how

these Neo-Ricans feel is seen in the following comments made by one Neo-Rican (Daily News, October 16, 1977): "You feel Puerto Rican all your life. So you want to come back to your roots. And one day you do, and then you get hit with all this. They tell you you're not really a Puerto Rican, just like they let you know up there that you weren't really an American."

2. Neo-Ricans show a cultural and political nationalism. These youngsters have lived and observed the struggles of their parents on the mainland, the poor housing, health and educational conditions and have demonstrated political aggressiveness toward the United States, a country that has not resolved their unique socioeconomic problems. They look to Puerto Rico with the hope that people in the Island will help them to fight for better political relations for them, and in some way this will improve their living conditions on the mainland. Therefore, the Neo-Rican sufferings, and their precarious conditions are demonstrated by an anti-American movement.

3. Some Neo-Ricans have problems speaking Spanish. It is strongly accented or limited. Spanish is the official language of Puerto Rico, and it is used in all domains. English is taught in school as a second language. A small part of the Puerto Rican population speaks English fluently. In 1977, Baltazar Corrada, Resident Commissioner in Washington from Puerto Rico to the Congress, appeared before a Senate Committee regarding Federal Aid to Elementary and Secondary Education, and he stated in answer to a question asked by Senator Pell about the fluency in English of the Puerto Rican high school graduate: "I would say that not all of them do; particularly those who are educated in private schools are, I would say, quite fluent. However, I do believe that those who graduate from our public school system do not have the kind of fluency in English that they ought to have." In other words, there are very few people in Puerto Rico to whom Neo-Ricans could speak.

Neo-Ricans use "Spanglish" (Mixture of Spanish and English which is used in Spanish speaking communities in the United States) for communication purposes. Acosta Belén (1975) summarized this phenomenon: "Since children born in the United States of Puerto Rican parents no longer have the same opportunity to learn Spanish (although bilingual education is beginning to change this situation) their vocabulary is less extensive and they learn the words that the previous generation borrowed or adapted from English, sometimes without knowing that they are not Spanish words. They also continue to borrow lexical items from their dominant language and incorporate them into Spanish when attempting to speak it." Neo-Ricans have the wrong idea that they are speaking Spanish (since this is the language spoken in their own community) and when they use these words in Puerto Rico they are criticized and ridiculed.

When many Neo-Ricans returned to Puerto Rico they found that since they do not speak Spanish well, and the Puerto Ricans do not speak English, there is no real communication between both groups, and they are not welcomed. The Neo-Ricans find themselves lost in a system where English is seldom used or never at all. They might even feel out of place in their English classes where pronunciation and drills, which they do not need, are emphasized.

4. Neo-Ricans cannot get jobs in Puerto Rico. The lack of professional skills in areas such as reading, conversational Spanish, the general lack of knowledge of Puerto Rican history and culture, and the high unemployment rate are factors that contribute to inability to get jobs. Neo-Ricans feel frustrated since the cost of living conditions in Puerto Rico is very high. These youngsters cannot earn enough money to satisfy those minimal needs of the every day life. Most of the time they have to depend on their parents' pockets for support.

5. Neo-Ricans are caught between two cultures: in their hearts they are Puerto Ricans, in their habits, Americans. Neo-Ricans have a different set of values and exhibit different patterns of behavior. They are struggling with Spanish traditions at the same time. Therefore, the mainland-born youth is seen as a cultural aggressor. One reason is that, historically, Spanish has been considered a key to the survival of the island's own personality; and Puerto Rican islanders see those mainland students as those who will bring the English language back to the Puerto Rican educational system.

What Has Been Done: What Could Be Done

Social and educational agencies in both Puerto Rico and in the United States have inadequately dealt with Neo-Ricans. These agencies should handle problems faced by Neo-Ricans and develop educational and social resources where they are acutely needed. The assumption is that language and employment more than any other factors are the greatest handicaps to the adjustment of mainland Puerto Ricans in Puerto Rico. The following are some recommendations toward the solution of the problem.

1. Puerto Rican youngsters on the mainland should study the language, history, and culture of Puerto Rico in addition to being aware of contemporary political developments on the Island. At present, Puerto Rico is a politically divided Island. Opposing ideas are affecting the economy, the culture and the morale of the Island. Neo-Ricans should get acquainted with the historical sites, geography and cultural centers of the island. If Neo-Ricans study about Puerto Rico on the mainland before moving to Puerto Rico, they can communicate their Island's knowledge with the people of Puerto Rico and the islanders will see them as Puerto Ricans. Therefore, Neo-Ricans will feel they are Puerto Ricans.

2. It is not a secret that English instruction programs have failed in the public schools of Puerto Rico. Bilingual education programs are needed in Puerto Rico and on the mainland. Puerto Rican children should be placed in bilingual schools, in which two languages are the medium of instruction. These bilingual education programs

must have a second language component: English as a second language. In both situations, the language of the home must be used as a medium for teaching part of the subject matter in addition to the second language.

Bilingual programs should have as one of their primary goals the maintenance of the child's native language and culture. In this way, students will be equipped to function in both the United States and Puerto Rico, although full bilingualism for all students is a near impossibility. In a Spring, 1977 report of the Office of Bilingual Education of the City of New York, it was stated that from 49,889 Spanish speaking students tested in the English Language Assessment Battery Test, 31,397 are at or below the 20th percentile. These numbers provide evidence of the lack of linguistic English skills attained by Spanish speaking people. Students need bilingual programs which will help them to improve skills, in both languages, to reduce the effects of the mainland Puerto Ricans' isolation by increasing their skills in understanding, speaking, reading and writing Spanish and English. Language isolation of these students has led to low academic achievement as reflected in low reading and mathematics scores. Therefore, special Federal aid programs should be increased, especially in Puerto Rico, to fund programs for language minority students. Title I and VII funds of the Elementary and Secondary Education Act (ESEA) should be increased. Puerto Rico's bilingual demonstration projects are scarce.

The educational goal of the United States and Puerto Rico must be to fully include all students. Neo-Ricans must also be included in these educational goals based on these principles:

a) The Neo-Rican can learn
b) Spanish is an effective tool for learning; therefore the learning and use of Spanish should be encouraged in the Neo-Rican
c) Cultural heritage is part of the resources of the curriculum and the school experience, and should be included in the curriculum
d) Teacher training is necessary to cope with the new language and curriculum trends and to have success working with this unique population.

Puerto Rican teachers on the Island, and American teachers on the mainland must be trained to understand the attitudes and values of the Neo-Ricans.

Baltasar Corrada (1977) has stated it very clearly: "It is a bilingual education that--in the reverse--we need in Puerto Rico. We believe that Puerto Rico should be a bilingual community and of course, that we should have command of both Spanish and English, but always retaining Spanish as our vernacular language." Puerto Rico's bilingual programs utilize a two-track system that lets the students select their own language of instruction. The second language, usually Spanish, is taken as a regular course, while subjects such as science and mathematics are taught in English. Classes are mixed so that students who are dominant in Spanish can learn in English and Neo-Ricans can get more conversational Spanish.

3. Since the majority of Puerto Ricans are concentrated in New York City, the Migration Division of the Puerto Rican Department of Labor should create a clear and definitively active role in helping Neo-Ricans residing in the United States who have ideas of moving to Puerto Rico. The Migration Division was established by the Puerto Rican Legislature for the purposes of aiding Puerto Ricans who migrate from the Commonwealth to the States adjust to their Puerto Rican neighbors. Extensive programs in employment, social services, education and other fields are carried out by the Migration Division. The Division could also establish similar programs to help these youngsters to adapt to the new social, cultural, and linguistic conditions on the mainland. The Division will also help to develop awareness of similarities and differences between Puerto Rican mainlanders and Puerto Rican islanders.

The picture does not look bad for all the Puerto Ricans returning to the Island. Many have found jobs and have adjusted to the mainstream of Puerto Rican life. Those Puerto Ricans who have had success and have seen the failure of others, have tried to organize sociocultural organizations to help them in returning to the Island. One of these organizations is New Yoricans in Puerto Rico, Inc. The 1977 president, Antonio Torres, a Neo-Rican and a computer school executive, explains the organization's goal: "We are going to try to create a more positive image for New Yoricans here." (Daily News, October 16, 1977.) We need more organizations like this one, to bridge the gap between these two cultural groups, since in the end, there is only one group--Puerto Ricans.

Bibliography

Acosta Belén, Edna, "Spanglish: A Case of Languages in Contact." In Burt, Marina and Dulay, Heidi C. (eds.), New Directions in Second Language Learning, Teaching and Bilingual Education, Washington, D.C., TESOL, 1975.

Asociación Puertorriqueña Pro Bienestar de la Familia, Unidos Ante Nuestro Problema Poblacional, San Juan, Puerto Rico: Tipografía Aldus, 1970.

Cebollero, Pedro A. A School Language Policy for Puerto Rico. San Juan: Imprenta Baldrich, 1954.

Cordasco, Francesco, and Eugene Bucchioni, eds. Puerto Rican Children in Mainland Schools. Metuchen, N.J.: Scarecrow Press, 1968.

Corrada del Río Baltasar, "Statement of the Honorable Baltasar Corrada, Resident Commissioner from Puerto Rico, to the Congress Subcommittee on Elementary and Secondary Education," 1977, pp. 26-40.

Cruz, Juan and Ricks, George R., "Some Aspects of Puerto Rican Adaptation to Mainland U.S.A.," In Ogletree, Earl J. and Gar-

cía David, (eds.), Education of the Spanish-Speaking Child.
Springfield, Illinois: Charles C. Thomas, 1975.
Daily News, "New Ricans: Unwelcomed in Two Worlds," October 16,
1977.
Fitzpatrick, Joseph, "Transition to the Mainland," in Puerto Rican
Children in Mainland Schools. Metuchen, N.J.: Scarecrow
Press, 1968.
López, Adalberto and Petras, James, Puerto Rico and Puerto Ricans.
New York: John Wiley and Sons, 1974.
Milán, William G., "New York City Spanish: Myths, Structure, and
Status," Paper delivered in the Chicano-Riqueño Lecture Series,
Indiana University, Bloomington, Indiana, 1976.
New York Times "Returning Migrants Find Puerto Rico Inhospitable,"
October 3, 1975, and June 23, 1977.
Nieves-Colón, Myrna and Acosta-Belén, "The Puerto Rican Child:
His Culture and his Language." In Muriel Saville, Troike,
Bilingual Children: A Resource Document. Washington, D.C.:
Center for Applied Linguistics, 1973.
Sierra-Berdecía, Fernando, La Emigración Puertorriqueña, San Juan,
Puerto Rico Editorial del Departamento de Instrucción Pública,
1956.
Stern, Michael, "Puerto Rico Pays Heavily for Mainland's Recession."
New York Times, March 22, 1975.
United States Commission on Civil Rights, Puerto Ricans in the Con-
tinental United States: An Uncertain Future. Washington, D.C.:
U.S. Commission on Civil Rights, 1976.
Varisco de García, Norma, "Education and the Spanish Speaking Woman:
A Sad Reality," Journal of the National Association for Biling-
ual Education, May, 1976.

THE GREAT METROPOLIS

As a nation founded on what there is that is human on earth,
it seems so insecure, dazzling only to the nearsighted, where
after three centuries of democracy, with one tilt of the law,
it can happen that the government is asked now to take upon
its shoulders the life of the poor masses. Where the sum
total of selfishness, driven mad by the pleasure of triumph
or the fear of misery, creates, instead of a people of one
firm weave, a doughy mass of individuals without support,
who divide among themselves and flee as soon as they no
longer feel the pull of the community of mutual benefits.
Where all the problems of hate from the old human continent have been transferred here, without that intimate and
soothing communion with the soil.

JOSE MARTI

According to the census of the United States, in 1974 the Puerto Rican
population residing in the United States climbed to a total of 1.5 million people, at least one million of whom, it is conservatively estimated, lived in New York City. [1] However, this total has been disputed not only by a recent study of the Puerto Rican Socialist Party
(Partido Socialista Puertorriqueño, PSP)--which concludes that there
are two million Puerto Ricans living in the United States, of whom
1,250,000 reside in New York--but also by a study of the United
States Commission on Civil Rights. [2] It seems to us that the number of Puerto Ricans residing in the United States--especially in New
York City--is greater than the total indicated by the federal census.
In any case, it is necessary to take into full consideration the magnitude of the problem: more Puerto Ricans reside in New York City
alone than in San Juan, the capital of Puerto Rico.

Reprinted by permission from The Emigration Dialectic: Puerto Rico
and the USA (New York: International Publishers, 1980, p. 69-82).

To what do we attribute the controversy over the exact number of Puerto Ricans who reside in New York City or in the rest of the United States? The question revolves around the problem of who is or is not Puerto Rican. On the island of Puerto Rico, the question does not seem to constitute a very complex problem: Puerto Ricans are all those who have been born in Puerto Rico, or who, having been born outside of the Island, are children of Puerto Rican parents. It should be noted that here the Puerto Rican is defined by purely geographic (born on the Island) or genealogical (Puerto Rican parentage) criteria. According to this definition, it matters little whether or not the person identifies with the fundamental characteristics of Puerto Rican national culture. That is reason enough for it to be preferable, perhaps, to say that the person who meets the criteria mentioned above is potentially a Puerto Rican, leaving to be determined in the future whether or not this person is to be integrated into the cultural currents that define Puerto Rico as a society belonging to the Latin American cultural family. In fact, the geographic and genealogical criteria mentioned above, granting that they are important, are nevertheless less important than the cultural criteria with respect to the definition of a nationality. From this perspective, not all those born in Puerto Rico or of Puerto Rican parents are Puerto Ricans when seen in light of their integration into the Puerto Rican national culture. We maintain, therefore, that the determining factor of whether or not a person is Puerto Rican lies in the cultural question as the definitive central element of his or her Puerto Ricanness.

Puerto Rico is a society with a national culture and it has therefore its own profile and definition, even when it is found to be subjected to a systematic process of cultural penetration and dissolution, which in another context we have called "The Siege of Puerto Rican Culture." In spite of this fact, the vast majority of those who reside on the Island identify themselves as Puerto Ricans when asked about their nationality. We do not want to brush aside the serious problem of the Puerto Rican's identity. We have first-hand knowledge of the cultural schizophrenia from which we suffer as a result of the ambivalent and subordinating relationship to which colonialism condemns us. In spite of that fact, however, there exists a cultural sediment, a basic substratum of experiences, habits, customs, language, etc., that define us as a people.

Let us look at the Puerto Rican community in the United States. The first thing to note here is an undeniable social fact: the Puerto Ricans who live in the United States live outside of the Puerto Rican national territory. They find themselves transplanted from their native country to another territory whose land does not belong to them, and is foreign to them (legally and existentially speaking). This is only insofar as geography is concerned. But the question cannot be limited to this aspect. Let us take things from a generational perspective. We have seen how the heaviest emigration to the United States takes place in the period immediately following World War II. Before this exodus there were only some 60,000 Boricuas in New York. Those people had emigrated for the most part before World War II.

Today, we can distinguish between various generations of Puerto Ricans in the United States. First of all, there are those who emigrated before 1940. These are people who are now elderly and who, when they arrived in the United States, were already formed culturally. Then we have the emigrants of the postwar period who, generally speaking, are today middle-aged people whose children are born in the United States. And lastly, we have those Puerto Ricans born in the United States, beginning approximately in 1950, whose parents are Puerto Rican. These younger people are already the parents of a new generation of Puerto Rican children who not only were born outside of the Island but have in general a very limited knowledge of the Island.

Let us concentrate on the first Puerto Rican generation born in New York after the mass emigration of the 1950s. The United States census classifies them as "of Puerto Rican origin" when one of their parents is of Puerto Rican origin. These youths have been born in, and have become part of the social fabric of the United States. Their parents are from Puerto Rico, speak Spanish among themselves, and maintain cultural and personal ties with the Island. Nevertheless, an important difference exists between a youth of Puerto Rican origin born in New York and one born in Puerto Rico. The former is born in a country where Puerto Rican nationality is found to be a minority nationality, where the vernacular language is English, and where one's vital experiences take place within the framework of U.S. culture. The latter, on the other hand, is born in a society with definite geographical contours, where the vernacular is Spanish and where the cultural context remains defined within the framework of Puerto Rican society. We repeat: the United States census defines "Puerto Rican" in purely genealogical, and to a lesser degree, geographic terms, whereas in Puerto Rico, we define it in cultural and social terms. The cultural question does not interest the metropolis because it is a matter of one more ethnic minority within U.S. society. For the metropolis, it is simply a matter of "Americans of Puerto Rican origin," or "Puerto Rican Americans." For us, however, what defines the Puerto Rican is fundamentally the cultural question, a contention that we will discuss more extensively in another chapter of this book. More than twice the number of Puerto Ricans live in New York City than in San Juan, the capital of Puerto Rico. In one borough alone of New York City--the Bronx--there is a Puerto Rican population that numerically exceeds that of many of the principal cities of the Island. There are also small towns bordering New York City with Puerto Rican communities which have been practically transplanted from the rural regions of Puerto Rico. In this sense, Puerto Ricans are found dispersed among many of the principal cities of the Eastern United States, and also with considerable concentrations in some cities on the Pacific Coast. [3]

New York City, that "great urban center," is what serves as magnetic pole for most Puerto Ricans. Puerto Ricans constitute ten percent of the city's residents. They make up the lowest rung of the social ladder, the most alienated from the power structures of the metropolis, among those who suffer with greatest intensity the process of exploitation suffered also by Afro-Americans, Native Americans,

Chicanos, Asian-Americans, West Indians, Dominicans, etc. Crowded into the dilapidated tenements of the South Bronx or Spanish Harlem ("El Barrio"), forced to live under subhuman conditions in Manhattan's Lower East Side, our people are pushed with greater intensity every day toward pauperism, dependency, and collective impotence.[4] These are not mere rhetorical phrases, but rather the bare reality that confronts the vast majority of Boricuas in the "great urban center."

Some general statistics might contribute to clear up the question. The same source quoted above--the United States census for 1974--indicates that of all the Spanish-speaking residents in the United States, Puerto Ricans are those with the lowest incomes. The 1975 Current Population Survey confirms this once again.[5] The average Puerto Rican income, for example, is $7,629 per family, in comparison to that of Chicanos ($9,498) and other minority groups ($11,500). Compare this to the average income of U.S. families ($12,836) and we see that the income of Puerto Rican families is only slightly more than half of the income of U.S. families. From this point of view, the situation in 1974 is not very different from what it was in 1970, when a study carried out in New York City showed that 32.6 percent of Puerto Ricans were found to be living below the poverty level.[6] This study also documents the difficult access of Puerto Ricans to education. For example, the average education for Puerto Ricans was eight and one-half years in 1970. For that same year, one out of every five Puerto Ricans over twenty-five had a high school diploma, while only one out of every hundred Puerto Ricans over twenty-five had a college diploma. It goes without saying that the access of our people to graduate and post-graduate education is even more limited than what we have indicated here.

Given these circumstances, it should not surprise us if Boricuas confirm the infamous and racist "self-fulfilling prophecy," that they do not progress because they lack education and that they lack education because they do not progress.

Let us take an additional index. We saw earlier that one of the characteristics of capitalist development is the hurling of thousands and thousands of people into the orbit of pauperism. That tendency is manifested among Puerto Ricans residing in the metropolis, especially in New York City. In a study done by Nicholas Kinsburg, consultant to New York Councilman Andrew J. Stein, it was found that approximately half of the Puerto Ricans residing in New York City were on welfare.[7] This fact is often taken as an index of the indolence and idleness of our people, when the truth is that the exploitation they suffer at the hands of bosses, landlords, bureaucrats, etc. forces the immense majority of them to swell the state welfare lists. Here, also, racial prejudice against the Puerto Rican community is unleashed, while the media babbles nonsense about the "parasitism" of our compatriots.

As if all this were not enough, a study done by Drs. Joseph P. Fitzpatrick and Robert E. Gould showed that the percentage of mental illnesses among Puerto Rican residents in New York City was "abnormally high," tripling the incidence of common mental illnesses in the rest of the population. For example, it was found that 102.5 of every 100,000 Puerto Ricans suffered from mental illnesses in contrast to 34.5 per 100,000 for the entire state of New York. Among the causes of these illnesses, the researchers mention "stress from migration, including uprooting, adjustment to a new way of life...."[8] But it is clear that this high incidence of mental illnesses is the product of intolerable situations created by the clash and conflict with a society that disowns and scorns us. It is worth the effort to stress the poisonous effects of extreme poverty and pauperism on these mental syndromes. It is not, therefore, due to the "mercurial" nature of Boricuas, nor because we are "tropical" and other such nonsense that we suffer to a greater degree from mental illnesses, but rather because of the alienating and inhuman character of the society, in which the structures created by imperialism press us down.

A larger number of Puerto Ricans is concentrated in the "great urban center" of New York City than in the capital of Puerto Rico itself. But as we have already seen, under terrible conditions. Our objective is not to evoke a Dantesque hell, but rather to describe with utmost precision the condition of Puerto Ricans in New York City. We could expand our discussion by using statistics on drug addiction, crime and juvenile delinquency among our people in New York. We could also offer the reader the other side of the coin: the Puerto Ricans who have "progressed," those who live in the suburbs of New York City or who are included among those who boast of being millionaires. The former cannot be understood without the latter, which is why it is imperative that we enter into the following considerations.

One of the characteristics of the ethics of capitalism is its insistence that social mobility is an individual action, perfectly attainable for all those willing to work hard and be frugal. Upward social mobility is, therefore, "proof" that a person has been able to overcome his or her limitations produced by impoverished living conditions, and has joined the company of those who had previously looked down on him or her. This ethic of capitalism, described with singular brilliance by Marx and Weber, has always been the ideology, the convenient reinforcement for the ruling class in its effort to incorporate--and therefore neutralize--the most prominent among the exploited classes, managing in this way to revive and sustain the myth of "equal opportunity." Those who succeed in "arriving" at certain posts or positions are immediately celebrated by the mass media which is at the service of the system.

It was merely a question of time before assimilation of emigrants of European origin would take place through the process which Glazer and Moynihan call nearing "the Anglo-Saxon center."[9] But when it came to "incorporating" Afro-Americans, Chicanos, Asians and Puerto Ricans, the tune has been a different one. In a society which is racist to the marrow, the groups classified as non-whites have to pay a higher, more costly price than that which emigrants of European descent had to pay when they took up the road of assimilation into U.S. society.

The Civil Rights Movement of the 1960s used the now familiar term "tokenism" in order to describe the practice of incorporating a single Black into the United States Supreme Court, or into a school for whites in Alabama, or some office previously all white, etc. in Boston. But "tokenism" is a racist ideological weapon, presented to us as "proof" that the system is open to talent and ability, that any Black youth who makes the effort and studies eagerly can capture the peak scaled by, for example, Judge Thurgood Marshall.

We Puerto Ricans fall precisely within that classification of non-whites, an objective definition which the system itself has given us and which has nothing to do with the desires of some Puerto Ricans to have it changed. And this is so not only because our population is in fact racially mixed, but because according to U.S. criteria, anyone who lives south of the Rio Grande in one way or another belongs to an inferior race. We Puerto Ricans are far from constituting an exception to that rule.

The fundamental racist character of U.S. capitalist society cements and reinforces prejudice against our people. The educational level or the economic advancement of some Puerto Ricans "chosen" as models of triumph against adversity matters little. These "chosen few" note immediately that they cannot escape the stereotypes deeply rooted in the U.S. monopoly-dominated environment. For example, a so-called form of "praising" a Boricua in the "great urban center" is by means of the phrase, hurled like a dart: "You don't look Puerto Rican." Of course, the fact that you might not "look Puerto Rican" is also a reflection of the virtues of a civilization that rejects us. To not look Puerto Rican becomes a categorical imperative of the racist system which associates "inferior" races with the most servile tasks within the social register.

In order for the Puerto Rican to "not look Puerto Rican," he or she has to adopt the norms and values of the society that denies his or her identity. For example, we have Mr. Manuel Casiano, Junior (Manny), whose accomplishments in the banking field have led him to amass a huge fortune. This Boricuan version of Horatio Alger has become one of the most fervent advertisers of the "American Way of Life." The system is open to anyone who will work hard and learn the rules of the game: so "Manny" Casiano seems to say, from his luxurious ten-room apartment on Park Avenue.

Also present on the New York scene is ex-Congressman from the Bronx and former Deputy Mayor of New York City, Attorney Herman Badillo. Hailing from the city of Caguas, Puerto Rico, Mr. Badillo was admitted to the bar in New York, culminating his political career with his election to the United States Congress. Badillo is a skilled person in the political machinery of New York City, having managed to bring about, at least up until now, an alliance between impoverished Puerto Ricans and a Jewish middle class, who gave him their votes for a seat in Washington representing the South Bronx.

It is no accident that both Badillo and Casiano have been presented to us as archetypes of the Puerto Rican community by New York Magazine. The issue in question is extremely interesting, in that it shows how many North Americans--including in this case the liberals--perceive us. Here, for example, is an excerpt from this magazine which presents the ruling class view in clearly racist tones.

Let us listen:

> These people were "Spanish." They came in swarms like ants turning the sidewalks brown, and they settled in, multiplied, whole sections of the city fallen to their shiny black raincoats and chewing-gum speech. We called them "mee-dahs," because they were always shouting "mee-dah, mee-dah," ["Mira" ("Look") in Spanish] with a presumptuous sense of wonder. Look at what? The subway, the sky, the Long Island Sound turned the color of dark rum by the sheer congestion of their bodies?
> I did not hate them or fear them or even feel disgusted by them. I only knew they grew in numbers rather than stature, that they were neither white nor black but some indelicate tan, and that they were here, irrevocably; the best you could do to avoid contamination was to keep them out of mind. And if they got too close--well, the smell of beans and beer, whole families eating chicken, gnawing down to the bone, pink walls and cockamamie music, endless bongos in the night--well, there would be this greaser with hair like an oily palm tree, and he'd be sitting next to you in the subway in his Desi Arnaz shoes and his silver sharkskin pants and his jukebox-bolero-shirt, and you just knew he had a razor up his sleeve. And his old lady with the Bueno Bargains ballgown and the breasts that spread like Staten Island: where were they going anyway, the two of them, at a time when all the decent people were either working the night shift or sitting home watching Your Hit Parade? We lived in the Projects, where everyone aspired to be above himself. Our Spanish neighbors spoke English to us, and they weren't on welfare. Still, I found myself wondering:
>
> > Do they have a parrot?
> > How can they fry bananas?
> > What was life like in the jungle?
> > Where do they sharpen their shoes?
>
> I never ventured to inquire. It was enough to know I was above them; that gave me a sense of noblesse oblige, so that I was quite friendly, as most WASPS are to me: aliens are to be appreciated for their "ethnic diversity." Or put another way: the lower classes got nice asses. [10]

Of course, after the racist insults, they have to present the brighter side of the picture. And that is where "Manny" Casiano and Herman Badillo come in. Puerto Rican young people of "El Barrio" and the South Bronx should not be discouraged, because if they apply themselves and work hard they can become millionaires like Casiano or congressmen like Badillo.   The problem lies, nevertheless, in the fact that the living conditions for the vast majority of Puerto Ricans in New York are such that the chances of their even being able to get out of the ghetto are extremely remote.   There exists, admittedly, a sector of middle-class Puerto Ricans who have migrated to the suburbs of New York City.   But their numerical importance is clearly clouded over by a Puerto Rican population which is eminently proletarian.

This is even more true when we compare the economic-social condition of Puerto Ricans residing in New York during three different historic periods.   Let us take first the situation in the 1930s, when--according to the first important sociological study on emigration to New York, that of Professor Lawrence Chenault--we are offered the following picture of Boricuas in New York:

> The social adjustment necessitated by the migration results
> from the abrupt change of people but slightly removed from
> the peasant class from a simple rural environment to the
> slum section of an enormous city.   The migration causes
> disintegrating forces to affect the family.   In addition to
> this painful adjustment, the worker and his family are ex-
> posed to conditions which have long been recognized as
> harmful to the happiness and well-being of all people re-
> gardless of background.   Often mixed with other families
> under extremely crowded conditions, without funds or em-
> ployment, and in many cases suffering from malnutrition
> or some chronic disease, it is not strange that the worker
> and his family feel the influence of the antisocial behavior
> which is prevalent in these neighborhoods.   Having come
> from an island where he has already acquired a feeling
> of mistreatment at the hands of the American people and
> their government, he [the Puerto Rican worker] is often
> resentful as a result of the clash in culture, racial antag-
> onisms, and the failure to realize many expectations because
> of what he feels are discrimination and indifference.[11]

It is worth the effort to observe that the total Puerto Rican population at the historic moment did not exceed 50,000 people, and that Professor Chenault considers us a relatively small Hispanic contingent.   It is important to observe, moreover, that because that was the decade of the depression, the flow and ebb of emigration is considerable.   We observe in the 1930s a tendency of many Puerto Ricans to return to the Island as a result of the adverse economic conditions found in the metropolis.   In the book just cited, we also find documentation of the serious problems of cultural adjustment suffered by Puerto Ricans, the eminently proletarian character of the majority of the emigrants, the fact that the majority of these workers are unskilled, etc.   In summary, Puerto Rican emigrants residing in New York during the 1930s lived under conditions of extreme poverty and dehumanization.

A little more than ten years later, a group of social science researchers from Columbia University, led by the great sociologist C. Wright Mills, did a study on Puerto Rican emigrants in New York City. Note that we are now dealing with the postwar period and that the study is done precisely when the Law of Industrial Incentives (1947)--"Fomento" in Puerto Rico--is passed. Let us listen to the descriptions by Mills and his colleagues of the Puerto Rican migrant:

> Occupational mobility of the Puerto Ricans in New York is quite restricted: they are concentrated in lower skilled jobs, and their chances to rise above them seem rather slim. In the journey to New York, most of the migrants do not experience a rise in the level of their job, many in fact are now at lower levels than they held in Puerto Rico. For some, this downward mobility is a new experience, for others it is a continuation of a downward mobility already experienced on the island from the occupational position of their fathers. Still others, who have risen in jobs in coming to New York, have only regained the job status once held by their fathers....
> As successive waves of immigrants have swept into Manhattan and elsewhere in America, a rather clear-cut pattern of their experience and of the reactions of native Americans has been established. Most of the newcomers are poor, and hence forced into the least desirable sections of the city, from two to ten families often living in accommodations built for one. They are uneducated; the ways of the new city are strange and complex; the ways of yet another culture add to their strangeness and complexity; they are exploited by native landlords and sharks, and by some of their own countrymen who already "know the ropes." Entering the labor market, unlearned, unskilled, they seem at the mercy of economic forces. If the business cycle is on the upturn, they are welcome; if it is on the way down, or in the middle of one of its periodic breakdowns, there is a savage struggle for even the low wage jobs between the new immigrants and the earlier ones who feel they have a prior claim. [12]

It is worthwhile to emphasize the phenomenon of "downward mobility" or descending mobility. The mythology of capitalism looks --in accordance with what we have already observed--to create in the exploited classes the feeling that social ascension is not really denied them. Nevertheless, the hard facts impose themselves over these pious myths.

Let us come closer to our present time. In 1970, a study done with all the methodology and categories of the positivist focus, was to inform us of the following: "Only 16.7 percent of the migrants are in white collar occupations, as compared with 32.9 percent of the Island inhabitants and 44.0 percent of the return migrants."[13] Another even more recent study, that of Kal Wagenheim, reinforces this thesis. The conclusions of this study--based on figures from the United States census--with respect to the level of incomes, education and unemployment, are the following:

    a. income level. In 1970, the federal government defined poverty as an income of $3,740 or less for a family of four, or $4,415 for a family of five. That year, 283,000 Puerto Rican New Yorkers were in poverty, and an additional ... 30,000 Puerto Ricans were in the near-poor category, with incomes only 25 percent above the poverty definition. This means that ... 45 percent of the Puerto Ricans in the city were either poor or near-poor. [14]
    b. education ... Puerto Ricans ... constitute 22.8 percent of the city's classroom enrollment. The city had only 978 Puerto Rican teachers--only 1.1 percent of the teaching staff. [15]
    c. unemployment. According to March, 1972 figures, Puerto Ricans have the highest unemployment rate of virtually all ethnic or racial groups in the United States. While 6 percent of all U.S. men were jobless, the figure was 7.4 percent for men of Spanish origin, and 8.8 percent for Puerto Rican men. Among women, unemployment was 6.6 percent nationwide, 10 percent for women of Spanish origin, and 17.6 percent for Puerto Rican women.
    These figures do not describe the true picture. It is worse. The rate of unemployment refers to that portion of the civilian labor force that is jobless. However, the "civilian labor force" is not synonymous with the entire working-age population. It includes only those persons who are working or actively seeking work. It does not include disabled persons. It does not include persons who, for various reasons (lack of skills, lack of opportunity in geographic area, and so forth) are not actively seeking work. In other words, the chronically unemployed, those who have lost hope, are not included in official unemployment statistics.
    For example, 86 percent of all Americans, ages 16 to 64, are in the labor force. Among Puerto Ricans, the figure drops to 76.6 percent. If Puerto Ricans participated in the labor force at the same level as the total population and the number of persons with jobs remained constant, unemployment among Puerto Rican men would be more accurately depicted--not at the "official" rate of 8.8 percent--but at the "adjusted" (and more realistic) level of 18.7 percent. Among Puerto Rican women, the "official" rate of 17.6 percent "adjusts" upward to 56.4 percent. For both men and women, the "official" rate of 12.6 percent soars to 33.0 percent. [16]

We are quoting from these studies somewhat extensively because we consider it essential that these incontestable statistics be known. Moreover, we want to establish that this happens within the city whose standard of living is higher than that of most of the cities of the world. The social inequality as it related to Puerto Ricans has not changed during the last thirty or forty years, in fact, it has been intensified. Reformist panaceas have simply intensified pauperism with all its resulting evils.

According to the U. S. census projections, the Puerto Rican population in the United States and on the Island will eventually match up. Within this context, the mammoth Puerto Rican population in New York City takes on a singular importance, since New York is a kind of giant mirror where all Puerto Ricans can look at ourselves. In that "great urban center," the problems of the Puerto Rican community stand out because of their very magnitude and profundity. We could say that New York City is a kind of giant mural where all the vicissitudes of our people are represented within an urban and highly industrialized setting.

Moreover, New York City itself is changing its face very rapidly. Besides the serious economic crisis that the city is facing at the present moment, we are observing--again as cause and effect of the same reality--an exodus of the most important manufacturing companies to the outskirts of the city, and a great population exodus of whites to the suburban areas of the city.

With respect to this exodus of businesses, Fortune magazine reported that 25 percent of the largest companies established in New York City had decided to move. A report on this very point indicates:

> A number of companies had moved to the area where many key employees--particularly the chief executives--live. Other considerations that are rarely mentioned, but sometimes considered when a movie is made ... are the number of blacks and Puerto Ricans in the city, crime against persons and property and a dislike of the physical environments. [17]

Still more, there exists such a pronounced tendency to abandon the main area of New York City, that according to a private organization studying this problem, it is conjectured that the city will be left "primarily with unemployed and the retired poor."[18] This would undoubtedly lead to the even greater displacement of the Puerto Rican work force in the city. New York is rapidly turning into a city which provides services. This tendency can only intensify the severity of the problem of Puerto Rican unemployment, especially if we keep in mind that our work force is principally unskilled or semi-skilled.

The enormous concentration of Puerto Ricans in New York City allows us to know firsthand the disastrous effects of a mass exodus which has placed them right in the neurological center of the great capitalist metropolis. In the "great urban center," all the sores of capitalism become more visible and throbbing. For the Puerto Ricans who live under subhuman conditions in the South Bronx, or on the Lower East Side, the "American Way of Life," more than being a propagandist slogan, constitutes a grotesque mockery in the face of their condition of pauperism. Prisoners of the ghetto, victims of harassment and racial prejudice, deprived of the most basic tools for their struggle for human dignity, the Puerto Ricans who live in New York daily resist the designs of the system to dehumanize them. But even more important is the fact that, unlike their compatriots on the Island, Puerto Ricans in "New York exile" come to know first-hand and directly what U. S. capitalist society really is. This knowledge gives them extraordinary revolutionary potential for the struggle for Puerto Rican liberation. The Puerto Ricans residing in New York have the potential and capacity to carry the revolutionary struggle to the very heart of the oppressor society. Just as the Algerians did in their day, or as the Irish have been doing for years, the Boricuas can be a battering ram capable of pounding away at the empire in its most vulnerable points.

In addition to this, the Puerto Rican proletariat of New York City can and should participate together with other ethnic groups who suffer exploitation (Blacks, Chicanos, Asian Americans, etc.) as well as with the most progressive sectors within the U. S. working class in a frontal attack on capitalism and on behalf of socialism. The one is not incompatible with the other. On the contrary, these are complementary actions.

Up until today, Puerto Rican emigrants in New York have successfully resisted all attempts directed toward the destruction of their national profiles. Just as on the Island, the Puerto Rican working class in the metropolis ought to play a dominant role in the struggle for national liberation and socialism. It is an internationalist struggle, but it should not, however, lose sight--as Lenin constantly warned us --of the fact that the weakening of imperialism through the successful struggle of national liberation movements is a categorical imperative for all revolutionaries. The support and solidarity for the national liberation struggle and the struggle for socialism in the metropolis are complementary, not conflicting strategies. To say that they are in conflict would be to deny the essential significance of the struggle for the liberation of our people.

References

1. The San Juan Star, August 7, 1974. According to the most recent computation, the total Puerto Rican population residing in New York City is 811,143, a figure strongly disputed by Puerto Rican leaders in New York. New York Times, October 2, 1972.
2. See the "Declaración de la seccional de Estados Unidos del Partido Socialista Puertorriqueño," which appeared in a special issue of the journal Nueva Lucha; also see the Report of the United States Commission on Civil Rights, Counting the Forgotten: The 1970 Census Count of Persons of Spanish Speaking Background in the United States, April 1974. A recent study of the Bureau of Applied Research of Columbia University contributes some interesting statistics on this subject. See A. J. Jaffe and Zaida Carreras Carleton, Some Demographic and Economic Characteristics of the Puerto Rican Population Living

on the Mainland U. S. A. (Columbia University: Bureau of Applied Research, November, 1974).

3. See the interesting article by Professor Raymond M. Otero Aurinaga, where he estimates that there are some 100,000 Puerto Ricans living in the state of California. "The Califorricans," The San Juan Star Magazine, April, 1974.

4. According to the latest census, the distribution of the Puerto Rican population by boroughs in New York City in 1970 was the following: Bronx (316,772 or 21.5% of the total); Brooklyn (271,769 or 10.4%); Manhattan (185,323 or 12%); Queens(33,141 or 1.7%) and Staten Island (4,838 or 1.6%). The figures are from the 1972 census and they indicate a total Puerto Rican population of 811,843 (10% of the city's population). (The New York Times, October 2, 1972). The figure, as we have said, is considerably greater, but the proportionate distribution by borough is accurate.

5. El Mundo, September 8, 1975.

6. Edward C. Burks, "Affluence Eludes Blacks, Puerto Ricans," The New York Times, August 18, 1972. An even more recent report by Kal Wagenheim confirms this tendency. See The New York Times, June 10, 1975.

7. The New York Times, October 25, 1971.

8. The New York Times, March 26, 1970.

9. Nathan Glazer and Daniel Patrick Moynihan, Beyond the Melting Pot, second edition (Cambridge: MIT Press, 1970), p. 20.

10. Richard Goldstein, "The Big Mango," New York Magazine, August 7, 1972, p. 24.

11. Lawrence R. Chenault, The Puerto Rican Migrant in New York City (New York: Russell and Russell, 1970), pp. 157-158. This book was published for the first time in 1938.

12. C. Wright Mills, et al., The Puerto Rican Journey (New York: Russell and Russell, 1967), pp. 73, 82. This book was originally published by Harper and Row in 1950. Its findings, however, cover essentially the period up to 1948.

13. Eva E. Sandis, "Characteristics of Puerto Rican Migrants to and from the United States," in Francesco Cordasco and Eugene Bucchioni (editors), The Puerto Rican Experience (New Jersey: Littlefield Adams, 1975), p. 138.

14. Kal Wagenheim, A Survey of Puerto Ricans in the U.S. Mainland in the 1970's (New York: Praeger, 1975), p. 41.

15. Ibid., p. 22. Actually, the so-called poverty line overlooks things that refer to the maldistribution of self-respect, educational opportunities, social mobility and participation in various forms of decision-making. See Bertram Gross in his review of Fox and Piven, Regulating the Poor, cited before, in Social Policy (New York), May-June, 1972, p. 58.

16. Ibid., pp. 27-28. Professor Bertram Gross has arrived at the conclusion that there are 25.6 million people unemployed in the United States, that is to say, 24.6% of the work force, if we truly take into consideration underemployment, non-apparent unemployment, the number of people who are no longer in the work force because they have tired from looking for work and not finding any. See Bertram Gross and Stanley Moses, "Meas-

uring the Real Work Force: 25 million unemployed," in <u>Social Policy</u>, September-October, 1972.

17. <u>New York Times</u>, September 21, 1972. Quoted in Wagenheim, <u>op. cit.</u>, p. 68.

18. <u>New York Times</u>, January 30, 1975.

Renato Poblete

ANOMIE AND THE "QUEST FOR COMMUNITY":
THE FORMATION OF SECTS AMONG
THE PUERTO RICANS OF NEW YORK

Immigration and assimilation of immigrants are sociological processes that have long been part of the American scene and have received their share of attention from sociologists. For some years after 1924, legislation restricting entrance to this country resulted in substantially lessening the importance of these phenomena in our midst. However, in recent years such problems have again come to the fore as a result of political conditions in Europe and the attraction of large numbers of migrants from the Commonwealth of Puerto Rico in the continental United States.

The migration of the Puerto Ricans introduces important new elements into the picture of cultural assimilation. First of all, these arrivals are citizens of the United States. Secondly, they arrive at a time when most other groups whose American origin goes back to a similar immigration experience have advanced far along the path of assimilation to general American culture patterns. Thirdly, despite their American citizenship, the Puerto Rican migrants come from a culture that is quite different from that of the people of the mainland. Thus to the discrimination that such arrivals usually meet is added the note of irony that they are in fact legally citizens of the Republic.

A fourth point is of considerable importance. Earlier immigrants clustered together in communities where adaptation to the new situation was eased by the preservation of important elements of the older culture. As time went on, more extreme ideas of rapid acculturation were replaced by the recognition of the vital role of the immigrant community in avoiding the worst effects of social and personal disorganization in the acculturation process.

Reprinted by permission from American Catholic Sociological Review, 21:18-36, Spring 1960.

"In view of this the concept of cultural pluralism became widely accepted. This helped scholars to recognize the importance of the culture of the immigrant, and to recognize that his loyalties and values and customs should be able to exist in America together with the other culture that we have come to call American."[1]

The Puerto Ricans, however, have been attracted chiefly to the eastern part of the country and in large numbers to New York. In New York City, which is our concern here, the Puerto Ricans have found themselves dispersed into almost every section of the city.

"There are noticeably large concentrations of them in East Harlem, in the South Bronx, on the Lower East Side and in downtown Brooklyn. But in considerable numbers they are scattering into almost every section of the city. This is reflected in the large number of public schools that have Puerto Ricans in attendance in large numbers, and in the parishes, so many of which require the assistance of a Spanish-speaking priest."[2]

There are many factors which are responsible for this dispersal. The city is built up and crowded. Public housing projects often replace older decaying tenements and disperse forming immigrant communities, and the criteria of admission to such projects when completed make impossible the development of a Puerto Rican immigrant community in them.

"In this situation, it is doubtful whether the Puerto Ricans will be able to form the type of community which earlier immigrants formed. If they do, they will have done it in circumstances much more difficult than those faced by earlier immigrant groups."[3]

The new arrivals come from a culture that may in certain respects be called "Catholic" and their reception by co-religionists here on the mainland is therefore of great significance. The official policy of the Archdiocese of New York has paralleled the conditions we have described. There has been no attempt to set up national parishes but rather to integrate the Puerto Ricans into the already existing parish structure. Yet in these circumstances "it is clearly acknowledged that an intermediate process must take place, that special services must be provided in Spanish, and opportunity given for the practice of traditional customs and devotions by the new parishioners."[4]

In this situation, then, the new arrivals experience cultural assimilation, a process that is already begun at home in the Commonwealth, for the island has been a United States possession for over half a century and the people have enjoyed citizenship for four decades. English was for a time the standard language of instruction and although that is no longer the case it is a compulsory subject at all levels of the educational system. Moreover, the political and also the business integration of the Commonwealth into the American community have opened other avenues of acculturation.

This paper is concerned with one element in that acculturation process, a response to conditions of social and cultural uncertainty in terms of religion. Any visitor to a densely populated Puerto Rican section of New York City will see a large number of what are often referred to as "store-front churches." These are religious groups that use as a place of meeting or worship stores formerly occupied by retail merchants. In one section in East Harlem, in 24 blocks (between First and Third Avenues, and between 100th and 105th Streets) there are 30 of these store-front churches. These sects will be our concern here, more specifically, the Pentecostal Sects or the "Asambleas de Dios."

Protestantism in Puerto Rico

First of all, however, let us look for a moment at the situation of Protestantism in Puerto Rico. Protestantism began its activities in that island about fifty years ago. The World Christian Handbook for 1952 mentioned 522 areas where Protestant activity was being carried on. Another publication, Midcentury Pioneers and Protestants, gives the number of Protestant church members who are actively communicants as 46,433 and the total size of the Protestant group seems to be about 160,000. The study states that at least ten per cent of the population could be characterized as Protestant and "probably eighty per cent of the island population would say they were Catholics if pressed with the question of religious orientation."[5] According to a study done at Columbia University in 1948, fifty-three per cent of the 5,000 persons who answered the question claimed that they were "religious in my own fashion."

Such, then, insofar as we know it, is the religious complexion of the Puerto Rican people before migration. Largely nominally Catholic, with a strong Catholic group and a minority of Protestants.

Protestantism Among Puerto Ricans in New York

The only information we have of a detailed kind on Protestantism among Puerto Ricans in New York City is found in a report made by the Church Planning and Research group of the Protestant Council of Churches of New York City in November, 1953. The survey covered 146 non-Roman Catholic churches in the seven areas of heavy Puerto Rican concentration. Fifty-four Negro churches responded saying that they had almost complete lack of contact with the Puerto Ricans. Fifteen other non-denominational churches said that Puerto Ricans were attending their groups and listed a total of 134 active members and 217 who only attend services. Fifteen of the 43 denominational churches had no contact at all with the Puerto Ricans in their neighborhoods. The survey revealed that the Protestant churches in the communities where Puerto Ricans reside were doing little to welcome them or to evangelize the "unchurched." The director of the survey has stated that the non-Spanish-speaking Protestant churches had only an infinitesimal contact with the Puerto Ricans.[6] This study is now six years old and the situation in these respects has changed because of the efforts made in an intense campaign to contact and attract Puerto Ricans, but no statistics are available. In a study of three Bronx communities [7] completed in November, 1956, we find fifteen per cent of the Puerto Rican population attending Protestant churches. The figure underestimates the actual state of affairs, since many of the small storefront churches do not turn in any reports of this kind.

What is the situation of the Spanish-speaking Protestant churches? It is in fact quite different.

The 1953 survey quoted above admits that it is almost impossible to arrive at an exact figure of the number of such churches and of their membership. It has been possible, the survey states, to draw up a list containing the names of 204 non-Catholic Spanish-speaking churches in New York City. Of these, however, only 169 provided sufficient data to permit meaningful study. Yet this figure was three times as large as the number located in 1947 by the Pathfinder Service. Despite the inadequacy of statistics, the fact of growth seems indisputable.

Of these churches reported by the Protestant Council, fifty-five per cent are classified as Pentecostal, but those listed under the category of "Independent" appear to be very similar and could without serious distortion of the situation be added to the total of the Pentecostal Movement. That would mean that probably seventy per cent of the Spanish-speaking churches can be classified in the Pentecostal category. This figure is impressive at first sight and a closer examination of what it involves reveals it to be particularly significant. For it is readily seen that "these two groups--Pentecostals and Independents--are largely a real indigenous expression of Protestant convictions. They receive no aid from denominational agencies ... they have a strong evangelical spirit and are willing to work with other Protestant Churches towards a limited number of specific short term goals. Generally they are reluctant to identify themselves with institutionalized efforts for Protestant cooperation. [8]

This striking phenomenon of vitality of the Pentecostal groups among people of a Latin culture is not something confined to New York Puerto Ricans. In Italy such groups had 120 places of worship in 1944. Ten years later they had 380 places of worship and comprised sixty per cent of all Protestant churches in the country. [9] In Chile the Pentecostals had around 182,000 adherents in 1955. [10] In fact the Pentecostals are the most numerous and active of all Protestant groups throughout Latin America.

In New York the Pentecostal churches have an average membership of 85 persons while the Independents have an average membership of 67 in each church group. The store-front churches have very little resemblance to the typical denominational church. The physical layout consists of a small store which is rented and transformed into a single large room with seats similar to those in a theatre. These seats face what had originally been the rear of the store but is now the front of the church. Here facing the congregation is a pulpit from which the Bible is read. Behind this, separated from the church by a curtain, is a small room in which members can go and pray in solitude and in silence. This is called the "cuarto alto," the upper room.

The Pentecostal groups are self-starting and self-sustaining. They are evangelical and missionary-minded. They stress a way of life rather than a creed: the emphasis is on intensity rather than universality and they tend to maintain uncompromisingly radical religious attitudes, demanding from their members the maximum in their relationships to God, to the world and to men. The moral standards are very high and there is a genuine austerity about their attitudes and patterns of living. This rigorism often expresses itself in external details: no smoking, no consumption of alcohol drink, no use of cosmetics for women. Membership is available only after a probationary period of from six months to one year and upon public confession of a personal religious experience. There is a high ratio of lay leadership and responsibility. Tithing is a common practice. One or two collections at one service are common. A community with 80 to 100 members supports a full-time minister. One survey found that of 96 churches reporting, forty-five have full-time pastors, that is to say, serving only one church and having no other employment. Thirty-six have pastors who work at other jobs during the week and fifteen share a pastor with another church. [11]

Theory on Sect and Church

It is interesting to recall here the classic definitions of sect and church deriving from the work of Ernst Troeltsch and Max Weber. Troeltsch declares, in his conclusion to his monumental study of church and sect in Christian history, that "the history of the Christian Ethos becomes the story of a constantly renewed search for ... compromise, and of fresh opposition to this spirit of compromise."[12] Park and Burgess, Simmel, Von Wiese, Becker, H. Richard Niebuhr and Liston Pope [13] have elaborated this basic idea. For these writers a "church or ecclesia is characterized by the following: (1) membership on the basis of birth; (2) administration of the means of grace and its sociological and theological concomitants--hierarchy and dogma; (3) inclusiveness of social structure, often coinciding with ethnic or geographical boundaries; (4) orientation to conversion of all; and (5) a tendency to compromise with the world. The sect, on the contrary, is characterized by (1) separatism and defiance of or withdrawal from the demands of the secular sphere, preferring isolation to compromise; (2) exclusiveness, expressed in attitude and social structure; (3) emphasis upon conversion prior to membership; and (4) voluntary election or joining."[14]

Moreover, the sect is always ascetic and usually attempts to implement the "priesthood of believers" in an egalitarian social structure. From these definitions it is quite clear that the church is usually associated with settled cultural and social conditions while the sect is a response of groups that do not for one reason or another fit into the going institutionalized religious bodies of the larger society. H. Richard Niebuhr has shown the social sources of denominationalism to be related to the position of deprived social classes in the total society and Liston Pope has studied the role of the sect in the adaptation of rural workers to industrial conditions.

In short, it may be said that the sect represents a response of the restructuralization of religious attitudes and orientations in a condition of what Durkheim has called anomie. For Durkheim anomie was characterized by two interrelated elements. First of all there is a breakdown of those social structures in which the individual found the psychological support and nurture requisite to personal and psychological security. Secondly, there is a loss of consensus or general agreement upon the standards and norms that previously provided the normative orientations and existential definitions in terms of which individual and group life were meaningful. Talcott Parsons has shown that the prevalence of anomie was positively related to rapid social change which brought about social differentiation and the upsetting of old standards and relationships in a changing situation, which prevents the crystallization of new attitudinal and social structures.

It is quite clear that the Pentecostal groups we have described meet most of the criteria of a sect put forward by the classical definitions. While the theological aspects of sectarianism are interesting and important, the sociological level of analysis seems to offer a more fruitful area of research for a fuller understanding of what these developments really signify. Over two decades ago Christopher Dawson suggested something similar with respect to the history of the Church. Said Dawson, "Most of the great schisms and heresies in the history of the Christian church have their roots in social and national antipathies, and if this had been clearly recognized by the theologians, the history of Christianity would have been a very different one."[15]

The Anomie Hypothesis

On the basis of the information which this preliminary and exploratory study has provided us so far we can safely conclude that the rise and development of the Pentecostal movement among the Puerto Rican migrants in New York represents a typical example of sectarian formation and development. That it is a serious religious phenomenon is clear to any informed observer. Moreover, historically such a development has been found to be associated with anomie and to be a form of the recrystallization of attitudes and the re-formation of solidarity in the face of such anomie. Since we are dealing here with people who all the available objective evidence would suggest are suffering the concomitant anxieties of social and cultural change encumbent upon migration and assimilation to a new culture, it seems a fruitful hypothesis to suggest that such movements represent precisely such a reaction to the anomie involved in migration.

It is necessary to recall that one important aspect of anomie for Durkheim was the disruption of existing social structures. Certainly removal to a new city under the conditions of dispersal would suggest that element in the present case. Moreover, Parsons, following Max Weber, has suggested that the "process of rationalization" by introducing impersonal relationships in the place of the more personal relationships of the older cultures played an important part in undermining personal securities and contributing to the anomique condition of the people involved. [16]

Sectarianism: A Response to Anomie

The hypothesis to be explored in the remainder of this paper may be stated as follows. The development of sectarianism among New York Puerto Ricans is a response to anomie. It is furthermore a response that represents a positive quest for community in the face of the loss of more traditional social structures and the impersonalization (universalism and functional specificity, in Parsons' terms) of modern American urban society.

The larger frame of reference in which this problem must be considered is one that includes western civilization as a whole. Modern man is haunted by the specter of insecurity in consequence of the many reasons which we have indicated above. "There is a decided weakening of faith in the inherent stability of the individual and in psychological and moral neutrality; individualism has become in recent decades a term to describe pathological conditions of society."[17] The release of the individual from the traditional ties of class, religion and kinship has made him free, but on the testimony of innumerable works of our age, this freedom is accompanied not by the sense of creative release, but by the experience of disenchantment and alienation. Erich Fromm has shown that it may be accompanied by intense psychological anxiety. [18] In fact the theme of uprooted man seeking fellowship is as frequent in our time as was the theme of the individual's emancipation from tribal or communal conformity in the past. Riesman speaks of a new need for "other directedness" among Americans, and popular magazines exploit the theme of "togetherness."[19] The loss of what Durkheim called consensus is what Nesbit has called a loss of moral certitudes and is followed by a sense of alienation from one's fellowman. [20] Industrial sociology has shown the importance of the work community for the morale of the individual workman. Drucker has commented upon the "end of the economic man." Since the larger framework of human orientation includes what Paul Tillich has called "the ultimate," that such a loss of solidarity and consensus has religious significance and that the response to it may take the form of a religious quest is not difficult to see.

Today there is visible a reaction against the heritage of the immediate past. Men seem to be seeking integration, status, membership; there is a desire for recognition, for the formation of small groups, for personal relationships. This is a reaction against the impersonalization of a technological society characterized by urbanism. Toennies saw the history of the West as the transformation of Gemeinschaft into Gesellschaft, what in Redfield's terms may be called the transition from a folk to an urban society. Today, American society seems to be reacting in an opposite direction. The much heralded and quite ambiguous revival of religion seems to be an associated phenomenon. [21]

If religion appears to offer a way out of this situation--especially to a people whose cultural background is characterized by important religious elements--the reverse is also true. Religious life requires the support and underpinning of social solidarity. André Brien emphasizes the need of small communities in order that Catholic people may be able to live the faith. [22] He refers to the proliferation of sects in the popular milieu as a sign of the importance of the formation of small communities in the urban world of today. These groups, characterized by enthusiasm in the 18th century meaning of that term, and sometimes to the point of fanaticism, are capable of evoking from the impersonalized man of our age a spirit of unity and sacrifice. The intense life of the group exalts the personality; the person caught up in the current of irresistible enthusiasm discovers in himself a force of life which previously had lain dormant. This gives the individual a feeling of participation and consequently of strength and worth.

The Quest For Community

What we have reviewed so far would suggest that anomie is a fairly general problem in modern urban society and that reactions against it--attempts to escape it--are far from uncommon. We are suggesting that a similar condition is characteristic of the Puerto Rican migrants in response to the concrete conditions of their migration. At this point, in view of our general characterization of this phenomenon as a quest for community, it will be helpful to consider recent theoretical discussions of the meaning of that term among sociologists.

George A. Hillery in his study of areas of agreement in the definitions of community used in sociological literature states that "a majority of the definitions include as important elements ...: an area, common ties and social interaction."[23] For MacIver a community is a social unity whose members recognize as common sufficient interest to permit the common activities and interactions of common life. [24] In his book Society, the same author states that we have community when the members live their lives wholly within the general group. He stresses community sentiment as the most important ingredient of community, since modern transport has made a territorial base relatively unimportant. For MacIver this community sentiment has three elements: "we-feeling," that is, a sense of collective participation in an indivisible unity, a sense of belonging to the group which can use the term "we" with the same referent; role feeling, a sense of status which consists in the fact that each person feels he has a part to perform, a function to fulfill in the reciprocal exchange, involving a subordination of the individual to the whole; and dependency feeling, closely associated with role-feeling involving the individual's

feeling of dependency upon the community as a necessary condition
for his own life. It involves either physical or psychological dependency since the community is the greater home which sustains him.
It is the refuge from solitude and the fears that accompany the individual isolation so characteristic of modern life. [25]

Toennies found the supreme form of community in what he
called the "Gemeinschaft of mind" implying "cooperation and coordinated action for a common goal."[26] August R. Hollingshead concluded that the term community was defined in at least three different
ways in current literature: (a) as a form of group solidarity, cohe-
sion and action around common and diverse interests; (b) as a geographic area with spatial limits; or (c) as a socio-geographical structure which combines the first two definitions. [27]

The elements of these classical and contemporary definitions
of most concern to us would appear to be those stressed in Toennies'
Gemeinschaft of mind and MacIver's community sentiment and represented in other terms in the other definitions.

A Test of the Anomie Hypothesis

Let us restate our hypothesis more fully at this point: The formation
of sects is one of the known ways out of anomie, and the facts of
Puerto Rican life in New York suggest the presence of such a condition among these new arrivals. The sect represents a search for a
way out of that condition and is therefore an attempt to redevelop the
community in the new urban situation.

In attempting to explore this hypothesis and to prepare for
some kind of observational testing of it, a small area in the Southern
Bronx was studied. This area coincides with St. Athanasius Roman
Catholic Parish. In this area we were able to locate ten store-front
churches and two larger churches of the same type, the Christian
Church of Juan 3:16, at Westchester Avenue, and the Independent
Church, Iglesia del Señor, with characteristics quite like those of the
Pentecostals.

These store-front churches did not have more than 60 members
each. They have almost daily meetings with an attendance of half to
two-thirds of the membership present. It is quite difficult to get reliable figures on the exact membership since there are always some
visitors at the services who either come from other store-front
churches or who may be just curious outsiders. Each evening's services are organized by a different sub-group, the men's group, the
women's group, or the youth group. The service begins around eight
o'clock in the evening and lasts until around ten. When a stranger
attends he is greeted immediately, given a song-book and offered a
seat. The amount of cordiality shown to the visitor is remarkable
to the field worker. The minister or some person from the congregation reads the Bible and explains what has been read. Accompany-
ing the words of the speaker there gradually develops a kind of spon-

taneous participation by the congregation. This takes the form of spontaneous ejaculations such as <u>Amen</u>, <u>Alleluia</u>, <u>Gloria a Dios</u>, <u>Gloria à Jesus</u>, <u>Dios todopoderoso</u>, and <u>Alabado Dios</u>. In this way the group actively participates even in that part of the service in which a leader has the structured ascendancy and initiative.

After the sermon, which is punctuated by such exclamations from the congregation, the whole community sings. Some of the melodies are old American folk songs with special religious Spanish text or are translated Protestant hymns. Frequently somebody volunteers to sing a solo or to play an instrument. The minister during this period invites people to speak a few words or relate their own religious experience or the history of their conversion. Some members of the congregation express gratitude for some favors received, or ask for prayers for some need. This is followed by more singing.

Then plans for evangelical work are proposed or reports of current activities are heard. At the end everybody prays in a loud voice and spontaneously. One can feel the enthusiasm and desire for the Spirit in the group. At times an individual manifests the reception of the Holy Spirit by "speaking with tongues." When that happens the members begin to shout incoherently or just to utter words. The speech of the person who has the gift of tongues may be "interpreted" by another member. Then the members of the community thank God and pray that all may receive these gifts.

On Sunday, service lasts for two hours. Here the minister, either the regular minister or a guest, will have a more important role. He will give instruction to the people on the Bible or upon moral precepts.

In addition to using what sociologists call "participant observation" of these groups, ministers and members were interviewed. We were able to interview 28 persons. The interviews were conducted in Spanish by the field worker, for whom Spanish is his native language. All but three of the twenty-eight were baptized Catholics. Yet these 25 did not have any real knowledge of the Catholic Church. There appeared to be no ground to assume that their conversion was in any intellectual sense a protest against the Catholic Church. The element of protest was not important in what they reported about themselves. Moreover, the interviews revealed that their knowledge of the ideology of the sect was rudimentary. The Bible is held to be the only norm of life, a point of view that involves a very fundamentalistic interpretation of the "Word." They all hold that we have been redeemed by Christ's death. They hold the importance of two baptisms, one of water and one of the spirit. There is much emphasis upon a total way of life involving brotherly love and the rejection of sin. There is no systematic doctrinal body of beliefs.

The people interviewed talked very frankly about their conversion. They consider the frank revelation of the history of their conversion as a "testimony": bearing of witness to the Holy Spirit. The form of such testimonies shows that despite the spontaneity of communal religiosity there is a degree of stereotyping. It would appear that each convert has heard many testimonies and makes the attempt to interpret and fit in his own experience into a normatively desired pattern. They usually go in this way. "I used to drink ... I was a drug addict ... I used to run around with women ... I was on the wrong path ... but one day I received the Spirit, I got to know the 'Word.'" They always attribute a great sinfulness to their previous life. The form of the testimony emphasizes a great experience of sinfulness and the religious experience of being possessed by the Spirit. And the latter appears to give them a certitude of regeneration.

The formal "design" of the testimony reveals consciousness of sinfulness--conversion--regeneration. While this is not a spontaneous product of subjective personal disposition unaffected by social confor-mation to an expected pattern, there is reason to suspect that subjec-tive experience lent itself readily to such conformation. That is to say, while these testimonies may be elicited in an interview situation without any direction suggested by the interviewer, the sectarian ex-pectations do in fact act to standardize them. Yet they also seem to reflect something important of the experience of conversion which seems in itself (as well as in its retelling) to have been shaped for subjective awareness by the sectarian stereotype. Moreover, the original need dispositions of the subjects appear to have lent them-selves to precisely this kind of standardization. Although it would be very difficult to separate the elements analytically and perhaps im-possible to observe them empirically, there appears a measure of congruence between the "primitive" experience and the content of the sectarian stereotype. This bears obvious resemblance to the general sectarian conviction of regeneration and to that aspect of the world religions that Max Weber referred to in his treatment of "salvation religions." These people feel saved from something incorporated into something new and clean and good.

Conversion--the classical phenomenon of religious psychology--is something that follows upon some months of attending services as spectators. When the interviewees were asked why they first became interested in the sect, their answers also revealed a degree of uni-formity, and possibly one less affected by a cultural stereotype. "The first time I went there, I was impressed by the way everyone shook hands with me and the way everybody said 'hello' to me." "I was sick, they came to my home to say a prayer for me." "I used to go to the Catholic Church, there nobody knew me ... now in my church they call me sister." A very typical answer was "Me sentí como en mi casa." (I felt at home.) "I was lost here in New York, a friend invited me and I like the way they sang and that we all could sing." "I like to read the Bible." "The first time I went, when the service was over, someone came to me and asked my name and invited me to come again." Participant observation at the meetings confirms the interpretation of warmth, welcome, and participation related by the converted.

The interviews strongly suggest that isolation is one of the things from which such people are saved by the salvation experience

of conversion. Isolation appears to be associated with a loss of orientation in life. Thus the material offered by those interviewed would
tend to support the contention that conversion offered a way out of
anomie, both in terms of providing social relationships and giving
meaningful orientations to the converted.

That the sect is a real community according to those elements
stressed in the sociological literature is confirmed by both the content
of the interviews and participant observation. For example the three
elements of community sentiment stressed by MacIver are present to
a high degree in the Pentecostal sect.

The presence of "we-feeling" is clearly evident in the way
members talk about the sect. The church to which they belong is
not something foreign or removed from them. The service is a common enterprise; the members support the group with great financial
generosity; there is a real conviction of membership in a brotherhood.
They all know each other by name: "hermano Juan," "hermana Maria," etc.

"Role-feeling" is also quite evident. Each member has a role
in the community and so marked is such participation that one report
concluded that "it is hard to know to what degree we can call these
churches a lay association."[28] The individual member has opportunities to direct the service, to tell his troubles, to recount his religious experiences, to ask for prayers and to give thanks for prayers
said, or to ask for help. The members not only participate in religious services in this way but also take part in such work as visiting
the sick. The minister of the East Harlem Protestant Parish, a parish divided into five small communities following the example of l'Abbé
Michoneau in France, stated to us that the activity of the layman was
in his opinion the clue to the success of these Protestant sects.

Moreover, MacIver's feeling of dependency is also present.
Each person knows that he is a part of the group, that he needs the
group in order to sustain his regeneration. He feels this dependency
at the service when the minister asks the names of those who are
sick, or the names of those whose birthdays fall in the coming week.
If a person give his name, the whole community prays for him.

It is important to note that the group solidarity appears to the
converted not as a loss of individuality but rather as a chance to develop his own personality--to experience a worthwhile fulfillment.

One indication of what has been said concerns the question of
size. It would seem that such close in-group sentiment requires
small groups and that a larger membership would inevitably introduce
secondary relationships with concomitant impersonalization. In this
respect it was interesting to find in the area of our study a large
Pentecostal church with a membership of 800. This church had been
founded in 1935 and began, as all such groups begin, as a small group
with a small meeting place. By 1954, it had grown to 500 members
and was able to purchase for $70,000 a reconditioned theatre with a

seating capacity of 1,800. Now two full-time ministers care for the community. At their weekly meetings they have between 200 and 300 persons. Though this figure in comparison with that of the total membership suggests a lower degree of participation, it is nevertheless remarkable to find there all the characteristics we found in the smaller bodies. H. Richard Niebuhr has developed the Troeltschian theory to show that sects in time also have to make some kind of compromise with the world in which they live and become routinized. Such a routinized sect he calls a denomination. This larger group in our area does not in the opinion of the observer show any impressive signs of such routinization, but our research has not proceeded far enough to answer the important questions in this respect.

While we do not consider our hypothesis unambiguously confirmed at this stage of the game, we do feel entirely justified in stating that a hypothesis based upon such a firm body of sociological theory as this one is provides a very helpful device for understanding the phenomenon with which we are dealing. Moreover, the evidence to date does bear a striking congruence with the hypothesis itself. Since the hypothesis is based upon a body of theory that has considerable congruence with religious life as it has been studied in a multitude of different concrete settings, the congruity of our preliminary material with it gives us greater confidence than would be the case were our hypothesis merely an ad hoc construction unrelated to a larger body of theory and empirical generalization.

Theoretical Suggestions

Following this provisory and tentative confirmation of our hypothesis several questions of importance arise in addition to the need for more data on the points discussed above. Many of them cannot be answered definitively by this study even when it is completed, but what we have uncovered so far makes their formulation possible and worthwhile.

1. Why do some people form specifically religious groups as a way out of anomie?

Some suggestions might be made here in relation to the general religious culture from which these people come. The Pentecostals bear a strong resemblance--and possibly an obscure historical relationship--to the Joachimite enthusiasm of the Middle Ages. First of all, there is the emphasis upon the Holy Spirit. Secondly, while the Joachimites expected the "rule of monks" in a third age of the world, the Pentecostals are in a certain sense monks in the world. Moreover, during the ages when religion was a dominant element in the culture of the West in a sense that has long ceased to be the case, many movements of social and even political significance found expression in religious forms and with a religious ideology, for example, the followers of Thomas Munzer in the German Peasant War. With secularization, such movements found socialistic or syndicalistic forms for expression. Certainly, the Communist Parties in their period of revolutionary opposition offer an analogue to the sect in the sphere of political life, while their becoming a ruling core of functionaries after they take power shows structural and functional equivalents to the transformation of a sectarian movement into a church. The Social Democratic Parties appear in many ways similar to denominations, with sectarian traditions accommodated to the present in a practical way. The Puerto Ricans, despite the remoteness of institutional Catholicism from many of their needs, would appear to come from a cultural situation more like that of Europe before secularization had proceeded very far, than like the culture of urban workers in Europe today. Hence their needs for orientation and personal security take on a religious form of expression and become a religious need.

2. If anomie is a result of migration, how do we explain the success of Pentecostal groups in Puerto Rico and in other Latin countries as well?

One might suggest that the relation of the institutional church to the needs of people in certain conditions of life in these countries is worth a good deal of study. It appears that institutional Catholicism fails to meet these needs and hence people turn elsewhere. The gap between them and the Church would appear to leave a void that involves some aspects of anomie. Yet the Church has kept them sufficiently Christian in their outlook so that they seek the answer in a Christian idiom.

3. How long does regeneration last? What about backsliding?

We have no real information on this important point. Backsliding has been an important and ubiquitous phenomenon in American Protestant revivalism, from which the term derives.

4. What are the sociological concomitants of the need for salvation, or as our interviewees express it, the sense of sinfulness?

Certainly isolation and the concomitant loss of meaningful orientation are important in this respect. But much more needs to be known. Certain conditions of life predispose people to certain needs and attitudes. Which of these are found associated with the sense of sin?

5. Do social mobility, status, and class, play a role in these sectarian movements? Does the frugal life of the sectary lead to worldly success as has so often happened with such groups? Does regeneration withstand worldly success?

We have as yet no information on these questions.

6. What about the suggested congruence between the stereotype of sinfulness--conversion--regeneration and the "primitive" experience of needing to be saved from something?

This question is largely a problem for religious psychology, but it is also important to the sociology of religion, for such experiences bear a relationship to socially structured and shared conditions. For, they are in part at least a response to anomie.

References

1. Joseph P. Fitzpatrick, "The Integration of Puerto Ricans," Thought, XXX, No. 118, (Autumn 1955), p. 406.
2. Ibid., p. 413.
3. Ibid., p. 415.
4. Ibid., pp. 415-416.
5. Meryl Ruoss, Midcentury Pioneers and Protestants. A survey report of the Puerto Rican migration to the U.S. mainland and in particular a study of Protestant expression among Puerto Ricans in New York City, Department of Church Planning and Research, Protestant Council of the City of New York, (New York, 1954), Second Edition, p. 2.
6. Ibid., p. 14.
7. Morrisania, Melrose, Mott Haven, Three Bronx Communities. Prepared by Department of Church Planning and Research, Protestant Council of the City of New York, (November 1956), p. 3.
8. Midcentury Pioneers, p. 16.
9. Revista Del Clero Italiano, Rome, (February 1950).
10. Ignacio Vergara, "Los Evangelicos in Chile," Revista Mensaje, Santiago, Chile, (August 1955).
11. Midcentury Pioneers, p. 22.
12. Ernst Troeltsch, The Social Teachings of the Christian Churches, Olive Wyon (London and New York: George Allen and Unwin, Ltd. and The Macmillan Company, 1931), II, pp. 999-1,000.
13. Cf. Robert E. Park and Ernest W. Burgess, Introductory to the Science of Sociology, (Chicago: University of Chicago Press, 1921), pp. 50, 202-3, 611-2, 657, 870-4. Howard Becker, Systematic Sociology: On the Basis of the "Beziehungslehre und Gebildelehre" of Leopold von Wiese: Adapted and Amplified. (New York: John Wiley and Sons, 1932), pp. 624-8. H. Richard Niebuhr, The Social Sources of Denominationalism, (New York: Henry Holt and Company, 1929), pp. 17 ff. And Liston Pope, Millhands and Preachers, A Study of Gastonia, (New Haven: Yale University Press, 1942).
14. Thomas F. O'Dea, "Mormonism and the Avoidance of Sectarian Stagnation: A Study of Church, Sect, and Incipient Nationality," The American Journal of Sociology, LX, (November 1954), 286.
15. Christopher Dawson, "Sociology as a Science," quoted from the republication in Cross Currents, IV, No. 2 (Winter 1954), 136.
16. Talcott Parsons, Essays in Sociological Theory, (Glencoe, Illinois: The Free Press, 1954), especially "Democracy and Social Structure in Pre-Nazi Germany," pp. 104-23 and "Some Sociological Aspects of Fascist Movements," pp. 124-41.
17. Robert A. Nesbit, The Quest for Community, (New York: Oxford University Press, 1953), p. 7.
18. Erich Fromm, Escape from Freedom, (New York: Farrar and Rinehart, 1941).

19. David Riesman, The Lonely Crowd, (New Haven: Yale University Press, 1950).
20. Nesbit, op. cit., p. 11.
21. Will Herberg, Protestant, Catholic, Jew, (Garden City, New York: Doubleday, 1955).
22. André Brien, "Les petits communautes soustenance de la Foi," Etudes, Paris, Vol. 279, (November 1953), 168-86.
23. George A. Hillery, "Definitions of Community: Areas of Agreement," Rural Sociology, XX, (June 1955), 111-123.
24. R. M. MacIver, Community, (New York: The Macmillan Company, 1936), pp. 110-31.
25. R. M. MacIver and Charles H. Page, Society, (New York: Farrar and Rinehart, Inc., 1939), p. 293.
26. Ferdinand Toennies, Fundamental Concepts of Sociology, tr. Charles Loomis, (New York: Monthly Review Press, 1940), p. 40.
27. A. B. Hollingshead, "Community Research: Development and Present Condition," American Sociological Review, XIII, (April 1948), 136-46.
28. Midcentury Pioneers, p. 20.

THE PUERTO RICAN COMMUNITY OF NEW YORK:
A STATISTICAL PROFILE.

One in five New Yorkers lives in poverty. Estimates based on the 1960 United States Census, taking into account budget requirements and family size, show that 875,000 whites, 490,000 nonwhites, and 315,000 Puerto Ricans are below the poverty line--a total of 1,680,000 persons. (Table 1.)

Deprivation is emphasized among Puerto Ricans and nonwhites relative to other whites (that is, whites other than Puerto Ricans). One of every two Puerto Ricans and two of every five nonwhites live in poverty. In comparison, one of every 7.5 other whites lives in poverty. (Table 2.)

Furthermore, Puerto Rican and nonwhite poverty are concentrated in large families. Of the Puerto Ricans living in impoverished circumstances, 61.9 per cent were in family constellations of five or more members. Of poor nonwhites 46.0 per cent were in similarly large families. But only 17.7 per cent of the poor other whites were in family groups of five or more. Among the other whites, 57.2 per cent of the deprived lived alone or with just one other related person. Only 25.4 per cent of the impoverished nonwhites and only 7.9 per cent of the Puerto Ricans were alone or in such small families. (Table 1.)

The statistics show that poverty among the other whites is primarily, but not exclusively, a problem of the aged.

For nonwhites, and even more for Puerto Ricans, poverty is a characteristic of family life--large families including children. It casts a shadow over the future of a generation of youth. ...

Table 1

Persons Living in Poverty, New York City,
By Size of Family and Ethnic Group
(Thousands)

Persons in Poverty

Ethnic Group	Persons in Families	Ethnic Distribution	One Person	Two Persons	Three and Four	Five	Six and Over
Total	1,680	100.0	320	330	455	195	380
Puerto Rican	315	18.7	5	20	95	60	135
Nonwhite	490	29.2	65	60	140	65	160
Other White	875	52.1	250	250	220	70	85

Persons in Poverty
Percentage Distribution by Family Size

Total			100.0	100.0	100.0	100.0	100.0
Puerto Rican			1.6	6.0	20.8	30.8	35.5
Nonwhite			20.3	18.2	30.9	33.3	42.1
Other White			78.1	75.8	48.4	35.9	22.4

Persons in Poverty
Percentage Distribution by Ethnic Group

Total			100.0	19.1	19.6	27.1	11.6	22.6
Puerto Rican			100.0	1.6	6.3	30.2	19.0	42.9
Nonwhite			100.0	13.2	12.2	28.6	13.3	32.7
Other White			100.0	28.6	28.6	25.1	8.0	9.7

Source: Based on United States Census and budget estimates derived from New York City Welfare Department, United States Bureau of Labor Statistics, and Community Council of Greater New York.

Newcomers to a complex urban society can accommodate to it most successfully if they arrive with or quickly achieve the cultural equipment that enables upward mobility in the new society. Certainly in the United States educational attainment is a vital part of that equipment, for it is usually educational preparation that enables occupational achievement in an industrial society. And because occupations normally are the chief source of income for urban individuals

Table 2

Total Population and Persons Living in Poverty[a]
(Thousands)

Ethnic Group	Total Population Number	Total Population Percentage	Population Living in Poverty Number	Population Living in Poverty Percentage
Total	7,780	100.0	1,680	21.6
Puerto Rican	613	7.9	315	51.4
Nonwhite	1,140	14.7	490	42.9
Other White	6,640	85.3	875	13.2

[a]Source: Based on United States Census, and budget estimates derived from New York City Welfare Department, United States Bureau of Labor Statistics, and Community Council of Greater New York.

and families, the link between education, occupation, and income constitutes a cycle of individual development of critical importance.

The cycle is significant between generations also. While family income and father's occupation are by no means perfect predictors of the educational and occupational future of children, they are significant predictors. That is, low occupational status and inadequate family income can constitute powerful deterrents to the subsequent achievements of children growing up in deprived circumstances. The adverse consequences for children and youth, moreover, are augmented when poverty and its associated conditions, such as poor health, housing, and delinquency, are rigidly concentrated in urban ghettos. For then they grow up in the shadows of failure and despair, isolated from the expectation of success generally characteristic of other parts of the American society.

It is appropriate that we look at the history of Puerto Ricans in the United States from the specific perspective of the education-occupation-income cycle. We will see if there is evidence of the structural mobility prerequisite to integration or acculturation, and examine indications of obstacles to full and productive contributions by Puerto Ricans to their fellow citizens in New York.

The Migration

In 1960, nearly 900,000 Puerto Ricans--born on the island or in the states to Puerto Rican parents--lived in the United States. Persons born in Puerto Rico were first recorded as residents of the states by the United States Census of 1910, when 1,500 were enumerated. Their numbers increased so that by 1940 almost 70,000 lived in the 48 states. However, the great migration began after 1940, with two subsequent censuses showing a very large increase in numbers. By 1950 Puerto

Table 3

Persons of Puerto Rican Origin,
Coterminous United States and New York City,
1910 to 1960

Nativity and Year	United States		New York City	
	Number	% Increase	Number	% of total
Puerto Rican birth:				
1960	615,384	172. 2	429,710	69. 8
1950	226,110	223. 2	187,420	82. 9
1940	69,967	32. 6	61,463	87. 8
1930	52,774	346. 8	a	-
1920	11,811	680. 6	7,364	62. 3
1910	1,513	-	554	36. 6
Puerto Rican parentage:b				
1960	272,278	261. 8	182,864	67. 2
1950	75,265	-	58,460	77. 7

a. Not available.
b. Born in the United States.
Source: U. S. Bureau of the Census-U. S. Census of Population:
1960. Subject Reports. Puerto Ricans in United States. Final
Report. PC(2)-1D. U. S. Government Printing Office, Washington,
D. C. , 1963. Table A, p. viii.

Rican born persons numbered 226,000, and over the decade to 1960
the net gain due to migration from the island amounted to nearly
390,000. (Table 3.)

The census of 1950 recorded the beginning of the second generation of Puerto Ricans in the United States--those born on the continent to parents who came from the island. They numbered 75,000
in 1950 and 272,000 ten years later. By 1960, three of every ten
Puerto Rican stateside residents were born on the continent. (Table
3.)

With the great migration began a reversal of the historic trend
of Puerto Ricans living in New York City. In 1910 only a little more
than a third of them in the states lived in New York City, but by 1940,
88 per cent made New York their home. Since then a dispersal to
other areas has occurred. The percentage in New York City for those
born in Puerto Rico dropped to 83 in 1950 and 70 in 1960. The dispersal probably is continuing, but at this time Puerto Ricans in the
United States still are overwhelmingly New Yorkers. More than two-
thirds of the migrants and their children live in New York. It is with
this population in excess of 600,000 Puerto Ricans that we are specifically concerned.

Age Groups

The Puerto Ricans are the newest, and the youngest, of New York City's populations. More than 47 per cent of the males and 45 per cent of the females were under 20 years of age in 1960. In contrast, only 38.8 per cent of the male and 34.9 per cent of the female nonwhites were in the same age category. The proportions of youth among the non-Puerto Rican whites were even smaller, being 28.6 per cent of the males and 26.0 per cent of the females.

The aged are few in the Puerto Rican community. Just 1.5 per cent of the men and 2.5 per cent of the women were 65 or over in 1960, while among nonwhites 4.5 per cent of the males and 4.9 per cent of the females were 65 years or older. New York's other whites are much older; 11.6 per cent of these men and 13.1 per cent of the women were 65 years of age and older in 1960.

As a result of the number of children among them, a relatively small part of the Puerto Ricans are at their best working ages. Only 51.1 per cent of the men and 52.4 per cent of the women were aged 20 through 64 in 1960. The nonwhites and other whites, in contrast, had higher proportions in the 20-64 age group. For the nonwhite men and women the comparable percentages were 56.7 and 60.2. About 60 per cent of both male and female other whites were 20-64 years of age. (Table 4.)

Only 7.9 per cent of New York City's population in 1960 was Puerto Rican. However, the Puerto Rican proportion among the younger population is more significant. In 1960, Puerto Ricans were 11 per cent of all youth aged 15 through 19, 11 per cent of the boys and girls 10-14 years old, 12 per cent of those 5-9, and 14 per cent of all children under 5. (Table 5.)

In other words, Puerto Ricans are an increasingly larger part of the upcoming age groups in our youth population. Moreover, large numbers of Puerto Ricans will be among the city's youth for the near future, unless a radically different migration flow occurs. The migration has selected young adults, and in 1960, 75 per cent of adult (20 years of age or older) female Puerto Rican residents were in the child-bearing age group of 20-44. There is a reasonable expectation that this proportion will increase. (Table 4.)

Educational Attainment

Puerto Rican adults have the lowest level of formal education of any identifiable ethnic or color group in New York City. Only 13 per cent of the Puerto Rican men and women 25 years of age and older in 1960 had completed either high school or more advanced education.[1] In other words, 87 per cent of them had dropped out without graduating from high school. Among New York's nonwhite (predominately Negro) population, on the other hand, nearly a third had

Table 4

Ethnic Groups, by Sex and Age,
New York City, 1960[a]

Age	Puerto Rican		Nonwhite		Other White	
	Male	Female	Male	Female	Male	Female
Total:						
Number	296,701	315,873	530,028	611,294	2,892,528	3,135,560
%	100.0	100.0	100.0	100.0	100.0	100.0
0-4 yrs	15.8	14.6	13.2	11.5	8.0	7.1
5-9 "	12.6	11.5	11.0	9.6	7.1	6.4
10-14 "	10.4	9.9	8.6	7.7	7.4	6.6
15-19 "	8.6	9.1	6.0	6.1	6.1	5.9
20-24 "	9.7	10.2	6.5	7.7	5.5	5.8
25-29 "	10.1	10.4	7.5	8.2	6.2	5.7
30-34 "	8.8	8.9	8.3	9.1	6.7	6.3
35-39 "	7.2	6.9	8.5	8.9	6.6	6.8
40-44 "	4.9	5.-	7.1	7.5	6.5	7.1
45-49 "	4.1	4.2	6.1	6.4	7.2	7.8
50-54 "	2.8	2.8	5.1	5.1	7.5	7.7
55-59 "	2.1	2.3	4.4	4.3	7.3	7.2
60-64 "	1.4	1.6	3.1	2.9	6.3	6.5
65 & older	1.5	2.5	4.5	4.9	11.6	13.1

a. According to the 1960 census, 24,871 Puerto Ricans--4 per cent
of the total--reported their color as nonwhite. Characteristics of
nonwhite and white Puerto Ricans were not tabulated separately for
New York City in 1960. To estimate the characteristics of whites
other than Puerto Ricans in this table and others which follow, all
the Puerto Ricans, including those who were nonwhite, were sub-
tracted from total whites. The nonwhite Puerto Ricans were not
eliminated from the total nonwhites. This introduced an error of 2
percent for nonwhites and less than a half of one per cent for whites
other than Puerto Ricans.

Source: U.S. Bureau of Census. U.S. Censuses of Population and
Housing: 1960. Census tracts. Final Report PHC(1)-104. Part 1.
U.S. Government Printing Office, Washington, D.C., 1963. Tables
P-2 and P-5.

at least completed high school; 68.8 per cent had left school prior
to high school graduation. The other white population (not including
Puerto Ricans) was in an even better position. Slightly more than
40 per cent had at least completed high school. (Table 6.)

The deficiency in the educational preparation of the Puerto
Rican population is perhaps more dramatically revealed by the num-
bers who had not even completed a grade-school education in 1960.[2]
More than half--52.9 per cent--of Puerto Ricans in New York City

Table 5

Age Groups, by Ethnic Background,
New York City, 1960

Age	Number	Percentages for Males + Females			
		Total	Puerto Rican	Nonwhite	Other White
Totals	7,781,984	100.0	7.9	14.7	77.4
0-4 years	686,717	100.0	13.6	20.4	66.0
5-9 "	505,847	100.0	12.3	19.6	68.1
10-14 "	575,321	100.0	10.8	16.2	73.0
15-19 "	486,851	100.0	11.2	14.2	74.6
20-24 "	482,522	100.0	12.6	16.9	70.5
25-29 "	513,629	100.0	12.3	17.6	70.2
30-34 "	542,769	100.0	10.0	18.3	71.7
35-39 "	546,966	100.0	7.9	18.2	73.9
40-44 "	524,381	100.0	5.8	15.9	78.3
45-49 "	550,310	100.0	4.6	13.0	82.4
50-54 "	534,526	100.0	3.2	10.8	86.0
55-59 "	499,493	100.0	2.7	10.0	87.3
60-64 "	428,825	100.0	2.2	8.0	89.8
65 and older	813,827	100.0	1.6	6.7	91.7

Source: U.S. Bureau of Census. U.S. Censuses of Population and Housing: 1960. Census tracts. Final Report PHC(1)-104. Part 1. U.S. Government Printing Office, Washington, D.C., 1963. Tables P-2 and P-5.

25 years of age and older had less than an eighth grade education. In contrast, 29.5 per cent of the nonwhite population had not finished the eighth year, and only 19.3 per cent of the other whites had so low an academic preparation. (Table 6.)

The lag in educational attainment of the Puerto Rican population is not entirely a commentary on New York City's educational establishment. The Puerto Rican population is heavily weighted with persons born on the island, many of whom undoubtedly ended school careers before coming to the states. The educational levels of Puerto Ricans born in the United States differ markedly from those of Puerto Ricans born in the Commonwealth.

Table 7 shows for 1960 the percentages of high-school dropouts among Puerto Ricans, 20 years and older, born in Puerto Rico and in the United States, further classified by age and sex. The males and females born in Puerto Rico at every age level exhibit very high percentages of school leavers. These range from 84 to 97 per cent. Those born in the United States, however, have considerably lower proportions of school leavers. In the youngest age group--25 through 34--the differential between the two generations

Table 6

Years of School Completed,
Persons 25 Years of Age and Over,
by Ethnic Background,
New York City, 1960[a]

Years of School Completed	Puerto Rican	Nonwhite	Other White
Total: Number	268,524	639,624	4,046,933
Percent	100.0	100.0	100.0
No School Years Completed	8.2	3.2	5.2
Elementary: 1-4 yrs	20.9	8.2	3.9
5-7 "	23.8	18.1	10.2
8 "	17.2	16.3	21.0
High School: 1-3 "	16.9	23.0	19.6
4 "	9.9	21.4	23.0
College 1-3 "	2.2	5.7	7.7
4 " or more	0.9	4.1	9.4

a. Includes persons in school at time of enumeration.
Source: U.S. Bureau of the Census. U.S. Censuses of Population
and Housing: 1960. Census tracts. Final Report PHC(1) 104.
Part 1. U.S. Government Printing Office, Washington, D.C., 1962.
Tables P-1 P-4, P-5.

Table 7

Percentages of Puerto Ricans 25 Years of Age
and Older Who Hd Not Completed High School,
by Age, Sex, and Place of Birth,
New York Standard Metropolitan Statistical Area, 1960[a]

Age	Place of Birth			
	Puerto Rico		United States	
	Male	Female	Male	Female
25-34 years	84.5%	84.0%	59.4%	50.0%
35-44 "	87.1	90.8	67.8	60.3
45-64 "	91.1	93.3	81.5	78.2
65 and over	94.5	96.8	90.2	84.5

a. Includes persons in school at time of enumeration.
Source: U.S. Bureau of the Census. U.S. Census of Population:
1960. Subject Reports. Puerto Ricans in the United States. Final
Report. PC(2)-1D. U.S. Government Printing Office, Washington,
D.C., 1963. Table 11.

is largest, amounting to 34 percentage points for females and 25 for males. Among this relatively mobile population, birth and present residence in the United States do not necessarily mean that all education was acquired in stateside schools. Moreover, an unknown number of Puerto Ricans educated in New York have returned to the Commonwealth. So differences in educational attainment by place of birth is probably not a satisfactory indicator estimate of the impact of New York's educational system. [3]

If the educational attainment of Puerto Ricans born in the United States is strikingly better than that of those born in the Commonwealth, it so far has small weight in the statistics for the total adult Puerto Rican community in New York City. The numbers in the second generation who have reached adult years is still small, only 6. 4 per cent of persons 20 years of age and older in 1960.

There is evidence that Puerto Rican youth, more than any other group, is severely handicapped in achieving an education in the New York City public schools. A 1961 study of a Manhattan neighborhood showed that fewer than 10 per cent of Puerto Ricans in the third grade were reading at their grade level or above. In comparison, 19 per cent of the Negroes in the same schools and 55 per cent of the others (mostly whites) were reading at grade level. Moreover, the degree of retardation of Puerto Rican youth was extreme. Three in ten were retarded one and one-half years or more and were, in the middle of their third school year, therefore reading at a level no better than appropriate for entry into the second grade. Only one-fifth of the nonwhite children and one in 14 of the others were so disadvantaged. (Table 8.)

By the eighth grade the degree of reading retardation was even more severe. While 13 per cent of the Puerto Rican youth were reading at grade level or above, almost two-thirds were retarded more than three years. In contrast, three in ten of the Negro youth were at least at grade level, with one-third retarded more than three years. More than one-half the others were at grade level, with only 13 per cent retarded more than three years. (Table 8.) City-wide studies are needed to measure reading ability in other neighborhoods.

Puerto Rican graduates with academic diplomas from New York City high schools still are rare in New York City. Of the nearly 21,000 academic diplomas granted in 1963, only 331 were to Puerto Ricans and 762 to Negroes. This is only 1. 6 per cent and 3. 7 per cent, respectively, of the total academic diplomas. In contrast, Puerto Ricans received 7. 4 per cent of the vocational school diplomas, and Negroes, 15. 2 per cent. As a result, only 20 per cent of the small number of Puerto Ricans completing high school in 1963 were prepared to begin higher academic education. Of the Negroes, 22 per cent received academic diplomas, as did 50 per cent of the other graduates. (Table 9.)

One critical issue for the Puerto Rican community is, then, the education of its children in the New York City public schools.

Table 8

Reading Retardation, by Grade and Ethnic Group, 1961
(Selected Manhattan Neighborhood)

School Grade and Ethnic Group	Total Number	Percentages by Degree of Reading Retardation[a]							
		Over 3 Years	2.5 to 3.0	2.0 to 2.5	1.5 to 2.0	1.0 to 1.5	0.5 to 1.0	0.1 to 0.5	At Grade Level or Above
Grade 3.5[b]									
Total	2,721		.49	6.68	16.60	25.86	14.23	15.68	21.58
Puerto Rican	1,490		.92	7.12	21.29	30.69	15.85	14.44	9.80
Negro	626		.16	5.43	15.97	27.00	15.02	17.73	18.69
Other	806			1.82	5.45	12.37	9.24	16.33	54.79
Grade 8.5[b]									
Total	862	30.74	3.94	8.24	4.06	6.26	3.83	4.76	38.17
Puerto Rican	235	64.68	2.98	7.66	1.28	4.79	2.55	2.98	13.19
Negro	138	33.33	5.80	11.59	3.62	7.97	3.63	5.07	28.99
Other	489	13.70	3.88	7.57	5.52	6.54	4.50	5.52	52.77

a. Since the academic year is 10 months, scoring intervals consist of five months each.
b. Tested midway through each of these grades.

Source: Research Center, Columbia University School of Social Work.

Table 9

High School Graduates, New York City Public Schools,
by Ethnic Background and Type of Diploma, 1963

Numbers

Ethnic Group	Total	Academic Diploma	Vocational Diploma
Total	38,304	20,729	17,575
Puerto Rican	1,626	331	1,295
Negro	3,434	762	2,672
Other	33,244	19,636	13,608

Percentages			
Total	100.0%	100.0%	100.0%
Puerto Rican	4.2	1.6	7.4
Negro	9.0	3.7	15.2
Other	86.8	94.7	77.4

Total	100.0%	54.1%	45.9%
Puerto Rican	100.0	20.4	79.6
Negro	100.0	22.2	77.8
Other	100.0	59.1	40.9

Source: New York City Board of Education.

Large numbers of Puerto Ricans are of school age, and they are an increasing proportion of the public school enrollment in New York City. In fact, Puerto Ricans accounted for about 20 per cent of public elementary school pupils in 1963, compared with 15 per cent in 1957. Of the junior high students 18 per cent were Puerto Ricans in 1963, up from 16 per cent six years before. In addition, 23 per cent in vocational high schools and 29 per cent in special schools (both upwardly trending proportions) were youth of the Puerto Rican community. The proportions in academic high schools were much smaller, changing from 4.6 per cent in 1957 to 7.2 per cent in 1963. (Table 10.)

Employment

Since the level of education of New York's Puerto Ricans is lower than that of any other group in the city and since educational attainment is prerequisite for entry into many kinds of jobs, employed Puerto Ricans are more than any other group concentrated in occupations with the lowest pay and status. In 1960, 70.6 per cent of the employed Puerto Rican males were in low-income occupations (operatives and kindred

Table 10

Pupils Enrolled in New York City Public Schools,
by Type of School, Fall of 1957-1963

Year	Number	Per Cent			
		Total	Puerto Rican	Negro	Other
Elementary					
1957	550,357	100.0	15.2	20.4	64.4
1958	558,749	100.0	16.3	21.9	61.8
1959	557,159	100.0	17.4	23.5	59.1
1960	567,613	100.0	17.9	24.9	57.2
1961	573,122	100.0	18.6	26.2	55.2
1962	581,755	100.0	19.1	27.3	53.6
1963	586,046	100.0	19.8	28.7	51.5
Junior High					
1957	169,123	100.0	16.1	18.9	65.0
1958	172,286	100.0	16.0	18.7	65.3
1959	186,595	100.0	16.1	19.2	64.7
1960	185,479	100.0	17.4	21.4	61.2
1961	186,113	100.0	18.3	23.6	58.1
1962	193,293	100.0	18.1	25.7	56.2
1963	208.177	100.0	17.9	26.9	55.2
Academic High					
1957	187,282	100.0	4.6	9.3	86.1
1958	192,409	100.0	4.7	10.0	85.4
1959	189,737	100.0	5.0	10.4	84.6
1960	188,795	100.0	5.2	10.7	84.1
1961	198,256	100.0	5.5	11.2	83.3
1962	205,971	100.0	6.2	12.5	81.3
1963	204,075	100.0	7.2	14.7	78.1
Vocational High					
1957	41,282	100.0	20.4	23.6	56.0
1958	39,111	100.0	21.1	23.4	55.5
1959	37,920	100.0	21.6	23.2	55.2
1960	38,697	100.0	20.6	22.9	56.5
1961	40,508	100.0	21.6	24.2	54.2
1962	40,223	100.0	21.3	24.5	54.0
1963	40,622	100.0	22.5	25.9	51.6

Table 10 (cont.)

Year	Number	Per Cent			
		Total	Puerto Rican	Negro	Other
Special Schools					
1957	4,574	100.0	25.1	32.7	42.2
1958	5,310	100.0	26.4	33.7	39.9
1959	6,120	100.0	26.6	37.0	36.4
1960	6,095	100.0	27.7	35.3	37.0
1961	6,266	100.0	29.1	36.9	34.0
1962	6,186	100.0	28.4	37.8	33.8
1963	6,634	100.0	29.1	38.6	32.3
All Schools					
1957	952,617	100.0	13.5	18.2	68.3
1958	967,865	100.0	14.2	19.0	66.8
1959	977,531	100.0	15.0	20.2	64.8
1960	986,679	100.0	15.6	21.5	62.9
1961	1,004,265	100.0	16.1	22.8	61.6
1962	1,027,428	100.0	16.5	24.0	59.5
1963	1,045,554	100.00	17.1	25.6	57.3

Source: New York City Board of Education

workers, non-household service workers, private household workers, and laborers), compared with 61.3 per cent of the nonwhite and 31.4 per cent of the other white males. [4] (Table 11.)

The differences in the occupations of employed females by ethnic group show the same pattern. Of the Puerto Rican employed women, 78.2 per cent worked in the low-status occupations. Among nonwhites and other whites the percentages were 66.6 and 26.8. Employed Puerto Rican and nonwhite women were concentrated in the low-status occupations to a greater degree than were Puerto Rican and nonwhite males. The other white females, compared to the males, had higher status jobs overall.

The Puerto Ricans employed by agencies of New York's city government also are in the least desirable jobs to a greater degree than are Negroes and others. Three of every four Puerto Rican city employees are at the level of operatives or below, while only three of every five Negroes and one of every three of the others are so employed. In other words, two-thirds of the others, 40 per cent of the Negroes, and only 25 per cent of the Puerto Ricans are employed as foremen, clerical workers, professionals, or officials on the city payroll. (Table 12.)

Furthermore, only 3 per cent of city employees are Puerto Rican, whereas 23 per cent are Negroes and 74 per cent, others.

Table 11
Occupational Status of Employed Civilian Labor Force,
by Sex and Ethnic Background, New York City, 1950 and 1960

Occupation	Puerto Rican 1950	Puerto Rican 1960[a]	Nonwhite 1960	Other White 1960
Employed Males:				
Number	49,860	127,384	233,584	1,601,904
Per cent	100.0	100.0	100.0	100.0
Professional, technical and kindred workers	2.6	2.2	5.2	13.6
Managers, Officials and Proprietors	5.4	3.7	5.0	14.1
Clerical, Sales and kindred workers	10.0	12.3	16.9	23.1
Craftsman, Foremen and Kindred workers	11.1	11.3	11.6	17.8
Operatives and kindred workers	37.2	44.1	28.4	17.2
Non-household service workers	28.4	20.5	21.1	9.4
Private household workers	0.1	0.1	0.9	0.1
Laborers	5.2	5.9	10.9	4.7
Employed Females:				
Number	34,685	67,518	181,942	860,722
Per cent	99.9	100.0	99.9	99.9
Professional, Technical and kindred workers	2.0	2.9	8.8	13.7
Managers, Officials and Proprietors	1.1	1.1	1.4	4.9
Clerical, Sales and kindred workers	9.2	15.9	21.8	53.1
Craftsman, Foremen and kindred workers	1.7	1.9	1.2	1.4
Operatives and kindred workers	77.5	69.7	25.9	15.8
Non-household service workers	5.9	6.9	18.8	8.2
Household service workers	1.6	0.8	21.2	2.6
Laborers	0.9	0.8	0.7	0.2

[a]Includes Nassau, Rockland, Suffolk and Westchester counties.

Source: U. S. Bureau of the Census. U. S. Censuses of Population and Housing: 1960. Census Tracts. Final Report PHC(1)-104. Part 1. U. S. Government Printing Office, Washington, D.C., 1962. Tables P-3, P-4, P-5; U. S. Bureau of the Census. U. S. Census

Table 11 (cont.)

of Population 1950. Special Report. Puerto Ricans in Continental
United States. U. S. Government Printing Office, Washington, D. C. ,
1953. Table 5. U. S. Bureau of the Census. U. S. Census of Population: 1960. Subject Reports. Puerto Ricans in the United States.
Final Report. PC(2)-1D. U. S. Government Printing Office, Washington, D. C. , 1963. Table 11.

As a result the Puerto Rican proportion in each occupational category
is small, the largest being 6. 4 per cent of service workers. The
most striking differences are between ethnic proportions of the crafts-
men-foremen and the managerial categories. Of the craftsmen and
foremen employed by New York City, only 3. 7 per cent were Negroes
and only six-tenths of one per cent were Puerto Ricans: 95. 7 per
cent of the influential category of officials were whites or other races,
only one-half of one per cent (44) were Puerto Ricans. (Table 12.)

Comparisons of 1960 with 1950 show modest changes in the
occupations of Puerto Ricans. In 1950, 37. 2 per cent of the employed
males 14 years old and over were operatives and kindred workers;
28. 4 per cent more were non-household service workers; 5. 2 per cent
were laborers. Among better-paying jobs, 11. 1 per cent of these men
were craftsmen, foremen, and kindred workers; 10 per cent were
clerical, sales and kindred workers; 5. 4 per cent were managers, officials, and proprietors; and 2. 6 per cent were professionals, tech-
nicals, and kindred workers.

The employed women in 1950 were even more highly concentrated in a few occupational categories. Of these, 77. 5 per cent
were operatives and kindred workers; 9. 2 per cent were clerical,
sales, and kindred workers; 5. 9 per cent were non-household service
workers; and 2 per cent were professional, technical, and kindred
workers. None of the other occupational categories employed as
many as 2 per cent of the Puerto Rican females. (Table 11.)

The percentage distribution of Puerto Ricans among major occupational groups in 1960 showed changes, even though they remained
predominantly in low-status jobs. For males 14 years and older the
per cent in non-household occupations declined from 28. 4 to 20. 5; the
percentage of managers, officials, and proprietors dropped from 5. 4
to 3. 7; professional, technical, and kindred workers declined slightly
as a proportion of the total. However, it should be remembered that
the number of Puerto Ricans in New York had increased considerably
between 1950 and 1960. Even though certain job categories showed a
drop in the proportions of Puerto Ricans in them, in every instance
the absolute number of persons increased. Among the males in 1960,
the percentage employed as laborers (5. 9) and as craftsmen, foremen,
and kindred workers (11. 3) remained about the same as in 1950.
Clerical, sales, and kindred workers showed a modest increase, from
10 to 12. 3 per cent. The greatest increase, however, was registered
in the category of operatives and kindred workers, in which 44. 1 per
cent of the Puerto Rican employed males worked in 1960, compared

Table 12

Occupations of New York City Employees, by
Ethnic Background, 1963[a]

Occupations	Puerto Rican	Negro	Other
Total: Number	5,404	40,946	130,848
Per cent	100.0	100.0	100.0
Officials	0.8	2.0	5.7
Professional, Technical and kindred workers	14.6	22.4	42.4
Clerical and kindred workers	8.6	14.1	8.6
Craftsman, Foremen and kindred workers	1.4	1.1	9.4
Operatives and kindred workers	5.3	3.8	4.4
Service workers	54.8	49.7	17.4
Laborers	14.5	6.9	12.1
Officials	0.5	9.9	89.6
Professional, Technical and kindred workers	1.2	14.0	84.8
Clerical and kindred workers	2.5	31.3	66.2
Craftsman, Foremen and kindred workers	0.6	3.7	95.7
Operatives and kindred workers	3.7	20.5	75.8
Service workers	6.4	44.2	49.4
Laborers	4.0	14.6	81.4

a. Figures do not include all City Departments. See source publication, Table 3.
Source: New York City Commission on Human Rights, The Ethnic Survey. (New York City Commission on Human Rights, 1964) Tables 1.1 thru 1.6.

with 37.2 per cent in 1950. In spite of these shifts, the occupational distribution of employed Puerto Rican males overall showed no improvement in the decade. In 1950, 70.9 per cent of them were in the lowest income occupations (operatives, private household workers, non-household workers, and laborers). In 1960 the comparable figure was 70.6 per cent. (Table 11.)

Changes through the decade between censuses were somewhat brighter for employed Puerto Rican females, though at both points in time they were employed in low-status jobs in greater proportions than were Puerto Rican males. In 1950, 85.9 per cent of the employed females were in the lowest income occupations (listed above) compared with 70.9 per cent of the men. By 1960, only 78.2 per cent of the females were so employed, compared with 70.6 per cent of the males.

Thus, the occupational differential between males and females narrowed from 15 to 7.6 percentage points during the decade. (Table 11.)

Improvement in the occupational situation of Puerto Rican women occurred chiefly through their employment as clerical, sales, and kindred workers. Of the total, 9.2 per cent were so employed in 1950; by 1960 the proportion in this category had increased to 15.9 per cent. A slight gain was also registered by professional, technical, and kindred workers. (Table 11.)

Examination of the separate data for the first and second-generation Puerto Ricans shows even more clearly an improvement of the occupational status of employed Puerto Rican women relative to Puerto Rican men. The employed men and women 14 years of age and older born in Puerto Rico were, of course, heavily employed in low-status occupations at the beginning and at the end of the 1950-1960 decade. Of the employed Puerto Rican-born men in 1950, 71.9 per cent were in low-status jobs (as defined above). The number changed only slightly--to 72.4 per cent--by 1960. The employed women born in Puerto Rico, however, improved their occupational positions to a more striking degree, even though they began (and remained) in a disadvantaged occupational situation relative to the men. In 1950, 89.1 per cent of these women were in the low-status occupational categories, but by 1960 the percentage had fallen to 82.3. Thus, due to improvement in the occupations of females the percentage-point difference between men and women born in Puerto Rico dropped from 17.2 to 9.9 over the decade. (Table 13.)

Among the employed Puerto Ricans born in the United States the females began with occupational distribution more favorable than that of the men in 1950 and they widened their advantage during the decade. However, the occupational situation of both men and women improved significantly. In 1950, 57.7 per cent of the men and 51.7 per cent of the women were in low-status occupations. By 1960 the figures had dropped to 49.4 per cent for the males and 34.2 per cent for the females. Thus the female occupational distribution improved to a greater degree than did that of the men. As a result, the female percentage-point advantage increased from 6.0 in 1950 to 14.2 in 1960. (Table 13.)

The occupational advance for both men and women of the second generation was achieved in similar ways--through increasing participation as professional, technical, and kindred workers, and as clerical, sales, and kindred workers. The proportion of men who were craftsmen, foremen and kindred workers also increased. The most dramatic increase was of women employed in clerical, sales, and kindred tasks, which rose from 39.4 per cent in 1950 to 56.0 per cent in 1960. The greatest percentage-point losses for the men were in the operative category--from 40.9 per cent in 1950 to 24.4 per cent in 1960. (Table 13.)

The occupational distributions do not tell the entire story, for of the 147,495 Puerto Rican males 14 years old and over in New York

Table 13
Occupational Status of Persons Born in Puerto Rico
and of Puerto Rican Parentage, by Sex,
New York City, 1950 and 1960

Occupation	Born in Puerto Rico		Puerto Rican Parentage	
	1950	1960[a]	1950	1960[a]
Employed Males:				
Number	46,275	118,288	3,585	9,096
Per cent	100.0	100.0	100.0	100.0
Professional, Technical and kindred workers	2.4	1.8	5.4	7.4
Managers, Officials and Proprietors	5.5	3.7	4.4	4.0
Clerical, Sales and kindred workers	9.2	11.4	20.5	23.8
Craftsmen, Foremen and kindred workers	11.0	10.8	11.9	16.3
Operatives and kindred workers	37.4	45.2	35.4	29.7
Non-household service workers	29.3	21.1	16.3	12.5
Household service	0.1	0.1	0.0	0.2
Laborers	5.1	6.0	6.0	6.0
Employed Females:				
Number	31,730	61,625	2,955	5,893
Percent	100.0	100.0	100.0	100.0
Professional, Technical and kindred workers	1.7	2.6	5.6	6.3
Managers, Officials and Proprietors	1.0	1.1	1.2	1.7
Clerical, Sales and kindred workers	6.4	12.1	39.4	56.0
Craftsmen, Foremen and kindred workers	1.7	1.9	2.0	1.7
Operatives and kindred workers	80.8	74.0	40.9	24.4
Non-household service	5.7	6.7	8.6	8.7
Household service	1.6	0.8	1.7	0.5
Laborers	1.0	0.8	0.5	0.6

[a] Includes Nassau, Rockland, Suffolk and Westchester counties.

Source: U.S. Bureau of the Census. U.S. Census of Population, 1960. Subject Reports. Puerto Ricans in the United States. Final PC(2)-ID. U.S. Government Printing Office, Washington, D.C., 1963. Table 11.

City's labor force in 1960, 14,507--or 9.9 per cent--were unemployed. Table 14 gives the unemployment rates for the Puerto Rican males, nonwhite males, and other white males, as they stood at the time of the censuses of 1950 and 1960. In both periods one in ten Puerto Rican men was unemployed and looking for work. Furthermore, the unemployment problem for the Puerto Rican was significantly worse than that of the nonwhite male or the much better off other white male.

This unemployment was heavily concentrated among youth. Of the Puerto Rican male labor force 14 to 19 years of age, 19.7 per cent were unemployed, as were 19.0 per cent of the nonwhite males of the same ages. (The figures for age groups are for New York City and Nassau, Suffolk, Rockland, and Westchester counties combined and probably understate the unemployment then prevalent in New York City.) Among females of the same age group, the unemployment rate of 14.7 for nonwhites was virtually the same as the Puerto Rican rate of 15.0. Unemployment was also high among the labor force 20 to 24 years of age: 10.7 per cent of the Puerto Rican males and 12.4 per cent of the females; for nonwhites, 9.7 per cent of the males and 9.2 per cent of the females. Rates of unemployment at older ages were smaller, but for no male Puerto Rican age group did it fall below 7.7 per cent. (Table 15.)

In summary, the occupational statistics for Puerto Ricans in New York City show that they largely occupied low-status, low-income occupations in 1950 and in general remained in them in 1960. The overall unemployment rate for Puerto Rican males has consistently exceeded that of any other racial or ethnic group in the city. A considerable upgrading is apparent in the occupations of the generation born in the United States relative to those who migrated here. However, the proportion of the second generation that has reached labor-force age is still small. Among both the first and second generation a trend is evident for the occupational status of employed women to improve relative to that of the employed men of the same generation. If the trend continues, it may have unfavorable implications for the stability of traditional Puerto Rican cultural patterns of family life.

Table 14

Male Unemployment, by Ethnicity,
1950 and 1960

Ethnic Group	Percent Unemployed	
	1950	1960
Puerto Rican	10.6	9.9
Nonwhite	8.4	6.9
Other White	5.1	4.3

Source: U.S. Bureau of the Census. U.S. Census of Population and Housing: 1960. Census tracts. Final Report PHC(1)-104. Part 1. U.S. Government Printing Office, Washington, D.C., 1963. Tables P-3, P-4, P-5.

Table 15

Unemployment Rates, for Puerto Ricans and Nonwhites, by Sex,
New York Standard Metropolitan Statistical Area, 1960

Persons 14 Years of Age and Over	Puerto Rican Male	Female	Nonwhite Male	Female
Total	9. 7	10. 6	6. 8	6. 5
14-19 years	19. 7	15. 0	19. 0	14. 7
20-24 "	10. 7	12. 4	9. 7	9. 2
25-34 "	8. 5	9. 5	6. 6	6. 7
35-44 "	8. 5	9. 3	5. 3	5. 8
45-64 "	8. 8	9. 5	5. 6	4. 7
65 years and older	7. 7	12. 3	7. 9	4. 6

Source: Manpower Report of the President, 1964. U. S. Government
Printing Office, Washington, D. C. , 1964. Table 33.

Income

In part, a consequence of the low educational attainment of the
Puerto Rican population and the consequently low-status jobs at which
they work, is the evident poverty of their families. Poverty is significantly more pronounced among Puerto Ricans than among any other
identifiable racial and ethnic group in New York City.

In 1959, 33. 8 per cent of Puerto Rican families had incomes
of less than $3,000, and more than half (53. 7 per cent) had less than
$4,000. The nonwhites in the city were better off, although not in
an enviable situation. In this group, 27. 1 per cent had incomes below
$3,000 and 43. 6 per cent had less than $4,000. The other whites
were least disadvantaged. Only 11. 8 per cent of their families had
incomes of less than $3,000; 19. 2 per cent had less than $4,000.
(Tables 16 and 17.)

Because of the youthfulness of the Puerto Rican population in
comparison with nonwhites and other whites, the children and youth
in the Puerto Rican communities are struck more severely than any
other group by massive conditions of poverty and deprivation.

Housing

As newcomers, Puerto Ricans entered the competition for housing
later than did the nonwhite and other white populations. This is reflected in the statistics on the year in which household heads moved
into the units where they resided in 1960. Among Puerto Ricans,
46. 6 per cent had moved in during the period from 1958 to March,
1960. Only 30 per cent of the nonwhites and 22. 8 per cent of the
whites had occupied their units so recently. Puerto Rican heads of
households were under-represented in the long-term occupants of

Table 16

Family Income, by Ethnic Group, New York City, 1959

| Income | Percentages of Families with Income[a] | | |
	Puerto Rican	Nonwhite	Other White
Under $3,000	33.8%	27.1%	11.8%
Under $4,000	53.7	43.6	19.2
$4,000 and over	46.3	56.4	80.8

a. Not additive. Families with less than $4,000 income includes those with less than $3,000 income.
Source: U.S. Bureau of the Census. U.S. Censuses of Population and Housing: 1960. Census Tracts. Final Report PHC(1)-104. Part 1. U.S. Government Printing Office, Washington, D.C., 1962. Tables P-1, P-4, P-5.

Table 17

Family Income, by Ethnic Group, New York City, 1959

| Income | Percentage of Families with Income | | | |
	Total Population	Puerto Rican	Nonwhite	Other White
Total: Number	2,079,832	140,389	263,963	1,675,480
Percent	100.0	100.0	100.0	100.0
Under $1,000	3.5	6.9	6.3	2.8
$1,000-$1,999	4.9	9.2	8.2	4.0
$2,000-$2,999	6.8	17.7	12.6	5.0
$3,000-$3,999	9.4	19.9	16.5	7.4
$4,000-$4,999	11.2	15.3	14.8	10.3
$5,000-$5,999	13.1	11.3	12.5	13.4
$6,000-$6,999	11.2	7.4	9.0	11.8
$7,000-$7,999	8.9	4.7	6.3	9.6
$8,000-$8,999	7.1	2.9	4.5	7.9
$9,000-$9,999	5.4	1.7	3.0	6.0
$10,000 and over	17.5	3.1	6.3	21.7

Source: U.S. Bureau of the Census. U.S. Censuses of Population and Housing: 1960. Census Tracts. Final Report PHC(1)-104. Part 1. U.S. Government Printing Office, Washington, D.C., 1962. Tables P-1, P-4, P-5.

housing units. While just 18.7 per cent of them had moved into their 1960 unit in 1953 or earlier, 41.1 per cent of the nonwhite and more than half (53.6 per cent) of the other white household heads were long-term residents. (Table 18)

Table 19

Tenure of Housing Units, by Ethnic Group,
New York City, 1960

| | | Percentages | |
Occupied Units	Puerto Rican	Nonwhite	Other White
Total: Number	156, 110	352, 554	2, 145, 781
Per cent	100. 0	100. 0	100. 0
Owner Occupied	4. 7	13. 2	24. 4
Renter Occupied	95. 3	86. 8	75. 6

Source: U.S. Bureau of Census. U.S. Censuses of Population and Housing: 1960. Census Tracts. Final Report PHC(1)-104. Part 1. U.S. Government Printing Office, Washington, D.C., 1962. Tables H-1, H-3, H-4.

In a city where owner-occupants of housing units are a distinct minority, families with household heads of Puerto Rican birth or parentage were least represented in the ownership group. Of the Puerto Rican families, 95.3 per cent rented the unit where they lived, compared with 86.8 per cent of those with nonwhite heads and 75.6 per cent of those with other white heads of households. (Table 19)

Table 20

Gross Rent, by Ethnic Group, New York City, 1960

| | | Percentages | |
Rent	Puerto Rican	Nonwhite	Other White
Total: Number	148, 714	305, 098	1, 624, 078
Percent	100. 0	100. 0	100. 0
Less than $20	0. 1	0. 1	0. 1
$20 to $39	7. 7	6. 4	4. 1
$40 to $59	36. 6	30. 2	20. 1
$60 to $79	37. 3	32. 3	29. 7
$80 to $99	11. 3	15. 9	18. 8
$100 or more	5. 1	12. 5	25. 4
No cash rent	1. 9	2. 6	1. 8
Median rent	$62. 00	$66. 00	$76. 00

Source: U.S. Bureau of the Census. U.S. Censuses of Population and Housing: 1960. Census Tracts. Final Report PHC(1)-104. Part 1. U.S. Government Printing Office, Washington, D.C., 1962. Tables H-2, H-3, H-4.

As the lowest-income population in the city, Puerto Ricans also paid less rent for renter-occupied units, but only slightly less than did the nonwhites. The median gross rent (the "middle" rent, with half the rents less and half exceeding it) for Puerto Ricans was $62; that for nonwhites was $66. In comparison, the other whites in general paid substantially higher rents. Their median was $76. (Table 20)

Table 21

Year Housing Structure Built, by Ethnic Group,
New York City, 1960

| Year Built | Percentages | | |
	Puerto Rican	Nonwhite	Other White
Total: Number	156,110	351,914	2,249,396
Percent	100.0	100.0	100.0
1950 to March 1960	8.8	10.9	13.5
1940 to 1949	3.9	5.1	7.3
1939 or earlier	87.3	84.0	79.2

Source: U.S. Bureau of the Census. U.S. Censuses of Population and Housing: 1960. Census Tracts. Final Report PHC(1)-104. Part 1. U.S. Government Printing Office, Washington, D.C., 1962. Tables H-1, H-3, H-4.

The Puerto Rican households are concentrated in the oldest residential structures in New York City. Of the households, 87.3 per cent were in structures built in 1939 or earlier, whereas 84 per cent of the nonwhite households and 79.2 per cent of the other white households were in the older buildings. (Table 21) The Puerto Rican homes also are more frequently in the structures with larger numbers of units than are the homes of the nonwhites and the other whites. Of Puerto Rican households, 85.4 per cent were in structures with five or more units, compared with 70.5 per cent for the nonwhites and 61.1 per cent for the other whites. (Table 22)

Though a significant number of Puerto Rican households are in the large, low-income public-housing projects where physical standards are maintained, 40.1 per cent of their households were in deteriorating and dilapidated structures. Thirty-three per cent of the nonwhites and just 11.0 per cent of the other whites were so badly housed. Furthermore, the differential among the ethnic groups is dramatic for units classified as "dilapidated"--housing that "does not provide safe and adequate shelter."[5] While 10.4 per cent of the Puerto Rican households and 8 per cent of the nonwhites lived in such units, only 1.8 per cent of the other whites were so housed. (Table 23)

Puerto Ricans residing in these households were crowded for

Table 22

Units in Housing Structures, by Ethnic Group,
New York City, 1960

Number of Units in Structure	Percentages		
	Puerto Rican	Nonwhite	Other White
Total	100. 0	100. 0	100. 0
1	2. 8	9. 5	14. 6
2	4. 2	9. 3	15. 8
3-4	7. 6	10. 7	8. 5
5 or more	85. 4	70. 5	61. 1

Source: U.S. Bureau of Census. U.S. Censuses of Population and Housing: 1960. Census Tracts. Final Report PHC(1)-104. Part 1. U.S. Government Printing Office, Washington, D.C., 1962. Tables H-1, H-3, H-4.

Table 23

Condition and Plumbing of Occupied Housing Units,
by Ethnic Group, New York City, 1960

Condition and Plumbing	Percentages		
	Puerto Rican	Nonwhite	Other White
Total	100. 0	100. 0	100. 0
Sound	59. 8	67. 0	89. 0
With all plumbing facilities	53. 8	57. 9	85. 2
Lacking all or some facilities	6. 0	9. 1	3. 8
Deteriorating	29. 7	25. 0	9. 2
With all plumbing facilities	24. 0	18. 6	7. 7
Lacking some or all facilities	5. 7	6. 4	1. 5
Dilapidated	10. 4	8. 0	1. 8

Source: U.S. Bureau of the Census. U.S. Censuses of Population and Housing: 1960. Census Tracts. Final Report PHC(1)-104. Part 1. U.S. Government Printing Office, Washington, D.C., 1962. Tables H-1, H-3, H-4.

space to a degree not true of the nonwhites and other whites. Of the households with a Puerto Rican head, 38.6 per cent were in units with 1.01 or more persons per room. Among nonwhite households, 22.1 per cent were crowded to this degree, compared to only 8.7 per cent of the other white households. (Table 24)

Thus, the information about the housing of Puerto Ricans parallels that characterizing their population. Just as they are the least educated, most frequently out of a job and looking for work, most concentrated in low-status occupations, and have the least family income of any identifiable ethnic population in New York City, so do

Table 24

Persons Per Room in Housing Units, by Ethnic Group,
New York City, 1960

Persons per Room	Percentages		
	Puerto Rican	Nonwhite	Other White
Total: Number of Units	156,110	352,554	2,145,781
Per cent	100.0	100.0	100.0
0.50 or less	11.9	28.6	36.7
0.51 to 0.75	17.7	20.1	28.5
0.76 to 1.01	31.8	29.2	26.1
1.01 or more	38.6	22.1	8.7

Source: U.S. Bureau of the Census. U.S. Censuses of Population
and Housing: 1960. Census Tracts. Final Report PHC(1)-104.
Part 1. U.S. Government Printing Office, Washington, D.C., 1962.
Tables H-1, H-3, H-4.

they live in housing units that are the most deteriorated or dilapidated,
and the most crowded. For this they pay slightly lower rents.

Health

Puerto Ricans in New York City, as reflected by public health records,
consistently maintain an intermediate rate relative to that of nonwhites
and other whites. This is shown by statistics on infant mortality,
active tuberculosis, and infectious venereal diseases. [6]

The mortality rate for Puerto Rican infants--the number of
deaths under one year of age per 1,000 live births--has hovered
around 30 for the past decade. The actual rate for 1963 was 28.4,
but annual fluctuations have produced almost this low a rate in prior
years, followed by higher rates. The nonwhite infant mortality rate
over the same decade has fluctuated around a rate of 40, the latest
being 38.9. The 1963 rate for the other whites was 19.5, continuing
the tendency to remain near 20 infant deaths per 1,000 live births.
Thus, the pattern for the decade has been a rate of about 20 for the
other whites, 30 for the Puerto Ricans, and 40 for the nonwhites.
(Table 25)

Similar relationships are pointed up in statistics on newly reported cases of active tuberculosis, all forms, in 1963. Puerto Ricans comprise 7.9 per cent of New York City's population, but they
comprise 13.8 per cent of new tuberculosis cases. Thus, the proportion of Puerto Rican cases was not quite twice the Puerto Rican
percentage in New York's population. The proportion of Negro tuberculosis cases was slightly more than three times their representation in the city's population. Of all new cases 46.5 per cent were
Negro, whereas Negroes account for 14 per cent of the city's population. In contrast, other whites contributed only 35.7 per cent of new

Table 25

Infant Mortality, by Ethnic Group
New York City, 1953-1963

| Year | Total | Deaths under 1 year per 1,000 live births | | |
		Puerto Rican	Nonwhite	Other White
1953	24. 4	29. 0	40. 5	20. 8
1954	23. 7	28. 8	37. 2	20. 2
1955	25. 8	34. 9	41. 0	21. 0
1956	24. 5	28. 8	38. 2	20. 3
1957	25. 0	30. 7	41. 9	19. 6
1958	26. 4	30. 8	43. 1	20. 8
1959	26. 5	32. 1	43. 3	20. 3
1960	26. 0	28. 4	42. 4	20. 3
1961	25. 6	30. 3	39. 7	19. 7
1962	27. 3	28. 2	43. 3	21. 1
1963	25. 9	28. 4	38. 9	19. 5

Source: New York City Department of Health. Summary of Vital
Statistics: 1962. The City of New York. Table 6; unpublished 1963
tabulation. New York City Department of Health.

Table 26

Newly Reported Cases of Active Tuberculosis, All Forms,
by Ethnic Group, New York City, 1963

Ethnic Group	Tuberculosis Cases	1960 Population
Total: Number	4,779	7,781,984
Per cent	100. 0	100. 0
Puerto Ricans	13. 8	7. 9
Negroes	46. 5	14. 0
Other whites	35. 7	77. 4
Other nonwhites	4. 0	. 7

Source: New York City Department of Health, unpublished 1963
tabulation.

tuberculosis cases--less than half their percentage of New York City's
population. As in infant mortality rates, then, Puerto Ricans are
between the other whites and the nonwhites in rate of new cases of
tuberculosis. (Table 26)

The much less adequate data on rates of infection with syphilis
and gonorrhea also show Puerto Rican rates in excess of those for
whites and lower than those for nonwhites. However, these statistics
should be interpreted as suggesting the possibility of ethnic differences
in true rates, not as establishing them. In the first place, the data

Table 27

Estimated Rates of Syphilis and Gonorrhea,
by Sex and Ethnic Group,
New York City, 1962[a]

Syphilis

Ethnic Group	Number of Cases		Rate per 100,000 Population	
	Male	Female	Male	Female
Spanish-sounding names	172	64	58.0	20.3
Nonwhites	1,079	525	186.1	78.6
Whites	1,267	192	40.7	5.6

Gonorrhea

Ethnic Group	Number of Cases		Rate per 100,000 Population	
Spanish-sounding names	824	125	277.7	39.6
Nonwhites	11,221	1,482	1,935.7	221.7
Whites	4,071	438	130.8	12.8

a. Cases based on public clinic diagnoses.
Source: Provided on request.

reflect only the cases diagnosed in public clinics. It is highly likely
that many such cases diagnosed by private physicians are not reported
and that this particularly minimizes the rates for whites. Second,
Puerto Ricans are identified only by a judgment that the name on the
record "sounds" Spanish. The degree of error thus introduced is
unknown and may be very large. It is safer merely to state that a
serious problem of venereal infection exists in New York City than
to emphasize differences in rates between ethnic groups. (Table 27)

A recent study indicates that a high rate of mental disability
may exist among Puerto Ricans in New York City. Based on responses to a list of symptoms, rather than past or present treatment
for disability, nearly half--48.8 per cent--of the sample of persons
born in Puerto Rico were classified as ranking in the highest of three
groups in degree of mental disability. In contrast, only 27.1 per
cent of the Negroes were so classified, and no other ethnic or religious group approached the Puerto Rican rate. (Table 28)

The authors of the study themselves state:

While one may question the validity of this instrument as a
measure of mental disability, especially when administered to a
Puerto Rican-born population, the size of the difference is such as
to strongly suggest that in our Puerto Rican population in New York
City we are dealing with a group that is experiencing difficult problems of psychological adjustment. [7]

Table 28

High Mental Disability Scores, by Ethnic Group,
Area of New York City, 1960-1961

Ethnic Group	Percentage with High Scores
Puerto Ricans (Born in Puerto Rico)	48. 8%
Non-Irish Catholics	37. 0
Jewish	33. 3
Protestants	27. 8
Negroes	27. 1
Irish	15. 5

Source: Edward A. Suchman, Raymond Maurice, Martin Goldman, and Daniel Rosenblatt, Sociocultural Variations in Illness and Medical Care. Unpublished manuscript, 1963, p. 14.

References

1. See Table 6, footnote a.
2. Grade school, as used here, refers to eight grades of education.
3. These figures are for the New York Standard Metropolitan Statistical Area and include 16,856 Puerto Ricans living in Westchester, Nassau, Suffolk, and Rockland Counties, in addition to those in New York City. Comparable data are not available currently for New York City alone. Puerto Ricans living outside the city limits have somewhat higher educational attainment than those within, so the percentages underestimate the dropout rates characteristic of New York City's Puerto Ricans. The numbers undoubtedly include a few persons still in school in 1960, but it is unlikely that the number of subsequent high-school completions would change the percentages greatly.
4. See footnote a, Table 11.
5. U.S. Bureau of the Census. U.S. Censuses of Population and Housing: 1960. Census Tracts. Final Report PHC(1)-104. Part 1. U.S. Government Printing Office, Washington, D.C., 1962.
6. Statistics for Puerto Ricans are available only when place of birth (or place of mother's birth on birth certificates) is a part of the record. For this reason the variety of statistics for color groups cannot be extended to the Puerto Rican population. Since place of birth is the basis of classification, these statistics are not entirely comparable to the census definition which, in addition to those born in Puerto Rico, includes as Puerto Ricans those born elsewhere but with one or both parents born in Puerto Rico.
7. Edward A. Suchman, Raymond Maurice, Martin Goldman, and Daniel Rosenblatt, Sociocultural Variations in Illness and Medical Care. Unpublished manuscript, 1963, p. 14.

Part III

PUERTO RICAN CHILDREN IN MAINLAND SCHOOLS

Eugene Bucchioni

THE DAILY ROUND OF LIFE IN THE SCHOOL

The curriculum is but one of many factors affecting life within the classroom. Daily, in the classroom, the teacher, in discharging her professional duties and responsibilities, attempts to implement the curriculum and its numerous provisions by making available the suggested experiences and activities, by utilizing the recommended materials and methods of instruction, and by observing the required time allotments. Children arrive early in the morning, their attendance is taken, and the acting out of the curriculum then begins.

Concurrently with the acting out of the curriculum, however, other things occur as well. Along with the mandated experiences and activities of the curriculum, children talk, become noisy, and are reprimanded accordingly. There are many requests for permission to get drinks or to use the toilets. The pencil sharpener and the waste paper basket become the crowded sites of frequent small meetings as children approach these locations, ostensibly to sharpen their pencils and discard paper but instead remain to chat or to laugh and play. Questions and answers, the playing of games, singing songs, recess periods for milk, classroom monitors performing their roles, the giving of homework assignments, fire drills, getting on line, standing up and sitting down are all significant components of classroom life.

The combination of the interaction of various curriculum requirements and these patterns of child behavior in the classroom result in an intricate round of life that is repeated daily, weekly and monthly in each elementary school. But this round of life, as varied and highly complicated as it is, becomes still more complex as Puerto Rican children interact with it and act out their several roles as chil-

Reprinted by permission from A Sociological Analysis of the Functioning of Elementary Education for Puerto Rican Children, (Unpublished Doctoral Dissertation, New School for Social Research, 1965), pp. 73-151.

dren in elementary school, and as young members of lower classes and participants in Puerto Rican culture.

Miss Dwight, the Curriculum, and los Niños Puertorriqueños[1]

Miss Dwight was seated at her classroom desk handscoring her fourth grade class's achievement tests when the 8:45 bell rang. She clipped the papers and arranged them in a neat pile on the metal file cabinet to her right, put out the room lights, and locked the door after her.

The third grade and other fourth grade teachers had begun to gather inside the side entrance to the building and took the opportunity to talk among themselves for a few minutes before admitting their lines of classes into the building.

Miss Dwight joined the group and said, "I've just been marking the achievement tests and I wish they hadn't been given."

"I know what you mean," said Mrs. Maran.

"How can almost everyone of the children miss a simple question like the one about musical instruments?"

"The Puerto Ricans seem to learn absolutely nothing--either here or at home."

"Yes," said Miss Dwight, "all they seem to care about is sleeping, eating, playing, and having parties."

"But you know ... the ones in my third grade class are very well behaved. Authority means something to them."

"Too bad they have to grow up!" said Miss Dwight. "Things sure take a turn for the worse then."

"Something's wrong somewhere," said Mrs. Maran.

"Well, we'd better get the children."

Miss Dwight moved to the door, beckoned her class to enter the building, and led the double line to their classroom. She held the keys out to Juan, who opened the door and switched the lights on quickly before another classmate, running to the switch, could beat him to it.

The children talked quietly among themselves as they went past the bookcase to hang their coats on the hooks in the closets. The two coatroom monitors took their stations in the closet at either end and saw that no one remained there longer than necessary. They also made certain that the children entered the closet at the left side and went out at the right.

Maria was watering the plants which sat on the long shelves built in front of the windows. She took particular care of the cactus plants and consulted with Miss Dwight as to the proper amount of water to be given them. Antonio adjusted the shades so that the bright morning sunlight did not streak across the desks and into eyes.

The bulletin board on the wall opposite the windows was filled with samples of children's written work, arranged in columns, some papers boasting glittering colored stars while others were devoid of similar commendation. To one end of the bulletin board were charts with colorful pictures illustrating words that begin with different consonants. The remainder of the bulletin board was devoted to a crudely drawn map, water-colored by the children, with street names indicated, of a twenty block radius around the school. Cracked, yellowed plaster hung from almost all of the room's wall space. The lighting for the room came from two rows of three huge globes that were suspended from the ceiling by long chains.

Miss Dwight finished looking over the plans she had written for the day's work. She took the classroom in with a glance and noticed that about half the class was already seated and ready for the day's work with a notebook and pencil on most desks.

"Children," she said, "please get to your seats now."

As the children moved to obey, some a little slowly, some more rapidly, Miss Dwight called the name of each child in the first seat across the room for the attendance of each row. The names of the boys and girls absent were called out and Miss Dwight made the appropriate notations in her attendance register.

As she closed the book, about to put it in its place in the metal file cabinet, Dolores and Jesús entered the room, late. Miss Dwight glanced at them, made the necessary corrections in her register, and asked, "Do you have a note for being late?"

Dolores replied breathlessly, "Maestra, el reloj despertador se rompió y ..."

"Dolores, speak in English please. You know that I don't understand Spanish."

"Sí, maestra. ¡Cómo no! Deh alarrme clock. Eet broken bery bad. My mama say ..."

"Please, Dolores. We've taken enough of the class's time for this. Furthermore, if it's not your alarm clock, it's having to go to the store, or helping dress your brother or some other excuse. You will have to learn to come to school on time. You too, Jesús! You have been coming to school long enough to realize that one of the important rules is to be early in the morning. And another thing, you are to bring a note each time you are late or absent. I expect a note from each of you tomorrow morning. And I'm tired of changing my attendance report every time you both come in late."

Miss Dwight turned to the class and asked for two volunteers to be Mr. and Mrs. America for the opening exercises. She looked at the many hands that were raised in her class of thirty-three children, and selected Alan and Carmen. Carmen smiled as she walked quickly to the front of the room. She joined Alan in asking the class to rise for the pledge of allegiance to the flag. Miss Dwight also rose, faced the flag, and helped to lead the class over such words as allegiance, republic, indivisible, and justice.

During the first few months of school the class sang America, but Miss Dwight had recently advanced them, after much drilling, to The Star Spangled Banner. Miss Dwight winced when she heard such phrases as "was so proudly we held" and "bought estripes and bri destars." Other words were also unintelligible: perilous, proof, ramparts.

Some of the children moved to seat themselves after the song. Miss Dwight stared in the direction of several of them, folded her hands, bowed her head, and followed Alan and Carmen as they led the class in prayer.

"Almighty God, we acknowledge our dependence on Thee. We beg Thy blessings on us, our parents, our teachers, and our country."

The children seated themselves and Miss Dwight looked at her planbook briefly. Some of the children talked with each other, a few looked through their desks for various papers and books, and others slumped down in their seats.

"Class, please open your number books to page 46. Henry, would you start reading the instructions at the top of the page."

Henry read the title, "'Learning more about subtraction.' These are problems that ask how many are left. To find the answer you must subtract."

"Helena, please read the first problem aloud."

"Dere were seex duckes esweemin een a pon. Two a dem eswam away. How many were lef?"

Miss Dwight said, "Helena, that's not quite right. You're not pronouncing the words correctly. Say, there were six ducks swimming in a pond. Two of them swam away. How many were left?"

Helena repeated the question incorrectly. Miss Dwight said, "That's better. Now, how many do you have left?"

Miss Dwight called on Juan. He tilted his head to the side and stared ahead, as Miss Dwight waited for an answer. Several children raised their hands to be called on, and others buried their heads in their books or rummaged through their desks.

"Juan, do you or don't you understand this problem?"

He did not answer. His grip tightened on the book as he continued to peer into it.

"Juan, I asked you a question and I expect an answer."

"Maestra, dees word I donno. Qué quiere decir?"

"Spell the word for us."

"S-w-i-m-m-i-n-g."

"That's swimming. To move in the water."

"Nadando," called out Manuel in explanation.

Juan looked into his book again and Miss Dwight waited in silence, keeping the class quiet by glancing around and resting her gaze on those who talked or fidgeted in their seats.

Manuel raised his hand and asked to go to the boys' room. "No, Manuel, you will have to wait until I take the entire class at ten o'clock."

Manuel turned to his neighbor, Pedro, and spoke rapidly and not too softly. "Pero tengo que ir al baño ahora mismo," Miss Dwight heard him say.

"No talking, Manuel! Juan please read the problem aloud to the class."

"Dere were seex duckes esweeming to...."

"To-geth-er," said Miss Dwight.

"...to-ged-der een a pon. Two a dem eswam away. How many were lef?"

"What is it, Juan?"

"Lef? No comprendo lef. What mean lef, teacha?"

"It means how many stayed together after the two ducks went swimming away."

"Ah, sí, ahora comprendo," he said rapidly, sitting taller in his seat.

He looked into his book and his lips began to move as he

reread the problem silently. Miss Dwight said, "Juan, we have taken a long time on this problem. Do you know how to solve it?"

"Seex ... takaway two."

Manuel shouted, "Seis menos dos."

"Quiet, Manuel," said Miss Dwight. Juan turned his head to the window. "Juan, please try to pay attention. Take out your squared material and work it out. And," she addressed the class, "if you do not have the answer, I want you to do the same."

The children, some quickly, and others more slowly, searched in their desks for the arithmetic materials. Books from overstuffed desks fell onto the floor and some children took this opportunity to walk to the basket with crumpled scrap paper they found in their desks. Others went to the pencil sharpener that was attached to the side of the bookcase where they conversed in soft tones.

"Get to your desks," called out Miss Dwight. "This moving about has got to stop!" When order was restored, she continued, "Class, how many ones' squares do you need to solve this problem?"

The same few hands that were raised previously went up again. Miss Dwight ignored these offers of assistance. The remainder of the class looked back into their books at the problem. More hands were raised.

"Juan, how many do you need?"

"Seex."

"Fine. Now take them out of your holder and place them separately on your desk. Now, how many should you take away?"

Again, heads turned to page 46.

"Two," Juan answered, as he picked up two squares of paper.

"How many are left?"

"Uno, dos, tres, cuatro," he answered as he tapped each square that remained.

"No, Juan. One, two, three, four."

Miss Dwight took a deep breath and adjusted her posture. She then read the second problem to the class. She called on Marvin for the solution and received an immediate correct answer.

"Children, these problems go on to the next page. When you have free time today, you are to do these two pages. Otherwise, they are part of your homework. Make an example of each one. And now, put all your arithmetic materials away. It's ten o'clock, and we must go to the lavatories and then to the basement for physical education. Row one, line up. No talking."

The children began to talk loudly. Miss Dwight said, "Sit down, children. We will have to stay here if you do not line up quickly and quietly. And Manuel and Pedro, school is no place for you to be leaping out of your seats and racing others to the front of the room. Behave yourselves."

"Now, let us try again. And keep quiet on line. Row one, stand. Walk to the front of the room. Row two."

Miss Dwight gave each row time to move slowly and then called the rest of the class in the same manner. She gave the keys to Juan, watched him lock the door and turn off the light switch, tried the door handle to make certain it was locked, and reminded him to pull the door closed after the class was out of the room. He nodded and gave her a grin as he said, "Sí, maestra."

Miss Dwight led the class to the end of the hallway and lined up the boys in front of the boys' toilet and the girls at theirs. "Hurry, boys, three at a time. Girls, four at a time. Please don't waste time as it's ten past ten and we have the basement only until it's ten thirty."

As a boy or girl came out of the lavatories, another child went in. Miss Dwight opened the door to the boys' room frequently and could see, through the mirror to the left, the boys standing at the urinals. "Wash your hands, boys, and if you are ready, come out so that the others might come in."

Antonio was out as fast as he had gone in. Miss Dwight felt his dry hands and sent him back to wash them. The girls were finished and standing on line. Miss Dwight said, "Girls, I'm sure you remembered to wash your hands. If anyone has forgotten, please go back and do it now."

Four girls returned to the girl's room and came out complaining that there was no soap in the dispensers. "Well, girls, we have soap in our room. You can wash your hands later. Now, class, let's be on our way."

Miss Dwight walked to the left of her class line and kept at about the middle. In this way, she was able to control the stragglers at the end of the line and watch for talking in the hallway. The line leaders stopped at the end of the next hall, waiting for instructions to make a turn to the left. There was some talking, but Miss Dwight restored silence and then instructed the line leaders to continue. She moved to the front of the line when they reached the staircase, and led them slowly down to the basement.

"Children, this morning we are going to continue with the

square dance. You remember that I explained that this is an early American dance that the first settlers in this country used to do. Today, many people still enjoy doing this kind of dancing. I need eight children; four boys and four girls for the first set."

Most of the children showed eagerness to participate by waving their hands and calling out, "Me!" or by shouting, "Pleez, teacha!" Some children hopped up and down and a few took their partners' hands and skipped about. Miss Dwight asked the class to calm down, selected some of the more eager children, and told the rest of the class to sit on the benches along the wall.

She arranged the four boys opposite the girls and gave brief instructions as to how to begin the dance. She put the Virginia Reel on the record player and started the record. The children danced in time to the rapid music. Miss Dwight took the arm of different children at times to help them with directions and to lead them to the new partners during the successive phases of the dance.

"Miss Dwight," complained Arthur, "Carmen doesn't know how to do this dance. She is always going the wrong way and getting me all mixed up."

"Arthur, be patient. You did this dance last year. And besides, Carmen is just learning our language. It is not easy to be new to everything all at once and maybe she doesn't understand directions."

Miss Dwight's attention was suddenly diverted to the children seated on the benches. They were talking, some were pushing and teasing others, some were laughing, and some were just moving about. She asked the children who had danced to sit down, then asked for quiet, and proceeded to select the next group of eight. She chose the children who had been making the most noise and disturbance, gave them the necessary instructions, and played the record once more. When the group had gotten halfway through the dance, another class entered the basement. Exclamations of annoyance came from those who had not yet danced. Miss Dwight lined up her class and spoke with Mrs. Frazier who had led her class to the benches.

"Hi, Mary. Boy! What a waste this morning has been. Two arithmetic problems and only half the class danced."

"Same here. All I do is give directions and explain, explain, explain! You'd think that by the time they get to the sixth grade they'd be able to read ten science pages by themselves."

"But we haven't even got enough tests, even if they could read them. It's a joke. I'm supposed to find time today for social studies, reading, language arts, writing, and health. Not to mention art and music."

"The third month of school and nothing across yet," said Mrs. Frazier.

"Yes, and I don't dare question most of the children about their work. I'm sure that most of what I say has gone out of the window. Most of them listen quietly and never ask a question, except now and then. Well, see you at lunch, Mary."

Miss Dwight reorganized her class and led them back to the classroom. Felipe came up to her at her desk and asked to go to the boys' room. "No, Felipe, you were there only twenty minutes ago."

"But, teacha, I deen have to make den."

"All right, but this will be the last time you leave the room this morning. And don't call me teacher. I have a name. Learn it!" Felipe left the room quickly. When he returned, the class was ready to begin a social studies discussion of the neighborhood.

"Yesterday, class," said Miss Dwight, "we talked of the block you live on. Many of you told us about your own block: what the houses look like, where you play, where you go to buy your groceries, drugs, and candy, and where your library, church, and police station are located. Today, let us talk about different neighborhoods right here in New York City and decide whether the differences make people live in different ways than you do. Who can tell me what the five boroughs of New York City are?"

Ronald, Frieda, and Stephen raised their hands. Some children opened their notebooks to find their listing of the boroughs, but other children went to the pencil sharpener or waste paper basket.

"Boys and girls, sit down and keep still." "Now what is the answer?"

Miss Dwight called on Frieda who answered, "Manhattan, Brooklyn, Queens, Bronx, and ..." She could not think of the fifth borough, and Stuart completed the answer with, "Staten Island."

"Children, please sit up tall," said Miss Dwight. "Your feet belong on the floor, and not on the rungs of your desks. And everyone should be listening. Some of you do not look as if you are paying attention. To continue, let us talk about the borough of Queens where I live. I'll write a list on the blackboard of points of comparison that we can make between your neighborhood and an average neighborhood or suburb of Queens. Now, what things can we compare?"

Many hands were raised, and a list was developed:

kinds of houses
places to shop for food and clothing
churches
schools
libraries
playgrounds

Miss Dwight explained, "Many of the houses in my neighborhood are two family houses. One family lives on the first floor and another family lives upstairs."

Jesús asked, "Each family--they have their own baño?"

Miss Dwight asked, "Baño?"

Jesús replied, "Sí, where you go to wash yourself."

"You mean bathroom," said Miss Dwight. "Yes, they do."

"Dees I like," said Jesús. "The same baño the odder people use, we use too. And sometimes I cannot get een dere neber. For dat, I am een the morning late."

María added, "I too. And mama rrush me when I trry to take a bat. Me she tell not to make people in the beeldeen wait. Dice que no tengo derecho a hacer que espere tanto a la gente."

"English, children," requested Miss Dwight. "You will find, children, that many families have houses all to themselves, with sometimes two bathrooms upstairs--one for each bedroom and one on the first floor too."

"Only bery rreech peepool leebe een doz places," said Juan.

"Not exactly rich, Juan. But they do work hard, and every day."

"My papa, he say he work hard, every day--eben on Sunday. Sometime he don habe to work on Sunday. He get a day to estay home." Juan added, "And heem I hear say, and my mama say too, neber weel we be able to move to a more better place to leebe."

"It is difficult, sometimes, to earn enough money to do everything we want. It's important for you to remember that your work in school will some day help you to get a better job, earn more money, and live in a good home. This is why I am here: to help you live better. But let us remember that while we work toward something better, we must accept what we have now and try to appreciate the good things we have. For instance, what do you have that is good in your way of living?"

Faces took on various expressions and mixed comments were made.

"A lot--we gotta a lot een weech to play."

"I habe a bedroom weed my brodder."

"And neber I am hungry like de oder keeds in my beeldeen who are bery hungry all dee days."

"Yes, when we have these basic comforts, we do have something to be thankful for. And that reminds me that it is time for our milk. Will the people we chose to give it out this week please do that now? And if you brought cookies, you may get them."

Miss Dwight sat at her desk and worked on the achievement tests while the children drank their milk and chatted. She overheard a few children make complaints about their living conditions. There was some talking in Spanish. When the milk containers had been discarded, she resumed their social studies lesson. Marvin began to tell of his cousin who lives on Long Island.

"My uncle drives my cousin, Raymond, to school every day. And I saw his school. It's not big like this one. And it's new. They have a gym with everything in it. They even have one of those things that they use in the circus to jump on. There's a big cafeteria and they have flowers and trees in front of the school. And the walls in the room are pretty colors."

"Long Island, children, is not in New York City. It is an island, almost 800 miles long, right outside of New York City. Many people have moved there because it is like the country, and they have built new modern schools and they have shopping centers where you have all the stores you need all together. There are very few apartment houses. Almost every family has its own house. The people who live near each other often get together for parties and dinner."

"Dat we'll do neber. My papa say eet ees too hard to change. Peepool won let you."

"No, Juan. That is not always true. If you study and work hard, and show people that you want to do what is right, they will let you improve yourself. It takes time and patience. We've seen today, children, that people in different places live in different ways, and I hope to continue this discussion tomorrow. For homework, I would like you to bring in pictures of houses, schools, churches, and playgrounds. And tomorrow, we will try to decide what kind of community these pictures fit into and compare them with your own. We have a half hour before lunch. Please open your notebooks to the English section and write a heading for today's work. I would like you to write a paragraph about our discussion today in social studies. Elsa, why is it taking you so long to find a page to write on?"

"An emty page, I cannot fin, teacha."

"How many times have I told you to keep at least five blank pages in each subject section of your notebook?"

"I don have no more paper."

"Well, why don't you ask your mother to buy you some?"

"I deed. Friday she say."

"But tomorrow is Tuesday. That means that you will have to borrow paper from a classmate for the entire week."

Several children were quick to offer Elsa paper. She accepted a few sheets and inserted the pages into her book. Miss Dwight walked around the room and stopped at many of the desks to help pupils in their work and to prod others to begin. Several children asked for the spelling of certain words. Miss Dwight stopped at Pedro's desk.

"Pedro, not 'Today we learn about new york.' It's 'learned' with an 'ed' ending to mean past time. Also New York is capitalized because it is the name of a place."

"I teenk New York ees only where I am."

"No, Pedro, you live in Manhattan which is only a small part of our state, which is also called New York."

Pedro shrugged his shoulders and Miss Dwight moved a few desks away and read, silently, the paragraph that Juan had written:

I libe in nu yor city and so do oder
many pipul who hab ril jauses
i wil not oways lib were I
lib because i wil studi in escool.

Miss Dwight smiled and pointed out the spelling, punctuation, and capitalization errors. "Juan, this is a very good beginning. I hope you will add a few details to show in what ways other people live differently than you do."

"Sí, maestra, cómo no." He took his pencil and proceeded to the next sentence.

"Tomás, please stop holding your head up and get your elbow off the desk. What time did you go to bed last night?"

"Carajo," whispered Tomás. "Twelve o'clock, teacha."

"Why so late?"

"My moder and fader had a party. Eet was een de room where I esleep."

"Well, couldn't you have slept in your parents' room until the party was over?"

"No, on de bed were too many coat. We don habe no room in de closet for de coat of de peepool."

"Well, Tomás, I hope you will go to bed early tonight so that you are rested tomorrow."

"Sí, maestra, I am bery tired."

"Children it is time to get ready for lunch. Will those children who are going home for lunch get their clothing?"

The children made much noise as they got their clothing and moved back to their seats. Most of the class remained in school for lunch, and Miss Dwight called them, row by row, to get their clothing. At the sound of the bell, she dismissed those who were leaving the building, and after having reminded them to go directly home and to be back before the late bell, then called the remainder of the class on line.

"Children, the principal made a definite point of telling the teachers that the behavior and noise in the lunchroom is terrible. I hope I can be proud of you and that you will behave as you should, get your food quietly, eat quickly, and clean your places before you leave."

Juan took care of the lights and door and Miss Dwight led the class through the crowded hallways to the lunchroom. She stopped at the entrance and observed the actions of many of the children as they pushed each other, called out to friends, approached their tables at a half run, and slammed the metal trays down. She saw many children who had already finished eating return their trays with salads and vegetables untouched. She turned to enter the teachers' room.

She poured herself a cup of coffee, chose a seat next to Mary Frazier, and began to unwrap her sandwich. The teachers' room was not large and was undecorated, except for a small bulletin board with leaflets tacked to it and notes and letters from teachers who had either left or were on leave. There was a brown leather couch along a small wall space and three matching easy chairs along another side. Teachers from all grades filled the three tables. Conversation ranged from fashions to housework to theater to curriculum.

"How was the rest of your morning, Frances?" Mary Frazier asked Miss Dwight.

"Not too bad. I did some social studies and a little English. But I must tell you about Juan."

"Before you do," interrupted Mary, "why not get your coffee and relax a little?"

Frances Dwight went to the small kitchen in the teachers' room and poured herself a cup of coffee. Edith, who sat opposite Mary said, "What's the use of worrying about these kids? Between their lousy way of living and their Spanish, we're lost before we begin."

Frances returned to the table in time to hear Edith's remark and said, "That's just what I mean about Juan. This morning we had a class discussion in social studies and he told how his father works so hard. His parents are sure they'll never get anywhere. It's sad."

"Well," said Mary, "how can they when they don't know anything, go anywhere, or read anything?"

"That reminds me," said Edith, "of a story I heard of a kid who had an assignment to collect pictures of colorful gardens from magazines. He came in the next day without any pictures. When his teacher asked why he replied, 'All we got home is love 'n murder.' Really, I can't wait to get away from these dirty kids. Sometimes, I could faint when I get close to them."

"Edith," said Mary, "let's face it. We are in a slum neighborhood, and as far as the Puerto Ricans go, only the lower class has migrated here."

"True," said Frances. "They're told about the wonderful opportunities for them in America. If they knew any better, they wouldn't live the way they do."

"They act like animals, too. But they're worse in high school. I wouldn't teach there if you doubled my salary."

"You'll have tenure this year, won't you?" Mary asked Edith.

"Yes, and then the hell with all this. No more of this for me."

"But," said Mary, "what if all the teachers felt the way you do. I get discouraged too, but they are in this country and we have a job to do. They are American citizens you know, and we have to teach them how to live here."

"So far, they've been useless," said Edith. "All you see in the newspapers are gang wars, dope addicts, and rapes. You know it is so dangerous here that we have to walk to the subway together."

"Oh, Edith, it's not really as bad as all that," said Frances.

"No, it's worse. It was bad enough when we had the Negroes. Now the goddamn spics too. Why even the Negroes despise these damn Puerto Ricans."

"Look," said Mary, "we've got them, so let's do the best we can."

"Another thing. What can you do with all this experience learning?" asked Edith. "If you fit in all these experiences, there's no time left to teach. These kids need good old-fashioned drill and lots of it. And what child can count from five to ten without fingers or one's strips?"

"What really bothers me," said Frances, "is all the talking in Spanish. And I'll flip if just one more child calls me 'teacha' today."

"When they speak Spanish, they really prattle like monkeys. I'm sure they're not even trying to learn English," said Edith.

"Wait," said Mary. "Remember that Spanish is natural to them. How would you like the pressure of learning a new language and new subjects all at the same time?'

"Mary," said Edith, "you're entirely too sympathetic. You live in a dream world. Do you really think for one minute that these kids will ever amount to anything? In ten years you'll be unable to recognize New York because there will be so many Puerto Ricans here."

"Well," said Mary, "I can't help feeling sorry for these people. They are so persecuted from all sides and they need help, and lots of it."

The bell rang and the teachers cleared their places at the table and filed out to the yard to get their classes. Miss Dwight called her class into the building, led them to the room and Juan opened the door. The children seated themselves and Miss Dwight called them, row by row, to put their clothing away. She attempted to keep the children quiet by alternately saying, "Quiet, boys and girls," or "Keep still, children."

"I noticed, children, that the lunch didn't go over too well to- day. I saw many salads and vegetables untouched. Would someone care to explain why?"

María raised her hand. "Sí, maestra, the corn eet habe no taste, and the sald was just lechuga."

"Lettuce," called out one of the children.

María continued, "My mama she make a sald dat taste so good."

"Well, we all do have different ways of preparing food so that it tastes good to us, but isn't it necessary to have a variety of foods each day?"

The class showed no response to this query. Miss Dwight continued, "Let us discuss a proper breakfast."

"Who has a suggestion?"

Roger and Antonio began to talk and Miss Dwight asked them to pay attention. They glanced at each other and smiled. Roger looked at the clock and then stared ahead, while Antonio picked up a pencil and started to scratch a groove deeper in his desk.

"Antonio, that is not your property that you are ruining. Many children will use that desk after you. I think you should leave it as you found it. Now put the pencil down and stop this nonsense. Do you hear?"

Antonio uttered a Spanish obscenity. He did not lower his voice when making this remark. Most of the children looked at one another, showing shock, and some giggled.

"Antonio, what did you say? In English!"

He repeated the obscenity.

"Antonio, stand up and tell me in English what you said."

Antonio did not answer. He looked away from her.

"I'm waiting for your answer, Antonio. What does that mean?"

He stared at Miss Dwight.

"Would anyone in the class care to translate for me?"

"Maestra, it ees a bad teeng he say. We cannot say."

"Thank you, Juan." Miss Dwight turned to Antonio and suggested, "Perhaps you would like to repeat it to your mother at a conference."

"No, teacha, I am bery sorry. I do not mean eet. No more will I say eet."

"All right, Antonio, I will believe you. And I hope you will control your feelings better in the future. People just don't burst out and call each other names whenever they feel like it. You must learn how to cooperate more with others. We have to live with many people in this world, and it's time you've learned that everything does not always go the way you want it to. Now sit down and behave yourself."

She turned to the class. "Now, what is a food that we should eat at breakfast time?"

Marvin said, "Cereal."

"Fine. What else should you have for breakfast?"

"Café," answered another child.

"Coffee? No, coffee does not nourish you. It doesn't help you to grow strong. What can you drink that is good for your bones and teeth?"

Several children called out, "Milk!"

"Yes, milk. Milk has calcium in it. There is one more thing you should have at breakfast time."

David interrupted, "Miss Dwight, what is calcium?"

"I'm glad you asked, David. Children, I wish more of you would ask me to explain words that you don't understand. Calcium is a mineral. Our bodies need minerals and vitamins, just as a car needs gas and oil. Without the different minerals and vitamins, our bodies would break down and become sick. Each vitamin has a special job to do. Calcium makes our bones and teeth strong. Now what else besides milk and cereal should we have at breakfast time?"

She paused for a suggestion. None came, so she added, "Orange juice. Orange juice is for vitamin C."

María raised her hand. "What ees beetameen C?"

"Each vitamin has a letter and that is a vitamin we get from citrus fruits. I'll make a list of these items on the blackboard while you are making a heading for today in the health section of your notebooks and copy the list. Perhaps you can show the list to mother so that she, too, will understand what the best foods are for you and the family. Now, what are other foods that we should eat each day?"

"Bread?"

"Yes, and whole wheat or rye bread is better than white because the flour has not been whitened. That means that there is more food value in these other breads."

"Meat?"

"Good. Each day you should have some meat or eggs or cheese. These are called protein foods and they help to build your bodies. What goes with meat?"

"Tomatoes?"

"Well, yes. Also, vegetables that are green. Can you name some?"

"Espeenach?"

"Peas."

"Fine. We have others, too, cabbage, stringbeans, broccoli, asparagus, and many more. Every day you should have a salad, too. If you have these foods each day, you are sure to be getting all the vitamins and minerals that your body needs and you will be healthier and stronger."

Manuel raised his hand. "Teacha, my mama she cook so deeferent. Our beshtabools are oways jellow and white, like corn and rrice. We habe beans, too. But mama don make doz oder teengs. Neber I heard of some of dem."

"This is why we are making a list, Manuel. Perhaps your mother will be interested in trying some of these foods. I think your family might find it fun to eat different foods. Children, why not ask mother to give you, each day, one of these foods on the list? And if you like it, she can serve it again. Little by little, you will have a balanced diet."

"It's almost one-thirty and we had better get into our reading groups. I'll work first with the Bluebirds. While I do that, I want the Little Red Group to finish the reading exercises you started yesterday, and the Thunderbirds can work on the paragraphs you started this morning in social studies. Bluebirds, bring your chairs and reading books up to the front of the room."

Some children pushed their chairs and Miss Dwight told them to carry them. Others who were talking were told to stop or they would be given additional homework assignments. Miss Dwight wrote a list of words on the board and said to the children, "Today we are going to read a story about a little boy and girl just your age who go with their uncle to a wharf. As I say the words on the board, you look at them and try to remember them. 'Wharf, trawler, pier, cabin, galley, stern, aft, salmon.' Now I want you to look these words up in the dictionary that is in the back section of your reading books and be prepared to tell me the meaning of each word."

She then addressed the children of the Little Red Group. Some were still working on the exercises in the reading workbooks. Three children who had finished this work were standing at the bulletin board before a world map and appeared to be discussing anything but geography.

"Will the children in the Little Red Group take your workbooks and chairs to the back of the room now?" The ten children followed directions and Miss Dwight started the review of the first exercise. "Vera, read the first sentence with your answer."

"'Fran has a ...' I don't know that word."

"'Ewe.' You pronounce it like the word 'y-o-u.'"

"'... ewe lamb.'"

"Yes, that is right. José, do the next."

"I couldn't do eet, teacha."

"Why not?"

"I deen read de story. I was home."

"Don't you know that you are supposed to catch up on your reading when you come back after being absent?"

"Sí, but I deen habe not enough time."

"Well, take the book and go to your seat and read it now."

Miss Dwight looked over the Bluebird group. "Bluebirds, if you continue to talk, I will have you write the meanings of those words and write them in sentences of your own. Continue your work quietly."

She turned back to the Little Red Group. "Susan, do the second one."

"The name of the ewe lamb is Fluffy."

"Correct. Antonio, the next."

"I don know what eet mean."

"Linda, read it please. Read it without the answer so then Antonio can answer it."

"'Jerry works in a ...'"

"Antonio, finish the sentence."

He looked into his notebook. Miss Dwight asked, "Antonio, do you know where he worked?"

"No."

"Get the book and look for the answer."

Antonio went to his desk for the book, came back to his chair, and turned the pages slowly, trying to find the story.

"Antonio, why don't you use the table of contents?" You can find the story very quickly this way."

He turned back to the table of contents, found the page number and after several moments, found the story.

"Now, look quickly," Miss Dwight said, "for the part that tells where Jerry works."

He used his finger to underline the sentences as he began to look methodically down the first page.

"Antonio, we read the story only yesterday. Can't you remember that the first few pages are about the lambs? You will find your answer further on in the story. There is no time to wait for you to find it now. Continue to look for the answer when you return to your seat. Children, we will finish this exercise tomorrow. Make sure that you have completed all the questions, so that we will be able to review this rapidly."

She spoke to the third reading group. "Thunderbirds, we have no time for reading today, I will start with your group in the morning. Bluebirds, go back to your seats now. We will start to read our new story tomorrow."

The children moved noisily. Miss Dwight ignored the momentary confusion while she continued to consult the planbook at her desk.

"We just have time before the bell rings to talk about our Christmas party. First, we need to divide the class into committees for entertainment, decorations, and refreshments. I'll write the committee titles on the blackboard and you decide which ones you want to be on."

Many children raised their hands. When Miss Dwight had finished writing on the board, she turned to see almost every hand waving energetically and voices grew louder as children began to call out. When Miss Dwight called for silence and asked each child for his and her preference, many more hands went up. The lists of names were noted on the blackboard.

"Each committee will have a special assignment and special things to do. Today, let's decide what the decoration committee will do."

Suggestions were shouted out from different parts of the room. The voices resounded. Miss Dwight raised her voice. "Children, if you continue to call out like this, we will have no party. We studied in our language arts lesson yesterday about how to hold a discussion. Please try to remember this discussion and all the rules we talked about, and be courteous so that you will all have a chance to be heard."

The class quieted down and Miss Dwight nodded to different children for their suggestions.

"Let's make baskets for our candy."

"I can make a Santa Claus for the door."

"Esnow for de weendo."

"Paper Christmas trees for the bulletin board."

"Fine. Those are enough ideas for now. Tomorrow, the

decoration committee can meet and plan the work to be done. Let us give the entertainment committee something to work on."

Again, there was much rapid talk while the children offered suggestions and decided upon a program. The class soon developed a long list of dancers and singers.

"I can see that we will need several more hours for our party than we have planned in order to fit in all of this entertainment. The bell is about to ring! I will write your homework on the blackboard after I explain the assignment. Copy it and be sure to take home all the books you need. Do spelling unit number ten, part B. Look at the new words carefully and write the answers to all the questions. If you did not finish your social studies paragraphs today, finish them for homework. And last, I want each of you to find at least three pictures from magazines and newspapers of different kinds of homes, schools, churches, and communities."

Miss Dwight called the class row by row to get their coats. When they were ready to leave, she asked the first person in each row to go down the row and point out papers and pencils left on the floor so that they might be picked up. She then walked around the room for a final check and called the class to line up. She led the children to the outside door where many wishes for a pleasant afternoon were exchanged between her and the children. The children burst through the door to the street where they shouted, talked, laughed, and ran.

The Culture of the Classroom

The preceding account of Miss Dwight's fourth grade class portrays the range of experience of Puerto Rican pupils and their teacher in an elementary school classroom. Extensive observations indicate that Miss Dwight and her class represent the typical situation encountered in Puerto Rican schools. The daily round of life is similar. In these schools, the acting out of the curriculum, the interaction of teachers and pupils as they act out their particular roles, and the contact with Puerto Rican culture traits and lower class social patterns form a culture that is characteristic of them.

The school day began with the arrival of Miss Dwight and, her pupils in the classroom. The children immediately placed their coats and other belongings in the closets at one side of the room. Whispering, loud talking in both Spanish and English, laughing and moving about characterized the informal opening moments of the day. Some children busily attended to certain housekeeping chores such as watering plants or dusting about the room. Other children worked on class assignments not completed the day before. Others read books that they had taken from the library table in the room. A few pupils just sat in their seats and stared out the window or at the teacher or other children.

Miss Dwight soon called her class to order. Attendance was taken and the routine opening exercises--the salute to the flag, the singing of the Star Spangled Banner, and the recitation of the Regents' Prayer--were held. Then the day's lessons and other activities began. They included arithmetic, recess, square dancing, social studies, milk time, English, lunch, health, reading, and discussion of plans for a party. Miss Dwight included these activities in her day's program because, as a teacher, it was her responsibility to assist her pupils to learn to read and write and acquire the other basic skills represented by the other lessons and activities held. Along with instruction in the fundamental academic skills, however, her pupils were learning other things.

They were learning, for example, to participate in certain rituals and ceremonies. In addition, Miss Dwight encouraged her Puerto Rican pupils to accept and internalize certain norms and values that were defined as appropriate by the teacher; her pupils were then expected to regulate their conduct in the classroom accordingly. Miss Dwight's pupils also learned that sanctions were applied to those who deviated from the moral rules and codes of behavior prescribed in the culture of the classroom. In short, the Puerto Rican pupils in Miss Dwight's class learned much that was not always explicitly formulated in her lesson plans for the day's instruction. They were learning, in general, the middle class definitions and interpretations of life and of the world.

Ritual Behavior in the Classroom

The elementary school includes, as a highly integral component of its culture, a wide variety of complicated and elaborate ritual behavior. Frequently, the recurring rituals can be defined and described by the teacher, and explanations of their manifest functions can be given without too much difficulty. Yet many of these rituals have functions and meanings other than those stated and recognized by the teacher, functions that are especially significant in the education of Puerto Rican children.

In Miss Dwight's classroom, children enter the class coatroom by the left door and leave through the right. Monitors are carefully stationed at each side to prevent children from deviating from the prescribed manner of entrance into and departure from the coatroom. Teachers state that this particular cultural arrangement, and others that are comparable, permit children to move quickly. Such an arrangement has certain pragmatic utility. Less time is wasted as each child enters one door, places his coat on his hook, and leaves by another door. This is a regular, orderly, and steady movement in one door and out the other.

This ritualistic behavior, however, does more than save time. The one-way traffic through the narrow coatroom prevents children from quarrelling and fighting with one another. It prevents the development of a critical situation that might occur if a child wishing to enter the coatroom and one wishing to leave arrive simultaneously at the same door. The ritualistic pattern of one way coatroom traffic from which deviation is not permitted functions to prevent the likely occurrence of conflict. A fight could result, there might be shouting and crying, and the teacher would then be responsible for terminating the fight, determining its cause, placing the blame, and administering appropriate punishment. A conflict of this kind and its consequences obviously threaten the social order of the classroom, a situation that most elementary teachers wish to avoid.

In the elementary school, equilibrium is ascribed a positive value, and teachers attempt to secure this equilibrium and preserve it at all costs. Furthermore, noise, disorder, and chaos--the probable consequences of a fight in the classroom--are difficult for the teacher to cope with, and yet class disorganization must be attended to immediately. The restoration of the stability of the social order in the classroom becomes the paramount aim. Both teachers and principals consider the breakdown of stability in the classroom, and the failure or inability to re-establish it, an indication of incompetency on the part of the teacher involved. Such a teacher is then likely to be criticized by other teachers or admonished by supervisors and principals.

The calling of the class row by row to line up, and the line itself pausing at specific locations in the halls to wait for the necessary permission before proceeding to its destination, represent another form of ritualistic behavior designed to avoid conflict among children and protect the highly valued social equilibrium of the classroom. Each child has his place on line. There is no pushing or fighting to be first on line because there are specially designated leaders. Line leaders have higher status in the culture of the classroom; children desire this status and consequently strive to be good, to live up to the expectations of the teacher, in order to be appointed leaders.

The stopping at fixed intervals for the required permission to proceed represents an act of deference to the teacher and her socially ascribed authority. Through the frequent stopping for permission to continue the trip through the corridors, the teacher impresses upon her class the significant fact that she is the possessor of important authority which must be respected by all.

The children, in stopping, recognize and acknowledge the superordinate status of their teacher; they obey the teacher by stopping and waiting, not only because it is the right and fitting thing to do in the culture of the classroom, but also because imminent misfortune--in the form of appropriate sanctions imposed by the teacher --threatens if they do not.

A threat to impose sanctions helps to secure the careful execution of complicated ritual behavior, behavior that contributes to the maintenance of the equilibrium of the classroom and the authority of the teacher. Authority is asserted frequently by elementary

teachers, for it is easily lost and weakened in the classroom, es-
specially through failure to assert and exercise it with sufficient
frequency.

The daily opening exercises in Miss Dwight's classroom constitute another important form of ritualistic behavior. It is legally
mandated that the salute to the flag be recited daily in elementary
classrooms. The singing of the National Anthem or some other appropriate song is also required. Teachers and principals say that
these procedures help children to develop and strengthen a feeling
of patriotism.

These rituals, however, become especially important when
lower class children or children of differing ethnic backgrounds are
in attendance. The salute to the flag and the singing of a suitable
patriotic anthem help to promote a sense of identification with the
society as a whole. Puerto Rican as well as other children participate in this unifying ceremony together, without regard to race,
color, religion or culture. In this manner, the ritual functions to
overcome, to some extent, ethnic group divisiveness. This ritual
also tends to obscure economic differences. Even those who are
poor are Americans. They too salute the flag and sing the National
Anthem in a ceremony that renders homage to the nation, a nation
in which even the poor are important participants.

Miss Dwight, in common with most elementary school teachers, holds various additional ceremonies throughout the school year
that honor the nation and its heroes. Lincoln's birthday, for example,
is commemorated. It is a school holiday, and in the days preceding this event, elementary school children are told about Lincoln,
Honest Abe; about how he gave his life for the nation and freed the
slaves; and about his rise to the presidency even though he was a
poor boy of humble origin who was born in a log cabin. The stress
upon this particular image becomes especially important in schools
attended by lower class children. They learn, in this manner, that
anyone can get ahead, if only he perseveres and works hard enough.

Celebrations of Washington's birthday, Armistice Day (now
called Veterans' Day in the schools), Memorial Day, and Thanks-
giving are also held. Through these celebrations and the periodic
retelling of the relevant national myths and legends, Puerto Rican
and lower class children are taught to identify with the nation, to
accept and respect its heroes, myths, legends, and values. By inculcating this sense of identification with the society as a whole, the
schools contribute to the development of an important and profound
sense of unity, one which tends to obscure and overcome divisiveness because of ethnic or social class differences and which, equally
important, precludes the development of conflicts arising from these
differences.

Rituals honoring the nation and its heroes are only one component of the daily opening exercises. Miss Dwight's class also recited the Regents' Prayer,[2] a prayer authorized for use in the public

schools by the New York State Board of Regents.* In this prayer, the class jointly affirms its dependence upon God. In this public affirmation of its dependence upon its deity, the class is almost like a society begging the blessings of its gods upon its ancestors (parents) and its ruler (teacher). Puerto Rican children, Negro children, Catholics, Protestants, and Jews, the indigent and those who can make ends meet, all pray together. All affirm jointly their dependence upon and the nearness of God. This collective expression of common social values symbolizes the unity of Miss Dwight's class and ultimately of the larger society.

Another type of ritual in Miss Dwight's classroom and in other elementary school classrooms is the morning trip to the toilet, followed by games or dances comprising the physical education period. During the course of the morning, children frequently request permission to go to the toilets. Occasionally, children are given permission immediately, while at other times, children are reminded that the entire class will be leaving the room for the toilets at a specified time and that they must wait until that time. There is no apparent consistency in the granting or withholding of permission.

The fixed daily toilet period represents more than time given to children to attend to their physical needs. Physical needs are secondary, for if they were otherwise, the permission needed to leave the room would probably be granted when requested; furthermore, it is highly unlikely that all children in a class will need to eliminate at a specified time during the school day.

During the school day, there are many reprimands and scoldings, lectures and warnings, all of which contribute to the building up of a considerable degree of tension in the classroom. Given the pressures inherent in the atmosphere of the elementary school classroom, any break in routine, even a hurried trip to the toilet, is welcome, and can function to provide much needed relief of the accumulated emotional and social tensions. Children and teachers are separated from the classroom and each other for several moments. Then they proceed to the basement for games and dances, a further break in the routine of the classroom. Children can laugh and talk and move about to a degree not permitted in class. Much of the informal conversation at such times is in Spanish, another illustration of the permissiveness that prevails at this time, in contrast to the situation in the classroom where the use of Spanish is discouraged.

During classroom observations, there was less general disorder in those rooms where the mid-morning trip to the toilet and the basement for physical education was a daily procedure. In these classrooms, children were sometimes warned that disobedience, disorder or noise of any kind would result in the cancellation of the recess period. In those classrooms where the mid-morning recess

---

*This was true at the time Dr. Bucchioni was writing. [Ed.]

was not observed, teachers stated that the failure to have recess was the result of a lack of time or of the imposition of sanctions.

Most teachers, including Miss Dwight, stated that the mid-morning recess provides welcome relief from the pressures of the morning. "It's a break from the rat race." "It gives me a breathing spell." One teacher explained that the recess provided her the opportunity to "recharge her battery because the long morning is such a drain of her energy." During the physical education period, Miss Dwight had the opportunity to speak to another teacher about the first half of the morning, providing additional relief of tension. Without the alleviation of the pressure and tension that accumulate very rapidly, it is quite possible that many teachers and children might not be able to function as expected for the remainder of the morning in school. Inattention, noise, disorder and restlessness might also develop more readily and the attempt to preserve order would result in a classroom climate even more punitive and repressive.

Social Behavior of Puerto Rican Pupils

The social behavior of Puerto Rican children in elementary school generally presents very little serious difficulty for the teacher insofar as classroom management and control are concerned. Puerto Rican children, for the most part, respect their teachers, do whatever they are requested to do, and generally attempt to be good in the sense of the word as used by teachers. There is little severe or uncontrollable disorder, few fights, and no attacks upon the teacher. Children strive to be good because they fear punishment by the teacher and their parents if they deviate to any great extent from the patterns of behavior expected in the classroom. Teachers do encounter some difficulties, however, and Puerto Rican children are frequently reprimanded. There are, for example, occasions of minor disorder, usually consisting of talking and the noise resulting from movement in and about the classroom; sometimes obscenities in Spanish are heard.

To a great extent, these difficulties encountered by the teacher derive from the conflict arising from differences in the values of middle class teacher and those of her slum dwelling pupils. The elementary school teacher is a transmitter of the culture, and she transmits, along with a variety of academic skills and other cultural traits, the values of the middle class group to which she belongs. When the elementary teacher teaches lower class pupils, as Miss Dwight does, value conflicts are likely to occur. The educational process then reflects the conflict in values both within the school and the social and cultural milieu of the surrounding community.

Most elementary school teachers are drawn from middle or lower middle class groups.[3] In these groups, the traditional values are emphasized. There is, for example, much emphasis placed upon success, especially success in school, and upon the belief that hard work and the deferment of immediate advantages and satisfactions are the means to its achievement.

Saving is stressed as well as the care of personal possessions and private property. Neatness, etiquette, and politeness are important. Respect for and obedience to authority are also important, and appropriate deference to the police, parents, and teachers is encouraged. The control of aggression, except perhaps in self-defense, is emphasized, and in most instances, when aggression does occur, it tends to be verbal. In general, middle class groups value their good reputation and conventionality and are quite concerned with what others think of them.

Lower class groups, in contrast, tend to prefer immediate satisfaction and gratification. There is little or no long range planning. Missing school is not always penalized and education is not generally ascribed much importance in the lower class scheme of things. It is important to get a job, and to get it early. There is no special emphasis upon neatness, politeness, or etiquette.

Early sex experience occurs with considerable frequency among lower class individuals, and there are few restrictions placed upon overt aggression either within or outside the family. Aggression tends to be physical rather than verbal. Lower class individuals tend to be hostile to middle class authority, to parents, teachers, and police. One achieves success through smartness and through the ability to get away with things. In general, lower class individuals tend to have little concern with the opinions of middle class individuals. These factors represent points of potential conflict with the middle class values that elementary school teachers attempt to transmit. Conflicts do occur, of course, but many teachers attempt to prevent the development and outbreak of conflict by consistently striving to maintain equilibrium or order through the establishment of a disciplinary ceremonial that is resorted to both before and after violations of the normative order occur.

Miss Dwight and the Normative Order

In Miss Dwight's classroom, as in almost all elementary school classrooms, certain recurrent requests or demands were observed. "No talking," "Quiet down," "Get back to your seats," were among the statements and commands made by Miss Dwight in defining and enforcing certain norms that she considered important in regulating the conduct of her pupils.

In attempting to avoid conflict and to prevent disruption of her classroom, Miss Dwight, in common with most elementary teachers of lower class Puerto Rican children, referred frequently to the framework of middle class values and norms that made up the normative order within her classroom. That is, Miss Dwight strived to affirm at all times, and in a variety of ways, the norms and moral rules of her classroom, and attempted to develop systematic, consistent, and methodical behavior which she considered fitting and proper in the culture of the classroom.

Like many other teachers, Miss Dwight displayed charts labelled, "How We Should Act in School," "Things We Should Do," and "Do's and Don'ts." In addition, in Miss Dwight's classroom, various rote procedures and rituals were emphasized. Spontaneity was not encouraged and was at a minimum. The general classroom atmosphere was impersonal and inflexible, and the children were kept under rigid control. Certain types of behavior were prohibited, while other kinds were encouraged.

After several observations in Miss Dwight's classroom, the following norms became evident, either through prominent display on the charts referred to previously, or because they were expressed through periodic statements, reminders, group discussions, reprimands, or lengthier scoldings:

No chewing gum
No speaking Spanish
No talking loudly
No talking when you're not supposed to
No pushing
No fighting
No fooling around
To speak English
No calling out
No throwing around books or anything else
To pick up paper or anything else on the floor
No copying
To raise hands during discussions
No passing notes
No writing on walls
No running in halls
No cursing
To say thank you and you're welcome
To come to school on time
Not to make noise
No taking things that don't belong to you
Not to interrupt when the teacher or someone else is talking
To get your work done on time
To do your work neatly and quickly
To pay attention to the teacher
To come to school neat and clean.

Many of the explicitly stated norms in Miss Dwight's classroom prohibit aggressive behavior, verbal or physical, as well as any other type of behavior that might result in conflict that would threaten the equilibrium in the classroom. Thus children are frequently reminded that pushing, fighting, fooling around, throwing things, and the like are proscribed. Other norms refer to the appearance of school work and the punctuality with which it is done. Still other norms are concerned with personal hygiene and cleanliness, care and appearance of the classroom, standards of courtesy, and prohibitions of swearing, obscene language and the use of Spanish.

Controls and Sanctions

The maintenance of order seems to be an essential prerequisite for a group to attain its objectives. The elementary school classroom is no exception in this respect in that the preservation of order is necessary if it is to function smoothly, continuously, and with a minimum of disruption. To prevent deviation from the patterns of equilibrium and order expected and demanded by the normative order of the elementary school classroom, various disciplinary measures are devised and utilized by teachers. Pupils are required to enter and leave the classroom in straight, double lines. If children wish to speak or use the toilets they must raise their hands and wait for recognition by the teacher. Spontaneous or otherwise unauthorized conversation among pupils is not usually permitted. Lengthy and involved reminders and discussions of the kind of behavior appropriate to the decorum of the classroom occur with considerable regularity. If there are no major disturbances in class, little noise or talking, and if children sit in an orderly and attentive posture, answer questions promptly, and if they express the respect and deference due to their teachers as people in authority, then there exists good, strong discipline in the frame of reference of the elementary school teacher. Inattention, talking, fighting, playing or any other indication of disorganization in the classroom or deviation from the prescribed norms shows poor control and weak discipline, a situation that could easily cast reflection upon the professional competency of the teacher.

When the continuance of the order and equilibrium of classroom is endangered through talking, playing, fighting, and the use of Spanish, or any other deviation from the expected patterns of behavior implicit in the established normative order, retribution is almost automatic and immediate. There are stern and frigid glances directed without delay at the offender. Sharp reprimands and long scoldings constitute a major portion of the sanctions applied, and children are frequently commanded to apologize for their offenses.

Sanctions may also include the isolation of the offending pupil. He may be sent to the classroom of a teacher of a lower grade, or he may be sent to stand in a corner of the classroom or outside the door of the room. There may be long classroom discussions on the ethics appropriate to the particular situation and grade level. Threats are made to notify the principal or to hold a conference with the parents of the offender. Elementary teachers frequently shorten or cancel recess periods or classroom parties when the normative order of the classroom is seriously violated. In some instances, teachers shake children, pull their hair, or humiliate them verbally in the presence of the entire class.

All the systems of control portrayed here involve domination

of the children by the teacher. Children must learn to respect authority. They must be obedient and carry out orders. Disobedience,
disorder, disruption of any kind must be punished with a degree of
severity appropriate to the offense. In the culture of the classroom,
consistent strictness and severity are essential, for if you give the
children "an inch, they'll take a yard." In light of the systems of
control used in most elementary school classrooms, the elementary
school appears to be a highly authoritarian organization where things
must be made tough, where the power and authority inherent in life
must be forcefully demonstrated, and where to "spare the rod, is
to spoil the child." In the elementary classroom, the social order
is established and maintained through coercion and force, and through
general domination by the teacher and submission by the children.

Teachers of Puerto Rican children operate within the framework of controls portrayed above. They state that rigid and inflexible regulations must be applied and enforced at all times if Puerto
Rican children are to be controlled, and if the business of teaching
and learning are to proceed properly and without undue interruption.
The resulting classroom atmosphere is essentially punitive and repressive in nature.

Miss Dwight's sanctions and controls were similar to those
characteristic of most elementary classrooms, although she was not
observed applying corporal punishment as a sanction. When Jesús
and Dolores arrived late as was their practice, Miss Dwight scolded:

> If it's not your alarm clock, it's having to go to the store,
> or helping dress your brother or some other excuse. You
> will have to learn to come to school on time. You, too,
> Jesús. You have been coming to school long enough to re-
> alize that one of the important rules is to be early in the
> morning. And another thing, you are to bring a note each
> time you are late or absent. I expect a note from each of
> you tomorrow morning. And I'm tired of changing my at-
> tendance report every time you both come in late.

During the mathematics lesson when some of the children
became restless and inattentive, Miss Dwight glanced at the class
and fixed her gaze upon those children who were the most obvious
offenders. At about the same time, Manuel volunteered, in Spanish,
the definition of the word swimming for Juan who did not understand
the word in English. Miss Dwight reprimanded, "No talking, Manuel!" A few moments later, when Manuel requested permission to
go to the boys' toilet, Miss Dwight said, "No, Manuel, you will have
to wait until I take the entire class at ten o'clock." This refusal
of a request is another type of control used by Miss Dwight, who
seems to be saying, in effect, that if you want certain privileges,
you must live up to the rules of the game.

Miss Dwight used many additional reprimands. She said to
inattentive Juan, "Juan, please try to pay attention." When several
children went to the pencil sharpener and waste paper basket during

the mathematics lesson, and some general noise broke out, Miss Dwight ordered, "Get back to your desks. This moving about has to stop." At recess, she commanded the class to "calm down." During the social studies lesson, when a short procession found its way once more to the pencil sharpener and waste paper basket as had happened during the mathematics lesson, Miss Dwight demanded, "Boys and girls, sit down and keep still." At the same time she ordered, "Children, please sit up tall. Your feet belong on the floor and not on the rungs of your desk. And everyone should be listening." When children spoke in Spanish, she reminded them, "English, children." "You know I don't understand Spanish." She told Tomás, who was resting his elbows on his desk and holding his head with his hand, "Please stop holding your head up and get your elbows off the desk. What time did you get to bed last night?"

Particularly sharp rebukes were directed at Antonio. When Miss Dwight caught him attempting to scratch a groove in his desk, she stated forcefully:

Antonio, that is not your property that you are ruining. Many children will use that desk after you. I think you should leave it as you found it. Now put the pencil down and stop this nonsense. Do you hear?

Antonio's rejoinder was to utter a most insulting Spanish obscenity. Miss Dwight did not know the meaning of this Spanish obscenity and ordered, "Antonio what did you say? In English!" She continued:

Antonio, stand up and tell me in English what you said! ... I'm waiting for your answer, Antonio. What does that mean?

After having been informed that it could not be translated because "eet is a bad teeng he say," and having received subsequently an apology from Antonio, Miss Dwight's scolding continued:

All right, Antonio.... And I hope you will control your feelings better in the future. People just don't burst out and call each other names whenever they feel like it. You must learn how to cooperate more with others. We have to live with many people in this world, and it's time you've learned that everything does not always go the way you want it to. Now sit down and behave yourself.

In addition to reprimands, scoldings, refusals of requests, and threats to inform parents, Miss Dwight also held group discussions about problem situations, such as the noise in the children's lunchroom.

Children, the principal made a definite point of telling the teachers that the behavior and noise in the lunchroom is terrible. I hope I can be proud of you and that you will behave as you should, get your food quietly, eat quickly, and clean your places before you leave.

A further technique of control was the threat to cancel recess, and later in the day, the threat to cancel the Christmas party.

Sit down, children. We will have to stay here if you do not line up quietly.

Children, if you continue to call out like this, we will have no party.

Miss Dwight also used the imposition of additional school work as a sanction. During the reading lesson, Miss Dwight threatened, "Bluebirds, if you continue to talk, I will have you write the meanings of those words and write them in sentences."

In Miss Dwight's classroom and others like it, the extremely meticulous attention given to sanctions, techniques of control, and other disciplinary measures, has, of course, its obvious pragmatic utility. Classrooms are expected to be quiet and orderly. Children are expected to accept and internalize the norms set before them, and the elaborate disciplinary ceremonial encourages them to do so, and penalizes them if they do not. But the sometimes complicated disciplinary reminders and rituals involving the expression of norms and the application of sanctions have other functions as well.

Most Puerto Rican children are not able to follow directions and classroom instruction quickly and accurately because of their lack of sufficient fluency in English. In addition, according to the elementary teacher, Puerto Rican pupils are limited in their intellectual abilities; their I.Q.'s are low, and they are, consequently, extremely slow in school work. Little seems to be accomplished in the classroom for one reason or another, and this fact is acknowledged by teachers of Puerto Rican children. Mrs. Maran, a colleague of Miss Dwight, stated that "Puerto Rican pupils seem to learn nothing--either here or at home." Miss Dwight agreed.

The elaborate disciplinary ceremonial, however, consumes much time; in a sense, it helps to pass time, and as such conveys the impression to all concerned that at least something is learned. While academically little is achieved, in terms of improved behavior much seems to be accomplished. This was acknowledged in a conversation between Mrs. Maran and Miss Dwight. When a brief discussion of the lack of academic progress had been brought to a conclusion, Mrs. Maran stated, "But you know ... the ones in my third grade class are very well behaved. Authority means something to them."

In the teacher's definition of the school and her own role in it, there is, or there ought to be, much teaching and learning; but in teaching Puerto Rican pupils, however, teachers observe that little learning occurs for a variety of reasons. Miss Dwight observed that Puerto Rican children do not learn because "all they care about is sleeping, eating, playing, and having parties." During lunch in the teachers' room, other teachers suggested possible reasons for the lack of academic progress. Edith, for example, referred to their "lousy way of living" and the use of Spanish. Another teacher expressed her conviction that Puerto Ricans will not "get anywhere," because "they don't know anything, go anywhere, or read anything."

The teacher's definition of the reality of the school situation and her own self-esteem are thereby challenged. She is supposed to teach her pupils; she at least attempts to teach them. She prepares her lessons, refers to her lesson plans, provides the necessary books and instructional materials, and becomes fatigued at the end of the day. Yet the children seem to have learned little as the result of her endeavors. She is seemingly a failure in her job.

In this situation, the elaborate disciplinary rituals function to resolve satisfactorily this challenge to the self-esteem and professional reputation of the teacher by making it appear that something is, after all, occurring, if only the frequent acting out of the various rituals that help to convey an impression of successful teaching and learning.

Use of Spanish in the Classroom

When Antonio was reprimanded by Miss Dwight because he had scratched a groove into his desk, he shouted out an obscenity. This use of obscenities in Spanish occurs in many instances, especially in the upper grades. It represents the defiance of a child who can no longer accept what he views as intolerable ... ***

The use of Spanish, however, is not restricted to the utterance of obscenities. Puerto Rican pupils also speak Spanish when they are embarrassed, nervous, or angry, or when they are reprimanded. When Dolores arrived late and Miss Dwight asked for an explanation or a note from her parents, she replied in Spanish, "Maestra, el reloj despertador se rompió y ..." ("Teacher, the alarm clock broke and ...") When Manuel was refused permission to go to the boys' room and was told by Miss Dwight that he would have to wait until ten o'clock when the entire class would have recess, he said, "Pero tengo que ir al baño ahora." ("But I have to go to the toilet now.") In discussing one and two family houses and their private bathrooms, Dolores explained rapidly and excitedly that when she tries to take a bath her mother tells her "not to make the people wait." Dolores then added quickly, "Dice que no tengo derecho a hacer que espere tanto a la gente." ("She says that I have no right to make the people wait so much.")

Spanish is also used when the required English words or phrases or answers to questions are unknown. During the mathematics lesson, Juan did not know the meaning of "swimming." He asked, "Que quiere decir?" ("What does it mean?") Manuel assisted him by calling out, "Nadando." ("Swimming.") When Juan did not understand the problem "six minus two," a neighbor suggested "seis menos dos." ("Six minus two.") In a health discussion María said that the salad at lunch consisted only of "lechuga." ("Lettuce.")

The primary function of language is communication, and in this sense, the use of Spanish by Puerto Rican pupils represents an attempt to communicate effectively when the alternative vehicle of communication is foreign, inadequately understood, and poorly spoken. The use of Spanish, however, in addition to serving as a means of communication and relatively safe way of expressing defiance and hostility, especially through the use of obscenities that are not understood, functions to assist Puerto Rican pupils in maintaining contact with the familiar in an unfamiliar, frequently hostile, environment.

Spanish is, for these Puerto Rican children, a symbol of their solidarity. As a means of communicating, the use of Spanish assists Puerto Rican children in sharing their experiences and thoughts with one another. But as a symbol of solidarity, the language helps to define the social situation in the classroom. It establishes a degree of rapport among the Puerto Rican children present physically in the classroom. Its use symbolizes the cultural understanding and unity of Puerto Rican pupils, especially when confronted by an outsider, one who is not a member of the group, and one who represents the imposed authority and control of a superordinate group. What is said in Spanish is not really important; the importance of its use lies in the fact that it is spoken in a hostile and unknown environment, and one's enemies cannot understand it.

In the classroom, the children speak Spanish while the teacher does not. They can use the language when they do not wish to have the teacher understand what they are saying. They are able to communicate with one another in a language known only among themselves. This use of another language distinguishes very sharply between the children who speak it and the teacher who does not. In this manner, language, as an important symbol of cultural differences, emphasizes the solidarity of the Puerto Rican pupils in the classroom.

When Antonio shouted out in defiance of Miss Dwight, Juan, in spite of the teacher's request, refused to translate the obscenity because "it was too bad to say." He was, of course, refusing to inform or "tattle." But this refusal to translate represented another significant factor: Juan was, in a sense, acknowledging his membership in a particular social group. He could not explain that the teacher and her mother, members of an out-group, were verbally attacked in a manner the full significance of which is known only to Puerto Ricans, in a manner representing intense hatred, utter scorn, and challenge. Even more significant, however, is the fact that the refusal to translate also symbolized the determination not to weaken the solidarity of the group by sharing its accumulated cultural understandings with outsiders. If Juan had explained the obscenity, assuming that he was capable of doing so, he would have permitted an outsider, an enemy, to share the secrets of his group, thereby weakening its solidarity and unity.

Puerto Ricans, Lessons, and Life Adjustment

The daily lessons in the elementary schools conform in both content and time allotments to the prescriptions of the authorized curriculum. Frequently, however, lessons are begun, but never completed; they are terminated abruptly when the scheduled time has run out. Thus Miss Dwight brought her arithmetic lesson to a sudden end when time was up.

> Children, these problems go on to the next page. When you have free time today, you are to do these two pages. Other- wise, they are part of your homework. Make an example of each one. And now, put all your arithmetic materials away. It's ten o'clock and we must go to the lavatories and then to the basement for physical education.

The reading lesson was concluded in the same manner, even though all of the children had not had the opportunity to read.

> Thunderbirds, we have no time for reading today. I will start with your group in the morning.

Questions and answers, and some discussion, composed Miss Dwight's teaching methods as they do for many elementary school teachers. A child is asked to read a passage in a book, and then he is asked one or more questions based upon his assigned reading. There is little or no explanation. Occasionally, concrete materials are used to clarify problems, such as in the arithmetic lesson which utilized squared materials, a mathematics device designed to help the child count, add, and subtract by actually performing these computa- tions with small squares of paper.

Teachers encourage Puerto Rican pupils to participate in these and other lessons, but when they wish to have the correct answer given immediately, perhaps to save time, perhaps because of impa- tience, they call upon non-Puerto Rican children.

There emerges from the subject matter and teaching methods a pattern of teaching based upon a concept of education as life adjust- ment, implying resignation to the prevailing conditions and pressures; also implied is a lack of self-reliant aggressiveness in meeting chal- lenges.

Children of elementary school age are generally very unself- conscious. They express quite candidly much dissatisfaction with their living conditions. Teachers, as Miss Dwight did, emphasize that "we must accept what we have now and try to appreciate the good things we have." Children are questioned as to what is "good in your way of living." In the culture of the classroom, there is something good in every child's life, something for which each child can be grateful. When Puerto Rican children are taught to appre- ciate and be thankful for what they have, they are taught to accept and adjust to the situation in which they find themselves. Even though the teacher states that she is in school "to help the children live better," there is much, nevertheless, for which to be thankful.

In the elementary school, a program of education based upon the conceptual framework of life adjustment and resignation to prevailing conditions does not emphasize the acquisition of the various academic skills essential to continued education. In addition, the subject matter and teaching methods are unrealistic; they do not motivate Puerto Rican children because of their irrelevance to the present status and general life experience of these pupils. Widespread discouragement and frustration occur, but are alleviated by the advice to accept and be thankful for what one has.

Observations indicate that many teachers, Miss Dwight included, have accepted life adjustment teaching. With the general acceptance of life adjustment teaching and the concomitant attitudes of acceptance and gratitude, education for failure, or alternatively expressed, education in attitudes of acceptance of failure, is the result. The teacher, in light of the general academic failure of Puerto Rican pupils, in reality attempts to appease and condition them to the point of resignation to their life situation. The teacher's objective then becomes that of sending her pupils into the world, resigned and adjusted, but also with the belief that if they but work hard enough, they will be able to improve their life chances.

What Do Puerto Rican Children Learn?

Academic learning among Puerto Rican children is limited, but these pupils do learn, in spite of the social, cultural, and other factors preventing successful academic progress, much that is not explicitly suggested in the curriculum or acknowledged by teachers. Much of the teaching during a typical day contains frequent allusions to the language of Puerto Ricans, to their food preferences, and to other characteristic social and cultural patterns. They speak Spanish. Their preferred foods are considered unhealthful. Their housing accommodations are drastically unlike the more desirable arrangements of middle class North Americans. These factors are frequently contrasted unfavorably with the social and cultural patterns of the North American middle classes. In this manner, Puerto Rican children develop a strong consciousness of themselves as Puerto Ricans and as members of a particular social group; thus, Puerto Rican children very quickly learn that they constitute a group apart from and different from North Americans.

As an essential component of this developing group consciousness, Puerto Rican pupils learn who their antagonists are: the teacher who constantly scolds and reprimands and the principal who supports the teacher in her attitudes, both of whom represent the dominant middle class groups. Furthermore, these other groups possess the highly desired symbols of the preferred and superordinate status. They have better schools, better housing, better jobs, and more money. They are the teachers and principals; and they control the schools in which Puerto Rican pupils are in attendance.

The Puerto Rican child must attend school because of compulsory attendance laws. But to continue to attend school when his ego is threatened and weakened by constant and often derogatory reference to his culture requires an adjustment by the Puerto Rican child that will enable him to survive the elementary school experience.

This adjustment, with a few notable exceptions, consists of a passive submission to and acquiescence in the school's demands. Puerto Rican pupils generally sit quietly in class. Teachers frequently complain that they are always "daydreaming." Puerto Rican children usually carry out whatever requests the teacher makes. They develop the technique of extreme, exaggerated courtesy as part of their social equipment for survival. The excessive courtesy helps the child to avoid further attacks upon his social and cultural status by his teacher, for teachers are less likely to reprimand or attack those who are polite and who accord them the proper deference.

Another technique of survival is the development and strengthening of group solidarity. Puerto Rican children do not inform upon their classmates. They do not reveal the names of children who may have caused some disturbance on the school playground, or in the classroom or lunchroom. If an obscenity is heard in the classroom, the translation, if requested, is not given. Puerto Rican children develop, in this manner, patterns of mutual aid and support when confronted by individuals of higher social status and differing cultural background.

Conclusion

The culture of the classroom represents a design for living, and it includes all the behavior patterns and thought ways of teachers and pupils. In Miss Dwight's classroom, pupils were guided to certain methods and techniques of accomplishing objectives. Children were also subject to certain rules, to certain do's and don'ts for living in the classroom. That is, the classroom culture provided for a complex of evaluations as to what is permitted or prohibited, appropriate or inappropriate, or good or bad in the elementary school scheme of living. This complex of evaluations, however, included consideration of ultimate values as well as immediate values, especially as manifested in various religious and patriotic rituals and ceremonies.

The elementary school can be considered the institution where the child learns to read and write and acquire other skills fundamental to literacy and continued education. Nevertheless, in a much broader sense, elementary education can be interpreted as socialization. Thus Miss Dwight's role can be viewed as including the guiding or directing the socialization process for her Puerto Rican pupils so that they might become accepted adults in middle class North American society. Miss Dwight provided her pupils with a set of definitions of various social and cultural situations, and these definitions included values and norms representing the general society and culture as well as those unique to the school and classroom. Miss Dwight's classroom, however, became the scene of a conflict in values, a conflict between the values of middle class North Americans and lower class Puerto Ricans. As a manifestation of this conflict, children became inattentive, uninterested, restless, talkative, and sometimes disorderly, and scoldings, repetitions, reprimands, reminders, moral rejoinders, and threats were commonplace and time consuming, In effect, much time, attention, and energy were given by Miss Dwight to the presentation, explanation, and enforcement of certain values and norms. Conversely, less time and attention were directed to the acquisition of academic skills and knowledge, also a phase of the socialization process. This differential time allotment is a factor affecting the academic achievement of Puerto Rican pupils.

References

1. The data presented in this chapter, including incidents within the classroom, teacher attitudes, etc. , were derived from an extensive series of observations made in various classrooms. Observations revealed the occurrence of similar events and incidents in each of the classes observed. Since curriculum content, teaching methods, and reactions to these were essentially similar in each of the classes, one such classroom was then selected for detailed discussion. Miss Dwight, her pupils, and the other teachers to whom reference was made are real persons; the names of both teachers and pupils were changed to conceal their identities. Several details concerning other incidents occurring within the classroom on the same day were eliminated in order to prevent a repetitive discussion; the details eliminated include classroom routines such as distribution and collection of materials, collection and correction of homework, several interruptions by children with messages from other teachers, much informal conversation among children during the transition from one subject to another and when lining up, and a fire drill.
2. The Regents' Prayer: "Almighty God, we acknowledge our dependence upon Thee. We beg Thy blessings upon us, our parents, our teachers, and our country." On June 25, 1962 the recitation of this prayer in the public schools was declared unconstitutional by the United States Supreme Court.
3. William Lloyd Warner, et al. , Who Shall Be Educated? New York: Harper and Brothers 1944, Chapter VIII. See also, Robin J. Williams, Jr. , American Society, New York: Alfred A. Knopf, 1951, p. 286 and Robert Riehey and William Fox, An Analysis of Various Factors Associated with the Selection of Teaching as a Vocation, Bulletin of the School of Education, Division of Research and Field Services, Indiana University, May, 1948.

Eugene Bucchioni

HOME ATMOSPHERE AND SUCCESS IN SCHOOL

Most Puerto Ricans in New York City live in the least desirable residential areas of New York, either in slums or in public housing projects that are rapidly deteriorating into slums.   Individuals who live
in a slum area and who are members of lower classes are apt to
have little orientation to success at school.   Frequently, residents
of slum areas, especially Puerto Ricans, encounter much discrimination socially and occupationally because of their ethnic origin, even
if they have secured some education.   This tends to discourage further
schooling.

Another important factor affecting home atmosphere and success at school is the fact that the integrated social norms of the larger
North American society do not function well in a slum; residents of
slum areas have their own norms, nevertheless they are expected to
accept the norms of more privileged groups in society and reflect
those norms in their behavior; yet the realities of the immediate social and cultural milieu and life chances of Puerto Ricans in slums
have resulted in norms and values that are at variance with and seemingly contradict the norms and values of other groups in the society.

What are the realities of life in a slum for Puerto Ricans?
What norms and values have developed that conflict with those of middle class groups?   Many Puerto Ricans live in crowded and dilapidated
old-law tenements; some live in low income housing projects that are
deteriorating rapidly.   High rates of unemployment and of unstable
employment as unskilled laborers result in chronic economic insecurity.   A disproportionate number of broken families is characteristic.   In Puerto Rican homes, there is likely to be an almost complete

Reprinted by permission from A Sociological Analysis of the Functioning of Elementary Education for Puerto Rican Children, (Unpublished
Doctoral Dissertation, New School for Social Research, 1965), pp. 55-
66.

absence of books, magazines, and toys for the children. Walls are frequently adorned with images of Christ in his various manifestations such as the Bleeding Heart, the Crucifixion, the Resurrection, or the Ascension. The Virgin Mary in her various manifestations, or the family's favorite saints are likely to appear either as pictures on the walls or as the focal point for a family altar. The normal home objects such as the family furniture, including usually a radio and television, however, generally furnish the main contents of a Puerto Rican home.

There exists a pattern of life for children that exposes them to a mere minimum of direct contact with the central issues of North American middle class culture. On the contrary, the everyday problems of living such as dealing with economic insecurity, coping with many children in a crowded apartment, cooking the various meals and making them stretch in order to provide for the family and unexpected guests, leave little time for adults to assist their children in exploring the local and the larger world and their relationship to it.

For many Puerto Rican children, the street becomes the playground where very much is learned. Fearlessness, bravery, daring physical prowess, machismo are among the norms learned in a Puerto Rican slum. One learns to be independent, tough, and to outsmart others, especially the police or other representatives of middle class authority. The authority figure becomes the hijo de puta (son of a bitch), the one responsible for having caused the individual to become jodido (screwed). A search for excitement, thrills, involving some degree of risk or danger, occurs with considerable frequency. Aggression is more often physical than verbal, and when it is verbal, obscenities in Spanish predominate. While the consequences of one's behavior are sometimes recognized, one's general situation is frequently attributed to la suerte (meaning both luck and fate) or to the will of God (como Dios quiera), or to the intervention or interference of a middle class authority.

The attitudes, values, and norms of the slum dweller are designed to strengthen, reinforce, and affirm his way of life. When these patterns are sharply different from the norms and values of middle class culture, they may be interpreted as malicious, evil, deliberately non-conforming and downright threatening by the middle class teacher. In school, the Puerto Rican child is expected to accept the conflicting norms of the larger society, and he is penalized if he does not. What is tolerated in a home in a slum is not always tolerated in other segments of the society, especially in school. Inappropriate behavior of the Puerto Rican child is penalized in many ways, and the resulting punitive atmosphere in school contributes to the lack of successful achievement.

An additional variable affecting success at school is the educational level of the parents and the image they have of the school. Mills found that most of the migrants in this sample were poorly educated.[1] The average number of years completed was 6.5. He also discovered that 8% of the total number of migrants in his sample were illiterate. The lack of sufficient parental education, coupled with the resulting inadequate understanding of the role of the school, hinders Puerto Rican children in their school careers. Parents are unable to assist their children with school work when necessary. In addition, parents are frequently unable to motivate their children or encourage them in their work at school because of their inadequate understanding of what the school is attempting to do.

Schools, in addition to teaching the traditional "Three R's" and providing instruction in the other subjects, also attempt to stimulate individuality in pupils, encourage self-assertiveness, initiative, self-expression, and creativity. These additional tasks of the school do not always coincide with the conceptions that Puerto Rican parents have concerning the role of the school. Puerto Rican parents expect their children to be quiet and submissive and respectful. Boys should develop into men of character and get an education that will enable them to get good jobs. This will help boys to become good parents and, later, persons respected by the family and others in their social group. A girl should develop into a quiet, modest, and virtuous woman, one who has some education so that she can secure employment if this should become necessary.

All this is part of the home atmosphere; and all this conflicts with what is taught in the schools and with what parents think should be taught. What is of importance here is the fact that parents believe the school should reinforce what they are teaching the children at home. This represents a conception of education that differs very sharply from that held by the teachers, principals, and the Board of Education.

Education has served as an instrument of upward mobility for many North Americans who were able to secure better employment and whose life chances were improved as a result of their education: children from these families were motivated to succeed in school because of the evident success of their parents. Puerto Rican children have no such motivation. Expressed differently, Puerto Ricans are not school-oriented because of the various factors discussed above; this lack of school orientation contributes to academic retardation and inadequate educational achievement. Inadequate educational achievement makes difficult, if not impossible, the continued education which could contribute to the improvement of the life chances of Puerto Ricans.

Home Atmosphere and the Curriculum

For Puerto Rican children there is little relationship between the curriculum and the complex of social and cultural patterns characterizing their lives. There can be little enthusiasm for the subjects and experiences of the curriculum, little motivation to succeed at school, when children are ill, hungry, poorly housed, from broken families, and when they do not speak or understand the language in which they are taught.

The school bears little relationship to the streets around it, where the policeman is the killer of Georgie Martinez, the milkman a legend of an older era of brownstone fronts and horse-drawn carts whose product is now too expensive for many of the families who live here largely on water and rice and beans. The children fed with those staples may qualify for the health class, where they take home lists of diets that are often impossible to fulfill.... The schools have been of little help to the children of Spanish Harlem in escaping the realities of its streets, or in changing those realities to something like the promise of the posters that smile from the classrooms. The schools, in fact, have blocked out the possibilities of the world beyond even more profoundly than the tenement buildings around them. [2]

This discrepancy between the realities of Puerto Rican life in New York and the school curriculum becomes especially clear when analyzed in terms of what Puerto Rican pupils learn on a day-to-day basis. Textbooks, for example, advise Puerto Rican children as to what they ought to eat:

Your food for the day should include foods from each of the seven groups you have already learned about. Can you name them? Let's review them. You know that milk makes a difference in health and growth. Milk and the many foods from milk are the best sources of calcium. They supply excellent protein and vitamin A.
The world's most wonderful engine--your body--runs well on the food energy from bread and cereal. Whole grains and enriched white bread and cereals supply vitamin B, phosphorous, and iron. They are a good source of protein, too. They are one of our cheapest foods. Meat and fish and eggs supply excellent protein and phosphorous.... Citrus fruits and tomatoes ... give us all the vitamin C we need.... Butter or fortified margarine is high in food energy and in vitamin A. A little fat goes a long way. We should not eat too much of it. [3]

Recommendations as to what specific meals should contain are also made:

Do you feel strong as a tiger or weak as a mouse? What kind of breakfast do you have at your house? You can't eat like a bird and work like a horse. Do you get that tired feeling before the morning is half over? Perhaps it is because you're a breakfast skipper. Do you have a 'four-star' breakfast every day? The four stars are (1) citrus fruit, (2) wholegrain or enriched cereal or bread or both, (3) milk, (4) butter or vitamin A margarine. If you have an orange or tomato, or half a grapefruit, at another meal, you may omit the citrus fruit for breakfast. [4]

A good lunch to take to school contains the Big Three--(1) cereal or bread, (2) milk or cheese, (3) fruit or vegetables. Your

lunch box might contain some food from each of the following
groups, which include the seven basic foods:
Group 1: Sandwiches having any of the following kinds of filling: finely chopped boiled eggs mildly seasoned; peanut butter;
dried fruit paste made by grinding raisins, dates, figs or other
fruits and nuts; chopped chicken liver; chopped meat; various
kinds of cheese....
Group 2: Fresh fruits of all kinds, ripe tomatoes, and pieces
of raw carrot are easily carried. Applesauce and other kinds
of stewed fruit may be carried in small jars with screw tops.
Group 3: A sweet such as a jelly sandwich, sponge cake,
cookies, cup custard, dates or figs, or fruit candy.
Group 4: A milk or fruit drink. If possible, bring a pint
bottle of milk or fruit juice or a thermos bottle of hot milk,
soup or cocoa. At least take a drink of water. [5]

The appropriate way in which to serve food is also part of
elementary school health instruction.

Food that looks and tastes good helps digestion. It "makes
the mouth water." The digestive juices in the mouth and in
the stomach, too, flow faster when the food looks good, smells
good, tastes good. If you were helping to get breakfast, dinner, or supper, what could you do to make the food look good?
Did you think of these things? See that the table cover is
clean. A clean, bare table, painted, is pretty, too. See that
the dishes and silverware are clean. Put the food neatly on
plates. Put a bowl of fruit or a small plant or freshcut flowers on the table. Serve hot foods hot and cold foods cold.
Plan to have some color in your meal--a green salad, orange
carrots, a red tomato. [6]

The above selections represent the kind of health teaching that
takes place in the elementary schools. Children learn during health
instruction about a balanced and nutritious diet, one containing a wide
variety of foods, many of which Puerto Rican children have not eaten
previously, nor would they eat such foods considering the cultural background of their parents and their economic status as well. Frequently,
children bring home detailed lists of foods that comprise a well-balanced
diet, lists which often must be signed by parents and returned to
school.

The social studies curriculum is equally unrelated to the Puerto
Rican experience in New York City. In classroom studies of different
communities within the United States, both farm and suburban life are
emphasized. In contrast, little attention is given to studies of urban
life.

The suburban community is especially stressed through a careful presentation of the suburbs as a complex of one family houses with
one or more bathrooms, one or more automobiles, supermarkets that
one drives to in order to make the necessary purchases, and trees,
lawns, flowers, and new modern schools. Puerto Rican pupils thus

learn early to desire these symbols of respectable middle class status. The unreality of this goal becomes most pronounced when considering the racial identification of Puerto Ricans that will probably prevent them, even if they secure adequate funds, from residing in such suburban communities.

Other social studies teaching includes studies of community helpers: the milkman, policeman, fireman, grocer, street cleaner, and the like, and their contributions to society. In the second grade, for example, the child should "develop the concept that the policeman is a friend and protector of children."[7] In order to develop this concept, the following basic experiences are prescribed: getting to know the policeman who serves the school; learning to call him by name; talking to him; making friendly gestures like writing notes; sending greeting cards; inviting him to visit class. [8]

The "community helpers" are generally depicted in a manner that bears little resemblance to the realities of the experience of Puerto Ricans with them. The policeman, for example, is idealized as one who helps and protects those in need of his assistance. Policemen assigned to slum areas, however, are not always sympathetic to residents, and in many instances, the Puerto Rican's experience with the police has been the reverse of the image presented in school.

Other social studies teaching is equally unrealistic. Puerto Rican children are taught that the United States provides them with many opportunities that are available in no other country in the world. The United States is the one nation where all people are free and equal, and where all people can get ahead if they work hard enough.

> The people of the United States have much to be thankful for. Most of them are living longer, healthier, and more comfortable lives than their ancestors did. Within their free nation Americans have made use of the knowledge, experience, and arts they inherited from Europe, to create their own art, music, literature--their own way of life. Because of their arts, natural resources, industries, skilled labor, and inventions, the people of the United States have more wonderful things and more time in which to enjoy them than any other people in the world. But greatest of their blessings are the freedoms of their democracy, which makes all other things possible. This democracy has been won, increased, and protected by the courage and hard work of many generations of Americans. The people of the United States will have to continue to work hard to keep and protect it. [9]

The curriculum, in calling for the kind of teaching illustrated above, excludes all reference to the realities of poverty, discrimination, and hostility which are the lot of many Puerto Ricans and their children. This type of teaching does not interest nor motivate Puerto Rican pupils who know through their experience and that of their families that often the reverse is true, especially where differences in race, color, and culture are involved.

References

1. C. W. Mills, The Puerto Rican Journey, New York: Harper, 1950, p. 32.
2. Dan Wakefield, Island in the City, New York: The Citadel Press, 1960, p. 157.
3. W. W. Charters, et al., Habits Healthful and Safe, New York: The Macmillan Company, 1955, p. 214.
4. Ibid., p. 215.
5. Ibid., p. 218.
6. Ibid., p. 221.
7. Resource Units for Classes With Puerto Rican Pupils in the Second Grade, p. 33.
8. Ibid., p. 33.
9. M. G. Mackey, et al., Your Country's Story. New York: Ginn, 1953.

Francesco Cordasco

BILINGUAL EDUCATION IN AMERICAN SCHOOLS
A CRITICAL OVERVIEW AND RESOURCE INVENTORY

Introduction

The growth of bilingual education in the United States invites attention
by the academic community. In this essay, I have provided a critical overview of the origins of bilingual education, contemporary bilingual educational practice, bilingual education theory, and the evolving controversy which surrounds the social contexts out of which bilingual education emerges. I have, also, provided an inventory of
those resources in bilingual education which are available to the in-
vestigator.

In its bicultural orientations, bilingual education is directly
related to the Black civil rights movement, and the new affirmations
of identity and proclamations of ethnic pride by Mexican Americans,
Puerto Ricans, Cubans, and by the progeny of earlier European im-
migrants--Italians, Greeks, Jews, Poles, Slavs, and others. In a
prescient foreword to Heinz Kloss's The American Bilingual Tradition,
William F. Mackey observes:

> The popular image of the United States as a nation united
> by one language and one culture has always been illusory.
> It was an ideal engendered by the now outmoded values of
> nineteenth century nationalism. Although the American
> melting pot has indeed fused millions of second- and third-
> generation immigrant families into unilingual English-speaking
> Americans, unmelted or partially melted millions have also
> survived whose isolation or regional dominance has permitted
> them to maintain their ethnic identity in their new and spa-
> cious land.

Professor Mackey's views are massively documented in Joshua A.
Fishman's Language Loyalty in the United States, an invaluable repository of formal language-maintenance resources and institutions
in American society. Fishman and his colleagues define the frame-

246

work of their investigations in very broad terms: the study of language loyalty in the United States encompasses American ethnic historiography; the twin processes of de-ethnization and the concomitant conflicts in the enforced acculturation that accompanies assimilation, and the history of immigrant language maintenance.

Some five million youngsters in the United States come from homes in which the generally spoken language is other than English. Estimates based on samplings in various states suggest that there are an estimated 3.6 million pupils in the country who need bilingual education to enable them to manage the regular school curriculum. Bilingual education is best defined as academic instruction in two languages, i.e., the child's language and English. Particular approaches used vary considerably, but most bilingual practice in the United States is transitional. Use of the child's native language as a medium of instruction will enable the student to learn cognitive skills in the language he understands, and prevent academic retardation; English taught as a second language will, in time, move the student to an English language proficiency, and end the need for instruction in the native language; and continuing attention to the child's heritage and culture (i.e., bicultural education) will build self-esteem, stimulating both comprehension and motivation.

Most introductory texts on American bilingual practice provide information on historical backgrounds, descriptive definitions of programs, and varying theoretical paradigms. Representative introductory texts include Cordasco, Bilingual Schooling in the United States; Henry T. Trueba and Carol Barnett-Mizrahi, Bilingual Multicultural Education and the Professional; Luis Ortega, ed., Introduction to Bilingual Education; and Francis W. von Maltitz, Living and Learning in Two Languages: Bilingual-Bicultural Education in the United States. A clear and forthright statement on transitional bilingual practice is the U.S. Commission on Civil Rights' A Better Chance to Learn: Bilingual Bicultural Education; and a lucid consideration of conflicting theories surrounding bilingual practice has been written by Christiana B. Paulston in Bilingual Education: Theories and Issues. The Center for Applied Linguistics has published a succinct multivolume Bilingual Education: Current Perspectives, intended to "answer some of the complex questions about bilingual education's past, present, and future": vol. 1 (Social Science); vol. 2 (Linguistics); vol. 3 (Law); vol. 4 (Education); vol. 5 (Synthesis).

Bilingual education is a promising pedagogical tool, but it is not without controversy. The passionate debate which accompanies the controversy derives from a complex set of factors. The implementation of bilingual programs is perceived as poor: and this charge is not easily rebutted; there have been few evaluation studies, and many bilingual programs were hastily undertaken without regard to the adequacy of staff training, the diagnosis of children's language needs, and appropriate curricular materials. Popular support for bilingual education has been lacking. In the past, public education has served as the chief vehicle for the assimilation of immigrant children into the mainstream of American society; English had always been the sole language of instruction in the schools. Bilingual education's use of native languages in the schools reversed what was perceived as a national policy; and to this there was (and continues to be) serious resentment by the progeny of earlier immigrants who see the new policy of bilingual education as the first step toward the official recognition of multilingualism extending from the schools across all public institutions of American society.

But the most dynamic element in the controversy surrounding bilingual education is the popular perception that it is a stratagem for ethnic employment not unrelated to the social, political, and economic aspirations of Hispanic minorities. Alan Pifer of the Carnegie Corporation of New York has, in his Bilingual Education and the Hispanic Challenge, addressed this issue directly:

> The programs have been strongly promoted by Hispanic organizations, and the educational, political, and administrative leadership for bilingual education has been mainly Hispanic. Indeed, bilingual education, as a vehicle for heightening respect and recognition of native languages and culture, for fighting discrimination against non English-speaking groups, and for obtaining jobs and political leverage, has become the preeminent civil rights issue within Hispanic communities. This development, coupled with the fact that Hispanics, through natural increase and immigration, are growing rapidly in numbers, has made the issue more visible and politicized than it might otherwise have been. Bilingual education is no longer regarded strictly as an educational measure but also as a strategy for realizing the social, political, and economic aspirations of Hispanic peoples. (p. 5)

Given this background, bilingual education cannot be considered without reference to larger frames in which it has evolved, and it remains vulnerable to political criticism with continuing need to justify itself educationally. In Language, Ethnicity and the Schools, Noel Epstein, critical of bilingual education, proposes a set of policy alternatives for bilingual-bicultural education; but Epstein's strictures should be evaluated alongside the views expressed by A. Bruce Gaarder in his Bilingual Schooling and the Survivial of Spanish in the United States; in the dimensional overviews afforded in Case Studies in Bilingual Education edited by Bernard Spolsky and Robert L. Cooper as well as in their companion volume, Frontiers of Bilingual Education; and in Francesco Cordasco, ed., Bilingualism and the Bilingual Child: Challenges and Problems.

Actually, bilingual education is not new in the United States: in a nation as diverse in origins as ours, this should not be surprising. English has not always been the only language used in American schools. School laws in the 1800s in Ohio (1839), Wisconsin (1846), Colorado (1867), Oregon (1872), Maryland (1874), and Minnesota (1877) dealt directly with the language issue in the curriculum either as a medium of instruction or as a subject to be taught.

German immigrants (whose progeny make up the largest ethnic group in America) established German-English bilingual schools in Cincinnati, Indianapolis, Hoboken, N.J. , Cleveland, and many other cities: these were public schools, and German was not only taught as a subject, it was used as a medium of instruction. Between 1880 and 1917, these schools flourished; they were eagerly supported by a powerful and socially-stratified German community. Only the political tensions of World War I ended their history. The rationale given by German immigrants to support the use of the German language in the schools of the 19th century is essentially that given to justify the existence of modern "maintenance" programs in bilingual education. They argued that German was important as an international language, and that its use in schools made sense for children from German-speaking families, and that it was also very enriching for children from English-speaking families. Leonard Covello advanced much the same views in recommending the use of Italian for Italian-speaking children in the New York City schools during the period of heavy Italian immigration (c. 1880-1920) and he outlined a program in his massive The Social Background of the Italo-American School Child. The German experience in American schools is extensively documented in Louis Viereck's German Instruction in American Schools which includes a wealth of material on the German bilingual public school systems in Cincinnati, Baltimore, Indianapolis, Cleveland, and other American cities. Viereck's report was originally published in The Annual Report (1900-1901) of the United States Commissioner of Education, and appeared in a German edition as well, Zwei Jahrhunderte der Unterricht in den Vereinigten Staaten (Braunschweig: Vieweg, 1903); it has been reprinted in Arno Press's core collection of texts, Bilingual Bicultural Education in the United States.

In Louisiana, French was used as the medium of instruction, and in New Mexico, Spanish was used. These were limited efforts and largely early and mid-19th century phenomena, but they confirm a bilingual tradition in America. In New York City, at different times and with differing commitments, the public schools taught children in Chinese, Italian, Greek, Yiddish, and French.

In a real sense, present-day efforts in bilingual education are a rediscovery of a respected and traditional American educational practice.

Bibliographies and General References

Information on the more than 100 ethnic groups who live in the United States (ethnically, the most heterogeneous nation in the world) is most conveniently available in the Harvard Encyclopedia of American Ethnic Groups which provides entries on the history, culture, and distinctive characteristics of each of the ethnic groups, and a series of thematic essays that clarify the key facets of ethnicity. Wayne Miller's A Comprehensive Bibliography for the Study of American Minorities includes 29,300 entries of English language materials for most American ethnic groups; a companion volume, A Handbook of American Minorities, reprints the preliminary bibliographical essays for each of the minority groups in the parent work. Additional useful general informational resources include: John D. Buenker and Michael C. Burkel, Immigration and Ethnicity; Francesco Cordasco, ed., A Bibliography of American Immigration History; Richard Kolm, ed., Bibliography of Ethnicity and Ethnic Groups; U.S. Cabinet Committee on Opportunities for Spanish Speaking People, The Spanish Speaking in the U.S.: A Guide to Materials; and Paul Wasserman and Jean Morgan, Ethnic Information Sources of the U.S. Francesco Cordasco's Immigrant Children in American Schools is a comprehensively dimensional bibliography of some 1500 titles, largely annotated, with selected source documents. In a broad frame of reference, Einar Haugen's Bilingualism in the Americas is a synthesis of the extensive literature in ten languages on the nature of the various languages in the Western hemisphere, contact among languages, the bilingual individual, and the bilingual community.

Bibliographies on individual ethnic groups abound. A few of the more useful (for research in American ethnic bilingualism) include: Enrique R. Bravo, Annotated Selected Puerto Rican Bibliography; Francesco Cordasco, Italian Americans: A Guide to Information Sources; Luis G. Nogales, ed., The Mexican American: A Selected and Annotated Bibliography; Henry Pochmann and Arthur Schultz, Bibliography of German Culture in America; Arnulfo D. Trejo, Bibliographia Chicana: A Guide to Information Sources; and Paquita Vivo, The Puerto Ricans: An Annotated Bibliography.

Over the last decade a number of bibliographical works dealing specifically with bilingualism and bilingual education have appeared. A massive annotated bibliography forms most of Volume I (pp. 149-243) of Theodore Andersson and Mildred Boyer's Bilingual Schooling in the United States. Francesco Cordasco and George Bernstein's Bilingual Education in American Schools: A Guide to Information Sources is intended "as a selective guide to the vast extant resources on bilingual education in the United States, its history, programs, curricula, administration, staff and teacher training, and the federal and state legislation which have governed its evolution, as well as the indices of tests, evaluation and measurement which have been employed." William F. Mackey has produced a basic bibliographical resource in Bibliographie Internationale Sur le Bilinguisme/International Bibliography on Bilingualism which is a computer printout of an alphabetized and indexed checklist of 11,000 titles; a Supplement lists an additional 9000 titles. Ivan Pinero's A Bibliography of Bilingual and Bicultural Education is a convenient register of recent materials (1970-1974); and Henry T. Trueba's Bilingual Bicultural Education for the Spanish Speaking in the United States: A Preliminary Bibliography is arranged by topical index categories which "represent the major disciplinary and theoretical concerns of scholars in the field of bilingual education."

Legislation: State and Federal Roles

The modern revival of public bilingual education in the United States did not originate in the area of foreign language teaching. It evolved within the context of minority rights which in various forms defined the critical social issues of the 1960s. As part of the social awareness inherent in the Johnsonian war on poverty, it was felt that ethnic poverty, exacerbated by unilingual teaching in English, seriously impaired the educational opportunities of non-English-speaking children; since education was a basic right, it was argued that the schools had an obligation to use the native languages of non-English-speaking children as the medium of instruction.

It was in a context of evolving equity-oriented legislation that the Bilingual Education Act of 1968 was passed by the Congress as Title VII of the amended Elementary and Secondary Education Act which had been enacted in 1965. The political support for the Bilingual Education Act came out of the large Mexican American community of the Southwest, and its sponsor was Senator Ralph Yarborough of Texas, eventually joined by others in the Congress. The aims of Title VII were modest; the Act provided funds for the planning and implementation of programs "designed to meet the special needs of children of limited English-speaking ability in schools having a high concentration of such children from families ... with incomes below $3000 per year." Hannah N. Geffert, et al., The Current Status of U.S. Bilingual Education, provides a complete overview of federal, state, and other "American" legislation in effect as of April 15, 1975, and updates Heinz Kloss's Laws and Legal Documents Relating to Problems of Bilingual Education in the U.S. which was published in 1971. Developments since Geffert's 1975 work can be traced in Abigail M. Thernstrom's "Language: Issues and Legislation" in the Harvard Encyclopedia of American Ethnic Groups.

The Bilingual Education Act was renewed in 1974 and again in 1978, and is due for renewal in 1983. Federal support has ranged from $7.5 million in 1969 supporting 76 projects reaching about 26,000 children to $107 million, supporting some 575 projects, and reaching some 315,000 children. Bilingual education has been strengthened by the decision in Lau v. Nichols (414 U.S. 563, 1974) in which the U.S. Supreme Court ruled that LESA children were entitled to some sort of remedial instruction; the Court held "under these state-imposed standards there is no equality of treatment merely by providing students with the same facilities, textbooks, teachers, and curriculum; for students who do not understand English are effectively foreclosed from any meaningful education." Lau v. Nichols was a class-action suit filed on behalf of some 1800 non-English-speaking Chinese students against the San Francisco Unified School District. The intricacies of the Lau decision and its effect on the 1974 bilingual amendments are detailedly studied by Susan G. Schneider in Revolution, Reaction or Reform: The 1974 Bilingual Education Act.

In 1971, Massachusetts was the first state to legislate the establishment of transitional bilingual programs; until that time no state had mandatory bilingual education legislation. By 1978, some ten states had enacted similar bilingual education statutes, but not without some considerable struggle and with continuing controversy. A vivid and painstaking account of the struggle in New York City by the Puerto Rican community in behalf of its children is chronicled in Isaura S. Santiago's A Community's Struggle for Equal Educational Opportunity: Aspira v. Board of Education.

English as a Second Language

ESL (or more properly TESOL, i. e. , "Teaching English to Speakers of Other Languages") is not, technically, bilingual education. In the United States, ESL has become an ancillary component of transitional bilingual programs. ESL is not unrelated to Americanization and immigrant naturalization programs in which English acquisition remained an integral part; as such, ESL is part of a tradition which, unfortunately, had as some of its major objectives the eradication of cultural differences, language suppression, and an ethnocentricism essentially inimical to immigrant aspirations. The structural-functional (S/F) approach is the position (if not explicit, almost always tacitly assumed) of the ESL advocates in the ESL vs. Bilingual Education controversy. Clearly, it is the position of the United States government. S/F theorists focus on the homeostatic or balancing mechanisms by which societies maintain a "uniform state." In such a paradigm ESL is an integral component of bilingual education programs.

The huge bibliographical resources of ESL theory and practice in Virginia F. Allen and Sidney Forman's English as a Second Language: A Comprehensive Bibliography (a subject-category listing of some 1500 titles) constitute the special English as a Foreign or Second Language Library in the Teachers College, Columbia University, Library. Wallace L. Goldstein's Teaching English as a Second Language: An Annotated Bibliography is a decennial review (1965-1975) which includes an author and a key-word index. Robert Lado's Annotated Bibliography for Teachers of English as a Foreign Language lists 750 items covering the period 1946 to 1953. A massive resource, Sirapi Ohannessian, and others, Reference Lists of Materials for English as a Second Language, includes annotated entries for (1) texts, readers, dictionaries, tests, and (2) background materials, and methodology; a Supplement, ed. by Dorothy Pedtke, should be consulted.

A wide range of texts on ESL theory and practice is available. The best introduction is that by Muriel Saville-Troike, Foundations for Teaching English as a Second Language. Saville-Troike (author of Bilingual Children: A Resource Document, and with Rudolph C. Troike of a widely used Handbook of Bilingual Education), is adamant in her assertion that "not only is ESL an essential component of bilingual education, but also instruction and explanation in the native language contribute significantly to the effectiveness of ESL." Practical strategies for ESL are available in Mary Finocchiaro's English as a Second Language: From Theory to Practice, and her Teaching English as a Second Language. Reference should also be made to Harold B. Allen's Teaching English as a Second Language, and to his Survey of the Teaching of English to non-English speakers in the

United States which describes teachers, teaching situations, aids and materials, and problems and needs in ESL. Useful additional references include Anne Newton, ed., The Art of TESOL; Marianne Celce-Murcia and Lois McIntosh, eds., Teaching English as a Second or Foreign Language; James E. Alatis and Kristie Twaddell, English as a Second Language in Bilingual Education; and Muriel Saville-Troike, ed., Classroom Practices in ESL and Bilingual Education. A valuable guide to training programs is Charles H. Blatchford, TESOL Training Program Directory.

The New York City Board of Education issued a number of pragmatic manuals for ESL of which the two most important are Teaching English to Puerto Rican Pupils in the Secondary Schools and Educating Students for Whom English is a Second Language; the Board's Puerto Rican Study was a heavily funded (one million dollars) four-year study of the problems of the education and adjustment of Puerto Rican children. The Study, and its related curriculum bulletins (Resource Units and Language Guide Series), furnished a detailed description of Puerto Rican children, devised a scale to rate English-speaking ability, and constructed a detailed program for the in-service education of teachers. Essentially an ESL document, the Study is the fullest examination ever made of the Puerto Rican educational experience on the mainland, and in a broader sense, it remains one of the most comprehensive statements yet made, not only of Puerto Rican school experience, but of the educational experience of the non-English-speaking minority child in the American school.

Evaluation, Tests, and Measurements

There is no dearth of evaluation instruments and tests for use in bilingual education. The Dissemination Center for Bilingual Bicultural Education has published Evaluation Instruments for Bilingual Education: An Annotated Bibliography whose 250 entries include material from commercial and nonprofit sources as well as from programs funded under Title VII. Instruments in eight languages, including English, are listed. How extensive and sustained the testing of bilingual children has been, and how obsessive the pursuit of intelligence-testing of bilingual children, is amply attested in Francesco Cordasco, ed., The Bilingual-Bicultural Child and the Question of Intelligence whose materials span a half-century and include investigations on the intelligence of immigrant children (and their parents); early hereditarian-oriented views; the perplexing issue of cross-cultural testing; the contemporary testing of Puerto Rican, Mexican, and other bilingual children; and, in a dimensional sense, the overall effects of bilingualism on intelligence.

A wide range of doctoral dissertations in the areas of evaluation, testing, and measurement in bilingual education have been completed, and these are noted (including abstracts) in Bilingual-Bicultural Education: Titles and Abastracts of Doctoral Dissertations. A number of these dissertations (by Robert R. Galvan, Solomon H. Flores, Amelia C. Medina, Juan C. Rodriguez-Munguia, Rosemary

Salomone-Levy, and Paul R. Streiff) have been published in the Arno Press core collection of materials entitled Bilingual-Bicultural Education in the United States.

In a very real sense, evaluation techniques have been enhanced by the sharpened perspectives of sociolinguistics which probes the interrelationships between language and social behavior and in which a recurring theme is the importance of social, linguistic, and psychological context to the effective understanding of speech and writing. The best introductions to the complexities of the linguistic domain for the student of bilingual education are Andrew D. Cohen, A Sociolinguistic Approach to Bilingual Education, and Joshua A. Fishman, Sociolinguistics: A Brief Introduction. The rich rewards of sociolinguistic orientations are illustrated in Einar Haugen's massive The Norwegian Language in America: A Study in Bilingual Behavior; in Eduardo Hernandez-Chavez, ed., El Lenguaje de los Chicanos; and in Lawrence Biondi's specialized monograph, The Italian American Child: His Sociolinguistic Acculturation.

Early materials developed by the New York City Board of Education are not without value, particularly the Board's Developing a Program for Testing Puerto Rican Pupils in the New York City Public Schools; and Herschel T. Manuel's Tests of General Ability and Reading and Development of Inter-American Test Materials are pioneer efforts in the testing of general ability and reading for the bilingual child.

It must be conceded that sophisticated techniques of evaluation and testing are available in the recent works by L. G. Kelly, Description et Mesure du Bilinguisme/Description and Measurement of Bilingualism; Robert J. Silverman, et al., Oral Language Tests for Bilingual Students; Bernard Spolsky, et al., A Model for the Description, Analysis and Evaluation of Bilingual Education; Stanley F. Wanat, ed., Issues in Evaluating Reading; and Randall Jones and Bernard Spolsky, eds., Testing Language Proficiency. Yet there is a compelling scarcity of hard data regarding the effectiveness of bilingual education programs, and the continuing vulnerability of bilingual education lies in this crucial area.

In 1976 the United States General Accounting Office (G. A. O.) issued its Bilingual Education: An Unmet Need. A report to the Congress, the G. A. O.'s study maintained that the United States Office of Education (U. S. O. E.) had made little progress in identifying effective means of providing bilingual education instruction, in the training of bilingual education teachers, and in developing suitable teaching materials. A damaging evaluation, commissioned by the U. S. O. E., extending over four years and examining the progress of 11,500 Hispanic students, was published in 1978. The evaluation was done by the American Institute of Research (AIR) and submitted under the title, Evaluation of the Impact of ESEA Title VII Spanish/English Bilingual Education Program: An Overview of Study and Findings. It concluded that most of the children did not need to learn English; that those who did were in fact not acquiring it; that with few exceptions the programs

aimed at linguistic and cultural maintenance; and that to the degree
that children were already alienated from school, they remained so.
The Center for Applied Linguistics published a Response to the AIR
Study, but the AIR evaluation forced the reorientation of bilingual programs as reflected in the renewed but amended Bilingual Education
Act of 1978. The amended 1978 Act placed a ceiling of 40 percent
on the number of English-speaking children who could be included in
the programs; placed a new stress on parental involvement; instructed
local schools to use personnel proficient in both the language of instruction and English; and described eligible participants as children
with limited English proficiency (as opposed to limited English-speaking
ability), thus expanding the meaning of linguistic deficiency to include
reading and writing. These 1978 modifications have not succeeded in
quieting the controversy which continues to surround bilingual education.

* * * *

The Bilingual Education Act is due to expire in 1983, and, at this
point, its future is uncertain. However, it would be a mistake, whatever the future of the Act, to believe that bilingual education will dis-
appear. A variety of other federal and state legislative acts fund bilingual education. Ten states have made bilingual education mandatory, and 16 others have enacted legislation that generally authorizes
the development of bilingual programs. Bilingual components are
parts of important and influential federal acts, among which are the
Emergency School Aid Act, the Vocational Education Act, the Adult
Education Act, and the Higher Education Act. The Lau remedies en-
tangle both judicial decisions and regulatory guidelines which make
even more complex any efforts to end, or even curtail, bilingual education programs. And there is little doubt that academicians are
unaware of the perilous state in which American bilingualism finds
itself, as is attested in the recent judicious overview of all aspects
of bilingual practice in James E. Alatis, ed., Current Issues in Bilingual Education.

At this juncture, the most salutary view may well have been
voiced by Alan Pifer: "What is needed, now, is a determined effort
by all concerned to improve bilingual education programs in the schools
through more sympathetic administration and community support, more
and better trained teachers, and a sustained, sophisticated, and well-
financed research effort to find out where these programs are succeeding and where they are failing and why."

References

ALATIS, James E. and Kristie Twaddell, eds. Teaching English as
a second language in bilingual education. TESOL, 1976.
ALATIS, James E., ed. Current issues in bilingual education.
Georgetown University Press, 1980.
ALLEN, Harold B. Teaching English as a second language. McGraw-
Hill, 1972.

_____. A survey of the teaching of English to non-English speak-
ers in the United States. National Council of Teachers of
English, 1966. Rep., Arno, 1978.
ALLEN, Virginia and Sidney Forman. English as a second language:
a comprehensive bibliography. Teachers College, Columbia
University, 1967. Rep., Arno, 1978.
AMERICAN INSTITUTE OF RESEARCH. Evaluation of the impact of
ESEA Title VII Spanish/English bilingual education program:
an overview of study and findings. AIR (Palo Alto, Ca.), 1978.
ANDERSSON, Theodore and Mildred Boyer. Bilingual schooling in the
United States. 2 vols. Southwest Educational Development La-
boratory, 1970. Rep. with introduction and supplementary bib-
liography by Francesco Cordasco. Blaine Ethridge, 1976.
BIONDI, Lawrence. The Italian American child: his sociolinguistic
acculturation. Georgetown University Press, 1975.
BLATCHFORD, Charles H. TESOL training program director, 1974-
1976. TESOL, 1975.
BRAVO, Enrique R. Annotated selected Puerto Rican bibliography.
Urban Center, Columbia University, 1972.
BUENKER, John D. and Nicholas C. Burkel, eds. Immigration and
ethnicity: a guide to information sources. Gale, 1977.
CELCE-MURCIA, Marianne and Lois McIntosh, eds. Teaching Eng-
lish as a second or foreign language. Newbury House, 1979.
CENTER FOR APPLIED LINGUISTICS. Bilingual education: current
perspectives. vol. 1 (Social Science); vol. 2 (Linguistics);
vol. 3 (Law); vol. 4 (Education); vol. 5 (Synthesis). Center
for Applied Linguistics, 1977.
_____. Response to AIR study. Center for Applied Linguistics,
1978.
COHEN, Andrew D. A sociolinguistic approach to bilingual education.
Newbury House, 1975.
CORDASCO, Francesco. Bilingual schooling in the United States: a
sourcebook for educational personnel. McGraw-Hill, 1976.
_____. Immigrant children in American schools: a classified and
annotated bibliography with selected source documents. Augustus M. Kelley, 1976.
_____, ed. Bilingualism and the bilingual child: challenges and
problems. Arno, 1978.
_____, ed. A bibliography of American immigration history: the
George Washington University project studies. Augustus M.
Kelley, 1978.
_____. Italian Americans: a guide to information sources. Gale,
1978.
_____, ed. The bilingual-bicultural child and the question of in-
telligence. Arno, 1978.
_____, advisory ed. Bilingual-bicultural education in the United
States. 37 vols. Arno, 1978.
_____ and George Bernstein. Bilingual education in American
schools: a guide to information sources. Gale, 1979.
COVELLO, Leonard. The social background of the Italo-American
school child: a study of the southern Italian mores and their
effect on the school situation in Italy and America. Edited
with an introduction by Francesco Cordasco. E. J. Brill,
1967. Rep. Rowman and Littlefield, 1972.

DISSEMINATION CENTER FOR BILINGUAL BICULTURAL EDUCATION. Evaluation instruments for bilingual education: an annotated bibliography. Dissemination Center for Bilingual Bicultural Education (Austin, Texas), 1975.

EPSTEIN, Noel. Language, ethnicity, and the schools: policy alternatives for bilingual-bicultural education. George Washington University, Institute for Educational Leadership, 1977.

FINOCCHIARO, Mary. English as a second language: from theory to practice. Simon and Schuster, 1964.

_____. Teaching English as a second language. Rev. ed. Harper and Row, 1969.

FISHMAN, Joshua A. Sociolinguistics: a brief introduction. Newbury House, 1971.

_____, ed. Language loyalty in the United States. Mouton, 1966. Rep. Arno, 1978.

FLORES, Solomon H. The nature and effectiveness of bilingual education programs for the Spanish-speaking child in the United States. Arno, 1978.

GAARDER, A. Bruce. Bilingual schooling and the survival of Spanish in the United States. Newbury House, 1977.

GALVAN, Robert R. Bilingualism as it relates to intelligence test scores and school achievement among culturally deprived Spanish-American children. Arno, 1978.

GEFFERT, Hannah, N., and others. The current status of U.S. bilingual legislation. Center for Applied Linguistics, 1975.

GOLDSTEIN, Wallace L. Teaching English as a second language: an annotated bibliography. Garland, 1975.

HAUGEN, Einar. The Norwegian language in America: a study in bilingual behavior. 2 vols. University of Pennsylvania Press, 1953.

_____. Bilingualism in the Americas: a bibliography and research guide. University of Alabama Press, 1956.

HERNANDEZ-CHAVEZ, Eduardo, ed. El lenguaje de los chicanos: regional and social character of language used by Mexican Americans. Newbury House, 1977.

JONES, Randall and Bernard Spolsky, eds. Testing language proficiency. Center for Applied Linguistics, 1975.

KELLY, L. G., ed. Description et mesure du bilinguisme/Description and measurement of bilingualism. University of Toronto Press, 1969.

KLOSS, Heinz. Laws and legal documents relating to problems of bilingual education in the United States. Center for Applied Linguistics, 1971.

_____. The American bilingual tradition. Newbury House, 1977.

KOLM, Richard, ed. Bibliography of ethnicity and ethnic groups. National Institute of Mental Health, 1973.

LADO, Robert. Annotated bibliography for teachers of English as a foreign language. G. P. O., 1955.

MACKEY, William F. Bibliographie internationale sur le bilinguisme/ International bibliography on bilingualism. Les Presses de Université Laval, 1972. Supplement, 1978.

MANUEL, Herschel T. Tests of general ability and reading: Inter-American test materials. University of Texas Press, 1963.

_____. Development of Inter-American test materials. University of Texas Press, 1966.

MEDINA, Amelia C. A comparative analysis of evaluative theory and practice for the instructional component of bilingual programs. Arno, 1978.

MILLER, Wayne, A comprehensive bibliography for the study of American minorities. 2 vols. New York University Press, 1976.

NATIONAL DISSEMINATION AND ASSESSMENT CENTER. Bilingual bicultural education: titles and abstracts of doctoral dissertations. California State University (Los Angeles), 1977.

NEW YORK CITY BOARD OF EDUCATION. Developing a program for testing Puerto Rican pupils in the New York City public schools. Board of Education, 1958.

_____. Teaching English to Puerto Rican pupils in the secondary schools. Board of Education, 1960.

_____. Educating students for whom English is a second language: programs, activities, and services for grades pre K-12. Board of Education, 1965.

_____. The Puerto Rican study, 1953-1957. Board of Education, 1958. Rep. with an introductory essay by Francesco Cordasco. Oriole Editions, 1972.

NEWTON, Anne, ed. The art of TESOL. 2 vols. Newbury House, 1978.

NOGALES, Luis G. , ed. The Mexican American: a selected and annotated bibliography. 2nd. ed. Center for Latin American Studies, Stanford University, 1971.

OHANNESSIAN, Sirapi, et al. Reference lists of materials for English as a second language. 2 vols. Center for Applied Linguistics, 1974-1966. Supplement, 1969.

ORTEGA, Luis, ed. Introduction to bilingual education. Las Americas, 1975.

PAULSTON, Christina B. Bilingual education: theories and issues. Newbury House, 1980.

PIFER, Alan. Bilingual education and the Hispanic challenge. Carnegie Corporation of New York, 1980.

PINERO, Ivan. A bibliography of bilingual and bicultural education. Bilingual Resource Center, New York City, 1975.

POCHMANN, Henry and Arthur Schultz. Bibliography of German culture in America. University of Wisconsin Press, 1953.

RODRIGUEZ-MUNGUIA, Juan C. Supervision of bilingual programs. Arno, 1978.

SANTIAGO, Isaura S. A community's struggle for equal educational opportunity: Aspira vs. Board of Education. Educational Testing Service (Princeton, N.J.), 1978.

SAVILLE-TROIKE, Muriel and Rudolph C. Troike. A handbook of bilingual education. Center for Applied Linguistics, 1971.

SAVILLE-TROIKE, Muriel. Bilingual children: a resource document. Center for Applied Linguistics, 1973.

_____, ed. Classroom practices in ESL and bilingual education. TESOL, 1973.

_____. Foundations for teaching English as a second language: theory and method for multicultural education. Prentice-Hall, 1976.

SCHNEIDER, Susan G. Revolution, reaction or reform: the 1974 Bilingual Education Act. Las Americas, 1976.

SILVERMAN, Robert J. et al. Oral language tests for bilingual students: an evaluation of language dominance and proficiency instruments. Center for Bilingual Education, Northwest Regional Educational Laboratory (Portland, Oregon), 1976.

SOLOMONE-LEVY, Rosemary. An analysis of the effects of language acquisition context upon the dual language development of non-English dominant students. Arno, 1978.

SPOLSKY, Bernard, and others. A model for the description, analysis and evaluation of bilingual education. University of New Mexico, Navajo Reading Study Progress Report, No. 23, 1974.

SPOLSKY, Bernard and Robert L. Cooper, eds. Frontiers of bilingual education. Newbury House, 1977.

_____, eds. Case studies in bilingual education. Newbury House, 1978.

STREFF, Paul R. Development of guidelines for conducting research in bilingual education. Arno, 1978.

THERNSTROM, Stephen, ed. Harvard encyclopedia of American ethnic groups. Harvard University Press, 1980.

TREJO, Arnulfo D. Bibliographia Chicana: a guide to information sources. Gale, 1975.

TRUEBA, Henry T. Bilingual bicultural education for the Spanish speaking in the United States: a preliminary bibliography. Stipes Publishing Co., 1977.

_____ and Carol Barnett-Mizrahi, ed. Bilingual multicultural education and the professional: from theory to practice. Newbury House, 1979.

U.S. CABINET COMMITTEE ON OPPORTUNITIES FOR SPANISH SPEAKING PEOPLE. The Spanish speaking in the United States: a guide to materials. G.P.O., 1971. Rep. with foreword by Francesco Cordasco. Blaine Ethridge, 1975.

U.S. COMMISSION ON CIVIL RIGHTS. A better chance to learn: bilingual-bicultural education. U.S. Commission on Civil Rights, 1975.

U.S. GENERAL ACCOUNTING OFFICE. Bilingual education: an unmet need. G.P.O., 1976.

VIERECK, LOUIS. German instruction in American schools. With an introduction by George Bernstein. Arno, 1978.

VIVO, PAQUITA. The Puerto Ricans: an annotated bibliography. Bowker, 1973.

VON MALTITZ, FRANCIS W. Living and learning in two languages: bilingual-bicultural education in the United States. McGraw-Hill, 1975.

WANAT, STANLEY F., ed. Issues in evaluating reading. Center for Applied Linguistics, 1977.

WASSERMAN, PAUL AND JEAN MORGAN. Ethnic information sources of the United States. Gale, 1976.

PUERTO RICAN CHILDREN IN AMERICAN MAINLAND SCHOOLS

The Migration and Mainland Experience: An Overview

In February 1971, the U. S. Census Bureau published its November 1969, sample-survey estimate that the fifty states and the District of Columbia had 1,454,000 Puerto Rican residents--811,000 born on the island, 636,000 born in the states and district, 1,000 in Cuba, and 6,000 elsewhere. In March 1972, the Census Bureau released pre-liminary and a few final state population totals from the 1970 census for three categories--persons of Spanish language, persons of Spanish family name, and Puerto Ricans. Puerto Rican counts were for three states only--New York (872,471; 5% of the state population); New Jersey (135,676; 2% of the state population); and Pennsylvania (44,535).

Puerto Ricans have been on the mainland for many years; in the 19th century, a small colony of Puerto Ricans, gathered largely in New York City, worked for the independence of the island. After the annexation of the island in 1898 by the United States, a continuing migration to the mainland began. In 1910 some 1,500 Puerto Ricans were living in the United States; by 1930, they numbered close to 53,000. The migration was reversed during the depression of the 1930s; and again was substantially impeded by World War II in the early 1940s. After the end of World War II (and concurrent with the advent of cheap air transport) it increased steadily until it reached its peak in the early 1950s (in 1953, 304,910 persons left the island and 203,307 returned, leaving a net balance of 74,603). The state of the economy on the mainland has always been an indicator of the migration. The decline in Puerto Rican migration to the mainland in 1970 and continuing across the 1970s was precisely due to eco-nomic hardship in the states. The pattern has not significantly changed between 1970-1980. A recent demographic study observes:

> Migration tends to decrease during periods of crisis in the United States and sometimes the current has reversed it-self; more than 280,000 people of Puerto Rican extraction have returned to Puerto Rico, and the current of returning

migrants seems to have increased considerably since 1970. An economy which depends on its ability to get rid of its excess population by means of migration cannot be expected to have great stability and finds itself on a very unsound base. (Vasquez Calzada, 1979: 235).

In a prescient book on Puerto Rican Americans, the Jesuit sociologist, Rev. Joseph P. Fitzpatrick, observes that Puerto Ricans have found it difficult to achieve "community solidarity" and suggests that they may work out adjustment "in very new ways" differing from those of past immigrants (technically, as American citizens, Puerto Ricans are migrants to the mainland United States); and Father Fitzpatrick cogently observes:

> A book about the Puerto Ricans in mainland United States, with a special focus on those in New York City, is very risky but also is very necessary. It is risky because the Puerto Rican community is in a state of turbulent change in a city and a nation which are also in a state of turbulent change. So many different currents of change affect Puerto Ricans at the present time that it is foolhardy to attempt to describe this group adequately or put them into focus. Nor is it possible to point out clearly any one direction in which the Puerto Rican community is moving in its adjustment to life on the mainland. Its directions are often in conflict, and no single leader or movement has given sharp definition to one direction as dominant over others.... What is most needed at this moment of the Puerto Rican experience, both for Puerto Ricans and other mainland Americans, is perspective: a sense of the meaning of the migration for everyone involved in that migration, for the new-comers as well as the residents of the cities and neighborhoods to which the Puerto Ricans come. (Fitzpatrick 1971: xi).

How varied the Puerto Rican experience on the mainland has been can be best indicated by the sharp contrasts provided in four juxtaposed excerpts from Puerto Rican reactions registered over a period of time.

In 1948, J. J. Osuna, the distinguished Puerto Rican educator, on a visit to New York City schools, observed:

> As far as possible something should be done in Puerto Rico to discourage migration of people who do not have occupations to go into upon their arrival in this country, or of children whose parents live in Puerto Rico and who have no home in New York. Too many people are coming, hoping that they may find work and thereby better themselves economically, and in the case of the children, educationally. It is laudable that they take the chance, but the experience of the past teaches us that as far as possible, people should not come to the continent until they have secured employment here. (Osuna 1948: 227).

In 1961, Joseph Monserrat, at the time Director of Migration
Division, Commonwealth of Puerto Rico, in speaking on "Community
Planning for Puerto Rican Integration in the United States," cautioned

> If all Puerto Ricans were to suddenly disappear from New
> York City, neither the housing problem nor other basic is-
> sues confronting the city would be solved.   In fact, without
> the Puerto Ricans, New York would be faced with one of
> two alternatives: either "import" people to do the work
> done by Puerto Ricans (and whoever was imported from
> wherever they might come would have to live in the very
> same buildings Puerto Ricans now live in for the simple
> reason that there is nothing else); or industries would have
> to move to other areas where there are workers, causing
> a severe economic upheaval in the city.   Obviously, neither
> one is a viable solution.   Nor will the stagnation of the past
> resolve our dilemma.... The Puerto Rican, although he
> comes from a close knit neighborhood in the Commonwealth,
> has found the best possibility for social action and self-
> improvement on the city-wide level.   The community of
> Puerto Ricans is not the East Side or the South Side.   It
> is New York City, Lorain, Chicago, Los Angeles, Middle-
> town.   City living is learned living.   The migrants must be
> helped to learn the facts of city life and how to function ef-
> fectively as a pressure group in a pressure group society.
> (Monserrat 1961:   221).

Both of these statements are in stark contrast to the ideology
of revolution and separatism evident in the animadversions which follow.   First, from a spokesman for "La Generación Encojonada":

> Violence is the essence of a colonial society.   It is estab-
> lished as a system in the interests of the ruling classes.
> Colonial society "is the meeting of two forces, opposed to
> each other by their very nature, which in fact owe their
> originality to that sort of substantiation which results
> from and is nourished by the situation in the colonies. Their
> first encounter was marked by violence and their existence
> together ... was carried on by dint of a great array of bay-
> onets and cannon."   Puerto Rican history has been witness
> to this violent confrontation between people and oppressor.
> We see it in daily events: in schools, churches, factories,
> the countryside, in strikes, demonstrations, and insurrec-
> tions.   As soon as an individual confronts the system, he
> feels its violence in the way of life colonialism imposes on
> him: the feudal-type exploitation in the countryside, the
> capitalist exploitation in the cities.
>   The lifeblood of every colonial society is the profit it
> offers to its exploiters.   Its basis is the authority of an
> exploiting system--not the authority that comes from a ma-
> jority consensus, but the paternal authority with which a
> minority tries to justify a system beneficial to it.   Around
> that system is built a morality, an ethic, rooted in the

economic co-existence of colonizers and colonized. Thus the system envelops itself in forms that create the illusion of sharing, of a brotherhood and equality that don't exist. The Puerto Rican elections held every four years exemplify this. We must not confuse the ox with the fighting bull, the causes with the problem, the root with the branches. (Silen 1971: 118-119).

And from a theoretician for the Young Lords' Party, spawned in the socio-pathology of the urban barrio:

> To support its economic exploitation of Puerto Rico, the United States instituted a new educational system whose purpose was to Americanize us. Specifically, that means that the school's principal job is to exalt the cultural values of the United States. As soon as we begin using books that are printed in English, that are printed in the United States, that means that the American way of life is being pushed ... with all its bad points, with its commercialism, its dehumanization of human beings.
> At the same time that the cultural values of America are exalted, the cultural values of Puerto Rico are downgraded. People begin to feel ashamed of speaking Spanish. Language becomes a reward and punishment system. If you speak English and adapt to the cultural values of America, you're rewarded; if you speak Spanish and stick to the old traditional ways, you're punished. In the school system here, if you don't quickly begin to speak English and shed your Puerto Rican values, you're put back a grade--so you may be in the sixth grade in Puerto Rico but when you come here, you go back to the fourth or fifth. You're treated as if you're retarded, as if you're backward--and your own cultural values therefore are shown to be of less value than the cultural values of this country and the language of this country. (Perez 1971: 65-66).

It is no accident that this strident voice registers anger particularly with the schools; for it is in the schools that Puerto Rican identity is subjected to the greatest pressures, and it is the educational experience on the mainland which, for Puerto Ricans, is generally bad and from which despair and alienation emerge. It is in mainland schools that the dynamics of conflict and acculturation for Puerto Ricans are best seen in clear perspective; and it is a grim irony that, generally, educational programs for Puerto Ricans have failed despite the multitudinous educational experiments encapsulated in those new attentions born in Johnsonian America to the culture of the poor and the massive programmatic onslaughts on poverty. In the Puerto Rican mainland communities, there has been a subtle shift (following Black models) from civil rights and integration to an emphasis on Puerto Rican power and community solidarity.

And the Puerto Rican poor in their urban barrios have encountered as their chief adversaries the Black poor in the grim struggle for antipoverty monies and for the participative identities in Community Action Programs (funded by the Office of Economic Opportunity) which are often the vehicles and leverages of political power in the decaying American cities; additionally, a Puerto Rican professional presence in schools and a myriad of other institutional settings has been thwarted by exiled middle-class Cuban professionals.

> Most of the Cubans are an exiled professional middle-class that came to the United States for political reasons. They are lauded and rewarded by the United States government for their rejection of Communism and Fidel Castro. The Cubans lean toward the political right, are fearful of the involvement of masses of poor people. Being middle-class they are familiar with 'the system' and operated successfully in this structure. They are competitive and upwardly mobile. They have little sympathy for the uneducated poor. (Hidalgo 1971: 14)

It is hardly strange that the Puerto Rican community has looked to the schools, traditionally the road out of poverty, as affording its best hope for successfully negotiating the challenges of a hostile mainland American milieu.

Non-English Speaking Children in American Schools: The Children of the Past

American schools have always had as students children from a wide variety of cultural backgrounds; and the non-English speaking child has been no stranger in American urban classrooms. If we are to understand the problems which Puerto Rican children encounter in mainland schools, it is instructive to look at the experience of other children (non-English speaking and culturally different) in American schools. A huge literature (largely ignored until recently) exists on the children of immigrants in the schools. No document on this earlier experience is more impressive than the Report of the Immigration Commission (1911) whose Report on the Children of Immigrants in Schools (vols. , 29-33) is a vast repository of data on the educational history of the children of the poor and the schools. By 1911, 57. 5% of the children in the public schools of 37 of the largest American cities were of foreign-born parentage; in the parochial schools of 24 of these 37 cities, the children of foreign-born parents constituted 63. 5% of the total registration. "To the immigrant child the public elementary school was the first step away from his past, a means by which he could learn to assume the characteristics necessary for the long climb upward. " (Thomas 1954: 253). And by 1911, almost 50% of the students in secondary schools were of foreign-born parentage. In American cities, the major educational challenge and responsibility was the immigrant child. (U. S. Immigration Commission Abstracts 1911: 2: 1-15).

In the effort to respond to the needs of the immigrant child, it is important to note that no overall programs were developed to aid any particular immigrant group. Although there was little agreement as to what Americanization was, the schools were committed to Americanize (and to Anglicize) their charges. Ellwood P. Cubberley's Changing Conceptions of Education (1909), which Lawrence A. Cremin characterizes as "a typical progressive tract of the era," saw the immigrants as "illiterate, docile, lacking in self-reliance and initiative, and not possessing the Angloteutonic conceptions of law, order, and government...," and the school's role was (in Cubberley's view) "to assimilate and amalgamate." (Cremin 1961: 263).

What efforts were made to respond to the needs of immigrant children were improvised, most often directly in answer to specific problems; almost never was any attempt made to give the school and its program a community orientation. The children literally left at the door of the school their language, their cultural identities, and their immigrant subcommunity origins. A child's parents had virtually no role in the schools, and the New York City experience was not atypical in its leaving the immigrant child to the discretion of the individual superintendent, a principal, or a teacher.

Against such a lack of understanding and coordinated effort in behalf of the children of the poor, it is hardly strange that the general malaise of the schools was nowhere more symptomatic than in the pervasive phenomenon of the overage pupil who was classed under the rubric "retardation" with all of its negative connotations. The Immigration Commission of 1911 found that the percentage of retardation for the New York City elementary school pupils was 36.4 with the maximum retardation (48.8%) in the fifth grade. The Commission observed:

> ... thus in the third grade the pupils range in age from 5 to 18 years. In similar manner pupils of the age of 14 years are found in every grade from the first of the elementary schools to the last of the high schools. It will, however, be noted that in spite of this divergence the great body of the pupils of a given grade are of certain definite ages, the older and younger pupils being in each case much less numerically represented. It may, therefore, be assumed that there is an appropriate age for each grade. This assumption is the cardinal point in current educational discussion in regard to retardation. If it were assumed that there is a normal age for each grade, then the pupils can be divided into two classes--those who are of normal age or less and those who are above the normal age. The latter or overage pupils, are designated as "retarded." (Report 1911: 32: 608-609).

At best, it is a dismal picture whose poignant and evocative pathos is etched in the faces of the children imprisoned in the cheerless classrooms of the era. It could have been otherwise: in the lower East Side of New York City the efforts of District School Superintendent, Julia Richman, at the turn of the century, pointed in the more rewarding directions of community awareness, of building on the cultural strengths which the child brought to the school; and the near quarter-century tenure (1934-1957) of Leonard Covello at Benjamin Franklin High School in New York City's East Harlem, dramatically underscored the successes of the community-centered school. But Julia Richman and Leonard Covello were the exceptions, not the rule; and it is hardly fortuitous that they came out of the emerging Jewish and Italian subcommunities, for these very identities help explain their responsiveness to the immigrant child.

Puerto Rican Children in the Schools: The Early Years

It is in the perspectives of these earlier experiences that the educational failures of the Puerto Rican child are to be viewed and understood. Committed to policies of Americanization, the schools neglected the cultural heritage of the Puerto Rican child, rejected his ancestral language, and generally ignored his parents and community. And these policies were in keeping with the traditional practices of the schools.

The Puerto Rican community in New York City is the largest on the mainland, and its experience would be essentially typical of other mainland urban communities. As early as 1938, the difficulties of the Puerto Rican child in the New York City schools are graphically (if passingly) noted:

> Many Puerto Rican children who enter the public schools in New York speak or understand little English. The children who are transferred from schools in Puerto Rico to those in New York are usually put back in their classes so that they are with children who are two or three years younger than they are. Americans who are teaching Puerto Rican children express the opinion that these children have had less training in discipline and in group cooperation than American children. Lacking the timidity of many of the children in this country, they sometimes act in an unrestrained and impulsive manner. One large agency in the settlement, which has dealt with Puerto Rican children for many years, reported that under proper conditions Puerto Rican children are responsive, easily managed, and affectionate. In contrast to this, another large institution said that for some reason which they could not explain the Puerto Rican children were more destructive than any group of children with whom they had had contact. All the evidence obtainable shows the relation of unsatisfactory home conditions to difficulties at school. During the past few years the desperate economic condition of these families has caused them to move so frequently that it has often been difficult to locate the children when they did not attend school. (Chenault 1938: 146).

In December, 1946, Dr. Paul Kennedy, then President of the New York City Association of Assistant Superintendents, appointed a committee "to study and report on the educational adjustments made necessary by the addition of the 400,000 Puerto Ricans who have lately become residents of this city." The surprisingly comprehensive report prepared by this committee considered native backgrounds; migration to the mainland; problems of assimilation; the education of the Puerto Rican pupil; and made a number of recommendations. That the report was anchored in the past is evident in its caution that "Although the Puerto Rican is an American citizen, the adjustment he must make in this city is like that of immigrants to this country from a foreign land." The report counted "13,914 pupils enrolled [June 1947; by October 1970, 260,000 were enrolled] in the public elementary and junior high schools of the city who originally came from Puerto Rico;" and further grimly observed

> there is no doubt but that many pupils coming from Puerto Rico suffer from the double handicap of unfamiliarity with the English language and lack or previous educational experience, sometimes approaching complete illiteracy. Malnutrition and other health deficiencies contribute to the educational problem of the schools. The overcrowding at home and the restlessness on the street carry over into the school in the form of nervousness, extreme shyness, near tantrums, and other behavior characteristics which are the more difficult for the teacher to understand because of the language barrier. (Report 1947: 38).

The Committee, also undertook the first study of "reading progress" among Puerto Rican pupils who were new admissions to the elementary and junior high schools; and it made a series of recommendations, chief among which was the establishment of special classes ("C" classes) for Puerto Rican children "for whom at least a year's time is needed for preliminary instruction and language work before they are ready for complete assimilation in the regular program." Although the report was generally neglected, it represented the first systematic study undertaken on the mainland to call attention to the needs of Puerto Rican children.

Attention has been called to J. J. Osuna's Report on Visits to New York City Schools in 1948. In 1951, a Mayor's Committee on Puerto Rican Affairs in New York City was convened and considered the needs of Puerto Rican pupils; and in 1953, Dr. Leonard Covello, then Principal of Benjamin Franklin High School in East Harlem, consolidated and articulated into schematic form for consideration the various proposals which had been made up to that time to deal with the needs of Puerto Rican children in the schools.

Finally, in 1953, the New York City Board of Education presented in booklet form the results of a study initiated by its Division of Curriculum Development. This brief report indicated a new awareness of the importance of using Spanish in instructing Puerto Rican children, of the need for knowledge of Puerto Rican cultural backgrounds, and of the need for bilingual teachers. But it equally made clear the critical need for a fully developed educational program for

Puerto Rican children; and it served as a prologue to The Puerto Rican Study which was initiated in 1953.

The Puerto Rican Study

The Puerto Rican Study was, for its time, one of the most generously funded educational studies ever undertaken. The Fund for the Advancement of Education provided a grant-in-aid of a half million dollars and "contributions equivalent in amounts authorized by the Board of Education made the study a vital operation in the school system" (Foreword). It was not completed until 1957, and it was finally published in April 1959. It is, unquestionably, the fullest study ever made of the Puerto Rican educational experience on the mainland; and, in a broader sense, it remains one of the most comprehensive statements yet made, not only of the Puerto Rican school experience, but of the educational experience of the non-English speaking minority child in the American school. As such it is an invaluable document in American educational historiography, with all of the contemporary relevancies which the 1960s have defined (and continuing across the 1970s) with reference to ethnicity, the minority child, the contexts of poverty, and the educational needs of the "disadvantaged" child. It is strange that, in the proliferating literature on the minority child and the schools, The Puerto Rican Study has been neglected; and its neglect may be due to its appearance before the advent of the Johnsonian antipoverty programs of the 1960s with their educational components, and to the inevitable fate of sponsored reports whose implementation and evaluation are seldom realized or avoided for a variety of reasons.

The Puerto Rican Study's objectives are clearly stated:

> In a narrow sense, The Puerto Rican Study was a four-year inquiry into the education and adjustment of Puerto Rican pupils in the public schools of the City of New York. In a broader sense, it was a major effort of the school authorities to establish on a sound basis a city-wide program for the continuing improvement of the educational opportunities of all non-English-speaking pupils in the public schools.
> While the Study was focused on the public schools in New York City, it was planned and conducted in the belief that the findings might be useful to all schools, public and private, that are trying to serve children from a Spanish-language culture. As the Study developed, it seemed apparent that it might have values, direct or indirect, wherever children are being taught English as a second language. (Study 1958: 1)

It sought answers to the following specific problems: (1) What are the most effective methods and materials for teaching English as a second language to newly-arrived Puerto Rican pupils? (2) What are the most effective techniques whereby the school can promote a more rapid and more effective adjustment of Puerto Rican parents and children to the community and of the community to them?

As the Study progressed, its staff developed two series of related curriculum bulletins--Resource Units organized around themes and designed for all pupils, and a Language Guide Series which provided the content and methods for adapting the instruction to the needs of the pupils learning English (the Study lists the Units and Series). The Study also furnished a detailed description of the Puerto Rican children; devised a scale to rate English-speaking ability; and constructed a detailed program for the inservice education of teachers (Chapter 17).

The Recommendations of The Puerto Rican Study

The Study's recommendations ("Where The Puerto Rican Study Leads") are both a blueprint and design for effectively meeting the needs of Puerto Rican children, and they impinge on all those facets of the experience of the minority child which are interrelated and which, if neglected, impede social growth and cognitive achievement. Simply listed (without the capsuled rationales which accompany them), they represent a skeletal construct as meaningful today as when they were formulated:

1. Accept The Puerto Rican Study, not as something finished, but as the first stage of a larger, city-wide, ever improving program for the education and assimilation of non-English-speaking children.
2. Take a new look at the philosophy governing the education of the non-English-speaking children in New York City schools.
3. Recognize that whatever is done for the non-English-speaking child, is, in the long run, done for all the children.
4. Use the annual school census as a basic technique in planning the continuing adaptation of the schools to the needs of the non-English-speaking pupils.
5. Recognize the heterogeneity of the non-English-speaking pupils.
6. Formulate a uniform policy for the reception, screening, placement, and periodic assessment of non-English-speaking pupils.
7. Keep policies governing the grouping of non-English-speaking pupils flexible. Place the emphasis upon serving the needs of the individual pupil.
8. Place special emphasis on reducing the backlog of retarded language learners.
9. Recognize "English as a second language" or "the teaching of non-English-speaking children" as an area of specialization that cuts across many subject areas.
10. Use the curricular materials developed by The Puerto Rican Study to achieve unity of purpose and practice in teaching non-English-speaking pupils.
11. Capitalize on the creative talent of teachers in finding ways and means of supplementing and of improving the program for teaching non-English-speaking pupils.

12. Recognize and define the school's responsibility to assist, counsel, and cooperate with the parents of non-English-speaking pupils in all matters pertaining to the child's welfare.

13. Take a new look at the school's opportunity to accelerate the adjustment of Puerto Rican children and their parents through advice and counsel to parents on problems normally considered to be outside the conventional functions of the school.

14. Staff the schools to do the job: to help the new arrival to make good adjustment to school and community; to help the non-English-speaking child to learn English and to find his way successfully into the main stream of the school's program.

15. Staff the proper agencies of the Board of Education to maintain a continuing program for the development and improvement of curricular materials and other aids to the teaching of non-English-speaking pupils.

16. Staff, also, the proper agencies of the Board of Education, and set in motion the processes to maintain a continuing assessment or evaluation of techniques, practices and proposals.

17. Take a new hard look at the psychological services provided for non-English-speaking children, especially for Puerto Rican children.

18. Through every means available, make it clear that the education of the non-English-speaking children and their integration in an ever-changing school population is the responsibility of every member of the school staff.

19. Maintain, improve, and possibly expand the program of in-service preparation initiated through The Puerto Rican Study for training special staff to assist in accelerating the program for non-English-speaking children.

20. In cooperation with the colleges and universities of metropolitan New York, create a dynamic program to achieve unity of purpose and more adequate coordination of effort in the education of teachers and of other workers for accelerating the program in the schools.

21. Use the varied opportunities available to develop an ever-improving cooperation between the Department of Education in Puerto Rico and the Board of Education in New York City.

22. In cooperation with the responsible representatives of the government of the State of New York, continue to explore the mutual interests and responsibility of the city and the state for the education and adjustment of non-English-speaking children and youth.

23. Think of the City of New York and the Commonwealth of Puerto Rico as partners in a great enterprise.

No full scale implementation of The Puerto Rican Study was attempted. Much of what the Study recommended appears again in the New York City Board of Education Educating Students for whom

English is a Second Language: Programs, Activities, and Services (1965), a pamphlet-review of subsequent programs which emphasized teacher training programs, particularly the exchange of teachers between New York and Puerto Rico. All kinds of reasons can be advanced for the failure to implement The Puerto Rican Study, and these might include teacher and Board of Education resistance; the struggles which were to ensue over community participation, and decentralization; the rapidly politicizing community/school contexts with their attendant ideological quarrels; the absence of qualified personnel; and the accelerating growth of the Puerto Rican community which simply overwhelmed many of the schools. Whatever the reasons (and no one reason or a combination of reasons provides an acceptable explanation), the Study was more than a million dollar white elephant. Its achievements (however incompletely implemented) included the following:

1. Developed two series of related curriculum bulletins-- Resource Units and Language Guides--for use in teaching English to non-English-speaking pupils. These are keyed to New York City courses of study but may be easily adapted to courses of study in other school systems. They are adapted to the maturity level of children, grade by grade in the elementary school, and in terms of need for special instruction in English during the early secondary school years.

2. Developed a guide for teaching science--resource units and sample lessons--to Puerto Rican pupils who are still trying to learn English; and a guide for teaching occupations to teen-age Puerto Rican pupils in high school who wish to qualify for occupational employment.

3. Developed a battery of tests, measures, and data-gathering techniques for use with Puerto Rican pupils in the mainland schools. Among these were a tape-recorded test for measuring the ability of non-English-speaking pupils to understand spoken English, a scale for rating ability to speak English, a bilingual test of arithmetic, and a process for screening new arrivals and for following their progress through periodic reviews.

4. Through an educational-ethnic-social survey of several thousand children in New York City elementary and junior high schools, obtained a profile of the characteristics of pupils of Puerto Rican background in relation to other pupils in the same grades and schools.

5. Through testing thousands of pupils, obtained estimates of the potential abilities as well as of the present performance of Puerto Rican pupils in relation to their peers i.e., other pupils of the same age and grade in the same schools.

6. Through a variety of studies of individual children from kindergarten through the tenth grade or second year of high school, gained revealing information concerning the problems of Puerto Rican children in achieving cultural-educational-social adjustment in New York City schools.

7. Through a survey of the relations of schools to Puerto

Rican parents, defined the problems confronting the schools, formulated criteria for determining the schools' role, and made some estimate of the cost in terms of personnel needed to help facilitate or accelerate the cultural adjustment of Puerto Rican parents.

8. Through analysis of previously established positions and of new positions established on an experimental basis, developed criteria for determining the necessity for special staff in schools to enable them to serve the needs of Puerto Rican and foreign-born or non-English-speaking children.

9. Through two years of experimentation with different procedures, developed proposals for an in-service program to reach all teachers required to teach non-English-speaking pupils.

10. Through participation in three summer workshops sponsored in part by the Board of Education of the City of New York at the University of Puerto Rico, formulated proposals for the development of the annual workshop as a continuing means of promoting better mutual understanding and cooperation between the school system of New York City and the school system of Puerto Rico.

11. Through the surveys and testing of thousands of children, devised a plan for obtaining a uniform census of all Puerto Rican and foreign-born children in the schools. Administration of census, through consecutive years, will give the Board of Education data for predicting with a high degree of accuracy pending changes in the ethnic composition of pupil population by school, school district, school level, borough and city.

12. The gradation of ability to speak English as defined by The Puerto Rican Study in its scale for rating ability to speak English was used by the Commissioner of Education of the State of New York in defining non-English-speaking pupils as a basis for the distribution of additional state aid appropriated by law.

In themselves, these achievements (and the recommendations) were to become the measuring criteria against which continuing needs were to be delineated.

The failure to implement The Puerto Rican Study led to great agitation and continuing demands from the Puerto Rican community. The first Citywide Conference of the Puerto Rican Community (April 1967) in its published proceedings (Puerto Ricans Confront Problems of the Complex Urban Society, New York City: Office of the Mayor, 1968) presented recommendations for the education of Puerto Rican children, essentially a repetition of those made by The Puerto Rican Study. And in 1968, Aspira (an organization founded in 1961 by the Puerto Rican Forum to promote higher education for Puerto Ricans) convened a national conference of Puerto Ricans, Mexican-Americans, and educators on "the Special Educational Needs of Urban Puerto Rican Youth." The conference's published report (Hemos Trabajado Bien. New York: Aspira, 1968), in its recommendations, reiterated most

of those of The Puerto Rican Study. The Aspira conference also
commissioned a report on Puerto Ricans and the public schools:
Richard J. Margolis, The Losers: A Report on Puerto Ricans and
the Public Schools (New York: Aspira, 1968). This brief report
chronicles visits to sixteen schools in seven cities and "makes no
explicit recommendations. Its purpose is to put the problem in
sharper focus and on wider display, not to promote any single set
of solutions." Margolis' report is a devastating indictment of those
schools which neglected Puerto Rican children, and of programs which
largely were encrusted with all the bitter abuses of the past: it appears inconceivable that the practices he describes could have been
occurring a decade after the publication of The Puerto Rican Study.

BEYOND THE PUERTO RICAN STUDY

The Bilingual Education Act

Much of the effort in behalf of the educational needs of Puerto Rican
children in the 1960s must be viewed and understood in the light of
the massive federal interventions in education largely initiated by the
enactment of the Elementary & Secondary Education Act of 1965, and
its subsequent amendments.

The passage by the Congress in 1968 of the Bilingual Education Act (itself, Title VII of the ESEA) reaffirmed and strengthened
many of the recommendations of The Puerto Rican Study even though
the Study had largely fallen into undeserved neglect. The struggle
for a national bilingual education act represented a continuing fight
against the ethnocentric rejection of the use of native languages in
the instruction of non-English-speaking children; and, in our view,
the successful enactment of the Bilingual Education Act represented
a movement away from the "ethnocentric illusion" in the United States
that for a child born in this country English is not a foreign language,
and virtually all instruction in schools must be through the medium of
English; even more importantly, the Act was a national manifesto for
cultural pluralism and bicultural education, and in this sense may
prove the most socially significant educational legislation yet enacted.

The Act recognized "the special education needs of the large
numbers of children of limited English speaking ability in the United
States," and declared "it to be the policy of the United States to provide financial assistance to local educational agencies to develop and
carry out new and imaginative elementary and secondary school programs designed to meet these special educational needs." The main
priorities of the Act are the provision of equal educational opportunities for non-English-speaking children; the strengthening of educational
programs for bilingual children; and the promotion of bilingualism
among all students. A great number of programs have come into
being as a result of the Act, and although the programs are of differing (and in some instances of dubious) quality, the programs affirm the practicability of meeting the needs of the non-English-speaking
child.

Amendments to the Bilingual Education Act in 1974 strengthened bilingual-bicultural programs, and clarified the Federal role and commitment to bilingual education, despite continuing controversy:

> The 1974 Bilingual Education Act represented the Federal response to the educational needs of limited English-speaking children. The researcher found that the 1974 Act resolved many philosophical issues concerning the Federal role in bilingual-bicultural education. Those resolutions permit a determination whether the Act itself constituted a revolution, a reaction or a reform of past practices.
> A continuing Federal role in assisting states and localities in meeting the needs of limited English-speaking students was contained within the 1974 Act. Although the Federal government was not committed by the legislation to provide direct services to all eligible students, it did expand the number of local classroom projects and institute a major new Federal role in providing the resources--teachers, paraprofessionals, curricula, research--to enable localities and states to provide those services.
> The 1974 Act diluted the transitional limitations of the previous 1968 law, permitting bilingual-bicultural education programs to be funded through high schools, although the emphasis remained on elementary school instruction. The Act also made a full bilingual-bicultural approach the likely outcome in all instances, and specifically denied the sufficiency of an English-as-a-second-language program. All of these resolutions of issues concerning bilingual-bicultural education contributed to understanding the nature and character of the Act. (Schneider 1976: 161-162)

Bilingual programs in American schools exist within the mandated provisions of Federal legislation. They are truly the progeny of Congressional responses to perceived needs.

The Realities of Program Implementation

In the last analysis, it is the program which addresses itself to the educational needs of the Puerto Rican child which must be evaluated with recommendations made for its continuing improvement. The evaluation of a particular program for Puerto Rican children in a large urban school district and the recommendations which were made for its improvement and expansion are, in themselves, instructive: they delineate the contemporary educational experience for the Puerto Rican child, and they point the way to meet the needs.

The recommendations which are subjoined derive from a study and evaluation of the educational programs for Puerto Rican students underway in the Jersey City (N. J.) school district in 1971-1972. Over 5,000 Puerto Rican pupils (out of a total school register of some 38,000) were in the city's schools. The recommendations provide a profile of contemporary Puerto Rican educational experience (practice that lends itself to improvement), generally encountered on the main-land. Most of the recommendations have been implemented across the 1970s.

Program Recommendations

ELEMENTARY LEVEL

1.   The basic recommendation to be made for the elementary schools involves the establishment of functional bilingual programs wherever there are Puerto Rican students in attendance.   The basic premise of bilingual education involves the use of Spanish to provide instruction in most curriculum areas when English is not the mother tongue of the children and when there is insufficient fluency in English to profit from school instruction in that language.   Thus, for example, instruction in basic curriculum areas such as mathematics, social studies, etc. would be in Spanish.   At the same time that instruction is given in the basic content areas in Spanish, an intensive program in the teaching of English as a second language must be conducted. As children develop greater fluency in English, additional instruction in the basic curriculum areas should be given in English.   This ap-proach would assist children in becoming equally fluent in both Span-ish and English, and at the same time it would also assist children to develop the appropriate knowledges and skills in curriculum areas other than Spanish and English.   Bilingual education should also pro-vide for the teaching of Spanish as a second language for those chil-dren who are dominant in English.   Such programs should begin in September 1972.
    At the present time in the bilingual classes in the Jersey City schools, this approach is not in widespread use.   Teachers who speak Spanish are used for the most part to interpret what the English speak-ing teacher has said, and (as noted above) often at the same time, a practice resulting in considerable confusion.   In addition, the practice of assigning two teachers to a room, one of whom functions as an in-terpreter, represents poor utilization of personnel, both educationally and financially.

2.   The bilingual program recommended by the evaluators would also necessitate the regrouping of participating children more care-fully.   In addition to using the traditional criteria for grouping in a bilingual education program, it is necessary to develop parallel classes or sections of children who are dominant in either English or Spanish. In developing bilingual programs, however, it is essential that priority be given in class assignment to children who are dominant in Spanish, rather than to those dominant in English, because the greatest immed-iate need exists for children who are dominant in Spanish and who cannot derive as much educational value as possible from school pro-grams conducted solely in English.

3.   It is recommended that two schools [perhaps, Public School No. 2 and Public School No. 16 in view of the very large number of Puerto Rican students in attendance] develop complete bilingual pro-

grams beginning with the kindergarten and including each grade in the school. In other schools, bilingual classes should be established as needed.

4. A committee on bilingual education at the elementary school level should be established immediately in order to plan for the development of bilingual programs in Public Schools Nos. 2 and 16, and in other schools of Jersey City where there are large Puerto Rican enrollments. The bilingual education committee will also give attention to the development of a bilingual curriculum encompassing the usual curriculum areas as well as the teaching of English as a second language, the teaching of Spanish as a second language, and the history and culture of Puerto Rico as an integral part of the elementary school curriculum. The present Hispanic Culture Committee is a beginning; but it must deal with a Puerto Rican studies curriculum and only ancillarily with Hispanic cultures in general. Membership on the committee should include parents, teachers, principals, and should also make provision for student input.

5. A city-wide Puerto Rican advisory council composed of parents, high school and college students and community leaders should be established. The advisory council can advise school officials on the needs, aspirations, sentiments and responses of the Puerto Rican community insofar as educational matters are concerned. The existence of a community advisory council will assist in making public schools with large number of Puerto Rican students "community schools," furnishing educational and other much needed services to the Puerto Rican community. Such an advisory council on a city-wide basis [and articulated with local advisory councils for specific schools] will provide much needed community participation in education in Jersey City for the Puerto Rican community.

6. Parochial schools with large numbers of Puerto Rican students should also participate in special programs funded with federal monies.

7. All communications from school officials to parents should be available in both English and Spanish.

8. Additional Puerto Rican personnel should be recruited for positions at all levels in the public schools including teachers, principals, school secretaries, a curriculum specialist, teacher aides, etc. Special attention should be turned immediately to the employment of a curriculum specialist in bilingual education.

9. At the present time, no city-wide coordinating effort involving existing bilingual programs is available in Jersey City. It is recommended, therefore, that a city-wide office at the level of coordinator for bilingual education be established. This office will have jurisdiction over planning, developing, implementing, supervising and evaluating all bilingual education programs, programs in the teaching of English as a second language, and other special service programs for Puerto Rican elementary school children and high school students. The office would also provide liaison with the Puerto Rican community.

10.   Bilingual classes as envisaged in recommendation #1 should also be made available in the Summer of 1972. [The period January 1972 to June 1972 should be used as a planning period for the bilingual programs to be established in the Summer and Fall of 1972.]

11.   It is recommended that provision be made for the establishment of a continuing consultancy in the implementation of the recommendations contained in this report.   Consultants would work with school officials and members of the Puerto Rican community in the implementation of the recommendations and would assist in the development of other programs and special services that may be needed by the children of the Puerto Rican community.

12.   Parent education programs conducted in both Spanish and English should be developed for the Puerto Rican community.

13.   An in-service program for teachers and other school personnel should be developed as soon as possible.   Current and past efforts in Jersey City in the areas of in-service courses include the offering of a course in "Teaching English as a Second Language" that was to be given in the 1970/71 school year, beginning in November, 1970 and a request to develop and finance an "In-Service Course Involving Philosophy, Approaches and Methodology of Bilingual Education," to be given during the 1971/72 school year.   In-service efforts should be expanded, and should include both professionals participating directly in bilingual programs or English as a second language programs as well as other professionals in the Jersey City public schools who may not be participating in special programs for Puerto Rican children but who do work with Puerto Rican children in regular classes. Such an extensive in-service program might be developed and offered during the regular school year, or might be given as a special summer institute for participating personnel.

14.   Greater numbers of Puerto Rican student teachers should be recruited from Jersey City State College.   An expanded student-teaching practicum drawn from the cadres of Puerto Rican students at Jersey City State College represents an important source for recruiting larger numbers of Puerto Rican personnel for employment in the Jersey City public schools.

15.   A continuing and expanded liaison between the Jersey City public schools and Jersey City State College is recommended.   Here, an important beginning and model [Title VII, at School No. 16] has been provided by Professor Bloom and Jersey City State College personnel.

SECONDARY LEVEL

1.   The city-wide Community Advisory Council described in recommendations for elementary schools should also turn its attention to secondary education and make recommendations relevant to the educational needs of Puerto Rican high school students in Jersey City.

2.   A testing and identification program should be developed at the secondary level.   Such a program would attempt to identify Puerto Rican students in need of intensive instruction in English as a second language or in other important school subjects such as reading.

3.   A special committee to deal with secondary education for Puerto Rican students should be established, with the membership drawn from teachers, principals, guidance personnel and other school professionals; and including parents and students from the Puerto Rican community. The committee should give special attention to the current basic offerings: industrial arts, college preparatory, business and general studies.   It should consider ways of increasing the holding power of the secondary schools so that greater numbers of Puerto Rican students remain in high school and graduate.

4.   Special work-study programs for Puerto Rican students might be developed in connection with the basic offerings now available. Such work-study programs could become a very significant phase of the industrial arts and business education programs, and should, consequently, carry high school credit.

5.   An immediate attempt should be made to increase the number of Puerto Rican students in the college preparatory program.   This can be done by teachers, guidance personnel and administrators. More information about current high school programs should be made available, and students should become familiar with the implications of selecting specific programs and the out-of-school consequences of enrollment in any given program.   In addition, talent-search programs might be initiated to increase the number of Puerto Rican students entering college.

6.   Secondary school teachers should participate in in-service programs dealing with the education of Puerto Rican students.

7.   It is recommended that high school students having little fluency in English be given basic instruction in Spanish in the various classes required in the four curricula.   Instruction in Spanish would be in addition to intensive instruction in reading, writing and speaking English as a second language.   When high school students have achieved a sufficient degree of fluency in English, they may then receive all or most of their instruction in English.   Bilingual education at the high school level at the present time is essential, and it is especially important when large numbers of students are dominant in Spanish rather than in English.   It should be remembered that it was not possible to secure from school officials data concerning the number of Puerto Rican high school students dominant primarily in Spanish.

8.   At present, a secondary school curriculum committee is working on a course of study in Puerto Rican history.   The work of this committee should be accelerated and a course of study in Puerto Rican history and culture should be developed as rapidly as possible. The committee might then turn its attention to the development of a course of study dealing with the Puerto Rican experience on the main-

land. At present, there are no student members of this committee. Students should be a significant and contributing part of this committee. Indeed, greater participation by high school students in the decisions affecting their school careers is vital, and it becomes especially crucial when there are large numbers of students dropping out of high school programs as is true for many Puerto Rican students.

9. The high schools should make available to all high school students without cost all special examinations such as the National Education Development Tests or the College Boards. Such examinations now require the payment of fees by candidates taking them. There may be many Puerto Rican and other students unable to take the examinations which require the payment of fees because of inability to afford the funds required.

10. The continuing consultancy referred to in recommendations for elementary schools should encompass secondary education as well as elementary education.

11. It is recommended that an experimental program involving independent study be instituted for those students who are considering leaving high school before graduation. This program would provide the opportunity for independent study under supervision, for which credit leading to a high school diploma would be given. Such a program would also provide for attendance in organized classes in the high schools, especially where remedial or advanced programs are required. Students would participate in developing their programs. Such supervised independent study programs could be related to jobs which students leaving high school before graduation may have secured.

12. It is recommended that additional Puerto Rican personnel be recruited for employment in Jersey City secondary schools. The two Puerto Rican guidance counselors at Ferris High School are an important beginning.

These recommendations were, essentially, reaffirmations of the cogency of those made years earlier in The Puerto Rican Study. One cannot help but wonder how differently meaningful educational opportunity for Puerto Rican children may have been had The Puerto Rican Study been implemented. In its cautions and admonitions, The Puerto Rican Study was prophetic: "A study, however good, never solves problems. At best, it finds solutions that will work. To translate proposed measures into practice is the greater task. At the very best it will take three to five years to translate the proposals of The Puerto Rican Study into an effective program.... The real question is, how rapidly can the school system move? ... there are thousands of Puerto Rican children in New York City schools who have been here two, three, four or more years and are still rated as language learners. The task is twofold--to salvage as many as possible of those currently retarded, and to reduce the numbers that thus far have been added annually to the list. The time to begin is now-- A year gone from a child's life is gone forever." (Study 1958: 237)

References

Aspira. (1968). Hemos trabajado bien. Aspira: New York
Banks, J. A. (1973). Teaching ethnic studies: concepts and strat-
    egies. Council for the Social Studies: Washington
Centro de Estudios Puertorriqueños (1979). Labor migration under
    capitalism: the Puerto Rican experience. Monthly Review
    Press: New York
Chenault, L. R. (1938). The Puerto Rican migrant in New York
    City. Columbia University Press: New York
Cordasco, F. and Covello, L. (1968). Studies of Puerto Rican chil-
    dren in American schools: a preliminary bibliography. Mi-
    gration Division, Commonwealth of Puerto Rico: New York
Cordasco, F. and Bucchioni, E., eds. (1972). The Puerto Rican
    community and its children on the mainland. Scarecrow Press:
    Metuchen, N. J.
Cordasco, F. (1973). "The children of immigrants in schools: his-
    torical analogues of educational deprivation," Journal of Negro
    Education, 42 3: 44-53
Cordasco, F. (1973). Teaching the Puerto Rican experience, in
    Banks (1973).
Cordasco, F. (1975). "Spanish-speaking children in American schools,"
    International Migration Review, 9 3: 379-382
Cordasco, F. (1976). Bilingual schooling in the United States. Mc-
    Graw-Hill: New York
Cordasco, F. (1978). "Bilingual and bicultural education in American
    schools: a bibliography of selected references," Bulletin of
    Bibliography, 35 2: 53-72
Cordasco, F. and Bernstein, G. (1979). Bilingual Education in
    American schools: a guide to information sources. Gale Re-
    search Company: Detroit
Covello, F. (1953). "Recommendations concerning Puerto Rican
    pupils in our public schools." Benjamin Franklin High School:
    New York City
Covello, L. (1967). The social background of the Italo-American
    school child. E. J. Brill: Leiden
Cremin, L. A. (1961). The transformation of the school. Alfred
    Knopf: New York
Cubberley, E. P. (1909). Changing conceptions of education.
    Houghton Mifflin: Boston
Fitzpatrick, J. (1971). Puerto Rican Americans: the meaning of
    migration to the mainland. Prentice-Hall: Englewood, N. J.
Gaarder, A. B. (1977). Bilingual schooling and the survival of
    Spanish in the United States. Newbury House Publishers:
    Rowley, Mass.
Hidalgo, H. (1971). The Puerto Ricans of Newark, New Jersey.
    Aspira: Newark, N. J.
Kloss, H. (1977). The American bilingual tradition. Newbury House
    Publishers: Rowley, Mass.
Margolis, R. J. (1968). The losers: a report on Puerto Ricans
    and the public schools. Aspira: New York
Mayor's Committee on Puerto Rican Affairs in New York City. (1951).
    "Puerto Rican pupils in American schools." Office of the
    Mayor: New York City

Monserrat, J. (1961). "Community planning for Puerto Rican integration in the United States," in Cordasco and Bucchioni (1972)
New York City Board of Education. (1947). "A program of education
for Puerto Ricans in New York City." Board of Education:
New York City
New York City Board of Education. (1953). "Teaching children of
Puerto Rican background in New York City schools." Board
of Education: New York City
New York City Board of Education. (1958). "The Puerto Rican study:
a report on the education and adjustment of Puerto Rican pupils
in the public schools of the City of New York." Board of Ed-
ucation: New York City
New York City Board of Education. (1965). "Educating students for
whom English is a second language: programs, activities, and
services." Board of Education: New York City
New York City: Office of the Mayor. (1968). "Puerto Ricans con-
front problems of the complex urban society." Office of the
Mayor: New York City
Osuna, J. J. (1948). "Report on visits to New York City schools,"
in Cordasco and Bucchioni (1972)
Palante. Young Lords' party. (1971). McGraw-Hill: New York
Perez, D. (1971). "The chains that have been taken off slaves' bod-
ies are put back on their minds," in Palante: Young Lords'
Party (1971)
Richman, J. (1910). "The social needs of the public schools,"
Forum, 43 2: 161-169.
Schneider, S. G. (1976). Revolution, reaction or reform: the 1974
bilingual education act. Las Americas: New York
Silén, J. A. (1971). The Puerto Rican people: a story of oppres-
sion and resistance. Monthly Review Press: New York
Thomas, A. M. (1954). "American education and the immigrant,"
Teachers College Record, 55 2: 253-267
United States Immigration Commission. (1911). Report of the Im-
migration Commission. 41 vols. Government Printing Office:
Washington
Vazquez Calzada, J. (1979). "Demographic aspects of migration,"
in Centro de Estudios Puertorriqueños (1979)
Wagenheim, K. (1975). A survey of Puerto Ricans on the U.S.
mainland in the 1970s. Praeger Publishers: New York

Francesco Cordasco and Eugene Bucchioni

STAFF DEVELOPMENT INSTITUTE FOR TEACHERS
OF PUERTO RICAN STUDENTS

Elementary and secondary school Puerto Rican students are confronted by the usual array of educational difficulties and emotional and social problems related to poverty or low-income status. In addition, Puerto Rican students demonstrate the life-styles, values and normative understandings and responses characteristic of Puerto Rican culture. The lack of specially trained teachers prepared to work specifically with Puerto Rican students is a major factor affecting the quality of the educational program offered to Puerto Rican students. Furthermore, teachers who are not specially trained contribute significantly to conflict in schools with large Puerto Rican enrollments. The lack of professional skills in areas such as remedial reading for Puerto Rican students, conversational Spanish, the teaching of English as a foreign language, guidance of Puerto Rican students, and the general lack of knowledge of Puerto Rican culture and of the Puerto Rican experience on the mainland, are additional factors contributing to unsuccessful school achievement and widespread academic retardation common among Puerto Rican students.

This proposed "Staff Development Institute for Elementary and Secondary School Teachers of Puerto Rican Students" is concerned consequently with the following areas:

1. The development of knowledge of and insight into Puerto Rican culture and the Puerto Rican experience in the United States.
2. Specific professional skills such as remedial reading for Puerto Rican students, methods and materials for the teaching of English as a second language, and specific guidance procedures to be used with Puerto Rican students.
3. Conversational Spanish as spoken within the Puerto Rican com-

Education Programs for Puerto Rican Students; Evaluation and Recommendations (Jersey City, N. J. , Board of Education, 1971), p. 40-45.

munity to enable teachers to relate to and communicate more effectively with both parents and children whose knowledge of English is very limited.
4. Bilingual Education: its philosophy, structure, objectives, curriculum, and methods and materials of instruction.

Structure and Organization of the Program

It is suggested that equal numbers of elementary and secondary school teachers participate in the program, together with other school personnel, forming teams of about four teachers from schools with high percentages of Puerto Rican students in attendance. The function of the team structure will be to provide a nucleus of individuals in selected schools so that a variety and diversification of professional skills will be available.

Each participant in the institute will take a seminar entitled, "Puerto Rican Students in American Schools" and "Aspects of Puerto Rican Culture and History." Each member of a school team will choose from the following offerings:

(1) Bilingual Education. Philosophy, Structure and Curriculum Methods and Materials of Instruction in Bilingual Education.
(2) Remedial Reading for Puerto Rican Students.
(3) Teaching of English as a Second Language.
(4) Conversational Spanish.
(5) Guidance of Puerto Rican Students.

Finally, a synthesizing seminar will be offered to each participant on the basis of level of teaching: elementary teachers will take "Elementary Education for Puerto Rican Children," and high school teachers will be expected to complete "Secondary Education for Puerto Rican Students."

The Program in Summary

Required of All Participants

1. Puerto Rican Students in American Schools.
2. Aspects of Puerto Rican Culture and History.
3. Elementary Education for Puerto Rican Children (Synthesizing Seminar) or Secondary Education for Puerto Rican Students (Synthesizing Seminar).

Participants Will Choose Two:

1. Remedial Reading for Puerto Rican students (both elementary and secondary levels will be set up).
2. Guidance of Puerto Rican students (elementary and secondary levels will be set up).
3. Conversational Spanish.

4. Teaching of English as a Second Language.
5. Bilingual Education: Philosophy, Structure and Curriculum.
6. Methods and Materials of Instruction in Bilingual Education (elementary and secondary sections will be set up).

The institute should be implemented through lectures, discussions, films, readings, field trips and with extensive contact with members of the Puerto Rican community. An important feature of the institute should be the inclusion of many Puerto Rican professionals and other members of the Puerto Rican community in the various offerings and activities of the program.

Suggested Criteria for Selection of Participants

It is suggested that some attention be given to the selection of participants in terms of the following criteria:

1. Reasonable competency and satisfactory service in a school.
2. General social and emotional maturity.
3. A commitment to the education of Puerto Rican students and to teaching in the Puerto Rican community.

Through interviews, letters of recommendation and examination of the professional history of the applicants, an attempt should be made to select only those teachers who have a firm commitment to the education of Puerto Rican students and who demonstrate the characteristics required for success in the institute and for implementation of learnings, skills, and knowledge derived from the institute in their respective schools. In addition, each participant selected should possess the leadership potential necessary for developing required charges as part of the team returning to each school. In this way, it is hoped that the impact of the institute will go beyond that of the participants alone, and will be extended to other members of the school staff who will be encouraged to use the members of the team completing the institute as leaders or resource people in the education of Puerto Rican students.

Costs for the institute may be defrayed in part by federal or by local funds depending upon budgetary exigencies. Title I (Elementary and Secondary Education Act) funds may be appropriately budgeted within existing guidelines; and where districts have applied for Title VII (ESEA) funds, the institute may be part of the program (within Title VII guidelines) for the education of non-English speaking children.

RECOMMENDATIONS CONCERNING PUERTO RICAN PUPILS
IN OUR PUBLIC SCHOOLS

A number of recommendations concerning the Puerto Rican Program in our public schools have been presented at various times by the following:

    I.   The Committee of the Association of Assistant Superintendents of the Board of Education of the City of New York. (August 1947) Dr. Clare C. Baldwin, Chairman.

    II.   The Committee of Puerto Ricans in New York City of the Welfare Council of New York City. (1948)

    III.   The report on "Education of the non-English speaking and bi-lingual (Spanish) pupils in the Junior High School of Districts 10 and 11 Manhattan submitted by Assistant Superintendent Clare C. Baldwin, June, 1952.

    IV.   The suggestions presented by Dr. Francisco Collazo, Associate Commissioner of Education for the Commonwealth of Puerto Rico. (1953)

    V.   Recommendations of the report of the Subcommittee on Education, Recreation and Parks of the Mayor's Committee of Puerto Rican Affairs. (1951) "Puerto Rican Pupils in New York City Public Schools" directed by Dr. Leonard Covello.

All of the most important recommendations are summarized below. The Roman numerals I, II, III, IV and V appearing in parentheses at the end of each recommendation indicate the source of the recommendation in accordance with the listing of the sources above.

Benjamin Franklin High School, May 1, 1953. (Mimeo.) Reprinted by permission.

You will note that these recommendations come from social agencies of the city and the supervisory and teaching staffs of our public schools--groups who are in daily contact with the problem and who are working actively with Puerto Rican children and their families.

Leonard Covello
Principal, Benjamin Franklin High School

I. School Organization:

A.   Special classes (C) should be allowed to schools in the ratio of a teacher for each 15 pupils newly admitted from Puerto Rico. (I)

B.   A special differential in class size should be provided in schools enrolling Puerto Rican pupils in proportion to the numbers on register. Class registers with a large representation of these pupils should not exceed 25. (I) (II) (III) (IV)

C.   Kindergarten opportunities should be provided for four and five-year-old children in schools located in Puerto Rican communities. (I)

D.   Junior High Schools should be reorganized as co-educational schools. (III)

E.   Fifteen and sixteen year old children who are new arrivals should be directly admitted to senior high schools without restrictions as to the length of time of previous schooling or reading achievement, or the tenth year should be added to the Junior High School for those children who are close to 16 and 17 years of age. (III)

F.   Eleven and twelve year old children who are new arrivals should be kept in the elementary schools until they are thirteen years old in order to ease the adjustment to new surroundings. (III)

G.   In the reorganization report in June, schools should be permitted to leave at least one class in each grade unfilled for the new admissions in September so that we may eliminate a condition which is virtually a reorganization in September. (III)

H.   No person licensed in Spanish should be appointed to the Junior High Schools unless requested by the principal. (III)

I.   Principals of Junior High Schools should be given the privilege of selecting all the teachers for their schools. (III)

J.   The allowance of teacher's time should be increased for remedial instruction in English and mathematics and for health counseling. (III)

K.   The by-laws should be waived to permit appointment to our schools of teachers licensed to teach English to foreigners to tide us over a critical period. (III)

L.   An additional assistant to principal should be provided for the supervision of teachers of non-English speaking children. (III)

M.   Additional clerks should be assigned to prepare stencils and to mimeograph materials made in the schools. (III)

N.   The Puerto Rican children should be placed in schools on an individual basis to effect a more satisfactory adjustment. (V)

II.   Textbooks and Supplies

A.   A special differential in textbooks and supply allotments should be made to schools enrolling Puerto Rican pupils in proportion to the numbers on register. (I)

B.   An increased allotment should be granted for auxiliary instructional materials such as projectors, film strips, recorders and players. (III)

C.   Report cards printed in Spanish should be made available for ordering from the general supply list. (III)

D.   A special study should be made to determine what allotment for textbooks and supplies should be authorized for schools with a large concentration of Puerto Rican students. (V)

III.   Curriculum

A.   Under the direction of the Division of Curriculum Research, a study should be made of existing curriculum materials and methodology with a view toward devising new courses of study and teaching materials appropriate to the instruction of Puerto Rican pupils on various school levels. (I) (V)

B.   There should be more English classes for all age groups. (II)

C.   The curriculum for children classified as CRMD should be reviewed by the department. (III)

D.   The curriculum should be broadened to include pre-vocational training for 15 and 16 year old pupils. (III)

E.   A program for the correction of foreign accent and improvement of slovenly speech should be planned by the Department of Speech for use with bi-lingual pupils. (III)

F.   Uniform teaching procedures should be used in the schools having a large number of beginners in English until such time as the need for special instruction in English is no longer so urgent. (III)

G.   There should be continuous teaching of English in the schools of Puerto Rico. (IV)

H.   There is a need for a curriculum bulletin for elementary, junior and senior high schools suggesting additional experiences, activities, procedures and practices for Puerto Rican children. (V)

IV. Tests and Measurements

A.   Under the direction of the Division of Educational Research, a study should be made of present tests of academic achievement and mental ability and appropriate instruments of measurement should be developed for Puerto Rican pupils. (I) (V)

B.   No standardized tests should be given to any children who have not had at least five years of attendance in our schools until such time as valid tests are available. (III)

C.   A program for aptitude testing should be introduced for the 15 and 16 year old students. (III)

V. Health

A.   Special medical services should be provided in schools having a large proportion of Puerto Rican pupils. (I) (V)

B.   A dental clinic should be set up in one of the schools for the exclusive use of junior high school pupils in each school district.

C.   Increased time should be given by the school nurse and doctor. (III)

D.   More welfare aides should be assigned as escorts for pupils to clinics. (III)

E.   More psychiatric services should be made available. (III)

VI. Registration

A.   Teachers who are expert interpreters of Spanish should be assigned during the period of registration to schools in the Puerto Rican neighborhoods to assist in the registration of new pupils. (I) (III)

B.   Spanish-speaking teachers should be used for all phases of the school program such as registration, for translation of forms and letters, as interpreters, as liaison with the community, etc. (V)

VII. Adult Education

A.   A study should be made to determine the adequacy of the present program of adult education for Puerto Ricans. (I)

B.   The special educational needs of the Puerto Rican people are
the following:

    a.   To learn English
    b.   To learn a marketable skill, trade or vocation if they ar-
        rive in New York without one and are beyond school age.
    c.   If they are parents they need to learn:
        (1) Nutrition and marketing facts.
        (2) Child care and child care facilities available to them
            in the city, such as baby health stations, playgrounds,
            school requirements and services.
    d.   To be oriented in urban living as to consumer problems,
        civic problems, sanitation and institutional assistance avail-
        able. (II) (IV)

C.   There should be local parent education on a full time basis. (II)

D.   There should be a vital adult education program in areas where
many Puerto Ricans live. (II)

E.   Personnel should be assigned for parent education and work
with mothers' clubs to meet during school hours and as part of the
regular work of the schools. (II)

F.   Instructions to parents on education and attendance laws should
be printed in Spanish and be made available to the schools. (III)

G.   There should be broader and more intensive instruction in
English in Puerto Rico for the prospective adult migrant. (IV)

H.   There should be more adequate information about living conditions in the continental United States in the social science program of
Puerto Rican schools. (IV)

I.   The prospective migrant in Puerto Rico should be provided with
graphic information on the entire United States by means of films on
life in all sections of the country in order to break down concepts
limited to the New York area alone. (IV)

VIII. Teacher Training

A.   Orientation courses for teachers on Puerto Rican culture and
in conversational Spanish should be organized. (I) (II)

B.   Courses for teachers in methodology and instructional materials for teaching non-English speaking pupils should be organized and
staffed by experts. (I)

C.   The eligibility requirements for all licenses should be expanded
to include at least one course in the principles and methods of teaching English as a foreign language. (III)

D.   In-service courses should be given in the techniques of selecting and writing materials for Puerto Rican pupils. (III) (V)

E.   During the year there should be a series of district-wide institutes of all teachers of the schools having large numbers of non-English speaking pupils with a view toward exchanging ideas, experiences, new materials and to improve our way of educating for citizenship. (III)

F.   The junior high school program of articulation with the elementary schools should be extended to include areas of methodology, materials, curriculum and community problems related to the education of non-English speaking children. (III)

G.   A committee of supervisors and teachers of the junior high and elementary schools should be organized to explore the possibilities for broadening the base for articulation and guidance and for exchange of experiences. (III)

H.   Special examinations should be given for the purpose of licensing people with a knowledge of Spanish to serve in the classroom and to assist with other special services. (V)

IX.   Guidance

A.   Insular, federal and city authorities should attempt to divert the flow of Puerto Rican emigrants from the overcrowded areas of New York into other sections of the city and elsewhere with some regard to the adequacy of housing accommodations and to occupational opportunities. (I)

B.   There should be more child guidance work in areas of special needs. (II)

C.   A Spanish-speaking teacher or social worker should be assigned to each school for work with parents and children. (II) (III)

D.   Pupils entering high school from Puerto Rico require special vocational and individual guidance. (II)

E.   Each school should be assigned a full time attendance officer. (III)

F.   Each school should be assigned a full time guidance counselor. (III)

X.   Community Relations

A.   A community relations teacher should be assigned to districts where there are major concentrations of Puerto Ricans. (I)

B.   There should be closer liaison between school and out of
school social agencies. (II) (IV)

C.   A publicity program should be initiated by the schools adver-
tising guidance and educational services available in this city.   This
should be in Spanish. (II) (IV) (V)

D.   Three pilot community centers should be established in Manhattan, Brooklyn and the Bronx under the Board of Education to include recreation, English classes, family case work, etc. (II) (III) (V)

E.   More outdoor play yards should be set up in Puerto Rican districts under the supervision of duly licensed teachers. (III)

F.   A youth council with pupil representation from each school
should be established with a view toward directing continuing attention to community problems and to affecting joint action in the improvement of the community. (III)

G.   A plan should be developed with social agencies for the coordination of activities. (III)

XI.   Vocational Training and Guidance

A.   Free vocational training should be provided beyond the age of
17 years. (II)

B.   The plants and teaching staffs of the vocational training schools
should be open at night for the training of young adults in vocations
for which there is a demand as indicated by the state employment
services. (II)

C.   There should be vocational training of prospective workers in
public and vocational schools and orientation of students towards useful and gainful occupation upon leaving school in Puerto Rico. (IV)

XII.   Coordination

A.   There should be coordination of the activities of the Department
of Education of Puerto Rico, the Board of Education of the City of
New York, and the Migration Division of the Puerto Rican Department
of Labor. (IV)

B.   There should be a continuous exchange of personnel between the
Board of Education of New York and the Department of Education of
Puerto Rico for on the spot study and training. (V)

Vera P. John and Vivian M. Horner

MODELS OF EARLY BILINGUAL EDUCATION

"A bilingual school is a school which uses, concurrently, two languages as a medium of instruction in any portion of the curriculum, except the languages themselves. The teaching of a vernacular solely as a bridge to another, the official language, is not bilingual education in the sense of this paper, nor is ordinary foreign language teaching."[1] Our working definition of bilingual education, restated in this quote from Gaarder, is more often the long-range goal rather than an actual description of current bilingual programs. The demand for a realistic and effective educational approach for non-English-speaking children has produced many new programs, but at present most schools are improvising with meager resources based on limited objectives. Those educators still committed to the English-only policies of the past are reluctant to engage in the major staff and structural changes necessary for the implementation of a truly bilingual system of education. Some members of the non-English-speaking communities themselves express ambivalence towards the idea of bilingual instruction. Speaking of one such community, Gil Murello observes:

> Frankly stated, bilingual education threatens the identification with the dominant group that some socially mobile Mexican-Americans maintain.... These same professionals dimly, if not explicitly, realize that to accept the concept of bilingual education for their Mexican-American students is to admit grave failure on their part over many years through the use of traditional materials and methods and an implicit "melting pot" philosophy. [2]

Even the administrators who agree that there is a need for bilingual education programs find themselves confronted by many problems: a shortage of bilingual teachers, a scarcity of appropriate cur-

Reprinted by permission from Early Childhood Bilingual Education (New York: Modern Language Association, 1971), p. 178-187.

riculum materials, limited opportunities for teacher training, and lack
of special funds. While the passage of Title VII of the Elementary
and Secondary Education Act, and the subsequent funding of experimental bilingual programs, has contributed to the moral and financial
support of bilingual education, the resources available for such programs continue to be limited. In addition to these problems, educators face the major decision of choosing a suitable model of bilingual
instruction.

A systematic exploration of the considerations that enter into
the selection of bilingual models has been developed by Mackey, based
on information gathered in the files of the International Center for Research in Bilingualism. [3] Mackey proposes four levels of dimensions
of varying bilingual educational settings: the learner in the home, the
curriculum of the school, the community (or area) in the nation, and
national language patterns. He notes that language is the basic component in each of these dimensions; that language "is itself a variable,"
and that "each language appears in each pattern at a certain degree
of intensity."

A useful illustration of this concept of intensity appears in Valencia's study of three Mexican-American communities of the Southwest. [4] Valencia compares the intensity and usage of the native language with English among children in Laredo, Texas; Pecos, New Mexico; and Albuquerque, New Mexico. He observes, for example, that
the child living in the border town of Laredo is exposed to and uses
a great deal more Spanish than the child living in Albuquerque. Valencia recommends, with Mackey, that the language competence of the
child be examined in the context of community patterns in language
use, and that the interaction of these and other variables be considered
in the planning of bilingual schools.

Most present programs of bilingual education, however, are
not organized with these socio-linguistic and demographic variables
in mind. While the importance of such research is recognized as
an aid to evaluation, it does not play a significant role in the current planning aspects of the education of non-English-speaking children.

Although we recognize the value of a deductive scheme for
classifying bilingual schools, we will limit ourselves, in this chapter,
to a simple and descriptive framework. Our approach is dictated by
the relatively meager information available on the use and functions
of language in the home of non-English-speakers in the United States.

A. The Informal Model

In a surprising number of classrooms throughout the country, two
languages are spoken. The native languages of American Indian and
Spanish-American children, and those of many other communities, co-
exist in the school with English as a means of communication, and,
occasionally, as a medium of instruction. This development is less
a reflection of recent community and educational interest in bilingual

education than an indication of certain organizational and ideological trends in anti-poverty programs. Office of Economic Opportunity-supported programs, whether of the Head Start or Follow-Through variety, have included from the very beginning the employment of members of the low-income communities which they serve. While in many classrooms, the activities of parents and community aids have been restricted to menial jobs (e.g., clean-up, cooking, and transportation), in some instances paraprofessionals have participated in the actual planning and execution of educational activities.

Parents and aids, by their very presence, have altered traditional pre-school education. This change is particularly significant in non-English-speaking communities, where these paraprofessionals have brought about an informal use of the child's native language in the classroom, a language usage often unplanned or accidental. Thus the Puerto Rican classroom aide in New York City, in helping to ease the Spanish-speaking child's difficult adjustment from home to school, explains school routines to the child and his parents in Spanish. Occasionally, she may be encouraged to present a lesson or an activity to the class in Spanish because the teacher is usually fluent in English only.

Communities in which such informal classroom experiences in two languages take place are large in number and different in character. Mackey's typology for assessing bilingual education offers one means of systematically identifying these community differences. Mackey refers to patterns of language usage in the home and identifies five types of "learners in the home." An illustration of one type of "learner" is the child from the monolingual home, where the language spoken is not that of the school, for example, a Navajo child living on the vast, isolated Navajo reservation. This child's pattern of language usage in the home would contrast sharply with that of a child raised in a Spanish-speaking home in a city with a bilingual tradition, such as Santa Fe. In spite of the differences in these two environments, the Head Start and Follow-Through programs conducted throughout much of the reservation are similar in their informal use of the native language and English to those in Santa Fe. These preschool programs often lack a clearly articulate policy toward the native language of the learner. A much-debated question here is whether the native language should be encouraged or should only be tolerated until the child acquires English.

A typical example of this ambivalence in classroom policy (and also of the mistaken belief that bilingual instruction consists of teaching the native language as a subject) is illustrated by the comments of a teacher participating in the Bureau of Indian Affairs kindergarten programs. "At first I did not consider this as a bilingual program, because we did not use materials published in the Navajo language, and were not attempting to teach it as a separate subject.... I now believe our efforts can be called bilingual and bicultural, and we are seriously considering extending bilingual instruction to other grades."[5]

A similar confusion is voiced by a very able Spanish-American aide in one of the leading Follow-Through programs in the Southwest, who reports he is neither encouraged nor discouraged from speaking Spanish to the children in the classroom; the Anglo teacher he works with is trying to learn Spanish and the children laugh good-naturedly at her pronunciation. However, the idea that learning to read in Spanish may be helpful to these children upsets him. In his own life and in that of his relatives, he has accepted the idea that Spanish is the language of oral communication, intimacy, and friendship, and that English is the language of literacy.

Much of the confusion in these informal programs derives from a lack of systematic planning in the instructional use of the two languages. While these programs cannot be considered bilingual education, as defined at the beginning of this chapter, they have increased the interest in bilingual instruction and have led to requests for more bilingual experiments.

B. The Supplementary Model

In a number of school systems throughout the country, limited attempts at using two languages as instructional media are in effect. These programs are supplementary in nature: some are organized in communities with scant resources for bilingual education (e. g. , Pecos, New Mexico); others are aimed at small numbers of non-English-speaking children in a primarily "mainstream" community (e. g. , Englewood, New Jersey).

A well-established supplementary program is found in Pecos, a community in northern New Mexico with limited resources for a bilingual program. All the children in the Pecos school, including the small number of native speakers of English, receive half an hour of Spanish instruction daily. In spite of limitations in staffing and time devoted to instruction in the native language, the Pecos program has been a pioneer in bilingual education in New Mexico. Since its establishment in 1965 with Ford Foundation funds, the program has served as a demonstration center. Recent and more ambitious programs in New Mexico are based upon the success of Pecos.

As Puerto Ricans continue to move into small communities on the Eastern seaboard, school systems count an increasing number of Spanish-speaking children among their pupils. In Englewood, New Jersey, the introduction of a non-graded multi-educational system offered an opportunity for educational innovation. Teachers work with children in small groups; bilingual tutors work with groups as small as two or three children. Their aim is to achieve a third grade proficiency in Spanish among the Puerto Rican children before moving them into reading in English.

In both the Pecos and the Englewood programs, instruction in the native language is limited to a small portion of the school day. The approach is similar to the "Spanish S" programs, familiar to many high school teachers. The inclusion of these efforts in our bilingual program descriptions is justified by their importance as starting points. Once a shift is made away from the English-only policy of public schools, no matter how minor the change may be, parents, educators, and community leaders become interested in exploring an alternative model of education for children in the non-English-speaking communities.

C. Transition Model

Mackey states that the long-range goals of bilingual schools are two-fold: the curriculum can be directed toward the language of the wider culture, thus promoting acculturation; or the curriculum can be directed toward the regional, national, or neo-national culture, thus promoting irredentism.

In most programs in this country there is no clear direction in language policy. The following recommendations of the Texas Educational Agency, while ascribing an important role to the Spanish language as a transitional medium leading toward acculturation, illustrate the general lack of a defined, long-range language policy:

> Non-English-speaking children needing special instruction to adjust successfully in school and to use the English language may be placed in a modified program which makes full use of the pupils' ability in the language they understand and speak when enrolled in public schools.... The modified program should have the following characteristics: The first language of the child is used as a means of instruction in developing the basic skills of reading, spelling, writing, and arithmetic.
> English is introduced as a second language; as the child becomes more proficient in understanding and speaking the second language, the use of the first language as a means of instruction should be decreased, while the use of English for this purpose is increased.
> The use of both languages as a medium of instruction is continued for a minimum of three years and thereafter until such a time as the child is able to comprehend and communicate effectively in English.
> To assure the development of a literate bilingual, the child is given the opportunity for continued study of the four basic skills of his first language (understanding, speaking, reading, and writing). [6]

Note that the last recommendation adds, almost as an afterthought, the phrase, "to assure the development of a literate bilingual." The student is offered the option of continuing his studies of (though not in) Spanish.

For many bilingual programs, the use of the native language serves mainly as a bridge to the national language. Mackey describes such a curriculum as the Transfer (T) type: He notes that "The transfer pattern has been used to convert from one medium to another.... In schools of this type, the transfer may be gradual or abrupt, regular or irregular, the degree of regularity and gradualness being available as to distinguish one school from another."[7]

The Follow-Through Project at Corpus Christi, Texas, is an example of a transfer program. Concepts are taught first in Spanish, then in English; at all levels the intensive language approach is aimed at developing proficiency both in English and in Spanish. The bilingual program ends after the third grade.

Bilingual educators, ideally, would like to develop in their students the skills of coordinate bilinguals; educators at Corpus Christi share these objectives. But frequently the funding available for pioneer programs (particularly before the passage of Title VII legislation) has imposed limitations on comprehensive planning. Follow-Through funds, for example, span only the K-grade 3 years of elementary instruction. Parent enthusiasm and community support have aided in expansion or reformulation of these early programs, but this process is just starting.

It is difficult to predict at this early stage of programmatic development of bilingual education in the United States how much interest students will display in the acquisition of literacy in Spanish. Educational programs affect as well as reflect language policy. During the three years that we have been engaged in the study of bilingual education, we have witnessed great variations, reversals of position, and significant new developments in the way in which the meaning of education in two languages has been interpreted by members of interested groups.

Some educators who doubted the wisdom of teaching children in their native languages modified their attitude after the publication of the Coleman report. The Coleman finding that a positive self-concept is a crucial attribute of the successful student has contributed to a re-evaluation of the role of the minority child's language and culture.[8] Bilingual education is now envisaged by an increasing number of administrators as one aspect of programmatic endeavors to increase the self-respect of children who are not part of the "mainstream."

The feelings and hopes of members of non-English-speaking communities toward the future of their language is difficult to assess. Some recent events may be of significance in this regard. Spanish-speaking students in high schools and universities are asking for Chicano studies, Puerto Rican studies, and a larger role for Spanish in these settings. In Spanish-speaking communities, the more militant members rely upon their native language increasingly in their publications, meetings, and press conferences. At the same time, others in these communities continue to emphasize assimilationist trends. Additional socio-linguistic studies, such as Fishman's Bilingualism in the Barrio, are needed to develop a fuller picture of the language aspirations existing in the diverse communities of America's minorities.

D. The Two-Way Model

Mackey, in his typology of bilingual schools, identified two major variants that we would categorize as two-way schools: the Dual Medium Differential Maintenance (DDM) and the Dual Medium Equal Maintenance (DEM). Mackey describes the DDM model as follows: "In maintaining two languages for different purposes, the difference may be established by subject matter, according to the likely contribution of each culture. Often the culture-based subjects like art, history, literature and geography are in the dominant home language."[9]

In our concern with early childhood bilingual education, this model is not quite as relevant as some of the others already described. However, the debates concerning this model are of interest. When the Rough Rock Demonstration School was first established on the Navajo reservation, it conformed to this description of the DDM model. Culture-based subjects (e.g., social science, tribal organization) were taught in Navajo, while more traditional academic subject matter was taught in English. Visitors from other Indian tribes, among them Robert Thomas, the Cherokee anthropologist, criticized the restricted role given to the Navajo language in the curriculum. Subsequently, Rough Rock's Board of Education, made up of Navajo elders, outlined a new policy with regard to the language, and many traditional academic subjects are now taught in Navajo.

Some sociologists, including Fishman, have argued in favor of the DDM model as the most accurate expression of the actual uses of the native and national languages in bilingual communities. On the other hand, others interested in the development of balanced bilinguals have argued in favor of a dual system characterized by equal treatment of the two languages. Mackey describes this system, the Dual Medium Equal Maintenance (DEM), in the following way: "In some schools ... it has been necessary ... not to distinguish between languages and to give equal chance to both languages in all domains. This is done by alternating on the time scale--day, week, month, or year from one language to the others."[10]

In the United States, the best-known example of a two-way bilingual school is the Coral Way Elementary School in Miami, Florida. Two important, long-range conditions of bilingual education are exemplified in this program: (a) equal time and treatment are given to two languages (Spanish and English), and (b) monolingual English-speaking children are integrated with Cuban immigrants into this bilingual system. The Miami experiment has been highly successful locally and nationally and is a much-admired exemplar of what bilingual education can become.

A few other school systems have tried to adopt the equal time and treatment approach. The comprehensive program developed in Las Cruces, New Mexico, with the aid of New Mexico State University, is one such attempt: "In the early stages of the program the day was divided in half, instruction in Spanish in the morning, and English in the afternoon. However, as the program developed, the teachers developed their own class schedules. While about half of the day continued to be spent in each language, individual instruction varied; in some classes both languages may be mixed in one lesson, or a lesson in English may directly follow a lesson in Spanish."[11]

E. Conclusions

Although theoretical concerns enter into the choice of a model for bilingual education, most bilingual schools develop their curriculum as a function of practical considerations. Basic research, the preparation of materials, and the training of teachers lag severely behind the needs of existing and projected bilingual programs. Consequently, administrators and parent advisory committees are often forced to choose programmatic models that fall short of the long-range goal of developing balanced bilinguals.

We have speculated earlier in this book that, once the prohibition against instruction in a language other than English is overcome, a series of new possibilities may be considered by individuals who have previously played a passive role in the education of their children. When bilingual programs are first started, they usually serve as demonstration programs only. The reactions of parents, of teachers in other schools, and of administrators often add the impetus necessary to implement comprehensive programs that include more than the beginning grades of school.

The participation of parents is a crucial aspect of bilingual education. Although many bilingual educators support this view, they fail to implement it. When programs are planned in isolation from the community, parents' contributions become merely incidental. Parental participation and community control do not guarantee relief from the shortage of qualified teachers, the lack of curriculum materials, limited funds, or from any other of the problems specific to bilingual education. Such participation and control do, however, provide support for and continuity to the school's efforts.

Educational innovations will remain of passing interest and little significance without the recognition that education is a social process. If the school remains alien to the values and needs of the community, if it is bureaucratically run, then the children will not receive the education they are entitled to, no matter what language they are taught in.

References

1. A. Bruce Gaarder, "Organization of the Bilingual School," Journal of Social Issues, 23 (1967), 110.
2. E. M. Bernal, Jr., ed., Bilingual-Bicultural Education: Where Do We Go from Here? San Antonio, Texas; sponsored by the Bureau of Educational Personnel Development, U.S. Office of Education, and St. Mary's Univ., 28, 29 March 1969.

3. William F. Mackey, "A Typology of Bilingual Education" (Quebec: International Center for Research on Bilingualism, 1969), mimeo.

4. A. A. Valencia, "Bilingual /Bicultural Education: A Perspective Model in Multicultural America," Southwestern Cooperative Educational Laboratory, April 1969.

5. See "Bureau of Indian Affairs Kindergarten Programs," p. 98-100.

6. Principles and Standards for Accrediting Elementary and Secondary Schools" (Austin: Texas Educational Agency, Spring 1967).

7. "A Typology of Bilingual Education," p. 8.

8. James S. Coleman, Equality of Educational Opportunity (Washington, D. C. : U. S. Office of Education, 1966), No. OE-38001.

9. "A Typology of Bilingual Education," p. 14.

10. "A Typology of Bilingual Education," p. 14.

11. See "Sustained Primary Program for Bilingual Students," Las Cruces, N. M. , pp. 39-42.

WHAT ARE THE EDUCATIONAL NEEDS OF PUERTO RICANS WHO COME TO NEW YORK?

I fully appreciate the invitation extended to me by the authorities of New York University to participate in this Conference on the education of the Puerto Ricans who migrate to New York City. For a long time I have devoted my life in the public service to the effort of raising the economic and cultural standards of my people. Now, as Secretary of Education of Puerto Rico, I am particularly pleased to speak before this group of distinguished educators and statesmen interested in discussing ways and means to help the Puerto Ricans realize their fullest potential.

On the subject of the educational needs of Puerto Ricans who come to New York, I can claim neither originality nor completeness. Other fellow-workers from Puerto Rico and from the mainland have made significant contributions in this field, in various forms, ranging from the formulation of possible basic policies to the study of specific problems in various areas, including the preparation of curriculum materials for teaching the Puerto Rican children in the States. Further, the subject is so vast that it precludes any attempt at full treatment before the job of full research is accomplished.

It would be presumptuous on my part to tell you specifically what the educational needs of Puerto Rican migrants are. Or, having suggested some or all of those needs, to try to come up with specific suggestions to take care of the needs. The case is similar to that of a patient who calls on a doctor. Through adequate examination the physician may be able to come up with an accurate diagnosis. After that, he may be in a favorable position to prescribe the required medical treatment. However, before starting on the physical examination the physician usually finds out what the clinical history

Address, New York University, January 14, 1961. Reprinted by permission.

of the patient is. If the patient cannot supply these answers, somebody ought to do it.

In connection with the educational needs of Puerto Ricans who
come to New York City, you are in a better position than we to make
the final diagnosis and prescribe the treatment. But we may help as
a source of facts in order for you to be able to write the full clinical
history of the patient. Hence, most of my talk today will be devoted
to supplying this type of information.

I shall first talk about the contributions made by the Puerto
Rican Study undertaken a few years ago under the sponsorship of the
Board of Education of the City of New York with a grant-in-aid from
the Fund for the Advancement of Education. At this time, I should
like to mention some of the steps that, according to the Report, must
be taken in order to accelerate the learning and adjustment of first
and second generation Puerto Ricans and other non-English speaking
pupils in New York City. They were:

> Recognize and define the school's responsibility to assist,
> counsel, and cooperate with the parents of non-English-
> speaking pupils in all matters pertaining to the child's wel-
> fare.

> Take a new look at the school's opportunity to accelerate
> the adjustment of Puerto Rican children and their parents
> through advice and counsel to parents on problems normally
> considered to be outside the conventional functions of the
> school.

> Staff the schools to do the job: to help the new arrival
> to make good adjustment to school and community; to help
> the non-English-speaking child to learn English and to find
> his way successfully into the main stream of the school's
> program.

> Take a new, hard look at the psychological services provided
> for non-English-speaking children, especially for Puerto
> Rican children.

One significant statement of basic policy of the Puerto Rican
Study was that we should accept it "not as something finished, but as
the first stage of a larger, city-wide, ever-improving program for
the education and assimilation of non-English-speaking children."

Those proposals cover some of the outstanding areas of research and action in which definite programs can be planned. They
embody original ideas and approaches for the solution of unique new
situations, yet not unlike similar ones that you faced in the past with
respect to other minority migrant groups.

I will not elaborate on the educational needs of Puerto Ricans
who migrate to New York and other parts of the mainland. This has

been the subject of numerous conferences and seminars both here and in Puerto Rico. Any account of such needs must, however, take into consideration the academic, social and vocational needs, and it must deal in part with the problems of adult education. I feel that you will be in a better position to discuss the subject by including an analysis of the social and cultural forces now prevailing in Puerto Rican life. As all of you know, Puerto Rico is at present undergoing a profound economic, social and cultural transformation. Although I may not be able to add any significant data to what has already come to your attention, I am sure you will readily understand how the Puerto Rican effort of the last twenty years is affecting in various forms the character, the culture, the education and the adaptive potential of the Puerto Ricans who will migrate to New York.

Under its Commonwealth status, Puerto Rico is a self-governing country in voluntary and close association with the United States of America based on common citizenship, common defense and free trade. In a historic resolution adopted by the General Assembly of the United Nations on November 3, 1953, this Commonwealth was solemnly recognized as a self-governing political body. The fact that it preserves its partnership with the Union represents a unique feature of world-wide significance and may eventually have its impact on the ways of dealing with international relationships. As a house of freedom it will necessarily have its imprint on the migrants who come to New York. It has been said that a good culture must be flavored with both local and world-wide values. It is, thus, quite understandable that an observer might say this is precisely what the Commonwealth of Puerto Rico is trying to do, as exemplified by the terms "free" and "associated." In the present day culture of Puerto Ricans the average child and the average adult are increasingly learning the lesson of democracy and will thus be able to contribute with their own values to the life of their fellow-citizens on the mainland. After all, we must never forget that, in spite of the so-much publicized cultural differences between New Yorkers and Puerto Ricans, we have much in common inherent in our common Western and Christian heritages.

The effort being made by the Commonwealth of Puerto Rico toward economic development will also affect the character of the Puerto Rican migrant. Due to its dynamic economic development program, Puerto Rico is no longer a predominantly agricultural country. In 1959-60 the net income from manufacturing was $289 million; that from agriculture $177 million. Income from manufacturing exceeded income from agriculture for the first time in 1955. The number of factories established with government help reached a total of 629 in June 1960. During the decade between 1949-50 to 1959-60 the Commonwealth's gross product rose from $750.5 million to $1,572.6 million. As a result of all this economic growth, the per capita income is now the highest in the Caribbean area and the second highest in all Latin America (exceeded only by oil-rich Venezuela). However, it is still only about one-half that of the poorest U.S. state.

One interesting feature of this economic growth is the fact

that it has been planned in a democratic climate. The Puerto Rico Planning Board, created by the Legislative Assemby, has been the basic instrument in this connection. This Planning Board has developed a master plan which includes a set of plans each dealing with a particular aspect of the island's development. This master plan continually adjusts its "guide lines" in accordance with the emerging needs and goals.

As a result of its economic development, Puerto Rico is undergoing a rapid transition from a rural to an urban way of life. The social transformation resulting from urbanization will be a factor in determining the educational needs of all Puerto Rican migrants. It will obviously increase the adaptiveness of the Puerto Rican to the patterns of living in New York.

This, gentlemen, is a tight summary of what is happening in Puerto Rico in the political, economic and social spheres. As to the impact of these recent developments on the Puerto Rican migrant, no one is better qualified to describe it than Governor Luis Muñoz Marin, who, in an address to a labor convention in Atlantic City, New Jersey, concluded:

> When you meet a Puerto Rican in the streets of New York, Chicago, Los Angeles, or on the farms of New Jersey, Connecticut or Minnesota, no matter how unadapted he may seem to his new environment, think of him as a member of a human group that is trying to be useful to freedom; remember that there is a little more to him than meets the eye. Back in his Commonwealth he has a background of democracy and kindliness, a simple and sincere regard for his fellow-beings--no matter of what race, color or nation. This may be invisible at first, but it also migrates with him.

Education, of course, has played a very significant role in the Puerto Rican transformation. At the present time well over a third of the island's population is receiving some kind of formal education, ranging from kindergarten to college and adult education. A United Nations publication (1957) reported this as the world's highest proportion, and this is undoubtedly a measure of Puerto Rico's faith in education. One-third of all government outlay is devoted to educational services of various kinds.

The stronger effort, just started, for the coming ten years has been very appropriately labeled "The Decade of Education." The economic, social and cultural goals adopted by the Commonwealth give rise to new demands and present new challenges to our educational system. These have to do not only with our manpower needs for further economic growth, but also with all the problems and needs generated by a rapidly changing society in a very exacting period of its history.

During the last twenty years, we have witnessed an unprecedented educational growth in quantitative terms. The number of class-rooms and teachers have increased spectacularly but are still insufficient. This has indeed been a remarkable achievement, but is only a first important stage. This effort must be continued but at the same time we have started on a new phase in which quality more than quantity will be our main concern. The present educational reform movement gives special attention to factors that condition the teaching effort. We have been able to make free, universal education a reality in Puerto Rico; we are now starting to consolidate this achievement by providing at least the minimum requisites for efficient instruction in all our schools.

At present, 61 per cent of all children in elementary grades attend schools organized under a double enrollment plan, which provides only 3 hours of instruction per day, and 10 per cent attend schools organized under an interlocking plan, providing for a 5-hour school day. At the junior and senior high school levels, 37 per cent and 18 per cent, respectively, are attending schools organized under the interlocking plan. Out of a total of 572,000 pupils in our public schools, 241,000 are in double enrollment. This means that over two-fifths of our students receive only three hours of schooling daily. It is thus obvious that our new reform effort needs to be directed toward the complete elimination of this inadequacy, representing, as it does, not only a handicap to the normal quality of performance but also a limit on the actual extension of educational opportunities. We have set this as a goal to be attained within the next four years.

Closely related to the quality of instruction is the problem of providing suitable textbooks and teaching aids in adequate quantities to meet the needs of all our students at all instructional levels. We have made considerable progress in this direction during the last ten years, thanks to the appropriations of our Legislative Assembly, but we still have a long way to go. We are producing a sizeable quantity of books especially designed to meet our educational needs and we have established our own printing facilities. We will continue to avail ourselves of United States textbooks, but we will also continue to produce increasing numbers of books, manuals, guides, courses of study and various other teaching materials adapted to our present day trends and conditions.

The number of pupils a teacher can handle in any ordinary teaching situation without impairing teaching efficiency is another problem receiving our attention. A heavy teaching load precludes the possibility of individual attention. This situation is responsible for a prevailing instructional pattern in which teaching is geared to the less than average performances, thus depriving the most capable students of the challenges to which they are entitled in a truly democratic educational system. We have, therefore, begun to organize special courses for talented students, including college level courses for twelfth grade students. We have also organized pilot classes for retarded but educable pupils.

We are strengthening our mechanisms for evaluating results.

For this we are preparing achievement tests to be administered at the various teaching levels to ascertain the degree of performance in terms of the goals previously set. The results of this evaluation will show us the deficient areas in which remedial action should be taken. In general, this will also be a concrete way of assessing the effectiveness of our public education for which so much money is being spent.

We have already started on other projects which, because of lack of time, I will not describe on this occasion. I have outlined only those which might be of special interest to you at this Conference. I should like to assure you that we in the Department of Education of the Commonwealth of Puerto Rico will give our wholehearted support to the recommendations made by the Fourth Migration Conference held in June 1960 here in New York. In that Conference it was recommended that the Board of Education of New York City and the Department of Education of Puerto Rico establish a joint committee to coordinate their activities in several areas of mutual concern; among these I mention the following: further implementation of the program for the teaching of English as a second language in Puerto Rico; the development of workshops for Puerto Rican teachers and supervisors to be held in New York; improvement of procedures for the exchange of pupil information and school records; exchange of information on methods of working with parents as part of community education and parent participation; continuation of efforts to develop valid tests to aid in the grade placement of pupils; re-activation of the program for the exchange of teaching personnel between Puerto Rico and New York; exchange and further development of teaching materials; and the continued development of educational and vocational guidance activities and of vocational training aimed at further encouraging Puerto Rican students to enter professional and technical fields.

This joint committee has already been organized and our permanent committee in collaboration with New York school authorities has currently under consideration a supervisory exchange proposal recommended by its sub-committee on the teaching of English as a second language. I hope soon to give special attention to matters concerning the joint action of this New York-Puerto Rico committee. In the meantime, we are continuing the projects that I have already outlined and these will eventually have their impact on the education of all Puerto Ricans, including the migrants to New York and other parts of the Union.

In closing, I would like to say that I have complete confidence in the results of this important conference sponsored by the educators of New York University. As co-workers we are rededicating ourselves to the unity of the Western Hemisphere. Puerto Rico and New York provide a remarkable example of what should be done on behalf of a better understanding among all the peoples of the world.

REPORT ON VISITS TO NEW YORK CITY SCHOOLS

On February 18, 1948, I visited the office of Superintendent of Schools Jansen and was given a general letter of introduction to district super-intendents and principals of schools. February 25 I called on Dr. Clare C. Baldwin, Assistant Superintendent, who gave me a list of schools which he thought I should visit. February 27 I called on Dr. Frank Whalen, Assistant Superintendent, 330 East 152 St., Bronx, who also suggested a number of schools with a large attendance of Puerto Rican children. March 2 I called on Miss Antoinette Riordon, Assist-ant Superintendent, 223 Graham Avenue, Brooklyn, who took me to visit two elementary schools in her district. Later Miss Riordon made arrangements for visits to other schools. Besides the schools suggested by the three Assistant Superintendents above, I visited other schools upon the suggestion of this office or through personal invitation on the part of the school principals or teachers. Altogether, I visited the following schools:

Bronx	P.S. 30 Elementary School
	P.S. 124 Elementary School
	P.S. 25 Elementary School
	P.S. 99 Elementary School
	P.S. 60 Junior High School (Girls)
	Morris High School
Harlem	P.S. 57 Elementary School
	P.S. 102 Elementary School
	P.S. 157 Elementary School
	P.S. 83 Junior High School (Boys)
	P.S. 120 Junior High School (Boys)
	P.S. 171 Junior High School (Boys)
	P.S. 101 Junior High School (Girls)
	P.S. 172 Senior High School (Boys)

Government of Puerto Rico. Department of Labor & Employment & Migration Bureau, (1948). (Mimeo.) Reprinted by permission.

<u>Lower Manhattan</u>   P. S. 188 Elementary & Junior High School
(Coeducational)

<u>Brooklyn</u>   P. S. 55 Elementary School (Annex)
P. S. 36 Elementary School
P. S. 168 Elementary School
P. S. 148 Junior High School (Boys)
P. S. 196 Junior High School (Girls)

Ten of these were elementary schools, one was elementary and junior high combined, seven were junior high schools, and two were senior high schools. It is supposed that these schools constitute a fair sampling of those schools in sections of the city where the Puerto Rican population is concentrated. The enrollment of Puerto Rican children in these schools varies from 90% in P. S. 57 to about 4% in P. S. 188. My visits to these schools were very brief, generally a day in each, hence I have not made a thorough study of conditions in them--I have visited briefly and jotted down observations.

I was cordially received in all of these schools by principals and teachers, and was given every opportunity to observe what was going on and what each school was trying to do in behalf of the Puerto Rican children.

The Puerto Rican children whom I saw in these schools may be classified into three groups: (1) those born in the United States of Puerto Rican parents; (2) those who came to this country very young and have resided here more than five years; (3) the recent arrivals. All things being equal, there should be no special educational problem with the first group, not any more than with any other group of native children of foreign parentage. Those who came very young, who have been here over five years, and who have gone through the kindergarten and first grades of the elementary school, should adjust very rapidly, almost as quickly as the first group.

The recent arrivals come from all parts of the island--quite a few from the inland towns such as Caguas, Cayey, Aibonito, Comerio. But the great majority of them come from the large city areas, San Juan being first and Ponce second; Mayaguez and Humacao follow. The large majority of the children I visited were recent arrivals, that is, generally two years or less in this country. With some exceptions, they come from the poor and under-privileged groups, economically, socially and educationally. The great majority of them have not enjoyed full advantage of school facilities in Puerto Rico. The older ones have attended school on an average of four years or less. I found a few fourteen and fifteen year olds who had attended school very little and who were illiterate in their vernacular.

Another phenomenon which must not be overlooked and which is very prevalent is the fact that a large number of these children have some home problem. A good number come from broken homes. Father and mother do not live together--in many cases the mother is here and the father in Puerto Rico or vice versa. In many cases

there has been divorce and remarriage, with one of either parents
being replaced by a stepfather or stepmother. In some instances the
child is an orphan and lives here with relatives. Or again, the parents are in Puerto Rico and the children live here with the grandmother, aunt, sister, or uncle, or what not--all sorts of combinations.
In many cases both parents are here, but they both work, and the
children are left to themselves all day long. They generally have
lunch in school or somewhere near the school. After school hours
they roam the streets or vacant lots playing and sometimes getting
into trouble. I mention these cases not only because of the emotional
strain under which these children live, which is bound to be reflected
in the school, but also because such situations lend themselves to
truancy and all the evils derived therefrom. I discovered these facts
casually, by talking to the children. I have not made a thorough study
of home conditions. It would be interesting to know just how many
broken homes are represented in the number of Puerto Rican children
attending the New York public schools. These recent arrivals, with
all the handicaps they bring from the island, plus the conditions under
which they are compelled to live in New York, constitute a real educational problem for the schools of the city.

What are the New York schools doing to meet these problems?
The report prepared by a Committee of the Association of Assistant
Superintendents entitled "A Program of Education for Puerto Ricans
in New York City" tells us what is being done educationally today for
the Puerto Rican population here, and makes recommendations for the
future. The report is thorough, comprehensive, and above all, most
sympathetic, showing genuine, sincere interest on the part of the
school authorities in the approach to and solution of the problem.
Parts III, IV and V are the most helpful insofar as my visits to the
schools are concerned. It is not necessary to repeat here the main
facts brought out in that report and the recommendations made therein
because copies of the report are available to this office. As far as
I have been able to observe in my visits to the schools, an earnest
effort is being made by public school authorities and teachers to carry
out the recommendations made in that excellent study.

After reading this report and visiting twenty schools among
the under-privileged population of the city, it seems to me that crit-
ics of the public schools here, including the so-called "Harlem Project," are very pessimistic. Anyone who knows anything about schools
knows that no school is perfect. The New York public schools no
doubt leave much to be desired--the schools I have seen could be improved greatly in many ways. (However, it is not my purpose to
describe here how these schools may be improved, the Superintendent
of Schools and his staff are aware of needed improvements.) But the
criticism that the public schools of the city are breeding places for
delinquency is very unjust. It happens that I have visited some of the
very public schools which have been the object of this criticism. After observing the communities where these schools are located, after
interviewing principals and teachers and observing the teaching in the
classrooms, and the behavior of the children, I have come to the conclusion that these schools, rather than breeding places for delinquency,

are the very institutions which are contributing most toward the prevention of delinquency. As usual, the public school must be the scapegoat and answer for the sins and shortcomings of the whole community, plus the neglect of other agencies.

As to the Puerto Rican children attending the public schools which I visited, I have found school authorities, principals and teachers genuinely interested in their problems. In many cases I have found real devotion on the part of principals and teachers toward helping the Puerto Rican children. After hearing so much adverse criticism, I was very pleasantly surprised at the intelligent way the problem is being attacked and the generally sympathetic attitude on the part of the school.

As may be observed in the report of the Assistant Superintendents, the problem of the education of Puerto Rican children in this city is a new problem for administrators and teachers. The city schools are trying various methods of approach and experimentation. The one outstanding concern is the language problem. The various methods being used in the teaching of English are described in the aforementioned report. These methods are being changed in accordance with experience. It is interesting to go from school to school, talk to teachers and hear their criticism of the methods being used in the teaching of English to Spanish-speaking children. It is interesting also to observe the changes these teachers are making constantly, and their explanations for the changes. This attitude shows the interest of the teachers and their desire to find out for themselves the efficiency of the methods recommended.

As I went from school to school, teachers and principals seemed anxious to discuss with me the work they were doing and the problems they were meeting. A perusal of the report of the Association of Assistant Superintendents will show that the New York school authorities are conscious of these problems and are planning intelligently for their solution. There is very little I can add to the recommendations made in this report. Nevertheless, I would like to comment briefly on some of the problems mentioned in this report, which the teachers wanted to discuss with me.

1. The Language Problem

Methods of teaching English to the Puerto Rican children in the schools are described in the report already mentioned. Some teachers do make variations on the methods recommended. Some principals and teachers are afraid of segregation and push their students so as to keep them in the special classes as short a period as possible. Others retain the children longer. As a general rule the policy is that a child should be placed in the regular grade as soon as he can benefit thereby. Of course, a great deal depends on the child's ability, and his previous schooling. I believe this practice is being handled very wisely.

Some teachers seemed troubled because their children speak Spanish at every opportunity they have. It is natural for children to use their vernacular among themselves, as it is natural for any group of people to use their mother tongue in preference to a foreign language. That should worry no one. A child learning a foreign language does not use it as a rule in place of the vernacular until he consciously feels the need to do so. This requires discipline on his part because he sees that it is absolutely necessary for him to learn the foreign language. This means that he must abstain from speaking his vernacular and accept the additional burden of speaking the more difficult medium. That resolution does not come to a child until the period of adolescence or later when he realizes the need for his learning the foreign language and the advantages that he will derive from the mastery of it. Then he makes the effort. The environment in which he lives has a great deal to do with the effort that he puts forth. An English-speaking environment would stimulate the effort. I do not think that too much pressure or constant urging helps very much--on the contrary, this may antagonize the child.

Another problem most discussed among teachers is the teacher herself. Should the teacher know Spanish herself? Some believe she should, and many teachers in New York City who teach Puerto Rican children are learning Spanish. In some schools as many as 50% of the teachers can use enough Spanish to get along with the children. Nevertheless, there are some teachers and administrators who feel that the teacher who teaches Spanish-speaking children need not know Spanish. They contend that when the teacher knows Spanish she uses it as a crutch. I have observed teachers who do not know Spanish and I have also observed those who know Spanish very well. In my visits, I have observed teachers without a knowledge of Spanish working very hard and very energetically in order to "put it over" as we often say. At the other extreme I observed a teacher who has an excellent command of Spanish and who used so much Spanish in the classroom that it was more an exercise in translation than an English class. These are the two extremes. On the other hand, in one of the public schools of the city, I visited a young, inexperienced teacher instructing Spanish-speaking children. No one could tell that she knew Spanish until she resorted to that language in order to clear up some slight point and avoid waste of time. In my opinion, this young teacher was using her knowledge of Spanish wisely, at the opportune moment. In the meantime, she used every possible device to make the children use English. Personally, I feel that a teacher teaching children whose native tongue is Spanish could do a better and more intelligent job if she were equipped with a knowledge of Spanish. Such a teacher would not only understand the child better, but would be able to appreciate his linguistic difficulties, because she can put herself in the child's place, and therefore should be able to understand him better than the teacher who does not know Spanish.

Due to the circumstances in the homes and the communities from which the children come, circumstances beyond the control of the school, the child hears and speaks more Spanish than English out of school. Hence the importance of his being in an environment of

English when he is in school. I agree that if the Spanish-speaking child in New York City is going to learn English he should be taught in that language. Spanish should be used only when necessary. However, this should not be an argument against the teacher's knowing Spanish as part of her teaching equipment. It is not her knowledge of Spanish which is a liability, but it is the misuse of Spanish as a crutch when it is not necessary. I think, therefore, that knowledge of Spanish on the part of a teacher who teaches children of Puerto Rican extraction is an asset rather than a liability.

2. Materials of Instruction

Another problem which seems to bother the teachers is the dearth of materials of instruction in English which may be used in the classes, especially in the junior high school where the children are retarded and the literature available is inadequate. Some resourceful principals and teachers are developing their own materials of instruction. This seems to be an excellent way to furnish the schools with reading material in the absence of appropriate literature. Some elementary and junior high schools have already gathered considerable material which should be mimeographed and improved in the hope that it will contribute to a fund of literature much needed for the Spanish-speaking population. The recommendation (4) made by the Report of the Association of Assistant Superintendents is most pertinent. Nevertheless, there should be adaptable material in the large amount of literature for children which is being published constantly by the various publishing firms. It seems to me that a committee of teachers, together with the school authorities entrusted with the selection of textbooks for the public schools, should get together and explore the field, find out what is being published and what might be appropriate in order to supply this need. I have examined several publications which should be interesting to children of Spanish speech. These deal primarily with Latin American topics. The New York public schools might have in stock material which may prove suitable. Bibliographies of children's literature issued by various companies and agencies may help. The Office of Puerto Rico in New York will be pleased to be of service in this regard.

3. Placement of Children

Another problem which concerns principals and teachers is placement of children upon their arrival from Puerto Rico. The teachers feel that there are no norms or diagnostic tests which might aid in the placement of these children in the city schools. Puerto Rico has an American system of education organized on the 6-3-3 plan, with the exception that Spanish is the medium of instruction in the elementary school. The content of the curriculum, including many of the textbooks, is the same as in the schools on the mainland. There is, therefore, sufficient similarity in organization and content so that when a Puerto Rican child transfers to the States, all things being equal, he should have a normal transfer. There is, nevertheless, the language difficulty which has to be met. At first the language difficulty seems an enormous barrier because the child apparently does not know English. Due to the fact that he has lived in a Spanish environment and has been taught in Spanish, he has had little opportunity to practice English; hence his ear is not educated to comprehension and his tongue is not educated to expression, and he may appear to know less English than he really does. It is my firm conviction that a child coming from Puerto Rico should, as far as possible, be given the opportunity of normal transfer. Then, in the special classes in English, he should have at least two hours a day studying the language. In six months he should be doing normal school work in his grade. This rule could apply both to the elementary and the secondary school levels.

The difficulty lies in the fact that the majority of the children in the schools which I have visited are recent arrivals, from underprivileged groups who have not had normal school facilities. They belong to the large group of children in the island who do not go to school long enough either to learn English or to receive much instruction of any kind. Generally, they are average, of secondary school level as far as school age is concerned, but very retarded in school achievement. It is difficult to place these children in New York City schools. I found many in junior high school, but actually doing primary grade work. This problem seems to trouble the teachers and they wonder whether Puerto Rico has a compulsory school attendance law, and why the children do not know more English when this language is taught from the first grade all through the public school system. Here, for teachers instructing recent arrivals from Puerto Rico, is the need for information about the lack of school facilities in the island; the problem of double enrollment; the tremendous increase in population; and the inability of the educational system to cope with the educational needs of the population. The visit of New York City teachers to Puerto Rico this summer will contribute a great deal toward the comprehension of this problem. The problem of these under-privileged retarded children is most serious, not only in New York, but also in Puerto Rico. It is difficult to make suggestions based on my brief visits. It is a problem which bears further and more extensive study.

4. Test of Academic Achievement and Mental Ability

Many teachers have spoken to me about diagnostic tests which might be used in placing children coming from Puerto Rico. Very little has been done in this field. The University of Puerto Rico has done some work in the preparation of a standard test for the public schools in Puerto Rico. Quite a great deal was accomplished in the thirties. Unfortunately, this activity has been neglected in recent years and the tests that we have today are not up to date. They may serve, however, as models in case a study of this kind is undertaken. The Office of Puerto Rico in New York will be glad to furnish copies of these tests to the school authorities in case they may help in the construction of new tests.

Copies of the following tests may be secured at the Office of Puerto Rico:

1. Spanish American test of English
    Form 1-A for Grades 2, 3, 4, 5.
2. "TEST" Hispanoamericano de Habilidad y Aprovechamiento
    Forma 1-A para grados 3, 4, 5.
3. Spanish American test of English
    Form II-A for grades 6, 7, 8, 9.
4. "TEST" Hispanoamericano de Habilidad y Aprovechamiento
    Forma II-B para grados 6, 7, 8, 9.
5. University of Puerto Rico
    General Ability Test for Grades 8-12
    Form A (Revised)
6. University of Puerto Rico
    General Ability Test for Grades 8-12
    Form B
7. University of Puerto Rico
    General Ability Test for Grades 8-12
    Form C
8. University of Puerto Rico
    General Ability Test for Grades 8-12
    Form X

California has done some work in the preparation of tests for children of Spanish speech. I am not acquainted with these tests but copies may be secured from the State of California, Bureau of Examinations, 5916 Hollywood Boulevard, Los Angeles, California. This test was translated into Spanish by the personnel of the Department of Education of Puerto Rico.

The Inter-American Test: The Committee of Modern Languages of the American Council on Education, of which Professor Robert H. Fife, of Columbia University, is chairman, has been interested in the construction of tests for children in bilingual situations. In 1940 Dr. Fife and Dr. H. T. Manuel of the University of Texas, visited Puerto Rico under the auspices of the American Council on Education. As a result of their visit it was decided that they should prepare a battery of tests which should be parallel in English and in Spanish for measuring achievements in these languages. With the cooperation of the Department of Education of Puerto Rico, the University of Puerto Rico, the Ministry of Education of Mexico and the University of Texas, the test construction project was begun. Copies of the test were completed in 1942.

The tests included general ability at the primary, intermediate and advanced levels; reading (vocabulary and comprehension) at the primary, intermediate and advanced levels; language usage (active vocabulary and expression); vocabulary and interpretation of reading material in the natural sciences; and vocabulary and interpretation of reading material in the social studies.

The test administration in Mexico and Texas began in 1943,

and in the spring of that year the tests were administered to nearly 20,000 pupils in the schools of Puerto Rico. The final test, revised and standardized, will be ready for use before the end of this year. Copies may be secured from the Educational Testing Service, Rosedale Road, Princeton, New Jersey, or from the American Council on Education, 744 Jackson Place, N.W., Washington, D.C. These tests should prove useful in New York.

Irrespective of what aid may be found in these tests mentioned above, I believe that the New York public school authorities should as soon as possible put into effect Recommendation No. 5, page 103, of the Report of the Association of Assistant Superintendents, and, that personnel be prepared in the construction and administration of tests to handle this situation; that other personnel be equipped with the linguistic preparation necessary to handle the problem and that the same personnel be attached to the Division of Test and Measurement of the Bureau of Reference, Research and Statistics of the Public Schools of New York. It is obvious that people doing this work should know Spanish well. It may be that the University of Puerto Rico would be willing to lend the services of a member of the staff of the Department of Educational Psychology to aid in the initiation of such a program. Dr. H. T. Manuel of the University of Texas has had a great deal of experience with children of Spanish speech and may be available for consultation.

4. Teacher Training Program

Inasmuch as the language problem is recognized by all to be the pivot point around which revolve many of the educational difficulties of the Puerto Ricans in New York, it would seem advisable to implement the recommendation of the Report of the Association of Assistant Superintendents to the effect that "courses for teachers in methodology and instructional materials for teaching non-English speaking pupils should be organized and staffed by experts." Much has been done in recent years in the preparation of teachers for the teaching of English as a modern foreign language. Several universities have recognized the need of preparing teachers to meet the language needs of non-English speaking children. The outstanding institution in this new field of language teaching has been the English Language Institute at the University of Michigan. Teachers College, Columbia University, has also established a program. New York University is planning to establish courses of this nature. It may seem advisable for the Board of Education, in accordance with the recommendation of the report already quoted, to establish a teacher-training program in the teaching of English as a foreign language, select those teachers who have been successful with Puerto Rican children and equip them with the knowledge and techniques necessary to meet the needs of the non-English speaking pupils.

5. The School and the Home.

In my visit to the public schools I took special interest in inquiring about the relationship between the school and the home and what is being done to bring the two together. All of the schools have Parent Teachers Associations. In some of them, such as P.S. 124, Bronx, the PTA is a strong organization. A Puerto Rican mother happens to be President. She has been instrumental in securing the cooperation of Puerto Rican parents. I was informed in other schools that Puerto Rican parents were members of the Board of Directors of their Parent Teachers Associations, but in many schools I found the PTA rather weak, and as a general rule the participation of Puerto Rican parents in the activities of the PTA was poor.

Housing and health conditions among the Puerto Rican population are substandard in many instances. The report cited, pages 25-27, gives a description of these conditions. Also the report "Puerto Ricans in New York City," prepared by a committee of the Welfare Council, gives (pages 30 and 33) a fine description of housing and sanitation facilities available to Puerto Ricans. Most of the parents living in these homes work and it is difficult for them to attend meetings. Mothers are overburdened with housework and large families, and this, plus the fact that the mothers as a general rule do not speak English and cannot understand what is going on, keeps them from attending the PTA meetings. It is not difficult to understand why Puerto Rican parents are not more active in the PTA in view of the above.

Some principals and teachers spoke about irregularity in school attendance on the part of Puerto Rican children. Sometimes they attend only half a day and sometimes they are absent all day. In some schools the problem is more serious than in others. The children play hooky and there is a need for someone to act as a connecting link between the home and the school. This person is generally a man and is called "Attendance Officer." Some devote all their time to this job, while others have other duties. The attendance officers whom I met are very fine men and some of them genuinely interested in the children. Yet the attendance officer is looked upon by the children more as a policeman, as the one that goes after the delinquent child, as the one who goes for the child after he has done something wrong. He is, therefore, someone to be afraid of, to be avoided, to run away from. Recommendation 13, page 107 of the report mentioned reads as follows:

> A community relations teacher should be assigned to districts where there are large concentrations of Puerto Ricans.
> School-community coordinators should be attached to the Assistant Superintendent's offices to facilitate adjustments and to further efforts for the establishment of more favorable school and community relations. These workers should be trained and supervised by the Bureau of Community Education. Their assignments should be made on the basis of local need in areas which have large numbers of Puerto Rican residents. The ability to speak Spanish should be one of the prerequisites in the selection of personnel for such assignments.

There is very little that I can add to this recommendation. The time
is ripe to have these community coordinators in sections where the
Puerto Rican population is concentrated, especially when the home
falls so far short of cooperating with the school. The present system does not prevent the child from becoming delinquent. The community coordinator or community relations teacher would prevent delinquency. The community coordinator would be an agent of adult
education among the parents. Benjamin Franklin High School already
has employed a fine young lady of Puerto Rican extraction with excellent command of both languages, well educated in one of the city
colleges. The services of this young lady are invaluable to Dr.
Covello, the Principal. He should have not only one community
coordinator but as many as the needs of the school demand. A
school such as P.S. 57, East Harlem, with a Puerto Rican enrollment of about 90%, could well use several community workers or
community coordinators. I am sure the Puerto Rican parents would
cooperate better if such a coordinator, with a knowledge of Spanish,
were to work among them. The Social Welfare section of this office
might well be of help in the selection, training and orientation of
community coordinators.

6. Vocational Guidance

Most of the Puerto Rican children attending public schools in New
York will leave school as soon as it is legally possible and will go
to work. The schools must have a vocational guidance program to
orient children in useful and gainful occupations upon leaving school.
The Board of Education also has a cooperative education program.
Boys and girls under eighteen years who visit our office seem to be
unaware of the existence of a guidance program. I have generally
referred the cases that have come to this office to the school principals. I would like to learn more about the vocational guidance
program of the public schools of New York City, the facilities available and the number of Puerto Rican children who take advantage of
these facilities. I have not had time to look into this part of the
school system. The majority of the boys and girls of Puerto Rican
extraction will either become unskilled, semi-skilled or skilled laborers. The school should be able to guide them into vocational
training in accordance with their abilities. I think that the section
of Education in this office should be equipped to cooperate with the
public schools in furnishing guidance to boys and girls who are preparing to learn a trade or profession.

Puerto Rico's Part

What should Puerto Rico do? As soon as a person from Puerto
Rico transfers to New York City and establishes his residence here,
he thereby becomes a citizen of New York and an heir to all the
privileges and responsibilities to be found here, and is no longer a
problem for Puerto Rico. Nevertheless, due to the unusual circumstances of population, migration, language, economic status and

problems of adjustment, Puerto Rico cannot lose interest in her citizens on the mainland who may be in need. To a certain extent Puerto Rico does have a responsibility, if only because of her population problem. She should cooperate with the States in the adjustment of her citizens who transfer to the continent. What should she do?

1. Children of School Age. - New York City has a compulsory school law whereby every child under eighteen years of age must attend school full time until he is sixteen years old, and part time under special arrangements during the last two years of compulsory school attendance. Therefore, the Department of Education of Puerto Rico could help the New York school authorities by facilitating school records and any check that the Department may have on the children's abilities, such as records of intelligence tests or any other pertinent information. It would help a great deal if children transferring to New York schools were informed about New York and the educational opportunities in the city. This should not be difficult for the Department, and the New York school authorities would no doubt be willing to furnish information for dissemination among those transferring to New York.

2. Materials of Instruction. Puerto Rico is beginning a new epoch in her educational history. For fifty years the Federal Government has actually set the pattern which Puerto Rico was to follow in her educational development. This year Puerto Rico will elect her own Governor who in turn will appoint a Commissioner of Education. In other words, Puerto Rico after fifty years since the American occupation, is going to take over the school system and run it her own way. She will be free to develop an educational philosophy and to implement it as she thinks best. An educational survey will soon be made of the school system. No doubt these events will be followed by much activity in the field of education. Puerto Rico has done little in the development of materials of instruction suitable to her peculiar problem in dealing with two languages and two civilizations. Great activity is already in progress. The results will no doubt encourage the development of materials of instruction and methodology. New York City is also working intelligently in the development of materials of instruction. There should be an exchange of materials and experience which will aid mutually in the solution of many problems.

3. Exchange of Personnel. This summer several teachers from New York City are visiting Puerto Rico and observing the schools at work. Puerto Rican educators have visited the New York schools and are interested in the education of their fellow citizens here. I believe the time has come to go further and think of exchanging personnel for a semester or a year. The people working on English at the Department of Education should spend a season in New York finding out what the schools here are doing, and some educators from New York interested in the problems of Puerto Rican children could spend half a year or a year observing what Puerto Rico is doing. This exchange of personnel should prove beneficial

to the two parties concerned. Members of the University of Puerto Rico staff may aid in this program.

4. The Teaching of English. Puerto Rico should intensify the teaching of English so that the transfer of children to the main- land and their adjustment here may be made easier. The Puerto Rican child should practice hearing and speaking English. He knows a great deal of English, but his ear does not catch on and his tongue is tied. Emphasis should be given to pronunciation.

5. Preparation for Migration. The Department of Education should facilitate as far as possible the preparation of workers, through courses in the public schools and vocational schools, either during the regular sessions or in evening classes and summer schools. The new School of Industrial Arts of the University can do much in this regard. There is a great demand for household services in this country. Candidates should be well selected and should be instructed in household work techniques of the mainland. There is a great de- mand on the continent for skilled laborers, who receive excellent wages. Intensive courses in English should be offered to those pre- paring to work in the states, with special emphasis on what we might call vocational English, i. e. , the English mostly used in connection with the trade or duties the migrants will perform upon their trans- fer to the mainland. I think the time has come for the Office of Puerto Rico in New York, in cooperation with industry, to take upon itself the responsibility of establishing adult education programs among Puerto Rican workers in the states and follow up work begun in Puerto Rico.

6. Control of Migration. As far as possible something should be done in Puerto Rico to discourage migration of people who do not have occupations to go into upon their arrival in this country, or of children whose parents live in Puerto Rico and who have no home in New York. Too many people are coming, hoping that they may find work and thereby better themselves economically, and in the case of the children, educationally. It is laudable that they take the chance, but the experience of the past teaches us that as far as possible, people should not come to the continent until they have secured employment here.

In closing I would like to express through you my deep ap- preciation to Superintendent Jansen, assistant superintendents, prin- cipals and teachers, for their courtesies and many acts of kindness during my visits to schools. They are all doing an excellent job worthy of Puerto Rico's gratitude.

PUERTO RICAN PUPILS IN AMERICAN SCHOOLS

There are numerous important nuclei of Puerto Ricans outside the familiar "barrio" (community) in East Harlem: Lower Bronx, north-western Manhattan, "south" Brooklyn, etc.

***

In the 75 schools under discussion (i. e. with the heaviest percentages of Puerto Rican pupils), there are over 25,000 pupils listed as Puerto Rican. There are, of course, thousands more in schools not included in this study.

The city has 8 assistant superintendents whose districts are included in this study; in the city over 26% of the entire school population is Puerto Rican. One superintendent's group of districts has over 49% Puerto Rican pupils; another has over 42%.

***

In the schools whose total school population is over 26% Puerto Rican, only 5% of the teachers claim any skill in use of Spanish. "In districts having 49% and 42% Puerto Ricans, we find that only 7. 6% and 6. 1 respectively of the teaching body can communicate with the pupils or their parents in a common language. "

"The need for teachers who can speak Spanish is urgent. If ... increased proportionately to the Puerto Rican school population, we should need approximately 1000 real Spanish-speaking teachers. ... "

Reprinted by permission from "Report of the Sub-Committee on Education, Recreation and Parks. " (New York, 1951), pp. 12-20. Mimeograph. Leonard Covello, Chairman.

"Almost one-third of schools reporting have no Spanish-speaking teachers."

"We disagree with the viewpoint that the teacher's use of Spanish in the classroom serves as a crutch. If we accept as our basic goal the child's adjustment to his new environment, it is important that he communicate ... in Spanish until he is able to express himself somewhat adequately in English." (It may be added that this is particularly true in the case of adolescents, recently arrived from Puerto Rico, who have attained some measure of mental and emotional maturity.)

***

"The Puerto Rican parent must be made to feel that his child is being accepted with the same status as that of the Continental child..., that his home life is not being held up to criticism."

"A special effort should be made to involve parents in the school program."

"All communications for parents should contain a Spanish translation." (It may be of interest to know that schools are beginning to use report cards in duplicate with translations in Spanish.)

***

"Active participation in the recreational life of the community will accelerate the Puerto Rican's acculturation.... It will give him a sense of belonging."

"Contact with other community groups in experiences which help relieve tensions will undoubtedly stimulate the desire to learn English."

"Schools should be kept open a maximum number of hours summer and winter for recreational and vocational purposes."

***

"The Elementary Division has appointed a group of 10 Puerto Rican (bi-lingual) teachers (Substitute Auxiliary Teachers) to schools having the largest concentration of Puerto Ricans ... to assist in the orientation of these children (and to) serve as liaison between the school and the community."

"If the purposes for which "C" classes were originally introduced ... are to be fulfilled, the register should not exceed 15." "C" classes are special classes required for non-English speaking pupils and new arrivals from Puerto Rico.

***

"The number of "C" classes is disproportionately small....
No school area has even half as many as it needs."

***

"There is need for a Curriculum Bulletin on each level ...
which will collate materials in existence." "The dearth of suitable,
adequate teaching and learning materials is a major problem."

***

"The kindergartens are crowded and there is an additional
40% waiting for admission."

***

"The attendance problems which are causing great concern
... will be appreciably lessened if an adequate mental hygiene policy
were pursued."

***

"Sixty of 75 schools ... find totally inadequate medical and
health resources, including those services offered by health agencies...." "The conditions under which they live (on the island and)
in New York City ... have made the Puerto Ricans more vulnerable
to disease."

***

Recommendations

This survey, encompassing all schools in the city with Puerto Rican
children and including all areas of the total school and community
program, has served to highlight the magnitude of the task which
confronts educational and social agencies in New York City.

On the basis of the responses to the survey questions, the
following recommendations are indicated.

I. Registration

A. The first contact between the school and the Puerto Rican parent should be made a pleasant experience. The Puerto Rican
parent must be made to feel that his child is being accepted with the
same status as that of the Continental child. He must be made to
feel that his home life is not being held up to criticism and to
scrutiny.

B. The attitude of principal, clerks and other school personnel acting as receptionists will set the tone for future rapport.

C.   There is no doubt that a Spanish-speaking person on the staff will facilitate this initial contact with the schools.   Many questions that arise in the mind of the parents concerning the school program, routines and special services offered by the school as well as many questions that arise in the minds of the school personnel concerning important aspects of the child's previous schooling and background, will be resolved through the medium of the foreign language.

D.   Short welcome booklets that explain the school program pictorially have been used effectively and should be made a universal practice.

E.   All pre-registration and registration forms should contain a Spanish translation.   These translations, however, do not obviate the necessity for a Spanish-speaking person since many parents cannot read or write.

II.   Placement

The emotional security and need for belonging that we recognize as fundamental for optimum school adjustment, are ensured to a great extent with the proper grade placement of the Puerto Rican child. Although more time-consuming, all placement done on an individual basis will effect more satisfactory adjustment.   The following factors should be taken into consideration in order of importance:

1.   The age of the child
2.   Social maturity
3.   Physical appearance (a child who is very small due to nutritional deficiency may be placed in a lower grade, where his classmates would most nearly approximate his stature)
4.   Previous schooling

When the grade has been determined on the basis of the four points listed above, the class chosen should be one where there are other Spanish-speaking children.   Criteria for selection of the teacher may include a knowledge of Spanish and an understanding attitude.

The above considerations obtain in cases of placement below the third year and where there are no "C" classes.

The child should remain with this group until he shows ability to adjust to a regular class.

III.   Organization

In schools where there are large numbers of Puerto Rican children, maximum registers in all regular classes in the school should not exceed 25.   For even after the initial period of orientation, there is still a great need for individualized instruction and guidance, e.g.

in the development of communication skills so that the child may participate more fully in class and school activities; in speech improvement and in intonation patterns.

If the purposes for which "C" classes were originally introduced into the school are to be fulfilled, the register should not exceed 15.

IV. Teachers

A. Use of Spanish-speaking teachers

We disagree with the viewpoint that the teacher's use of Spanish in the classroom serves as a crutch, retarding the child's English language development. If we accept as our basic goal the child's adjustment to his new environment, it is important that he communicate with others in Spanish until he is able to express himself somewhat adequately in English.

The objection that the child will not feel the need of learning English if the teacher understands his Spanish, is not a valid one; the child's desire and interest in learning the second language will be stimulated by participation in meaningful classroom experiences and activities.

The Spanish-speaking teacher may be utilized in all phases of the school program:

1. For registration
2. For translation of forms and letters
3. As interpreter for parents and children
4. As teacher of "C" or Remedial Language classes
5. As liaison with the community
6. As school guidance counselor
7. As speaker at parents meetings
8. As instructor of Spanish In-Service Courses
9. To advise parents and children in the areas of health, safety, nutrition, sanitation and community resources.
10. To assist school, district and city personnel, who come to render special services (Bureau of Child Guidance, Attendance Coordinators, Psychologists, etc.)

It is suggested that special examinations be given for the purpose of licensing people with a knowledge of Spanish, to serve both in the classroom and in the capacity stated above.

B. The Orientation of Teachers

Teachers should be assisted in meeting the challenge of this latest migration. The following minimum suggestions are offered:

1. The principal should arrange for faculty conferences

dealing with the background of the Puerto Rican and with problems of Puerto Rican adjustment here. Resource people should be invited to contribute the benefit of their experience.

2. Workshops should be set up in each school to examine existing materials and to develop additional units of work.

3. A Spanish-speaking teacher in the school or in a neighboring school should give instruction in Conversational Spanish.

4. There should be a center which would serve as a clearing house for ideas, units, materials of instruction that have been found useful. This project would serve as a means of articulation between the different levels of the system.

5. There must be time set aside for periodic conferences between the Remedial Language (O. T. P.) and the regular teacher. Learnings, knowledges, skills and attitudes as they are gained in one class may be reinforced in the other by a mutual exchange of ideas and materials.

6. Teachers who are known to have evolved special procedures and techniques with Puerto Rican children, should be encouraged to give demonstration lessons for other teachers.

7. Provision should be made for inter- and intra-visitation.

8. Bulletins dealing with the bilingual children from other sections of the country should be studied and evaluated for adaptation to the New York City situation.

V.   Textbooks and Supplies

Summaries of the answers to this question show such wide variations in the amount of extra money made available to the schools for the Puerto Rican program as well as in what the schools actually required that a special study is evidently needed in this area.

VI.   Teaching and Learning Materials

The dearth of suitable, adequate teaching and learning materials is a major problem confronting supervisors and teachers.

There is a need for a Curriculum Bulletin for elementary, junior and senior high schools.

1. This Bulletin should represent the cooperative effort of teachers of Puerto Rican children, of Curriculum Research Assistants, of personnel from special divisions at the Board of Education and Community Agencies.

2. This Bulletin should suggest additional experiences, activities, procedures and practices for the Puerto Rican children.

3. The Bulletin should be based on the principles of child growth and development which are the foundations of the current school program in New York City.

4. The Bulletin should emphasize the experiences, activities and concepts which the Puerto Rican child will find useful in his daily life, in the home, school and community.

5. The Bulletin should evaluate carefully such methods as the Ogden Method, or the Fries Method, adapting these to the situation of Puerto Ricans in New York City. These methods might assist teachers to supplement and vary certain aspects of the teaching situation.

6. The Bulletin should make suggestions for all teachers of Puerto Rican children. The regular teacher with some Puerto Rican children has as much need for this type of material as the "C" or Remedial Language teacher.

There is need for materials in all areas geared to the social maturity level of the children but with a vocabulary level simple enough for their limited knowledge of English. Material may be prepared locally.

Audio-visual materials which develop and fix concepts and which vitalize instruction should be part of the regular school equipment. Existing audio-visual materials should be examined in light of these children's needs.

Strip films and slides which allow for informal, spontaneous discussion during their showing are to be preferred to more elaborate movies.

A special differential should be allowed not only for texts, but also for craft and art supplies, for manipulatory activities and art experiences which contribute to the emotional security of the Puerto Rican child. These offer to the Puerto Rican child the opportunity: 1. to express himself in media other than language and 2. to utilize his native abilities. He will thus acquire status in the eyes of his classmates.

VIII. Methods of Instruction

All formal learning should be deferred until the child feels secure. The development of learning should follow the pattern suggested below:

1. Utilization of the child's background.
2. Provision for experiences which familiarize him with the

school and community and which stimulate the desire to learn English.

3. Utilization of the language arts program of the natural sequences of communication arts: activities--oral communication--reading--writing.

The approach to formal reading should be through experiential charts.

All means of expression, music, art, puppetry, dramatic play should be an integral part of the school day.

IX. Tests and Measurements

Tests for these children should be developed and standardized according to our knowledge of their background in Puerto Rico and the emerging cultural pattern in the new environment.

The tests, to be conducted by trained Spanish-speaking personnel, should be administered in small groups and in an informal atmosphere so that the maximum potentialities of the child can more accurately be gauged.

Results of group standardized tests should not be the decisive factor in grade placement. Wherever questions arise, individual non-language tests should be given.

X. Health

An intensified health program for children and adults is vitally important. Instruction in the areas of sanitation, nutrition and safety should be emphasized through actual experiences in and out of the classroom. Discussions and actual demonstrations on these and similar topics should be held for parents. Spanish translations of available health materials should be made. Home visits by social and welfare personnel, although very costly in time and money, are desirable. Parents should be made aware of existing public or private health services.

It would be advisable to carry on a "readiness" program which would help the child to accept the foods served in the school lunch program. One effective means of doing this would be to introduce new foods together with the familiar foods.

XI. Mental Health or Child Guidance

Every school should have a well-planned guidance program with fixed responsibility, resting upon a person assigned for that specific purpose. This person should speak Spanish. The entire staff, however, should be made aware of the problems facing the children and of the necessity of adapting the curriculum to meet the special needs of these children.

The attendance problems which are causing great concern at the present time will be appreciably lessened if an adequate mental hygiene policy were pursued.

XIII. Recreational Facilities

All city agencies should be involved in planning for adequate recreational facilities.

Many Puerto Rican mothers work because it is easier for the woman to find work than the man. Provision for all-day care of children at all age levels should be made to insure the health and safety of the children and to eliminate any incipient juvenile delinquency.

Summer camp facilities should be extended.

In all cases, the personnel should be especially trained to work effectively with these children.

Schools, strategically located and equipped for adult afternoon and evening programs, should be kept open a maximum number of hours summer and winter for recreational and vocational purposes.

XIV. Community Relations

A.   Efficient and responsible operation of the program requires fixed responsibility. Trained personnel should be licensed to assume full charge of community centers.

B-1.   Optimum functioning requires a procedure where tested experiences could be reported to a central agency, and guidance funneled out from central headquarters to all workers in the field. This can be the case only if one agency, such as the Board of Education, assumes responsibility for the appointment of all the Puerto Rican field or staff workers recommended above.

B-2.   Uniform qualifications for service should be established in terms of the needs of such a position rather than depending on the haphazard selection now evident.

B-3.   Part-time or on-the-run responsibility cannot cope with a problem of the magnitude of the Puerto Rican orientation and assistance program. There is need for a full-time staff worker distributing his time among teaching Puerto Rican students, serving as a counsellor to this group, and working with parents and community agencies for the welfare of these people.

C.   While the indicated attempt to convey the aspects of the Puerto Rican program to parents and community is commendable, there is no evidence of a procedure to evaluate most effective techniques developed for such purposes. Here, too, a central overall responsibility in the Board of Education might be able to set up central evaluation procedures.

XV.   Adults

A special effort should be made to involve parents in the school program so that they will understand the aims and the functions of the schools. One effective means of obtaining parent cooperation is to assist them.

Group meetings of parents should be so arranged that the Puerto Rican parents are made to feel an integral part of the proceedings. Topics for discussion at these meetings should be carefully selected on the basis of an awareness of their needs--needs as we may see them and as they express them. There is no doubt that other participating groups will profit from discussions of nutrition, health, employment opportunities and community resources.

All communications for parents should contain a Spanish translation.

XVI.   Teacher Training

In addition to the recommendations of the Subcommittee, the training of teachers is one of the basic areas which should be developed and strengthened. Accordingly, the following four recommendations should receive the special attention of the educational system and the teacher-training institutions:

1.   Separate training and examination for bilingual teachers with ability to speak Spanish fluently, and with knowledge of Puerto Rican social backgrounds and special methods of teaching English to Puerto Ricans.

2.   Stimulation at all teacher-training institutions for above qualifications for use in student-teaching, with credit for practice teaching.

3.   Stimulation for all teacher-trainees looking toward teaching careers to take majors in Spanish and guidance.

4.   Intensification of In-Service credit courses for teacher-training in the above services.

THE CRISIS IN EDUCATION

Data in the previous chapter showed that mainland Puerto Ricans
have lower incomes than whites, blacks, and other Hispanic minorities in the United States. The same relationship is evident in
terms of education. The typical white American adult has graduated
from high school and has had a taste of college; the typical black
has completed 9.8 years of school; and the typical mainland Puerto
Rican has completed only 8.7 years.[1]

Recent census figures (1975) also show clear differences in
education among major Hispanic groups (Puerto Ricans, Mexican
Americans, and Cubans), with Puerto Ricans generally at the lowest
rung of the ladder. There is a sharp difference, for example, between the educational picture for Cubans and Puerto Ricans. As for
Mexican Americans, while they are less likely than Puerto Ricans
to have completed 5 years of school, they are more likely to have
graduated from high school. In the younger age brackets (25 to 29
years) Puerto Ricans have made notable progress in education, but
still lag behind other groups. (See Tables 27 and 28.)

School Enrollment and Dropout Rates

Between 1960 and 1970 the dropout rate for school-age Puerto Ricans
fell, particularly for young adults. But a severe dropout problem
persists.

During the elementary school years (age 5 to 13), the staying power of Puerto Rican children is quite comparable to the national
average: 72 percent of all youngsters age 5 to 6, and 97 percent of
those age 7 to 13, are enrolled in school.

The dropout problem becomes evident in the age 14 to 17 group.
Nationwide, 93 percent of all youngsters in this age group remain in
school, compared with 85 percent of Puerto Rican youngsters.

(Washington: United States Commission on Civil Rights, 1976,
p. 92-143).

Table 27

Percent of Persons (25 Years Old and Over)
Who Have Completed Less Than 5 Years of School

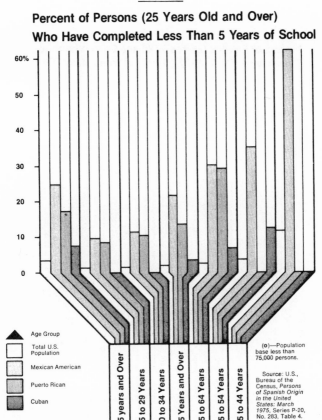

The difference grows more acute in the age 18 to 24 group. Nationwide, while 37 percent of young males remain in school, only 18 percent of the Puerto Rican males are still enrolled (the figures are comparable for women). In other words, young adult Puerto Ricans are only half as likely to be in school as their peers. (See Table 29.)

In a study conducted in Chicago, the dropout rate for Puerto Ricans in grammar and high school was 71.2 percent. The study indicated that 12.5 percent dropped out in grammar school, while 58.7 percent dropped out in high school.[2]

Students drop out of school for a variety of reasons. While some drop out because they cannot keep up academically, this is by no means the sole reason. Of the 30 percent of U.S. high school students who drop out each year, one-third are in their senior year and have already completed most of the required courses. Most

Table 28

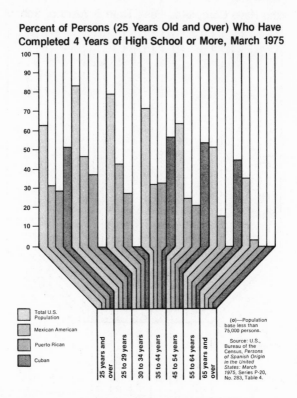

Percent of Persons (25 Years Old and Over) Who Have Completed 4 Years of High School or More, March 1975

Total U.S. Population

Mexican American

Puerto Rican

Cuban

25 years and over

25 to 29 years

30 to 34 years

35 to 44 years

45 to 54 years

55 to 64 years

65 years and over

(o)—Population base less than 75,000 persons.

Source: U.S., Bureau of the Census, *Persons of Spanish Origin in the United States: March 1975*, Series P-20, No. 283, Table 4.

dropouts are bored, find the school unresponsive to their cultural backgrounds, or feel compelled to obtain a job. [3]

By examining several aspects of the Puerto Rican student's experience in school, the multiple reasons for dropping out become clear.

Language and Culture

More than 30 percent of the 437,000 Puerto Rican students enrolled in mainland schools are born in Puerto Rico. Each year thousands of children transfer from schools in Puerto Rico to those on the mainland. (See Table 30 for student transfers between Puerto Rico and New York City.) Spanish is the mother tongue of a major segment of the Puerto Rican school-age population (and is the language used most often in the home, even for those students born on the mainland.).

Table 29

School Enrollment of the Total U.S. and Puerto Rican Populations Age 5 to 34 Years: United States—1960 and 1970 (by percent)

	Puerto Rican Residents of the U.S.							
	Total in U.S.		Total		Born in Puerto Rico		Born in U.S.	
Age	1960	1970	1960	1970	1960	1970	1960	1970
5 and 6 years old	63.8	72.4	66.4	72.4	64.7	67.5	67.0	73.7
7 to 13 years old	97.5	97.3	94.9	94.9	94.2	93.2	95.7	95.6
14 to 17 years old:								
Male	87.8	93.2	75.8	85.5	73.7	78.5	83.5	90.7
Female	87.1	92.7	72.5	83.7	69.5	75.8	84.9	90.0
18 to 24 years old:								
Male	27.8	37.5	10.9	18.4	9.5	13.3	21.4	32.6
Female	18.4	27.2	8.4	14.3	7.6	10.3	13.6	26.3
25 to 34 years old	4.6	6.3	3.3	2.5	3.1	1.9	5.5	6.8

Table 30

Transfers of Public School Students Between Puerto Rico and New York City

School Year	Came from Puerto Rico	Moved to Puerto Rico	Net Migration to New York[1]
1954-55	9,496	3,662	5,834
1955-56	11,727	3,934	7,793
1956-57	12,905	5,020	7,885
1957-58	11,505	5,557	5,948
1958-59	10,737	6,491	4,246
1959-60	10,315	7,806	2,509
1960-61	9,414	7,688	1,726
1961-62	8,777	8,428	349
1962-63	7,942	8,508	−566
1963-64	8,245	7,849	396
1964-65	8,496	8,179	317
1965-66	9,232	7,986	1,246
1966-67	11,191	8,193	2,998
1967-68	13,706	8,696	5,010
1968-69	14,840	10,095	4,745
1969-70	12,586	12,254	332
1970-71	11,466	12,752	−1,286
1971-72	8,482	14,079	−5,597
1972-73	8,445	13,434	−4,989
1973-74	9,892	10,771	−879
10-year totals,			
1954-1963	101,063	64,943	36,120
1964-73	108,336	106,439	1,897
5-year totals,			
1969-1973	50,871	63,290	−12,419

[1] A minus sign (−) denotes net return migration from New York City to Puerto Rico.

In New York City in 1970, of 362,000 Puerto Ricans under age 18, nearly one-fourth (80,370) had been born in Puerto Rico. About one-fourth (nearly 80,000) of the Puerto Rican and other Hispanic students in New York City's public schools speak poor or hesitant English.[4] Birthplace is, obviously, a major determinant of ability to speak English.

It is also clear that birthplace, language ability, and dropping out are closely intertwined. Great disparities exist in the dropout rates of island-born and U.S.-born Puerto Rican youngsters. Those born on the mainland tend to enroll earlier in school and tend to drop out less frequently.

About 47 percent of all mainland Puerto Ricans age 3 to 34 are enrolled in school. But this overall average is misleading: 67 percent of the mainland-born Puerto Ricans in that age group are enrolled, compared with only 28 percent of those born in Puerto Rico. The disparity is very pronounced in the age 18 to 24 group. Among males of this age group, for example, 33 percent of the U.S.-born were still in school, compared with only 13 percent of the island-born. Among males age 16 to 21, about 12,000 of the U.S.-born are not enrolled in school, compared with 32,000 island-born youngsters. (See Table 31.)

These figures indicate that the dropout rate is more severe among Puerto Rican youngsters born on the island than among those

Table 31

School Enrollment of Mainland Puerto Ricans, by Birthplace, 1970

	Mainland Puerto Ricans	Born in Puerto Rico	Born in U.S. Mainland
Total enrolled, age 3-34	437,863	134,501	303,362
Nursery School	5,439	928	4,511
Kindergarten	29,112	5,747	23,365
Elementary (Grades 1-8)	294,785	81,006	213,779
High School (Grades 9-12)	90,822	37,279	53,543
College	17,705	9,541	8,164
Percent enrolled, age 3-34	46.8	27.7	67.4
3 and 4 yrs. old	10.6	11.4	10.4
5 and 6 yrs. old	72.4	67.5	73.7
7 to 13 yrs. old	94.9	93.2	95.6
14 to 17 yrs. old:			
Male	85.5	78.5	90.7
Female	83.7	75.8	90.0
18 to 24 yrs. old:			
Male	18.4	13.3	32.6
Female	14.3	10.3	26.3
25 to 34 yrs. old	2.5	1.9	6.8
Male 16 to 21 yrs. old	81,056	49,387	31,669

youngsters of Puerto Rican parentage born on the mainland. Island-born youngsters are more likely to have problems communicating in English, more likely to be unemployed or underemployed, and more likely to be doomed to a life of poverty.

While the education problems of mainland Puerto Ricans are certainly not limited to the island-born, this group is more adversely affected by inadequate schooling. Language is often the key factor that makes them different from other Puerto Rican students, many of whom may sit in the same classroom, or may even be siblings. The fact that these language-handicapped students achieve less and drop out more is compelling evidence that the school's response to the problem has been inadequate.

One Puerto Rican parent expressed his dismay at the lack of special instruction for his children:

> ... They are practically wasting their time because they are not learning anything. First of all, they don't understand the language. What good does it do to sit there in front of the teacher and just look at her face? It is wasting their time. They don't learn anything because they don't understand what she is saying. [5]

Achievement Levels

In a sample taken by the New York City Board of Education, schools with heavy Puerto Rican enrollment had much lower reading averages than predominantly black or white schools. At every level sampled, Puerto Rican students were behind the other two groups in reading. [6]

In 1972 two-thirds of the elementary schools in New York City that contained 85 percent or more students reading below grade level had a student population which was more than 50 percent Puerto Rican. [7]

In Chicago, 1970-71 test scores in reading and mathematics indicated a much lower achievement rate for Puerto Rican students than the citywide median. The lag increased with each succeeding grade. [8]

Testing

The use of standardized achievement tests contributes to the failure of public schools to teach Puerto Rican students. IQ and achievement test scores often are used as guides in assigning students to ability groups and to classes for the educable mentally retarded (EMR).

Since most tests are given in English, many children are programmed for failure. In Philadelphia, a school official acknowledged that psychological tests are often given only in English and that they form the basis for assessing the mental and emotional states of Puerto Rican students. [9]

> Commenting on this point, a Philadelphia psychologist said:

> > In my clinic, the average underestimation of IQ for a Puerto Rican kid is 20 points. We go through this again and again. When we test in Spanish, there's a 20 point leap immediately--20 points higher than when he's tested in English. [10]

Some school systems have attempted to overcome the language gap by translating standard IQ tests into Spanish, but these tests are often designed for Mexican American children. (Although Spanish is common to both Mexico and Puerto Rico, there are many colloquialisms peculiar to each area.) A few school systems have experimented with tests developed in Puerto Rico, but testing continues to be a major linguistic and cultural barrier for many Puerto Rican students.

Student Assignment Practices

School systems frequently place underachieving students in low-ability groups, or in classes for the educable mentally retarded, or retain them in grade. Recent arrivals from Puerto Rico are often assigned to lower grades. The rationale for such practices is that students will benefit from special instruction in low-level classes, but the correlation between such placement and improved academic performance is dubious. In fact, the lower level of curriculum and the absence of stimulation from higher-achieving students may be negative factors that further retard the student. [11] If anything, the stigma attached to being labeled a "slow learner" can result in a loss of self-esteem and reinforce the student's sense of failure. [12] Rather than progress out of EMR classes or low ability groups, students tend to remain there, be assigned vocational (rather than college-bound) curricula, or drop out altogether. [13]

> A former president of the New York City Board of Education has testified:

> > Historically, in New York City we have had two school systems, one school system for those youngsters who are expected to achieve, and one for the youngsters who were not expected to achieve, and don't achieve. And most of the minority group youngsters are in that second school system, and the system is pretty much set up to see to it that they don't succeed. And I think that's why they drop out of schools. [14]

The Office for Civil Rights (OCR) of the U.S. Department of Health, Education, and Welfare (HEW) has investigated ability-grouping practices in several school districts that have large Puerto Rican student populations. In East Chicago, Indiana, for example, these practices resulted in racially identifiable "tracks": students appeared to be assigned arbitrarily to a group with no apparent pedagogical justification. The school district was required by HEW to develop new assignment policies.[15] The Philadelphia school system has reported that its practice of using achievement tests as the basis for placing students in "tracking systems" has resulted in a disproportionate number of black and Puerto Rican students in low ability groups.[16]

Placement in educable mentally retarded classes is also largely determined by a child's score on a standardized IQ test given in English or upon subjective teacher evaluation. In New York City, almost 30 percent of the students in special classes for children with retarded mental development have Hispanic backgrounds. It has been suggested that faulty analysis of test results (by psychologists who do not speak the same language as the children) is responsible.[17]

The Office for Civil Rights had documented that the school district in Perth Amboy, New Jersey, assigned language-minority students to EMR classes on the basis of criteria that essentially measured English language skills, even though it appeared that the majority of the Hispanic students had difficulty with the English language. OCR also found that some regular classroom teachers were more inclined to refer Puerto Rican children to the department of special services for EMR placement than Anglo children "because they do not know how to deal with the behavioral problems of these children."[18]

The New York State Commissioner of Education has reported that non-English-speaking children are sometimes placed in classes for slow learners or EMR classes without sufficient justification. Some students were judged to be mentally retarded because they were quiet in class.[19]

These types of practices result in a high number of "over-age" Puerto Rican students in the schools. In New England, it has been reported that 25 percent of the Hispanic children have been held back at least three grades in school and that 50 percent have been held back at least two grades. Only 12 percent were found to be in the correct grade for their age group.[20] A field survey in Boston found that nearly 75 percent of the Hispanic high school students were in classes behind students of their own age.[21]

The problem is particularly acute among transfer students from Puerto Rico. A witness at the Massachusetts Advisory Committee's open meeting testified:

> They came from Puerto Rico, they're in the 10th, 11th, or senior year of high school, and they're 17, 18, 19 years old.... They came to Boston and they placed them

in the 6th and 7th grades. You're wondering why they
dropped out. A person who does not feel his identity is
lost right there.... Here's a kid trying to learn and he
automatically gets an inferiority complex and quits.[22]

Programs for Language-Minority Children

During the 1960s two types of approaches emerged to overcome the
linguistic barriers of language-minority children.[23] One approach,
English as a Second Language (ESL), teaches students to communicate in English as quickly as possible. The programs provide instruction and practice in listening, speaking, reading, and writing
English. Students are taken from their regular classrooms for 30
to 40 minutes per day for this special help, but otherwise remain
in their regular classes for content matter instruction.

By themselves, ESL programs are very limited since they
use only English to teach literacy and communication rather than
the student's native language to transmit concepts and skills (which
might facilitate the learning of English). ESL students inevitably
fall behind in the regular classroom, where content courses are
being taught.[24]

The second approach, slowly growing in acceptance, is bilingual-bicultural education. A program of bilingual education is:

(4)(A) ... a program of instruction, designed for children
of limited English-speaking ability in elementary or secondary schools, in which, with respect to the years of
study to which such program is applicable--

(i)there is instruction given in, and study of, English and,
to the extent necessary to allow a child to progress through
the educational system, the native language of the children
of limited English-speaking ability, and such instruction is
given with appreciation for the cultural heritage of such
children, and with respect to elementary school instruction,
such instruction shall, to the extent necessary, be in all
courses or subjects of study which will allow a child to
progress effectively through the educational system....[25]

This attempt at a total approach includes the teaching of English as a second language, development of literacy in the mother
tongue, and the uninterrupted learning of subject areas. It is based
on the principle that learning should continue in the mother tongue
rather than be postponed until a new language has been acquired.
Teaching a child to read first in the language that he or she speaks
makes it easier to read and write in a second language, since the
basic skills are transferable from one language to another. The
inclusion of curriculum materials on the student's culture and background experience also heightens interest in the subject matter.[26]

Hernan LaFontaine, a Puerto Rican educator and the executive administrator of the Office of Bilingual Education for the New York City Board of Education, has noted:

> Our definition of cultural pluralism must include the concept that our language and our culture will be given equal status to that of the majority population. It is not enough simply to say that we should be given the opportunity to share in the positive benefits of modern American life. Instead, we must insist that this sharing will not be accomplished at the sacrifice of all those traits which make us what we are as Puerto Ricans.[27]

Personnel

School personnel have profound influence over the success or failure of students. Not only do they make decisions to promote or retain students in school programs, but also their attitudes and expectations often are reflected in student performance.[28] When they perceive low expectations on the part of teachers, for example, students tend to do less well on tests.[29]

In its investigation into Mexican American education, the Commission found that Anglo teachers tended to favor Anglo children over Mexican Americans in their praise, encouragement, attention, and approval. Predictably, it was also found that Mexican American students participated in class less than Anglo students.[30] No similar study of Puerto Rican students has been carried out, but it is reasonable to assume that the results would be the same.

The impact that teachers and administrators have on the learning environment for students underscores the need for school personnel who reflect the background of students and thus are more likely to relate positively to them. As the Educational Policies Commission noted:

> Despite their better judgment, people of another background often feel that disadvantaged children are by nature perverse, vulgar, or lazy. Children sense quickly the attitudes of school people toward them, and they retaliate against condescension or intolerance with hostility, absenteeism, and failure.[31]

The Office for Civil Rights recognized the influence of school personnel on equal educational opportunities in its memorandum of January 1971, "Nondiscrimination in Elementary and Secondary School Staff Practices." School superintendents were informed that discrimination in hiring, promotion, demotion, dismissal, or other treatment of faculty or staff serving students had a direct adverse effect on equal educational services for students and was therefore prohibited by Title VI of the Civil Rights Act of 1964. Since that year, OCR has required school districts to submit affirmative action plans in cases where minority faculty is underrepresented.

Despite the importance of having Puerto Rican teachers and administrators in districts with large numbers of Puerto Rican students, none of the districts surveyed by the Commission had an adequate representation.[32] Few school systems gather data on the number of Puerto Rican students and teachers, nor is such data now required by the Federal Government. The data that are collected usually refer to "Spanish surnamed" students or teachers, which includes other Hispanic Americans. Table 32 reflects the percentage of students and teachers of Spanish origin in several cities with large concentrations of Puerto Ricans.

New York City has the single largest concentration of Puerto Rican students in its public schools. In fiscal year 1974, nearly 300,000 Hispanic children were enrolled in the public schools, including 256,000 Puerto Rican students. Hispanics accounted for 27.0 percent of total school enrollment (23.1 percent Puerto Rican and 3.9 percent other Hispanic). (See Table 33.) Despite the fact that more than one-fourth of the student body was Hispanic, only 2.5 percent of the total number of school teachers were of Spanish origin. Only 1,391 of the 56,168 teachers in New York City had Spanish surnames. This figure is considerably larger than the 0.8 percent share 5 years previous, but the disparity between the percentage of teachers and students remained enormous (see Table 34).[33]

One study has estimated that at least 13,700 more teachers of Spanish origin would need to be hired to approach equitable representation in the New York City public schools. This would be nearly 10 times the number in 1973.[34]

The situation is no better in other major cities where Puerto Ricans live. In Chicago (1972), there were 27,946 Puerto Rican

Table 32

Spanish-Surnamed Students and Teachers in Selected Cities: 1972

City	% Spanish-Surnamed Students	% Spanish-Surnamed Teachers
New York	26.6	2.2
Philadelphia	3.4	0.0
Bridgeport	21.2	1.9
Hartford	21.5	3.7
New Haven	9.8	1.6
Boston	5.3	0.7
Springfield	7.7	1.3
Camden	16.8	1.8
Elizabeth	19.9	3.9
Hoboken	56.8	3.3
Passaic	31.5	1.4
Paterson	22.1	2.1
Perth Amboy	49.2	4.6
Union City	64.6	7.1
Rochester	5.6	1.4
Chicago	11.1	1.2

Table 33

Puerto Ricans and Other Spanish-Surnamed-Students in New York City Public Schools: 1973-74

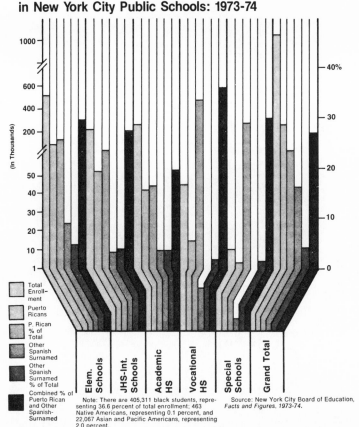

Note: There are 405,311 black students, representing 36.6 percent of total enrollment; 463 Native Americans, representing 0.1 percent, and 22,067 Asian and Pacific Americans, representing 2.0 percent.

Source: New York City Board of Education, *Facts and Figures. 1973-74.*

students, but only 91 Puerto Rican teachers in the entire system. Of 1,706 administrative and supervisory personnel, only 17 were Puerto Rican. No statistics were available for the number of Puerto Rican counselors.[35]

In Boston (1972), only 5 of the city's 4,729 teachers were Puerto Rican, and not one guidance counselor could speak Spanish. In Springfield, Massachusetts, there were only 5 Puerto Rican and 5 other Hispanic teachers for 1,485 Puerto-Rican students.[36] In Philadelphia, less than 1 percent of the teachers were Puerto Rican; only 2 of 532 guidance counselors were Puerto Rican, about 1 for every 4,750 Puerto Rican students.[37] In Bridgeport, Connecticut (1971), the board of education employed only 10 Puerto Rican teachers for nearly 4,000 Puerto Rican students. None of the 23 full-time counselors was Puerto Rican. A plan to recruit more teachers of Spanish origin was vetoed by the school board.[38]

Table 34

Staff of New York City Public School System, Including number and percentage of Spanish-Surnamed Staff, 1968, 1972, 1973

Job Category	Fall 1968			Fall 1972			Fall 1973			Fall 1974		
	Total	Spanish Surnamed	%	Total	Spanish Surnamed	%	Total	Spanish Surnamed	%	Total	Spanish Surnamed	%
Principals	893	1	0.1	940	20	2.1	962	31	3.2	981	39	4.0
Assistant principals	1,841	6	.3	2,600	40	1.5	2,645	38	1.4	2,705	48	1.8
Teachers	54,908	522	1.0	55,242	1,158	2.1	56,168	1,391	2.5	55,415	170	3.1
Other professional staff	–	156	2.6	–	–	–	–	–	–	–	–	–
Other instructional staff	–	–	–	4,110	220	5.4	4,038	232	5.7	4,120	227	5.5
Full-time Clerical office staff	–	–	–	3,465	165	4.8	898	26	2.9	–	–	–
Part-time professional staff	–	–	–	2,217	37	1.7	2,371	46	1.9	–	–	–

Source: New York City Board of Education, Division of Teacher Personnel.

Note: In spring 1975 the New York City Board of Education began laying off thousands of teachers and other staff. Statistical information reflecting the current situation in New York City is not yet available.

Counseling

Many Puerto Rican students perceive their non-Hispanic teachers and counselors as indifferent or insensitive. One student in Connecticut testified:

> I feel that the teachers don't care about the students.... A Spanish-speaking student comes into the room, immediately that person is considered dumb without even being given a chance.[39]

A Puerto Rican student in Camden, New Jersey, echoed the belief that counselors are insensitive to Puerto Rican students:

> The attitude that a lot of counselors had with a lot of friends of mine, because a lot of the individuals that graduated with me from high school are now shooting drugs and doing time in jail [is] to generalize and tell me that my people are dumb, that we make good dishwashers. We can't manipulate our minds, but we're good with our hands, and we are docile.... [40]

Another Puerto Rican student told the Pennsylvania Advisory Committee of her efforts to be admitted to an academic course and of the repeated warnings of guidance counselors that "I should not aim too high because I would probably be disappointed at the end result."[41]

Few Puerto Rican students are encouraged by high school counselors or teachers to think about college. The president of Hostos Community College in Bronx, New York, cited several instances in which counselors told Puerto Rican high school students that they were not "college material." One girl, who, according to this official, eventually completed her junior and senior years in 1 year at Queens College, allegedly had been removed from a college preparatory curriculum in high school and put into a secretarial course.[42] A counselor at Temple University (Philadelphia) said, "A lot of Puerto Rican kids don't think of college. They're not exposed to the right counselors in high school. They're in the wrong programs: most are in nonacademic courses."[43]

Parent and Community Involvement

Families exercise great influence on student attitudes toward education. By working in concert with parents, schools maximize chances that students will effectively participate in public education.[44]

In their open meetings, the Commission's State Advisory Committees heard testimony that Puerto Rican parents and community leaders were frequently excluded from participation in school matters. In Massachusetts, it was found that "poor communication, if any, exists between the local school districts and the Puerto Rican

community."[45] A major reason was difficulty with the English
language. Often, parents could not communicate with authorities
because of this language barrier; school notices generally were in
English.

In Illinois, a parent representative on a Title I advisory
council said that meetings were sometimes incomprehensible to her.
The council's agenda and related information were always prepared
in English.[46]

In Bridgeport, Connecticut, 89 percent of the Puerto Rican
parents surveyed said that they had difficulty in communicating in
English, but only 20 percent received written notices in Spanish.[47]

Puerto Rican parents have been frustrated in attempts to join
councils and organizations representing the school community. They
often do not participate in PTA organizations, whose meetings are
conducted in English.[48] Community involvement in advisory councils to Federal programs, such as those under Titles I and VII of
the Elementary and Secondary Education Act, has also been limited,
despite the requirement that communities be involved in decision-
making. Although Puerto Ricans were about 5 percent of the student enrollment in Boston, the Title I advisory council of 66 members
and 42 alternates had no Puerto Rican representatives.[49]

In Chicago, most of the six Hispanic members of the citywide
advisory council were employees of the school system. This would
appear to create some difficulty over their ability to function as im-
partial advisers to school programs.[50]

Decentralization

Because advisory groups have been unable to influence unresponsive
school districts, Puerto Rican and other minority communities have
in recent years demanded decentralization and community control of
schools which serve their children. For Puerto Ricans, this demand
has been most vehement in New York City.

In the wake of the 1968 teachers' strike in New York City,
the State passed a decentralization law.[51] It established the central board of education; created the position of chancellor to replace
the superintendent of schools; and established a system of 32 elected
community school boards. Decision making was split between the
central board and the community boards, with the central board retaining much of the final authority.[52]

Community boards are comprised of, and elected by, parents
who have resided in the district 1 year, are U.S. citizens, over 21
years of age, and are registered voters. Within their attendance
zones, the boards have jurisdiction over elementary through eighth
grade education. They appoint a community superintendent; oversee
instruction of students;[53] assign, promote, and dismiss principals

and teachers; prepare operating budgets; and apply for State and Federal grants.[54]

The central board determines district boundaries and conducts elections of local school board members. All high schools and special schools are centrally controlled.

The central board, the chancellor, and the board of examiners[55] have residual powers over the local districts as follows: First, local boards are limited in that personnel decisions and policies may not conflict with any collective bargaining agreement; such agreements are negotiated by the central board. Second, teachers and supervisors are selected (under a civil service system) from among those passing competitive or qualifying examinations administered by the board of examiners. Third, the central board determines minimum educational and experience requirements for teachers and supervisory personnel.[56] And, fourth, regulations concerning staff dismissals and cutbacks due to budget reductions and declining enrollments continue to be promulgated by the central board.

Decentralization is intended to open the way to greater parental involvement in operating the schools. But in New York City problems remain unsolved. For example, the central board is responsible for supplying technical aid to community boards in the preparation of project proposals to the Federal and New York State governments, but the board has been lax in this duty.[57] Problems are most acute in the design of proposals for Title I and State urban education financing and in applications for education projects under other Federal programs. In 1972, for example, community boards were given only 2 days notice to submit Title I proposals. Title VII proposals were prepared by local boards without any consultation with staff of the central board.

The benefits to date of decentralization appear mixed as far as Puerto Ricans are concerned. Recent modest increases in Puerto Rican teachers and administrators in New York City may be partially due to decentralization, but parental involvement in important school decisions remains limited.

The Government's Role in the Education of Puerto Rican Public School Students

The Federal Government has traditionally provided leadership to equalize educational opportunity for students from minority groups. Federal attention was first focused on the issue of school desegregation when several States and local school boards resisted implementation of desegregation laws. The Federal role was later extended to meet the special needs of language-minority students and to enforce laws that provide them with equal access to education.

State governments have also increasingly concerned themselves with development of special programs for disadvantaged and language-minority students.

Federal Special Aid Programs: The Elementary and Secondary Education Act (ESEA) of 1965 was the first comprehensive legislation designed to support programs for low-income students with special educational needs.[58] The act contains eight titles, three of which--Titles I, VII, and VIII--can fund programs for language-minority students.

Title I provides the bulk of ESEA funding. In fiscal year 1974, school districts received $1.6 billion to support compensatory education for low-income students. Funds are disbursed to States according to the numbers of low-income students and may be utilized for a variety of purposes, including early childhood education, reading, mathematics, ESL, and bilingual programs.

Title I has enormous potential for meeting the needs of language-minority students. In fiscal year 1971, Congress appropriated $1.8 billion under Title I, of which New York State received $192 million. Although about 23 percent of New York City's students were Puerto Rican, only $4 million (3.2 percent) of the $125 million allocated to the city went to Title I programs serving them. A total of $673,213 was spent on bilingual programs. In 1972 funding for bilingual programs increased to more than $3 million, while $503,322 was allocated for ESL programs. Approximately 14,400 students benefited from Title I language programs, the majority of whom were Hispanic.

Title I funds were also utilized to recruit and train teachers of Spanish origin. The program recruits native Spanish-speaking graduate and undergraduate students and trains them for teaching in New York schools. Nearly half of the Puerto Rican teachers now in the public school system are products of the program. Title I funds also help underwrite programs to motivate pupils who have dropped out of school.[59]

Title VII, also known as the Bilingual Education Act, funds demonstration projects to meet the special needs of low-income children who speak limited English.[60] Unlike Title I, the program could not meet the needs of all or even most needy children because of its limited funding. In fiscal year 1971, for example, proposals for Title VII funds submitted by local districts in New York City alone totaled $70 million, yet the appropriation of funds for the entire nation was only $25 million. New York State received slightly more than $1 million.[61]

Most of the projects funded by the U.S. Office of Education served Mexican American children in California and Texas. In 1971 New York received $1.2 million, California received $17.3 million, and Texas received $12.5 million.[62]

Increased Federal funding is needed for curriculum development, nationwide teacher training programs, and research into evaluation measures for bilingual education.[63] A combination of these activities and techniques, along with experience gained in demonstra-

tion programs, could increase the nation's capacity to provide quality education for all children.

Title VIII provides funds to local educational agencies for developing school dropout prevention programs. Since language difficulties are a major cause of dropouts among Puerto Ricans, Title
VIII can be used to support language programs. Like Title VII,
Title VIII projects are designed for demonstration purposes and support must later be assumed by the local school district. Schools
qualifying for Title VIII aid may be located in urban or rural areas,
must have a high percentage of low-income children, and must have
a high proportion (35 percent or more) of children who do not complete their elementary or secondary education.

Funding for Title VIII has never exceeded $10 million nation-
wide, and thus has had little impact on the dropout problem among
Puerto Ricans. Only 19 school districts had received Title VIII
grants by 1972. In New York State, where the majority of mainland
Puerto Ricans live, only one district, Fredonia, had received a Title
VII grant.[64]

Since 1972 funds have been available for bilingual education
under the Emergency School Aid Act (ESAA), program designed to
help school districts in implementing desegregation plans. In addition to a fiscal year 1974 appropriation of more than $236 million,
ESAA provides $9 million as a set-aside for bilingual education pro-
grams; 47 programs have been so funded. Most were in Texas.
New York received the second largest amount of bilingual set-aside
funds.[65]

State Governments: School districts receive most of their
financial support from their State governments. State agencies set
academic standards and credential requirements, and influence policy
and practice at all levels in local districts. States have fought to
protect their jurisdiction over local education and therefore have
major responsibility for ensuring equal educational opportunity for
language-minority students. Several States have passed legislation,
authorized funds, or issued policy regulations that address the needs
of language-minority students.

In Massachusetts the 1971 Transitional Bilingual Education
Act has involved the State and local school districts in a comprehensive program. The bill mandates that transitional bilingual education programs be implemented in each district with 20 or more children of limited English-speaking ability in one language classification.[66] It provides for supplemental financial aid to help school
districts meet the extra costs of such programs.[67]

In Illinois bilingual education is supported almost exclusively
by State funds. State funds for bilingual education in the 1972-73
school year totaled approximately $2.4 million. Public Law 78--727,
which became effective in September 1973, mandates bilingual education by July 1, 1976, in attendance zones having 20 or more students

whose first language is other than English.[68] However, Illinois school districts are making little progress to prepare for bilingual education. Efforts to recruit bilingual personnel still have not been fully undertaken. The Chicago board of education has no affirmative action plan with goals and timetables for hiring Hispanic teachers.[69]

In New Jersey, an office for Hispanic affairs in the division of curriculum and instruction at the State department of education assists in allocating State resources more effectively to meet the needs of students of Spanish origin.[70] In January 1975 the State legislature passed a compulsory bilingual education bill that requires school districts with 20 or more children of limited English-speaking ability to provide bilingual education programs.

Ironically, New York State, home of the great majority of mainland Puerto Rican students, has no law mandating bilingual education. Its "English only" law has been amended to permit 3-year programs of bilingual instruction in the public schools.[71]

In lieu of a legislative mandate for bilingual education, the Board of Regents of the University of the State of New York stated that they "believe it is the duty of the school to provide programs which capitalize on the strengths of the non-English-speaking child and his family."[72] Less commitment to the needs of language-minority children is inherently discriminatory, according to the board.

The regents directed increased use of Title I ESEA and State Urban Education funds for bilingual education and ESL programs, and defined the responsibility of local school districts in New York State as follows:

> In any case, where there are approximately 10 or more children of limited English-speaking ability who speak the same language and are of approximately the same age and level of educational attainment, every effort should be made to develop a bilingual rather than second language program.[73]

The New York State Department of Education has also established an office of bilingual education to oversee programs for non-English-speaking children. Under the auspices of that office, according to the regents, the State will actively press for adherence to the guidelines established in the May 25 memorandum of the Office for Civil Rights, HEW.[74]

In Pennsylvania, the State secretary of education directed school districts to provide bilingual education in every district having 20 or more non-English-speaking students in a language category.[75] New guidelines stipulate that basic State subsidy money must be used by the districts to teach children in their dominant language:

> ... every school district with 20 or more students whose
> dominant language is not English ... will have to use its
> basic per pupil instructional subsidy plus its Title I per
> pupil allocation plus whatever other categorical funds are
> available to educate its Puerto Rican students. This
> means basic instruction--not just supplementary help. [76]

Moreover, the Pennsylvania education department says it will use
its authority to force school districts, through the threat of fund
cutoffs, to provide Puerto Rican children with an adequate education.

Although several States have demonstrated concern over the
quality of education received by Puerto Rican students, school districts have claimed that they lack funds to implement new programs.
Additional funds are needed to extend these programs to thousands
of Puerto Rican students. [77]

School districts currently receive millions of dollars each
year to educate children in their attendance zones. Per-pupil expenditures are virtually wasted on Puerto Rican and other language-
minority children unless they can be redirected for compensatory
language training and other special programs.

States could require, as a necessary first step, that local
districts survey the language dominance of students; the achievement
test scores of language-minority students; placement of language-
minority students in low-ability groups or educable mentally retarded
classes; and dropout rates for language-minority students. Based
on such data, schools and districts could prepare operating budgets
and requests for special State and Federal funds. States could also
evaluate district budgets to monitor the extent to which a good faith
effort is being made.

The Courts and Language-Minority Children

The continued unresponsiveness of school districts to the needs of
language-minority students has stimulated court action. In Lau v.
Nichols the Supreme Court of the United States ratified HEW guidelines contained in the May 25, 1970, memorandum known as the
"May 25th Memorandum." The Court decided that:

> Basic English skills are at the very core of what these
> public schools teach. Imposition of a requirement that
> before a child can effectively participate in the educational
> program, he must already have acquired those basic skills
> is to make a mockery of public education. We know that
> those who do not understand English are certain to find
> their classroom experiences wholly incomprehensible and
> in no way meaningful. [78]

The decision in Lau v. Nichols found that a monolingual educational policy does violate HEW guidelines. The Court did not rule

on whether the private plaintiffs had a constitutional right to bilingual education. While finding the school district to be in noncompliance with Title VI of the 1964 Civil Rights Act, the Court explicitly declined to state what an appropriate remedy for such a violation may be. As of September 1976, Federal district court in San Francisco was reviewing a master plan for bilingual-bicultural education submitted by the school district.[79]

Aspira of New York, Inc. v. Board of Education of the City of New York [80] was the first major case concerning equal educational opportunity for Puerto Rican children.[81] Puerto Rican students and their parents, ASPIRA of New York, Inc., and ASPIRA of America, Inc. [82] brought action against the Board of Education of New York City individually and on behalf of a class comprising an estimated 182,000 Spanish-speaking students in New York City public schools.

The suit alleged that the school system had failed either to teach Spanish-speaking children in a language that they understood, or to provide them with the English language skills needed to progress effectively in school. Plaintiffs charged they were faced with unequal treatment based on language, and thus were denied equal educational opportunity as compared with English-speaking students.

After the Lau decision, plaintiffs moved for a summary judgment. The court, in ruling on the motion, asked both parties to submit plans which, in their view, satisfied the mandate of Lau as applied to Puerto Rican and other Spanish-speaking students in New York City's public schools.[83]

Negotiations followed the submission of these plans. With the approval of the court, the parties entered into a consent decree on August 29, 1974,[84] which provided that:

> 1. The board of education would identify and classify those students whose English language deficiency prevents them from effectively participating in the learning process, and who can effectively participate in Spanish.

> 2. By September 1975, the defendants were to provide all the children described above with: (a) a program to develop their ability to speak, understand, read, and write English; (b) instruction in Spanish, in such substantive courses as mathematics, science, and social studies; (c) a program to reinforce and develop the child's use of Spanish, including a component to introduce reading comprehension in Spanish to those children entering the school system, where an assessment of reading readiness in English indicates the need for such development. In addition to, but not at the expense of, the three central elements of the required program, entitled students were to spend maximum class time with other children to avoid isolation from their peers.

3. By the beginning of the second semester of the 1974-75 school year, the defendants were to provide all elements of the program to all children within the defined class at pilot schools designated by the chancellor. By September 1975 the program was to encompass all children within the defined class.

4. The board of education was to promulgate minimum educational standards to ensure that the program would be furnished to all children within the defined class, and ensure that the program would be provided in each of the community school districts. (On July 21, 1975, after lengthy negotiations, the minimum educational standards were issued by the chancellor.)

5. The defendants were obligated to use their maximum feasible efforts to obtain and expend the funds required to implement the program. If there are insufficient funds to implement the program, defendants were to notify plaintiffs' lawyers. (As of March 1976, they had not yet notified the Puerto Rican Legal Defense and Educational Fund, Inc. that there were insufficient funds or insufficient staff. [85])

In addition to these stipulations, the consent decree included agreements regarding the use, development, and dissemination of appropriate materials and tests, and the recruitment, training, or retraining of adequate staff.

The decree also set specific timetables for completing each task. The defendants were required to consult with plaintiffs concerning the development and implementation of all items in the consent decree. The court retained jurisdiction to hear and settle disputes concerning the adequate implementation of the decree.

Implementing the Decree: The chancellor for the city school district of New York is ultimately responsible for implementing the consent decree. [84] He has set up a project management team to monitor the progress of the program and to coordinate the different divisions of the board of education. [87]

The decree required that an improved system of student identification and eligibility for the program was to be developed. A complete battery of tests was designed in the fall of 1974. This is commonly referred to as the L. A. B. (Language Assessment Battery). The board of education agreed to use the results of that test to place children in those special classes provided for by the consent decree. The L. A. B. was administered in the spring of 1975 (the only previous test was an assessment of oral language skills in English). [88]

Not until September 1975 were procedures established to monitor adherence to the standards and to the decree. The minimum educational standards included:

1) English language instruction;
2) Subject area instruction in the pupil's dominant language;
3) Reinforcement and development of the child's use of Spanish, including development of reading and writing skills;
4) Opportunity for spending maximum time with other pupils in order to avoid isolation and segregation from peers without diluting or abrogating the above mentioned three elements.

Forty schools (including elementary, junior high, and senior high schools) were designated as "pilot schools" to serve as models and training centers in preparation for full implementation in September 1975. Their selection was based on whether or not the schools were already implementing one or more phases of the program. [89]

An evaluation of the pilot schools was undertaken by the Community Service Society of New York. [90]

The chancellor has emphasized that, for the most part, basic city tax levy funds (rather than State or Federal funds) would be utilized to implement the consent decree. The district also receives $11 million in supplementary tax levy funds, and an increased amount is being requested by the board to help implement the decree. [91]

The city school district also receives funds from State and Federal sources, and is exploring the possibility of using some of these funds to implement the decree.

On July 11, 1975, Judge Frankel settled another dispute generated by this lawsuit, ruling that parents of Hispanic students found entitled to the program could withdraw their children. Appended to the court's memorandum and order were the forms of notice to school administrators and letters to Hispanic parents which established the opting-out procedures. As described by the court, the form letters and notice were intended to "permit opting-out while refraining from encouraging it." The form letters and notice were agreed to by counsel for the plaintiffs only after negotiations, and even then outstanding differences had to be finally resolved by the court. [92]

On September 9, 1975, the court ordered the defendants to provide certain information essential to determining the degree of compliance with the program. As of that month, there appeared to be sufficient numbers of adequately trained persons available to implement one aspect of the decree, the hiring of trained personnel. But certain schools had not yet hired staff to implement the program. On December 22, 1975, plaintiffs' lawyers moved to hold the chancellor and members of the board of education in civil contempt for failing to fully implement the decree. [93]

In his response to this report, Chancellor Anker stated that "The larger part of the effort briefly described here had taken place before the Consent Decree was signed in August of 1974. Although it is true that the impact of the decree had obviously accelerated many of these activities we certainly feel that recognition should be given to our willingness to address a major educational problem in an innovative and responsible manner."

This view conflicts considerably with that of Federal District Judge Frankel, who heard the case and approved the consent decree. In an opinion granting attorney's fees to the plaintiffs, Judge Frankel said:

> Nevertheless, however positive we may wish to be and whatever the naivete of judges, the defendants must surely recall the long and sometimes bitter times before the era of good feelings set in. This is not a subject the court desires to dwell upon now or, if possible, ever. It should be sufficient to remind everyone, without detailed documentation, that even though 18 or 20 months of struggle and a motion for summary judgment led to negotiations for a consent decree, there were bargaining sessions when the court was driven to speak as more than a "mere moderator," [citations omitted] ... occasions when the Board was chided for what seemed tardy and grudging concessions, and a penultimate stage at which the Board's adversary passion led to blatant infringement of first amendment rights. To the very end, it must be said, steady and energetic pressure by plaintiffs' attorneys was required so that pertinent information and responsive proposals would be forthcoming on a reasonably prompt and orderly schedule. (Aspira of New York, Inc. v. Board of Education of the City of New York, 65 F.R.D. 541, 544 (S.D.N.Y. 1975)).

Although the consent decree has not yet been fully implemented, it is viewed as a vital step in achieving equal educational opportunity for Puerto Rican students in New York City's public schools, and a basis for protecting the rights of other non-English-speaking children in the city. [94]

Puerto Ricans and Higher Education

An estimated 25,000 mainland Puerto Ricans were enrolled as full-time college undergraduates in 1972. [95] This figure reflects vigorous growth in recent years. In New York City, for example, 1970 census data showed that there were only 3,500 Puerto Rican college graduates (compared with 2,500 in 1960). That year, only 1 percent of the Puerto Rican adults in New York City were college graduates, compared with 4 percent of black adults and 13 percent of white adults.

The City University of New York (CUNY) had 5,425 Puerto Rican undergraduates in 1969. By 1974 CUNY had 16,352 Puerto Rican undergraduates. This is not only a substantial leap in numerical terms, but also a sign of growing Puerto Rican participation in higher education. In 1969 Puerto Ricans at CUNY represented 4.0

Table 35

Ethnic Composition of CUNY Undergraduates by Numbers and Percentages: Fall 1969-1974

Group	1960	1970	1971	1972	1973	1974
White	77.4% (104,974)	74.0% (117,566)	71.8% (129,232)	64.0% (125,804)	58.2% (121,887)	55.7% (123,079)
Black	14.8 (20,072)	16.9 (26,850)	19.5 (35,098)	22.4 (44,031)	25.8 (54,033)	25.6 (56,568)
Puerto Rican	4.0 (5,425)	4.8 (7,626)	5.9 (10,619)	6.9 (13,563)	7.5 (15,707)	7.4 (16,352)
Other Spanish-Surnamed American[1]	N/A	N/A	N/A	1.8 (3,538)	2.3 (4,817)	3.0 (6,629)
American Indian	0.4 (543)	0.2 (318)	0.3 (540)	0.3 (590)	0.3 (628)	0.4 (884)
Oriental	2.0 (2,713)	2.1 (3,336)	2.0 (3,600)	2.1 (4,128)	2.2 (4,607)	2.6 (5,745)
Other	1.4 (1,899)	2.0 (3,177)	0.5 (900)	2.5 (4,914)	3.7 (7,749)	5.3 (11,711)
Total	100.0% (135,626)	100.0% (158,873)	100.0% (179,989)	100.0% (196,568)	100.0% (209,428)	100.0% (220,968)

[1] The ethnic category "Other Spanish-Surnamed American" was not required by HEW until 1972.
Source: City University of New York.

Table 36

Ethnic Composition of Matriculated First-time Freshman by Numbers and Percentages, Fall 1969-1974

Group	NEW YORK STATE						Estimated 1974 New York City U.S. Graduates
	1969	1970	1971	1972	1973	1974	
Black	13.9% (2,815)	17.3% (6,144)	21.3% (8,370)	21.8% (8,340)	26.9% (10,221)	28.8% (12,087)	22.2% (15,595)
Puerto Rican & Spanish-Surnamed American[1]	6.0 (1,215)	7.8 (2,769)	8.7 (3,332)	11.8 (4,514)	14.1 (5,358)	13.4 (5,624)	14.8 (10,396)
Other[2]	80.1 (16,223)	74.9 (26,598)	70.0 (27,509)	66.4 (25,402)	59.0 (22,419)	57.8 (24,259)	63.0 (44,255)
Total	100.0% (20,253)	100.0% (35,511)	100.0% (39,211)	100.0% (38,256)	100.0% (37,998)	100.0% (41,970)	100.0% (70,246)

[1] Figures were derived by applying the ethnic distribution of New York City public and non-public 12th graders to the actual numbers of New York City graduates of public and nonpublic high schools.

[2] Includes whites, Asian Americans, Native Americans, and others.

Source: New York State Education Department, Information Center on Education.

percent of total enrollment; by 1974, they were 7.4 percent of the undergraduates. (See Table 35.)

In 1974 Puerto Ricans and other Hispanics (defined as Spanish-surnamed Americans) represented 13.4 percent of the first-time freshmen in the CUNY system, compared with 6.0 percent 5 years previous. (See Table 36.) Further growth of Puerto Rican college enrollment is an immediate possibility since in the 1974-75 school year Puerto Ricans represented 16.1 percent of all students in New York City's academic high schools (the pathway to college), and other Hispanics represented another 4.9 percent. (See Table 37.)

While there is reason for optimism, the growth trend rests on shaky foundations. Much of the increased enrollment is due to the "open enrollment" policy of the CUNY system and fluctuating levels of federally-funded financial aid and support services. The New York City fiscal crisis has profoundly affected CUNY. On June 1, 1976, Chancellor Robert Kibbee closed CUNY for two weeks owing to lack of funds. On June 12, the Board of Higher Education, under intense pressure from State and city officials, voted to charge tuition for the first time. The cost is $775 a year for freshmen and sophomores and $925 for upperclass students. As part of the $27 million State aid package, $3 million was authorized for the educational needs of Spanish-speaking students in Hostos Community College. [96]

Figures are not yet available to ascertain how many Puerto Rican students are dropping out due to academic or financial problems. Nor are figures available to show how many Puerto Ricans are actually graduating from college, in comparison with previous years.

In the absence of these data, the only reliable source that offers means of comparison is the limited information supplied by the 1970 census. These data show that, although more Puerto Ricans are going to college, they are much less likely to attend college than are high school graduates from other racial or ethnic groups. In 1970, 45 percent of college-age youths in the U.S. were reported to be engaged in higher education, compared with 15 to 20 percent of blacks, and only 5 percent of Puerto Ricans. [97]

Among college freshmen there has been a smaller percentage of Puerto Ricans than of blacks, Mexican Americans, Asian Americans, or Native Americans. Between 1971 and 1973, the percentage of black freshmen dropped from 8.6 to 7.6 percent, and of Puerto Rican freshmen from 0.6 to 0.4 percent. [98] At the other end of the academic spectrum, Puerto Ricans constituted only 0.01 percent of all minority group doctoral degree recipients in 1973. (Of 2,884 minority group recipients that year, only 37 were Puerto Rican, with 2 from Puerto Rico.)[99]

The limited data available, and results from Commission field research in New York, Philadelphia, Newark, and Chicago, suggest the following composite of the mainland Puerto Rican college student:

Table 37

Total, Puerto Rican and Spanish-Surnamed Student Enrollment in New York City Public Schools, 1974-75.

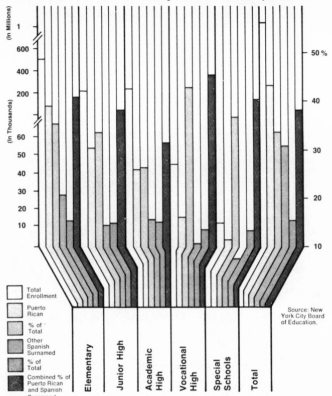

Source: New York City Board of Education.

The student is more likely to be male than female and from a low-income family. [100] He is the first in his family to go to college and is somewhat older than the average student, as he may have worked or completed military service prior to entering college.

He is likely to be a first-year student at a relatively low-cost, 2-year or community college, or at a college or university with open enrollment policies. He commutes to class in an Eastern metropolitan area or in Chicago. He is receiving financial aid, probably from a variety of sources. He is majoring in the social sciences, perhaps education, Spanish, or social work, rather than the physical sciences. He is severely handicapped by earlier educational deficiencies, particularly in communication skills.

The following profile of Puerto Rican college students was offered in 1970:

This new population in higher education comes to the university with some very special problems and concerns. They are all concerned with the fact that they are the survivors ... of an educational system which has succeeded in eliminating 50 percent of their group before they completed school. They are all concerned about the extent of racism in our society.

In a group with a varied racial background, sometimes white, black or, more commonly, some shade in between, they struggle with racial identity and its consequences. They are also concerned with the future status of Puerto Rico and the questions of the time--whether "Puerto Rico is a slave colony of the United States," or "A Showcase for Democracy."

They enter college in a period of general disaffection with the university, its purpose and role in our society. They make increasing demands for courses and programs in the field of Puerto Rican studies and at the same time are anxious that their education pay off in a job which will break the bonds of poverty. [101]

The Puerto Rican student is unlikely to complete his or her education in the normal 2- or 4-year period, but will drop out for a semester or more and return later. Even over the long run, the student has less than a 50-50 chance of graduating. If a Puerto Rican manages to survive the high dropout rate in high school, he or she then must face the steep cost of college and the difficulty of securing financial aid. [102]

Not all Puerto Rican students have access to the open enrollment City University of New York system. Even at CUNY, the cost of fees and related expenses has risen dramatically. Going to a private college is prohibitive for the majority of Puerto Rican students. (Average yearly costs for various types of colleges are shown in Table 38.)

Given the impoverished circumstances of the mainland Puerto Rican community, college costs can be met by very few Puerto Rican families, since median family income for mainland Puerto Ricans in 1974 was only $6,779. Tuition alone at Ivy League schools, which averages more than $3,800 per year, is more than half the annual income of most Puerto Rican families. For the 1975-76 school year, fees are $387.50 per semester at Hostos Community College (part of the City College of Chicago), $21 per credit hour at Essex County Community College in Newark, and $242 per semester at Philadelphia Community College. But not all needy students have access to such low-cost institutions.

Shortage of Colleges in the Cities: A shortage of colleges in large cities reduces the opportunities for Puerto Ricans and other low-income students, who can only afford to attend if they live at home.

Table 38

Average Total Expenses for Resident and Commuter Students at Postsecondary Institutions 1975-76

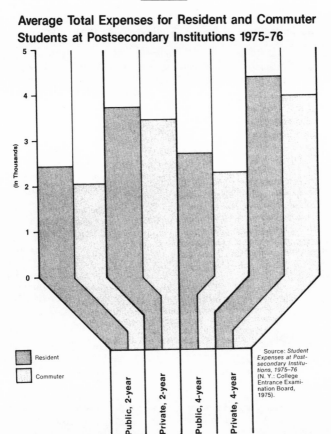

Resident

Commuter

Public, 2-year

Private, 2-year

Public, 4-year

Private, 4-year

(In Thousands)

Source: *Student Expenses at Post-secondary Institutions, 1975–76* (N. Y.: College Entrance Examination Board, 1975).

In 1970 the Carnegie Commission found:

> ... a major deficit in two types of institutions--community colleges and comprehensive colleges in metropolitan areas, especially those with a population over 500,000. The inner cities, in particular, are not well served. Higher education has not adequately reflected the urbanization of America. Deficits in North Jersey and the eastern side of Chicago are illustrative. [103]

Puerto Rican populations are largest in the Northeastern States and in the Chicago area, both of which were net exporters of college students in 1970. The Carnegie Commission called for 175 to 235 new community colleges in the United States by 1980, 80 to 125 of them to be located in metropolitan areas. [104] It also called for 85 to 105 new comprehensive colleges by 1980, with 60 to 70 of them in large metropolitan areas.

Another study found that nearly three-fifths of the nation's total population does not live near (within 45 minutes drive, one-way) a "free access" college, and that metropolitan residents are only somewhat better served by such colleges than those living in rural areas. [105]

All of these factors have shaped Puerto Rican perceptions about educational opportunities beyond high school. They have combined to reinforce each other, from one generation to the next, so that to the Puerto Rican junior or senior in high school, college is likely to be an alien or remote institution.

Despite this prevailing noncollege orientation, however, many low-income Puerto Rican parents will "sacrifice tremendously" to obtain for their children the highest possible degree of education. They have learned that social and economic mobility depends heavily upon academic credentials. The Puerto Rican student who graduates from high school tends to be very "hardy" and "fiercely determined to enter the mainstream of American society."[106]

Financial Barriers: While financial aid for college students is more plentiful than it was 10 years ago, Puerto Rican applicants and their parents still must shoulder a heavy share of the cost. In Illinois, for example, after Federal and State financial sources have been used, the remaining unmet need for students of Spanish origin averages $1,097, a very high percentage of family income. [107] In New Jersey, the comparable figure is $337. [108]

Several sources complain that student aid funds allocated to colleges have remained the same, or have been cut, despite enrollment increases. Only about one-third of the 55,000 students who need Federal aid at CUNY are expected to receive it in fiscal year 1976. [109]

The "red tape" involved in getting or renewing aid is often a greater problem than the availability of aid. At Hostos Community College in the Bronx, New York, staff said that "No one knows" when aid might be stopped or cut back, and, partly because some aid programs are so new, "You can't get any straight information on them."[110]

Lack of Information: Since so few mainland Puerto Ricans have attended college, important information concerning applications, forms, required statements, curricula, special programs, financial aid, and so forth may not be available from relatives or friends.

College counseling staffs are usually limited, and few have Puerto Rican or other Hispanic counselors. The City College of New York (CCNY) has only one Puerto Rican or Spanish-speaking counselor and one Puerto Rican financial aid counselor for about 1,350 Puerto Rican students. [111] Puerto Rican students frequently complain of the lack of counseling aid, both in high school and in college. It is felt, for example, that more Hispanic counselors are needed at CUNY to reinforce the "self-image" of Puerto Rican students there. Some Puerto Ricans feel that non-Hispanic counselors tend to be more rigid and "go by the book," when more sympathetic and imaginative advice is needed. [112]

A faculty member at the University of Illinois Chicago Circle campus charges that counseling there is "poisonous." He asserts that counseling helped Puerto Ricans to survive "by teaching them tricks, pacifying them, and showing them easy courses." That is one reason, he said, why nearly three-fourths of Puerto Ricans drop out of college, leaving only a minuscule number of graduates. [113]

Puerto Ricans also lack adequate counseling with reference to graduate school opportunities. Furthermore, many counselors are unable to appreciate the "overwhelming" health and financial crises and "intense" emotional problems that face many Puerto Rican students. [114] One observer stated that counseling for Puerto Ricans in college was superior to that which they received in high school: In high school they were told not to attend college. [115]

Admission Standards and Examinations: Largely because of the poor quality of education received in city schools and the failure of educational system to meet their needs, Puerto Ricans frequently graduate from high school with low grade point averages. They also tend to score lower on college entrance examinations, such as the Scholastic Aptitude Test (SAT).

In 1965 the estimated median achievement test score (non-verbal, reading, math, and general information) for 12th grade Puerto Rican students was 43.1 compared with 52 for white students. [116] An official at the Educational Testing Service (ETS) which designs most college entrance tests, feels that the lack of college experience among most minority group families probably explains their lower SAT scores. [117] Thus, the "B" grade average or high SAT scores required by many colleges are beyond the reach of the typical Puerto Rican high school graduate.

At Essex County Community College in Newark, New Jersey, an estimated 85 percent of the Puerto Rican students require ESL (English as a Second Language) training. [118]

At Northeastern Illinois University, 90 percent of all Hispanic students (including Puerto Ricans) need language assistance, according to a counselor. "Most of the Latin American students here are products of the Chicago school system. Their difficulties are not always one of language, but of inadequate preparation and indifferent educational techniques," he said. [119]

A New York educator said that many Puerto Ricans (as well as other students) continue to graduate from high school ill-equipped for college work. [120] Since Puerto Rican students often are not encouraged to follow a college preparatory program, they may not be as adept at preparing for tests or writing term papers as their white counterparts. A college may have to teach them not only subject matter, but also how to write a term paper. [121]

Tutoring and Remedial Services: Few tutors are available to assist Puerto Rican students who have difficulty with college-level work. A teacher at Essex County Community College in Newark, commenting upon teacher overload, noted that he teaches seven courses and so has no time for counseling or tutoring. Many Puerto Ricans "still cannot function" after 2 years because programs of assistance at the college are so limited and ineffective, he said. [122]

Many of the remedial courses designed to upgrade essential skills reportedly fail to achieve their purpose. At Temple University, Puerto Ricans "were thrown into a remedial English course along with other non-English-speaking minority students," and few profited, according to one observer. "They needed a Spanish-speaking teacher." [123]

Speaking of support services at the college level, a Rutgers official said that, "Kids are brought in like cattle" and then "dumped." Students tend to drift and have to counsel each other. [124]

Student Alienation: Largely because of inadequate support services, low-income students often feel like "intruders" in a traditionally white, middle-class environment. [125] Having managed to ride into college on "the coattails" of black students, Puerto Rican students are often "an anonymous entity" in affirmative action programs. [126] Receiving little attention from college staff, sometimes living away from home for the first time, noting the absence of Puerto Rican administrators, faculty, and even clerical staff, many are often "lost in the shuffle." Finding the college atmosphere "cold" and "rigid," the temptation to drop out looms large. [127]

For these reasons, Puerto Rican students at most colleges and universities have formed student unions. Unlike the traditional student union, which is primarily involved in planning dances and social events, Puerto Rican groups often perform administrative functions such as student recruiting and tend to devote themselves to key issues concerning their education. These issues include: demands for more Puerto Rican administrators, faculty, and admissions and recruitment staff; increased or continued funding for support programs for Puerto Ricans; support for or creation of Puerto Rican studies programs or departments; greater recruitment efforts aimed at Puerto Rican students in the surrounding community; the alleged channeling of Puerto Rican students into certain curricula and departments; and the steady rise in tuition costs.

Many Puerto Rican students and faculty members perceive themselves on the defensive, as objects of discrimination, fearing that the broadened access to higher education in recent years is now narrowing, and that minority programs face extinction. These views have provoked demonstrations by Puerto Rican students at City College in New York, [128] Yale, [129] the University of Illinois Chicago Circle

Campus, [130] and Macalester College in Minnesota. [131] Tension and unrest over feared cutbacks in minority programs and staffs exist at other schools, such as Temple, Lehman College in New York City, and Rutgers' Livingston College. [132]

Many Puerto Rican students assume that, unless they relentlessly press college administrators, they will be neglected. A common sentiment is that the administration "distrusts the legitimacy of Puerto Rican needs and will only respond to pressure." [133] Whatever small gains have been achieved are done by the students themselves with Puerto Rican staff support. Thus, a decision to dismiss an English teacher considered especially effective in developing the writing skills of Latino students at Northeastern Illinois University was rescinded after Latino protests. [134] Macalester College announced it would not terminate its Puerto Rican program after Puerto Rican and other minority students seized an administration building to protest budget cuts in the school's minority program. [135]

The perspective from which some Puerto Rican students view college administrators and policies is shaped, at least in part, by what one faculty member termed an "anti-colonial" attitude and a strong need among many Puerto Rican youth to maintain their cultural and linguistic identity. [136] They are bitter that their language is considered detrimental and a "handicap" in college; they resist what they perceive to be the destruction of their individuality in what they see as the "melting pot" approach to higher education. They want desperately to develop skills that will enable them to live useful, rewarding lives, but they want to do so without having their values and heritage ridiculed or denied.

Government's Role in Education of Puerto Rican University Students

Federal expenditures for university student aid rose from $941 million in 1966 to an estimated $5 billion in 1972. About $3.9 billion of this amount was used to pay tuition and fees, with the remainder applied to cover living costs. [137]

The Education Amendments of 1972 extended many of the existing Federal aid programs. The amendments added a new program of basic student grants for every high school graduate who wants to continue his or her education but lacks the resources to do so, and encouraged establishment of new planning structures at the State level to improve all forms of planning for postsecondary education. [138]

Federal financial aid for college students consists of grants, loans, and work-study funds. Most of the grant and scholarship aid given up to 1973 was provided by the Veterans Administration (VA) and the Social Security Administration (SSA).

The largest Federal student aid program was the G. I. Bill,

which allows up to 36 months of full-time schooling or on-the-job training for eligible veterans and military personnel. Expenditures for the program by the VA were nearly $1.8 billion in fiscal year 1972. In the same fiscal year, the Social Security Administration provided $475.3 million in benefits to 432,863 students who were children of retired, disabled, or deceased social security beneficiaries. [139]

The principal student grant program administered by the U.S. Office of Education in fiscal year 1972 was the education Opportunity Grant (EOG) program. Federal funds of up to $1,000 were granted to college students with "exceptional financial need." Colleges administer the program, which has varying definitions of need. The college must match each grant with other Federal or non-Federal aid. EOG grants of $210.3 million were obligated in fiscal year 1972 to participating institutions. [140]

The Basic Education Opportunity Grant (BEOG) program created in 1972, allows low-income students even greater access to higher education. Administered by the Office of Education, BOG provides direct grants that help qualified undergraduates finance their postsecondary education.

BEOG differs from EOG in that it is an entitlement program with a standard definition of need. Both full- and part-time students are eligible for up to 5 years of study.

In fiscal year 1975, BEOG provided a maximum of $1,050 each to about 700,000 first- and second-year students. [141] When fully funded, it is to provide annual grants of up to $1,400 (minus expected family contribution) but not more than one-half the total cost of college attendance. The Carnegie Commission has estimated that 500,000 to 1 million additional students "might be induced to attend college if BOG were fully funded."[142]

The two principal Federal loan programs are the National Direct Student Loan program (NDSL, formerly the National Defense Student Loan Program) and the Guaranteed Student Loan program, authorized by the Higher Education Act of 1965.

State Aid: In fiscal year 1973, the 50 States spent an estimated $348 million for undergraduate student aid in the form of scholarships and grants, plus a substantial sum for gauranteed and direct loans, tuition waivers and reductions, and various restricted grants to special categories of students. [143] Despite recent increases in such aid, State spending for these programs accounts for no more than 4 or 5 percent of total measurable State and local support for postsecondary education. [144] Six States--California, Illinois, New Jersey, New York, Ohio, and Pennsylvania--account for 78 percent of the total student-aid financing and 67 percent of the student recipients. Most State programs cover only tuition, or tuition and mandatory fees, but a few now provide aid primarily for disadvantaged students from low-income families and/or with marginal records of achievement.

One such program is the Educational Opportunity Fund (EOF), which aided 13,000 students (including 1,050 Puerto Ricans) at public and independent institutions in New Jersey and other States in fiscal year 1974. [145]

Under EOF in New Jersey, State funds go directly to students via grants and to institutions to maintain supportive services (tutoring, developmental courses, counseling, diagnostic testing, and full-time summer programs). Three-fourths of EOF students are from families earning less than $6,000 per year. [146] The average family income of the EOF student is $4,464, compared to $11,082 for the average New Jersey family. The average EOF grant is $817. This covers half the cost of attending a community college, and less than a third of the cost of attending a State college or Rutgers University.

Lack of data on Puerto Rican participation in both Federal and State student aid programs prevents efforts to ensure that they are in fact receiving their fair share. Some Puerto Rican educators believe that a disproportionately large share of that aid goes to Mexican American students west of the Mississippi River. [147]

Many Puerto Ricans believe that much student aid is not based on financial need. This has been confirmed in at least one study by the College Entrance Examination Board:

> A cherished myth of educators and the general public is that student financial aid today is primarily based on relative need. However, when the source and application of all aid funds (including the G.I. Bill, Social Security, athletic grants, and scholarships from restricted funds) are considered, the greater amount of student aid appears to be beyond institutional control and is commonly awarded on the basis of criteria other than need. ... [148]

Similarly, the Carnegie Commission pointed out that:

> Because many students from upper-income families attend institutions with tuition charges that are far below costs (true in the case of many private colleges and universities, as well as public institutions), these educational subsidies are not distributed as effectively as might be the case if minimizing the financial barrier to attendance were the primary goal. For example, of the total monetary outlays on higher education, students and their families on the average contribute about 37 percent of the total ($8.1 billion out of $22 billion in 1970-71). [149]

Special Admissions and Support Programs: A number of new policies and programs that focus on the needs of low-income, disadvantaged students have been established in recent years. These have permitted access to college for a significant number of Puerto Rican students.

The introduction of open admissions at the City University of New York in 1970 played a major role in increasing Puerto Rican college attendance in the system. Under this policy, admission to a college within the CUNY system was guaranteed to all New York City high school graduates. Puerto Rican undergraduate enrollment at CUNY increased from 5,425 (4 percent of total enrollment) in 1969 to 15,707 (7.5 percent) in 1973.

Other schools have also instituted open admission programs. The Temple Opportunity Program (TOP) at Temple University, Proyecto Pa'lante at Northeastern Illinois University, and the Equal Education Opportunity(EEO) program at Macalester College, among others, offer (to a limited number of Puerto Rican and other low-income, minority students) admission based only on indications of potential and motivation. These programs provide counseling and academic tutoring services, and help students put together financial aid packages.

One of the oldest special programs for low-income students is the College Discovery Program (CDP), created at CUNY in 1964. Its purpose was to:

> demonstrate that students who were then being excluded from college because of the existing admissions criteria could, with the proper supportive services, attain a college degree. From the beginning, it was understood that students fail not only because they are underprepared but also because they are economically disadvantaged. For this reason, stipends for books, fees and personal expenses were made available to the student as was intensive counseling, remediation and tutoring. [150]

Since 1964 CDP has expanded its enrollment from 231 students at two community colleges to well over 4,000 students in eight programs at seven community colleges. Thirty percent of CDP enrollment is Puerto Rican. [151]

Special Services for Disadvantaged Students (SSDS)[152], a Federal program created in 1965, offers remedial and other supportive services to disadvantaged students with academic potential who need such services to commence or continue higher education. Grants are made on the basis of proposals submitted by eligible applicants on a competitive basis. In 1973-74, Puerto Ricans numbered 3,945 of participants in SSDS. This was 5.3 percent of all participants, compared to 5 percent of participants in 1972-73 and 4 percent in 1971-72. [153]

Open admissions and special academic support programs for low-income minority students are so new that it is difficult to evaluate their effectiveness. A study at CUNY, however, found that the university has not become the "revolving door" which some had expected with the advent of open admissions, and that attrition rates under open admissions were, overall, about the same as the national average. [154]

EOF students in New Jersey "continually perform at a respectable level of achievement, and although they come to college with lower SAT scores than their regularly admitted counterparts, they quickly close the gap."[155]

As the result of help provided by Proyecto Pa'lante at Northeastern Illinois University, the Proyecto director expects as many as 60 percent of Latino students to graduate. [156]

References

1. According to the 1970 U. S. census, among persons aged 25 years and above, whites had a median of 12. 1 school years completed, blacks had 9. 8 school years, and mainland Puerto Ricans had 8. 7 school years.
2. Isidro Lucas, "Puerto Rican Dropouts in Chicago: Numbers and Motivations" (Manuscript, 1971), p. 23. Research conducted under grant no. OEG-5-70-0037(509) for the Office of Education, U. S. Department of Health, Education, and Welfare.
3. Daniel Schreiber, ed. , The School Dropout (Washington, D. C. : National Education Association, January 1964), pp. 3, 18-19.
4. City of New York, Board of Education, Community School Profiles, 1973-74. According to a study undertaken for the Board of Education of the City of New York, in May 1974 there were more than 65,000 Hispanic school children with severe or moderate difficulty in English comprehension. Of this number, more than 47,000 were Puerto Rican children. The study concluded that "English language disability among pupils of Hispanic origin is substantial, encompassing about a third of Puerto Rican pupils...." See Donald Treiman, Thomas Di Prete, and Kermit Terrell, "Preliminary Report on a Survey of Educational Services for Hispanic Pupils with English Language Difficulty, Conducted in the New York City Schools, May 1974" (Center for Policy Research, mimeograph, July 1, 1974), Table 1 and p. 16.
5. Testimony of Antonio Candido Martinez in Hearing Before the United States Commission on Civil Rights, Hearing Held in New York, N. Y. , Feb. 14-15, 1972, p. 43 (hereafter cited as New York Hearing).
6. Data are from the Metropolitan Reading Achievement Test (April 1968), Table H, which contains city and borough average reading scores for 2nd, 5th, and 8th grades.
7. Bureau of Educational Research, Board of Education of the City of New York, "Ranking of Schools by Reading Achievement," attachment to amicus curiae brief for the Puerto Rican Legal Defense and Education Fund in Lau v. Nichols, 414 U. S. 563 (1974).
8. Illinois Advisory Committee (SAC) to the U. S. Commission on Civil Rights, Bilingual/Bicultural Education--a Privilege or a Right? (May 1974), p. 42. (hereafter cited as Illinois SAC Report).
9. See testimony of Dr. Marechal-Neal Young, Associate Superin-

tendent for Special Education, in Pennsylvania Advisory Committee (SAC) to the U. S. Commission on Civil Rights, Transcript of Open Meeting, June 7, 1972, vol. II, pp. 433-57 (hereafter cited as Pennsylvania SAC, Transcript of Open Meeting).

10. Testimony of Braulio Montalvo, Psychologist, Philadelphia Child Guidance Clinic, in Pennsylvania SAC, Transcript of Open Meeting, pp. 415-16.

11. Warren G. Findley and Miriam M. Bryan, Ability Grouping: 1970--Status, Impact, and Alternatives (University of Georgia), p. 25.

12. David N. Aspy, "Groping or Grouping for Teachability," Contemporary Education, Vol. 41, No. 6, May 1970, pp. 306-10.

13. U. S., Commission on Civil Rights, Toward Quality Education for Mexican Americans, Report VI: Mexican American Education Study (February 1974), pp. 25, 31.

14. Testimony of Joseph Monserrat in New York Hearing, pp. 122-23.

15. John R. Hodgdon, Regional Civil Rights Director, OCR/HEW, Region V, letter to Dr. Robert Krajewski, Superintendent, East Chicago Public Schools, June 9, 1972 (hereafter cited as Hodgdon Letter).

16. Pennsylvania Advisory Committee, In Search of a Better Life--The Education and Housing Problems of Puerto Ricans in Philadelphia (1974), pp. 23-6 (hereafter cited as Pennsylvania SAC Report).

17. "Children With English Language Difficulties," The Fleischman Commission Report, Part III, Vol. II, reprinted from the Fleischman Commission, A Report of the New York State Commission on the Cost, Quality and Finance of Elementary and Secondary Schools, 3 Vols. (1972), p. 8.

18. Westry G. Horne, Chief, Elementary and Secondary Education Branch, Region II, memorandum to Dr. Lloyd Henderson, Director, Education Division, Office for Civil Rights, Apr. 30, 1973.

19. Testimony of Ewald B. Nyquist, President, University of the State of New York and Commissioner of Education, in New York Hearing, p. 519.

20. New England Regional Council, Overview of the Problems Encountered by New England's Spanish-Speaking Population, (July 7, 1970), pp. 14-15.

21. Adriana Gianturco and Norman Aronin, Boston's Spanish Speaking Community: Findings of a Field Survey (Boston, Prudential Insurance Co., 1971), p. 45. Prepared under a grant from the U. S. Department of Labor.

22. Massachusetts Advisory Committee to the U. S. Commission on Civil Rights, Issues of Concern to Puerto Ricans in Boston and Springfield (February 1972), p. 9.

23. "Language-minority" children speak a non-English native language and belong to an identifiable minority group of generally low socioeconomic status.

24. Nancy Modiano, "National or Mother Language in Beginning Reading: A Comparative Study," Research in the Teaching

of English (1968). For a thorough discussion of the ESL approach, see Mary Finocchiaro, Teaching English as a Second Language in Elementary and Secondary Schools (New York, 1969) and Harold B. Allen, ed., Teaching English as a Second Language (New York, 1965).

25. 20 U.S. C. § 880(b)-1(4)(A)(Supp. IV 1974).

26. For a detailed discussion of the bilingual education approach, see Muriel Saville and Rudolph Troike, A Handbook of Bilingual Education (Washington, D. C., 1971) and Theodore Andersson and Mildred Boyer, Bilingual Schooling in the United States, Vols. I and II (Austin, Texas, January 1970).

27. Hernan LaFontaine, "Bilingual Education for Puerto Ricans: Sí o No?" in Introduction to Bilingual Education, Bilingual-Bicultural Educational Series, ed. Luis Ortega (Anaya Las Americas: New York, 1975) (unpaged).

28. Ray C. Rist, "Student Social Class and Teacher Expectations: The Self-Fulfilling Prophecy in Ghetto Education," Challenging the Myths: The Schools, The Blacks, and The Poor (Cambridge, Mass.: Harvard Educational Review, 1971), p. 70. See also, Clarence Senior, "Newcomers, Strangers, and Schools," in Schreiber, The School Dropout.

29. Ronald J. Samuda, "Racial Discrimination through Mental Testing: A Social Critic's Point of View," IRCD (Information Retrieval Center on the Disadvantaged) Bulletin, May 1973.

30. U. S., Commission on Civil Rights, Report V: Mexican American Education Study, Teachers and Students (March 1973), p. 43.

31. National Education Association and American Association of School Administrators, Educational Policies Commission, Education and the Disadvantaged American, p. 19, as cited by Clarence Senior in Schreiber, The School Dropout, p. 112.

32. Cities investigated by the Commission and its State Advisory Committees included Boston, Mass.; Chicago, Ill.; New York, N. Y.; Bridgeport, Conn.; Springfield, Mass.; and Philadelphia, Pa.

33. According to a recent New York Times article, Hispanics (Puerto Ricans and other Spanish origin groups) comprised 27.7 percent of the 1974 student population in the New York City public school system (grade and high school) while Hispanic teachers were 3.1 percent of all teachers in the school system. "Laid-Off Teachers Tell About Broken Careers," New York Times, June 24, 1976, p. 36M.

34. "Statistical Projection of Need for Spanish-Speaking Teachers: 50 States and 18 Leading Cities," paper presented by Samuel B. Ethridge, Director, Teacher Rights, National Education Association, before the National Bilingual Institute, Albuquerque, N. M., Nov. 30, 1973.

35. Illinois SAC Report, pp. 7, 13, and 15.

36. Massachusetts SAC Report, pp. 9 and 95.

37. Pennsylvania SAC Report, pp. 5 and 8.

38. Connecticut Advisory Committee to the U. S. Commission on Civil Rights, El Boricua: The Puerto Rican Community in Bridgeport and New Haven (January 1973), p. 22.

39. Ibid., p. 19.
40. New Jersey Advisory Committee to the U.S. Commission on Civil Rights, Transcript of Open Meeting, Camden, N.J., July 12, 1971, p. 125.
41. Testimony of Lydia Corcino in Pennsylvania SAC, Transcript of Open Meeting, p. 570.
42. Candido de Leon, President, Hostos Community College, interview in New York City, N.Y., Nov. 22, 1974 (hereafter cited as De Leon Interview).
43. Mike Fucili, Counselor, Temple Opportunity Program, Temple University, interview in Philadelphia, Pa., Dec. 3, 1974. For additional comments on the negative role of some guidance counselors in the Philadelphia public school system, see the Pennsylvania SAC Report, pp. 11-13.
44. John H. Niemeyer, "Home-School Interaction in Relation to Learning in the Elementary School," in The School Dropout, p. 122.
45. Massachusetts SAC Report, p. 16.
46. Illinois SAC Report, p. 53.
47. Sylvia Ortega, "Some Needs of the Spanish-Speaking Child in Bridgeport, Connecticut" (West Hartford, Conn.: University of Hartford, 1970), cited in Perry Alan Zeikel, An Evaluation of the Effectiveness of Selected Experimental Bilingual Education Programs (1972), p. 29.
48. Illinois SAC Report, p. 17.
49. Massachusetts SAC Report, p. 17.
50. Illinois SAC Report, p. 52.
51. N.Y. Education Law § 2590.
52. For a discussion of the Decentralization Law of 1969, see U.S., Commission on Civil Rights, Public Education for Puerto Rican Children in New York City, Staff Report, printed as Exhibit 5 in New York Hearing, pp. 305-319 (hereafter cited as Staff Report: Education).
53. This includes selection of textbooks and other educational materials, provided that materials have been approved by the chancellor.
54. Staff Report: Education, in New York Hearing, p. 317.
55. The Board of Examiners is the body which qualifies all candidates for positions in the New York City school system.
56. N.Y. Education Law §§ 2590-e, g, j (McKinney 1970).
57. The Board of Education of the City of New York states: "Since September 1972 there has been an Office of Bilingual Education at the Central Board which has responsibility for providing such technical assistance." Irving Anker, Chancellor of the Board of Education of the City of New York, letter to John A. Buggs, Staff Director, U.S. Commission on Civil Rights, June 18, 1976, p. 4. It appears likely that the office of bilingual education was created in response to the criticisms such as those voiced at the Commission's hearing in New York City in February 1972.
58. 20 U.S.C. § 236 et seq. (1970).
59. Staff Report: Education in New York Hearing, p. 377-380.
60. 20 U.S.C. § 800(b) et seq. (Supp. IV 1974).

61. Staff Report: Education in New York Hearing, p. 379. According to Hernan LaFontaine, executive administrator of the Office of Bilingual Education, New York City Board of Education, $4 million were received by the city for Title VII programs for the school year 1973-74. See Hernan La Fontaine, "Introduction to Bilingual Education," in Urban, Social, and Educational Issues, eds. Dr. L. Golubchick and Dr. B. Persky (Kendall Hunt: Dubuque, Iowa, 1974), p. 26.

62. Staff Report: Education, pp. 380, 382.

63. See Statement of the U.S. Commission on Civil Rights on Bilingual Bicultural Education before the General Education Subcommittee of the House Education and Labor Committee, Apr. 17, 1974. The Commission strongly supported the extension and expansion of Title VII, with increased appropriations for research, teacher training, and curriculum development. The Commission supported similar measures before the Senate Committee on Labor and Public Welfare, Oct. 31, 1973.

64. Staff Report: Education in New York Hearing, p. 383-384.

65. Larry Kaseman, staff member, Bureau of Equal Educational Opportunities, U.S. Office of Education, HEW, interview in Washington, D.C., July 8, 1974.

66. In these programs, national origin minority children are grouped in transitional classrooms away from the regular classes in a school. This separation can last up to 3 years.

67. The Commonwealth of Massachusetts General Laws, Chapter 71A. 1971.

68. Illinois SAC Report, p. 64.

69. Ibid., p. 66.

70. Diego Castellanos, Perspective, The Hispanic Experience in New Jersey Schools, New Jersey State Department of Education, (January 1972), p. 8.

71. However, "The New York State law actually permits six years of bilingual instruction if the local school administrators apply for approval of three years beyond the initial three year period." Irving Anker, Chancellor of the Board of Education of the City of New York, letter to John A. Buggs, Staff Director, U.S. Commission on Civil Rights, June 18, 1976.

72. "Bilingual Education, A Statement of Policy and Proposed Action by the Regents of the University of the State of New York" (1972), p. 10. The Regents of the University of the State of New York is the policymaking body for the State Educational system.

73. Ibid., p. 7.

74. Ibid., p. 11.

75. School Administrator's Memorandum 491 of Mar. 10, 1972, cited in Pennsylvania SAC Report, p. 21.

76. Ibid., p. 22.

77. Statement of Ewald B. Nyquist, President, University of the State of New York and Commissioner of Education in New York Hearing, p. 521. In Chicago, more than 60 percent of the 40,800 students who spoke Spanish as a first language received no special English language assistance. Only 4,000 received any form of bilingual-bicultural instruction. Another

12,000 are estimated to be enrolled in ESL programs. (Illinois SAC Report, pp. 46-47).

78. 414 U.S. 563, 566 (1974).

79. Paul Berdue, attorney, San Francisco Neighborhood Legal Aid Foundation, Chinatown office, telephone interview, Sept. 3, 1976.

80. Aspira of New York, Inc. v. Board of Education of the City of New York, 72, Civ. 4002 (S.D.N.Y., Sept. 20, 1972).

81. This chapter was submitted to the Board of Education of the City of New York for review and comment prior to publication. See letter from Chancellor Anker to John A. Buggs, Staff Director, U.S. Commission on Civil Rights, June 18, 1976.

82. ASPIRA of America, founded in New York City in 1961, is an educational nonprofit organization which provides counseling and leadership development programs for Puerto Rican youth. Funded by Federal and State governments and by various private foundations and corporations, ASPIRA has affiliates in New Jersey, Pennsylvania, New York, Illinois, and Puerto Rico.

83. A motion to dismiss the complaint had been filed by defendants on November 15, 1972. On January 23, 1973, the court denied that motion in all respects, and the defendants filed an answer to the complaint on February 9, 1973. After lengthy pretrial discovery, plaintiffs in February 1974 moved for summary judgment, asking the court to render a decision on whether a violation of law existed, without a trial of disputed facts. The defendants opposed summary judgment, stating that adequate supportive services were being provided to plaintiffs. Plaintiffs argued that, in actuality, there were students not receiving services. (See "History of Bilingual Suit," Aspira of New York, Inc., pp. 1-3.)

84. Consent Decree at 2, Aspira v. Board of Education, 72 Civ. 4002 (Aug. 29, 1974). By consenting to the entry of the decree, plaintiffs did not waive any rights they have under the 14th amendment, and defendants did not admit to having committed any violations.

85. Richard J. Hiller, staff attorney, Puerto Rican Legal Defense and Education Fund, Inc., interview in New York, N.Y., Mar. 3, 1976 (hereafter cited as Hiller Interview).

86. Dr. Murray Hart, Superintendent, Board of Education of the City of New York, interview in New York, N.Y., Dec. 11, 1974 (hereafter cited as Hart Interview).

87. Dr. Michael Costelloe, Director, Project Management Team, Office of the Chancellor, Board of Education of the City of New York, interview, Dec. 11, 1974 (hereinafter cited as Costelloe Interview).

88. The L.A.B. has been the subject of some dispute between the parties, and was eventually brought before the court for consideration. See 394 F. Supp. 1161 (S.D.N.Y. 1975). The court ruled that the English L.A.B. was to be administered to all Hispanic students. Those who fell within the bottom 20th percentile were to be given the Spanish L.A.B. Those

who scored better in Spanish than in English were members of the class, and were entitled to the program.

89. Marco Hernandez, Assistant Director, Office of Bilingual Education, Board of Education for the City of New York, interview, Dec. 10, 1974 (hereafter cited as Hernandez Interview).

90. Community Service Society of New York, Report on Bilingual Education: A Study of Programs for Pupils With English-Language Difficulty in New York City (June 1974).

91. In addition to its basic per capita allowance from tax levy funds, the district receives supplementary tax levy funds, for funding special programs. The basic tax levy funds are city funds allocated to the school districts on a formula basis. They amount to the per capita allocations which are disbursed to the districts.

92. Hiller Interview.

93. Ibid. The Board of Education commented that "in fairness it should be made clear that the Board of Education is more than 90% in compliance with the Consent Decree. This is a remarkable achievement considering the fact that more than 60,000 eligible children had to be identified, tested, and programmed." See letter from Chancellor Anker to John A. Buggs, Staff Director, U.S. Commission on Civil Rights, June 18, 1976.

94. Victor Marrero, Chairman of the Board, and Herbert Teitelbaum, Legal Director, Puerto Rican Legal Defense and Education Fund, Inc., Press Release, Aug. 29, 1974, p. 2.

95. This figure was reached by estimating the percentage of Puerto Ricans included in the Spanish-surnamed total enrollment in several States for fall 1972 (from HEW's Racial and Ethnic Enrollment Report). The percentages of total Puerto Rican student enrollment (85 percent in New York and Connecticut, 90 percent in New Jersey, 45 percent in Illinois) were based on estimates by HEW, Aspira, and various higher education officials in the different States.

96. See New York Times, June 13, 1976.

97. Hearings before the Select Committee on Equal Education Opportunity for the U.S. Senate, 91st Congress, Part 8, Equal Opportunity for Puerto Rican Children (November 1970), p. 3796.

98. American Council on Education, The American Freshman: National Norms, reports for fall 1972 and 1973 (Washington, D.C.).

99. National Academy of Sciences, Commission on Human Resources, Summary Report 1973: Doctorate Recipients from United States Universities (Washington, D.C., May 1974), p. 4.

100. Of 337 students placed in college by ASPIRA of Illinois in 1972-73, half came from families receiving public assistance, and the remainder from families earning less than $7,000. ASPIRA of America Annual Report, 1972-73 (New York), p. 23.

101. Statement of Louis Nunez, ASPIRA of America, in Senate Hearings on Equal Education Opportunity for Puerto Rican Children, p. 3796.

102. Elizbeth W. Suchar, Stephen H. Ivens, and Edmund C. Jacobson, Student Expenses at Postsecondary Institutions, 1975-76 (New York: College Entrance Examination Board, 1975), p. 41.
103. The Carnegie Commission on Higher Education recommended that 29 to 41 new community colleges and 19 to 26 comprehensive colleges be established in the major cities of the eight States with largest Puerto Rican population: New York, New Jersey, Pennsylvania, Massachusetts, Illinois, Connecticut, California, and Florida. See New Students and New Places: Policies for the Future Growth and Development of American Higher Education (New York: McGraw Hill, 1971), pp. 142-44.
104. "Free access" higher education is defined to include "low cost, admission of 'the majority' of high school graduates, and an absence of geographical and psychological barriers." (College Entrance Examination Board, Barriers to Higher Education (New York, 1971), p. 11.
105. DeLeon Interview.
106. Isidro Lucas, Chicago Regional Office, Department of Health, Education, and Welfare, interview, Nov. 19, 1974 (hereafter cited as Lucas Interview).
107. Illinois State Scholarship Commission (1974).
108. New Jersey Department of Higher Education, The Educational Opportunity Fund, Fourth Annual Report, 1973-74 (Trenton, N.J.).
109. Pat O'Reilly, Office of Student Financial Aid, CUNY, New York City, telephone interview, Jan. 14, 1975.
110. DeLeon Interview.
111. Yolanda Sanchez, Office of the President, City College of New York, telephone interview, Jan. 10, 1975 (hereafter cited as Sanchez Interview).
112. Frank Negron, Director of Affirmative Action Program, CUNY, interview in New York City, N.Y., Nov. 26, 1974.
113. James Blout, Geography Department, telephone interview, Nov. 20, 1974.
114. DeLeon Interview, and Estella McDonnell, Aspira of New Jersey, interview, Nov. 26, 1974.
115. Aleda Santana, counselor, City College "Seek" Program, New York City, telephone interview, Jan. 16, 1975.
116. U.S. Department of Health, Education and Welfare, Digest of Educational Statistics, 1971, p. 137.
117. Bob Smith, ETS, Princeton, N.J., telephone interview, Dec. 12, 1974.
118. Jerry Lieberman, Department of Behavioral Science, Essex County Community College, interview in Newark, N.J., Nov. 26, 1974 (hereafter cited as Lieberman Interview).
119. Maximino Torres, Proyecto Pa'lante Director, Northeastern Illinois University, Chicago, interview, Nov. 19, 1974 (hereafter cited as Torres Interview).
120. Carmen Puigdollers, Puerto Rican Studies Department, Lehman College, New York City, interview, Jan. 13, 1974 (hereafter cited as Puigdollers Interview).

121. Samuel Betances, Political Science Department, Northeastern Illinois University, interview in Chicago, Ill., Nov. 19, 1974 (hereafter cited as Betances interview).
122. Lieberman Interview.
123. Russell Daniel, former director, Student Resource Center, Temple University, interview in Philadelphia, Pa., Dec. 3, 1974.
124. Maria Blake, Department of Community Education, Newark-Rutgers University, N.J., interview, Nov. 26, 1974.
125. DeLeon and Betances Interviews.
126. Manuel del Valle, Puerto Rican Legal Defense and Education Fund, interview in New York City, N.Y., Nov. 22, 1974.
127. Elaine Girod, Office of Admissions, Temple University, Philadelphia, Pa., interview, Dec. 3, 1974 (hereafter cited as Girod Interview).
128. Puerto Rican students seized the college's administration building in the spring of 1973.
129. "Puerto Rican Students Claim Yale Hiring Bias," New Haven Register, Mar. 28, 1974, p. 60; "Puerto Ricans Stage Protests Against Institutional Racism," Yale Daily News, Apr. 3, 1974, p. 1.
130. Latin Community Advisory Board, "Circle Campus vs. the Latin Community of Chicago," (mimeograph, October 1973), cited in Samuel Betances, "Puerto Ricans and Mexican Americans in Higher Education," The Rican: Journal of Contemporary Puerto Rican Thought, May 1974, p. 27.
131. "Students Protesting Cut in Minority Program Occupy Macalester Building," Minneapolis Tribune, Sept. 14, 1974, p. B-8; "Minorities Occupy 77 Mac; Compromise Reached on Budget Cuts," Macalester Today (October 1974), p. 2.
132. Girod, Puigdollers, and Nieves Interviews.
133. Torres Interview.
134. Northeastern Illinois University, Print, Oct. 21, 1974.
135. Macalester College, Macalester Today, October 1974; Michael O'Reilly, Puerto Rican Program, Macalester College, letter to James Corey, U.S. Commission on Civil Rights, Dec. 11, 1974.
136. Maria Calanes, Spanish Department, Temple University, Philadelphia, Pa., interview, Dec. 6, 1974.
137. National Commission on the Financing of Postsecondary Education, Financing Postsecondary Education in the United States (December 1973), p. 114. (hereafter cited as Financing Postsecondary Education).
138. 20 U.S.C. § 1070c (Supp. IV 1974).
139. Financing Postsecondary Education, p. 115.
140. Ibid., p. 116.
141. Data from the Bureau of Postsecondary Education, HEW.
142. Carnegie Commission on Higher Education, Higher Education: Who Pays? Who Benefits? Who Should Pay? (New York: McGraw, 1973), p. 41 (hereafter cited as Higher Education: Who Pays?).
143. Financing Postsecondary Education, p. 95.
144. Ibid., p. 96.

145. New Jersey, The Educational Opportunity Fund, Fourth Annual Report, 1973-74, pp. 1 and 8.
146. Ibid., Table 2.
147. Girod and Fucili Interviews.
148. College Entrance Examination Board, New Approaches to Student Financial Aid: Report of the Panel on Financial Need Analysis (New York, 1971), p. 9.
149. Higher Education: Who Pays?, p. 41.
150. CUNY, College Discovery Program Fact Sheet (February 1974).
151. Ibid.
152. 20 U.S.C. § 1070d (Supp. IV 1974).
153. U.S. Department of Health, Education, and Welfare, Bureau of Postsecondary Education, Division of Special Services for Disadvantaged Students.
154. David E. Lavin and Barbara Jacobson, Open Admissions at the City University of New York: A Description of Academic Outcomes After Three Semesters (April 1973).
155. New Jersey, The Educational Opportunity Fund, Fourth Annual Report 1973-74, p. 8.
156. Torres Interview.

Patricia Sexton

SCHOOLS: BROKEN LADDER TO SUCCESS

School administrators have been under fire in East Harlem and elsewhere. In New York's lower East Side, school principals locked
horns with the area's Mobilization for Youth project; charges and
demands for resignation were made on both sides. The principals
claimed they were being harassed by the parents.

Such parent arousal is new to these schools. Formerly,
the word of the school authorities was gospel. The new vocal chords
that parents in slum schools are exercising are hard to manage.
The new voice comes out loudly at first, louder than intended as
the bottled up complaints burst forth. Then parents learn to speak
in normal tones. In the meantime schoolmen will probably continue
to take a verbal beating and perhaps worse. Many have asked for
it; some have not.

Parents blame the school for the child's failure to achieve.
The school blames the parents, directly or by implication. In some
cases the blame is harsh: "They (the poor) are animals. They
don't care about their children. How can we be expected to do anything?" More often the "blame" takes the form of pity rather than
accusation: "They are so poor and deprived and apathetic that they
can't do anything. The families are broken, the children have no
fathers. What can the school do?"

Both pity and accusation have the same effect: the abandonment of hope and responsibility for achievement and change. While
some schoolmen have now turned from low IQ scores to conditions
and "deprivation" in the home as explanations of failure, few have
turned to the school for explanations. Those asking for change have
favored a "different" program of instruction for the poor. A good

Reprinted by permission from Spanish Harlem: Anatomy of Poverty,
New York: Harper & Row, 1965, pp. 47-70. Copyright © 1965 by
Patricia Cayo Sexton.

idea, but what it has often meant in practice is "easy learning" or detours around mastery of academic skills.

A composition written by a sixth grade Puerto Rican boy in East Harlem, and reproduced exactly as written, reveals the size of the problem:

> I would like to have good teachers because some teachers like to hit the children so the children don't come to school because of that. Some of the classmates like to pick on the children that don't like to fight so the classmates pick on them. Some school don't give good lunch and some of the window are broken. The chairs aren't good the desk are bombing and you can't write on it and some of the hallway are written with chalk or crayon. Some teachers don't teach us in every subjects. So the children don't learn a lot. So the teachers leave them back.

We, the Puerto Rican people, in our way of life, do not practice separation of race either by law, by custom, by tradition or by desire. Notwithstanding this and suspectedly because of this, in the nomenclature of race relations on the Continent, we are designated neither White nor Negro, but a special group denominated Puerto Ricans.

This objectivity, aggravated by our distinctiveness of culture, has made us the victims of the same type of discrimination and social persecution that is visited upon the Negro group of this Country. The result has been to make us more conscious of the justice and righteousness of the cause of the Negro in America today. We therefore, feel impelled to identify ourselves with the Negro's struggle and lend him our support, while at the same time conserving our own cultural integrity and our way of life.

We, therefore, launch ourselves into the arena of today's struggles for a full and complete education alongside the Negro with the full knowledge that by so doing we are advancing our own cause.
-- Preamble to the "Draft Resolution on the Education of the Puerto Rican Child in New York City," issued by The National Association for Puerto Rican Civil Rights, February 6, 1964.

East Harlem schools are segregated schools in the sense that, in all but four schools, 90 per cent of the students are Negro and Puerto Rican. They are not segregated in the sense that Central Harlem's schools are segregated. The Puerto Ricans, a large percentage of them light skinned, make the difference. East Harlem's schools do not look segregated. Indeed, if the "nomenclature of race relations" designated Puerto Ricans as white, the schools in East Harlem would be fully integrated.

The Puerto Ricans' feelings about segregated schools are very different from the Negroes'. They do not have the history and the sense of exclusion that Negroes have, and, because many of them are in fact white, they have much less trouble "integrating."

When the first city-wide school integration boycott in New York came along, the citizens' school committee of East Harlem hesitated. Puerto Ricans were not strong for protest or integration, the feelings of whites were mixed, and strong Negro sentiment was not forthcoming for various reasons. After lengthy debate, led mainly by whites on both sides, the school committee finally supported the boycott. On the day of the boycott, its support was, like Central Harlem's, more than 90 per cent effective.

Whatever else it did, the boycott sparked parent and community interest in East Harlem. Parents and youths poured into the preboycott rally, and the older hands who had been begging parents to attend meetings asked, "Where did they all come from?" They came to protest. They had grievances, and they came to air them. For many of these parents it was the first time at a school meeting. Few Negro or Puerto Rican men attended, but the women came, and a number of white men.

School integration achieved by busing, a method championed in New York mainly by middle-class Negroes in the ghetto, has had less appeal in East Harlem than in other places. Puerto Ricans have held back from the integration and civil rights struggle, and many whites in East Harlem school groups feared that busing would remove the active parents from the schools. These whites seem to have one object: to build East Harlem into a real community. Both urban renewal and bused integration run contrary to their goal when they threaten to disrupt the community and remove the more "participating" citizens.

When East Harlem turned out for the integration boycott it was the first time in the community's history, or the city's, that Puerto Ricans joined with Negroes in protest and pursuit of a common goal.

Even the militant CORE youths, committed to organizing and building in the neighborhood, were lukewarm to busing anyone out of the community. They wanted to upgrade the neighborhood schools and tended to read citizen sentiment as also indifferent to bused integration. One Negro organizer said:

The people in the community are not interested in integration. They just want better schools and better teaching for their kids. In Central and West Harlem there are many people who have a slightly better income level, slightly better earning capacity, and are more articulate than people in East Harlem and want integration.

And a white organizer joined in:

The integration issue is irrelevant if you're trying to beat
the rats off your children at night. We're not up to that
point yet. You have to be above the survival level--I
shouldn't speak not being black--you haven't got much energy
left. Not only that, integration is a horrible experience for
people. If your children are limited in the education they
get, you really put them through a terrible experience by
sending them elsewhere.

Still, East Harlem went all out for New York's first integration boycott ... but not for the second.

A powerful argument for school integration is found in the
transfer of eighty-three students from East Harlem to white, middle-
class Yorkville.

"We found children who improved in many ways following
transfer," a report said. [1] "In one, or two, just a handful of
cases, there was little noticeable change, but in the majority of
cases the children showed dramatic improvement in their school
work, in their attendance and, generally, they showed renewed vigor
and interest in school."

After parent protest, these East Harlem children had been
bused to white schools to relieve overcrowding and promote integration. Only 7 per cent of eligible children in one school and 2 per
cent in the other signed up to transfer. Of these, fifty-eight were
Negroes, twenty-two were Puerto Ricans, and three were Chinese.

Both the parents and children were far from being the most
destitute in these schools. Of the 83 who transferred, 34 were
reading on or above grade level. Most parents set high educational
goals for their children. Sixty-seven parents planned that their children complete high school; 39 that they attend college; and another
14 favored college if other conditions were met. Only 16 had not
attended parent meetings in school. Fifty of the parents had attended high school, 21 were high school graduates, and 4 had some
college. Fifty-two of the children had fathers at home: forty-one
did manual labor, 11 had professional or white collar jobs. Only
10 mothers were employed full time.

What happened to student conduct at the integrated school?
There were 13 changes reported, all improvements. As for interest
in school, 47 showed an increase, one a decrease. There were 13
changes in attendance records, all improvements. There were 52
changes of "work habits;" 51 were improvements and one was a decline. Only 5 parents said they were disappointed with the transfer;
11 were "pretty well satisfied;" and 55 said that they were "well
satisfied."

Some people complained that the most interested parent leadership "had bused their children out and were lost to East Harlem's
schools." For this reason they opposed further bused integration.

It appears much easier to integrate schools that are not co-educational. In 1959 East Harlem's Benjamin Franklin High School was all boys. It was 29 per cent Negro, 28 per cent Puerto Rican, and 43 per cent "other," i. e. white. When it became coeducational, in 1960, the "others" dropped from 43 per cent to 20 per cent. Catholic schools that are sexually segregated are, for this reason, easier to integrate racially.

Increasingly, both whites and Negroes are leaving the public school integration crisis and transferring to Catholic parochial schools. Both go to escape mounting Negro enrollment in public schools. Before World War II, one in twelve students in the United States was enrolled in Roman Catholic schools; now the ratio is one in eight. Catholic school enrollment between 1945 and 1962 increased 129 per cent (to 5. 5 million students), while public school enrollment grew only 69 per cent (to 38. 8 million students). The integration conflict seems to be swelling parochial schools.

Some Catholic schools in East Harlem provide a common meeting place where racially mixed youth groups have relatively familiar contact. There are few such places in East Harlem.

The Catholic schools are strictly disciplined, and parents are virtually required to attend school meetings. East Harlem's St. Cecilia's Church bulletin, in a message to parents, said, "After a short business meeting the parents will meet the teachers and receive their report cards. " Report cards are one insurance that parents will come. The Catholic school is better able to handle integration than the public school for at least three reasons; segregation of the sexes in many Catholic schools, the natural and sometimes arbitrary controls of ethnic mixture, and centralized church authority.

In New York about half of all Negro and Puerto Rican children go to public schools that are at least 10 per cent "other" (white). It is not known what proportion of these integrated minority children are Negro. In New York the biggest integration hurdle is the primary school. Secondary school students can travel on their own to integrated schools. Small children cannot, and their parents (both Negro and white) are often reluctant to have them bused outside the neighborhood. A state education department report proposed educational parks as a long-range integration solution and, for the short term, an integrated "middle school," starting in the fifth grade (5 through 8), to which children would be bused if necessary. The purpose of these proposals is to make integration possible by drawing students from a larger and more heterogeneous area. The feasibility of these parks is unknown since few people have much experience with them.

The Quality Issues

We're asking for a new school. It will be a ghetto school, but we can improve the educational level and move them

downtown. For four years they say, "Well, you'll have your
school this year." Then they say, "We can't fit it into the
city budget."

They said they had no money for repairs. Then after three
boycotts, they sent some men around to build a garbage bin
and they also built some partitions around the toilets. They
think that way! You bug them and they put up a board around
the toilet which is in the lunchroom.

> --An eighteen-year-old CORE organizer.

Education is said to be a ladder for the poor to climb up,
but in East Harlem it is rickety and many steps are missing. Of
the sixteen elementary schools in East Harlem, twelve have over-
capacity enrollment. Four out of five junior high schools are overcrowded. [2] The result is a short school day for students who should
have a long one.

Educators stress nursery and early childhood education. Yet
only a few of East Harlem's schools had a full five-hour first grade.
About one out of three or four children, it is estimated, enter first
grade without kindergarten. Space for kindergarten classes has been
in short supply, and the schools have seldom recruited among parents for enrollment. Often there has been a long waiting list for
kindergarten. In New York children who have gone to kindergarten
are usually put automatically in top "ability groups" in first grade,
where they tend to stay throughout school.

New schools in East Harlem came slowly and never kept up
with demands made by new housing projects and population. Schools
should be included in the ground floors of new projects in order to
keep pace with population growth and integrate the school into the
community.

"Tear down the armory, and put up a school" was the slogan
of an East Harlem mass demonstration. The site demanded was an
"integrated" one within white territory to the south. The armory
has been used, among other things, as a polo ground by wealthy
East Siders and as a police stable. Citizen demands have persuaded
the board to earmark funds for a school on the site.

One school that would send pupils to the proposed new school,
had three different principals in five years and a 90 per cent turnover of teachers. While the average teacher-turnover in New York
City as a whole has been 10 per cent, the turnover in East Harlem
has been 20 to 25 per cent.

In one recent year, 57 per cent of East Harlem's school
teachers had permanent licenses, 25 per cent were substitutes, 18
per cent had probationary licenses. In the junior highs, 44 per cent
had permanent licenses and 43 per cent were substitutes. Many licensed teachers in junior highs taught subjects they were not licensed
to teach. Many with only elementary licenses were teaching in junior
highs. [3]

Reading and IQ scores of East Harlem children decline with age. In the third grade, students in one district scored 2.8 on a reading test compared with the city average of 3.5. By the eighth grade, the East Harlem students were two full years below grade level.

By the eighth grade their IQ score was 83.2, compared with 103.4 for the city. In the third grade it had been 91.2, compared with 98.8 for the city.

In the junior high schools, 12 per cent of students were reading above grade level, 8 per cent on grade level, 10 per cent one year below grade level, and 70 per cent more than one year below grade level.

As for what the children think about school, the compositions of sixth grade students, quoted exactly, describe some of their wishes and needs: A Puerto Rican girl wrote:

> I would like to be change is to have a better playground where the children could enjoy. Or perhaps a big swimming pool and around it many fountains. Or to have better clean Bathrooms and to have better teachers that could teach you all different languages, all maybe a better auditorium where many people of all over the world could come and make us happy, and in the auditorium could have better comfortable seats, all maybe better hallways.

A Negro girl wrote:

> I would like to have more teachers in the school where the children could have different subjects everyday. And the school need more bathrooms because they have one each bathroom on each floor, they need at least three bathrooms on each floor. And they need a bigger auditorium because this auditorium is too small for this many children that they have here.

The children are inclined to blame themselves for their failure to learn. And, on the top of their mind always is fear or concern about physical abuse. Sixth graders commented:

> Suppose you were the teacher and you explained something and I said, "I wasn't listening" and you explained it again, and I wasn't listening again. You would get mad, right? Some of the kids are real bad. Some of the teachers don't know how to hit kids. You hit with a ruler. You should see the Catholic school. You talk to somebody and the sister she tell you to stand up and she takes the ruler and she hits you real hard two times on each hand.

> If a person wants to learn, he will concentrate, and he wouldn't get whipped, because by whipping a person he'll

just go on and do it again. Like my brother, he's real bad.
He do everything in his classroom. He pull up girls' dresses.
He knock down chairs. This teacher hit my brother, and he
was all black and blue and he was bleeding. The teacher has
no right to hit no child, they should send for his mother.

My father says if I get too much unsatisfactory, he's gonna
whip me. Because if my mother waste her time getting up
at 7 o'clock to wake me up, for me to do nothing, it's my
fault. I admit it. I don't listen to nothing what my teacher
says.

I think the teachers should treat us better, you know. We're
young, we don't hardly know nothing. You know, when you
tell them something, they say, "Where'd you get that strange
story or something." You tell them the truth but they don't
believe you or nothing. But I think it's not the teacher's
fault. It's up to you. True.

Teachers' Comments

Some teachers try and succeed. Others try and fail. Some don't
try, at least not very hard; they give up almost before they start.
One East Harlem teacher of a "medium slow" fifth grade (not a
"bottom" class) was having trouble and, like many others, was at
the point of throwing in the sponge:

> I won't try to teach them something like social studies. They
> don't have the basic concepts. This is true even in reading.
> You can't relate to them. When they do hit a story that means
> something there is a dramatic difference in their comprehen-
> sion. I can't say why some stories mean something and
> others don't. Social studies is a complete loss. Probably
> the only thing you can do is tell them social studies through
> a story, but this is not social studies. It is nothing like how
> laws are made or why a railroad was built in a certain place.
> You shouldn't call story telling social studies....

This teacher had found one clue to her pupils' learning--that
there was a "dramatic difference in their comprehension" when a
story meant something to them, but she didn't know where to take
this clue, how to find stories and social studies material that had
meaning.

Another teacher of a "slow" sixth grade had found many other
clues and had a different approach and attitude to her students:

> By demanding correct speech at all times I have found their
> Spanish accents have just about disappeared by now. Their
> vocabularies have begun to enlarge. They must give reports
> orally, without a paper. They must know what they have
> written so well that they can remember the main ideas. At

the beginning of the year I read aloud to them a great deal
of the time, pointing out to them what I thought about pitch,
timbre, pace, etc. Then we used a tape recorder and immediately they became self-critical, saying things like "That
isn't me, is it?" and "I didn't say it that way, did I?" I
didn't let them do any written work at first. After a few
trips we would start to have open discussions. For a few
weeks we did almost only talking. I tried to move them from
specifics to abstracts. ... Then we were ready for writing
... During the Panama crisis they did sequential pictures of
why we went there in the first place, how the situation grew
during the years, and how things began to deteriorate. I put
the pictures up for a week. Then we discussed what the pictures meant. We had discussed the Panama crisis so thor-
oughly that the students seemed to feel personal about it by
the time they sat down to divide up the topic for the illustrations.

Though this teacher had a "bottom" group, she had succeeded,
according to her story, in teaching the children something about social studies, even in such remote places as Panama, and she had
successfully modified their accents. Another teacher said:

Things just don't make an impression on these children. We
haven't found the way to teach them. For some reason they
don't relate to school. The reason is that their whole culture
is different. The only way to teach them is to repeat things
25 times unless for some reason it means something to them.
They are not motivated at home. They can't learn unless they
see the specific reason for doing something.

Another teacher feels the children have a problem of "how to
get along," and that they are learning this even up until the third
grade. Not until the fourth grade are they ready to learn concepts.
"They play too much. Discipline of themselves is a problem--per-
haps it is at the root."

One East Harlem teacher felt that "Negroes and Puerto Ricans
have incorrect perception. They probably see only vague outlines.
This would explain why they do so poorly in reading."

Many teachers complain about administrators and say that
they stand in the way of learning. One said: "Administrators are
my main problem as a teacher. They are not creative. They think
the slow child won't get things. I don't think this is fair. For example: going to the World's Fair. Only the top three classes will
go. The children feel this and think they should live up to the expectations that they won't catch on to things."

Another teacher complains that beginning teachers are not
properly briefed, that they should be told "how far down these children are." Teachers have to keep "starting over at a lower level."
New teachers never get "concrete help." Administrators give teach-

ers the wrong books; "the books are too high;" and many are "worth-less." There is no communication between teachers; there should be "some way for new teachers to get rex-o-graphed materials that more experienced teachers have drawn up."

One experienced and highly rated teacher in an East Harlem school explains her monitor system for keeping order, her attitudes toward the children and the rewards they need:

> I appoint monitors at the beginning of the year. I make it clear that I will change an appointment if they are not worthy. I give awards each month based on conduct, grades, appear-ance, and manners. I jot down things that are outstanding for each child--good or bad. I used to give an assembly award for dressing but now the whole class dresses right so I had to give it up. They must be given recognition. For instance, right now I have left them alone for this interview. It lets them know that I trust them. I don't have monitors to take names. There is no tattletaling in my class. One way I helped build up this spirit was by taking them on trips and doing things together. They know they must act a certain way in order to do these things.

Knowledge, at its most useful, is an accumulation of wisdom and experience from the past. Teachers, custodians of this accumu-lated knowledge, have virtually no access to the accumulated exper-ience of the thousands of other teachers who have been out in combat with the same problems, and who have through trial and failure worked out some successful methods. Neither the colleges of education nor the school administrators have done much to help the novice teacher who leaves her middle class cocoon to venture out into the slum school. The schools of East Harlem are filled with these novice teachers, most of them eager but lost.

Dr. Kenneth Clark has said: "The concept of the culturally deprived child is a new stereotype, a new excuse, a new rationali-zation for inadequate education of minority group children. Instead of those responsible for their education being made to teach them, all sorts of alibis are provided. The only thing that will really mat-ter is the total reorganization of the educational system in these communities."

"On the evidence available to date," he went on, "one is forced to conclude that the major reason why an increasing number of Central Harlem pupils fall below their grade levels is that sub-standard performance is expected of them. For this, the schools, principally its administrators, must shoulder the major responsibility, although the community must share some of the blame."[4]

Dr. Clark cited the data below in support of his statement (see next page):

Table 2

Assessment of Pupil-Potentials in Central Harlem

	Principals	Assistant Principals	Teachers
1. Per cent reporting that one-fourth or less of the pupils have college level potential.	45	62	53
2. Per cent expecting one-half or fewer of their pupils to finish high school under present conditions.	32	57	46
3. Per cent expecting one-half or fewer of their pupils to finish high school under conducive conditions.	4	19	3
4. Per cent stating that greater learning potential in their students was a major change necessary to carrying out professional duties.	9	14	4

The Rev. Milton Galamison, leader of New York's school boycott, has contended that "in the Negro school the child is not being taught. The basic problem we are fighting in the segregated school is one of attitude, which expresses itself in low expectations on the part of middle-class teachers whose concept of a human being is not met by these children. The most liberal teacher will say, 'If the Negro child had an equal economic, cultural and social background, he could learn as well as other children.' This if-ism results in 'not much teaching and not much learning.'"

Puerto Ricans have also reacted to the schoolman's concept of "cultural deprivation," but in a different way. The Puerto Ricans are proud of their culture. Joseph Monserrat, of the Commonwealth of Puerto Rico, asks:

Is a culture that has for four centuries been able to maintain the individual dignity, value and worth of all its members (despite differences in race and class) a deprived or disadvantaged culture when compared with one that has been striving to achieve these values and has as yet not been able to do so?

Some of the dispute has to do with word meaning. The term "culturally deprived" suggests the negative aspects of low income culture. In some cases, as in Dr. Frank Riessman's excellent book, The Culturally Deprived Child,[5] the positive aspects of this culture are stressed. This emphasis tends to boost rather than depress teacher morale and expectation.

Another version of the deprivation theme has entered the

arena, put there by psychoanalysis. The school gets the child too late, the argument goes, after the early, formative years, and therefore can do very little either by integrating or improving the quality of education for the disadvantaged. While the argument has strong points, suggesting that much more attention should be given to nursery schools and the child-rearing education of parents, it also suggests what is not proven, that most Negroes and other disadvantaged adults are deficient in the affection, care, or instruction they give to infants. It also ignores the achievements of older children under ideal school conditions and the regenerative effect on older youths and adults of civil rights activity.

What is observed in East Harlem and other slum schools is that children compare favorably in their achievement until the third and fourth grades, when they begin a relative decline. This might indicate that the critical period for the child is in these years rather than the preschool years.

Recognizing the importance of the infant years, however, it is essential that the schools reach not only the child but the mothers as well. On the assumption, true or not, that there are remediable deficiencies in parental care, the parent becomes as much an object of instruction as the child. One hypothesis that should be examined is that the children of the poor are typically put out on their own and given weighty responsibilities at an early age. The parents are burdened, and they are forced to pass on these burdens to young children. Families are often large, and children follow fast after one another. The mother of the large, impoverished family has no help with her chores and no time for the child who is no longer an infant who needs her continuous attention. The child is put on his own and given responsibilities for the care of other children. In short, the child may not be given the individual attention he needs for growth. He becomes a small adult at an age when more advantaged children are just beginning to emerge from infant dependency.

In this sense also, "deprivation" has a double edge. The "deprived" child, because of his early adulthood, knows a great many things that the advantaged do not, too much perhaps. If the schools were able to make use of this knowledge, the "deprived" child might be at an advantage rather than a disadvantage in school.

East Harlem is split into two school districts, as it is split into two police precincts and two political (assembly) districts. The district in the north section also includes schools in Central Harlem. The southern district includes many white, middle class schools, and Martin Mayer, one of the country's leading writers on the schools, has been chairman of its local school board, a group whose functions and powers are rather like those of parent-school groups. Both boards are said to be hard-working and close to the people. They have formed a closer link between citizen and school.

Whites tend to dominate East Harlem schools. All school

principals are white and so are almost all administrators. Negroes and Puerto Ricans, in fact, have little to say officially about what goes on in East Harlem's schools. Even unofficially, as parents, they take a back seat and are usually silent. The chairman of the East Harlem Schools Committee, the main citizen group, has been a white woman whose Negro husband operates a small business. Whites usually do most of the talking and leading in the committee.

There is little true integration in parent groups. "In every school," says Mrs. Nora Bowens (a white woman who works full time on schools for the East Harlem Project), "there is one major ethnic group dominating the parent groups. There is seldom a mixture." In recent years a number of Negro and Puerto Rican leaders have come forth, and active parent groups are found in some schools.

The Schools Committee, from its inception in 1954, had spurts of energy. Until the first integration boycott, the committee was for a time at low ebb. It did not know what to do next. Its initial job had been to get new schools for East Harlem. Now many feel the committee should branch out into the troubled area of curriculum, an area that has in the past been held as the exclusive jurisdiction of schoolmen.

In East Harlem the major parent demand on curriculum is that the children improve reading and academic skills. They do not ask for dreary drills or any particular "method" of instruction. They want only improved learning. The schools are touchy about instrusions into curriculum. According to Preston Wilcox of the East Harlem Project, the worst verbal beating he has gotten from the schools came after he asked the question at a meeting: "How can we get parents involved through curriculum?"

The Parent-Teacher Associations are criticized by many active people in East Harlem because they seldom take on any real issues. Some feel that the PTA's do only what the principal tells them to do--money-raising, cake sales, socials--and are upset when curriculum is raised.

Ellen Lurie gave much of the initial drive to the Schools Committee in the early 1950's. The first act of the committee was to petition for new schools. Ninety parents gathered and went to the Board of Estimate with proposals. "Women sat up nights working on their speeches; and Negro and Puerto Rican parents did things they never thought they could do," said Mrs. Lurie. The new schools came, but they did not automatically bring quality education. Hence, the new desire of East Harlem parents to take up curriculum and quality issues. The committee's demands for quality include: academic achievement, smaller class size, preschool programs, full five-hour first grades, remedial reading in grades 3 to 6 rather than junior high, "gifted child" classes in each school rather than in one separate school, separate classes with "positive programs" for children who are discipline problems, involvement of parents in the educational process as school aides. [6]

Negores and Puerto Ricans also want the history of their people to be taught in the schools, and not just to their own children. One young Negro CORE organizer put it this way: "I said to the history teacher, 'Why are you showing me a book where there's only one paragraph about Negro history. You mean to tell me 400 years, with only one paragraph.' The teacher told me, 'Sit down. Lincoln freed the slaves and you should be glad you're in this part of the book.' Look in the index and look at page 389, one paragraph, 'Negroes.' The kids don't like this at all. Some books don't even have a paragraph. They just put down a few people like Joe Louis and Marian Anderson."

Some citizens in East Harlem are now raising questions, not only about curriculum but about the "power structure" of the schools. They want more Negro and Puerto Rican representation at high levels in the schools. As it is, of more than 1,200 top-level administrative posts in New York's school system, only about four are held by Negroes. Of some eight hundred principals, only several are Negro. Out of a nine-man city school board, only one is a Negro; and there is no Puerto Rican member--in a city where 40 per cent of public school children are Negro and Puerto Rican.

What do East Harlem's children think about school? They are seldom asked. When they are, they express little interest in what they are learning in school. The reasons they give for going to school and doing well almost always bear on future prospects, not on the rewards of learning but on other rewards that school can offer. These remarks of sixth grade Negro and Puerto Rican boys are typical:

> You go to school to get an education so when you grow up you can get a decent job, and you can have a high school diploma. You can go to a decent junior high, and then you can go to a decent high, and go to a decent college, and get a decent job. When we grow up it'll be the nuclear age, and we couldn't do the jobs our fathers do. They'll be done by machines.

> If you don't go to school you'll be a nobody. You'll be a drifter all your life.

> School's OK, cause when you get a job you got to count things in your mind, not on your fingers. If you don't go to school you grow up to be dumb. You won't be able to get a job.

> Whenever I wake up I say, you better study, you know, to get a better education. If you study now, you could become something big. When you grow up you get a good job.

A Perspective

Citizen unrest usually moves in an upward spiral. Among the poor it has moved in the past few years, during the peaks of the civil rights revolt, from apathy to agitation, then back to some midpoint of constructive criticism and interest.

In New York City--big, anonymous, and noisy--a person with a grievance must make a loud noise to be heard. The school boycotts and the rent strikes were that loud noise. They made the conditions of the poor at last visible and audible. But the momentum of the revolt (the agitation cycle) was slowed by many related factors and may not move on again for some time. Among these factors were: a presidential election, the civil rights and poverty bills, the summer ghetto riots that injured only Negroes but frightened everyone, the inability of Negro leaders to bargain their demands and to work in unity, the white backlash, the fatigue of Negro and white activists who wearied of danger and street demonstrations, the northern liberal retreat when the demonstrations came into the back yard, the failure of the demonstrations to produce immediate and visible results.

More than anything, the school boycotts and the demands for bused integration of de facto segregated students in New York brought the civil rights struggle to the door of the white middle class liberal and caused him to withdraw support from direct action and demonstration. These liberals, most of whom genuinely seek equality and integration, balked at busing and dropped away from groups like CORE, leaving their future as exclusively direct action groups in doubt.

The loudest and most racist "busing backlash" came from conservative organizations (Parents and Taxpayers) in middle class Queens. A quieter, more moderate, and sadder backlash came from sections of the Jewish community, which more than other groups in New York, have been in contest with Negroes and Puerto Ricans over scarce facilities in the public schools. Many liberals have, furthermore, been reluctant to acknowledge the presence of unequal educational opportunities for Negroes and Puerto Ricans in the North. Their response has been: We did it despite discrimination, why can't they?

Having reached this cyclical plateau, very little mass agitation over schools can be expected in the nation's northern ghettos. This will not mean much in East Harlem since it was a reluctant partner in the boycotts in the first place, and since the Puerto Ricans keep it from being a Negro ghetto.

The integration boycott has undoubtedly had a positive effect on the schools of East Harlem. It has brought public attention and extra aid to the schools. It has clearly informed schoolmen that parents are dissatisfied with the progress of their children in school. Above all, it aroused parents and citizens in East Harlem to a new interest in the schools and showed them that they could through their own actions, influence school policies. Schoolmen have traditionally complained that parental apathy is responsible for low achievement

in slum schools. The boycott aroused many parents from this
"apathy."

Insofar as East Harlem has held back from direct action in
the schools, however, it seems likely to get less from the schools
and from new aid programs than Central Harlem, Brooklyn, and
other more "militant" communities. The wheel that squeaks loudest
usually gets the most grease.

East Harlem schools need a lot more grease. New schools,
relief from crowding, experienced teachers, preschooling, a suitable
curriculum and texts, belief in the children, contact with parents,
small classes--all are visible needs. Integrationists claim it is impossible to have quality education in segregated schools. This may
be true, but the claim is unproved, either way. The effect of quality education on achievement in ghetto schools is unknown because
it is virtually untried. Only in the last few years has much serious
experimentation with teaching methods and curriculum for the disadvantaged been tried. And only now are some suitable reading materials being prepared.

Concentrated research and development in education, comparable to the R&D that in the technological and scientific worlds are
regarded as essential to progress, should be supported by public
and foundation funds. This educational R&D should pull together
available knowledge about successful methods in educating the disadvantaged, and develop new techniques and curriculum.

It is unlikely that quality education can be brought to the
slums until members of disadvantaged minorities are brought into
the schools--many of them, at high and low levels, as board members and as educational aides either in the schools or outside them.

The schools need new ideas and new energy. One way to get
them is to democratize decision-making and bring in teachers, parents, and children on decisions and planning. The organization of
teachers into unions and parents into citizen groups is already beginning to bring the knowledge and wisdom of these two vital groups
to bear on educational decision-making. Their participation so far
has mainly taken the form of protest, brought on by their general
exclusion from school decision-making.

In the money-versus-method controversy, some experts say
that only money, lots more of it, will make any difference in slum
schools. On the other hand people like Martin Mayer say that money
will make little or no difference, that new methods and new approaches
must be found. Both money and methods are needed. About half as
much money is being spent on New York's slum child as on the child
in the better suburbs of New York. With such expenditures, the poor
could, without question, be given quality education. The point is,
money will not be forthcoming in such amounts, even though the nation can afford it. So the question becomes: What are the most
efficient and economical ways to give top-quality education to the poor?

The complaint made by Negro leaders that the schools expect too little of Negro and Puerto Rican students is well taken. Many schoolmen do not really expect that the poor could, with proper instruction, learn as much and do as well as middle class students. This may, indeed, be the major flaw in the slum school: low expectations on the part of administrators, teachers, children, parents. This does not mean, however, that the disadvantaged can always start at the same place as the advantaged. The imposition of impossibly difficult texts and assignments on children inevitably leads to frustration and failure. But, with suitable methods and extra help, these children ought to be able to end at the same place as other children.

In East Harlem and similar communities there are, then, at least three routes to change in the schools: (1) change of attitude, motivation, expectation from failure to success; (2) new instructional and organizational methods; (3) community arousal and the power and pride it can provide to impoverished citizens.

One solution to the teacher shortage and the general shortage of educated leadership in the slum community would be to offer special housing buys to teachers in the neighborhood schools. If the housing offered were good enough, it would not only attract and hold teachers in the community, but would provide a needed link and understanding between school and community. These teachers would also provide community leadership. In East Harlem, for example, one of the most active minority group leaders and two of the most active white parents are also teachers who live and work in East Harlem. For the most part, however, teachers in slum schools are "absentee professionals" who leave the school and neighborhood promptly at three o'clock.

A very heavy burden has been put on slum schools. It is put there because there are so few other services and institutions in the slum community. So the school must tend to the intellectual, emotional, recreational, organizational, etc. needs of children and adults in the community--or at least it is asked to try. Other groups and agencies should be brought in to help carry this heavy weight. In particular, a massive volunteer program of youths and adults, recruited from the community, universities, women's clubs, church groups, etc., should be drawn in to help with tutorials, trips, and other instructional needs.

Though the problems of East Harlem's schools are glaringly visible, it should be said that in many schools the impression is one of health, not sickness. Teachers can be found in every school who are creative and effective and who like and respect the children. Most of East Harlem's children seem to like school, and most are well treated. Moreover, most of the children appear well dressed, clean, happy, and healthy. It is striking to the stranger who may be expecting tattered urchins or a scene from Oliver Twist or The Blackboard Jungle. This is perhaps the neglected part of the story. The better known and more tragic part is that so much is wrong; so much is needed and so little received.

It is the same as in the neighborhood. Health and disease live alongside each other--great strength and serious weakness. We tend to pick on the soft spots, the weaknesses, because they need attention. At the same time the strengths need to be seen, credited, and built upon.

References

1. Releasing Human Potential, prepared by the East Harlem Project and the New York City Commission on Human Rights, 1961.
2. The total overload is 2,700 in the elementary schools and 440 in the junior highs as of the end of 1963.
3. Source: Bureau of Educational Research, Board of Education.
4. Harlem Youth Opportunities Unlimited, December 12, 1963.
5. New York: Harper & Row, 1961.
6. At the time of the first school boycott, a new Puerto Rican civil rights group issued its first detailed manifesto of school demands. Its five stages of demands were:

Language: Spanish should be part of the curriculum of all elementary schools, and all teachers should have a working knowledge of Spanish. High schools: Vocational high schools as they currently exist should be abolished, along with the general course diploma. All junior highs should be integrated within a year. Reading retardation: A five-hour daily instruction period should be guaranteed; IQ tests should be abolished; changes should be made to "reflect the specialized learning problems of Puerto Ricans;" a "positive image of the Puerto Rican child and his culture must be fostered to enhance the child's motivation for learning."

Teacher training and recruitment: Since there are only 230 Puerto Rican teachers out of 40,000 intensive recruitment should be undertaken, teachers with Spanish accents should be accepted. Teachers should be taught greater understanding and appreciation of Negro and Puerto Rican culture, "not in sterile terms of Brotherhood but aimed at handling specific situations that destroy the dignity and morale of the Puerto Rican youngster."

Puerto Rican Representation: "Neither white dominant groups nor the Negro minority can speak for the Puerto Rican who must speak for himself." An effort should be made "to insure Puerto Rican parent participation in the process of decision-making which will influence at all levels the future of his child's education, and that such participation be received in a courteous, dignified manner." A Puerto Rican should be appointed to the next school board vacancy.

PUERTO RICAN STUDY RECOMMENDATIONS

I. Introduction

The Puerto Rican Study is a four-year inquiry into the education
and adjustment of Puerto Rican pupils in the public schools of the
City of New York.

People want to know:
> How to assess their ability to learn English?
> How to group for instruction?
> How to teach them English?
> How to reach their parents?

The Study's objectives are summed up in three main problems:

First--What are the more effective ways (methods) and materials
for teaching English as a second language to newly arrived
Puerto Rican pupils?

Second--What are the most effective techniques with which the schools
can promote a more rapid and more effective adjustment of
Puerto Rican parents and children to the community and the
community to them?

Third--Who are the Puerto Rican pupils in New York City's public
schools?

II. What are the effective methods and materials for teaching English as a second language to newly arrived Puerto Rican pupils?

A. The study found such a great diversity in approach toward teaching English that it decided to experiment to determine which ap-

Reprinted by permission from Puerto Rican Study for the Program
in New York City Schools." Board of Education, City of New York.
1958. (Mimeo.)

proach was best. Three methods are singled out for experimentation, the vocabulary method, the structured or language patterns method, and the functional situations or experimental method.

The conclusions arrived at were:
1. The experiential approach leads to greater gains in ability to <u>understand</u> English than does the vocabulary approach.
2. The vocabulary and structural approach lead to greater gains in ability <u>to write</u> English than does the experiential approach.
3. The vocabulary approach leads to greater gains in ability to <u>speak</u> English than does the experiential approach.
4. <u>None of</u> the methods leads to significant gains in ability <u>to</u> <u>read</u> English.

The <u>Puerto Rican Study</u>, therefore, recommends an integration of all three approaches plus a more direct attack on reading.

B. To integrate the several methods described above the <u>Puerto Rican Study</u> developed two series of related curriculum bulletins, keyed to the prescribed New York City course of study. These are the series of nine Resource Units and the four Language Guides. Each Resource Units bulletin contains three or more resource units.

The units and guides for use in the Junior High Schools were prepared on a needs rather than on a grade basis. These are the orientation, extended orientation and transition stages.

The need for continuous evaluation of these bulletins with an eye towards their revision and improvement is strongly emphasized. Also emphasized is the need to develop pupil reading material keyed to these Resource Units.

The bulletins, "A Doorway to Science," and "A Guide to the Teaching of Science," are supplements to the course of study in Science in the Junior High Schools for use with Puerto Rican pupils not ready for the regular stream, who are still in the process of learning to read English. They are geared to help these children adjust to their new environment and cover such basic areas as safety, health, and nutrition.

The Junior High School bulletins are also recommended for use with orientation pupils in the High Schools. In addition, to meet the needs of orientation pupils in High Schools, the "Resource Units for Puerto Rican Pupils in Teaching Occupations" were developed.

For the kindergarten class, the Study experimented with the bulletin, "Directing Language Learning in Early Childhood." Further development or revision of this bulletin as experimental use might dictate was left to the Bureau of Curriculum Research.

C. In 1955, it was decided that more precise information was needed as to the numbers, characteristics of Puerto Rican pupils, distribution by age, grade, and need for instruction in English. Forms were prepared and filled out. From these a seven-point rating scale as to English ability, A to G, was developed. This scale has a high degree of validity for use in formulating city-wide policy and programs for improving the educational opportunities of Puerto Rican pupils.

D. Practices helpful to adjustment and learning of non-English-speaking Puerto Rican children in the primary grades are:

1. Themes should be closely related to children's own experiences.
2. Pupils need physical and motor activity.
3. Children need time to explore the classroom and to use materials and equipment.
4. Children need to hold and manipulate objects. Possession means so much.
5. Occasional periods of silent watching and socializing are needed.
6. Where children's initiative, spontaneity and active interest are at a high level, they make great strides in language learning.
7. Cultural differences in the interest in toys and games exist. Puerto Rican children need toys and games, but different ones, sometimes, than mainland children. Teachers must bridge these cultural differences.
8. There is need for a continuity of experiences between kindergarten and first grade, first grade and second grade.
9. A great deal can be done within the classroom to improve cultural social adjustment if the teaching load is not overwhelming and if teachers are given additional help.
10. Sympathetic school supervisors and warm, understanding teachers are crucial to the success of the program.

E. Further conclusions and recommendations to achieve continuing improvement of methods and materials are listed below:

1. The elements of vocabulary, structure, quality of speech and experiences in learning English as a second language are interrelated.
2. The aural-oral approach is essential until the child gains some skill in the oral use of English.
3. A daily period of direct teaching of English in an experiential setting plus continuing attention to pupils' use of English throughout the school day are two elements of method essential to learning.
4. Non-English-speaking children learn much from their peers, therefore, the content and method of instruction should be organized to promote learning through association with English-speaking children.
5. Knowledge of Spanish is useful but not essential to the successful teaching of English to non-English-speaking classes.

6. The resource units are designed for use in mixed classes as well as in classes made up wholly of non-English-speaking pupils.

7. In addition to the need for preparing informational and recreational type reading material for non-English-speaking pupils, there is a need to gather audio-visual aids such as tape-recordings (for use with individuals and groups to improve speech), films, film strips, radio and television. There is also the need to develop a guide to the social and cultural background of all non-English-speaking pupils as cultural information for pupils and teachers.

8. The use of the core program (combining the English and Social Studies periods) is recommended for non-English-speaking pupils in High Schools. Additional Resource Units, keyed to the maturity and experiential background of pupils, should be developed for the High Schools.

III. There is a need to formulate a uniform policy for the reception, screening, placement and periodic assessment of non-English-speaking pupils. The alternative is to continue the present high rate of retardation and perennial orienteeism.

A. Instruments for assessment:

1. The Study found the following instruments useful and suggests that they be used regularly in screening and assessing progress of non-English-speaking pupils until such time as the Bureau of Educational Research may find or develop better tests or tests of equal value:
   a. The USE test--Ability to understand spoken English
   b. The Gates Reading test--Primary and Advanced
   c. The Lorge-Thorndike Non-Verbal Test.

2. Forms were developed to help screen and place non-English-speaking pupils.

B. The Puerto Rican Study proposes three broad categories of class organization.

1. The regular class--mainland pupils and bilingual pupils rated A or B on the Scale of Ability to Speak English. Bilingual pupils rated C, who have demonstrated ability to carry the work of the regular class, may be admitted.

2. The mixed class--mainland pupils and non-English-speaking pupils rated C, D, E or F on the Scale of Ability to Speak English.

It is desirable that these classes should not exceed 25 in ADA (average daily attendance) and that the non-English-speaking group should not exceed from one-fifth to one-third of the class register (that is from 5 to 9). In general, provision should be made to transfer pupils who show marked improvement to regular classes. Such transfer may be made at any time during the year.

3. The orientation class--made up entirely of non-English-speaking pupils needing aural-oral instruction in English, that is, pupils rated C through G.

Here, too, it is desirable that the class register should not exceed 25 or 22.5 ADA. Should the majority of this class fall in E-F-G categories, a class standard not to exceed 20 ADA is recommended.

Opportunities must be provided pupils in orientation classes to associate with mainland children. This is partly achieved through the daily use of the curriculum materials prepared by the Puerto Rican Study. The goal may be further achieved through association with mainland children in the lunchroom, the gymnasium, the playground, club activities, assembly programs, and other school activities that cut across class and grade lines.

C. Other types of special class organizations approved by the Puerto Rican Study are:

1. The CRMD class for the educable mentally retarded pupils. It is assumed that non-English-speaking children would qualify for admission to these classes in about the same proportion as do mainland children.
2. The reception or C class--to serve only the needs of the newly arrived non-English-speaking pupils.

These classes should be set up only where a school has a considerable number of new arrivals. Only C through G rated pupils should be assigned. The teaching should be highly individualized and pupils transferred out as rapidly as they show evidence of ability to carry the work of the regular classes.
3. The transition class--for retarded language learners.
4. The core class--for non-English-speaking pupils in the High Schools. These are double period classes, combining social studies and language arts, taught by a single teacher.

D. Staffing

Schools with non-English-speaking pupils must be adequately staffed. The Puerto Rican Study found the use of Substitute Auxiliary Teachers (SAT's), Puerto Rican Coordinators, School-Community Coordinators and Other Teaching Positions (OTP's) in both elementary and junior high schools essential. The functions of the OTP to be stressed are specifically defined.

In the Senior High Schools, teachers of English to non-English-speaking children and Guidance Counselors are needed.

After describing the service the holders of these positions may be expected to perform, the Puerto Rican Report specifies that when an Elementary School has 100 non-English-speaking pupils or 10% of its total registration is non-English-speaking, an SAT should be assigned. If the school has less, then it should be provided with the services of an SAT on a part-time basis. If the school has more, a coordinator of the program for non-English-speaking pupils is needed. As the number of non-English-speaking children increases other OTP pisitions will be required. When a junior high school has 75 or more non-English-speaking pupils rated C-G, a Coordinator should be assigned. When such schools have 500 or more non-English-speaking pupils, a School-Community Coordinator should be assigned to them as well as OTP personnel.

To help the district superintendents' office counsel and assist schools with their problems as well as to coordinate the services, a coordinator from the Bureau of Community Education should be assigned to the office. The Study suggests that this be tried in three districts.

At headquarters, the Puerto Rican Study recommends the continuation of the Puerto Rican Planning Committee; the placing of responsibility for the smooth operation of the Puerto Rican Program in the hands of the associate superintendent in charge of the Curriculum Division; the assignment of a Puerto Rican Coordinator in each of the three operating divisions--Elementary Schools, Junior High Schools, High Schools.

Following are proposals affecting the staffing of bureaus:
1. A full-time staff member, qualified in audio-visual instruction and in the education of non-English-speaking pupils, be added to the Bureau of Audio-visual Instruction.
2. WHYE should be staffed to develop radio programs specifically keyed to the resource units and language guides prepared by the Puerto Rican Study for use in teaching non-English-speaking pupils.
3. The Bureau of Child Guidance needs a minimum of three terms of two persons each--one a psychologist, the other a social worker of Hispanic background, to examine those difficult cases where language is a barrier between examiner and pupil.
4. The Bureau of Community Education will need one or more additional supervisors to develop a more adequate program (method and content) for teaching English to Puerto Rican adults, in addition to the junior high school-community Coordinator and the assistants in the offices of the district superintendents for the development of leadership and social affiliation of ethnic groups.
5. In the Bureau of Educational and Vocational Guidance is needed personnel to provide the High Schools with competent counseling and testing by bilingual examiners working in close cooperation with teachers. Such personnel should be assigned to each High School on a full or part-time basis.

6. The Bureau of Educational Research must provide two types of service not now available to schools. One is in the area of testing non-English-speaking children, the other is an expansion of the Bureau's psychological service. This calls for additional personnel.

E. Problems of Teacher Education. The Puerto Rican Study recommends:

1. A carefully organized series of seminars for training teachers assigned to work with non-English-speaking pupils.
2. Summer workshops in Puerto Rico to promote a better understanding of Puerto Rico.
3. A re-examination and revision of in-service credit for teachers who work and help carry out the Puerto Rican program.
4. Coordinating efforts of colleges and universities within the metropolitan area in cooperation with the Board of Education to achieve greater unity of purpose and effort in developing both undergraduate and graduate programs for teachers who will work with non-English-speaking pupils, and to promote the mutual interests of Puerto Rico and New York City in developing a program that will be helpful to people everywhere confronted with similar problems of education and social assimilation.

IV. What are the most effective techniques with which the schools can promote a more rapid and more effective adjustment of Puerto Rican parents and children to the community and the community to them, and
Who are the Puerto Rican pupils in the New York City Public Schools?

A. The Puerto Rican Study, through an ethnic survey, obtained a profile of characteristics of pupils with Puerto Rican background. The findings were publised in 1956 and repeated in this final report.

B. A considerable amount of up-grading and down-grading of pupils transferring from Puerto Rico was found in New York City classes. These pupils present so many different patterns of educational history in relation to their age that they present serious problems in identifying, screening and placement to our schools. Schools must have a diversity of educational programs to meet the needs of so heterogeneous a group.

C. The Study divides pupils into four categories, (A) island-born, island-schooled, (B) island-born, mainland-schooled, (C) mainland-born pupils of Puerto Rican parentage, and (D) mainland-born pupils of non-Puerto Rican parentage. This includes pupils one or both of whose parents were born in a foreign country or whose parents were mainland born.

The Study concludes that there is a steady, progressional change from group to group as measured by the time spent in New York City or on the mainland, with respect to intactness of the family unit, the employment status of the father, reduction of crowded living quarters, and in the percentage of homes where English is used wholly or in part.

The apparent differences between the groups may be credited primarily to changes taking place in the social-cultural outlook of the home. Therefore, one potential means of accelerating the social-cultural adjustment of Puerto Rican pupils is to find ways and means of helping to facilitate the social-cultural adjustment of the parents.

D. Widespread public opinion holds the incidents of poor attendance, truancy, disciplinary problems, and welfare status of Puerto Rican pupils to be most discouraging. Frequently, analysis of school records produces quite a different picture. The Study concludes that:

1. Like other children, Puerto Rican children tend to become about as good or as bad as the children or youth with whom they associate.

2. While the proportion of Puerto Rican pupils who get free lunch exceeds the proportion of non-Puerto Rican children, we must keep in mind that free lunch is part of the educational pattern in Puerto Rico and that it is not a true measure of need or reliance on public welfare.

3. The record of school attendance in New York City of Puerto Rican children is quite comparable to that of mainland children. This is a great credit to them when we consider the degree of cultural deprivation under which so many of them live--the language barrier, the different climate in New York City as compared to Puerto Rico and the fact that there is no compulsory education law in Puerto Rico. Yet, when they become truants, they are more inveterate truants.

4. Illness is not the major cause of absence among Puerto Rican children.

5. Truancy is more prevalent in Junior High Schools than in Elementary Schools.

6. Non-Puerto Rican children exceed Puerto Rican children in the number of court referrals.

E. Findings of special studies on adjustment in schools made by Puerto Rican pupils follow:

1. Many newly arrived Puerto Rican pupils were not participating in classroom activities, were not learning but were quietly and unobtrusively "sitting-out" their allotted school time.

2. There are no shortcuts to understanding the progress of the individual child. No simple background factors can be isolated as explaining a child's difficulty or ease in adjusting

to school or neighborhood. Many areas must be studied. Included among these are inter-family relations and the personality structure of the child.

3. Can the Puerto Rican pupils learn English?

The records show that they can be expected to repeat the experience of other migrant groups and become well assimilated by the third generation. Their performance tends to improve each succeeding year spent in New York City schools. The rate of improvement decreases after the fourth year. Even their I.Q. goes up--which shows they adapt to our culture in time. The third generation should be able to compete on equal terms with their peers of like socioeconomic background. Their progress would be accelerated if the best that we know were applied in teaching and guiding them.

But even with the best teaching and guidance in the school, there would still be need for obtaining the active cooperation of the home in learning English and for helping children at all levels to find social acceptance.

F. On the relation of Puerto Rican parents to schools, the Puerto Rican Study holds that because Puerto Rican parents are preoccupied with problems of learning English, finding apartments, finding employment, and with problems of providing their families with food, clothing, and proper health protection, they are not ready to set a high priority on their children's school problems. The schools can't wait until they are ready. The Study ran into varied responses to its questions as to how far schools should be expected to help the parents.
The Study states the following:

1. The schools are important to the newcomers. They do come to school for guidance and such help as referrals to hospitals, clinics, welfare agencies, to get letters written for them and for advice on family problems.
2. The Puerto Rican parents tend to transfer the anxieties of living in new surroundings to fears and suspicion of their neighbors--even Puerto Rican neighbors.
3. Puerto Rican parents are timid rather than aggressive. They are not responsive to notices of parent meetings and school functions. Those who do attend are shy and nonparticipating. Meetings as usually conducted do not meet their needs.
4. Puerto Rican parents must be dealt with individually rather than in groups.
5. Puerto Rican parents come to see their children perform in assembly programs and to give help with trips, bazaars, cake sales, health drives, clerical work, sewing, as resource persons, and as interpreters. A few become leaders.
6. When meetings are well advertised and have Puerto Rican speakers, Puerto Rican parents attend.

7. Clubs are more successful than big meetings.
8. Schools have tried to work with parents in many ways.
They have tried using a school-community coordinator and
extending the services of SAT's. These have found personal, informal contact of most help. From this beginning,
they have developed mothers' clubs and gotten them to work
with parent associations on school functions. Given time
and scope to work informally, they can build friendly relations with the schools.

G. On factors in financing the education of non-English-speaking
children, the Puerto Rican Study reports that in 1956 the state
legislature voted additional state aid for this purpose. The
State Education Department accepted the Puerto Rican Study's
Scale of Ability to Speak English. A rating of C or below
makes one a non-English-speaking child. The additional costs
in educating non-English-speaking pupils justifying state aid are
described:

1. Cost of special staff (SAT, Puerto Rican Coordinators,
School-Community Coordinators, OTP's, SAT Officers,
High School Counselors).
2. Cost of special classes with lower registers.
3. Cost of keeping accurate additional records and follow-up
measures necessitated by high mobility.
4. Cost of producing special teaching material.

The Commissioner of Education recognized three types of special classes:
a. A class with 100% non-English-speaking children
b. A class mixed with 50% non-English-speaking children
c. A class that meets for special instruction one period a day,
but in other periods these children are in regular classes.

The 100% non-English-speaking class must be composed of fewer
than 25 ADA (Average Daily Attendance), which means 27 as an
average class register. All must be in C-G category on the
rating scale and must work as a class group the full day or at
least 80% of the school day under a single teacher or several
departmental teachers.

Classes of fewer than 10 may be included with special permission of the Commissioner.

The Board of Education may fix a minimum class standard between 10 and 25 ADA. This helps in setting up classes with
open registers for reception or orientation of new arrivals anticipated in June.

The 50% mixed class must have fewer than 25 ADA, half of
whom are non-English-speaking. This type of class should be
used with discretion because during its three years of experimental work the Puerto Rican Study found that where there are

1, 2, or 3 non-English-speaking children in a class, they are forgotten. As the concentration approaches 50 per cent, the teacher tends to divide the class in half, leading towards segregation. A concentration of thirty to thirty-five per cent was considered best. Therefore, there is need to have the Commissioner change the fifty per cent in ADA to allow for twenty or thirty per cent and still get one-half of the state aid.

V. Next Steps: Where The Puerto Rican Study Leads
Like other groups that have entered New York City, the Puerto Ricans, in the normal course of events, will become socially and educationally assimilated by the third generation. Neither we nor the Puerto Ricans can afford to wait that long. We must find ways and means of accelerating the learning and adjustment of first and second generation Puerto Rican and other non-English-speaking pupils. Twenty-three lines of attack on many fronts towards the aforementioned goal are listed:

1. Accept the Puerto Rican Study, not as something finished, but as the first stage of a larger, city-wide, ever-improving program for the education and assimilation of non-English-speaking children. To translate proposed measures into practice will take three to five years at the very best.

2. Take a new look at the philosophy governing the education of non-English-speaking children in New York City schools. Does educating them involve helping them to forget the language of their fathers? Does it involve creation of barriers between them and their parents? What attitudes are we inculcating?

3. Recognize that whatever is done for the non-English-speaking child is, in the long run, done for all the children. The schools' program must be adapted to the ability and the need of each individual.

4. Use the annual school census as a basic technique in planning the continuing adaptation of the schools to the needs of the non-English-speaking pupils. The probabilities are that the characteristics of Puerto Rican pupils will change within a decade or generation and that these changes will prove even more challenging to educational planning than their increase in number and distribution.

5. Recognize the heterogeneity of the non-English-speaking pupils. Part of the difficulty in learning English and in assessing their abilities stems from their different cultural background. This needs to be explored further.

(The Puerto Rican children are heterogeneous with respect to their native intelligence, prior schooling, aptitude for learning English, general scholastic ability, etc.) This heterogeneity must be taken into account in almost every contact the school has with the pupil.

6. Formulate a uniform policy for the reception, screening,

placement, and periodic assessment of non-English-speaking pupils. Putting the proposals made by the Study into effective operation in all schools is a major undertaking.

7. Keep policies governing the grouping of non-English-speaking pupils flexible. Place the emphasis upon serving the needs of the individual pupil. Discourage the practice of grouping new arrivals with grossly retarded language learners. Encourage the practice of a reception class for new arrivals where each pupil is given individual attention and is helped to achieve his best. These classes will require small registers, and teachers skilled in teaching and guidance of non-English-speaking pupils. Every teacher of a non-English-speaking child has a right to a profile of his prior schooling, his achievement, and his potential abilities.

Practices and proposals for grouping vary with different school levels.

8. Place special emphasis on reducing the present backlog of retarded language learners.
9. Recognize "English as a second language" as an area of specialization that cuts across many subject areas. It starts with the aural-oral approach leading gradually into reading and writing.
10. Use the curricular materials developed by The Puerto Rican Study to achieve unity of purpose and practice in teaching non-English-speaking pupils.
11. Capitalize on the creative talent of teachers in finding ways and means of supplementing and of improving the program for teaching non-English-speaking pupils. Develop materials to supplement those prepared by the Puerto Rican Study. Set in motion processes that will improve future editions of established courses of study.
12. Recognize and define the school's responsibility to assist, counsel and cooperate with parents of non-English-speaking pupils in all matters pertaining to the child's welfare. There is too wide a range of theory and practice on this issue.
13. Take a new look at the school's opportunity to accelerate the adjustment of Puerto Rican children and their parents through advice and counsel to parents on problems normally considered to be outside the conventional functions of the school.
14. Staff the schools to do the job.
15. Staff the proper agencies of the Board of Education to maintain a continuing program for the development and improvement of curricular materials and other aids to the teaching of non-English-speaking pupils.
16. Staff the proper agencies of the Board of Education, and set in motion the processes to maintain a continuing assessment or evaluation of techniques, practices and proposals.
17. Take a new, hard look at the psychological services provided for non-English-speaking children, especially for Puerto Rican children.

18. Through every means available, make it clear that the education of the non-English-speaking and their integration in an ever-changing school population is the responsibility of every member of the school staff.

19. Maintain, improve and possibly expand the program of in-service preparation initiated through the <u>Puerto Rican Study</u> for training special staff to assist in accelerating the program for non-English-speaking children.

20. In cooperation with the colleges and universities of Metropolitan New York, create a dynamic program to achieve unity of purpose and more adequate coordination of effort in the education of teachers and other workers for accelerating the program in the schools.

21. Use the varied opportunities available to develop an ever improving cooperation between the Department of Education in Puerto Rico and the Board of Education in New York City. Maintain the practice of operating summer workshops, consider more effective use that might be made of participants, develop a system of exchange of teachers between New York City and Puerto Rico, hold annual conferences of officials alternately in New York City and in Puerto Rico to examine practices, common interests and generally to promote the educational program for the Puerto Rican pupil.

22. In cooperation with the responsible representatives of the government of the State of New York, continue to explore the mutual interests and responsibility of the city and state for the education and adjustment of non-English-speaking children and youth.

23. Think of the City of New York and the Commonwealth of Puerto Rico as partners in a great enterprise.

PUERTO RICANS ON THE UNITED STATES MAINLAND:
A SUMMARY IN FACTS AND FIGURES

A. GENERAL POPULATION DATA

1. Number of Puerto Ricans in U.S. Mainland

In March, 1979, there were 12.1 million persons of Hispanic origin in the United States mainland: 7.3 million Mexican-Americans; 1.7 million Puerto Ricans*; 800,000 Cubans; 2.2 million Central and South Americans and persons of other Spanish origin.[1]

From 1970 to 1978, the Puerto Rican population grew by 27.5 percent.[2] In March, 1978, there were an estimated 1,823,000 Puerto Ricans in the U.S. mainland, compared to the 1970 census count of 1,429,396.[3] While Hispanics lead the minorities in growth rate,[4] the Puerto Rican community is the fastest growing Spanish-origin ethnic group.[5]

*Puerto Ricans have generally been undercounted in the census, and more dramatically so in estimates based on population samples. [Statement, page 3, Bureau of Census, Persons Of Spanish Origin in the United States, March, 1979, (Advanced Report), Series P-20, No. 347]

2. Age of Mainland Puerto Rican Population

The Puerto Rican ethnic group is the youngest ethnic group in the mainland U.S. In March, 1979, the median age of Puerto Ricans was 19.9 years, compared to 29.8 years for the total U.S. population, 22.0 years for all Hispanics, 21.1 years for Mexican Americans, 36.3 years for Cubans, 25.5 years for Central and South Americans, and 30.4 years for individuals not of Spanish origin.[6]

The Puerto Rican population has a heavy concentration of young people, particularly young males. In March, 1978, the median age of Puerto Rican males was 17.9 years, compared to 28.5 years for the total U.S. male population, 21.4 years for all Hispanic males, 21.2 years for Mexican-American males, 35.5 years for Cuban males, and 25.9 years for Central and South American males.[7]

The median age of Puerto Rican females was 22.4 years, compared to 30.6 years for the total U.S. population, 22.8 years for all Hispanics, 21. 3 years for Mexican-Americans, 37. 7 years for Cubans, 27. 3 years for Central and South Americans, and 23. 4 years for other Spanish origin. [8]

In March, 1979, the Puerto Rican community in the mainland was comprised of 935,000 females (54. 2%) and 813,000 males (45. 8%). [9]

Of Puerto Rican males, in March, 1978, 39. 0 percent were under 13 years of age; 17. 1 percent were between 14 and 21 years of age; 29. 1 percent were between 22 and 44 years of age; 45. 3 percent were over 21 years of age. [10]

Of Puerto Rican females, the same years, 34. 8 percent were under 13 years of age; 14. 6 percent were between 14 and 21 years of age; 35. 8 percent were between 22 and 44 years of age; 51. 8 percent were 21 years of age or older. [11]

Overall, in March, 1978, the age distribution of the Puerto Rican population of an estimated 1,823,000 persons was: 11. 3 percent under 5 years of age; 25. 4 percent between 5 and 13 years of age; 12. 9 percent 14 to 19 years of age; 24. 2 percent 20 to 25 years of age; and 26. 3 percent over 35 years of age. 65. 4 percent of the total Puerto Rican population were 29 years of age and younger, compared to 40. 6 percent for the total U. S. population. [12]

Given the special problems faced by youths, it is important to note that in March, 1979, 52. 3 percent of the Puerto Rican population were 21 years of age and younger, in contrast to 34. 6 percent of the total U. S. population, 47. 7 percent of the total Hispanic population, 49. 5 percent of the Mexican-American population, 32. 4 percent of the Cuban population, 40. 3 percent of the South and Central American population, and 33. 9 percent of non-Hispanic populations.

3.   Distribution of Puerto Ricans in U. S. Mainland

The majority of Puerto Ricans reside in the central cities of metropolitan areas.   In March, 1975, over 62 percent of the mainland Puerto Ricans resided within a 400-mile radius of New York City, but shifts in Puerto Rican populations have established new settlements and expanded older ones.   In 1970, there were 872,471 Puerto Ricans in New York State, 105,262 in New Jersey, 86,482 in Illinois, 44,555 in Pennsylvania, 36,305 in Connecticut, 24,394 in Florida, 6,769 in Michigan.   However, Puerto Rican communities have been established or expanded in most major cities and towns in the Eastern Seaboard, Central, Southwestern and Southeastern States. [13]

B.   FAMILY DATA

1.   Residence of Puerto Rican Families

In March, 1979, there were 434,000 Puerto Rican families in the mainland United States: 95. 8 percent resided in metropolitan areas; 79. 2 percent resided in central cities in those areas. In contrast, 66. 7 percent of all U. S. families resided in metropolitan areas and 27. 0 percent in central cities. Mexican-American families were distributed as follows: 85. 4 percent resided in metropolitan areas; 51. 1 percent resided in central cities; 14. 6 percent resided in non-metropolitan areas. [14]

2. Marital Status

In 1978, of the 504, 000 males and 650, 000 females 14 years of age and over in the mainland Puerto Rican community, 55. 3 percent of the males and 56. 4 percent of the females were married; 38. 7 percent of the males and 27. 2 percent of the females were single; 1. 6 percent of the males and 10. 6 percent of the females were divorced. [15]

3. Puerto Rican Familes, U. S. Mainland: Size and Composition

Besides being younger, Puerto Rican families had a lower median family income and a higher rate of poverty than all U. S. families and all Spanish-origin families as well.

In March, 1978, the mean number of Puerto Rican persons per family was 3. 78: 24. 3 percent of Puerto Rican families consisted of 2 persons; 22. 3 percent of 3 persons; 24. 1 percent of 4 persons; 17. 3 percent of 5 persons; 5. 8 percent of 6 persons; and 6. 2 percent of 7 or more persons. In comparison, 34. 2 percent of U. S. families consisted of 2 persons, 19. 5 percent of 3 persons, 18. 5 percent of 4 persons, 13. 1 percent of 5 persons, 6. 7 percent of 6 persons, and 8. 0 percent of 7 persons or more. [16]

In March, 1978, 41. 0 percent of Puerto Rican families were headed by females. While 39. 5 percent of all Puerto Rican families were in poverty, 74. 6 percent of Puerto Rican families headed by women were in poverty. (See section on "Women Data" for comparisons of Puerto Rican families to other families.)[17]

C. EDUCATION DATA

Persons of Puerto Rican origin had a significantly lower educational level of attainment than other persons in the U. S. and Hispanic populations.

1. Attainment

In 1978, whereas 31. 9 percent of the Puerto Rican population 14 years old and over were high school graduates, 38. 9 percent of Hispanics, 34. 1 percent of Mexican-Americans, and 52. 6 percent of other Hispanics 14 years old and over were high school graduates. [18]

Also, of 1,154,000 Puerto Ricans 14 years old and over, 10.9 percent completed 0 to 4 years of elementary school, 15.1 percent completed 5 to 7 years of elementary school, and 13.2 percent completed 8 years of elementary school. A slightly larger percent, 28.9 percent, completed 1 to 3 years of high school, 21.5 percent completed 4 years of high school, 10.4 percent completed high school and one or more years of college, 7.3 percent completed 1 to 3 years of college, 3.2 percent completed 4 years of college. [19]

2. Barriers to Employment and Education

In March, 1978, of 301,000 Puerto Rican males in the labor force, 33.8 percent completed 8 years or less of elementary school, 26.5 percent completed 1 to 3 years of high school, 28.8 percent completed 4 years of high school, 7.3 percent completed 1 to 3 years of college, and 3.6 percent completed 4 or more years of college. [20]

In March, 1978, of 171,000 Puerto Rican females in the labor force, 27.5 percent completed 8 years or less of elementary school, 18.1 percent completed 1 to 3 years of high school, 42.1 percent completed 4 years of high school, 8.2 percent completed 1 to 3 years of college, and 4.1 percent completed 4 years or more of college. [21]

In 1977, among Puerto Rican heads of families 25 years of age and over (400,000) a large percentage, 48.4 percent, completed only 8 years or less of elementary school, compared to 22.2 percent of U.S. heads of families in poverty, 29.2 percent of similar Hispanic heads of families, 25.6 percent of Mexican-American heads of families, and 27.6 percent of other Spanish-origin heads of families who completed only 8 years or less of elementary school. [22]

On the whole, compared to other groups, a significantly larger percentage of Puerto Rican heads of families in poverty had no high school education, or completed only a few years of high school. 43.5 percent of Puerto Rican heads of families in poverty completed only 1 to 3 years of high school, compared to 19.9 percent of similar U.S. heads of families, 26.4 percent of similar Hispanic heads of families, 23.5 percent of Mexican-American heads of families, and 15.9 percent of other Spanish-origin heads of families. [23]

3. Language Barriers: Education Related

While 10 percent of persons (ages 14 to 25) with English-language backgrounds were high school dropouts, 40 percent of those in this age group with language-minority backgrounds and who usually speak their native languages were high school dropouts. [24]

Hispanics who usually speak Spanish dropped out at a higher rate (45 percent) than persons in the aggregate of other language minorities who usually speak their native languages (30 percent). [25]

Compared with that of persons with English-language backgrounds, the dropout rate was 4. 5 times as high for Hispanics who usually speak Spanish, and 3 times for those of other language backgrounds who usually speak their native languages (30 percent). [26]

The dropout rate for persons with non-English-language backgrounds who usually speak English (12 percent) was close to the rate for those with English-language backgrounds (10 percent), but differed substantially from the rate for those who usually speak their native languages (40 percent). [27]

D.   INCOME DATA

In March, 1979, the median income of Hispanic families ($12, 566) was significantly lower than that of non-Hispanic families ($17,912), and the median income of Puerto Rican families ($8,282) was lower than for all other groups. [28]

1.   Income of Families

In March, 1979, the median income of Puerto Rican families was $8,282, compared to $17,640 for all U.S. families, $10,879 for all Black families, $12,566 for all Hispanic families, $12,835 for Mexican-American families, $15,326 for Cuban families, and $14,272 for other Spanish-origin families. [29]

In March, 1979, 15. 8 percent of Puerto Rican families had incomes of less than $4,000, compared to 5. 6 percent of all U.S. families, 9. 6 percent of all Hispanic families, 9. 3 percent of Mexican-American families, 5. 0 percent of Cuban families, 6. 8 percent of other Spanish-origin families, and 5. 3 percent of all non-Hispanic families. [30]

28. 2 percent of Puerto Rican families had incomes of $4,000 to $6,999, compared to 8. 7 percent of U.S. families, 14. 2 percent of all Hispanic families, 11. 7 percent of Mexican-American families, 10. 6 percent of Cuban families, 11. 5 percent of other Spanish-origin families, and 8. 4 percent of all non-Hispanic families. [31]

In 1977, 27. 7 percent of Puerto Rican families had incomes of less than $5,000.   Of all Puerto Rican families with incomes of less than $5,000, 64. 7 percent had no wage earners, 12. 0 percent had one wage earner, and 2. 4 percent had two wage earners. [32]

39. 4 percent of Puerto Rican families had incomes of less than $10,000.   Of all Puerto Rican families with incomes less than $10,000, 35. 3 percent had no wage earners, 46. 9 percent had one wage earner, and 12. 5 percent had two wage earners. [33]

In the same year, 55. 6 percent of Puerto Rican families had incomes of less than $15,000.   Of all Puerto Rican families with incomes of less than $15,000, 23.0 percent had one wage earner and 32.4 percent had two wage earners.[34]

In 1959, Puerto Rican family earnings were 71 percent of the national average, but by 1974, Puerto Rican family earnings dropped to only 59 percent of the national average, and continued to drop. By 1979, Puerto Rican family earnings were 47 percent of the national average. In 1959, 45 percent of Puerto Rican families had two wage earners, but by 1970, 20 percent had no earners, and by 1977, 35.3 percent had no wage earners. Generally, Puerto Rican families were worse off in 1979 than ten years earlier.[35]

2. Income of Workers

In 1977, the median income of Puerto Rican persons, 14 years old and over, was $5,445. At the time, 46.4 percent of Puerto Ricans had incomes of less than $5,000, 78.8 percent had incomes of less than $10,000, and 89.7 percent had incomes of less than $15,000.[36]

The median income of Puerto Rican males was $8,051: 29.4 percent had incomes of less than $5,000; 59.7 percent had incomes of less than $10,000; and 80.2 percent had incomes of less than $15,000.[37]

The median income of Puerto Rican females was $4,179: 62.2 percent of Puerto Rican females had incomes of less than $5,000; 92.8 percent had incomes of less than $10,000; and 99.1 percent had incomes of less than $15,000.[38]

E. LABOR FORCE PARTICIPATION DATA

Compared to other groups, Puerto Ricans had a lower rate of participation in the labor force. While adult Puerto Rican males in the labor force enjoyed employment rates approximating other ethnic groups, they had longer durations of unemployment and a higher rate of unemployment than other groups.[39]

1. Total Labor Force Participation

In 1979, 50.7 percent (512,000) of the Puerto Rican population were in the labor force. In comparison, 63.9 percent of the U.S. population, 64.2 percent White, 61.2 percent Black, 63.9 percent Hispanic, 66.9 percent Mexican-American, and 65.2 percent Cuban, were in the labor force.[40]

2. Males in the Labor Force

78.5 percent (285,000) of the Puerto Rican male population 20 years and over were in the labor force, compared to 79.5 percent of the U.S. male population, 80.0 percent White, 76.1 percent Black, 85.1

percent Hispanic, 87.7 percent Mexican-American, and 84.9 percent Cuban. [41]

3. Females in the Labor Force

36.4 percent (179,000) of the Puerto Rican female population 20 years and over were in the labor force, compared to 51.7 percent of the U.S. female population, 51.0 percent White, 56.0 percent Black, 48.6 percent Hispanic, 49.1 percent Mexican-American, and 54.5 percent Cuban. [42]

4. Youths in the Labor Force

31.2 percent (48,000) of the Puerto Rican youth population 16 to 19 years were in the labor force. In comparison, 55.8 percent of U.S. youth population, 59.2 percent White, 36.2 percent Black, 51.2 percent Hispanic, and 58.1 percent Mexican-American were in the labor force. [43]

F. EMPLOYMENT DATA

In 1979, the employment rate of Puerto Rican workers was less than in 1978. In comparison, all other groups had more workers in 1979 than in 1978.

1. Rate of Employment

In 1978, 470,000 Puerto Rican workers 16 years and older were employed; in 1979, there were 458,000. In 1978, 287,000 Puerto Rican male workers 20 years old and over were employed; in 1979, there were 284,000. In 1978, 184,000 Puerto Rican female workers were employed; in 1979, there were 179,000. In 1978, 48,000 Puerto Rican youths 16 to 19 years were employed; in 1979, there were still 48,000. [44]

2. Occupations and Employers

In 1979, of the 458,000 Puerto Rican workers, 90,000 were government employees, 347,000 were in private industries, and 16,000 were self-employed. 397,000 workers worked full-time, 13,000 worked part-time for economic reasons, and 48,000 worked part-time for non-economic reasons. [45]

Compared to the total U.S. population, Puerto Ricans had a higher rate of employment as operatives and laborers, and had a higher incidence of seasonal employment and a longer duration of unemployment.

In 1979, of the 458,000 Puerto Rican workers employed, 9 percent were professional, technical and kindred workers, 5 percent were managers and administrators, 4 percent were sales workers, 19 percent were clerical workers, 22 percent were operatives, 9 percent were craft and kindred workers, 6 percent were laborers, 3 percent were transport equipment operators, and 22 percent were service workers. [46]

In comparison, of 98,049,000 U.S. workers, 16 percent were professional, technical and kindred workers, 11 percent were managers and administrators, 7 percent were sales workers, 18 percent were clerical workers, 11 percent were operatives, 13 percent were craft and kindred workers, 5 percent were laborers, 4 percent were transport equipment operators, and 13 percent were service workers. [47]

Of 512,000 Puerto Rican workers in the labor force, 38 percent were white-collar workers, 40 percent were blue-collar workers, and 22 percent were service workers. In comparison, of 98,049,000 U.S. workers, 51 percent were white-collar workers, 33 percent were blue-collar workers, and 13 percent were service workers. [48]

In 1978, 293,000 Puerto Rican males 16 years old and over were employed: 26.2 percent were white-collar workers; 52.3 percent were blue-collar workers; 19.8 percent were service workers; and 1.7 percent were farm workers. [49] In comparison, 53,865,000 U.S. males were employed: 51.7 percent were white-collar workers; 32.3 percent were blue-collar workers; 13.5 percent were service workers; and 2.6 percent were farm workers. [50]

In 1978, 173,000 Puerto Rican females 16 years old and over were employed: 56.3 percent were white-collar workers; 30.9 percent were blue-collar workers; 11.9 percent were service workers; and 0.9 percent were farm workers. [51] In comparison, 38,099,000 U.S. females were employed: 63.9 percent were white-collar workers; 14.5 percent were blue-collar workers; 20.5 percent were service workers; and 1.1 percent were farm workers. [52] However, only 36.4 percent of the Puerto Rican female population are in the labor force, compared to 51.7 percent of the U.S. female population. (See section on "Labor Force Participation Data: Females in the Labor Force.")

G. UNEMPLOYMENT DATA

In 1979, Puerto Rican men, women, and youth, were less likely to be employed than their counterparts. Unemployment for these segments of the Puerto Rican population exceeded the national employment rate, and Puerto Ricans had the highest rate of unemployment among Hispanic groups.

1. Total Unemployment

In March, 1979, of 512,000 Puerto Rican workers 16 years old and over in the labor force, 10.5 percent were unemployed. In contrast, 5.6 percent of U.S. workers, 4.9 percent White, 11.4 percent Black,

8. 6 percent Hispanic, 9. 1 percent Mexican-American, and 6. 6 percent Cuban, were unemployed. [53]

2. Male Unemployment

In 1979, of 285,000 Puerto Rican males 20 years old and over, 7. 2 percent were unemployed, compared to 4. 0 percent of U. S. males, 3. 5 percent White males, 8. 8 percent Black males, 5. 8 percent Hispanic males, 5. 8 percent Mexican-American males, and 4. 7 percent Cuban males. [54]

3. Female Unemployment

In 1979, of 179,000 Puerto Rican females 20 years old and over, 10. 6 percent were unemployed, compared to 5. 5 percent of U. S. females, 4. 8 percent White females, 9. 9 percent Black females, 9. 8 percent Hispanic females, 11. 2 percent Mexican-American females, and 6. 6 percent Cuban females. [55]

4. Puerto Rican Youth and Adult Unemployment

In March, 1978, the unemployment rate of Puerto Rican persons 16 years old and over was 11. 7 percent, compared to 6. 6 percent for the total U. S. population, 9. 5 percent for Hispanics, 9. 6 percent for Mexican-Americans, 6. 9 percent for Cubans, and 9. 0 percent for other Spanish-origin persons. [56a]

In March, 1978, the unemployment rate of Puerto Rican males 16 years old and over was 11. 5 percent, compared to 6. 3 percent for U. S. males, 9. 0 percent for Hispanic males, 8. 6 percent for Mexican-American males, 8. 6 percent for Cuban males, and 8. 7 percent for other Spanish-origin males. [56b]

Also in March, 1978, the unemployment rate of Puerto Rican females 16 years old and over was 12. 2 percent, compared to 7. 0 percent for U. S. females, 10. 4 percent for Hispanic females, 11. 4 percent for Mexican-American females, 4. 4 percent for Cuban females, and 9. 5 percent for other Spanish-origin females. [56c]

5. Youth Unemployment

In 1979, of 48,000 Puerto Rican youths 16 to 19 years old, approximately 29 percent were unemployed. In 1978, of an estimated 59,000 Puerto Rican youths, 29. 2 percent were unemployed. [57] In comparison, 15. 7 percent of U. S. youths were unemployed in 1979, 13. 6 percent White youths, 35. 8 percent Black youths, 19. 5 percent Hispanic youths, and 19. 2 percent Mexican-American youths. [58]

H. POVERTY AND WELFARE DATA

The rate of poverty among Puerto Ricans was higher than that of other Hispanic and non-Hispanic groups.

1. Individuals in Poverty

In 1977, there were 707,000 individuals of Puerto Rican origin living below the poverty level. This constituted 38.8 percent of the Puerto Rican population, compared to 11.6 percent of the U.S. population living below the poverty level, 8.9 percent of the White population, 31.3 percent of the Black population, 22.4 percent of the Hispanic population, 21.1 percent of the Mexican-American population, and 15.8 percent of the Spanish-origin population. [59]

74.6 percent of persons in families headed by Puerto Rican women were in poverty, compared to 36.2 percent of persons in U.S. families, 56.7 percent of persons in Hispanic families, 49.7 percent of persons in Mexican-American families, and 44.7 percent of persons in other Spanish-origin families. [60]

In metropolitan poverty areas, 75.6 percent of individuals in Puerto Rican families headed by females were in poverty, compared to 60.1 percent of U.S. families headed by females, 54.2 percent of similar White families, 62.3 percent of similar Black families, 66.6 percent of similar Hispanic families, and 58.7 percent of Mexican-American families headed by females. [61]

2. Families in Poverty

39.5 percent of Puerto Rican families were in poverty, compared to 10.2 percent of U.S. families, 7.5 percent of White families, 30.5 percent of Black families, 21.9 percent of Hispanic families, 20.5 percent of Mexican-American families, and 14.7 percent of other Spanish-origin families. [62]

49.7 percent of Puerto Rican families with related children under 18 years of age were in poverty, compared to 16.0 percent of similar U.S. families, 11.4 percent of similar White families, 41.6 percent of similar Black families, 28.0 percent of similar Mexican-American families, and 18.3 percent of similar other Spanish-origin families. [63]

Of Puerto Rican families in metropolitan areas, 41.2 percent lived in poverty, compared to 9.1 percent of U.S. families, 6.3 percent of White families, 27.9 percent of Black families, 21.7 percent of Hispanic families, 19.4 percent of Mexican-American families, and 14.1 percent of other Spanish-origin families. [64]

In metropolitan areas, there were 593,000 Puerto Rican families headed by females; 75.8 percent of Puerto Rican female heads of families were in poverty, compared to 30.7 percent of U.S. female heads of families, 23.0 percent of White female heads of families, 48.8 percent of Black female heads of families, 64.3 percent of Hispanic female heads of families, and 57.2 percent of Mexican-American female heads of families. [65]

86.4 percent of children under 18 years of age in Puerto Rican families headed by females inside metropolitan areas were in poverty, compared to 48.8 percent of similar U.S. children, 38.7 percent of similar White children, 62.9 percent of similar Black children, 77.6 percent of similar Hispanic children, and 71.4 percent of similar Mexican-American children. [66]

3. Welfare Recipients

The data on Aid to Families with Dependent Children (AFDC) are available for Puerto Ricans and Hispanics in New York State. However, comparisons can be made using these data because, in 1979, over 50 percent of the Puerto Rican population resided in the New York area. Additionally, in 1977, 41.2 percent of the Puerto Rican families in metropolitan areas were in poverty, and 75.8 percent of Puerto Rican families headed by females were in poverty. [67]

In May, 1979, the number of AFDC families in the nation was 3,502,931, the number of recipients was 10,311,622, and the number of children was 7,192,252. In New York State, there were 364,046 AFDC families, 111,309 AFDC recipients, and 771,459 AFDC children. [68]

In 1977, Puerto Ricans constituted 33.4 percent of the AFDC caseload in New York City and 24.5 percent of the caseload in New York State. [69]

21.7 percent of recipients in the city were Hispanic; 49.4 percent of Hispanic welfare recipients, including 29.146 adults, were available for employment. [70]

21.9 percent of Hispanics in the city were unemployed; 33.9 percent of disadvantaged Hispanics were unemployed. [71]

In New York City, in 1978, 16.5 percent of Hispanics applied for unemployment insurance benefits; in New York State, 23.8 percent applied. [72]

I.   WOMEN DATA

There were 935,000 Puerto Rican women in the continental United States in March, 1979. The Puerto Rican female population is 54 percent of the total Puerto Rican population and 15.2 percent of the total Hispanic population. [73]

1. Age and Marital Status

In March, 1978, the median age of Puerto Rican women was 22.4 years, compared to 17.9 years for Puerto Rican males, 30.6 years for the total U.S. female population, 22.8 years for all Hispanic females, 21.3 years for Mexican-American females, 37.7 years for Cubans, 27.3 years for Central and South American females, and 23.4 years for other Hispanic females. [74]

Because the Puerto Rican population was very young, there was a high concentration of young women. 42. 3 percent were under 18 years of age and 72. 9 percent were under 35 years. Comparatively, 28. 1 percent of U. S. women and 40. 0 percent of Hispanic women were under 18 years of age; 46. 3 percent of U. S. women and 71. 7 percent of Hispanic women were under 35 years.

Of the 650,000 Puerto Rican women 14 years old and over, 27. 2 percent were single, 56. 4 percent were married, 5. 8 percent were widowed, and 10. 6 percent were divorced. [75]

2. Female Heads of Families

In March, 1978, 41 percent of the 437,000 Puerto Rican families were headed by women, compared to 10. 2 percent of all U. S. families (1977), 20 percent of all Hispanic families, and 16 percent of Mexican-American families. [76]

Of all Puerto Rican families headed by females, 97. 7 percent resided in metropolitan areas and 89. 3 percent resided in central cities. [77] In March, 1975, 38 percent of the 477,000 Puerto Rican heads of household were women, compared to 23 percent of all Hispanic heads of household. [78] In 1977, 70. 3 percent of all Puerto Rican female heads of families were in poverty, and 74. 6 percent of Puerto Rican families headed by women were in poverty. [79] (See section on "Poverty" under this heading, for comparisons with other groups.)

3. Educational Attainment

In 1978, 32. 5 percent of Puerto Rican women were high school graduates, compared to 38. 2 percent of Hispanic women, 32. 4 percent of Mexican-American women, and 52. 4 percent of other Spanish-origin women. [80]

Of 650,000 Puerto Rican women 14 years of age and over, 12 percent completed 0 to 4 years of elementary school, 15. 8 percent completed 5 to 7 years, and 12. 5 percent completed 8 years of elementary school. 27. 1 percent completed 1 to 3 years of high school and 23. 5 percent completed 4 years or more of college; 32. 5 percent completed high school and 9. 0 percent completed high school and 1 or more years of college. [81]

4. Labor Force Participation

32. 5 percent of Puerto Rican women 20 years of age and over were in the labor force in March, 1978, a considerably lower percentage than that of other women. 49. 6 percent of the total U. S. female population were in the labor force, including 48. 7 percent of White women, 55. 4 percent of Black women, 47. 1 percent of all Hispanic women, 48. 5 percent of Mexican-American women, and 56. 1 percent of Cuban women. [82]

5. Employment and Occupations

In March, 1978, of all Puerto Rican female workers, 12. 2 percent were unemployed, compared to 7. 0 percent of all U. S. women, 10. 4 percent of all Hispanic women, 11. 4 percent of Mexican-American women, and 4. 4 percent of Cuban women. [83]

In 1970 (latest data available), Puerto Ricans were the least likely of all Hispanic women to have had work experience. 34 percent of Puerto Rican wives and 24 percent of female heads of families worked at some time in 1970, as compared to 42 percent of all Hispanic wives and 47 percent of female heads of families. [84]

In 1978, of 173,000 Puerto Rican women 16 years of age and over, 28. 4 percent were employed, compared to 50. 1 percent of U. S. women, 40. 6 percent of Hispanic women, 41. 6 percent of Mexican-American women, and 46. 9 percent of Cuban women. [85]

Of the 173,000 Puerto Rican women employed in 1978, 56. 3 percent were white-collar workers (34. 4 percent were clerical workers), 30. 9 percent were blue-collar workers, with a high concentration (27. 3 percent) in operative jobs, 11. 9 percent were service workers, and 0. 9 percent were farm workers. [86]

In comparison, 64. 9 percent of all U. S. women and 48. 1 percent of all Hispanic women were white-collar workers, 14. 5 percent of all U. S. women and 28. 2 percent of Hispanic women were blue-collar workers, 20. 5 percent of U. S. women and 22. 6 percent of Hispanic women were service workers, and 1. 1 percent of U. S. women and 1. 1 percent of Hispanic women were farm workers. [87]

6. Unemployment

In March, 1979, of 179,000 Puerto Rican females in the labor force, 10. 6 percent were unemployed, compared to 5. 5 percent of U. S. women, 4. 8 percent of White women, 9. 9 percent of Black women, 9. 8 percent of Hispanic women, 11. 2 percent of Mexican-American women, and 6. 6 percent of Cuban women. [88]

7. Income

In 1977, the median income of Puerto Rican women was $4,179, 62. 2 percent of Puerto Rican women earned less than $5,000, 92. 8 percent earned less than $10,000, and 99. 1 percent earned less than $15,000. [89]

8. Poverty

In 1977, 41 percent of Puerto Rican families were headed by women. 74. 6 percent of families headed by Puerto Rican women were in poverty, compared to 36. 2 percent of U. S. families headed by women, 26. 8 percent of similar White families, 55. 3 percent of similar Black families, 56. 7 percent of similar Hispanic families, 49. 7 percent of

similar Mexican-American families, and 44. 5 percent of other Spanish-origin families headed by women.   Also, 70. 3 percent of Puerto
Rican females who headed families were in poverty, compared to
24. 0 percent of White females, 51. 0 percent of Black females, 53. 6
percent of Hispanic females, 45. 9 percent of Mexican-American females, and 45. 8 percent of other Spanish-origin females who headed
families. [90]

82. 2 percent of female-headed Puerto Rican families with related
children under 18 years of age were in poverty.   In comparison,
52. 0 percent of female-headed U. S. families with related children
under 18 years of age, 40. 3 percent of similar White families, 65. 7
percent of similar Black families, 68. 6 percent of similar Hispanic
families, 65. 7 percent of similar Mexican-American families, and
54. 4 percent of similar other Spanish-origin families, were in poverty. [91]

J.   YOUTH DATA

Because the Puerto Rican population is younger than the population
of other groups, there is a larger concentration of youths among
Puerto Ricans than among other groups.   In March, 1979, the median age of Puerto Ricans was 19. 9 years and in March, 1978, when
the median age of all Puerto Ricans was 20. 3 years, the median age
of Puerto Rican males was 17. 9 years.   The median age of Puerto
Ricans, in 1979, was lower than in 1978, which indicates that there
is a greater concentration of youths than before.

In March, 1979, 52. 3 percent of the Puerto Rican population were
under 21 years of age, compared to 34. 6 percent of the U. S. population, 47. 7 percent of the total Hispanic population, 47. 5 percent
of the Mexican-American population, 32. 4 percent of the Cuban population, 40. 0 percent of the Central and South American population,
51. 0 percent of other Hispanic populations in the continental United
States, and 33. 9 percent of the non-Hispanic population. [92]

1.   Youth Heads of Families

In 1977, of the 37,000 Puerto Rican families headed by individuals
14 to 24 years old, 51. 4 percent (19,000) were in poverty, compared
to 24. 2 percent of all U. S. families headed by individuals 14 to 24
years of age, 18. 3 percent of similar Mexican-American families,
and 28. 8 percent of similar families of other Spanish origin. [93]

2.   Education of Youth-In-School and Youth-Out-of-School

In March, 1978, 7. 1 percent of Puerto Rican youths 14 to 19 years
of age completed 4 years of high school, compared to 12. 2 percent
of Hispanic youths and 12. 2 percent of Mexican-American youths. [94]

Only 7. 5 percent of Puerto Rican male youths 14 to 19 years of age

completed high school, compared to 10. 2 percent of Hispanic male
youths and 10. 6 percent of Mexican-American male youths.   6. 7
percent of Puerto Rican female youths 14 to 19 years of age completed 4 years of high school, compared to 14. 2 percent of Hispanic
female youths and 13. 7 percent of Mexican-American female youths. [95]

In October, 1978, 57. 1 percent of all Hispanic youths, 58. 2 percent
of Hispanic male youths, and 55. 2 percent of Hispanic female youths
who were not in school, were not high school graduates.   In comparison, 27. 1 percent of all U. S. youths, 27. 9 percent of U. S. male
youths, and 26. 1 percent of U. S. female youths who were not in
school, were not high school graduates; and 33. 0 percent of all Black
youths, 32. 0 percent of Black male youths, and 34. 2 percent of Black
female youths who were not in school, were not high school graduates. [96]

National figures for Puerto Rican youths who were out-of-school,
non-high school graduates are not available.   However, it can be
deduced that the figures for Puerto Rican youths are even higher
than those for Hispanic youths.   12. 2 percent of all Hispanic youths
--10. 2 percent males, and 14. 2 percent females--completed 4 years
of high school in March, 1978.   However, only 7. 1 percent of all
Puerto Rican youths--7. 6 percent males and 6. 7 percent females--
completed high school.   The figures for Hispanic youths who were
not in school and were not high school graduates were 57. 1 percent
for all Hispanic youths, 58. 2 percent males and 55. 2 percent females.   Therefore, the figures for Puerto Rican youths who were
not in school and who were not high school graduates must be even
higher. [97]

3.   Labor Force Participation of Youth

In 1978, 37. 3 percent of all Puerto Rican youths 16 to 19 years of
age were in the labor force.   In comparison, 58. 0 percent of U. S.
youth, 61. 0 percent of White youth, 40. 8 percent of Black youth,
49. 6 percent of Hispanic youth, 52. 3 percent of Mexican-American
youth, and 29. 0 percent of Cuban youth, were in the labor force. [98]

4.   Youth Unemployment

In 1977, of 59,000 Puerto Rican youths in the labor force, 29. 2
percent were unemployed, compared to 15. 4 percent of U. S. youths,
38. 6 percent of Black youths, 20. 6 percent of Hispanic youths, and
19. 4 percent of Mexican-American youths. [99]

5.   Youths in Poverty

In Puerto Rican families headed by females, 82. 6 percent (303,000)
of children under 18 years of age, lived in poverty, compared to
68. 6 percent of children in U. S. families headed by females, 62. 6
percent of children in Mexican-American families headed by females,
and 54. 4 percent of other Hispanic children in families headed by
females. [100]

In Puerto Rican families headed by females, 91 percent (108,000) of children under 6 years of age, were in poverty, compared to 76.1 percent of all children, and 73.4 percent of Mexican-American children. [101]

K. HEALTH DATA

1. Health and Economic Opportunity

Racial minorities have almost twice the infant mortality of Whites.

The birth rate of the total U.S. population has been declining in recent years, but at a much faster rate among the White population than among racial minorities. The birth rate of racial minorities was one and a half times that of Whites in 1975, and it was higher than that experienced by Whites as long ago as 1940. [102]

Health care was made an important part of the War on Poverty because poor health was seen as an obstacle to economic opportunity. [103]

The most comprehensive health data on Puerto Ricans were available for New York City. Comparisons can be made for the national Puerto Rican population, because over 50 percent of the Puerto Rican population resided in the New York area.

2. Mortality Rates

In New York City, although the chief causes of death among Puerto Ricans and the total city population from 1969 to 1971 were heart diseases and malignant neoplasms, there was a higher mortality rate from cirrhosis of the liver, accidents, and diabetes among Puerto Ricans than among the total population. The average annual mortality rates from cirrhosis of the liver, accidents, and diabetes among Puerto Ricans were 45.4, 29.3, and 17.7 per 100,000 population, respectively, compared to 36.5, 27.8, and 25.4 among the total New York City population. The percentages of death from cirrhosis of the liver, accidents, and diabetes were 7.5, 4.9, and 2.9 percent, respectively, for Puerto Ricans, compared to 3.3, 2.5, and 2.3 percent, respectively, for the total New York City population. [104]

The average annual mortality rates from accidents, homicides, bronchitis, influenza, and pneumonia, were higher for Puerto Ricans under 15 years old than for the total population under 15. The average annual mortality rates from homicides, drug dependence and accidents, were higher for Puerto Ricans in the age group 15 to 44 than for the total New York City population, and equal for cirrhosis of the liver. [105]

3. Selected Health Problems

The rates per 100,000 population of admissions to community mental health and mental retardation facilities for all psychiatric diagnoses were 2270.5 for Puerto Ricans, 2113.1 for Blacks, and 1067.9 for Whites,[106] whereas the rates for mental retardation were 85.7 for Puerto Ricans, 53.3 for Blacks, and 21.4 for Whites.[107]

From January 1 to September 30, 1971, the incidence of lead poisoning was 23.2 percent for Puerto Ricans, 60.2 percent for Blacks, 4.0 percent for others, and 12.6 percent unknown.[108]

4. Utilization of Health Services

Of those who visited outpatient departments of hospitals in the Southern New York Region in 1974, 28.8 percent were Hispanics, 36.9 percent were Blacks, and 31.8 percent were Whites. Of those who visited emergency rooms, 18.6 percent were Hispanics, 34.5 percent were Blacks, and 45.8 percent were Whites.[109]

References

1. Persons of Spanish Origin in the United States: March, 1979, (Advanced Report): Population Characteristics, Current Population Reports, U.S. Department of Commerce, Bureau of Census, Series P-20, No. 347, (Issued October, 1979). p. 1, Figure 1.

2. Persons of Spanish Origin in the United States: March, 1978: Population Characteristics, Current Population Reports, U.S. Department of Commerce, Bureau of Census, Series P-20, No. 339, (Issued June, 1979). p. 15, Table L.

3. Ibid.

4. Newman, Morris J., "A Profile of Hispanics in the U.S. Work Force," Monthly Labor Review, December, 1978, U.S. Department of Labor, Bureau of Labor Statistics.

5. Ibid.

6. Persons of Spanish Origin in the United States: March, 1979. (Advanced Report): Population Characteristics, Current Population Reports, U.S. Department of Commerce, Bureau of Census, Series P-20, No. 347, (Issued October, 1979). p. 4, Table 2.

7. Persons of Spanish Origin in the United States: March, 1978: Population Characteristics, Current Population Reports, Series P-20, No. 339, (Issued June, 1979). p. 17, Table 2.

8. Ibid.

9. Persons of Spanish Origin in the United States: March, 1979, (Advanced Report): Population Characteristics, Current Population Reports, U.S. Department of Commerce, Bureau of Census, Series P-20, No. 347, (Issued October, 1979). p. 4, Table 1.

10. Persons of Spanish Origin in the United States: March, 1978: Population Characteristics, Current Population Reports, Series P-20, No. 339, (Issued June, 1979). p. 18, Table 3.

11. Ibid.
12. Ibid.
13. 1970 Census Report, Department of Commerce, Bureau of Census.
14. Persons of Spanish Origin in the United States: March, 1979, (Advanced Report): Population Characteristics, Current Population Reports, U. S. Department of Commerce, Bureau of Census, Series P-20, No. 347, (Issued October, 1979). p. 5, Table 3.
15. Persons of Spanish Origin in the United States: March, 1978: Population Characteristics, Current Population Reports, U. S. Department of Commerce, Bureau of Census, Series P-20, No. 339, (Issued June, 1979). p. 20, Table 5.
16. Ibid. p. 37, Table 18.
17. Ibid.
18. Ibid. p. 23, Table 8.
19. Ibid.
20. Newman, Morris, J., "A Profile of Hispanics in the U. S. Work Force," Monthly Labor Review, December, 1978, U. S. Department of Labor, Bureau of Labor Statistics.
21. Ibid.
22. Characteristics of the Population Below the Poverty Level: 1977: Consumer Income, Current Population Reports, U. S. Department of Commerce, Bureau of Census, Series P-60, No. 119, (Issued March, 1979). p. 185, Table 43, and p. 24, Table 5.
23. Ibid.
24. "The Educational Disadvantage of Language--Minority Persons in the United States, Spring 1976," National Center For Education Statistics Bulletin, U. S. Department of Health, Education, and Welfare, Education Division. 78 B-4, p. 3.
25. Ibid.
26. Ibid.
27. Ibid.
28. Persons of Spanish Origin in the United States: March, 1979, (Advanced Report): Population Characteristics, Current Population Reports, U. S. Department of Commerce, Bureau of Census, Series P-20, No. 347, (Issued October, 1979). p. 5, Table 4.
29. Ibid.
30. Ibid.
31. Ibid.
32. Persons of Spanish Origin in the United States: March, 1978: Population Characteristics, Current Population Reports, U. S. Department of Commerce, Bureau of Census, Series P-20, No. 339, (Issued June, 1979). p. 49, Table 30.
33. Ibid.
34. Ibid.
35. Persons of Spanish Origin in the United States: March, 1979, (Advanced Report): Population Characteristics, Current Population Reports, U. S. Department of Commerce, Bureau of Census, Series P-20, No. 347, (Issued October, 1979). p. 5, Table 4.

36. Persons of Spanish Origin in the United States: March, 1978: Population Characteristics, Current Population Reports, U.S. Department of Commerce, Bureau of Census, Series P-20, No. 339 (Issued June, 1979). p. 28, Table 12.
37. Ibid.
38. Ibid.
39. Newman, Morris J., "A Profile of Hispanics in the U.S. Work Force," Monthly Labor Review, December, 1978, U.S. Department of Labor, Bureau of Labor Statistics.
40. Employment and Earnings: January, 1980, U.S. Department of Labor, Bureau of Labor Statistics, Vol. 27, No. 1, pp. 68-69, Tables A-59, A-60.
41. Ibid.
42. Ibid.
43. Ibid.
44. Ibid. p. 69, Table A-60.
45. Ibid. p. 71, Table A-62.
46. Ibid.
47. Ibid. p. 70, Table A-61.
48. Ibid. p. 71, Table A-62.
49. Persons of Spanish Origin in the United States: March, 1978: Population Characteristics, Current Population Reports, U.S. Department of Commerce, Bureau of Census, Series P-20, No. 339, (Issued June, 1979). p. 26, Table 10.
50. Ibid.
51. Ibid.
52. Ibid.
53. Persons of Spanish Origin in the United States: March, 1979, (Advanced Report): Population Characteristics, Current Population Reports, U.S. Department of Commerce, Bureau of Census, Series P-20, No. 347, (Issued October, 1979). p. 5, Table 4.
54. Employment and Earnings: January, 1980, U.S. Department of Labor, Bureau of Labor Statistics, Vol. 27, No. 1, pp. 68-69, Tables A-59, A-60.
55. Ibid.
56a. Persons of Spanish Origin in the United States: March, 1978: Population Characteristics, Current Population Reports, U.S. Department of Commerce, Bureau of Census, Series P-20, No. 339, (Issued June, 1979). p. 26, Table 10.
56b. Ibid.
56c. Ibid.
57. Employment and Unemployment During 1978: Analysis, Special Labor Force Report 218, U.S. Department of Labor, Bureau of Labor Statistics. p. A-40, Table 45.
58. Employment and Earnings: January, 1980, U.S. Department of Labor, Bureau of Labor Statistics, Vol. 27, No. 1, pp. 68-69, Tables A-59, A-60.
59. Characteristics of the Population Below the Poverty Level: 1977: Consumer Income, Current Population Reports, U.S. Department of Commerce, Bureau of Census, Series P-60, No. 119, (Issued March, 1979). p. 181, Table 42: pp. 13-15, Table 1.

60. Ibid. p. 181, Table 42; p. 39, Table 9.
61. Ibid. p. 181, Table 42; p. 41, Table 9.
62. Ibid. p. 181, Table 42; pp. 13-15, Table 1.
63. Ibid. p. 181, Table 42; p. 35, Table 8.
64. Ibid. p. 181, Table 42; p. 40, Table 9.
65. Characteristics of the Population Below the Poverty Level: 1977: Consumer Income, Current Population Reports, U. S. Department of Commerce, Bureau of Census, Series P-60, No. 119, (Issued March, 1979). p. 181, Table 42; p. 40, Table 9.
66. Ibid.
67. Ibid.
68. Public Assistance Statistics: May, 1979, U. S. Department of Health, Education, and Welfare, Social Security Administration, Office of Policy, Office of Research and Statistics, (October, 1979). HEW Publication No. (SSA) 80-11917. p. 9, Table 4.
69. Characteristics of AFDC Families, March, 1977, Program Analysis Report No. 64, September, 1979, Department of Social Services, Bureau of Data Management and Analysis, p. 7, Chart 1.
70. Public Assistance Summary Data, "The Quarterly Data Report For January--March, 1979." Division of Policy and Economic Research, The City of New York Human Resources Administration, (November, 1979). p. 17.
71. Ibid. p. 18.
72. Ibid. p. 21.
73. Persons of Spanish Origin in the United States: March, 1979, (Advanced Report): Population Characteristics, Current Population Reports, U. S. Department of Commerce, Bureau of Census, Series P-20, No. 347. (Issued October, 1979). p. 5, Table 1.
74. Persons of Spanish Origin in the United States: March, 1978: Population Characteristics, Current Population Reports, U. S. Department of Commerce, Bureau of Census, Series P-20, No. 339, (Issued June, 1979). p. 17, Table 2.
75. Ibid. p. 3, Table C.
76. Ibid. p. 37, Table 18. Population Profile of the U. S.: 1977: Population Characteristics, U. S. Department of Commerce, Bureau of Census, Series P-20, No. 324, (Issued April, 1978). p. 20, Table 10.
77. Ibid. p. 37, Table 18.
78. Persons of Spanish Origin in the United States: March, 1976: Population Characteristics, Current Population Reports, U. S. Department of Commerce, Bureau of Census, Series P-20, No. 310, (Issued July, 1977).
79. Characteristics of the Population Below the Poverty Level: 1977: Consumer Income, Current Population Reports, U. S. Department of Commerce, Bureau of Census, Series P-60, No. 119, (Issued March, 1979). p. 181, Table 42.
80. Persons of Spanish Origin in the United States: March, 1978: Population Characteristics, Current Population Reports, U. S. Department of Commerce, Bureau of Census, Series P-20, No. 339, (Issued June, 1979). p. 24, Table 8.

81. Ibid.
82. Employment and Unemployment During 1978: An Analysis, Special Labor Force Report 218, U.S. Department of Labor, Bureau of Labor Statistics. p. 181, Tables 44, 45.
83. Persons of Spanish Origin in the United States: March, 1978: Population Characteristics, Current Population Reports. U.S. Department of Commerce, Bureau of Census, Series P-20, No. 339, (Issued June, 1979). p. 26, Table 10.
84. Women of Puerto Rican Origin in the Continental United States, U.S. Department of Labor, Employment Standards Administration, Women's Bureau. p. 2.
85. Persons of Spanish Origin in the United States: March, 1978: Population Characteristics, Current Population Reports, U.S. Department of Commerce, Bureau of Census, Series P-20, No. 339, (Issued June, 1979). p. 26, Table 10.
86. Ibid.
87. Ibid.
88. Persons of Spanish Origin in the United States: March, 1979, (Advanced Report): Population Characteristics, Current Population Reports, U.S. Department of Commerce, Bureau of Census, Series P-20, No. 347, (Issued October, 1979). p. 5, Table 4.
89. Persons of Spanish Origin in the United States: March, 1978: Population Characteristics, Current Population Reports, U.S. Department of Commerce, Bureau of Census, Series P-20, No. 339, (Issued June, 1979). p. 28, Table 12.
90. Characteristics of the Population Below the Poverty Level: 1977: Consumer Income, Current Population Reports, U.S. Department of Commerce, Bureau of Census, Series P-60, No. 119, (Issued March, 1979). p. 184, Table 43; pp. 13-15, Table 1.
91. Ibid.
92. Persons of Spanish Origin in the United States: March, 1978: Population Characteristics, Current Population Reports, U.S. Department of Commerce, Bureau of Census, Series P-20, No. 339, (Issued June, 1979). p. 18, Table 3.
93. Characteristics of the Population Below the Poverty Level: 1977: Consumer Income, Current Population Reports, U.S. Department of Commerce, Bureau of Census, Series P-60, No. 119, (Issued March, 1979). p. 184, Table 43; pp. 23-31, Table 5.
94. Ibid. p. 23, Table 8.
95. Ibid. pp. 23-24, Table 8.
96. School Enrollment--Social and Economic Characteristics of Students: October, 1978: Population Characteristics, Current Population Reports, U.S. Department of Commerce, Bureau of Census, Series P-20, No. 346, (Issued October, 1979). p. 12, Table 1.
97. Persons of Spanish Origin in the United States: March, 1978: Population Characteristics, Current Population Reports, U.S. Department of Commerce, Bureau of Census, Series P-20, No. 339, (Issued June, 1979). p. 23, Table 8.
98. Employment and Unemployment During 1978: An Analysis,

Special Labor Force Report 218, U.S. Department of Labor, Bureau of Statistics. p. A39-40, Tables 44, 45.

99. Ibid.
100. Characteristics of the Population Below the Poverty Level: 1977: Consumer Income, Current Population Reports. U.S. Department of Commerce, Bureau of Census, Series P-60, No. 119, (Issued March, 1979). p. 181, Table 42; pp. 13-15, Table 1.
101. Ibid. p. 181, Table 42.
102. Health Status of Minorities and Low-Income Groups, U.S. Department of Health, Education, and Welfare, Public Health Service, Health Resources Administration, Office of Health Resources Opportunity, DHEW Publication (HRA) 79-627. pp. 5-6.
103. Ibid. p. 5.
104. Alers, Jose Oscar, Puerto Ricans and Health Findings From New York City, Monograph No. 4 Hispanic Research Center, Fordham University, Bronx, New York, 1978. p. 6, Table 3.
105. Ibid. p. 8, Table 4.
106. Ibid. p. 17, Table 8.
107. Ibid. p. 22, Table 11.
108. Ibid. p. 29, Table 15.
109. Ibid. pp. 32-33, Tables 16, 17.

ADDENDUM

Puerto Ricans in New York City

New York City data are not as current as national data and, therefore, direct parallels cannot be drawn on a year to year basis.
Nonetheless, data from the 1970 Census for New York City, in most
cases the only data available, reflect the same profiles and patterns
about the New York City Puerto Rican community evident in later
national data.

Since conditions overall have worsened over the years, the lack of
current New York City data distorts the local profiles. Data which
can be correlated with national data indicate that the two studies,
local and national, reflect the same status and conditions, especially
since over half of the nation's Puerto Ricans in the mainland reside
in New York City.

The parallels are further distorted by the population base used in
different years, in local and national census data. For instance,
in 1970 the Bureau of Census reported that there were 1,379,000
Puerto Ricans living in the mainland United States, with 811,800
living in New York City. Responding to charges of undercounting,
in March, 1979, the Bureau reported that there were 1,748,000
mainland Puerto Ricans. In 1978 the Bureau showed a nationwide
count of 1,823,000, and reduced that number to 1,748,000 in 1979.
The figures for 1980 are unknown at this time.

Puerto Ricans are the youngest (19.9 years) ethnic group in the
mainland United States, as reported in March, 1979. Similarly,
all research and counts in New York City indicate that the Puerto
Rican community is the youngest (21 years in 1970) ethnic group in
the City.

The birth rate among Puerto Ricans nationwide and locally is the
highest for all ethnic groups and, therefore, the community's median age has been dropping since 1970. The Puerto Rican community
in New York City is about ten years younger than the national average, and even younger in terms of New York City overall population
data. Latest (1970) New York City data showed that over half the

432

Puerto Rican population was under 30 years of age. In 1978, nationwide census data showed 65. 4 percent to be 29 years of age or
younger.

The latest data (1970 Census) on New York City indicated that 29
percent of Puerto Rican families were headed by females. National
data (March, 1978) note that 41. 0 percent of Puerto Rican families
were headed by females, with 74. 6 percent of them in poverty. The
New York City data in 1970 noted that 58 percent of Puerto Rican
families headed by females were in poverty. Because there has been
a sharp increase in the number of families headed by females in the
United States, the differential can easily be accounted for between
national and local data and base years. Welfare and AFDC (Aid to
Families with Dependent Children) data in New York City indicate
that the number of Puerto Rican families with female heads is the
same percentage as throughout the entire Puerto Rican community
in the mainland United States. Further, since economic conditions
in New York City and rates of unemployment reflect a serious loss
of jobs over the years, the number of families with female heads
must reflect, in terms of employment and poverty, local economic
patterns.

In the 1970 Census it was reported that 49 percent of all Puerto Rican males aged 16-21 in New York City were not in school and not
employed. National figures for Puerto Ricans are not available for
comparison, but in 1978 only 37. 3 percent of all Puerto Rican youths
aged 16-19 were in the labor force, and 57. 1 percent of all Hispanic
youths were not in school. Overall, national data have shown that
Puerto Rican youth employment has not changed over the years,
while positive changes occurred in other ethnic sectors. In terms
of new jobs created, this means that Puerto Rican youth employment
decreased, and in New York City, with serious unemployment problems, it decreased more than the national averages.

In 1970, Puerto Ricans in New York City schools had an 80 percent
dropout rate, in contrast to 49 percent for the total New York City
population. Nationally, in 1978, Puerto Ricans 14 years of age and
older had only a 31. 9 percent rate of high school graduation. Data
(1979) from the New York City Board of Education indicate that Puerto
Ricans still have the highest dropout rate of all ethnic groups in New
York City.

Unemployment figures for New York City are distorted, as are national figures, since they are based on those in the labor force and
not upon those of working age. For instance, the number of Puerto
Rican women over 14 years of age in the labor force is roughly half
that of other ethnic groups. To say that there is a 10 percent unemployment rate among Puerto Rican females distorts the truth.
All those who are not in the labor force but should be, including
large percentages of female heads of household and displaced home-
makers, are not counted in labor force figures or unemployment
data. Consequently, comparative data have no meaning.

The same can be said for youth employment and unemployment. In New York City, where youth unemployment represents a formidable problem, the number of youths who withdrew from the labor force is concealed in references to labor force counts. Nationally, in 1978, of the 608,000 Puerto Rican women 16 years of age and over, only 197,000 were reported in the labor force. The other 411,000 were not reported in the labor force.

Figures for poverty developed in recent national censuses apply as well to local communities. The poverty figures for Puerto Rican New Yorkers have always been extremely high. The loss of family earners and employment has increased the number of unemployed and, therefore, the number of Puerto Rican families that receive public assistance.

Overall, New York City data, while older than national data, establish that conditions for New York City's Puerto Ricans are as bad as or worse than national averages. Further, they are consistent with the argument that the Puerto Rican community is the worst off, both nationally and locally and therefore the community most in need.

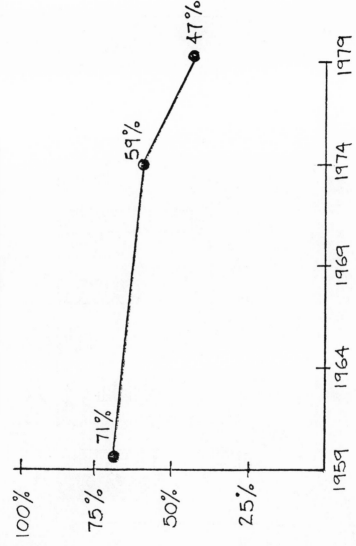

MAINLAND PUERTO RICAN FAMILY EARNINGS

PERCENT OF NATIONAL
AVERAGE

FAMILIES IN POVERTY (March, 1979)

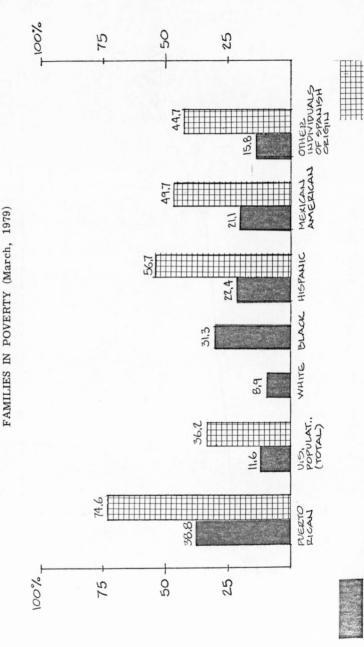

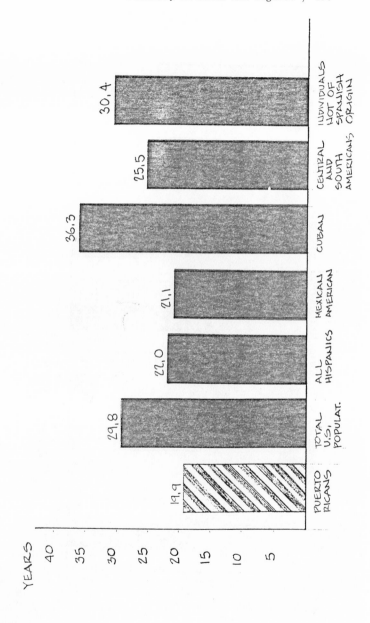

MEDIAN AGE (March, 1979)

FAMILIES WITH CHILDREN IN POVERTY (March, 1979)

PERCENTAGE OF FAMILIES WITH RELATED CHILDREN UNDER 18 YEARS OF AGE (IN POVERTY)

PERCENTAGE OF WOMEN WHO HEAD FAMILIES WITH RELATED CHILDREN UNDER 18 YEARS OF AGE (IN POVERTY)

PUERTO RICAN — 81.2 / 49.7

SIMILAR U.S. FAMILIES — 52.0 / 16.0

WHITE — 40.3 / 11.4

BLACK — 65.7 / 41.6

MEXICAN AMERICAN — 65.7 / 28.0

OTHER FAMILIES OF SPANISH ORIGIN — 54.4 / 16.3

SIMILAR HISPANIC FAMILIES — 68.6

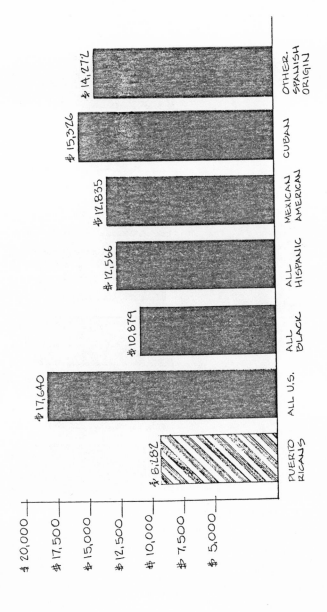

MEDIAN FAMILY INCOME 1979

INCOME

$ 20,000
$ 17,500
$ 15,000
$ 12,500
$ 10,000
$ 7,500
$ 5,000

PUERTO RICANS — $ 6,282
ALL U.S. — $ 17,640
ALL BLACK — $ 10,879
ALL HISPANIC — $ 12,566
MEXICAN AMERICAN — $ 12,835
CUBAN — $ 15,326
OTHER SPANISH ORIGIN — $ 14,272

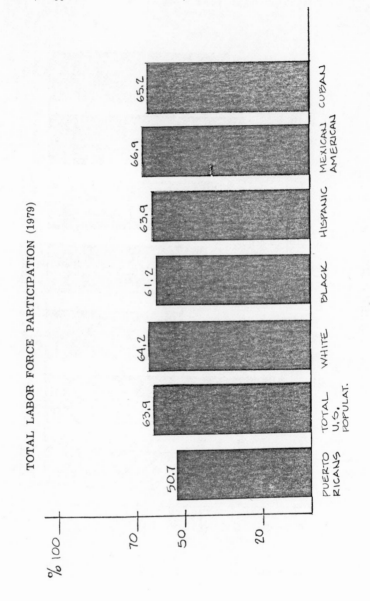

TOTAL LABOR FORCE PARTICIPATION (1979)

GENERAL BIBLIOGRAPHY

Babson, Sara, comp. The Education of Puerto Ricans on the Mainland: An Annotated Bibliography. New York: Institute for Urban and Minority Education, Columbia University, 1975.

Bravo, Enrique R., comp. Annotated Selected Puerto Rican Bibliography. New York: Columbia University, Urban Center. 1972.

Cordasco, Francesco and Leonard Covello. Studies of Puerto Rican
Children in American Schools: A Preliminary Bibliography.
New York: Department of Labor, Migration Division, Commonwealth of Puerto Rico, 1967. (Some 450 entries). Also published in Education Libraries Bulletin, Institute of Education,
University of London, #31, Spring 1968, pp. 7-33; and in Journal of Human Relations, vol. 16, 1968, pp. 264-285.

_____. Puerto Ricans on the United States Mainland: A Bibli-
ography of Reports, Texts, Critical Studies, and Related Materials. Totowa, N.J.: Rowman and Littlefield, 1972.

_____, ed. The Puerto Ricans: Migration and General Bibliog-
raphy. New York: Arno Press, 1975.

_____. Bilingual Education in American Schools: A Guide to
Information Sources. Detroit: Gale Research Co., 1979.

Dessick, Jesse. Doctoral Research on Puerto Rico and Puerto Ricans. New York: New York University, School of Education,
1967. A classified list of 320 doctoral dissertations completed
at American mainland universities.

Herrera, Diane, ed. Puerto Ricans and Other Minority Groups in
the Continental United States: An Annotated Bibliography. Austin, Texas: Dissemination Center for Bilingual Bicultural Education, 1973. Reprinted with a New Foreword and Supplemental
Bibliography by F. Cordasco. Detroit: Blaine Ethridge, 1979.

Jablonsky, Adelaide, comp. The Education of Puerto Rican Children and Youth: An Annotated Bibliography of Doctoral Dissertations. New York: Columbia University, ERIC Clearinghouse on the Urban Disadvantaged, 1974.

Miller, Wayne C., et al. A Comprehensive Bibliography for the Study of American Minorities. 3 vols. New York: University Press, 1976. "Puerto Rican Americans," vol. II, pp. 757-771.

Padilla, Amaldo M. and Paul Aranda. Latino Mental Health: Bibliography and Abstracts. Washington: Government Printing Office, 1974.

Parker, Franklin and Betty June Parker, comps. Education in Puerto Rico and of Puerto Ricans in the U.S.A.: Abstracts of American Doctoral Dissertations. San Juan: Inter American University Press, 1978.

Pedreira, Antonio S. Bibliografia Puertorriqueña: 1493-1930, Madrid: Imprenta de la Libreria y Casa Editorial Hernando, S.A., 1932. Reissued with a New Introduction by Francesco Cordasco. New York: Burt Franklin, 1974.

"The Puerto Rican Experience on the United States Mainland." The International Migration Review, vol. 2, Spring 1968. Includes "An annotated bibliography on Puerto Rico and Puerto Rican Migration." pp. 96-102.

The Spanish Speaking in the United States: A Guide to Materials. Washington: The Cabinet Committee on Opportunity for the Spanish Speaking, 1971. Reissued with a New Introduction by Francesco Cordasco. Detroit: Blaine Ethridge, 1975.

Status of Puerto Rico. Report of the United States--Puerto Rico Commission on the Status of Puerto Rico. Washington: Government Printing Office, 1966. Includes "Selected Bibliography" (Legal-Constitutional; Political; Economic; Social-Cultural-Historical; Government Publications) with some annotation.

Status of Puerto Rico. Selected Background Studies Prepared for the United States--Puerto Rico Commission on the Status of Puerto Rico. Washington: Government Printing Office, 1966. Includes Clarence Senior and Donald O. Watkins, "Toward A Balance Sheet of Puerto Rican Migration: Bibliography."

Vivo, Paquita, ed. The Puerto Ricans: An Annotated Bibliography. New York: R. R. Bowker Company, 1973.

SELECTED REFERENCES

Alers, Jose Oscar. Puerto Ricans and Health: Findings From New

York City. New York: Hispanic Research Center, Fordham University, 1978.

Aspira. Hemos Trabajado Bien: A Report on the First National Conference of Puerto Ricans, Mexican-Americans, and Educators on the Special Needs of Urban Puerto Rican Youth. New York: Aspira, 1968.

Bearle, Beatrice B. Eighty Puerto Rican Families in New York City: Health and Disease Studied in Context. New York: Columbia University Press, 1958. Reissued with a New Foreword by the Author. New York: Arno Press, 1975.

Bourne, Dorothy D. and James R. Bourne. Thirty Years of Change in Puerto Rico. New York: Praeger, 1966.

Brameld, Theodore. The Remaking of a Culture: Life and Education in Puerto Rico. New York: Harper, 1959.

Bucchioni, Eugene. A Sociological Analysis of the Functioning of Elementary Education for Puerto Rican Children in the New York City Public Schools. Unpublished Doctoral Dissertation, New School for Social Research, 1965.

Cafferty, Pastora S. J. and Carmen Rivera-Martinez. The Politics of Language: The Dilemma of Bilingual Education for Puerto Ricans. Boulder, Colorado: Westview Press, 1981.

Canino, Ian A., et al. The Puerto Rican Child in New York City: Stress and Mental Health. New York: Hispanic Research Center, Fordham University, 1980.

Carcino, Lydia, et al. The Puerto Ricans: A Resource Unit for Teachers. New York: Anti-Defamation League of B'nai B'rith, 1974.

Castro, Francisco. The Politics of Local Education in New York City: A Puerto Rican View. Unpublished Doctoral Dissertation, Rutgers University, 1973.

Cebollero, Pedro. A School Language Policy for Puerto Rico. San Juan, 1945.

Center for Applied Linguistics. Bilingual Education: Current Perspectives. 5 vols. Arlington, Va.: Center for Applied Linguistics, 1977. Vol. 1: Social Science; Vol. 2: Linguistics; Vol. 3: Law; Vol. 4: Education; Vol. 5: Synthesis.

Chenault, Lawrence. The Puerto Rican Migrant in New York City. Columbia University Press, 1938. Reissued with A New Foreword by F. Cordasco. New York: Russell & Russell, 1970.

Cintrón, Celia and Pedro Vales. A Pilot Study: Return Migration to Puerto Rico. Rio Piedras: Centro de Investigaciones Sociales de La Universidad de Puerto Rico, 1974.

Collazo, Francisco. The Education of Puerto Rican Children in the Schools of New York City. San Juan: Department of Education Press, 1954.

Commonwealth of Puerto Rico. Department of Labor, Migration Division. New York City. "A Summary in Facts and Figures: 1979-80 Edition." Migration Division. Revised annually. Irregular.

Cordasco, Francesco. "Spanish Harlem: The Anatomy of Poverty." Phylon: The Atlanta University Review of Race & Culture, vol. 26 (Summer 1965), pp. 195-196.

_____. "Studies in the Disenfranchised: The Puerto Rican Child." Psychiatric Spectator, vol. 3 (November 1966), pp. 3-4.

_____. "Puerto Rican Pupils and American Education." School & Society, vol. 95 (February 18, 1967), pp. 116-119.

_____. "The Challenge of the Non-English Speaking Child in the American School." School & Society, vol. 96 (March 30, 1968), pp. 198-201. On the proposal for the enactment of the Bilingual Education Act, Title VII, Elementary and Secondary Education Act with, historical background.

_____ and David N. Alloway. "Spanish Speaking People in the United States: Some Research Constructs and Postulates." International Migration Review, vol. 4 (Spring 1970), pp. 76-79.

_____ and R. Galatioto. "Ethnic Displacement in the Interstitial Community: The East Harlem (New York) Experience." Phylon: The Atlanta University Review of Race and Culture, vol. 31 (Fall 1970), pp. 302-312. Discussion of Jewish, Italian, Black, and Puerto Rican subcommunities.

_____ and Eugene Bucchioni. The Puerto Rican Community of Newark, N.J.: An Educational Program for Its Children. Newark: Board of Education, 1970.

_____ and Eugene Bucchioni. Education Programs for Puerto Rican Students. Jersey City Public Schools. Evaluation and Recommendations. Jersey City: Board of Education, 1971.

_____ and Eugene Bucchioni. "A Staff Institute for Teachers of Puerto Rican Students." School & Society, vol. 100 (Summer 1972), pp. 308-309.

_____. The Puerto Ricans, 1493-1973: A Chronology and Fact Book. Dobbs Ferry, N.Y.: Oceana Publications, 1973.

_____. "Teaching the Puerto Rican Experience" in James A. Banks, ed., Teaching Ethnic Studies: Concepts and Strategies. Washington: Council for the Social Studies, 1973, pp. 226-253.

_____ and Eugene Bucchioni. The Puerto Rican Experience. Totowa, N.J.: Littlefield, Adams & Co., 1973.

_____. "The Children of Immigrants in Schools: Historical Analogues of Educational Deprivation." Journal of Negro Education, vol. 42 (Winter 1973), pp. 44-53.

_____. "Spanish-Speaking Children in American Schools." International Migration Review, vol. 9 (Fall 1975), pp. 379-382.

_____, ed. Puerto Ricans and Educational Opportunity. New York: Arno Press, 1975.

_____, advisory ed. The Puerto Rican Experience. 33 vols. New York: Arno Press, 1975. A collection of texts, documents, and materials which provide a basic reference source for the study of the island, the migrations, and the varied and still evolving responses to the continental milieu in which Puerto Ricans find themselves.

_____. Bilingual Schooling in the United States: A Sourcebook for Educational Personnel. New York: McGraw-Hill, 1976.

_____. "Bilingual and Bicultural Education in American Schools: A Bibliography of Selected References." Bulletin of Bibliography, vol. 35 (April-June 1978), pp. 53-72.

_____. "Images of Puerto Ricans in American Films and Television." Melus, vol. 5 (Summer 1978), pp. 61-62.

_____, ed. Bilingual Education in New York City: A Compendium of Reports. New York: Arno Press, 1978. Includes texts of A Program of Education for Puerto Ricans in New York City, 1947; The Puerto Rican Pupils in the Public Schools of New York City, 1951; and Bilingual Education in New York City, 1971.

Council on Higher Education. Estudio del Sistema Educativo de Puerto Rico. Rio Piedras: University of Puerto Rico Press, 1962.

Covello, Leonard. The Heart is the Teacher. New York: McGraw-Hill, 1958. Also published as Teacher in the Urban Community: A Half Century in City Schools. With an Introduction by F. Cordasco, Totowa, N.J.: Littlefield & Adams, 1970. Autobiography of Leonard Covello (1887-) who served as principal of Benjamin Franklin High School, East Harlem, New York City, for almost a quarter century. See F. Cordasco, "Leonard Covello and the Community School," School & Society, vol. 98 (Summer, 1970), pp. 298-299.

[Covello, Leonard]. "Interview with Leonard Covello." Urban Review, vol. 3, 1969, pp. 13-19.

Cripps, L. L. Puerto Rico: The Case for Independence. Cambridge, Mass.: Schenkman Publishing Co., 1974.

Cruz Monclava, Lidio. Historia de Puerto Rico. 3 vols. Rio Piedras: Editorial Universitaria, 1957-1962.

Epstein, Erwin H. Politics and Education in Puerto Rico: A Documentary Survey of the Language Issue. Metuchen, N.J.: Scarecrow Press, 1970.

Estades, Rosa. Patterns of Political Participation of Puerto Ricans in New York City. Rio Piedras: Editorial Universitaria, 1978.

Fitzpatrick, Joseph P. Puerto Rican Americans: The Meaning of Migration to the Mainland. Englewood Cliffs, N.J.: Prentice Hall, 1971.

Fitzpatrick, Joseph and Douglas T. Gurak. Hispanic Intermarriage in New York City. New York: Hispanic Research Center, Fordham University, 1979.

Gallardo, José M., ed. Proceedings of the Conference on Education of Puerto Rican Children on the Mainland. Santurce, Puerto Rico: Department of Education, 1970. Reprint: New York: Arno Press, 1975.

Glazer, Nathan and Daniel P. Moynihan. Beyond the Melting Pot: The Negroes, Puerto Ricans, Jews, Italians, and Irish of New York City. 2nd. ed. Cambridge, Mass.: M.I.T. Press, 1970.

Hauberg, Clifford A. Puerto Rico and the Puerto Ricans. New York: Twayne Publishers, 1974.

Herbstein, Judith H. "Rituals and Politics of the Puerto Rican Community in New York." Ph.D. Dissertation, City University of New York, 1978.

Hernandez Alvarez, José. Return Migration to Puerto Rico. Berkeley: University of California Press, 1967.

History Task Force, Centro de Estudios Puertorriqueños. Labor Migration Under Capitalism: The Puerto Rican Experience. New York: Monthly Review Press, 1979.

Howard University. Symposium: Puerto Rico in the Year 2000. Washington: Howard University Press, 1968.

Jaffe, A. J., et al. The Changing Demography of Spanish Americans. New York: Academic Press, 1980.

Jennings, James. Puerto Rican Politics in New York City. Washington, D.C.: University Press of America, 1977.

John, Vera P., and Vivian M. Horner. Early Childhood Bilingual Education. New York: Modern Language Association, 1971.

Johnson, Roberta A. Puerto Rico: Commonwealth or Colony? New York: Praeger, 1980.

Kantrowitz, Nathan. "Social Mobility of Puerto Ricans: Education, Occupation, and Income Changes Among Children of Migrants, New York City, 1950-1960." International Migration Review, vol. 2 (1968), pp. 7-102.

Lewis, E. Glyn. Bilingualism and Bilingual Education: A Comparative Study. Albuquerque: University of New Mexico Press, 1980.

Lewis, Gordon K. Puerto Rico: Freedom and Power in the Caribbean. 2nd. ed., New York: Monthly Review Press, 1974.

_____. Notes on the Puerto Rican Revolution. New York: Monthly Review Press, 1974.

Lewis, Oscar. La Vida: A Puerto Rican Family in the Culture of Poverty--San Juan and New York. New York: Random House, 1966.

_____. A Study of Slum Culture: Backgrounds for La Vida. New York: Random House, 1968.

Lopez, Adalberto and James Petras, eds. Puerto Rico and Puerto Ricans: Studies in History and Society. New York: Schenkman Publishing Co., 1974.

Lopez, Alfredo. The Puerto Rican Papers: Notes on the Re-Emergence of a Nation. New York: Bobbs Merrill, 1973.

Maldonado-Denis, Manuel. Puerto Rico: Una Interpretación Histórico-Social. Mexico City. Editores Siglo XXI, 1969.

_____. The Emigration Dialectic: Puerto Rico and the U.S.A. New York: International Publishers, 1980.

Manrique Cabrera, Francisco. Historia de la Literature Puertorriqueña. Rio Piedras: Editorial Cultural, 1965.

Mapp, Edward, ed. Puerto Rican Perspectives. Metuchen, N.J.: Scarecrow Press, 1974.

Margolis, Richard J. The Losers: A Report on Puerto Ricans and the Public Schools. New York: Aspira, 1969. A report on visits to a number of schools with description and evaluation of programs for Puerto Rican children.

Marques, René. "El puertorriqueño docil." Cuadernos Americanos. Vol. 21, No. 1 (Enero-Febrero 1962), pp. 144-195.

Martin, George. Ethnic Political Leadership: The Case of Puerto Ricans. San Francisco: R&E Associates, 1978.

Mills, C. Wright; Clarence Senior; and Rose Goldsen. The Puerto Rican Journey: New York's Newest Migrants. Harper, 1950. Reissued, New York: Russell & Russell, 1967.

Mintz, Sidney W. Worker in the Cane: A Puerto Rican Life History. New Haven: Yale University Press, 1960.

Morales, Carrion Arturo. Puerto Rico and the Non-Hispanic Caribbean. Rio Piedras: University of Puerto Rico Press, 1952.

Morrison, J. Cayce, Director. The Puerto Rican Study: 1953-57. New York City Board of Education, 1958. Final report of the most complete study of the impact of Puerto Rican migration on the public schools of New York City, and how schools were affecting Puerto Rican children and their parents. Reissued with an introductory essay by F. Cordasco. New York: Oriole Editions, 1972.

National Puerto Rican Forum. A Study of Poverty Conditions in the New York Puerto Rican Community. New York: Puerto Rican Forum, 1970.

_____. The Next Step Toward Equality: A Comprehensive Study of Puerto Ricans in the United States Mainland. New York: The Forum, 1980.

Negrón de Montilla, Aida. Americanization in Puerto Rico and the Public School System, 1900-1930. Rio Piedras: Editorial Edil, 1971.

Nieves Falcon, Luis. Los Emigrantes Puertorriqueños. Rio Piedras: Editorial Edil, 1974.

Osuna, Juan José. A History of Education in Puerto Rico. Rio Piedras: University of Puerto Rico Press, 1949. Reissued, New York: Arno Press, 1978.

Padilla, Elena. Up From Puerto Rico. Columbia University Press, 1958.

Paulston, Christina B. Bilingual Education: Theories and Issues. Rowley, Mass.: Newbury House Publishers, 1980.

Pedreira, Antonio S. Insularismo. San Juan: Biblioteca de Autores Puertorriqueños, 1942.

Pico, Rafael. Nueva Geografía de Puerto Rico: Física, Económica, y Social. Rio Piedras: University of Puerto Rico Press, 1969.

Pietri, Pedro. Puerto Rican Obituary. New York: Monthly Review Press, 1974.

Protestant Spanish Community. Report on the Protestant Spanish Community in New York City. New York: Protestant Council of the City of New York, 1960.

Puerto Rican Children. "Education of Puerto Rican Children in New York City." The Journal of Educational Sociology, vol. 28 (December 1954), pp. 145-192. A collection of articles.

Puerto Rican Forum. The Puerto Rican Community Development Project: A Proposal for a Self-Help Project to Develop the Community by Strengthening the Family, Opening Opportunities for Youth and Making Full Use of Education. New York: Puerto Rican Forum, 1964.

Rand, Christopher. The Puerto Ricans. Oxford University Press, 1958.

Ravitch, Diane and Ronald K. Goodenow, eds. Educating an Urban People: The New York City Experience. New York: Teachers College Press, Columbia University, 1981.

Recio, Juan-Luis. Family as a Unit and Larger Society: The Adaptation of the Puerto Rican Migrant Family to the Mainland Suburban Setting. Unpublished Doctoral Dissertation, City University of New York, 1975.

Roberts, Lydia J. and Rosa L. Stefani. Patterns of Living in Puerto Rican Families. Rio Piedras: University of Puerto Rico, 1949.

Rodriguez Pacheco, Osvaldo. A Land of Hope in Schools: A Reader in the History of Public Education in Puerto Rico, 1940-1965. San Juan: Editorial Edil, 1976.

Rogler, Lloyd. Migrant in the City. New York: Basic Books, 1972.

Sandis, Eva E. "Characteristics of Puerto Rican Migrants to, and from the United States." The International Migration Review, vol. 4 (1970), pp. 22-43.

Santiago, Isaura S. A Community's Struggle for Equal Educational Opportunity: Aspira v. Bd. of Ed. Princeton: Educational Testing Service, Office for Minority Education, 1978.

Seda Bonilla, Edwin. "Cultural Pluralism and the Education of Puerto Rican Youth." Phi Delta Kappan, vol. 53 (January 1972), pp. 294-296.

Senior, Clarence. The Puerto Ricans: Strangers--Then Neighbors. Chicago: Quadrangle Books, 1965.

Sexton, Patricia. Spanish Harlem: Anatomy of Poverty. New York: Harper & Row, 1965.

Sissons, Peter L. The Hispanic Experience of Criminal Justice. New York: Hispanic Research Center, Fordham University, 1979.

Steiner, Stan. The Islands: The Worlds of the Puerto Ricans. New York: Harper & Row, 1974.

United States Commission on Civil Rights. Puerto Ricans in the Continental United States: An Uncertain Future. Washington: The Commission, 1976.

Vivas, José Luis. Historia de Puerto Rico. New York: Las Americas Publishing Co., 1962.

Wagenheim, Kal. Puerto Rico: A Profile. New York: Praeger, 1970.

Wagenheim, Kal, with Olga Wagenheim. The Puerto Ricans: A Documentary History. New York: Praeger, 1973.

_____. A Survey of Puerto Ricans on the U.S. Mainland in the 1970's. New York: Praeger, 1975.

Wakefield, Dan. Island in the City: Puerto Ricans in New York. Houghton Mifflin, 1959.

Weinberg, Meyer. A Chance to Learn: The History of Race and Education in the United States. New York: Cambridge University Press, 1977. Part I: Chapter 6, "Puerto Rican Children."

Wells, Henry. The Modernization of Puerto Rico. Cambridge: Harvard University Press, 1969.

Young Lords' Party. Palante. New York: McGraw-Hill, 1971. A portfolio of photographs by Michael Abramson with text by the Young Lords' Party and Michael Abramson. "Palante" is the Spanish equivalent of "Right On."